INTERNATIONAL ECONOMIC LAW SERIES

General Editor: John H. Jackson

FRESH WATER AND INTERNATIONAL ECONOMIC LAW

Fresh Water and International Economic Law

Edited by

EDITH BROWN WEISS

LAURENCE BOISSON DE CHAZOURNES

and

NATHALIE BERNASCONI-OSTERWALDER

OXFORD
UNIVERSITY PRESS

OXFORD
UNIVERSITY PRESS

Great Clarendon Street, Oxford OX2 6DP

Oxford University Press is a department of the University of Oxford. It furthers the University's objective of excellence in research, scholarship, and education by publishing worldwide in

Oxford New York

Auckland Cape Town Dar es Salaam Hong Kong Karachi Kuala Lumpur Madrid Melbourne Mexico City Nairobi New Delhi Shanghai Taipei Toronto

With offices in

Argentina Austria Brazil Chile Czech Republic France Greece Guatemala Hungary Italy Japan Poland Portugal Singapore South Korea Switzerland Thailand Turkey Ukraine Vietnam

Oxford is a registered trade mark of Oxford University Press in the UK and in certain other countries

Published in the United States by Oxford University Press Inc., New York

First published 2005

British Library Cataloguing in Publication Data
Data available

Library of Congress Cataloging in Publication Data

Fresh water and international economic law / edited by Edith Brown Weiss, Laurence Boisson de Chazournes, and Nathalie Bernasconi-Osterwalder
p. cm.—(International economic law series)
Includes bibliographical references and index.
ISBN 0-19-927467-3 (hardback : alk. paper)
1. Water resources development—Law and legislation. 2. Sustainable development—Law and legislation. 3. Water resources development—Economic aspects. I. Weiss, Edith Brown, 1942– II. Boisson de Chazournes, Laurence. III. Bernasconi-Osterwalder, Nathalie. IV. Series: International economic law series (Oxford, England)
K3498.F74 2005
346.04′691—dc22 2005013745

Typeset by Newgen Imaging Systems (P) Ltd., Chennai, India
Printed in Great Britain
on acid-free paper by
Biddles Ltd., King's Lynn

ISBN 0-19-927467-3 978-0-19-927467-3

1 3 5 7 9 10 8 6 4 2

General Editor's Preface

Water is an essential but also deceptively simple product. In a very timely book, the editors, Edith Brown Weiss, Laurence Boisson de Chazournes, and Nathalie Bernasconi-Osterwalder, have authored and edited an extraordinarily thorough and extensive volume to probe the international economic law aspects of fresh water. It is truly remarkable how complex this inquiry can be, involving the WTO in a number of ways (trade in water as a product, services and GATS, subsidies, agriculture, etc.), as well as other matters such as investment and water disputes. Complementing all this are several chapters exploring broader contexts such as the economics of water, and principles of good governance such as transparency and public participation.

The book, derived partly from a conference and containing many chapters by many outstanding experts on the subject, will clearly be a definitive work. The editors have brought a broad—as well as a deep—perspective to this volume. For example, they note that the '"economization" of the management of water raises cross-cutting issues, especially the challenges for managing water as an economic, social, cultural, and ecological good'.

It is a privilege and a pleasure for the Oxford University series on International Economic Law, to count this book as one of its 'members'.

JOHN H. JACKSON*

* *University Professor of Law*, Georgetown University Law Center (GULC), Washington, DC; *Director*, Institute of International Economic Law, GULC; *General Editor*, International Economic Law Series, Oxford University Press; *Editor in Chief, Journal of International Economic Law*, Oxford University Press.

Acknowledgements

In writing this book, the editors have benefited from the support and assistance of many people. The project began when the Carnegie Corporation of New York awarded a small grant for research on Water, Trade, and Investment to Georgetown University Law Center. Two seminars were held to explore the issues. The first, on 29 October 2002, took place at Georgetown University Law Center and was co-hosted by the Institute for International Economic Law. Participants included scholars and representatives from the International Joint Commission between Canada and the United States, the World Bank, several U.S. government departments and agencies, nongovernmental organizations, and law firms.

The second meeting was an international workshop on Fresh Water and International Economic Law, held on 3 March 2003 at the Graduate Institute of International Studies in Geneva, Switzerland, and co-sponsored by the University of Geneva Law Faculty. Participants, who were from many different countries, included scholars, officials from international intergovernmental organizations, officials of the Swiss Government, representatives of nongovernmental organizations, and lawyers from local and international law firms. The decision to publish this book emerged from the latter workshop. The editors are exceedingly grateful to the Carnegie Corporation for the grant which made these programs possible.

The editors also express their deep appreciation to the participants in the workshops for their insights and comments, and to Georgetown University Law Center and to the Graduate Institute of International Studies in Geneva for hosting the meetings.

Thanks are also due to the many people who assisted with the preparation of this book. Mara Tignino of the University of Geneva deserves special thanks for her very fine research and editorial assistance in preparing the book for publication. We are also grateful to Makane Moise Mbengue, James Donnelly, Susan Maslen, and Tracy Stitt, who assisted with research in various stages. Special thanks must also go to Georgetown University Law Center and the Institute for International Economic Law, the University of Geneva Law Faculty, and the Center for International Environmental Law for their support in so many ways, which made the preparation of the book possible.

Edith Brown Weiss and Laurence Boisson de Chazournes express their deep personal thanks to Nathalie Bernasconi-Osterwalder for her dedication and great skill as a co-editor in editing material and ensuring timely publication.

Contents

List of Tables, Figures, and Maps

Tables

Figures

Maps

List of Acronyms and Abbreviations

AfDB	African Development Bank
ADB	Asian Development Bank
AMS	Aggregate measurement of support (agriculture)
AsDB	Asian Development Bank
ASEAN	Association of South East Asian Nations
BIT	Bilateral investment treaty
CAFTA	Central America Free Trade Agreement
CAO	Compliance Advisor Ombudsman (IFC, MIGA)
CEC	Council of the Commission for Environmental Cooperation (NAAEC)
CESCR	Committee on Economic, Social and Cultural Rights
CP	Civil and Political Rights
CVD	Countervailing duty (subsidies)
DSB	Dispute Settlement Body (WTO)
DSM	Dispute settlement mechanism
DSU	Dispute Settlement Understanding (WTO)
EBRD	European Bank for Reconstruction and Development
EC	European Communities
ECHR	European Court of Human Rights
ECJ	European Court of Justice
ECOSOC	Economic and Social Council (UN)
EEC	European Economic Community
EEC Treaty	Treaty Establishing the European Economic Community, 1957
EIA	Environmental impact assessment
EPA	United States Environmental Protection Agency
ESC	Economic, Social and Cultural Rights
EU	European Union
FAO	Food and Agriculture Organization of the United Nations
FCCC	Framework Convention on Climate Change
FTA	Free trade agreement
FTAA	Free Trade Agreement of the Americas
GATS	General Agreement on Trade in Services
GATT	General Agreement on Tariffs and Trade
GDP	Gross domestic product
IBRD	International Bank for Reconstruction and Development

ICESCR	International Covenant on Economic, Social and Cultural Rights
ICJ	International Court of Justice
ICPR	International Covenant on Civil and Political Rights
ICSID	International Centre for Settlement of Investment Disputes
IDA	International Development Association
IDB	Inter-American Development Bank
IFC	International Finance Corporation
ILA	International Law Association
JPC	Joint Public Committee (NAAEC)
MAI	Multilateral Agreement on Investment
MEA	Multilateral environmental agreement
Mercosur	Mercado Común del Sur
MFN	Most-favoured-nation
MIGA	Multilateral Investment Guarantee Agency
NAAEC	North American Agreement on Environmental Cooperation
NAFTA	North American Free Trade Agreement
NGO	Non-governmental organization
OECD	Organization for Economic Cooperation and Development
OHCHR	Office of the High Commissioner for Human Rights
OSPAR	Convention for the Protection of the Marine Environment of the North-East Atlantic
PCA	Permanent Court of Arbitration
PCIJ	Permanent Court of International Justice
PWC	Permanent Water Commission (Senegal Water Charter)
RTA	Regional trade agreement
SADC	Southern African Development Community
TRIMs	Agreement on Trade-Related Investment Measures
TRIPS	Agreement on Trade-Related Aspects of Intellectual Property Rights
UN	United Nations
UNCED	United Nations Conference on Environment and Development
UNCHR	United Nations Commission on Human Rights
UNCITRAL	United Nations Commission on International Trade Law
UNCTAD	United Nations Conference on Trade and Development
UNDP	United Nations Development Programme
UNECE	United Nations Economic Commission for Europe
UNEP	United Nations Environment Programme
WB	World Bank
WHO	World Health Organization
WSSD	World Summit on Sustainable Development (2002)
WTO	World Trade Organization

Notes on Contributors

Al-Dbiyat, M. : Mohamed Al-Dbiyat is researcher at the Institut Français du Proche Orient, Damacus, and at the Maison de l'Orient Méditéranéen, Lyon, and consultant for the Water Management Program of the Aga Khan Development Network. His research concentrates on the urban transformations in Syria and on the history and human occupation of the arid margins of the Fertile Crescent. Recent publications include *La ville en Syrie et ses territoires: héritages et mutations* (J.C. David and M. Al Dbiyat, eds, Bulletin d'Etudes Orientale, IFEAD, No. 52, Damascus) and *L'exploitation des eaux de subsurface des marges arides de Syrie: dégradation ou transformation?* (in *Sécheresse*, 13(1) No.1, Vol. 13, 2002).

Bernasconi-Osterwalder, N. : Nathalie Bernasconi-Osterwalder is managing attorney of the Geneva office of the Center for International Environmental Law (CIEL), where she is working primarily on issues relating to trade, investment, and sustainable development. She is a former fellow of the Institute of International Economic Law in Washington D.C. She previously worked in Hanoi, Vietnam, for a legal reform project of the United Nations Development Programme (UNDP), as well as for the Australian law firm Phillips Fox. Earlier, she was at the Justice Department in Berne, Switzerland, in the Section for International Law. Recent publications include articles on the trade and environment linkage, WTO dispute settlement, and reform of international financial institutions.

Boisson de Chazournes, L. : Laurence Boisson de Chazournes is Professor of International Law and Director of the Department of Public International Law and International

Organization at the Faculty of Law of the University of Geneva. She is also Visiting Professor at the Graduate Institute of International Studies (Geneva) and the University of Aix-Marseille III. She is a consultant and a member of groups of experts with various international organizations, including the World Bank, WHO, UNDP, and ILO. Between 1995 and 1999, she was Senior Counsel with the Legal Department of the World Bank, in charge of international law, institutional and natural resources management issues. Professor Boisson de Chazournes is the author of a large number of publications dealing with public international law, international organizations, international humanitarian law, and international environmental law and natural resources law. Recent publications include: *International Organizations and International Dispute Settlement: Trends and Prospects* (with C. Romano and R. Mackenzie, eds), published by Transnational Publishers in 2002; *National Sovereignty and International Watercourses* (with B. Charrier and F. Curtin), Green Cross International, World Water Vision, 2000; and *International Law, the International Court of Justice and Nuclear Weapons* (with P. Sands, eds), Cambridge University Press, 2000.

Brown Weiss, E. : Edith Brown Weiss is Francis Cabell Brown Professor of International Law at Georgetown University Law Center in the USA. In 2002, she was appointed to the Inspection Panel at the World Bank, and in 2003 became the Panel's Chairperson. She has been President of the American Society of International Law, Special Legal Advisor to the North American Commission on Environmental Cooperation, a member of the highest bodies of the U.S. National Research Council and the board of editors of the American Journal of International Law, the Journal of International Economic Law, and Environment Magazine, among others. From 1990–1992, she served as Associate General Counsel at US EPA, where she established the division on international law. Professor Brown Weiss has published widely, including the books *In Fairness to Future Generations*, by UNU and Transnational Publishers, 1989 (translated in five languages); *Engaging Countries: Strengthening Compliance with International Environmental Accords* (with Harold K. Jacobson), by MIT Press, 1998; and *Reconciling Environment and Trade* (with John H. Jackson, eds), by Transnational Publishers, 2001.

Cossy, M. : Mireille Cossy is Counsellor in the Trade in Services Division of the World Trade Organization. Her areas of specialization include energy and environmental services. She joined the World Trade Organization's Trade and Environment Division in March 1995, and worked on the various aspects of the interrelationship between trade and the environment. She also acted as a panel secretary in three environment-related trade disputes, the so-called *Gasoline*, *Shrimp*, and *Asbestos* cases. Previously, Ms Cossy worked for the Swiss Ministry of Economic Affairs, where she participated in various negotiating groups during the Uruguay Round negotiations and then performed two humanitarian missions, in Colombia and Tajikistan, with the International Committee of the Red Cross.

Cullet, P. : Philippe Cullet is a Senior Lecturer in International Environmental Law at the Law Department of the School of Oriental and African Studies (SOAS), University of London, where he teaches environmental law and intellectual property. He is also a Research Programme Director at the International Environmental Law Research Centre (IELRC) in Geneva. He studied law at the University of Geneva, King's College London, SOAS, and received a doctoral degree in international environmental law from Stanford Law School, Stanford University. He has published widely in the fields of international environmental law, comparative environmental law, and intellectual property rights. Recent publications include: *Differential Treatment in International Environmental Law,* Ashgate, 2003; *Key Materials in International Environmental Law*, (with A. Gowlland-Gualtieri, eds), Ashgate 2004; *Intellectual Property Protection and Sustainable Development*, Butterworth, 2005.

Ducrey, O. : Olivier Ducrey studied law the University of Fribourg (Switzerland) and holds a Master of Advanced European Studies from the Europa Institut of the University of Basel in 2002. He is currently an associate in the Geneva office of the international law firm Baker & McKenzie.

Gowlland-Gualtieri, A. : Alix Gowlland-Gualtieri holds a Ph.D. from Oxford University and an LL.M from UC Berkeley in the field of international environmental law. She is a Research Fellow at the International Environmental Law Research Centre in Geneva, and has worked at the Environmental and Human Settlements Division of the United Nations Economic Commission for Europe. Her main area of interest, apart from international environmental law, is human rights. Publications include: *The Environmental Accountability of the World Bank to Non-State Actors: Insights from the Inspection Panel*, 72 *British Yearbook of International Law*, 2001, p. 213; and *Key Materials in International Environmental Law* (edited with P. Cullet), Ashgate, 2004. Her doctoral thesis on the environmental accountability of the World Bank to non-state actors will be a forthcoming publication of Hart Publishers.

Jaubert, R. : Ronald Jaubert is Professor at the Graduate Institute of Development Studies, Geneva, and at the Department of Geosciences and Environment of the University of Lausanne. His research concentrates on water resource management, agricultural policies in dry regions, and economic instruments for sustainable development. Recent publications include *Alternative Perceptions of Authority and Control: The desert and the Ma'moura of Syria* (D. Chatty and R. Jaubert, eds, Arab World Geographer, Vol. 5, No. 2, Toronto, 2002) and *Land Use and Vegetation Cover, Semi Arid and Arid Areas of Aleppo and Hama Provinces, Syria* (Jaubert et al., Monde Arabe Contemporain, Hors Série, Maison de l'Orient, Lyon, 1999.)

Luterbacher, U. : Urs Luterbacher is Professor at the Graduate Institute of International Studies in Geneva, where he has taught political science since 1973. He is also a member of ProClim, the Forum for Climate and Global Change of the Swiss Academy of Sciences, and of the Consultative Organ on Climate Change, a committee set up by the Swiss Academy of Sciences to advise the Swiss government on climate change. He is currently involved in an international research project concerned with the peaceful allocation and distribution of fresh water resources in the Middle East. Professor Luterbacher is the author/co-author of *Dynamic Models of International Conflict, Cooperative Models in International Relations Research and Pathways of Understanding: The Interactions of Humanity and Global Environmental Change* and numerous articles on international political and environmental problems. *The International Politics of Climate Change* (co-authored with Detlef Sprinz) was published by MIT Press in 2001.

Mbengue, M.M. : Makane Moïse Mbengue is PhD Candidate and research assistant at the Faculty of Law of the University of Geneva, Department of Public International Law and International Organization. Previously, Mr Mbengue served as External Collaborator for the International Labour Organization (ILO) and Legal Assistant for the 'Tobacco Free Initiative' at the World Health Organization (WHO). His publications include articles on *Amicus Curiae* in the WTO Dispute

Settlement System, on water issues (particularly on the status of the Senegal River), as well as other articles on trade and environment.

McCaffrey, S.C. : Stephen C. McCaffrey is Distinguished Professor and Scholar at the University of the Pacific, McGeorge School of Law in Sacramento, California, USA. He served as a member of the International Law Commission of the United Nations (ILC) from 1982–1991 and chaired the Commission's 1987 Session. He was the ILC's Special Rapporteur on the Law of the Non-Navigational Uses of International Watercourses from 1985 until 1991, when the Commission provisionally adopted a full set of draft articles on the topic. The ILC's draft articles formed the basis for the 1997 United Nations Convention on the same subject. Among other activities, he currently serves as Legal Counsel to the Nile Basin Initiative. Professor McCaffrey's publications include *The Law of International Watercourses: Non-Navigational Uses*, published by Oxford University Press in 2001.

Ostrovsky, A. : Aaron Ostrovsky is pursuing his studies at the University of Michigan Law School. Recent publications include *The European Commission's Regulations for Genetically Modified Organisms and the Current WTO Dispute—Human Health or Environmental Measures?*, 15 COLO. J.INT'L ENVT'L L. & POL'Y 209 (2004) and *The New Codex Alimentarius Standards for Food Created with Modern Biotechnology—Implications for the EC GMO Framework's Compliance with the SPS Agreement*, 25 MICH. J. INT'L L. 813.

Pannatier, S. : Serge Pannatier is Attorney-at-Law with the international law firm Baker & McKenzie in Geneva. He practices in the areas of international trade regulation and customs as well as general employment law. Mr Pannatier's Ph.D. thesis relates to the trade and natural resources linkage.

He is also Visiting Professor at the World Trade Institute, Berne, Switzerland.

Smets, H. : Henri Smets is an International Consultant working, *inter alia*, for OECD, UNEP, and the Water Academy. He is also Director of the Catalan Institute for Scientific Research in Paris and Member of the Board of the Association for the Development of Environmental Law and Economics (ADELE). Henri Smets served at the OECD's Environment Directorate, Paris, from 1972–1998, where he focused on environmental economics and law, and environmental performance, and where he was Principal Administrator. He also taught at the University of Paris I—Panthéon-Sorbonne, at Liège University (Belgium), University of Paris XII, and Ecole Nationale des Ponts et Chausées, Paris. Mr Smets' latest publications include the books: *Le droit à l'eau* and *La solidarité pour l'eau potable*, published by the Water Academy in 2002 and 2003. He also wrote *The cost for meeting the Johannesburg targets for water* which was published in 2004 by the Water Academy, and in 2005 the report, '*Pour un droit effectif à l'eau potable*,' available at www.academie-eau.org.

Speed, R. : Robert Speed is an environmental lawyer from Australia who specializes in water resources law and management. Mr Speed has worked in environmental law in commercial, government, and non-government sectors in Australia, Ecuador, Sri Lanka, The Maldives, and Switzerland. He presently works in the water reform unit for the Queensland Department of Natural Resources and Mines.

Tarlock, A.D. : A. Dan Tarlock is Professor at Chicago-Kent College of Law. He is also a Special Legal Advisor to the North American Commission on Environmental Cooperation in Montreal. Professor

Tarlock is the co-author of casebooks on both water law and environmental law, and chaired the U.S. National Research Council's Committee which looked at water markets in the West.

Tignino, M. : Mara Tignino is a Ph.D. Candidate at the Graduate Institute of International Studies and assistant at the Department of Public International Law and International Organizations, in the Faculty of Law at the University of Geneva. Previously, Ms. Tignino has served as consultant for the Basel Convention Secretariat. Her publications include articles on water in time of armed conflicts and in the Middle East.

Tuerk, E. : At the time of writing, Elisabeth Tuerk is a staff attorney in the Geneva Office of the Center for International Environmental Law (CIEL), where she works in the Trade and Sustainable Development Program. Ms Tuerk focusses on WTO rules on trade in services, WTO dispute settlement, and on questions relating to the regulation of international investment. Currently, Ms Tuerk is a member of UNCTAD's Trade Negotiations and Commercial Diplomacy Branch. In 2004, she worked on UNCTAD's World Investment Report, *The Shift Towards Services*. Previous publications include: *Necessity Revisited—Proportionality in WTO Law after Korea-Beef, EC-Asbestos and EC-Sardines*, which was published in the Journal of World Trade in 2003 (co-authored with J. Neumann); and *The WTO Negotiations on Services: The Regulatory State up for Grabs*, which was published in Canada Watch in 2002 (co-authored with R. Howse).

Wiegandt, E. : Ellen Wiegandt holds a Ph. D. in social anthropology from the University of Michigan. Her main research domain is the analysis of institutional aspects of environmental and natural resource management, and of demographic processes. She was Director of the Human Dimensions Programme on Global Environmental Change and currently teaches at the Graduate Institute of International Studies in Geneva, where she gives a seminar on interdisciplinary issues of international environmental problems. She also directs research at the University Institute Kurt Bösch in Sion, Switzerland. In 2003 she received the Moppert Prize in Sustainable Development for her work on water management. Dr Wiegandt is the author of numerous articles on institutions, demography, and resource management in Alpine regions, and is the editor of *Mountains: Sources of Water, Sources of Knowledge*, Kluwer, forthcoming and *The Darkening Peaks: Glacial Retreat in Scientific and Social Context*, to be published by University of California Press in 2006.

Ziegler, A.R. : Andreas Ziegler is Professor at the University of Lausanne, Switzerland, and Of Counsel in the Zurich-based law firm of Blum Attorneys-at-law. He is also a Fellow of the Tim Fischer Centre for Global Trade and Finance in Sydney. Professor Ziegler previously served as a legal adviser to the Ministry of Defence, the Ministry of Foreign Affairs, and the Ministry of Trade in Switzerland, and as a senior officer in the Secretariat of the European Free Trade Association (EFTA) in Geneva. He is the author of *Trade and Environment in the European Community*, which was published by Clarendon Press in 1996, as well as of many articles on international, European, and Swiss public law.

Introduction

Fresh water is essential for our survival and for the health of the planet. Water has many values: ecological, social, cultural, and economic. As the demand for water has increased worldwide, the challenges for managing it effectively for multiple uses have also grown. Not surprisingly, the approaches to water resource management and to the supply of water and sanitation services have evolved significantly over the past decades to respond to these challenges. As in centuries past, the availability of adequate water supplies is important not only for economic development and ecological robustness but also, importantly, for safeguarding international peace and security. This book focuses on the implications of the use of water as an economic good, the implications of commodification of fresh water, and the bearing of international economic law on water issues. At the same time, it examines the application of other areas of law, such as human rights, and analyzes the implications for the economic uses of water.

On the economic front the calls are increasingly vocal for privatization of formerly public services, and trade and investment liberalization in all sectors, including that of water. The economic concerns also relate to agricultural subsidies and other subsidies, some of which have a direct impact on how water is managed and sometimes wasted. International investment agreements affect domestic water resource management and regulation of water quality. This 'economization' of the management of water raises cross-cutting issues, especially the challenges for managing water as an economic, social, cultural, and ecological good. This book analyzes these issues primarily through the prism of law, but it also integrates relevant learning from economics and political science. It is intended as an introduction to the many interfaces between the protection and the management of fresh water and international economic law.

The book is divided into five parts. Part I addresses the transboundary management of fresh water, with a particular focus on exports of fresh water under international trade law and related geopolitical and economic issues. Part II covers services related to water and highlights the WTO's General Agreement on Trade in Services (GATS). It addresses access to water services and the claim for a human right to water, as well as the privatization of water utilities. Part II also examines how the GATS and human rights instruments might be reconciled so as to favor access to water for all. Part III analyzes the use of agricultural subsidies and their effects on water management and efficiency. Special attention is dedicated to environmental protection. Part IV concentrates on investment issues and the potential impact of international investment regimes on domestic water management policies and environmental regulation. This part also focuses on the involvement of local communities in water-related investment projects. Lastly, Part V deals with dispute settlement in relation to water and economics issues, and with the contribution of public participation and transparency in resolving these disputes.

Part I: Trade of fresh water: geopolitics, law, and economics

In a context in which water resources might appear scarce, proposals to export or remove water across national boundaries, whether by diversion, surface bulk transport, marine tankers, pipeline, or as ballast water, have increased. Trade agreements, including the General Agreement on Tariffs and Trade (GATT) and the North American Free Trade Agreement (NAFTA), may have serious implications for these water movements. If fresh water falls under the disciplines of international trade law, efforts to keep waters for local use or to manage them in a sustainable way may falter. This has become an area of concern for civil society, as well as for international and domestic policy makers; however, the topic of international trade in fresh water has received little attention so far in the legal literature.

Part I addresses issues associated with the transfer of fresh water at both the international and the domestic levels. Chapter 1, by Luterbacher and Wiegandt, sets the stage by analyzing how water conflicts can emerge and by looking at specific international river basins. Taking into account the peculiarities of the resource itself and distributional questions related to its very nature, the authors provide an analytical framework for addressing the more specific issues of transboundary exports of fresh water. They also consider the potential use of water rights and allocation uses—while highlighting the shortcomings of these measures when ill-defined—and the possibilities trade in fresh water may have for lessening political tensions in water-scarce areas of the Middle East.

Chapter 2, by Tarlock, concentrates on domestic water markets and water management and how these relate to the international economic system. The chapter focuses on water markets in the U.S., and in particular on efforts to engage in transboundary water markets between Canada and the U.S., and on the Rio Grande between Mexico and the U.S. It compares U.S. constitutional law regarding the commerce clause (as it applies to 'water marketing' between states in the U.S.) with relevant provisions of international trade law. Where appropriate, the chapter highlights legal provisions affecting water markets in other countries.

Transfers, or 'water marketing', have been endorsed as a fair and relatively cheap way to relocate water, and as a preferable alternative to the continued construction of carry-over storage reservoirs. There have always been water rights transfers, but as the number and size has increased, so has opposition. The transfer of water threatens to deprive areas of origin of political power, future development options, and the loss of control over the resource. The debate turns on the question of water being (or not being) a commodity. The reconciliation of competing views depends on the recognition that water transfers are not an end in and of themselves, but are one of a suite of policy instruments to achieve environmentally sustainable water use.

Part I ends with a chapter by Brown Weiss, who sets forth the different ways that fresh water moves across borders, from international rivers, to pipelines and tankers, to bottles of water, examines relevant international and regional legal arrangements, and analyzes the application of international trade law to the various means. The author addresses the potential conflicts between the need for sustainable management of water resources and associated ecosystems and the goal of removing barriers to an open economic trading system. The chapter provides an in-depth analysis of the legal question whether and at what point fresh water becomes a 'product' or a 'good', subject to international trade disciplines, and examines the relevance of the de facto exclusion of oil resources from the GATT. Brown Weiss proposes an approach of anticipatory caution as an extension or complement to the precautionary approach as applied to transboundary movements of fresh water.

Part II: Water services, the GATS, and related issues

Access to water and to adequate sanitation has become a key issue on the international agenda. As an example, the WSSD Implementation Plan, adopted at the World Summit on Sustainable Development (WSSD) held in Johannesburg, South Africa in 2002, commits the world community, by the year 2015, to halve the proportion of people globally who do not have access to safe drinking water and adequate sanitation, while not specifically referring to a human right to water.

The United Nations Committee on Economic, Cultural and Social Rights, in November 2002, for its part, formally declared that safe and secure drinking water is a human right, and stated that 'water should be treated as a social and cultural good, and not primarily as an economic commodity'. Stating that '[t]he human right to water entitles everyone to sufficient, affordable, physically accessible, safe and acceptable water for personal and domestic uses', the General Comment implies that the countries that are bound by the provisions of the Covenant 'have a constant and continuing duty' progressively to ensure that everyone has access to safe and secure drinking water and sanitation facilities—equitably and without discrimination.

Trade liberalization and privatization may be answers to these quests. However, concerns have arisen that the trend to liberalize and privatize essential services sectors, such as health, education, and water, might endanger certain human rights obligations that a state may have under international and domestic laws on human rights and the environment. Particular fears have been expressed with respect to the implications of the GATS for domestic policy-making, including on services relating to the supply of water.

Part II of the book begins with an overview of the development of the human right to water. McCaffrey argues in Chapter 4 that a human right to water could be inferred from existing human rights law and highlights some of the implications of such an entitlement. The chapter shows that pressure on the world's fresh water resources is growing and that governments have experimented with methods of increasing the efficiency of water delivery systems. These phenomena have led to an increasing recognition of the human right to water. McCaffrey reviews the background of the human right to water and explores some of the issues raised with regard to current conditions. Smets, for his part, provides an overview of some of the latest developments at the international level regarding the human right to water, with a particular focus on the Third World Water Forum held in Kyoto, Japan, in 2003.

The discussion of the human right to water naturally leads to a discussion of water-related services and, more particularly, how this right relates to the rules of the international trade in services. It focuses on legal issues arising from the application of the GATS, one of the three pillar agreements of the WTO, to water distribution and sanitation services. The GATS establishes a legal framework for trade in services with the goal of progressively liberalizing such trade. WTO Members are currently pursuing this goal through a set of far-reaching negotiations covering effectively all services sectors, including the provision of water.

Cossy's chapter examines to what extent water-related services are covered by the GATS. The author assesses the existing WTO classification instruments, which currently only refer to sewage services, and examines differences in the treatment of private and public services. Cossy elaborates on the implications of specific commitments for water-related services and reviews the pattern of specific commitments on sewage services which have been undertaken so far by forty WTO Members. In particular, Cossy considers how the characteristics of water-related services—existence of natural monopolies, decentralization of management, use of the public domain, etc.—affect the implementation of specific commitments.

Tuerk, Ostrovsky, and Speed's chapter responds to civil society's concerns about the privatization of water services, against the backdrop of water's status as a basic human right. As private sector participation in water services increases, the authors explain that WTO Member States must carefully design their specific commitments under the GATS to ensure that regulatory control of water services remains with the State. The authors review the wording of those existing specific commitments under the GATS that relate to various forms of privatization. This review aims to determine how to ensure that current negotiations on specific commitments will not constrain vital regulatory flexibility.

The authors conclude that, while privatization of water services may be a useful tool for improving water services, future GATS specific commitments with respect to privatization must leave sufficient policy space to regulate flexibly and to ensure privatization is not simply done for its own sake.

PART III: WATER, SUBSIDIES, AND AGRICULTURE

Agricultural water use accounts for about 70–75% of the total water use worldwide. Recent studies indicate that water-related subsidies lead to misuse of water for agricultural and other purposes. Instead of encouraging the conservation of existing water supplies, subsidies may nurture wasteful practices, such as excessive irrigation. Too much irrigation often leads to additional environmental problems, including the water-logging and salinization of irrigated croplands. Moreover, society-at-large often has to pay for damage caused to rivers and lakes through the polluting activities of farmers and industry.

While subsidies and their effects are being discussed in several inter-governmental fora, including the Organization for Economic Cooperation and Development (OECD) and the UN Food and Agriculture Organization (FAO), States have primarily agreed on disciplines regarding subsidies within the WTO. Disciplines under the WTO aim mainly to reduce subsidies in order to promote international trade. They do not focus on disciplining the use of subsidies for conservation or environmental protection.

Given the importance of the agricultural sector in the context of water use, Part III of the book centers primarily on agricultural subsidies. It begins with a chapter by Jaubert and Al-Dbiyat on water use efficiency in agriculture, and addresses questions raised by the dominant standard approach to water management. Through the analysis of a case study in Syria, the authors consider the divergent definitions of water use efficiency (or divergent objectives regarding water management) and the highly variable contexts in which water management strategies are implemented. The authors also highlight the relation between water use efficiency and developing countries' capacities to export agricultural products, as well as the obstacles caused by the current international agricultural subsidies regime.

The chapter by Bernasconi-Osterwalder examines whether international trade rules regarding subsidies, cover water-related agricultural subsidies, and whether they offer a framework that is useful for reducing and eliminating environmentally harmful water subsidies. The author analyzes the two main agreements of the WTO dealing with agricultural subsidies: the Agreement on Agriculture and the Agreement on Subsidies and Countervailing Measures. The author assesses the scope of coverage of the two agreements and the reduction commitments of members to reduce their 'domestic support', with a focus on the question whether these commitments require WTO Members to reduce subsidies that are leading to water waste. The author also looks at the complex issue of exemptions and at the relationship between the two agreements.

The chapter ends with an overview of the transparency requirements relating to subsidies and provides options for how the international community could address water-related problems arising from the use of subsidies in agriculture.

Part IV: Water and investment

Over the last two decades, the international framework on foreign investment has changed significantly. While no global investment agreement exists to date, there are now well over 2,000 bilateral investment treaties worldwide, in addition to a host of regional agreements covering transnational investment aiming at investment liberalization and investor protection.

Rules on foreign investment contained in bilateral and regional treaties grant broad rights and enforcement powers to investors investing abroad. In so doing, international investment rules restrict the ability of national and local governments to regulate the activities of foreign investors to meet local environmental and social priorities, including those relating to water resource management and the provision of water distribution and sanitation.

Part IV provides an analysis of the investment rules and how they relate to water resource management and environmental protection. In recent years, the European Union (EU) and the European Free Trade Association (EFTA) have begun to include investment-related provisions in the comprehensive trade agreements they have concluded on behalf of their members with countries such as Mexico, South Africa, Chile, and Singapore. European negotiators are increasingly facing questions regarding the effect of pre- and post-establishment investment disciplines on fresh water supply.

Chapter 10, by Ziegler, focuses on EFTA and EU third country agreements. The author looks at the motives and basic structures regarding water-related services of these bilateral free trade agreements. He points out how the approach of integrating GATS-type services chapters with a traditional Bilateral Investment Treaty (BIT)-style protection of investments may pose new challenges within the global trading system.

The following chapter by Bernasconi-Osterwalder and Brown Weiss describes the rules of NAFTA's investment chapter and how the investor guarantees or rights could affect domestic water resource management policies and regulation. The authors examine relevant cases decided under NAFTA and assess their implications for future disputes. Given that most bilateral and regional investment regimes contain similar provisions, the experience gained under NAFTA is relevant not only for the three North American States, but beyond. It is especially important to integrate the lessons learned from NAFTA into the ongoing negotiations on the Free Trade Agreement of the Americas (FTAA) and other regional agreements.

Pannatier and Ducrey's chapter looks at national water concessions attributed to private corporations that rely on bilateral investment treaties protecting foreign investments. Through a specific case study, the Compañía de Aguas del Aconquija, S.A. and Compagnie Générale des Eaux case brought before the International Centre for the Settlement of Investment Disputes (ICSID), the authors show the relevance of bilateral investment treaties as means to settle water disputes dealing with the grant of national water concessions.

Cullet and Gowlland-Gualtieri's chapter focuses on the evolving rights to environmental information, participation in decision-making processes, and access to justice for local communities. The authors assess the application of prior informed consent to water service investments, which goes one step further in giving local communities input into decisions concerning their water supplies and services. In their analysis, the authors examine the case law of international and regional human rights bodies, as well as the practice of the World Bank and the International Labour Organization, which contribute significantly to the development of participatory standards for local communities.

Part V: Resolution of water disputes, with special emphasis on economic issues

International fresh water-related disputes have been settled under the auspices of a wide array of international bodies, including, *inter alia*, the International Court of Justice (ICJ), the European Court of Justice (ECJ), the European Court of Human Rights (ECHR), and the Inter-American Commission of Human Rights. Water-related disputes may also be resolved through arbitration and through economic dispute settlement mechanisms and procedures.

The number of trade and investment disputes has increased significantly during the past decade. This increase, as well as the lack of transparency and participation in proceedings, has raised concerns among civil society and governments regarding the adequacy of dispute settlement mechanisms and procedures, particularly with respect to cases involving the protection of human rights, health, and the environment. Several investor-to-State disputes have involved fresh water. An important issue is participation by non-State actors in, if not access to, these dispute settlement proceedings.

Part V of the book focuses on the growing role of water protection and management issues in dispute settlement mechanisms and procedures, and on questions relating to public participation and transparency in the related procedures.

Boisson de Chazournes's chapter considers the impact of the multiplication of dispute settlement mechanisms and procedures on the resolution of water disputes. The existence of various dispute settlement mechanisms and procedures gives the opportunity to States and other actors to bring their complaints forward. In this context, the author looks at water-related disputes brought before inter-State dispute resolution mechanisms, as well as before dispute settlement mechanisms and procedures that are accessible to non-State actors. The author draws attention to the complex nature of water disputes involving issues of investment protection, human rights, and trade policies. The opening of dispute settlement mechanisms to a wide array of actors and the emergence of specialized universal and regional dispute settlement bodies represent key elements in the development of a corpus of norms and principles with respect to water management disputes.

The chapter by Mbengue and Tignino examines the concepts of public participation and transparency as means of water-disputes avoidance. It also looks at the role of such concepts in the dispute settlement context. The authors argue that effective public participation, contributing to public awareness of environmental issues, increases the accountability and transparency of the dispute settlement mechanisms. The chapter also analyzes the role of *amici curiae* briefs as means of public participation before dispute settlement bodies, and the issue of transparency in arbitration proceedings. Lastly, the chapter highlights the role of the newly-established compliance mechanisms by several international financial institutions as vehicles for strengthening public participation in water disputes.

PART I

TRADE OF FRESH WATER: GEOPOLITICS, LAW, AND ECONOMICS

1

Cooperation or Confrontation: Sustainable Water Use in an International Context

URS LUTERBACHER and ELLEN WIEGANDT

1. International water problems

'The world is incurring a vast water deficit. It is largely invisible, historically recent, and growing fast.'[1] It is also critical because it has far-reaching consequences, touching all sectors of society. Impending water scarcities can exacerbate social conflict, lead to food shortages, and cause or aggravate diseases. Assuring access to sufficient water resources throughout the globe is a thus major challenge for the international community. The problem is even more pressing and complex because future quantity and quality of water are linked to other critical issues such as climate change, property rights, and economic development. Numerous regions of the world are particularly at risk of potential shortages due either to physical or social causes, or because of uncertainties about access generated by rapid and far-reaching political changes. The Middle East immediately comes to mind because water shortages are invariably linked to the broader conflict in which water has become a weapon. This area may be a harbinger of similar conflicts to come in other parts of the world. River systems such as the Mekong in Southeast Asia, the Syr and Amu Daria in Central Asia, the Nile in Africa, or the Colorado in North America are shared by countries whose needs are evolving and whose riparian States have unequal power relations. Competition for water in these regions is already, or can potentially become, linked to other political and economic developments to reinforce existing differences. The current international regime is insufficient to deal with these emerging issues.

Historically, conflicts over international waterways were mostly about navigation, which created its own geographic dynamic. In this context, the strategic position was the mouth of the river, creating particular power hierarchies and

[1] Brown, Lester R., *Water Deficits Growing in Many Countries: Water Shortages May Cause Food Shortages*, EARTH POLICY INSTITUTE: ECO-ECONOMY UPDATES, August 6, 2002, available at http://www.earthpolicy.org/Updates/Update15.htm.

confrontations. The evolution of international agreements has gone a long way to regulate numerous issues in order to assure unimpeded transport and commerce. Within Western Europe the international conventions for navigation on the Rhine (1816) and the Danube (1856) are largely credited not only for presenting attractive solutions to international transport and trade questions, but also as constituting the first real international organizations.

Guaranteeing access to the water resource itself for various forms of consumption poses new and very different problems. While it may be agued that there is no absolute shortage of water globally, its regional distribution is problematic. Some regions have large water surpluses, while others cannot cover their needs from internal sources. Nine countries hold 60% of the world's water resources, while others depend significantly on water resources outside their national borders (for example: Turkmenistan 96%, Egypt 96%, Syria 84%).[2] There are also enormous discrepancies in the per capita consumption of water across the globe and some populations have access, for geographic and political reasons, to far less than the generally agreed minimum of 500 cubic meters per capita. This figure is in any case most approximate, because definition of need depends on far more factors than the amount required for mere survival.

The division of the globe into humid, semi-arid, and arid regions is only part of the distribution problem. Even in relatively well-endowed regions there can be important differences of access between upstream and downstream users, which are cause and consequence of asymmetries ranging well beyond water and create very different power relations than those defined by transport issues. Moreover, seasonal requirements can produce water shortages even in situations of relatively abundant supply. Water is not always available when it is needed, and there is often too much of it when not needed. Seasonality constraints are at the origin of the numerous elaborate irrigation systems found in many mountain regions of the world. Needless to say, irrigation systems can lead to conflicts if rights of passage questions are not dealt with properly.

Changing uses of water accompanying economic development are another factor that can exacerbate the potential for conflict. Competition exists not only among geographic regions, but also among types of users. Agriculture, industry, energy production, and domestic use all place growing demands on a resource whose supply is being modified by climate change and by various forms of pollution generated by overuse. International efforts to address these complex issues must recognize the multiple facets of water use, including its increasing definition as a product, to be regulated in the context of trade agreements.

It might seem that trade in water would be an appropriate solution to equalize access and smooth differences in levels of consumption. However, the characteristics of the resource itself and the associated management and conflict-resolution strategies reveal significant challenges to achieving efficient and equitable use of water at the international level.

[2] World Bank, 2001 World Development Indicators, p. 142.

To address the very broad and comprehensive problems falling under the heading of international trans-boundary water issues, we will first lay out an analytical framework that takes into account the particularities of the resource itself and distributional questions related to its very nature. We will then illustrate our theoretical remarks with two examples that illustrate different water scarcity and conflict situations—the Middle-East and Central Asia.

2. Characteristics of Water Resources: Special Problems for Management and Regulation

Because water is essential for survival and nothing can be substituted for it, societies have always been concerned with allocation issues. In some regions and during some historical periods, quantities were plentiful enough that water could be considered a pure public good; that is, consumption by one user did not affect the consumption of another. This is still largely the case in some Western European countries such as Norway and Switzerland, where seasonal variations can nevertheless cause temporary deficits (or excess supply leading to flooding). These are limiting cases, however, and it is therefore relevant to consider some general characteristics underlying resource allocation and the inherent characteristics of water that pose particular management problems.

In a most general sense, growing water shortages have launched a debate pitting two apparently contradictory views of this indispensable resource. On one side are those who emphasize the symbolic value of water because of its life-giving qualities. According to this perspective, one of the basic human rights is the right to water, and therefore it should have no price. An opposing view recognizes the scarcity aspects of water and thus its intrinsic value in an economic sense. It does have a price and it has a cost, including costs of extraction and maintenance, as well as opportunity costs and externalities associated with its use. From this point of view, efficiency criteria demand setting the correct price, otherwise the resource will not be used in an optimal way. Too high prices will deprive poorer users; too low prices will encourage overuse. In neither case will the right of every person to have access to sufficient quantities of water be realized. Thus, we see that there is in fact a link between the symbolic and the economic qualities inherent in water. Society must therefore devise norms, rules, and institutions that provide incentives to achieve equitable and efficient use of this vital resource. In this context, property rights emerge as a fundamental mechanism determining how resources will be exploited and distributed. As a set of entitlements which specify the rights, privileges, obligations, and limitations related to use of an entity, property rights act in effect as quotas that control access and limit quantities used, so that exploitation will not hit diminishing returns and the resource will continue to meet needs across space and through time with greatest efficiency. Different forms of ownership exist, including open access (which is the object of Hardin's 'tragedy of the commons' argument),[3] common property, and private property. There is now a vast literature debating the viability and efficiency of various types of property systems, which we allude to only briefly here.

Prevailing views in economics have long argued that private property rights are superior because they lead to greater efficiency of resource use. This point is contradicted by both theoretical and empirical work. Dasgupta and Heal,[4] for example, argue that the competitive markets for externalities, which Coase[5] demonstrated would lead to efficient use of resources, may not emerge under certain conditions. A fundamental pre-condition is the existence and enforcement of property rights. Dasgupta and Heal show that property rights may be either difficult to define, or difficult to enforce. Flowing water, for example, cannot be treated as a separate commodity because is in a 'constant state of diffusion' or of movement,[6] and a precise unit thus cannot be allocated to a single individual. In the case of pools of underground water, property rights can be defined as an area of land above them, but it will not be clear whether the water extracted really comes from the area below this surface because of the fluid nature of the resource. Pumping from another area of land may in fact be extracting the water underneath another owner's patch of ground.

The very nature of some types of resources, such as water, and of specific factors associated with their use, has led to the definition of certain conditions under which common rather than private property is more likely to obtain:

(1) The nature of the resource itself is important. Private property requires clear definition of the entity. Water cannot easily be divided into clearly defined units. Moreover it has fugitive aspects, because use implies previous 'capture' through pumping or other forms of collection.
(2) Economies of scale favor common property management, as in the case of grazing lands or fishing zones.
(3) Resources that require expensive maintenance or large capital investment favor collective ownership as a way of mobilizing necessary capital or labor resources. This is the case for irrigation works, dams, or pumping systems.
(4) Private property rights must be protected and guaranteed. Enforcement costs may be too great to be carried by individual owners.

There are also problems of information associated with monitoring behavior of multiple users. How is it possible to know if ground water or oil is being extracted from the pool owned by a particular extractor, or rather from an adjacent source owned by another? And how is it possible to prevent such behavior without some institutional superstructure? There is another clear

[3] Hardin, Garrett, *The Tragedy of the Commons*, 162 Science 1243 (1968).

[4] Dasgupta, Partha & Heal, Geoffrey, Economic Theory and Exhaustible Resources (Cambridge University Press 1979).

[5] Coase, Ronald, *The Problem of Social Cost*, 3 Journal of Law and Economics 1 (1960).

[6] Dasgupta, Partha & Heal, Geoffrey, Economic Theory and Exhaustible Resources (Cambridge University Press 1979).

advantage to common property: risk sharing. This applies specifically to the case of water resources. Again, the example of pools of water under property defined at the surface is relevant. For each individual owner of the surface properties, digging a well might not be worth it because of the risks associated with the prospect of not finding any water under a particular property. Yet, as shown by Dasgupta and Heal,[7] risk sharing in a common property arrangement tremendously increases the possibility of deriving benefits from digging wells in a coordinated fashion. In fact, the greater the number of participants in the risk sharing operation, the lower the costs associated with the enterprise and thus the higher the benefits for each individual owner. Similar reasoning can be made with respect to irrigation: it represents a kind of insurance scheme for agricultural producers, who can then make use of it in case of drought. Thus even risk-averse individual owners have an incentive to enter such an insurance scheme, which renders the costs of risk-bearing negative.[8]

Often these different factors favoring common property management are interdependent. The combination of the resource's inherent characteristics, technological features, and the institutional configurations related to its management underlies arrangements to prevent some groups or individuals from over-using water resources at the expense of others. Frequently the solution has been to define water as common property and to have a collective or central management structure. This form of management has its own special problems, the major one being the familiar 'free-rider' problem. Collective users have incentives to maximize the benefits of the common resource without paying their fair share of the costs. Without socially imposed limits, the end result is overexploitation and dissipation of the resource, as illustrated in Figure 1.1 (see p. 16).

As one can see in the graph, production of a given natural resource type good (the y axis) depends on the number of producers willing to share in its supply (the x axis). In order to ensure benefits in production, there must exist a relatively large number of producers, leading initially increasing returns to scale. As more and more producers join, however, diminishing returns set in. This is illustrated by the S-shaped aspect of the production curve. If each producer incurs a unit fixed cost, then the total cost of production can be represented by a solid straight line. This straight line crosses the production curve in two points: at A, where the number of producers is sufficient to initiate profitability, and at C, where too many producers have completely dissipated profits or surpluses. This also corresponds to the dissipation of the scarcity rent associated with the natural resource.[9] Quite clearly the optimum lies at B, which maximizes surplus production over costs. This optimal situation can be maintained by limiting the number of producers entering the process either by exclusion or by taxes, which increase the fixed costs of each entrant. A solution of the problem involving taxes is presented by the straight line parallel to the cost line and tangent to

[7] *Id.* [8] *Id.* [9] Hardin, Garrett, *The Tragedy of the Commons*, 162 SCIENCE 1243 (1968).

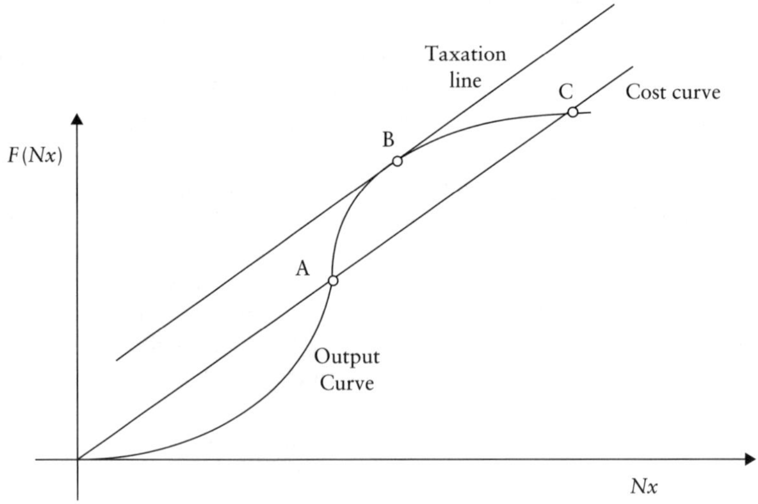

FIGURE 1.1. Water as Common Property—Collective or Central Management Structure

SOURCE: Authors

the production curve in B : A correct taxation of each entrant limits their number and assures maintenance of the scarcity rent.

There are additional problems posed by the public good aspects of water resources. The distribution systems associated with them often create 'network externalities'. For example, water networks are often dependent on individuals or small groups who occupy crucial positions within them, or who own land through which the water flows. Such situations have been called 'weakest link' systems by Hirshleifer,[10] because each individual's contribution is essential to prevent the collapse of the overall system and they therefore require a high degree of cooperation. In these cases, free-riding must be kept to a minimum as it threatens the whole society. While some of these features can make the supply of the collective good easier to achieve, since they provide opportunities for private benefits even under conditions of public ownership, they can also, under some circumstances, enhance inequalities and create conflict.

We can identify common property water management systems throughout history and across the globe, which attests to their ability to resolve some of the key problems associated with water use and allocation. Difficulties associated with common property management nevertheless raise important questions, notably about how communities come together and develop rules and technologies that produce efficient and equitable water management, that is, how they avoid dissipation of the resources and free-rider problems that plague all

[10] Hirshleifer, Jack, *From Weakest Link to Best Shot: The Voluntary Provision of Public Goods*, 41 PUBLIC CHOICE 371 (1983).

cooperative human endeavors. Moreover, given the distinctive qualities of water resources we have evoked so far, we also observe that when conflicts do erupt, they are often associated with a characteristic set of conflict resolution strategies, also linked to the special nature of the resource itself.

3. Water conflicts

It is important to identify both the specificities of water conflicts and their resolution. This is best achieved through reference to general aspects of conflict. In this way, we can identify conflicts as they emerge out of initial situations of cooperation (or absence of hostilities). In this context, we distinguish two types of social relations (which include conflict): those in which participants are relatively equal and those involving inequalities. In systems of social relations based on relative equality among participants (at the domestic as well as at the international level), the possibility for agents to retaliate against each other to prevent free riding and defection always exists. In unequal situations, however, participants are rewarded for actions they take before others. Or, given the inequality, they can simply take advantage of the particular position they enjoy at the moment if their first move (or possibly the second move) gives them a superior outcome. In this case, retaliation by the other parties is not effective because it will make their position worse. Game theorists have formalized these relations by specifying conditions under which first mover advantage, and thus competition for first move, exists or is absent. They (in particular Moulin)[11] have established that absence of such first move competition derives from the existence of a particular Pareto optimal set whose cooperative outcomes can be enforced by credible threats (such as the tit for tat threat in a Prisoner's Dilemma game). If dominating strategies are equally available to each agent, they ensure the existence of such a set. In the case of an open access production system, according to Dasgupta and Heal, no dominating strategy is available to participants or producers. Without dominant strategies, there is thus strong competition for the first move.

The Pareto optimal set associated with the absence of competition for first move, is not empty, according to Moulin,[12] if each agent can reach a utility level that is at least as great as the one he could reach by realizing his best position in an asymmetric Nash equilibrium.[13] A game of Chicken, where players have no dominating strategies and where the asymmetric equilibrium payoffs favor the leader, indicates that the set is not empty. However, as also shown by Moulin, if each agent has a dominating strategy, the existence and non-emptiness of the set is guaranteed. Problems of strong competition for first move will occur only if no agent has, or only a few agents have, dominating strategies, since they are then

[11] Moulin, Hervé, Game Theory for the Social Sciences (1986).

[12] *Id.*

[13] This is what is called a Stackelberg equilibrium.

powerless against abuses of the collective good by first movers. This can lead to authoritarian arrangements at the domestic level and to conflicts at the inter-State level. In general, the use of relatively open and inexpensive formal structures, such as dispute settlement mechanisms, is a way of preserving and consolidating widespread retaliatory powers and to ensure the existence of the Pareto optimal set.

Open access situations often lead to first mover advantage since they lack the dominant strategies as specified above. First mover advantage conditions can even be enhanced by geographic or technological circumstances, such as an upstream position or the capacity to pump more water out of a common pool. These characteristics of resource use underline the importance of formal structures such as international agreements or dispute settlement mechanisms, to reduce first mover advantages.

4. The nature of resource conflicts

Resource conflicts are embedded in open access and first mover advantage questions. James Fearon[14] carried out a classical analysis of ordinary inter-State conflicts within a rational choice framework. One of his main conclusions is that when the possibility of sharing a resource, such as a territory, exists, there are always peaceful bargaining possibilities that will dominate incentives for armed conflict outcomes. In this perspective, the only reason for armed conflict between two parties lies in misunderstandings they might have about each other's willingness to resist demands. Such misunderstandings might be corrected by the exchange of clear signals about the resolve to resist. As shown by Fearon, however, the impact of such signals, even if they are relatively costly for the party that sends them, is ambiguous.[15] They can sometimes prevent, but also sometimes enhance, the possibility of armed conflict. This conclusion can also be applied in the other direction, that is, when two States try to bargain to avoid armed conflict and send signals to show a greater willingness to cooperate. To what extent, especially if they are costly for the emitter, can such signals then be interpreted as signs of weakness, or as a willingness to give up essentials? The effect might be the opposite of what is intended. Even low-cost concessions may be difficult to make because of potential misunderstandings, but also because some issues associated with possible concessions tend to acquire symbolic values. This is the case with natural resource questions, because they often come to be associated with what are considered basic attributes of sovereignty. Examples include being independent in food production or water as the basic element of life. This will be the case even if the economic value of these goods is relatively low.

[14] Fearon, James, *Rationalist Explanation for War*, 49 International Organization 3, 379 (1995).

[15] *Id.*

As outlined earlier, we can easily extend some of Fearon's analyses to natural resources to examine if what has been called 'the bargaining model of interstate conflict' also applies. Given that Fearon's perspective on signaling and the resulting considerations about the symbolic aspects of natural resources are clearly relevant, we can expect that water and other environmental goods will present additional problems of conflict resolution. We have already mentioned the fact that first mover advantages are present whenever one has open access to natural resources, and that such disparities are sometimes compounded by geographic (for instance upstream–downstream) or technological inequalities. Therefore, all of a sudden taking advantage of such first mover positions may place current users in a difficult position, giving them the feeling that something that they have had (sometimes for centuries) is taken away from them. The associated bargaining space will therefore be significantly reduced, and conflict therefore becomes more likely. Conflict also can erupt more easily because one party perceives gains that do not necessarily obtain for the other party. An upstream State which constructs a dam to develop water resources in the form of irrigation or power generation, for example, sees the expected gains from the project. The downstream party, on the other hand, will interpret such developments as an irrevocable change that leaves it with a permanent loss.

5. Water resources and conflicts: examples from the Middle East and Central Asia

The Middle East is a particularly striking example of the tensions and open conflicts that can evolve out of competition for vital resources, especially water. Geography and history have shaped the region's basic features, but complex environment–society interactions through time have exacerbated its problems. This interplay between natural and social forces leads us to reflect on general aspects of resource availability and use. The region is semi-arid; Jordan receives 271 mm, Syria 173 mm, and Israel 550 mm of rainfall annually. Moreover, much of this water is lost immediately to evaporation.[16] Water distribution further aggravates these differences and relative scarcities. All these trends lead to a growing deficit in terms of sustainability of water use. This water deficit has seemingly existed since 1985 and continues to this day. World Bank figures for 1999 indicate that Israel (including the West Bank and Gaza) has freshwater withdrawals of 1.7 billion cubic meters, which corresponds to 180 cubic meters per capita per year. Forty-five per cent of this water came from outside Israel proper: 42% is from the Golan Heights and Gaza; the remainder from Lebanon, Jordan, and Syria. This translates into a per capita consumption for Israelis in

[16] Isaac, Jad & Selby, Jan, *The Palestinian Water Crisis—Status, Projections and Potential for Resolution*, 20(1) Natural Resource Forum 17 (1996).

Israel proper of an average of 370 cubic meters per year, while a Palestinian uses 107–156 cubic meters per year and a Jewish settler in the territories uses 650–1,714 cubic meters per year.[17] The last figure in particular highlights the high volumes of water that are used for agriculture. Israel overall uses 64% of its water withdrawals for agriculture; but in terms of land surface Palestinians irrigate roughly 11% of their cultivated lands, while Israel irrigates more than 50% of its cultivated land.[18] In total, then, Israelis use around 483 million cubic meters per year from the West Bank waters, while Palestinians are using only 118 million cubic meters per year of their own waters.

These differences are dramatically illustrated in satellite photographs of the Jordan River system, which show green vegetation on the Israeli side and brown desert in the West Bank, evidence of the inseparability of physical and social components of water resources. In this perspective, resources are the societal definition of environmental goods, and can thus become part of explicit political strategies to strengthen allies and weaken opponents. Hence water resources play a crucial strategic role in the political rivalries between Israel and the Palestinian territories.

From its creation, Israel, like many other countries and irrespective of their geographic conditions, has developed a strong agricultural sector that exports a large part of its production abroad. For Israel, as elsewhere, agriculture has a symbolic dimension, reinforced by its particular history and position within a hostile political environment. Obviously water, which is vital for agriculture in this region, also takes on a deeper importance. Concessions to other potential users are thus not only viewed in economic terms, but become seen as a surrender of sovereignty itself.

The Jordan River basin (see Map 1.1) has a long history of water management problems with political overtones. After the first Arab–Israeli war, Israel decided to promote agriculture, and thus proceeded to install the necessary irrigation facilities. It started the National Water Carrier in 1953, which took water from the Lake of Tiberias in the North to the Negev area in the South. The National Water Carrier carries the flow through open canals, tunnels, and water reservoirs. Allegedly the system also channels water for artificial and underground storage, which means that mostly during the winter, water from the Jordan conduit is recharged into the aquifers in the central region of Israel. This project went on despite heavy protests from Israel's Arab neighbors and almost led to a military conflict. The occupation of the West Bank and the Gaza strip in 1967 gave Israel control over the main aquifers of the region, and some additional pumping and irrigation projects were initiated. These efforts, together with a rise in the standard of living, generated big water consumption increases in Israel.

[17] Gleick, Peter, WATER IN CRISIS (Oxford University Press 1993); Isaac, Jad, et al., 'Water Supply and Demand in Palestine', ARIJ (1994) (unpublished, on file with the Harvard Middle East Water Project).

[18] World Bank, 2001 World Development Indicators.

MAP 1.1. The Jordan River Basin

SOURCE: Map reproduced courtesy of the University of Alabama.

Similar issues plague relations between Turkey and Syria concerning the Euphrates River. The case of the Euphrates presents us with the relatively intractable problem of upstream–downstream use (see Map 1.2). Turkey occupies the upstream position: 88–89% of the total Euphrates River basin flow

Map 1.2: Euphrates and Tigris River Basins with highlighted Kurdish Territories

Source: Map reproduced courtesy of the University of Texas Libraries, the University of Texas at Austin.

originates within its territory. Syria controls only between 11–12% of the water flow, and Iraq none.[19] Because of its dominant position, Turkey has launched a Southeastern Anatolian Water Project (Gêneydogu Anadolu Projesi, or GAP), which has led to the construction of several dams (most notably Keban in 1973, Karakaya in 1987, and Ataturk in 1992). These dams, and the associated agricultural production and power generation, are mostly found in territories dominated by Turkey's Kurdish minority. This has caused resentment because of a massive influx of newcomers. The underlying tension has led to the emergence of separatist movements such as the PKK, a factor that Syria tried to use to its advantage.

Syria feels particularly concerned by these developments because the constructions have had, and continue to have, a significant impact on the Syrian water supply, and Syria has therefore reacted very strongly. Turkey, potentially, would be able to reduce by 70% the volume of water in the Euphrates River, and by 40% that in the Tigris which flows from Turkey to other regions. Given that Syria depends on outside sources for 84% of its water use,[20] this control is a major factor both in the relations between these countries and their domestic opponents, and it shapes their alliances at the international level and determines strategies in regional disputes. The potential for conflict becomes apparent when the opposing positions are quantified. Syria is demanding a flow quota from the Euphrates of at least 700 cubic meters per second, whereas Turkey is willing to grant it at most 500 cubic meters per second. Moreover, the GAP project will not be completed until 2030. By then, the Syrian share could drop to as little as 300 cubic meters per second, because a significant amount of the Euphrates waters will be diverted by the low pressure dams of the GAP project. In addition to these problems about quantity, quality issues will bring additional disagreements. The increased agricultural activity in Southeastern Anatolia has been and will be accompanied by the greater release of pesticides into the Euphrates, and this will in turn affect Syrian access to safe water.

The Euphrates River basin conflict is complicated to resolve because it depends to a large extent on wider regional problems, such as the respective status of the Syrian and Iraqi political system and their relations, as well as on the willingness of the United States to force one of its major allies, Turkey, into a settlement on the water question—an unlikely possibility for the moment. Analyzed in more formal terms, a Chicken or War of Attrition sequence best describes the Euphrates situation in which Turkey's superior position as an upstream power allows it to impose its solution, at least for the moment. Obviously, no country would be satisfied with such an inferior outcome. Syria is thus resorting to other means to pressure Turkey. In this it has adopted two

[19] Daoudy, Marwa, *Entre le Tigre et l'Euphrate: Une négociation en eaux troubles*, LES CAHIERS DE L'ORIENT 44 (4th Trimestre 1996); Güner, Serdar, *The Turkish-Syrian War of Attrition: The Water Dispute*, 20(1) STUDIES IN CONFLICT AND TERRORISM 105 (1997).

[20] World Bank, 2001 World Development Indicators.

types of strategies. On the one hand, it has supported insurrectional movements against Turkey such as the Secret Army for the Liberation of Armenia (ASALA) and, especially, the Partiya Kerkarani Kurdistan (PKK). Under strong military pressure from Turkey, this strategy seems to have been momentarily abandoned. On the other hand, Syria has reasserted its claim over the Sandjak of Alexandretta or Hatay, a formerly Syrian possession that was detached from the French Syrian mandate in 1939 and given to Turkey. In other words, the asymmetric position in which Syria finds itself, leads it on occasion to enlarge the conflict by finding other ways to pressure Turkey, but at the expense of regional security concerns. So far neither country is willing to give in. With the current volatile situation in Iraq, a Syrian–Iraqi coalition against Turkey could emerge, because Iraq is even more harmed by Turkish water policies than Syria. Such a coalition could be effective against Turkey, which might need Iraqi support in conflict with the Kurds.

The Central Asian case is different both in the level of tension and with regard to causal factors. Current tensions are high, but so far there is no overt conflict resembling that of Israel and the Palestinian territories, or strategic coalition building like that between Syrians and Kurdish populations against the Turks. What characterizes the Central Asian case is the evolution of a political structure in which internal relations managed by a strong central authority have become international relations between upstream and downstream countries, where other asymmetries also play an important role (see Map 1.3).

Reports from Central Asia regularly alert the international community to worsening ecological conditions, the dire social and economic status of its population, and the ensuing potential for serious civil and inter-State conflict. The situation is particularly complex and delicate, because familiar problems of over-extensive irrigation agriculture and population increase have become mixed with inter-State politics as a result of the collapse of the USSR, as a consequence of which, 'a very complex water management problem became a very complex *transboundary* water management problem'.[21]

Riverine water resources, especially from the Amu Darya and Syr Darya Rivers, play essential roles in the economy and society of the Central Asian States of Kyrgyzstan, Tajikistan, Turkmenistan, Uzbekistan, and Kazakhstan, all dependent in varying degrees on irrigated crops for survival. Cotton, for example, the most important irrigation crop, is the major source of income and employment in Turkmenistan and Uzbekistan. Its production was encouraged under the Soviet system as a source of hard currency. Over-use of water resources for irrigation is responsible for the drying of the Aral Sea, whose surface and volume have declined by 35% and 58% respectively since the mid-1980s. This water that was used in agriculture was then unavailable to

[21] Veiga da Cunha, Luis, *The Aral Sea Crisis: A Great Challenge in Transboundary Water Resources Management*, NATO Advanced Research Workshop on Transboundary Water Resources Management: Technical and Institutional Issues, Skopelos, Greece, May 1994.

Map 1.3: Central Asia

Source: Map reproduced courtesy of the University of Texas Libraries, the University of Texas at Austin.

upstream countries of Kyrgyzstan and Tajikistan, who rely on hydropower for 50% of their electricity production.

These competing water uses are aggravated by demographic pressures which saw the population grow by 140% between 1959 and 1989,[22] projected to increase between 35% and 50% in most of the States between now and 2050 (see Figure 1.2).[23]

Although tensions over water allocation are not new, they have taken on new significance since the collapse of the Soviet Union. Previously managed from Moscow by a centralized administration, water systems have suddenly come under the control of separate sovereign States that have no history of agreements or coordination structures. This poses important allocation problems because of the nature of water resources and the weakness of new State institutions in the Central Asian republics.

[22] Horsman, Stuart, in Water in Central Asia: Regional Cooperation or Conflict? (Roy Allison and Leana Jonson, eds, 2001), 70.

[23] Population Reference Bureau, 2002 World Population Data Sheet, available at http://www.prb.org/pdf/WorldPopulationDS02_Eng.pdf.

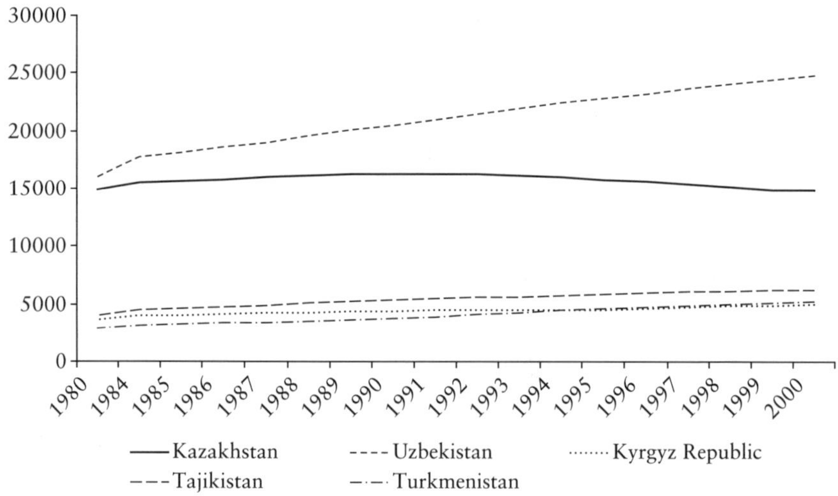

FIGURE 1.2. Central Asia—Population Growth

SOURCE: World Bank Development Indicators, World Bank, 2002.

Indeed, important downstream/upstream issues have emerged since the regions have gained the status of independent republics. Upstream States, Kyrgyzstan and Tajikistan need water for hydroelectric production as well as for irrigation, while Kazakhstan and Uzbekistan use water mostly for irrigation. The upstream republics have held up release of water, or threatened to charge for delivery downstream, in order to pressure downstream users to compensate for energy production forgone when water is released for downstream irrigation. It is important to note that despite their control over the source of water, upstream States are party to allocation schemes that oblige them to provide water downstream.

It is common wisdom that resources whose allocation proves problematic because of the difficulty of assigning clear, unambiguous property rights are generally managed through common or centralized property institutions. This was the case under Soviet rule when the whole region was controlled from Moscow and agriculture, industrial, and energy production were part of national policy. The central State was able to enforce exchanges of water and energy between upstream and downstream users.

At present, the previous patterns are maintained, having been reaffirmed in the Alma Alty agreement of 1992, but they are not perceived to be equitable. The arrangements reflect the favored status that downstream countries had achieved during the Soviet era. Kyrgyzstan and Tajikistan would like to expand irrigation agriculture as well as electricity production. However, even their dominant upstream position does not permit them to achieve their goals because of their political weakness in the face of the downstream users' control over coal

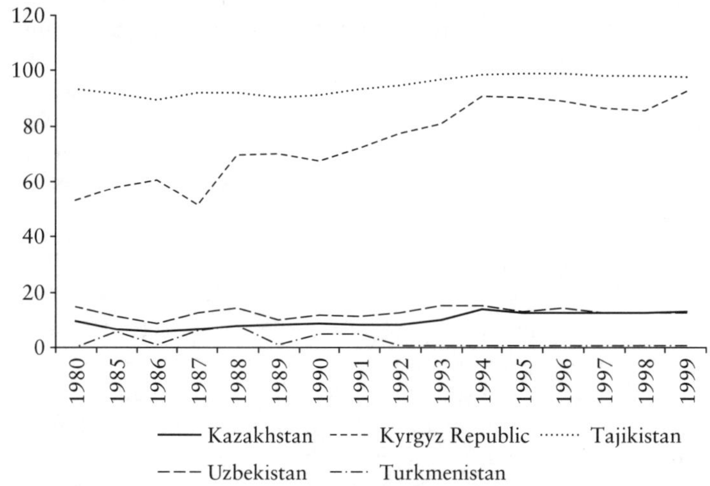

FIGURE 1.3. Central Asia—Electricity Production from Hydroelectric Sources

SOURCE: World Bank Development Indicators, World Bank, 2002.

and gas and the energy produced by these fuels.[24] Indeed, after independence, Uzbekistan and Kazakstan introduced market prices for gas and coal. Kyrgyzstan could not pay these higher prices and its response was to increase electricity production in order to augment revenues. This meant that the amount of water available for downstream irrigation in Uzbekistan and Kazakstan was reduced. As a consequence, agreements were not respected. In breaching their commitments, upstream States thus become vulnerable to reprisals from downstream States, which have refused to provide energy in the form of natural gas and coal in return for water.

The case of Central Asia illustrates two important aspects of water resource allocation. The first is the nature of the asymmetries associated with its allocation. In contrast with the Middle East, various forms of dominance do not overlap but rather cross-cut each other. There is thus no obvious power hierarchy. Upstream republics can control quantities of water sent downstream, but they are subject to reprisals because they do not control other critical resources like gas and coal. The shift from the status of regions in a single State to that of independent republics highlights the weakness of international regimes to regulate transboundary waters. No authority is empowered to impose a distribution system.

However inequitable an upstream/downstream relation may be, it will be stable unless the downstream user has other resources or power with which to

[24] Horsman, Stuart, in WATER IN CENTRAL ASIA: REGIONAL COOPERATION OR CONFLICT? (Roy Allison and Leana Jonson, eds, 2001), 70.

pressure those upstream who control access to water. The asymmetric distribution of resources in the Central Asian republics is just such an example of an unstable relationship between users of a same natural resource with unclear property rights and cross-cutting powers or access. In this case, there is no obvious solution that is both equitable and efficient. Management schemes must therefore be negotiated.

6. Water use as a problem of cooperation and negotiation

Crucial interactions between geographic and climatic aspects of water distribution and the economic and political aspects of its use make competition and conflict a likely outcome in regions where water is scarce and other divisions characterize relations. In order to study the dynamics of these linkages, they have been expressed within a dynamic simulation model adapted to the particular case of the Middle East for the conflict in the Jordan River basin. It allows for the exploration of competition, conflict, and possible cooperation between regions and nations in the context of resource use and allocation, particularly water use. We make the argument that cooperative strategies and conflict resolution schemes can be effective in achieving sustainable water management in this volatile region. The simulation model explicitly represents demographic and economic trends, as well as physical factors affecting water availability, and is able to show that, despite population increase and industrial development leading to increased levels of water use, cooperative strategies can succeed in redistributing resources in a significantly more sustainable way. The model allows also for the representation of a bargaining process based on game theoretical notions. Optimal strategies resulting from such a process can be calculated through the following steps:

(1) Each Middle Eastern region in the Jordan River system, with the exception of Israel, is represented in terms of an industrial (urban) part and a rural traditional part. Israel is represented as an industrial sector only (including its agriculture, which is considered an industrial, modern type of cultivation system).

(2) The agricultural production functions of all the regions specified in the model are influenced directly by water consumption in both the industrial and agricultural regions.

(3) Maximization over time of utility functions, defined as the difference between agricultural production and costs of water consumption (implicit or explicit even if the end consumer is subsidized), is postulated for each region. Each utility function is defined as the difference between agricultural production produced locally minus the total cost of water consumption, defined as the per unit price of water in each region multiplied by physical consumption of local water (imports from the other region are subtracted).

Sequential maximization of the respective utility functions of each region can be achieved in this way.

(4) Limits to water consumption are introduced as the result of a dynamic bargaining process: the regions will progressively agree to maintain their agricultural water consumption within some bounds dependent on the other region's water use.

Maximizing the utility functions defined in point (3) above with respect to the constraints defined by the bargaining process specified in point (4), defines a differential game similar to a sequential or repeated Prisoner's Dilemma game, leading to a Nash solution[25] in which regions will minimize their water use. Our analysis leads to a result which is somewhat similar to the one of the *Folk Theorem*.[26] However, if the regions are too asymmetric in their access to water resources, as in an upstream–downstream relationship, the dynamic bargaining process mentioned above will not work.

Results from this modeling and optimization procedure are outlined in the two graphs in Figure 1.4 for a two-region case. They depict base runs in water consumption in the industrial and marginal regions. The graphs show that cooperative limitation of water consumption will slow down water demand in the industrial region (a). As a consequence, some reserves will be maintained longer and the decrease in water availability in the rural region (b) will be less steep despite increasing drought. These outcomes suggest a sequential response to the water problems in the Middle East and confirm the results presented in Figure 1.4: if Israelis and Palestinians and Jordanians initiate a cooperative approach characterized by voluntary quantitative restriction schemes that could be put into place at a relatively high level by Israel on the one hand and, to a lesser degree, by the Palestinians and Jordanians on the other, a sustainable water resource policy could progressively be established.[27] Such restrictions could make sense initially because the current conflictual relations between the various parties make it difficult to envisage the establishment of rules demanded by more complex schemes, such as the establishment of a water market. This makes the otherwise interesting proposals examined by Franklin Fisher,[28] about trading water, problematic, at least for the moment. After some cooperative moves are initiated, such as voluntary restraint measures, water-trading schemes such as the one he develops can improve the positions of participants significantly. However, either the general political climate must evolve, or small cooperative

[25] A *Nash equilibrium* corresponds to an outcome from which no participant has an unilateral incentive to withdraw. It is often not the Pareto optimal outcome of a social interaction. Moreover, several *Nash equilibria* might exist for a given interaction. However, here, the Nash equilibrium corresponds to a Pareto optimal outcome because both parties can retaliate.

[26] Fudenberg, Drew & Tirole, Jean, Game Theory (MIT Press 1992).

[27] The Palestinians and Jordanians consume significantly less water.

[28] Fisher, Franklin, *The Economics of Water Dispute Resolution*, Project Evaluation and Management: An Application to the Middle East Water Resources Development 11, 4 (1995).

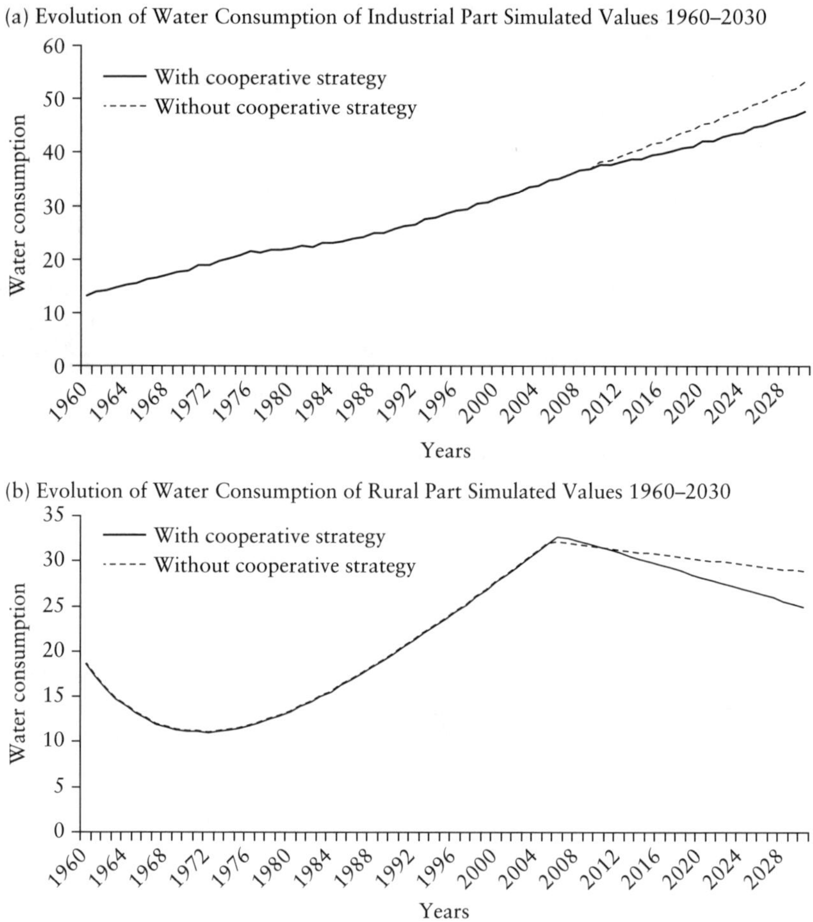

FIGURE 1.4. Achieving Sustainable Water Management through Cooperative Strategies

SOURCE: World Bank Development Indicators, World Bank, 2002.

endeavors in a single sector (like voluntary restraints in the water sector) must be put in place before a fully-fledged water market could be envisaged.

Elsewhere, we have examined the bargaining conditions necessary for the successful negotiation of an agreement in which parties would accept voluntary restraints on their water consumption while maintaining a goal of maximizing agricultural production,[29] and present the details of this methodology in the various appendices. It is worth mentioning that the bargaining analysis results presented in Figure 1.4 imply that mutual restrictions hold, despite trends that

[29] Luterbacher, Urs & Wiegandt, Ellen, *Social dimensions of resource use: The freshwater case*, 1(4) SWISS POL. SCI. REV. 131 (1995).

could otherwise offset them, such as population or agricultural production increases.

In particular, our approach allows us to compare the merits of three proposed solutions to the Jordan River basin problems. These solutions are not necessarily exclusive of each other:

(1) Water could be traded between areas according to market mechanisms. This is a solution that has been proposed by Fisher[30] and Schechter.[31] However, standard results concerning market equilibria show that market mechanisms and trading might lead to inefficient and environmentally damaging outcomes when property rights are ill defined, absent, or difficult to establish, as in the case of externalities associated with common pool resources (refer to the beginning of the chapter and the discussion of commons).[32] Also, since trading concerns a vital common pool resource, a certain degree of trust[33] must prevail between the various participants to such a process, in particular as far as the establishment of clear-cut property rights is concerned. Quite clearly, once trust is established and rights and obligations are clearly set, trade in water between regions constitutes an attractive solution to water shortages.

(2) Technological solutions could enhance water supply. Various schemes have been proposed, ranging from pipelines from Turkey to desalination of sea water. All of them are very expensive.

(3) The voluntary quantitative restriction schemes presented above could be introduced. These have the advantage of being (a) relatively inexpensive, (b) not too demanding in terms of institutional arrangements, in that they would require a minimal number of formal agreement structures, and (c) not too complex as an initial step.

Therefore, the common pool problem that characterizes use of water resources requires a set of rules for their use, even in peaceful situations, to prevent over-extraction by some users at the expense of others since, in the absence of regulation, each individual has an incentive to over-use common pool resources.[34] Developing such rules in conflictual situations poses additional problems. Cooperative strategies and conflict resolution schemes can nevertheless be elaborated, and can be effective in such instances.

[30] Fisher, Franklin, *The Economics of Water Dispute Resolution*, Project Evaluation and Management: An Application to the Middle East Water Resources Development 11, 4 (1995).

[31] Schecter, Mordechai, Becker, N., and Zeitouni, N., *Reallocating Water Resources in the Middle East through Market Mechanisms*, 12(1) Water Resources Dev. 17 (1996).

[32] Coase, Ronald, *The Problem of Social Cost*, 3 Journal of Law and Economics 1 (1960); Chichilnisky, Graciela, *North-South Trade and the Global Environment*, 84(4) American Economic Review 851 (1994).

[33] The importance of this factor should not be exaggerated, however. One must note that the existence of Hong Kong always depended on the supply of water from Communist China.

[34] This is the 'tragedy of the commons' described by Hardin: Hardin, Garrett, *The Tragedy of the Commons*, 162 Science 1243 (1968).

In a multi-country situation, common resources may be used by several populations or labor forces. If countries try to maximize their surplus independently of each other, they will each end up in a suboptimal position. It should be noted that if countries act in isolation, they will ignore each other's extraction efforts in their maximization calculations. Such behavior reduces each country's long-term surplus, since its management occurs without considering the other country's actions. It is quite clear that an agreement between all of them would improve the utility of all parties. Establishing extraction quotas or a pricing scheme that would put countries' surpluses above their purely competitive values, for example, would eliminate each country's negative externality. This situation is a kind of Prisoner's Dilemma, because to extract more than the other who obeys the agreement increases the surplus and, therefore, the utility of the over-extracting country above the agreement level. If, however, as in Prisoner's Dilemma situations, retaliatory strategies exist and are in the interest of parties to implement when other parties cheat, a cooperative scheme can be maintained and improved upon over time. This can occur even in the face of population or resource trends that would seem to threaten the existence of the agreement. In the case of the Middle East and the Jordan River basin, we have shown that such strategies leading to the maintenance of a cooperative arrangement are possible and could be implemented. Central Asia is, as previously noted, a more difficult case to solve because of the upstream–downstream relations among the different republics. However, the asymmetry is not as pronounced as between Turkey and Syria, where the relationship is accentuated by economic, demographic, and military disparities. In Central Asia the asymmetry in access to waters could be compensated by industrial and agricultural developments that could in the end benefit all countries concerned.

In general, therefore, voluntary restraint strategies can work because they depend on decisions by regional or national authorities implicated in the problem. They do not imply commitments to complex institutional settings such as markets, which might be quasi-irrevocable, but appear more open to renegotiation. Moreover, they tend to de-emphasize symbolic signaling effects attached to water issues in terms of sovereignty, since sovereignty is formally maintained. This approach can therefore be considered a good starting strategy to improve difficult relations and to mark a first step in mastering scarcities at a transboundary level. The only drawback is that such strategies work less well for the completely asymmetric situations characterized by upstream–downstream positions. In this case, we have emphasized the negative aspects and the potential for conflict enlargement because of detrimental spillover effects. We find such cases in the Syrian strategy of supporting Turkish opposition movements, or the interruption of the delivery of fossil fuels in Central Asia. There might also be favorable spillover effects, where two countries or regions could share in the advantages created by the development of water resources in one region by specializing in complementary activities. This might consist of developing industry in the area less suitable for agricultural development and taking advantage of the cheaper electric power made available by dam construction in an upstream country. This dam development need not be limited to run of river low-pressure constructions. High altitude countries can develop the kind of high-pressure dams known in the Alpine areas, which are much less harmful for the downstream regions. These also have the advantage of providing large amounts of electric power under peak load conditions. They can then serve the industrial needs of firms located relatively far away from their particular location, and thus be useful beyond the boundaries of a given country. Central Asia could be an example of such cooperation in power generation. The high altitude but relatively poor countries of Kyrgyzstan and Tadjikistan could benefit from such schemes. In these cases, existing international organizations such as the World Bank would be appropriate institutions to devise policies that favor such positive spillovers, and thus help to resolve otherwise intractable asymmetric water conflicts.

7. Conclusion

We have suggested that freshwater use generates many complex interactions among various users. Often such situations lead to water conflicts. These water-based conflicts themselves have the power to escalate because they often become enmeshed with other confrontations and acquire symbolic weight, which makes them even more difficult to solve. An important part of the problem comes from the link between water and agriculture. Agricultural production is by far the biggest user of fresh water. In certain regions, agricultural production would be impossible without a substantial amount of irrigation. Even in places where some cultivation is feasible, crops are produced that could not grow without important fresh water inputs. This occurs because farmers often use water that is subsidized, or the costs of which are improperly calculated, artificially lowering production expenses. Agriculture prevails in regions with scarce water resources for reasons of national sovereignty and autonomy of food production, and because of the political strength of agricultural lobbies. This position is contested more and more as competition among sectors and regions intensifies. In recent years, traditional agricultural water use is in competition with water requirements for power generation. Upstream–downstream positions tend to accentuate this competition, which can lead to shortages, and thus increasingly to trans-boundary resources conflicts. Attempting to solve water shortages and disputes via trading schemes will not necessarily be effective because property rights in water are often difficult to define and thus to attribute, both in pool type and in upstream–downstream river situations. An essential precondition for markets is the clear and unambiguous definition of property rights to the goods to be traded. Informal and voluntary arrangements might be better suited to such situations, but we previously suggested that while mutual voluntary usage restrictions might work quite well as conflict resolution schemes in shared pool conditions, they are more difficult to implement in upstream–downstream situations. In the latter cases, a new organization of production processes, with redistribution of benefits resulting from a better use of comparative advantages of regions, might also be effective.

More generally, the close association between agriculture and irrigation needs further investigation. Agricultural production should be primarily organized in regions that are most suitable for it. These include those with high rainfall, or those that benefit from the availability of natural pools such as large fresh water lakes that are easily replenished. Countries should also begin to realize that agricultural and food self-sufficiency are no longer necessarily indispensable goals. Good access to transportation might be just as important these days. Therefore, the cheapest way to organize a water trade would consist of importing food and other agricultural products. This would liberate water in arid regions to meet needs in the domestic, industrial, and tourism sectors. However, the path to achieve these goals is fraught with obstacles and likely to be long and complex. It will take considerable time to persuade governments and populations that regional food security can be achieved through exchanges with more productive regions elsewhere. And indeed, the current political and economic landscape makes such goals a utopian vision. There are nevertheless small steps that can be taken at present. It is important to understand current water uses and the factors that influence them, to develop predictors of future availability under conditions of climate change, to evaluate the present legal framework that regulates transboundary use, and to evaluate the effectiveness of certain circumscribed initiatives to foster cooperation and exchange. These issues will be addressed in the chapters to follow.

2

Water Transfers: A Means to Achieve Sustainable Water Use

A. DAN TARLOCK

1. Introduction: From Supply Augmentation to Reallocation

The United States and many other countries are entering a new era of water allocation: environmentally sustainable water use.[1] This standard is not a simple river preservation concept because any national water policy must accommodate a wide range of sustainable, non-wasteful consumptive uses.[2] It is a more complex standard that recognizes that it is no longer possible to meet new demands for consumptive and non-consumptive uses by relying exclusively on the historic solution to increased water demand, supply augmentation through the construction of large, new carry-over storage reservoirs[3] and trans-basin diversions which bring water from areas of origin to more arid areas of demand. The case for large dams and trans-basin diversions has been partially undermined by the potential impact of global climate change on water resources, the report of the World Commission on Dams,[4] and the increased worldwide emphasis on the restoration of ecosystem degradation caused by the large-scale modification of the hydrologic regimes of rivers and lakes during the previous century. Thus, it will often be necessary to reallocate existing supplies.

[1] There are many definitions of sustainable water use. All agree that it must include an environmental protection component. A leading United States student of water policy, Peter Gleick, posits that sustainable water management must include (1) a human right to the minimum amount of water to sustain human health, (2) the recognition of the need for water to maintain and restore ecosystems, (3) the decreased reliance on structural solutions such as supply augmentation, (4) the application of efficiency principles to water use, (5) the more efficient design of new water supply and distribution systems, and (6) increased NGO and stakeholder participation in decision making. Peter H. Gleick, *The Changing Water Paradigm: A Look at Twenty-First Century Water Resources Development*, 25 Water International 127, 131 (2000).

[2] This definition of sustainability was endorsed by the Western Water Policy Review Advisory Commission. Water in the West: Challenge for the Next Century 32–33 (1998).

[3] *See* Water Science and Technology Board, National Academy of Sciences/National Research Council, Water Transfers in the West: Equity, Efficiency, and the Environment (1992).

[4] World Commission on Dams, Dams and Development: A New Framework for Decision-Making (2000). *See* generally A. Dan Tarlock, *What the Report of the World Commission on Dams Might Mean for the United States Water Community*, 5 U. Denver Water Law Rev. 225 (2001).

The end of the river basin development era means that in the future the competition for water resources will become more rather than less intense. Rapidly growing cities are competing with irrigated agriculture for limited supplies, and environmental interests are competing with all major consumptive uses, as well as the hydroelectric power industry, for increased in-stream flows or more 'natural' hydrologic regimes.[5] The possibility that the 'greenhouse' effect will alter traditional snow pack and run off patterns adds an additional element of uncertainty to the competition. In many areas, run offs may occur earlier in the year, and increased evaporation will decrease available supplies and base flows during periods of peak summer demand.[6]

The net result of the shift to reallocation is to increase the need for water transfers, especially from existing to new uses, to meet new demands caused by continued population growth and the rise of new societal values, primarily environmental protection. Most modern transfers will move water relatively short distances. They will not be massive interregional and international schemes which were often proposed by visionary engineers and politicians in the past. Nonetheless, many of these transfers will be extremely controversial because they threaten to disrupt established economic and cultural patterns, stress ecosystems,[7] and raise long-standing fears about the monopolization of water.[8] Transfers, broadly defined, have long been part of water law and policy. Today, they are becoming more controversial because they are increasing in number, and we care more about their third party impacts as well as the broader societal impacts than we once did.[9] The most controversial transfers are those that remove water from the watershed of origin, or shift water from agriculture use to urban and environmental uses. This chapter examines the pros and cons of transfers and the law that governs the transfer process. At the present time, neither the United States federal government nor any of the individual federal states has a uniform approach to the assessment of proposed transfers. Instead, we rely on markets which are both encouraged by piecemeal promotion laws and checked by uncoordinated assessment laws, as well as on the political

[5] *See* ICUN, FLOW: THE ESSENTIALS OF ENVIRONMENTAL FLOWS (Megan Dyson, Ger Bergkamp, and John Scalon eds, 2003).

[6] Office of Technology Assessment, PREPARING FOR AN UNCERTAIN FUTURE: SUMMARY 32 (1993). Subsequent scenarios based on new research and modeling are consistent with this basic prediction.

[7] The California rice industry in the Central Valley illustrates the third party impact problem. In the past decade, the rice industry has become an 'eco-friendly' industry by combining rice farming with the maintenance of a large amount of bird habitat. However, rice growers only use about 70% of their state water entitlements and sell some of the surplus water to southern California. Environmentalists are concerned that further transfers, which would require land fallowing, could jeopardize the existing wildlife habitat. Seth Hettena, *State's Rice Farmers Evolve From Foe to Friend*, Associated Press, December 12, 2003.

[8] WATER HEIST, HOW CORPORATIONS ARE CASHING IN ON CALIFORNIA'S WATER, available at www.citizen.org/california/water/heist.

[9] For example, WATER HEIST, *supra* note 8, argues that a large water bank in the Southern San Joaquin Valley is being used to support both corporate agriculture and continued urban sprawl in southern California.

process. Some states have addressed specific barriers to transfers, such as the legal status of water saved through conservation,[10] and we use a variety of water, environmental, and common law theories as 'handles' to assess the consequences of transfers, particularly interregional ones. In some cases, such as the Great Lakes, we have developed a special legal regime for selected large transfers with high perceived environmental and social costs.[11]

2. Water transfers: pros and cons

2.1 What is a water transfer?

The term 'water transfer' is a generic term, but it has become a value-laden one because of concerns about the social and environmental costs of many transfers. A water transfer can refer either to the acquisition of new entitlements, or to the reallocation of existing ones that result in the movement of water from the watershed of origin or the place of original use to a more distant location. In popular parlance, the term is also often used interchangeably with water marketing, but marketing technically refers only to the sale or donation of an exiting entitlement.[12] Water law has traditionally referred to the initial removal of water from a stream or lake for use within or outside the watershed of origin as a withdrawal or diversion, and has reserved the term 'transfer' for changes in use or point of use of an existing entitlement. This chapter uses the broad term 'transfer' to include any movement of water; from an international pipeline, to the sale of water from an agricultural district to a nearby growing urban area. It discusses a variety of controversial movements of water, with an emphasis on the sale of existing entitlements for new uses.

Two recent transfers, one proposed and one in the process of implementation, illustrate the controversies that modern transfers can raise. In 1998, a company proposed to extract 160 million gallons of water from Lake Superior, the purest of the Great Lakes, and ship it in bulk to Asia.[13] The proposal triggered a bi-national review of water diversions from the Great Lakes.[14] The transfer died after fierce objections about its cumulative impacts. The debate is an example of an 'area of origin' objection which was raised to protect the integrity of an aquatic ecosystem. The recently concluded political deal to shift a large block of

[10] California Water Code §§ 1010–1111 (1991). [11] See notes 62 to 73, *infra*.

[12] In 1994, a coalition of business interests prepared a Model Water Transfer Act for California. Section 202 stated that the Act applied to 'voluntary changes in surface water rights, voluntary transfers of surface rights, and voluntary transfer of water'. The Act and commentary can be found in 4 Hastings West-Northwest J. Envir. L. and Policy, No. 1 (1996).

[13] *See* Mark Squillace & Sandra Zellmer, *Managing Interjurisdictional Waters Under the Great Lakes Charter Annex*, 18 Natural Resources & Environment 8 (No. 2, Fall 2003).

[14] International Joint Commission, Final Report to the Governments of Canada and the United States, Protection of the Waters of the Great Lakes (2000), available at http://www.ijc.org/boards/cde=finalreport/finalreport.html.

water dedicated to irrigated agriculture from the Imperial Valley in southern California to urban Los Angeles and San Diego, is an example of a shift of use transfer which was concluded only after a wide range of social and environmental third party impacts in the original place of use were addressed.[15]

2.2 Why water markets

a. The case for markets

The increasing reliance on water markets to meet societal water demands can be traced to an influential 1973 Report of the National Water Commission,[16] which argued that the 'ur'norm of all water use should be the principle of economic efficiency. The Report applied the sustained criticism advanced by neoclassical economists, that market allocation is almost always superior to the government allocation of scarce resources.

The basic idea behind current water reallocation policy is that the market rather than water administrators (bureaucrats) should determine the comparative value of alternative water uses. From an economic perspective, water is simply another commodity to be bought and sold with the lowest possible transaction costs. Economists have long argued that too much water is devoted to low value uses and thus water allocation patterns are inefficient. The difference between the value of water for irrigated agriculture and alternative uses remains the primary economic rationale for water marketing. A 1996 United States National Academy of Sciences/National Research Council report explains the marginal position of irrigation concisely: '[t]he value of water in agriculture is generally less than in industrial and municipal uses ... [and] [b]ecause it is so expensive to develop additional water supplies, only the higher-value water uses are likely to be justified economically'.[17]

Until the past twenty years, water marketing was primarily a theoretical policy prescription to move water from low to high value uses.[18] Both cities and farmers were opposed to transfers, or preferred not to use them. In the mid-1980s, the idea of water marketing was endorsed by some mainline environmental groups as a means to two ends: stopping new dams and restoring minimum flows in stressed stream systems.[19] However, until the early 1990s, the logical proponents of water marketing, urban water suppliers in places like

[15] *See* notes 80 to 82, *infra*.

[16] Water Policies for the Future: Final Report of the National Water Commission 260–70 (1973).

[17] Committee on the Future Demands of Irrigation in the Face of Competing Demands, Water Science and Technology Board, National Research Council/National Academy of Sciences, A New Era for Irrigation 67 (1996).

[18] L. Hartman & D. Seastone, Water Transfers (1970); National Water Commission, Water Policies for the Future 260–61 (1973).

[19] Zach Willey, Economic Development and Environmental Quality in California's Water System (Institute of Governmental Studies, 1985).

California, rejected the idea because it would erode powerful political coalitions forged with irrigated agriculture for subsidized water projects. But, as the federal government has retreated from its traditional role of backstopping water rights by constructing large carry-over storage reservoirs, urban water suppliers have been forced to accept marketing. Ironically, the legacy of this subsidized water development makes sophisticated marketing physically possible in many places. Buyers and sellers can use a combination of natural river channels and canals to transport water long distances at competitive costs.

Transfers are likely to increase because water politics are very different in the 21st century than they were for much of the 20th century. Up to the mid-1970s, federal and state water agencies and the major water users controlled the water agenda, but this is no longer the case. This tight control depended on the politics of distribution practiced by the federal government and a few states such as California. The politics of distribution led to the 'pure doctrine of river basin management', which posited the need to construct and manage comprehensively planned, integrated federal projects (dams, reservoirs, and canals) on the nation's large rivers to promote regional development.[20] Proponents of comprehensive watershed and river basin planning assumed that large-scale water resources projects were necessary to promote the efficient (non-wasteful) use of water through multiple-purpose projects which would provide widespread benefits to the nation. During the 'Big Dam Era',[21] transfers played a limited role because supply augmentation was the norm to meet new demands. Federal largesse is now shrinking. The downward trend of Bureau of Reclamation and Corps of Engineers[22] budgets has been constant in both Republican and Democratic administrations and Congresses for over three decades.

The shrinking fiscal support for water development and the devolution of federal power have created a more fluid water policy environment. Neither

[20] *See* John Krutilla & Otto Eckstein, MULTIPLE PURPOSE RIVER BASIN DEVELOPMENT (1958).

[21] The 'Big Dam Era' refers to the 1930s through 1960s, when the construction of large, multiple purpose dams and reservoirs was a national political priority. The best example was the construction of six mainstem dams on the Missouri River. *See* John R. Ferrell, THE BIG DAM ERA: A LEGISLATIVE AND INSTITUTIONAL HISTORY OF THE PICK-SLOAN MISSOURI BASIN PROGRAM (1993).

[22] The federal Bureau of Reclamation and the United States Army Corps of Engineers are the two major federal water resources development and management agencies. For historical reasons, there is no single ministry of water or a single federal agency. Instead, there are two major federal agencies that often compete for the exclusive right to construct and operate a project. The Corps of Engineers, which traces its origins to the Revolutionary War, brought the French idea of large-scale military public works to the United States and applied them first to navigation improvement and later to flood control. The Corps constructs multiple purposes projects, primarily for flood control and navigation enhancement, throughout the country. *See* Beatrice H. Holmes, A HISTORY OF FEDERAL WATER RESOURCES PROJECTS, 1800–1960 (U.S. Dept. Of Agriculture, Misc. Pub. No. 1233, 1972). In the 1890s, proponents of the settlement of arid and semi-arid areas of the United States urged that the West develop as an irrigation society. By the beginning of the 20th century, it became clear that private capital and state support would not induce the desired level of irrigated acreage. In 1902, Congress passed the Reclamation Act of 1902, which provided federal support for irrigation projects. The best histories are Donald Pisani, TO RECLAIM A DIVIDED WEST: WATER, LAW AND PUBLIC POLICY, 1848–1902 (1992) and WATER, LAND, LAW IN THE WEST: THE LIMITS OF PUBLIC POLICY (1996). The Bureau's authority is limited to the 17 Western states.

irrigated agriculture nor municipal water suppliers will be able to control the policy agenda as they did in the past. Power is now more diffused, and the institutions that have managed and allocated this country's water resources are less able to perform their historic function of mediating competing demands for water and buffering all major uses against the vagaries of climate. All old and new interests or stakeholders now demand a seat in the multiparty bargaining processes that characterize many allocation conflicts, and have undermined the old idea of static water plans which were often project construction blueprints or wish lists.[23] The federal agencies have responded by changing their missions from project construction to management. The Bureau of Reclamation has formally changed its mission from water development to water management, and budget priorities reflect this change.[24] The United States Army Corps of Engineers is undergoing a similar but more complex and uneven transition, and is pinning its hopes for future survival on playing a large role in restoring degraded aquatic ecosystems.[25]

b. The case against water markets

Two primary objections have been raised against water markets. The first asserts that water marketing is sound in theory, but there are many legal institutional barriers which increase the transaction costs of such transfers. Thus, water markets will not deliver the promised new supplies. The second asserts that water marketing is immoral. Water marketing advocates argue that reduced transaction costs will promote more transfers. Proposals to reduce the transaction costs of transfers include streamlining existing processes and creating incentives to conserve and transfer the saved water.[26] However, studies indicate that the transaction costs are low enough to support many transfers. A major study of water transfers in six states concludes that—with the exception of lawyer-dominated Colorado—the current transaction costs of water transfers are not excessive.[27]

The coldly rational economic view of water is vigorously opposed by a wide variety of people, from present users, especially farmers,[28] to some NGOs.

[23] Highly water stressed states such as New Mexico have begun the difficult process of confronting the question of whether reliable, available supplies pose real limits to future growth. *See* Lora Lucero & A. Dan Tarlock, *Water Supply and Urban Growth in New Mexico: Same Old, Same Old, or New Era*, 43 NAT. RES. J. 803 (2003).

[24] *See* United States Bureau of Reclamation, RECLAMATION'S STRATEGIC PLAN: A LONG-TERM FRAMEWORK FOR WATER RESOURCES MANAGEMENT, DEVELOPMENT AND PROTECTION (June, 1992).

[25] *See* National Research Council, U.S. ARMY CORPS OF ENGINEERS WATER RESOURCES PLANNING: A NEW OPPORTUNITY FOR SERVICE (2004).

[26] ORE. REV. STAT. § 537.455(2) (1993). *See* Larry J. MacDonnell, *Transferring Water Uses in the West*, 43 OKLA. L. REV. 119 (1990).

[27] Larry J. MacDonnell, THE WATER TRANSFER PROCESS AS A MANAGEMENT OPTION FOR MEETING CHANGING DEMANDS (Natural Resources Law Center, University of Colorado School of Law, 1990).

[28] The position of farmers varies, often depending on the scale of the transfer and the crop raised. For some farmers, it is a source of supplemental income; but for others, water transfers are an exit

The objection rejects the premise that water is just another commodity and asserts that it is not even a mere commodity but a resource with higher, transcendent, generally community values.[29] In arid regions, control of water means political power, and power is not something that is ever surrendered with low transaction costs. For this reason, reallocation decisions are becoming more complex, because non-water right holders are increasingly and successfully asserting a greater stake in water appropriation and transfer proceedings than they have in the past. These claimants generally represent community or environmental interests.[30]

Many water rights transfers remove water from agricultural use and dedicate it to urban use. Many communities object to being de-watered and to the consequent loss of political and economic power and viability that follows, as well as to the erosion of the rural way of life. Water law has traditionally provided little protection for these communities beyond the political process, but this process has proved increasingly successful, even after reapportionment, and communities have achieved direct legislative protection for their interests. Nostalgia for a mythic past is a powerful political weapon worldwide. These community interests will be asserted in the courts as well. In response to such concerns, a number of *ad hoc* mechanisms are being included in the water transfer process to address and mitigate environmental and social equity issues.

3. The law of water rights with special emphasis on transfers

The law of water rights both promotes and retards transfers. Water rights are a form of property rights, and thus the general presumption of free alienability applies. However, water rights are different from land and other forms of property; they reflect a web of connected interests that often makes it hard to move water away from the watershed of origin.[31] Water rights are correlative rather than exclusive property rights; a user's right to use the resource is a function of the impact of the use on other uses. Two mature water rights systems, administered by the 50 states, exist in the United States due to the wide climatic variability of her land mass. In addition, federal water rights

strategy for an economic activity that is no longer viable. *See* e.g., *Farmers Turning Into Water Brokers: Tracy at Forefront of Growing Trend*, San Joaquin Record, December 28, 2003.

[29] *See* e.g., Eric Freyfogle, *Water Rights and the Common Wealth*, 26 Envtl. L. 27 (1996).

[30] *See* Joseph L. Sax, *Understanding Transfers: Community Rights and the Privatization of Water*, 1 Hastings West-Northwest J. Envir. L. and Policy 13 (1994) and Santos Gomez & Penn Loh, *Communities and Water Markets: A Review of the Model Transfer Act*, 4 Hastings West-Northwest J. Envir. L. and Policy 63 (1996).

[31] *See* Craig Anthony Arnold, *The Reconstruction of Property: Property as a Web of Interests*, 26 Harv. Envtl. L. Rev. 281 (2002).

exist to promote social equity for Native American Tribes and to protect the public lands.[32]

State systems were developed to promote the consumptive use of water through the construction of both small and large-scale diversion projects and reservoirs. The East adopted the common law of riparian rights. The common law limits the right to use water to those who own land which touches a stream. The West rejected the common law as unsuited to an arid rather than humid climate, and replaced it with the doctrine of prior appropriation. Prior appropriation created relatively certain rights to a fixed quantity of water and provided a high degree of security for early users. During droughts, the most recent or junior rights can be curtailed to ensure the older 'senior' water holders receive their full right. There is no equitable sharing as there can be under the common law.[33] In addition, water may be used outside the watershed of origin. Much has been made of the differences between the two systems, but in reality they share a common characteristic that makes large-scale transfers both legally and politically difficult. They both assume that water would be perpetually used close to its watershed of origin or place of initial use.

3.1 The common law of riparian rights

The common law of water rights is conventionally characterized as a land-based water allocation system which limits water use to land adjacent to a stream system. A riparian right is a natural usufructuary property right to use a portion of the flow of a watercourse; riparian rights are limited to the ownership of land which abuts a stream.[34] Riparian rights are correlative because the reasonableness of a use is a function of its impact on other users. Historically, the core idea of riparianism was that in situ uses are the norm and ex situ ones the exception.[35] For example, a riparian originally had a right only to make use of the natural flow. Thus, all consumptive uses, as opposed to non-consumptive

[32] These rights were first recognized by the United States Supreme Court in Winters v. United States, 207 U.S. 564 (1908) (water for irrigation impliedly reserved when reservation created to turn Indians into 'civilized' pastoral people). These rights were originally limited to on-reservation uses, but in recent years Congress has enacted a series of laws settling reserved right claims for individual reservations. These settlements often allow water marketing subject to various conditions. *See* A. Dan Tarlock et al., WATER RESOURCE MANAGEMENT: A CASEBOOK IN LAW AND PUBLIC POLICY 898–902 (5th edn 2002).

[33] In practice, there is often no sharing under the common law of riparian rights. *See* Edmondson v. Edwards, 111 S.W.3d 906, 910 (Mo.App.S.D. 2003) (injunction against an upstream recreational dam which dried up a stream used by downstream riparian for livestock watering because '[t]he use to which [the upstream] defendants sought to put the stream was not reasonable in that it diverted the natural watercourse on defendant's property to the exclusion of its long-standing use on plaintiff's property.').

[34] *See* Roberts v. Martin, 77 S.E. 535 (W. Va. 1913) ('The right exists *jure naturae* as parcel of the land.').

[35] *See* Lynda Butler, *Allocating Consumptive Water Rights in a Riparian Jurisdiction: Defining the Relationship Between Public and Private Interests*, 47 U. PITT. L. REV. 95 (1987).

ones such as mill power, were per se illegal. In addition, the watershed rule limited uses to those within a stream's watershed to protect downstream users by guaranteeing them return flows.

Over time, the common law has become less rigid, but it still remains a land-based law of water allocation. The common law has been modified by judicial decisions and legislation to allow water to be used consumptively, and in some cases away from the river corridor when there is no substantial injury to other users.[36] Today, almost no states follow the natural flow theory.[37] It has been replaced by a judicially administered reasonable use, or by regulated riparianism which is a de facto priority rule. The modern reasonable rule is an open-ended balancing test, similar to the test used to determine if a land use is a common law nuisance, which, in theory, permits the weighing of the comparative utilities of inconsistent uses to determine how what will be shared. In practice, courts generally find the balancing test too incoherent or unfair; instead, they often choose to protect the prior user.[38]

The watershed rule is also being replaced by tort rules that focus on the injury, if any, caused by use outside the watershed. The rule was eroded by two important Supreme Court precedents. The Court first held that there is no watershed limitation in the rule of equitable apportionment which allocates the right to use inter-state rivers among riparian states. Thus, a state can use its fair share of a river for a trans-basin diversion.[39] Iowa Hydro-Electric Cooperative v. Federal Power Commission (FPC)[40] held that the Federal Power Act impliedly preempted state water law, and thus Iowa could not apply a watershed protection statute to bar an FPC licensee from making a trans-watershed diversion.

[36] E.g. Pyle v. Gilbert, 265 S.E.2d 584 (Ga. 1980). However, the watershed rule continues to surface in new contexts. In 1994, Florida created a commission to review its water management law, which has liberal trans-basin transfer rules. Water-rich counties convinced the commission to recommend to the legislature that local sources be favored. Before a trans-basin diversion could be authorized, the water management district with authority to authorize the transfer would have to consider the proximity of the source to the proposed destination and the availability of alternative sources of water. Two commentators have characterized the recommendation as 'a partial revival of the common law rule that prohibited the diversion of water to use on nonriparian lands'. Marcia Penman Parker & Sally Bond Man, *Water Management: Mission Impossible?*, 70 Florida Bar J. 20, 28 n. 9 (1996).

[37] There is no right to the natural flow under the reasonable use theory. Recreational use and a limited right to view are reasonable uses but, to prevail against other users, a riparian must prove that there has been a total destruction of the use. City of Los Angeles v. Aitken, 52 P.2d 585 (Cal.App. 1935), *hearing denied* (loss of view). Under the reasonable use theory, a riparian may not claim a right to the natural or uninterrupted or unaltered flow for recreation use or view. Dunlap v. North Carolina Power & Light, 195 S.E. 43 (N.C. 1938); Intracoastal North Condominium Ass'n v. Palm Beach County, 698 So.2d 384 ((Fla.App. 1997), *review denied*, 703 A.2d 746 (Fla. 1997); Application of Buttolph, 527 A.2d 1147 (Vt. 1987). But see Alburger v. Philadelphia Electric Co., 535 A.2d 729 (Pa. Commw. Ct. 1988).

[38] Jacob Beuscher, *Appropriation Water Law Elements in Riparian Doctrine States*, 10 Buffalo L. Rev. 448 (1961).

[39] Connecticut v. Massachusetts, 282 U.S. 660 (1931).

[40] 328 U.S. 152 (1946). The result was foreshadowed in Phillips v. Guy F. Atkinson Co., 313 U.S. 508 (1941), which held that Congress could construct a multi-purpose reservoir with disproportionate benefits to the downstream rather than upstream state.

More recently, some states have replaced per se prohibitions on trans-watershed or basin diversions with statutes that permit diversions after a rigorous review of the need for the transfer and of its environmental impacts. However, many states do not have a formal procedure in place, and thus transfers are challenged both in the political process and through the invocation of state and federal environmental laws.[41]

3.2 Prior appropriation

The arid and semi-arid western states rejected the common law as unsuited to the promotion of mining and irrigation economies in the arid West and replaced it with the doctrine of prior appropriation.[42] Prior appropriation rests on three foundational principles:

(1) priority;
(2) the separation of entitlements from land ownership; and
(3) the requirement that the right to use water depends on its continuous application to beneficial use.

The common law watershed limitation was rejected because it prevented the movement of water to areas of demand. Equitable sharing was also rejected because it provided insufficient protection for investments in water diversion systems.

Prior appropriation can be understood as a drought risk management system.[43] It creates quasi-exclusive property rights which allow all available resources to be used to the point of exhaustion wherever they can be transported. The western states ultimately had to accept more regulation of entitlements and posited that water was not owned by individuals but by the state in trust for the public. State ownership normally asserts:

(1) that water rights are limited to the privilege to use water as opposed to individual ownership of streams and aquifers;
(2) that access to water requires state permission in the form of a permit or license;[44] and

[41] *See* Joesph L. Sax et al., LEGAL CONTROL OF WATER RESOURCES 63–76 (2000) for examples of such conflicts and law suits.

[42] The leading case is Coffin v. Left Hand Ditch Company, 6 Colo. 443 (1882). The United States Supreme Court validated the substitution of prior appropriation for the common law in California-Oregon Power Company v. Beaver Portland Cement Company, 295 U.S. 142 (1935).

[43] *See* A. Dan Tarlock, *Western Water Law: Global Warming, and Growth Limitations*, 24 LOYOLA OF LOS ANGELES L. REV. 979 (1991).

[44] *See* Food and Agricultural Organization of the United Nations, PREPARING NATIONAL REGULATIONS FOR WATER RESOURCES MANAGEMENT: PRINCIPLES AND PRACTICE, FAO LEGISLATIVE STUDY NO. 52 (1994). The study concludes that the non-regulated uses 'represent an ever shrinking minority of water allocation decisions overall'.

(3) that access can be denied if the state determines that there is a higher or more efficient alternative use of the water.

The key elements of prior appropriation are priority and beneficial use. Rights are allocated according to the date that the water was put to a beneficial use. In times of shortage, junior rights can be curtailed to guarantee that senior right holders obtain their full entitlement. There is no formal equitable sharing as there is under the common law of riparian rights. Thus, each user knows in advance the extent of his right and the risks of curtailment in times of shortage. A beneficial use is a non-speculative or non-wasteful use. The standard has not played a major role in promoting the efficient use of water, although the beneficial use requirement promotes some sharing because it limits the right to use water to non-wasteful uses. Beneficial use plays an important role in transfers; it is the measure of the right and thus defines the amount that can be transferred. A user cannot simply transfer his or her paper entitlement but must establish the amount of water that has actually and historically been continuously used.

Prior appropriation can be described as a watershed destruction rule, but a new quasi-riparianism is emerging from the various attempts to block out of stream or basin transfers. Native American Tribes and environmental groups are demanding that the impacts of transfers be subjected to increased public interest scrutiny. Federal laws such as the Endangered Species Act create federal regulatory rights to minimum flows necessary to protected, listed, threatened, and endangered species, which have the potential to displace state-created rights. The California[45]–Hawaii[46] public trust doctrine allows a court to curtail a vested water right or block the reallocation of an abandoned one to fulfill public trust purposes which include the preservation of viable aquatic ecosystems. The celebrated Mono Lake case invoked the public trust to reduce the Los Angeles Department of Water and Power's diversions from a tributary of the lake,[47] and Hawaii invoked it to limit potentially Honolulu's use of water from an abandoned sugar ditch. In the end, the trust is likely to be invoked only if a prior use threatens to destroy an entire aquatic ecosystem subject to the trust.[48]

[45] National Audubon Society v. Superior Court, 658 P.2d 709 (Cal. 1983), *cert. denied*, 464 U.S. 977 (1983).

[46] *In re* Water Use Permit Applications for Interim Instream Flow Standard Amendments, and Petitions for Water Reservations for the Waiahole Ditch, 9 P.3d 409 (Haw. 2000). *See* Carol Wilcox, SUGAR WATER: HAWAII'S PLANTATION DITCHES 98–112 (1996) for a history of the ditch.

[47] Mono Lake is a natural closed lake like the Dead Sea east of Yosemite National Park. The salinity levels in the lake created a simple but unique ecosystem which supports a large bird habitat. By the 1970s, the Los Angeles Department of Water and Power's diversions from tributary creeks, dating from the 1940s, threatened to lower the levels to those beyond which the ecosystem could sustain itself. Ironically, the diversions also caused the growth of unique calcium carbonate formations, Tufa Towers, which attracted worldwide attention to the area. The litigation eventually resulted in reduced withdrawals which will eventually stabilize the lake's ecosystem. *See* John Hart, STORM OVER MONO: THE MONO LAKE BATTLE AND CALIFORNIA'S WATER FUTURE (1996).

[48] Consolidated Special Proceeding Special Title (Rule 15550(b)), State Water Resources Control Board Cases, Case No. JC 4118, Superior Court of the State of California, February 27, 2003

Riparian rights and prior appropriation are often portrayed as inconsistent systems, but in fact there is considerable convergence between the two. The adoption of any permit system will require the protection of prior uses. Florida's Water Management Act expressly makes non-interference with the presently existing uses one of the three criteria for the issuance of a permit. A Florida intermediate court of appeals substantially reduced the amount of water granted to an agricultural user to protect pressure levels in an existing well field from a 1.7 foot drop. Existing users enjoy superiority over new applicants.[49]

3.3 The transferability of water rights

a. Riparian rights

Transfers of riparian rights remain problematic even under the liberalized law of riparian rights. In contrast to appropriative rights, a riparian does not have a right to a fixed quantity until the right has been adjudicated. Even an adjudicated riparian right is theoretically vulnerable to the subsequent claims of other riparians who were not subject to the adjudication. A riparian cannot bind other riparians.[50] Thus, a riparian can convey the right to use its share of a watercourse,[51] but it is an inchoate or undefined right, which may be challenged by other riparians not party to the agreement. Only the transferor is estopped to assert any riparian rights.[52]

b. Prior appropriation

Appropriative water rights have always been transferable (marketable), but the rules are different when compared with other commodities. As are riparian rights, appropriative water rights are correlative usufructuary rights; they must be exercised with regard to their impact on other uses. The most concrete manifestation of this idea is the protection of junior rights.[53] Unlike other property rights, which can be transferred without regard to the effect on other property holders, except in unusual cases, an appropriative water right cannot be transferred unless there is no injury to junior water right holders. This means that the senior right holder can only transfer the amount of water that it consumed rather than the amount of water it originally diverted. The increment that returned to

(court should only invoke the public trust when no responsible body has assessed the impact of diverting the entire flow of a navigable water body).

[49] Harloff v. City of Sarasota, 575 So.2d 1324 (Fla.App. 1991). *See also* Edmondson v. Edwards, 111 S.W.3d 906, 910 (Mo.App.S.D. 2003) (upstream riparian who dried up a stream liable because it diverted 'the natural watercourse ... to the exclusion of [a] long-standing use').

[50] Duckworth v. Watsonville Water & Light Co., 110 P. 927 (Cal. 1910); State v. Apfelbacher, 167 N.E. 244 (Wis. 1918).

[51] Pyle v. Gilbert, 265 S.E. 2d 584 (Ga. 1980).

[52] Duckworth v. Watsonville Water & Light Co., 110 P. 927 (Cal. 1910).

[53] *See* A. Dan Tarlock, Law of Water Rights and Resources § 5.05(2) (1988); George Gould, *Water Rights Transfers and Third-Party Effects*, 23 Land & Water L. Rev. 1 (1988).

the stream as return flow does not belong to the senior right holder. This long-entrenched rule can be a major barrier to transfers because the range of affected water right holders, the amount of water actually used, and the amount of water that junior water right holders are using must be identified and adverse effects mitigated. In practice, the rule does not bar transfers, but it does add to their cost. However, in most cases, the transaction costs are not excessive enough to discourage transfers. A major study of water transfers in six states concludes that—with the exception of lawyer-dominated Colorado—the current transaction costs of water transfers are not excessive.[54] The real barriers are political not legal.[55] Historically, water districts that control large blocks of water have been reluctant to sanction transfers because of the accompanying loss of political power.[56]

There are other third party protections. For example, the legal status of saved water is uncertain. There are cases holding that this water once again becomes state owned or public and is open to appropriation by other users in the system. Historically there has been little incentive for water users to conserve and market the saved increment. Proposals to reduce the transactions costs of transfers include streamlining existing processes and creating incentives to conserve water and to transfer the saved water,[57] and several states allow water right holders to do this. Utah is the first State Supreme Court to allow a water right holder who increases the efficiency to his use to enjoy the fruits of the investment. Courts had long followed a confusing distinction between return flow, which was available to other water right holders, and captured water that never reached a stream, which remained the property of the original user. For the first time, the court held that the state's policy of water conservation required that the saver retain the right to any water conserved by the application of new technology, even if some of the saved water reached a stream.[58] Several states have passed legislation that awards all or a portion of saved water to the saver.[59]

4. Water transfer regimes

Many different types of water transfer regimes are currently operating in the United States. The variety is a reflection of the different functions that transfers play and of the competing third party and societal interests. The regimes range

[54] Larry J. MacDonnell, The Water Transfer Process as a Management Option for Meeting Changing Demands (Natural Resources Law Center, University of Colorado School of Law, 1990).

[55] *See* Barton H. Thompson, Jr., *Institutional Perspectives on Water Policy and Markets* 81 Cal. L. Rev. 671 (1993).

[56] *Id.*

[57] Ore. Rev. Stat. § 537.455(2) (1993). *See* Larry J. MacDonnell, *Transferring Water Uses in the West*, 43 Okla. L. Rev. 119 (1990).

[58] Estate of Steed v. New Escalante Irrigation Co., 846 p.2d 1223 (Utah 1992).

[59] E.g., Ore. Rev. Stat. § 537.455(2) (1993).

from markets which operate within state law regimes, to regimes where it is very difficult to use the market. The common threads that link the regimes together are:

(1) they generally adopt some form of a watershed protection rule to constrain market-dictated transfers which pose serious environmental risks or do not mitigate third party impacts;
(2) transfers are not ends in and of themselves but a means to achieve a broader social objective; and
(3) thus they are often part of a political solution to broader resource allocation conflict.

Many new state and federal water laws may be used to restrain transfers to protect the area of origin or the status quo among existing users. Collectively, these new laws may pose significant constraints on transfers, and perhaps on the efficient reallocation of water resources. At a minimum, these laws may also greatly increase the costs of transfers and make them politically unattractive.[60] This section examines four types of transfer barriers:

(1) resource regimes which highly constrain transfers;
(2) true purchases and sales;
(3) water banks and other short-term transfers; and
(4) 'treaty transfers', transfers of specific resources which are the result of a legislative or other settlement among the major stakeholders, that address a wide range of transfer-related issues.

4.1 Highly constrained transfers

Historically, society assumed that streams, lakes, and aquifers were destined for consumptive use. However, a water resource can be dedicated primarily to in situ uses. In this case transfers are prohibited or highly constrained. For example, the level of Lake Tahoe, a beautiful, deep, clean mountain lake between the states of California and Nevada, is fixed by an Act of Congress, and thus there is a high floor on diversions out of the lake.[61] The emerging legal regime that governs the use of the Great Lakes, a shared Canadian–United States resource, is an example of a regime that attempts to limit transfers to small intra-basins, or to inter-basin transfers within a basin state. International trade may undermine these constrained regimes, although this result is unlikely.

[60] *See* A. Dan Tarlock, *New Water Transfer Restrictions: The West Returns to Riparianism*, 27 WATER RESOURCES RESEARCH 987 (1991).

[61] The Lake is the source of the Truckee River which supports the urban area of Reno-Sparks, Nevada, an irrigation district, and ultimately empties into a closed lake which is home to an endangered fish venerated by a local Indian tribe. The decision to maintain the level of Lake Tahoe for environmental reasons has led to a complex downstream allocation regime. *See* WATER TRANSFERS IN THE WEST, *supra* note 3 at 119–35.

The Great Lakes states and Canadian provinces have developed a 'soft law' regime to limit diversions from the lakes. In 1985, the Great Lakes governors and premiers of Ontario and Quebec adopted the Great Lakes Charter. This is a non-binding agreement that allows any governor or premier to veto a proposed diversion from the lakes. In the first litigation to consider it, a federal district court described it as

> a kind of gentlemen's agreement between the Governors of the Great Lakes States and the Provinces of Ontario and Quebec that the parties to the charter should not make any new diversion of Great Lakes waters averaging more than 5 million gallons per day over a 30-day period without the notification, consultation and approval of all the parties to the charter.[62]

Several basin states implemented the Charter by enacting legislation that prohibited out of basin diversions.[63] This type of legislation is unconstitutional under Sporhase v. Nebraska, which held that flat prohibitions on the transfer of water out of state violate the Dormant Commerce Clause[64] because they are 'protectionist' and block inter-state trade.[65] However, the Charter can be applied in the United States, because federal legislation waives the Dormant Commerce Clause and allows any basin state governor to veto a trans-basin diversion.[66] In 2001, the states and provinces adopted Annex 2001,[67] which commits them to develop a binding, bi-national regulatory regime to allow small out-of-basin diversions for cities that lie just outside the watershed, which is often a narrow line in some states. Regardless of the regulatory regime, if any, that emerges, the core principle of the 'Law of the Great Lakes' is that

[62] Little Traverse Bay Bands of Odawa Indians v. Great Springs Waters of America, Inc., Case No. 1:02-CV-127 (Western District of Michigan, May 28, 2002).

[63] E.g., MICH. COMP. LAWS ANN. § 324.32703 (West 1999).

[64] The Dormant Commerce Clause is a judge-made doctrine, derived from the so-called affirmative Commerce Clause. The affirmative Commerce Clause is an express grant of constitutional power to Congress to regulate inter-state and foreign commerce: United States Constitution, Article I, Section 8. The Court has inferred from this grant and its history that state laws that discriminate against inter-state commerce undermine the goal of the creation of national markets unburdened by state parochialism. E.g., states cannot prevent the export of energy resources. New England Power Co. v. New Hampshire, 455 U.S. 331 (1982).

[65] Sporhase v. Nebraska ex rel. Douglas, 458 U.S. 941 (1982). El Paso, Texas applied for a permit to export New Mexico groundwater; New Mexico denied it because state law prohibited out of state transfers. To defend the constitutionality of its law, the state raised a sophisticated 'conservation' defense based upon confusing language in Justice Stevens' opinion in Sporhase that suggested that states could hoard in cases of necessity. No immediate shortages existed in the state, but New Mexico argued that it could retain all water within its borders to protect future generations' community value defense. 'Outside of fulfilling human survival needs, water is an economic resource.' City of El Paso v. Reynolds, 563 F. Supp. 379, 389 (D.N.M. 1983). No 'demonstrably arid' state can meet this narrow standard, so New Mexico amended its statute to permit extensive public interest review of both intra- and inter-state appropriation and transfer applications. N.M. STAT. ANN. §§ 72-6-3 and 72-12B-1.

[66] The Water Resources Development Act of 2000, 42 U.S.C. § 1962d-20, requires that each Great Lakes governor approve an out-of-basin export.

[67] Annex to the Great Lakes Charter, June 18, 2001, available at www.cglg.org/1pdfs/Annex2001.pdf.

consumptive uses of the lakes should be small and limited to those in the watershed, or in close proximity to it.[68] This principle is reflected in an International Joint Commission[69] Reference, which concluded:

> If all interests in the basin are considered, there is never a 'surplus' of water in the Great Lakes system; every drop of water has several potential uses, and tradeoffs must be made when, through human intervention, waters are removed from the system. Environmental interests, for example, require fluctuations between high and low levels to preserve diversity.[70]

A great deal of water is allocated by inter-state compacts. This water could be a new source of urban and environmental supply. However, parties to a compact view compacts as incorporating a form of watershed protection rule: a state must use its entitlement within the state. For example, the damming of the Colorado River has shrunk most of the once vibrant Colorado River Delta. There are proposals to restore the Delta through upstream water transfers. However, inter-state compacts may limit the ability of states to transfer their entitlements. Non-governmental organizations (NGOs) trying to restore the Delta are confronted by the problem that the Colorado Compact prevents a state from transferring part of its share to instream uses because such a use is not a beneficial use.[71] However, they argue that the Compact does not bar the transfer of state-created water rights consistent with a state's treaty allocation. Thus, it is possible that a United States NGO could acquire United States water rights for use in the Delta since no state is denied its allocation and each remains free to limit uses to those specified in the Compact.

Utah illustrates the possibility of inter-state trades of compact allocations. The state has never been able to put all her allocated water under the Colorado Compact to use. Traditionally, slower developing, upstream states such as Utah have tried to block developments which would foreclose future uses of its entitlement, even though the ability of the state eventually to put the water to use was slight. However, in 1996 Utah's legislature created a committee to explore

[68] *See* International Joint Commission, INTERNATIONAL WATER USES REVIEW TASK FORCE, PROTECTION OF THE WATERS OF THE GREAT LAKES: THREE YEAR REVIEW (November 2002) for an assessment of the legal and scientific problems of the Annex 2001 Process. *See also* Mark Squillace & Sandra Zellmer, *Managing Interjurisdictional Waters Under the Great Lakes Charter Annex*, 18 Natural Resources & Environment 8 n. 2 (2003).

[69] The International Joint Commission (IJC) was created by the Boundary Waters Treaty of 1909 between Great Britain and the United States. Treaty Between the United States and Great Britain Relating to Boundary Waters and Questions Arising Between the United States and Canada, 36 Statute 2448 (1909). The IJC is a six person bi-national body which has jurisdiction over all obstructions and diversions that effect the natural level of flow of any boundary water between Canada and the United States. See Stephen J. Toope & Jutta Brunee, *Freshwater Regimes: The Mandate of the International Joint Commission*, 15 Arizona J. Int. & Comp. L. 273 (1998).

[70] International Joint Commission, PROTECTION OF THE WATERS OF THE GREAT LAKES: FINAL REPORT TO THE GOVERNMENTS OF CANADA AND THE UNITED STATES, March 21, 2000, available at http://www.ijc.org/boards/cde/finalreport/finalreport.html.

[71] Robert J. Glennon & Peter W. Culp, *The Last Green Lagoon: How and Why the Bush Administration Should Save the Colorado River Delta*, 28 ECOLOGY L.Q. 903 (2002).

water marketing options, and the committee concluded that the state could better control its destiny and generate revenue by considering selling its entitlements to more rapidly growing downstream Nevada and California.

International trade regimes such as GATT and the NAFTA introduce a new potential constraint into water transfers.[72] Non-governmental organizations and some legal commentators suggest that any national effort to prohibit the export of water from its territory is illegal under GATT or NAFTA. This is an unlikely result, because there is a crucial difference between a country's sovereign right to decide whether to put a resource into the stream of international commerce and its power to discriminate among users once it has made the decision to allow trade in the resource. The NAFTA countries have addressed this issue by declaring that raw water is not a good,[73] which is consistent with the general understanding that a product is the result of some transformation of raw materials, and thus raw water is not a product subject to the anti-discrimination principles of trade law.

4.2 True purchases and sales

Water rights are frequently purchased on the open market. In prior appropriation states, water is separate from land, and thus a water right can be detached from the land on which it was used. Originally appropriative rights had a riparian feature because they were appurtenant to the land where they were first applied, but this rule has been abolished or relaxed in most states. In riparian jurisdictions, the most frequent method of purchasing a riparian right is to

[72] See Chapter 3 of this volume by Edith Brown Weiss.

[73] The text provides in part:

> The NAFTA creates no rights to natural water resources of any party to the Agreement unless water, in any form, has entered into commerce and become a good or product. And nothing in NAFTA would oblige an NAFTA Party to either exploit its water for commercial use, or to begin exporting water in any form. Water in its natural state in lakes, rivers, reservoirs, aquifers, water basins and like is not a good or product, is not trade, and therefore is not and never has been subject to the terms of any trade agreement. [Webmaster@scics.x400.gc.ca]

Canada's North American Free Trade Implementation Act, R.S.C. 1993, c. 44, similarly provides that water in packages, products or tanks is a good but that natural surface or groundwater is not. This 'soft' declaration does not, of course, settle the issue.

All Canadian provinces, with the exception of Quebec, have agreed to a ban on bulk water removal from the Canadian portion of the country's major drainage basins (Accord for the Prohibition of Bulk Water Removal From Drainage Basins). The policy will be implemented by each province and contains several exemptions and exclusions such as bottled water, water packaged in small, portable containers, water used in food production, water to meet short-term safety, security, or humanitarian needs, 'and other purposes as determined by individual jurisdictions to meet environmental and other management needs consistent with the objective of the Accord'.

purchase riparian land, but riparian rights can be severed from the land, as can appropriative rights. In appropriation jurisdictions, transfers are subject to administrative scrutiny. In brief, the amount of the transferable right must first be determined. Some states limit transfers to the historical beneficial use rather than the decreed amount;[74] others allow the amount of water presently being put to beneficial use to be transferred.[75]

Transfers usually promote the efficient use of water by moving water to a higher valued use. They can also be used to temper the rigid enforcement of priorities. For example, the Northern Colorado Conservancy District, which gets water from the Colorado Big Thompson project, is located in eastern Colorado and serves a large agricultural and urban population. However, its water right is junior to many western slope water rights across the Front Range of the Rocky Mountains. It is concerned that a power plant which holds a senior right will make a call in a low water year and deprive the project of needed upstream water. The project and the city of Denver have offered to pay the power plant's owner for loss energy to avoid the call.[76]

4.3 Water banking and other temporary transfers

Temporary transfers generally involve leases or water bank deposits. Leases are viewed by some users as an interim source of supply. Leasing activity increases during droughts. United States drought policy assumes that droughts are relatively short-term weather 'abnormalities', to be dealt with by victim compensation and ad hoc reallocations. The prolonged drought of the late 1980s and early 1990s stimulated interest in temporary transfers and the creation of water banks. In any given year a water right holder may have excess water, or find it rational not to plant a crop. Water banks are a useful way of moving 'surplus' or 'excess' water to areas of need during a drought and form one of several temporary transfer policy instruments. They are also useful in providing water necessary to comply with environmental mandates.[77] Even during a drought many users have entitlements to more water than they can use. Water banks have been created to allow these holders to profit from this excess water and

[74] E.g., Orr v. Arapaho Water and Sanitation Dist., 753 P.2d 1217 (Colo. 1988); Santa Fe Trail Ranches Property Owners Assoc. v. Simpson, 990 P.2d 46 (Colo. 1999).

[75] United States v. Alpine Land & Reservoir Co., 687 F.2d 851 (9th Cir. 1983); United States v. Alpine Land & Reservoir Co., 983 F.2d 1487 (9th Cir. 1992) (reminding state engineer that he or she cannot rely on the original 'paper' entitlement because beneficial use must first be calculated).

[76] Northern Colorado Water Conservancy District, Water News.

[77] In the Klamath Basin, the maintenance of reservoir levels and downstream flows to support endangered fish has resulted in the cut-off of water deliveries to irrigators. *See* Holly Doremus & A. Dan Tarlock, *Fish, Farms, and the Clash of Cultures in the Klamath Basin*, 30 ECOLOGY L.Q. 279 (2003). A National Academy of Sciences committee has endorsed the Bureau of Reclamation's efforts to create a 100,000 acre foot per year water bank to provide the necessary water in future years. National Research Council, ENDANGERED AND THREATENED FISHES IN THE KLAMATH RIVER BASIN: CAUSES OF DECLINE AND STRATEGIES FOR RECOVERY 267 (2003).

benefit society at the same time. Water banking is a technique to tap underused water rights and temporarily reallocate them. The prior appropriation rule that an appropriated right may be abandoned or forfeited by non-use creates perverse incentives to waste water. Water banking seeks to counter the 'use it or lose it' rule by allowing temporary transfers which do not impair the underlying right.

Water banking was pioneered in Idaho on the Snake River and adopted by California during the drought of the late 1980s and early 1990s. In early 1991, California was facing the fifth consecutive year of drought. Major reservoir storage was 54% of average. To meet the gap between available supplies and demand, the state created a Drought Water Bank. Emergency legislation was enacted to allow water suppliers the authority to enter into contracts with the Bank and to provide that any temporary transfer would not affect the supplier's water rights. In its first year, the Bank acquired 820,000 acre feet of water at $125.00 per acre foot, which it sold at $175.00 per acre foot. The water was primarily acquired from San Joaquin-Sacramento Delta farmers who fallowed their land, as well as from suppliers with water entitlements from the Yuba and Feather Rivers. Approximately 390,000 acre feet were delivered to districts in the San Francisco Bay Area, the San Joaquin Valley, and Los Angeles, with the Metropolitan Water District of Southern California receiving about 55% of the total allocations. Through August 12, 1992, the second year of operation, the California Water Bank acquired 155,000 acre feet, mainly due to conservation measures and dumped groundwater, at $72.00 per acre foot.[78] An evaluation of the program concludes that it meets the objective of providing emergency supplies but that established procedures for the protection of third party interests were bi-passed.[79] Water transfers now account for 3% of California's water use.[80] Cities are buying water from Central Valley farmers and public agencies are buying water for instream flows. Most transfers are short term, but about 20% are long-term or permanent agricultural to urban transfers.

4.4 'Treaty transfers'

Many large-scale water transfers are not simple market transactions but the product of an agreement between private and public parties that addresses a

[78] WESTERN STATES WATER, Issue No. 957 (September 18, 1992). *See* THE 1991 DROUGHT WATER BANK (California Department of Water Resources, January, 1992). Richard Howitt et al., A RETROSPECTIVE ON CALIFORNIA'S 1991 EMERGENCY DROUGHT WATER BANK: A REPORT PREPARED FOR THE CALIFORNIA DEPARTMENT OF WATER RESOURCES (March, 1992), concludes that the net gains to agricultural and urban users were positive although there were severe individual losses from decreased farming.

[79] Brian E. Gray, *The Role of Laws and Institutions in California's 1991 Water Bank*, SHARING SCARCITY: GAINERS AND LOSERS IN WATER MARKETING 133 (Harold O. Carter, Henry Vaux, Jr., and Ann F. Securing eds, 1994).

[80] Ellen Hanak, WHO SHOULD BE ALLOWED TO SELL WATER IN CALIFORNIA? THIRD PARTY ISSUES AND THE WATER MARKET (Public Policy Institute of California, 2003).

wide range of issues raised by a transfer. The agreement usually takes the form of state or federal legislation. Legislative ratification is necessary both to compel the necessary transfers and to provide funding to deal with the costs of the transfer. The movement of water from the Imperial Valley of California, a source of winter vegetables, fruits, and other crops to urban southern California, is an example of such a transfer. California is entitled to 4.4 million acre feet annually of the Colorado River:[81] 3.85 million acre feet are used for agriculture in the deserts of the Imperial and Coachella Valleys. For decades the federal and state governments have argued that the Imperial Irrigation District (IID) uses too much water in relation to its irrigation needs, and thus this wasteful use is non-beneficial. The IID had the political power to rebuff these allegations, and the state of California had little incentive to press the waste issue because it was able to use the surplus entitlements of Arizona and Nevada to supply southern California.

By the 1990s, IID's position became economically and politically unsupportable as the disparity between the value of water for irrigation and municipal and industrial uses in urban southern California and the environmental impacts of its use increased. High value winter fruits and vegetables are grown in the Imperial Valley, but a great deal of acreage is in low value alfalfa. Concurrently, the states of Arizona and Nevada had the ability to use their full compact shares, making California's surplus use legally unsustainable.

In the late 1990s, the Department of Interior issued Colorado River rules that limited California to its compact entitlement of 4.4 million acre feet, as opposed to the 5 million plus that it actually diverted.[82] The federal government put additional pressure on IID to consent to the transfer in 2002, when the Department of Interior ruled that a portion of IID's use was non-beneficial and thus contract deliveries would be curtailed. After intense multiparty negotiations, the state of California has agreed to buy 1,600,000 acre feet of IID's water and sell it to the Metropolitan Water District of southern California at a higher price. The difference will be used to help restore the Salton Sea, an artificial body of water created by an earlier California flood.

5. Third party impact protection laws

5.1 Large-scale inter-basin transfers

A major problem with most transfers, especially large ones, is the protection of 'third party' claims. There is no general legal framework in the United States for the evaluation of transfers. Many large-scale transfers would be directly

[81] The long history of the inter-state compacts and other legislation that control the use of 'America's Nile' is summarized in Sax et al., *supra* note 41, at 692–719.

[82] The formal legal document is Colorado Water Delivery Agreement: Federal Quantification Settlement Agreement for Purposes of Section 5(B) of Interim Surplus Guidelines (2003).

constructed and operated by the federal government. Other state-constructed or private transfer facilities will require some form of federal approval. Most transfers would therefore be subject to the National Environmental Policy Act of 1969.[83] There are many leverage points for transfers that require federal approval. For example, the federal Environmental Protection Agency (EPA) has the statutory authority to veto a permit to deposit dredge and fill material in a wetland issued by the United States Army Corps of Engineers.[84] This power has been sparingly used to veto proposed dams and inter-state pipelines. The EPA has no duty to balance the economic benefits of the foregone project against the environmental benefits of the veto.[85]

5.2 Small-scale transfers

One of the major problems associated with water transfers is protecting the interests of those in the area of origin. Junior water right protection rules recognize the long-standing expectation among users that water should be shared among similar users to the maximum extent possible, but the potential compass of protected interests is larger. Because the earliest water rights are generally along streams, this rule functions as a form of watershed protection rule, and is the conceptual basis for protecting both water right and non-water right holders. Junior protection rules are being augmented by broader area-wide protection claims. Many water rights transfers remove water from agricultural use and dedicate the right to urban use. Non-water right holders are asserting a greater stake in water appropriation and transfer proceedings to prevent or condition these transfers.

These claimants are generally 'community welfare' claimants or environmental interests. Rural communities consider themselves at risk from these transfers because the community's economic base and way of life are

[83] The Garrison Diversion Project illustrates the strengths and weaknesses of NEPA to review the environmental impacts of trans-basin diversions. In brief, North Dakota lost almost 900,000 acres when the Pick-Sloan Project, a series of flood control and navigation support dams, was constructed on the Missouri River. The state was promised over 1,000,000 acres of replacement irrigated land, but only 9,000 acres were actually developed.

For years North Dakota pursued a large scale irrigation project, the Garrison Diversion Project, and Canada objected because it would introduce exotic Missouri River biota into the Hudson Drainage. The irrigation component of the project was formally terminated in 2000, but a smaller version of the project, the Northwest Area Water Supply Project, is being constructed to serve 14 small rural communities. An Environmental Assessment, which is a truncated environmental impact analysis, was prepared for the downsized project. Manitoba has sued North Dakota and the Department of Interior to require a full EIS. The Province of Manitoba v. North and State of North Dakota, Civ. No, 1:02CV2057 (RMC), United States District Court for the District of Columbia. In June 2003, the government of Canada filed an amicus brief supporting Manitoba. For a history of the Garrison Diversion, *see* Brian Keith Russell, The Promise of Water: The Legacy of Pick-Sloan and Irrigation in North Dakota, available at http://www.nd-humanities.org/html/russell.html.

[84] 33 U.S.C § 1344 (1987).

[85] James City County v. Environmental Protection Agency, 12 F.3d 1330 (4th Cir. 1993), *cert. denied*, 513 U.S. 823 (1994).

threatened.[86] It is difficult to assert these claims as property claims. With the exception of the junior right holder protection rule, property owners who transfer their property have no duty to consider the impact of the transfer on third parties. Water law provides no direct protection for these interests, but these claims are increasingly being asserted both through litigation and the political process.[87] In addition, traditional water right holders, especially agricultural users, have increasingly adopted the rights-based rhetoric of the Native American Rights movement. Water users once adequately protected by the law and politics of water allocation must now often argue that higher, intangible values, such as rural community stability, should prevail over monetary values, to preserve the status quo.

5.3 Three examples of third party protection

The most spectacular example of the possibility of judicial protection for community values occurred in Northern New Mexico. A state trial judge held that a proposed change of use from livestock and early season flood irrigation to a ski resort was invalid, even though there was no proof of any injury to vested rights. The trial judge found that the change was contrary to the public interest because

> [t]he Northern New Mexico region possesses significant history, tradition and culture of recognized value, not measurable in dollars and cents; the relationship between the people and their land and water is central to the maintenance of that culture and traditions and the imposition of a resort-oriented economy in the Ensenada area would erode and likely destroy a distinct local culture that is several hundred years old.[88]

The decision was reversed on by an intermediate appellate court appeal because the New Mexico transfer statute at the time did not allow public interest considerations in transfers.[89] The precedent is not as dead as one might think, because New Mexico law now allows the public interest to be considered in transfers. Despite the appellate opinion, the story has a happy ending for the plaintiffs, because the Albuquerque ski resort developers went bankrupt. As of 1993, the water was still flowing into the ditches and not into the ski resort.

[86] Cy Oggins & Helen Ingram, Does Anybody Win? The Community Consequences of Rural-to-Urban Water Transfers: An Arizona Perspective (Udall Center Issue Paper No. 2, 1990).

[87] *See* F. Lee Brown & Helen Ingram, Water and Poverty in the Southwest (1988).

[88] Ensenada Land & Water Ass'n v. Sleeper, 760 P.2d 787 (N.M. 1988), *cert. quashed*, 759 P.2d 200 (N.M. 1988), reprinted in Charles J. Meyers et al., Water Resource Management 434–35 (3rd edn, 1988).

[89] *Id. See also* Shannon Parden, *The Milagro Beanfield War Revisited in Ensenada Land & Water Association v. Sleeper: Public Welfare Defies Transfer of Water Rights*, 29 Nat. Resources J. 861 (1989). *Sleeper* has led some to suggest that communities be given a veto over major water rights transfers. *See* Charles T. DuMars & Michele Minnis, *New Mexico Water Law: Determining Public Welfare Values in Water Right Allocation*, 31 Ariz. L. Rev. 817 (1989).

Rural third parties have also used nostalgia for country life to muster strong legislative support to protect them from trans-basin diversions. The Arizona legislature's response to the unintended regional consequences of groundwater conservation is an interesting example of the ability of rural interests to obtain legislative protection long after judicially mandated legislative reapportionment. In 1980, Secretary of the Interior, Cecil Andrus, and the Carter administration forced Arizona to enact a groundwater conservation law in order to obtain federal funding for the Central Arizona project. Arizona did pass the legislation and received favorable worldwide publicity for doing so. However, one of the unanticipated effects of the resulting limitations on pumping was to set off a competition among the fast-growing suburbs of Phoenix to obtain additional water supplies in rural areas of the state. A very innovative provision in the law provides that new subdivision developments will not be approved without a guaranteed hundred-year water supply. A number of fast-growing communities began to buy up 'water farms' in the rural areas not subject to the Groundwater Management Act.[90] Residents of these areas have raised both lifestyle and fiscal objections to the possible transfer of water to Phoenix.[91] Prior to 1991, Arizona's groundwater law did not require prior approval of the transport of groundwater from non-regulated areas, but the Act now limits transfers of groundwater from rural to urban areas to allotments based on the percentage of land owned in the basin, and conditions them on the payment of transportation fees and 'in lieu' contributions to the local area infrastructure.[92]

There are many efforts to create greater incentives for agricultural users. Water is power, and many rural areas fear that transfers can turn the area into a wasteland. For example, Congress has begun to remove transfer barriers to encourage transfers, but has stopped short of creating an unregulated market in federally subsidized water. The Central Valley Project Improvement Act of 1992,[93] authorizes the transfer of four classes of water service contracts held by beneficiaries of the California Central Valley Project (CVP) to 'any other California water use or water agency, State or Federal Agency, Indian tribe or private nonprofit organization'.[94] The transfers are subject to standard transfer conditions, developed by the Bureau of Reclamation, as well as a number of specific conditions. The standard conditions include:

(1) Secretary of the Interior review;
(2) the transferees' proposed use must be for a CVP project use, *or* be beneficial under California law;

[90] The statute only limits pumping in Active Management Areas. With one exception, these zones are limited to the state's major urban areas.

[91] McEntire, *Water Farms and Transfer Conflicts in Arizona, USA: A proposed Resolution Process*, 13 Envtl. Mgmt. 287 (1989).

[92] Ariz. Rev. Stat. §§ 45-522-556 (1983).

[93] Central Valley Project Improvement Act of 1992, Pub. L. 102-575, 106 Stat. 4600.

[94] *Id.* § 3405.

(3) the transfer must be consistent with state law; and
(4) the transfer will not impair the Secretary's ability to deliver water to other CVP contractors.

The most interesting feature is the equity limitation on the amount of water that can be transferred. To preserve the agricultural economy created by the project, only 20% of the water held by a district served by the CVP may be transferred without the approval of the district and the Secretary of the Interior.

Water marketing can also be used to shift water from agricultural to environmental uses. A large reallocation experiment is occurring on the Truckee and Carson Rivers in eastern Nevada. A small, old and marginal irrigation district is stressed from two sources. To the north, Pyramid Lake requires more water for native fish species. It is stressed to the east by efforts to preserve and restore remnant desert wetlands in the Stillwater Wildlife Refuge. The Carson River empties into a sink which is the site of a World Heritage wildlife refuge that has become polluted from run off from upstream marginal irrigation. As part of a comprehensive settlement of a number of water disputes in the region, in 1990 Congress directed the Secretary of the Interior to preserve 25,000 acres of wetlands in the Stillwater Wildlife Refuge and to support the wetlands through the purchase of irrigation water rights: 125,000 acre feet of water will be required to meet this objective.[95] The 1996 environmental impact statement recommended that 75,000 acre feet of existing water rights be purchased from farmers in the irrigation district, and that the additional water be obtained through a variety of strategies, including leases and the use of treated sewage effluent. The acquisition process is complex since the Fish and Wildlife Service must assure that the purchased water right is 'wet'—that the holder has actually perfected an appropriative right by applying water to a beneficial use—and that the water will actually reach the refuge when the land to which the right attached is retired from production.

6. Conclusion

Water transfers are powerful policy instruments to improve the reallocation of water, but it is essential to realize that transfers are ultimately only one of the available strategies that a country can follow to promote the more efficient and equitable use of water to accommodate new demands. They are not an end in and of themselves but a means to an end: the sustainable use of scarce water resources. Water marketing works best in developed countries that are likely to

[95] U.S. Department of Interior, Final Environmental Impact Statement, Water Rights Acquisition for Lahontan Valley Wetlands, Churchill County, Nevada, Vol. 1, 1–5 (September 1996).

have surplus waters dedicated to agricultural use; but the lessons learned from developing countries apply equally to developed ones. As a leading United States water expert cautions, 'unregulated or monopolistic water markets can lead to over-exploitation of water sources, inequities in water distribution, and exploitative prices'.[96]

[96] Sandra Postel, DIVIDING THE WATERS: FOOD SECURITY, ECOSYSTEM HEALTH, AND THE NEW POLITICS OF SCARCITY 60 (1996). For a detailed analysis of the problems with the introduction of water markets in Chile, *see* Carl J. Bauer, SIREN SONG: CHILEAN WATER LAW AS MODEL FOR INTERNATIONAL REFORM (2004).

3

Water Transfers and International Trade Law

EDITH BROWN WEISS[1]

Fresh water is vital to human life and to the sustainability of Earth. There is no known substitute for fresh water. People have strong emotional ties to water, whether for health, nature, soil productivity, religious, or other reasons. Historically water has not had a price, only the costs of extracting, using, or purifying it. But within the last half of the twentieth century, water increasingly acquired a price, entered into the market, and was subject to international trade. These developments have raised the question of the extent to which international trading regimes apply to transboundary fresh water transfers.

To encourage more efficient use of water and meet water needs, various entities, from cities to agricultural users, are buying and selling water. The market takes the form of often large-scale transfers of specific quantities of water not only within countries (or within a state or province), but also in some cases, between countries. In the previous chapter Tarlock described the water market in North America, primarily in the United States, and the issues that water markets have raised domestically. This chapter focuses on the nascent international market in water and the efforts by some countries to keep water within their own borders free from export.

The conflicting trends reflect differences within the international community about how water should be viewed. Some argue that fresh water is a commodity, which ought to have a price, and that the price ought to be high enough to ensure that water is used efficiently.[2] This is even more important where fresh water is scarce and the demands many. Others view the commodification of water as inappropriate and regard fresh water as a public good, or as the common heritage of humankind. They point to the essential role of water in ecosystems and to a basic human right to water.[3] This, they argue, counters or constrains the

[1] The author thanks Tracy Stitt for her research assistance and Jane Bradley for her comments.

[2] *See*, e.g., SHARING SCARCITY: GAINERS AND LOSERS IN WATER MARKETING (Harold O. Carter, et al. eds, 1994); CONTINENTAL WATER MARKETING (Terry L. Anderson, ed., 1994); Gary D. Libecap, RESCUING WATER MARKETS: LESSONS FROM OWENS VALLEY (2005).

[3] *See*, e.g., Stephen C. McCaffrey, chapter 4 in this book; Salman M. A. Salman & Siobhán McInerney-Lankford, THE HUMAN RIGHT TO WATER (2004).

market perspective. The seeming clash between environmental and human rights concerns and the trade disciplines bears analysis.

This chapter addresses the extent to which the trade disciplines apply to transboundary movements of fresh water. It does so primarily by examining the 1994 General Agreement on Tariffs and Trade ('GATT 1994')[4] and, secondarily, relevant experience with the North American Free Trade Agreement ('NAFTA').[5] It concludes that while the trade disciplines may conceptually apply at the point where water is removed from its natural state, they should in practice generally be applied only after fresh water has been removed from its bulk status and transformed into traditional products, such as bottled water and other drinks, which are already subject to the trade disciplines. Products containing water, such as agricultural produce, are also already subject to trade disciplines. In the case of bulk transfers of fresh water, private contractual remedies negotiated between the parties or remedies available in public international law, rather than remedies provided for in trade agreements, should be used to address disputes.

1. The characteristics of fresh water

Fresh water is a unique resource, because all forms of life need it, and there are no known substitutes. The actions we take today influence the amount and quality of fresh water available in the future. Human-induced climate change affects the amount and distribution of precipitation, and hence the quantity of water available in watercourses and rechargeable aquifers.[6] Temperatures affect evaporation rates of water in lakes, rivers, and other bodies of water. The withdrawal of ground water in excess of the rate at which the aquifer is recharged leads to depletion of the aquifer. Withdrawal of fossil ground water (namely, water that is not recharged and not connected to surface watercourses) removes water forever from that location. Land use practices that cover over the porosity of the land in the recharge area of an aquifer, as with pavement and buildings, prevent normal recharge of water in that aquifer, and can deplete the aquifer and linked surface watercourses. Toxic pollution can lead to effectively irreversible contamination of aquifers and long-term contamination of lakes.

Water is oblivious to national boundaries. Countries share international rivers, lakes, and sometimes ground water aquifers. The hydrological system for

[4] General Agreement on Tariffs and Trade, April 15, 1994, 1867 U.N.T.S. 3, available at http://www.wto.org/english/docs_e/legal_e/ursum_e.htm#General (last visited January 18, 2005) [hereinafter GATT 1994].

[5] North American Free Trade Agreement, December 17, 1992, U.S.-Can.-Mex, available at http://www.nafta-sec-alena.org/DefaultSite/index_e.aspx (last visited January 18, 2005) [hereinafter NAFTA].

[6] *See* Intergovernmental Panel on Climate Change (IPCC), *Third Assessment Report, Climate Change 2001: Impacts, Adaptation and Vulnerability*, Ch. 4.3.2 Precipitation (2001), available at http://ww.grida.no/climate/ipcc_tar/wg2/index.htm (last visited January 18, 2005).

any given water basin may reside in more than one country. This means that actions by one country in a river basin, even on a distant tributary, may influence the quantity and quality of water available to another country in the river basin. Land use practices in one country that restrict the seeping of water through the land into an aquifer may affect the long-term availability of water supplies in a shared river, because aquifers and surface watercourses are linked.

The international community has generally viewed fresh water as a unique resource, which by itself does not have a value expressed in market prices. This perception is changing as countries focus on water as an economically scarce resource, and view water pricing and water transfers as a way to use water more efficiently. This means that water at a certain point assumes the economic characteristics of a good that could be subject to the disciplines of international trade.

The characteristics of fresh water differentiate fresh water from other tradable natural resources such as timber, fish, or fossil fuels. Our dependency on fresh water now and in the future must condition the application of international trade law to this essential resource.

2. Transboundary transfers of water

Water crosses national boundaries in at least three different forms: by natural or artificial flows in rivers, streams, or aquifers; by bulk transfers, which require the removal of water into pipelines, tankers, or other conveyance vehicles; and by incorporation into products, whether as drinking water, agricultural produce, or other items. The first form should not, and I argue does not, invoke trade disciplines, while the last clearly does. The legal treatment of bulk transfers of water across national borders has yet to be resolved.

2.1 Water flowing in its natural state across national borders

Most fresh water flows between countries as international rivers, shared lakes, or shared ground water aquifers. It is then diverted from its natural state for use within the country. There is a long history of international law related to international watercourses. In the last three centuries, countries have concluded over 2,000 international water agreements.[7] While many of the early conventions addressed boundary and navigation issues, in the twentieth century most addressed at least in part the allocation and management issues. Some address pollution control and ecosystem protection. Rules of customary international law regarding allocation and use of international rivers have also emerged. The 1997 United Nations Convention on the Law of Non-Navigational Uses

[7] Edith Brown Weiss, *International Water Agreements*, The Evolution of International Water Law (forthcoming) (database on file with author).

of International Watercourses sets forth a comprehensive legal framework for international rivers and their associated water basins.[8] While this agreement has not yet gone into effect, and indeed may never go into effect, some important provisions may reflect customary international law, and thus be binding on all countries.[9] Other provisions may become rules of customary international law.

The 1997 UN International Watercourse Convention provides for general principles in which States must use the international watercourse in 'an equitable and reasonable manner' (Article V) and must 'take all appropriate measures to prevent the causing of significant harm to other watercourse States' (Article VII).[10] Article V notes that a State must use and develop an international watercourse 'with a view to attaining optimal and sustainable utilization thereof and benefits therefrom, taking into account the interests of the watercourse States concerned, consistent with adequate protection of the watercourse'.[11] Article VI elaborates seven factors that States must consider in determining whether the use of a watercourse is reasonable, including the existing and potential uses of the watercourse, the social and economic needs of the watercourse States, and the availability of alternatives of comparable value to a specific planned use.[12]

If water flowing in its natural state in an international watercourse were to be subject to international trade rules, it would insert yet another criterion in determining whether such use was reasonable and equitable, and that criterion might override the others. At the moment, Articles V and VI anticipate that the factors enumerated will be balanced against each other in making the determination of whether a given action constitutes reasonable and equitable use. The situation is further complicated by the fact that the demand for reasonable and equitable use may be seen sometimes to conflict with the obligation not to cause significant harm. Scholars have written widely on this perceived conflict, with the majority arguing that the reasonable and equitable use has more force in the event of a clear conflict, or that the two can be reconciled and are indeed compatible.[13] If the trade rules were to apply, then they might either determine the outcome, or in some cases lend greater weight to the obligation not to cause significant harm. Most importantly, if the trade rules were to apply, decisions in disputes about international watercourses could be decided by trade dispute bodies. This would contradict countries' intentions in negotiating the

[8] Convention on the Law of Non-Navigational Uses of International Watercourses, May 21, 1997, U.N. Doc. A/51/869, available at http://www.un.org/law/ilc/texts/nonnav.htm# (last visited January 8, 2005) [hereinafter 1997 UN International Watercourse Convention].

[9] *See*, e.g., Stephen C. McCaffrey, The Law of International Watercourses: Non-Navigational Uses (2001); Hilal Elver, Peaceful Uses of International Rivers (2002).

[10] 1997 UN International Watercourse Convention, *supra* note 8.

[11] *Id.*, Art. V.

[12] *Id.*, Art. VI.

[13] *See*, e.g., McCaffrey, *supra* note 9; Elver, *supra* note 9; Ibrahim Kaya, Equitable Utilization: the Law of the Non-Navigational Uses of International Watercourses (2003); Attila-Tanzi & Maurizio Arcari, The United Nations Convention on the Law of International Watercourses (2001) (arguing that there is no conflict between the two principles and that Arts. V–VII are primarily aimed at providing guidance for mutually agreeable implementation on a case-by-case basis by the States concerned: p. 179).

1997 UN International Watercourse Convention and the hundreds of regional and bilateral international water agreements.

If international water agreements governing access to, allocation of, and use of fresh water contain trade-related provisions, the debate in the World Trade Organization ('WTO') about how to treat multilateral environmental agreements ('MEAs') that contain trade-related measures becomes relevant. (While it is unclear whether many such water agreements would be considered as MEAs, at least those agreements focused on water quality and ecosystem protection should be.) The Trade and Environment Committee of the WTO has been studying the treatment of MEAs, but has yet to reach agreement on the issues.[14] The parties to the NAFTA addressed the issue by providing in the agreement that countries could list MEAs containing trade-related provisions, which, subject to certain constraints, essentially 'trump' or override any conflicting provisions of the NAFTA.[15] Since the three countries party to the NAFTA have not deemed it necessary to list the transboundary water agreements that apply as among and between them, it seems likely that they do not consider them as potentially in conflict with any of the provisions of the NAFTA. The separate statement by the

[14] At the Doha Ministerial Conference of November 2001, representatives decided to begin negotiations on the relationship between existing WTO rules and specific obligations set out in various MEAs. Special sessions of the WTO Committee on Trade and the Environment have convened for this purpose. WTO, TRADE AND ENVIRONMENT AT THE WTO (2004). For recent reports, *see* PRESS/TE/036; PRESS/TE/039, *inter alia* of this committee at http://docsonline.wto.org (last visited January 8, 2005). As of January 2005, no disputes had come to the WTO regarding trade restrictions contained in a MEA. However, the Convention on Trade in Endangered Species (CITES), which protects against trade in endangered species, was discussed in the Shrimp-Turtle case before the WTO's Dispute Settlement bodies. United States–Import Prohibition of Certain Shrimp and Shrimp Products, W.T.O. case 58, Report of the Panel, May 15, 1998, WT/DS58/R; Report of the Appellate Body, October 12, 1998, WT/DS58/AB/R (which contains the specific discussion of CITES); Recourse to Article 21.5 of the D.S.U. by Malaysia, October 22, 2001, WT/DS58/AB/RW; *see also* Andres Rueda, *Shrimp and Turtles: What About Environmental Embargoes Under NAFTA?*, RECONCILING ENVIRONMENT AND TRADE 519 (Edith Brown Weiss & John H. Jackson eds, 2001). If an international water agreement restricts transfer, allocation, or use of fresh water in its natural state or in bulk, and fresh water were considered a tradable commodity under GATT, disputes could arise over the implementation of the MEA, especially with States that were not party to the agreement. *See* Bradley Condon, *Multilateral Environmental Agreements and the WTO: Is the Sky Really Falling?* 9 TULSA J. COMP. & INT'L L. 533 (2002).

[15] NAFTA, *supra* note 5, Art. 104. The multilateral agreements included in the NAFTA are: the Convention on International Trade in Endangered Species of Wild Fauna and Flora, March 3, 1973 (amended June 22, 1979), 993 U.N.T.S. 243, available at http://www.cites.org/eng/disc/text.shtml (last visited January 18, 2005); the Montreal Protocol on Substances that Deplete the Ozone Layer, September 16, 1987 (amended June 29, 1990), 1522 U.N.T.S. 3, available at http://www.unep.org/ozone/Treaties_and_Ratification/2B_montreal_protocol.asp (last visited January 18, 2005); the Basel Convention on the Control of Transboundary Movements of Hazardous Wastes and Their Disposal, March 22, 1989, available at http://www.basel.int/index.html (last visited January 18, 2005); the Agreement Between the Government of Canada and the Government of the United States of America Concerning the Transboundary Movement of Hazardous Waste, October 28, 1986 (amended November 25, 1992), 2120 U.N.T.S. 97, available at http://www.ec.gc.ca/tmb/eng/tmbcanusaag_e.html (last visited January 18, 2005); and the Agreement Between the United States of America and the United Mexican States on the Cooperation for the Protection and Improvement of the Environment in the Border Area, November 16, 1983, 1352 U.N.T.S. 67, available at http://www.usembassy-mexico.gov/eLapaz.html (last visited January 18, 2005).

parties to the effect that water in its natural state is not intended to be covered by the NAFTA, as discussed below and as set forth in Appendix D of this book, further supports this position.[16] While international water agreements might prevail against trade agreements to the extent of the inconsistency, it is not clear how rules of customary international law regarding the allocation, access and use of fresh water would fare if they were deemed inconsistent with provisions in trade agreements.

2.2 Export of water products or products containing water

Water is itself a product when it is bottled and sold, or, combined with other elements, packaged and sold. Most juices and soft drinks, for example, are based on water. In these cases, water resembles any other product that enters the market place, and is subject to the international trade disciplines. Similarly, products that are produced with water are subject to the international trade disciplines. These include the rules of the WTO/GATT 1994 and, in North America, the NAFTA.[17] There is already a very substantial literature on the generic issues that this category of use of fresh water poses for international trade law.

One of the emerging issues of concern is the export and import of agricultural produce containing significant amounts of water, or requiring large volumes of water to produce. Scholars have pointed to the very substantial export of 'virtual' water that occurs through such exports, or to the efficiency of importing products such as grain that require much water to produce. To date, the international trade disciplines have not addressed the water content of agricultural produce. As fresh water supplies become increasingly scarce, attention is turning to the very significant category of water export and imports associated with agricultural products, and to the relevance of the trade disciplines.[18] Similarly, there has been some discussion about water subsidies as an agricultural subsidy and the application of international trade law to such subsidies.[19] These increasingly important issues are the subject of relatively little jurisprudence and deserve further attention.

2.3 Export of bulk water

Bulk transfers of fresh water raise the most difficult issues for the application of trade agreements. Bulk water removal may be defined as removal by

[16] *See* discussion *infra*, '3. Water as a Good or Product'; 1993 Statement by the Governments of Canada, Mexico and the United States, *available at* http://www.scics.gc.ca/cinfo99/83067000_e.html#statement (last visited January 8, 2005).

[17] E.g., Canada exports several hundred million liters of bottled water to the U.S. annually. These products are recognized by the government as tradable commodities under NAFTA, and are thus excepted by the country in its attempt to ban bulk water exports. *See* Cynthia Baumann, Note, *Water Wars: Canada's Upstream Battle to Ban Bulk Water Export*, 10 MINN. J. GLOBAL TRADE 114, 119 (2001).

[18] *See*, e.g., Lester R. Brown, Janet Larsen, & Bernie Fischlowitz-Roberts, THE EARTH POLICY READER (2002). The authors note that it takes '1,000 tons of water to produce 1 ton of grain,' which means, in the context of China, 'that importing grain is the most efficient way to import water'. *Id.*, at 208.

[19] *See* Bernasconi-Osterwalder, chapter 9 in the present book.

human-made diversions, including canals, tanker ships, trucks, or pipeline.[20] Governments may transfer from one State to another; private parties in different States may contract for the transfers; the transaction could involve a government exporter and a private importer, or even a private exporter and a government importer. The relations between the parties are contractual in nature, and even if executed by governments, may not take the form of treaties. This category of transfer raises the most difficult issues, because it clearly pits environmental and ecological concerns against free trade concerns. These issues are addressed in detail below. The chapter concludes that while technically these bulk transfers may constitute goods in trade, the precautionary approach in international law as developed and applied to fresh water makes it important to exclude them from the reach of trade law, as least for now until more experience is gained with them. Were this position adopted, bulk transfers for a specified purpose, i.e. for hydroelectric power, could be excepted from this general exclusion if necessary.[21]

3. Water as a Good or Product

At what point does water become a good or a product subject to the WTO/GATT 1994?[22] If water is a good subject to the GATT 1994, it will be considered a good subject to the NAFTA. The NAFTA defines a 'good' subject to its provisions as 'domestic products as these are understood in the General Agreement on Tariffs and Trade'.[23] The GATT 1994 contains no definition of 'good' or 'product'. However, the World Customs Union's Harmonizing Commodity Description and Coding System, which identifies products for tariffs purposes under the GATT 1994, covers water in various forms.[24] Heading 22.01 includes 'waters, including natural or artificial mineral and aerated waters, not containing added sugar or other sweetening matter nor flavored; ice and snow'.[25] An explanatory note adds 'ordinary water of all kinds (other than sea water)'. The subheadings cover 'Mineral waters and aerated waters' and 'Other'.[26] While it may seem odd to include 'ice', in the nineteenth century the sale of ice was a major enterprise in the northeastern part of the United States.[27] Heading 22.02 covers 'Waters,

[20] *See Canadian Government: Strategy [to] Prohibit the Bulk Removal of Canadian Water, Including Water for Export*, M2Presswire, February 2, 1999, available at 1999 WL 12604553. Removal for bottling would not qualify.

[21] Quebec Water Resources Preservation Act, R.S.Q. P-18.1, sec. 2, para. 1 (1999), available at http://www.canlii.org/qc/laws/sta/p-18.1/20041104/whole.htm (last visited January 18, 2005).

[22] For detailed analysis of alternative approaches in answering this question, see Robert J. Girouard, *Water Export Restrictions: A Case Study of WTO Dispute Settlement Strategies and Outcomes*, 15 Geo. Int'l L. Rev. 247 (2003).

[23] *See* NAFTA, *supra* note 5, Art. 201, available at http://www.nafta-sec-alena.org/DefaultSite/index_e.aspx (last visited January 8, 2005).

[24] World Customs Organization, Harmonized Commodity Description and Coding System: Explanatory Notes (3rd edn, 2002).

[25] *Id.*, at 186, Heading 22.01.

[26] *Id.* Explanatory note (A).

[27] James M. Utterbach, Mastering the Dynamics of Innovation 146–157 (1994).

including mineral waters and aerated waters, containing added sugar or other sweetening matter or flavored and other nonalcoholic beverages, not including fruit or vegetable juices of Heading 20.09.'[28] Heading 25.01 covers 'salt (including table salt and denatured salt) . . . ; sea water'.[29] The Canadian Department of Foreign Affairs and International Trade notes that because Canada's (and most other countries') tariff schedule includes 'natural waters' as a tariff heading, some commentators have suggested that this means that all water must be considered as a good. But the Department concludes: 'This is a mistaken view of the purpose of the tariff schedule. . . . it does not tell us if and when water is a good; it only tells us that when water is classified as a good, it falls under a particular tariff heading.'[30]

From this classification of goods for tariff purposes, nonetheless, some might argue that the GATT 1994 covers any diversion of water from its natural state, whether from the surface or by extension from an aquifer. This could extend to all diversions of water or pumping of water for any purpose, since the water would be removed from its natural state. Should the diversion or pumping cross national borders, it would be subject to the trade disciplines.

However, one might distinguish further between diversions such as damming, flooding, or altering watercourses to force water to flow to a targeted destination from other means of diversion, such as conveyance by pipeline.[31] The latter would then qualify as a good, while the former would not. Others have suggested that the criteria should include whether there has been human intervention to extract the water and put it into a form that could be introduced into commerce, or whether there are agreements relating to the price of the water delivered.[32]

The broad interpretation of the definition of 'good' and of 'product' to cover water in its natural state is arguably inconsistent with the intent and the language of the GATT 1994 regarding tariffs. In any case, it is unwise. The description for purposes of the Harmonized Tariff Schedule refers to water when it has entered into trade as a commodity. It is doubtful that the authors of the Tariff Schedule contemplated covering, or intended to cover, water in its natural state or large-scale bulk transfers of water. There is no tariff binding yet on water. Moreover, it is not clear that any State has established a schedule for water. In October 2001, Mexico circulated a Notification to the Committee on

[28] World Customs Organization, *supra* note 24 at 187, Heading 22.02.

[29] *Id.* at 210, Heading 25.01.

[30] *Bulk Water Removals and International Trade Considerations: Document from the Canadian Department of Foreign Affairs and International Trade, Nov. 16, 1999*, International Joint Commission, Protection of the Waters of the Great Lakes: Final Report to the Governments of Canada and the United States, February 22, 2000, p. 67, available at http://www.ijc.org/php/publications/html/finalreport.html (last visited January 18, 2005).

[31] Scott Philip Little, *Canada's Capacity to Control the Flow: Water Export and the North American Free Trade Agreement*, 8 Pace Int'l. L. Rev. 141 (1996).

[32] Esther J. de Haan, *Balancing Free Trade in Water and the Protection of Water Resources in GATT*, in The Scarcity of Water: Emerging Legal and Policy Responses 248–9 (Edward H. P. Brans et al., eds, 1997).

Technical Barriers to Trade ('TBT') of its draft Mexican Official Standard regarding sanitary specifications for water and ice for human consumption, 'either pre-packaged or in bulk, except for water consumed directly from supply systems'.[33] However, a Notification under the Technical Barriers to Trade Agreement of the WTO is completely separate from the Tariff Schedule. It does suggest, though, that at the point when bulk water becomes subject to human consumption, such as for drinking water, it becomes a good or product for purposes of the TBT.

The GATT 1994 does not expressly define the term 'product'. According to the *Oxford Compact English Dictionary*, 'product' originates from the Latin word meaning 'something produced', and can be defined as 'a substance produced during a natural, chemical, or manufacturing process'.[34] This suggests that something must be done to water to make it a product, and that mere diversion, pumping, or transfer does not suffice. As long as it remains in its natural state or source, water could not be a 'product'. Water is mobile, it seeps into the ground, evaporates into the air, flows in sometimes unpredictable ways, 'dries up' or inundates land areas. When it is maintained as instream flow (as for recreational, fisheries, or tourist uses), or diverted or transferred in earthen canals, similar physical processes take place, which makes it difficult to characterize it as a product.

Canada, Mexico, and the United States addressed the issue of fresh water in relation to the NAFTA. In 1993, the three governments issued the following statement regarding the application of the NAFTA to water:

> The NAFTA creates no rights to the natural water resources of any Party to the Agreement.
>
> Unless water, in any form, has entered into commerce and become a good or product, it is not covered by the provisions of any trade agreement including the NAFTA. And nothing in the NAFTA would oblige any NAFTA Party to either exploit its water for commercial use, or to begin exporting water in any form. Water in its natural state in lakes, rivers, reservoirs, aquifers, water basins and the like is not a good or product, is not traded, and therefore is not and never has been subject to the terms of any trade agreement.[35]

The U.S. Deputy Trade Representative reaffirmed this position in a 1999 letter to the International Joint Commission in connection with the Commission's deliberations on diversion of water from the Great Lakes. The letter noted that '...the WTO simply has nothing to say regarding the basic decision by governments on whether to permit the extraction of water from lakes and rivers in their territory,' although it did observe that '[t]his is not say that WTO rules

[33] World Trade Organization, Committee on Technical Barriers to Trade, Notification, Doc. G/TBT/N/Mex/8 (October 3, 2001).

[34] Oxford Compact English Dictionary (2003), available at http://www.askoxford.com/dictionaries/compact_oed/ (last visited January 18, 2005).

[35] 1993 Statement by the Governments of Canada, Mexico, and the United States, available at http://www.scics.gc.ca/cinfo99/83067000_e.html#statement (last visited January 8, 2005). The text is available in Appendix D of the present book.

could never apply to water which has been extracted from a watercourse and actually traded in international commerce.'[36] The Canadian Department of Foreign Affairs and International Trade was equally explicit:

> Water in its natural state can be equated with other natural resources, such as trees in the forest, fish in the sea, or minerals in the ground. While all of these things can be transformed into saleable commodities through harvesting or extraction, until that crucial step is taken they remain natural resources and outside the scope of the trade agreements.[37]

In its 2000 report on 'Protection of the Waters of the Great Lakes', the International Joint Commission between Canada and the United States reaffirmed the governmental positions that water in its natural state is not a good. But the Commission noted that '[w]hen water is "captured" and enters into commerce, it may, however, attract obligations under the GATT, the FTA, and the NAFTA'.[38]

The question remains: at what point is water deemed to be captured and to enter into commerce? Are bulk transfers across national borders included? Should they be?

4. The relevance of the GATT 1994 to bulk transfers

International agreements specific to particular international river basins may provide rules of allocation and use that determine whether transfers in bulk of fresh water from the river basin are legal. Alternatively, there may be no relevant international water agreements; only national, provincial, or local laws may govern the legality of the transfer. In the absence of legal constraints, such transfers would be permitted. International trade law comes on top of this existing framework of regulation.

4.1 The applicable trade provisions

Three articles of the GATT 1994 contain the provisions most readily applicable to transboundary water transfers: Articles I, III, and XI. Of these the last is likely the most relevant.

[36] *Letter from the Deputy United States Trade Representative, November 24, 1999*, International Joint Commission, Protection of the Waters of the Great Lakes: Final Report to the Governments of Canada and the United States, February 22, 2000, p. 65, available at http://www.ijc.org/php/publications/html/finalreport.html (last visited January 18, 2005).

[37] *Bulk Water Removals and International Trade Considerations: Document from the Canadian Department of Foreign Affairs and International Trade, Nov. 16, 1999*, International Joint Commission, Protection of the Waters of the Great Lakes: Final Report to the Governments of Canada and the United States, February 22, 2000, p. 67, available at http://www.ijc.org/php/publications/html/finalreport.html (last visited January 18, 2005).

[38] International Joint Commission, Protection of the Waters of the Great Lakes: Final Report to the Governments of Canada and the United States, February 22, 2000, Section 8, Law & Policy, International Legal Context, available at http://www.ijc.org/php/publications/html/finalreport.html (last visited January 18, 2005).

Article XI(1) provides the substantive rule on export and import restrictions:

> No prohibitions or restrictions other than duties, taxes or other charges ... shall be instituted ... on the importation of any product ... or on the exportation or sale for export of any product destined for the territory of any other contracting party.[39]

Article XI(2)(a) provides an exception to this general prohibition for '[e]xport prohibitions or restrictions temporarily applied to prevent or relieve critical shortages of food stuffs or other products *essential* to the exporting contracting party'.[40]

Whether Article XI applies depends initially on whether a bulk transfer of fresh water is considered a product. If it is not, Article XI does not apply. If it is a product, then a State's ban on the export (or import) of fresh water would violate Article XI, unless it were covered by the exception in Article XI(2) or other general exception under Article XX. In certain cases, such as drought, unexpected contamination of water supplies as by accidents or natural disasters, or other such emergencies, temporary restrictions on exports could be justified under the exception. The shortage would need to be critical and essential to the exporting country, but presumably, in certain emergencies, fresh water would qualify. However, the export restrictions could only be temporary. The exception would not be available to support restraints on the export of fresh water when water shortages were not critical.

Countries may want to restrict exports not only to provide fresh water to people and to their industries, but also to protect ecology and river basin ecosystems. Fish and other wildlife and flora depend upon fresh water resources. If fresh water were to be viewed as a product even in its natural state, and the river basin ecosystem as essential to the country, then the exception in Article XI(2) might become relevant should the ecosystem be threatened.

Article III provides for national treatment of international taxation and regulations for both domestic and imported products. Article III(4) provides that the imported products 'shall be accorded treatment no less favourable than that accorded to like products of national origin in respect of all laws, regulations and requirements affecting their internal sale, offering for sale, purchase, transportation, distribution or use'.[41] If bulk transfers of water were to be treated as 'like products', the requirements of national treatment would apply. Issues might arise in the context of regulations over the quality of imported water, but it is not clear why countries would want to regulate the quality of water transfers domestically, as treatment of water for a given quality is generally considered as a separate issue. Similarly, it is difficult to see why a country would not want to import water if it could.

However, discrimination issues could arise in the context of foreign investment in water resources or water services in a country, and the application of

[39] GATT 1994, *supra* note 4, Art. XI(1).

[40] *Id.*, Art. XI(2) (emphasis added).

[41] *Id.*, Art. III(4).

national or local laws and regulations. These are pursued in Part IV Water and Investment, later in this book.

Article I might also be relevant to bulk transfers. Article I provides for general most favoured nation treatment, which requires that any of the specified categories of 'favors' granted by one country to any product originating in or destined for any other country be accorded 'immediately and unconditionally to the like product originating in or destined for the territories of all other contracting parties'.[42] Were the GATT 1994 to apply to bulk transfers, and were a country to receive bulk water transfers from more than one country or export such water to more than one country, the disciplines of Article I could restrain countries from discriminating among 'receivers or senders' in the favors granted.

If a country were to violate Articles XI, III, or I, then the exceptions in Article XX(b) and (g) become relevant. Article XX provides as follows:

> Subject to the requirement that such measures are not applied in a manner which would constitute a means of arbitrary or unjustifiable discrimination between countries where the same conditions prevail, or a disguised restriction on international trade, nothing in this Agreement shall be construed to prevent the adoption or enforcement by any contracting party of measures:
> (b) necessary to protect human, animal or plant life or health;
> (g) relating to the conservation of exhaustible natural resources if such measures are made effective in conjunction with restriction on domestic production or consumption.

According to the WTO Appellate Body in the Reformulated Gasoline Case[43] and to practice, the first test is whether one of the exceptions in Article XX applies, and if it does, the next test is whether the chapeau language of Article XX is satisfied.

Prohibitions or restraints on water exports could qualify under the Article XX(b) exception if they were in fact 'necessary to protect human, animal or plant life or health'. This would presumably cover measures necessary to reserve water for the robustness of ecosystems, animal populations, and drinking water and sanitation supplies. One might conceivably argue that it should extend to agriculture on the grounds that agriculture produces food essential to human and animal health, though this argument has not been made. Much of agriculture is destined for export. The Article XX exception presumably would not reach measures that are intended to restrain bulk transfers of water to ensure sufficient supplies for agriculture.

It may be possible to argue that all restraints on the export of fresh water are measures to ensure that there is enough water locally to maintain the ecosystem and to provide adequate urban and rural water supplies to people. Since future climate is uncertain and the vagaries of weather ever more extreme, this argument would hold that it is important to take a cautious approach and maintain fresh water supplies within a country, unless the water flows in international watercourse systems.

[42] GATT 1994, *supra* note 4, Art. I.

[43] *See World Trade Organization Appellate Body: Report of the Appellate Body in the United States—Standards for Reformulated and Conventional Gasoline* (adopted May 20, 1996), W.T.O. Doc. WT/DSZ/AB/R.

Article XX(g) provides an exception for measures that relate to the conservation of exhaustible natural resources, but only if such measures are made effective in conjunction with restrictions on domestic production or consumption. Technically fresh water is not an exhaustible natural resource, unless it is contained in fossil ground water aquifers. It merely changes form. However, in any particular location, fresh water can be an exhaustible natural resource in the sense that a decrease in supply may result in essentially irreversible ecological changes. If oil and natural gas are considered exhaustible natural resources, fresh water supplies also should be. A restraint on exports, however, satisfies the paragraph (g) exception only if it is made in conjunction with domestic production or consumption. Prohibitions on exports designed to protect ecosystems might then need to be accompanied by bans on shipments of water out-of-basin. Thus, unless a country (in reality a local or provincial government) was willing to restrict out-of-basin transfers of water, it could not satisfy the international requirements for the exception. There is precedence for this domestically in the United States, where the Supreme Court has prohibited restraints on the export of ground water between states as violations of the Constitution's Commerce Clause, unless the restrictions are part of a state's own conservation plan which limits use within the state.[44]

Assuming that the measures came either within (b) or (g), they must still satisfy the conditions in the chapeau language,[45] namely that the measure not 'constitute a means of arbitrary or unjustifiable discrimination between countries where the same conditions prevail, or a disguised restriction on international trade'. Interpreting whether a given measure is 'arbitrary or unjustifiable,' assumes an ability to 'second guess' the country on the need for water supplies to protect the ecosystem now and into the future. For fresh water, one can argue that the second phrase 'where the same conditions prevail' should be decisive. Since all ecosystems are inherently different from each other, the same conditions never prevail between countries. Hence, measures that restrict exports in order to protect ecosystems could not be viewed as between countries where the same conditions prevail. This would make it easy to bypass the chapeau language. However, the focus in interpreting this language has always been on 'arbitrary or unjustifiable discrimination', and not on where the same conditions prevail. Thus, it is not clear how the phrase would be interpreted. Moreover, the measures would still have to satisfy the criterion that they not be 'a disguised restriction on international trade'. This directly pits those concerned with managing international trade against those concerned with managing fresh water resources, with the trade community deciding on the legitimacy of the measure.

[44] *See* Sporhase v. Nebraska, 458 U.S. 941 (1982). A Nebraska statute forbade the transfer of water across state lines without a permit. The Court found that ground water was an article of commerce subject to the Commerce Clause of the United States Constitution, and that the Nebraska statute impermissibly burdened inter-state commerce.

[45] For an in-depth discussion of the Art. XX chapeau as it relates to environmental policy and trade, see Sanford Gaines, *The WTO's Reading of the GATT Article XX Chapeau: A Disguised Restriction on Environmental Measures*, 22 U. Pa. J. Int'l Econ. Law 739 (2001).

The discussion below examines the several different types of bulk transfer arrangements between countries, and highlights the efforts of some countries to control such exports. The subsequent section explores the pros and cons of applying or not applying the GATT 1994 to these transfers.

4.2 The bulk water transfer arrangements

Bulk transfers of water occur between different kinds of actors and in different modes. The most traditional is between governments in the form of treaties. But governments may also enter into contractual arrangements for the export and sale of bulk water. In some cases, the export arrangements are between a government (or its agency) and private companies in another country, or between private parties in both the exporting and importing country. The identity of the actors affects the relevance of the trade law disciplines.

The mode of transfer also differs. Sometimes the water is shipped in bulk in ocean tankers; at other times it is conveyed by pipeline, or conceivably other conveyances. In some cases, it would be possible to convey it by artificial canal or similar earthen mechanism. The mode of transfer should not, however, affect the application of the trade law disciplines.

a. Government to government transfers by treaty

Sometimes large-scale transfers of water take place pursuant to a treaty. For example, the water-rich Kingdom of Lesotho sells water by treaty to the Republic of South Africa. In return for providing a reliable source of water, the South African government guarantees millions of dollars in payment to Lesotho.[46] The recently completed $2.5 billion Katse Dam, which is the first phase of the Highlands Water Project, catches water from Lesotho's highlands and ferries it via an elaborate system of dams and underground tunnels to South Africa.[47] The project transfers about 910 cubic feet of water per second from Lesotho to six of South Africa's nine provinces. The treaty between the two countries created several entities that are charged with jointly implementing the project. The project, which is partially funded by the World Bank, is a prototype for other water resource development projects.

The Kingdom of Lesotho is under no obligation to reach agreement with other neighboring countries to provide fresh water. Lesotho could also decide not to comply with its obligation to provide the water, and the remedies would be

[46] Treaty on the Lesotho Highlands Water Project, October 24, 1986, Lesotho-S. Afr., *cited in* Fred. O. Boadu, *Relational Characteristics of Transboundary Water Treaties: Lesotho's Water Transfer Treaty with the Republic of South Africa*, NAT. RESOURCES J. 381 (1998). The treaty has not yet been registered with the United Nations. *See also* Salman M. A. Salman, *Legal Regime for Use and Protection of International Watercourses in the Southern African Region: Evolution and Context*, 41 NAT. RESOURCES J. 981 *et seq.* (2001).

[47] For more information on the project, see http://web.worldbank.org/WBSITE/EXTERNAL/NEWS/0,,contentMDK:20018028~menuPK:34460~pagePK:64003015~piPK:64003012~theSitePK:4607,00.html (last visited January 8, 2005).

those available under the treaty, with the funding entity, or generally in public international law.

One could argue that water is certainly a good here, that it has a price, and that the receiving country would suffer should Lesotho decide to ban the export of water from Lesotho. Moreover, neighboring countries, such as Mozambique, are not happy about the water exports going to South Africa. While all of this may be true, there is still no obligation in trade law for a country to sell its water outside its border, nor, I would argue, should trade disciplines affect the choice of importer. Moreover, in this case, under the rules of the Vienna Convention on Treaties, the treaty between the two countries should prevail.[48]

b. Government to government contractual transfers

Israel and Turkey have signed a ten-year contractual agreement in which Israel is to buy 50 million cubic meters of water annually from the Manavgat region of Turkey. The agreement is for twenty years.[49] The water will be shipped in bulk by sea to Israel. A spokesman for the Israel Foreign Ministry said that the agreement was a landmark, which turns water into an internationally accepted 'commodity'.[50]

Other water exports between countries are planned or already occurring. Turkey reportedly plans to sell water to countries, such as Malta, Cyprus, and the Gulf countries, where fresh water is very scarce.[51] Iran reportedly may enter into a thirty-year contract with Kuwait to export water from her rivers to supply Kuwait's needs, and there are reports of plans to supply water to Qatar and Saudi Arabia.[52] In Southeast Asia, Malaysia sends untreated water to Singapore, which treats it and sells some of it back to Malaysia for a profit.[53]

c. Transfers between government and foreign private party

The transfers between countries may also take place between the national government (or a branch of it) and foreign companies. For example, Bolivia permits the export of water by the government to foreign users. In November 2001, the Bolivian Parliament approved its Water Export Law, which permits the Bolivian Water Resources Corporation (COBOREH) to export water.[54] The

[48] Vienna Convention on the Law of Treaties, May 22, 1969, 1155 U.N.T.S. 331.

[49] Joshua Brilliant, 'Israel to Import Water from Turkey', *United Press International*, March 20, 2002; William M. Turner, 'Water Export from Manavgat, Turkey', April 1, 2004, at http://www.waterbank.com/Newsletters/nws23.html (last visited January 18, 2005).

[50] Turner, *supra* note 49. When the agreement was signed, the price was reportedly still being negotiated, and payment for the water might be partly in military hardware. *Id.*

[51] 'Turkey Plans Water Export to Gulf States', March 29, 2004, at http://www.turks.us.article (last visited January 18, 2005).

[52] 'Iran Says It Will Export Water to Kuwait: Daily', July 31, 2000, at http://www.payvand.com/news/00/jul/1134.html (last visited January 18, 2005).

[53] *See* Brian D. Anderson, *Selling Great Lakes Water to a Thirsty World: Legal, Policy & Trade Considerations*, 6 Buff. Envt'l. L. J. 245 (1999).

[54] *See* William M. Turner, 'Bolivia Permits Bulk Export of Water to Chile', at http://www.waterbank.com/Newsletters/nws39.html (last visited January 18, 2005). If the COBOREH could be viewed as a state trading enterprise, it may invoke the trade disciplines of Art. XVII of the GATT 1994.

immediate export project is to mining companies in Chile. Plans called for initial export of 800 liters per second, rising to 3,000 liters per second at the end of the project's third year.[55]

d. Transfers between private parties in different countries

In the future, many water exports may be by a company in the exporting country to a company or other user in another country. In Alaska, a private company plans to ship water by tankers to Hong Kong, where it goes to a plant bottling water for market. The Alaska government must approve the sale of water and the exporter must pay a user's fee.[56] Similarly, a private company in British Columbia company sold water to a US company for making bottled water, with the permit obtained from the provincial government, until the government banned the export of bulk water.[57]

4.3 National and local efforts to limit exports of water

At the same time that some countries, such as Bolivia or Turkey, are initiating exports of bulk water, other countries are limiting exports of water, both at the national and provincial or local levels. Canada provides an excellent example of limitations on bulk water export at both the federal and provincial level. The Canadian Constitution makes it clear that many water issues, including flow regulation, authorization of water use development, and the authority to legislate in areas of water supply, pollution control, and thermal/hydroelectric power development, remain under provincial control.[58] However, a federal water policy also exists.[59] The federal policy seeks to implement a strategy of cooperation with provincial governments on water management issues and dictates that all possible measures will be taken to prohibit the export of water from Canada through inter-basin transfers. Canada also amended the International Boundary Waters Treaty Act in 2001 to prohibit removing boundary waters outside the water basin.[60] This follows on the recent regulations which

[55] Royalties will be paid on the water exported. The Chilean mining companies scheduled to use the water include both larger and smaller mining companies.

[56] *See* Anderson, *supra* note 53 at 243.

[57] Sun Belt Water, a United States company, issued a notice of intent to sue Canada under Chapter 11 of the NAFTA after British Columbia banned the bulk export of water, for damages over $200 million for the loss of a contract to ship Canadian water to California. Sun Belt viewed water as a commodity and British Columbia's ban of bulk exports as providing preferential treatment to Canadian companies in violation of the NAFTA. *See* Sun Belt Water, Inc. v. Gov't of Canada, November 27, 1998, available at http://www.dfait-maeci.gc.ca/tna-nac/disp/sunbelt_archive-en.asp (last visited January 10, 2005).

[58] Environment Canada, *Water Policy and Legislation: Jurisdictional Responsibilities*, at http://www.ec.gc.ca/water/en/policy/coop/e_juris.htm (last visited January 18, 2005).

[59] Canadian Federal Water Policy, available at http://www.ec.gc.ca/water/en/info/pubs/fedpol/e_fedpol.htm (last visited January 18, 2005).

[60] *An Act to Amend the International Boundary Waters Treaty*, December 18, 2001, 2001 S.C. ch. 40, available at http://www.canlii.org/ca/as/2001/c40/sec1.html (last visited January 18, 2005).

many provinces have passed prohibiting the export of bulk water outside their province, which have the effect of prohibiting transfers outside Canada.

Nearly every province in Canada has instituted some type of limitation on bulk water transfers, whether in the form of a provincial policy or actual legislation (see Table 3.1). British Columbia's 1996 Water Protection Act provides a good example of provincial legislation regulating bulk water transfers. The Act prohibits the removal of water from British Columbia, except if the water is packaged in containers 20 liters or less in volume, and bans large-scale transfers of water between major watersheds in the province.[61] Provinces such as the Northwest Territories and Nunavut, which have not enacted legislation on bulk water exports, have adopted provincial policies forbidding the export of water in containers greater than 40 liters in volume. Because under the Canadian Constitution the provinces have primary authority over water development and control, these provincial measures are especially important. The Federal government has attempted unsuccessfully to reach accords with the provincial governments to prohibit exports.[62]

The locus of authority for water resources at the provincial level has important implications for implementation of the GATT 1994. If only a country's subnational units attempted to limit international exports of water from their borders, any of the GATT 1994 obligations discussed above that could apply to prevent such restraints might not be enforceable beyond the country's federal government. Specifically, because the GATT 1994 in Article XXIV(12) requires a contracting party to take 'reasonable measures ... to ensure observance of the provisions of this Agreement ... within its territory', a national government might not breach its GATT 1994 obligations as long as it does 'everything within its power' to win compliance from its states or provinces, regardless of whether or not it succeeds.[63]

5. Evaluating the application of WTO/GATT 1994 to bulk transfers

Whether the GATT 1994 applies to bulk transfers of water has important policy implications for international trade, water and agricultural policy, and ecosystem protection. This chapter examines both the reasons to apply the GATT 1994 and those reasons which caution against doing so.

[61] British Columbia, Water Protection Act, R.S.B.C., ch. 484, sec. 4, 5, 6 (1996), available at http://www.qp.gov.bc.ca/statreg/stat/W/96484_01.htm#section4 (last visited January 18, 2005).

[62] For more information on Canada's water export policy, see Gary Fritz and Matthew J. McKinney, *Canadian Water Export Policy and Continental Water Marketing*, Continental Water Marketing 71-92 (Terry L. Anderson ed., 1994). The conflict between humanitarians and economists, who see people to be helped and money to be made, versus the conservationists, who see fresh water as Canada's most precious resource, must also be considered. *See* Anderson, *supra* note 53, at 215 for a discussion of cultural, political, and human rights implications of a ban on water exports from Canada.

[63] *See* John H. Jackson et al., Legal Problems of International Economic Relations 242–4 (4th edn, 2002).

Table 3.1: Canadian Provincial Bulk Water Legislation

Province	*Bulk Water Legislation*	*Title*	*Year*	*Out of Province Transfers*	*Out of Basin Transfers*	*Allowances*
Alberta	Yes	Water Act	1999	Transfer from province out of Canada Prohibited	Prohibited	
British Columbia	Yes	Water Protection Act	1996	Prohibited	Prohibited	Containers 20L or less
Manitoba	Yes	Water Resources Conservation and Protection Act	2000	Prohibited	Removal from Hudson Bay basin Prohibited	Containers 25L or less; vehicle*; transport food/products; humanitarian purposes^, water used to manufacture or produce products transferred out of basin
New Brunswick	No					
Newfoundland/Labrador	Yes	Water Resources Act	2002	Prohibited	Permitted	Containers 30 L or less; vehicle; to transport food/products; humanitarian purposes^
Northwest Territories	No**					
Nunavut	No***					
Nova Scotia	Yes	Water Resources Act	2000	Prohibited	Prohibited	Containers 25 L or less; vehicle*; transport food/products; humanitarian purposes^;

Table 3.1: Canadian Provincial Bulk Water Legislation (cont)

Province	*Bulk Water Legislation*	*Title*	*Year*	*Out of Province Transfers*	*Out of Basin Transfers*	*Allowances*
Ontario	Yes	Water Transfer Control Act; Water Resources Act	1990 (amended 1993); 1999	Prohibited	Prohibited	Containers 20L or less; vehicle*; water used to manufacture products transferred out of basin
Prince Edward Island	Yes	Environmental Protection Act	2001	Prohibited	Prohibited	Containers 25L or less for drinking; vehicle*; transport of products; humanitarian purposes^
Quebec	Yes	Water Resources Preservation Act	1999	Prohibited	Permitted	Containers 20L or less for drinking; vehicle*; removed to produce electric power; potable water for border communities; humanitarian purposes
Saskatchewan	No****					
Yukon	No*****					

^With Minister Approval. * The vehicle allowance permits the removal of water in a vehicle for the ordinary operation of that vehicle and for the use of the people in the vehicle while they are transporting it. ** The Northwest Territories announced a policy to prohibit bulk water transfers in 2003 with an allowance for containers 40L or less in volume. *** Nunavut announced a policy prohibiting bulk water exports similar to that of the Northwest Territories in 2003. **** In 1999, Saskatchewan implemented an export policy requiring that water be removed only for drinking purposes and in containers 10L or less in volume. In 2001, the Water Corporation Act was amended to prohibit the water corporation from allowing out of basin transfers. However, the Water Corporation Act was subsequently repealed in 2002, and the new statute does not mention prohibitions of bulk water transfer. ***** Yukon only recently took control over the management of its waters from the Federal government (April 1, 2003).

5.1 Reasons to apply the GATT 1994

The reasons for extending the application of the GATT 1994 to fresh water resources relate to water's economic value and to the need to reduce barriers to trade among States. Several reasons are discussed below.

a. Recognizes the status of water as a commodity

When fresh water is transferred in bulk across a national boundary, it is generally for the purpose either of turning it into products, such as bottled water or other drink, or of using it to produce products, including agricultural produce. In theory it could also be transported for the purpose of generating electricity. Conceivably it could also be done to protect tourist areas, natural habitats, or ecosystems that have been threatened by drought. Except for the last, all of the above uses mean that bulk water is being exported and imported because of its value as an economic good. This argues for treating bulk transfers as other articles of commerce, i.e. for subjecting them to the trade disciplines. Bottled water or similar products containing water, or fertilizers to assist agriculture, are subject to such disciplines. In the absence of a compelling reason to the contrary, water should not be treated differently.

Moreover, if water were not to be treated as a commodity subject to the trade disciplines, it would open a 'slippery slope' for other natural resources, such as timber, to escape the trade disciplines. The trading regime should be expanding its coverage, not knowingly contracting it.

b. Levels the playing field for trade in water resources

If bulk water is subject to the trade disciplines, exporters in one country cannot favor one importing country over another. Similarly, importers cannot discriminate in favor of water from one country over that from another by imposing differential tariffs or quantitative limitations. This would in theory protect against bulk water being used to gain a competitive advantage. However, in many, if not most, countries water does not by itself have an economic price. The cost of bulk transfers will vary markedly depending upon mode and cost of transport and ease of extraction, i.e. it may be arbitrary and not a good guide to comparative advantage.

c. Protects against disguised barriers to trade

Limitations, or outright bans, on the export of water across national boundaries, or even bans on transferring water out of a river basin within countries, raise the possibility that such actions are intended to protect domestic water supply for economic reasons rather than to protect the ecosystem, or for some other environmental or health reason. Export restraints may be imposed in order to hold onto water so that it can be used for agriculture, thus arguably subsidizing agriculture and ensuring cheaper produce for markets. The export controls may be justified as protecting the productivity of the land. It may be difficult to determine when they are required for protecting the environmental integrity of an area, and when they provide cheap agricultural subsidies and constitute a disguised barrier to competitive trade.

All of the above considerations support subjecting bulk transfers of fresh water, at least initially, to the trade disciplines.

5.2 Reasons not to apply the GATT 1994 to water in its natural state or to bulk transfers

The reasons against applying the GATT 1994 focus on the affront to a country in exercising its national sovereignty to allocate, use, and protect its fresh water resources, and on the need for an anticipatory cautionary approach in addressing water issues.

a. Constrains a State's ability to protect ecological systems

Fresh water is essential for satisfying human needs and for protecting ecosystems and river ecology. One of the functions of governments is to be able to ensure that sufficient water is available to protect the integrity and diversity of ecosystems. Weather and climate, coupled with land use practices, largely determine how much fresh water is naturally available in any given season within a river basin. While dams and reservoirs affect quantities made available for specific uses, the underlying natural phenomena may yield marked variations over time in precipitation and ground water recharge. Governments need to be able to impose restrictions in times of scarcity to ensure that sufficient water is available to meet basic needs and to protect ecosystems.

If bulk transfers are subject to the trade disciplines, it will make it more difficult to take the measures required to meet basic needs and protect ecosystems. While the exception in Article XI(2)(a) might be available, the trade community would determine whether the measures qualified for the exception. If such measures are not subject to the trade disciplines, States could restrict the transfer of water resources more freely. Whether the importer, or the private investor in a State's water resources must be compensated is then a matter of domestic legislation. In the North American context, compensation to investors would also be subject to the provisions of the NAFTA, discussed later in this volume.

b. Makes long-term management of water resources more difficult

It is inherently difficult to predict adequately the long-term demand for and supply of water resources. This is particularly so in the face of climate change. This makes long-term management of water resources inherently difficult. While the water resources may be sufficient at one time to satisfy economic needs and protect ecosystems, they may not be in the future. When greater need for the water arises, out-of-basin diversions or contracts for the export of water may be difficult to suspend or cancel. Yet continuing to export water could stunt economic growth at home, or, worse, lead to arid, unproductive lands that lack water.

States or provinces may want to limit the export of fresh water to other countries because it is difficult to calculate future demand for the water. Once the water importer has a right, prior appropriation takes effect in practice against the subsequent need. Canceling the contract or agreement can be costly. These situations exist today. However, they would be made much more difficult if bulk transfers, or transfers of fresh water in its natural state, were subject to the trade disciplines. This is because such decisions would be subject to the additional scrutiny of whether they could be regarded as distortions of trade in violation of the GATT 1994. Governments need to be able to exercise caution with regard to exporting (and importing) water resources, without the trade community deciding whether there is sufficient scientific evidence to justify the trade restriction.

c. Gives trade considerations a significant voice in reconciling conflicting uses of water

If bulk transfers, or natural flow transfers, were subject to the trade disciplines, it would mean that within countries, those public officials charged with implementing the trade agreements would have a voice in determining whether actions affecting the allocation and use of water resources could be taken. This would have important negative effects.

First, it could make it more difficult to take the necessary actions to protect ecosystems in times of emergencies, or especially in times when shortages are forecast on the basis of hydrological and meteorological data. Trade considerations could delay decision-making and make the deliberations more complex. If bulk transfers were subject to the GATT 1994, those public officials responsible for complying with international trade agreements would have an important voice in determining whether actions nationally or locally to protect water resources could be taken. The national agency responsible for trade would be empowered in relation to those concerned with water resources in ways that do not exist today.

In countries where provincial governments hold the primary authority for decisions regarding water resources, such as Canada, national concerns about trade agreements could engender national–provincial conflicts. A provincial government might want to ban transfers in a manner that the trade ministry would regard as contravening the trade agreements. Under one scenario, conservation interests would need to push their interests at the national level, and the national government might not be willing to support the provincial government (for political reasons or otherwise). The environment or natural resources ministry might press for water conservation, but lack power to do so against pressures from the trade ministry to the contrary.

d. Gives trade dispute settlement mechanisms authority to resolve water claims

If bulk transfers, or natural flow transfers, were subject to the trade disciplines, the dispute resolution mechanisms set up under the trade agreements would be available to resolve disputes over such transfers. This could mean that the same disputes could come before different bodies, depending upon whether they arose under a multilateral or bilateral water treaty, or only under a trade agreement. Disputes that arose under international water agreements would be subject to the dispute resolution mechanisms provided in the treaty, under public international law, in domestic courts, or in other forums of dispute resolution,[64] while other disputes involving similar transfers could go before the trade dispute settlement bodies. This could encourage forum shopping and result in very different decisions for similar disputes. Moreover, it would mean that disputes about the allocation and use of water, and about the legitimacy of measures to protect ecosystems and river ecology, could be made by trade bodies. Many would argue that the latter lack the requisite expertise to decide such disputes and would be inappropriate fora.[65]

5.3 Striking the balance

As reflected above, there are competing interests in the transboundary transfer of bulk water. On the one hand, some countries, especially those in the developed world, want to limit the export of water, in good part for ecological reasons. In other cases, they may wish to protect their fresh water resources to further their own economic development. Developing countries, especially the least developed countries, or middle-income countries with abundant water resources, may find the export of fresh water attractive, for they earn revenue from it. Moreover, since water stimulates development, they may view efforts of developed countries to prevent the export of water as unfair on their part, since they have already achieved development. These arguments could be, and have been, raised in many international environmental issues.

In striking the balance for fresh water, it is essential to consider that water is different from other natural resources. It is a unique resource. Fresh water is essential for human life and for ecosystems, and there are no known substitutes for water. Moreover, people have strong emotional ties to water. Thus, it would be prudent to adopt an approach of 'anticipatory caution', to strike the appropriate balance between the need to conserve water resources and the need to ensure a level playing field in trading relationships. Anticipatory caution means that in the face of uncertainty about the future, a country should be able to exercise its sovereign authority to maintain its fresh water resources without having to convince the trade community of the legitimacy of its actions. This is especially important because of the difficulty of predicting water demand and water supply, and of anticipating adequately the natural variations that will affect water availability and the stability and integrity of the Earth's ecosystems. Anticipatory caution is an extension of, or complement to, the precautionary

[64] Resolution of International Water Disputes: Papers Emanating from the Sixth P.C.A. International Law Seminar, Nov. 8, 2002 (Int'l Bureau of Permanent Court of Arbitration ed., 2003) (providing comprehensive review of issues, methods, and fora).

[65] *See*, e.g., Boisson de Chazournes, chapter 14 of the present book.

approach, which is well reflected in international law.[66] While this approach justifies taking action in the face of scientific uncertainty, anticipatory caution justifies retaining flexibility for responding to uncertainty about the future and protects against becoming locked into actions that would undermine such flexibility. It is especially relevant to the management of fresh water resources.

Exempting bulk transfers together with water in its natural state from trade agreements would be consistent with the de facto status of oil resources under the trade agreements. For historical reasons, oil has not been subject to the GATT 1994. This is because many of the countries who are the largest producers of oil were not contracting parties to the GATT 1947, prior to the WTO, and some still are not members of the WTO. Of those countries that each produce more than approximately 2% of the world's oil, only Brazil, Canada, Indonesia, Kuwait, Nigeria, Norway, the United Kingdom, the United States, and Venezuela were party to the former GATT prior to the WTO. Only four member countries in OPEC were party to the prior GATT,[67] and only ⅔ were members of the WTO/GATT 1994 as of January 1, 2005.[68] Saudi Arabia, Iran, Iraq, and Algeria, members of OPEC, were not members of the WTO.

While trade in oil would conceptually be subject to the trade disciplines as oil is considered a product in the market place, the failure to subject it to the trade disciplines provides strong precedent for not subjecting bulk transfers of water across national borders to the trade disciplines. Moreover, unlike oil,[69] fresh water is a resource for which there are no known substitutes, and it serves vital functions for both people and the Earth's ecosystems.

6. Alternatives for Implementing the Balance

If bulk transfers and water flowing in its natural state are to be considered normally exempt from the GATT 1994, the question is how best to accomplish this. One set of options relates to measures that a country might take at the national level that are legal under the GATT 1994 to discourage bulk transfers. These include water extraction quotas and export taxes. A country could also

[66] *See*, e.g., Rio Declaration on Environment and Development, June 1992, Principle 15, U.N. Doc. A/CONF/151/5/Rev.1, 31 I.L.M. 874 (1992), available at http://www.unep.org/Documents/Default.asp?DocumentID=78&ArticleID=1163 (last visited January 23, 2005); *see also* Arie Trowborst, Evolution and Status of the Precautionary Principle in International Law (2002); James Cameron, *The Precautionary Principle in International Law*, in Reinterpreting the Precautionary Principle 113 (Tim O' Riordan, James Cameron & Andrew Jordan, eds, 2001); Charles Weiss, *Scientific Uncertainty and Science Based Precaution*, International environmental agreements: politics, Law and Economics 137–66 (2003).

[67] Member Countries, OPEC, available at http://www.opec.org (last visited January 15, 2005). A significant difference between OPEC and non-OPEC countries is that OPEC countries produce most of their oil for export.

[68] Member Countries, WTO, available at http://www.wto.org (last visited January 15, 2005).

[69] In the transportation sector, however, there is still no economically viable substitute for oil available on a large scale.

try for tariff negotiations. The second set of options relates to those measures provided in Articles IX and X of the Marrakesh Agreement Establishing the WTO for clarifying, interpreting, and amending the agreement, or providing a waiver under it. Both sets of options are elaborated below.

6.1 The national measures to discourage exports

Countries have national sovereignty over the water resources within their territory, subject to any international agreements to which they are a party or to rules of customary international law. Thus, countries could adopt limits on extracting water resources, whether from surface watercourses or ground water aquifers, consistent with the GATT 1994. The extraction limits used by OPEC do not violate the GATT 1994. States or provinces could adopt such extraction limits, and indeed already do by their permit systems for the allocation and use of water. A country could also adopt an export tax on water, and put it at a level high enough to discourage bulk transfers of water across national borders. While this measure could be attractive for those concerned about quantitative restrictions under Article XI of the GATT 1994, it could raise domestic legitimacy problems. For example, the United States Constitution prohibits the use of export taxes, as demonstrated when the United States Supreme Court invalidated the Harbor Maintenance Tax.[70] Countries could also renegotiate tariffs to increase the price of exported water and discourage exports, but renegotiation could require compensation under Article XVIII.

The advantage of relying on such measures is that only those countries that wish to discourage or to prohibit the export of fresh water would be involved. Those that want to transfer water for revenue could do so. The problem with export taxes or tariffs is that it is difficult to set the tax or tariff at a level that will be effective in ensuring the needed water conservation. Moreover, export taxes would not respond quickly to a requirement to conserve fresh water for immediate needs.

6.2 The alternatives for applying the agreement

The Marrakesh Agreement Establishing the WTO[71] sets forth four ways for clarifying the application of the WTO/GATT 1994: by decision, by interpretation, by waiving its application in specific cases, or by amending the agreement.[72] These will be considered in reverse order.

[70] U.S. v. United States Shoe Co., 523 U.S. 360 (1998).

[71] Marrakesh Agreement Establishing the WTO, April 15, 1994, 1915 U.N.T.S. 103, available at www.wto.english/docs_e/legal_e/04-wto_e.htm (last visited January 18, 2005).

[72] For explanation and analysis, see John H. Jackson, William J. Davey & Alan O. Sykes, Jr., International Economic Relations 223–6 (4th edn, 2002); Dencho Georgiev, *The Decision-Making Process in the World Trade Organization*, Essays on the Future of the WTO: Finding a New Balance 25–46 (Kim Van der Borght, ed., 2003).

a. Amendment

One approach would be to try to amend the GATT 1994 to provide that bulk transfers of fresh water and natural water flows are not covered by the Agreement. Alternatively, an amendment could create a new exception in Article XX to cover all measures for the conservation of water resources. This would make it clear that even if bans on the export of fresh water contravened provisions of the GATT 1994, they could still be justified under Article XX, provided that they also satisfied the chapeau in Article XX, which requires that the measures not 'constitute a means of arbitrary or unjustifiable discrimination between countries where the same conditions prevail, or a disguised restriction on trade'. As discussed earlier, disputes could arise over the application of the chapeau language. The requirements in the chapeau would in practice subject the actions taken to protect fresh water resources to the scrutiny of the trade disciplines.

The Marrakesh Agreement sets forth in Article X the procedures for amending the WTO. An amendment must be approved by the WTO Ministerial Conference by a two-thirds vote of the whole membership. The WTO Members may by consensus propose the submission of an amendment to the GATT 1994. If consensus is not available, a two-thirds vote of all Members is needed to submit the amendment to the Ministerial Conference for consideration. Amendments come into force when approved if they do not affect Member rights and obligations. Otherwise they generally come into force only for those Members approving them. The amendment procedures make it difficult for Member States to amend the WTO. It is unlikely that countries would use the procedure for an amendment to exempt bulk transfers and water in its natural state from the GATT 1994.

b. Waiver

A second option is for Member States to agree to waive the application of particular obligations of the GATT 1994 to all bulk transfers of fresh water between countries and to all water in its natural state flowing across national boundaries. Under the GATT 1947, waivers were used, primarily for agricultural trade. While there was some concern under the GATT 1947 that waivers might be used as an implicit substitute for amending the agreement, the concern did not materialize. The waivers generally extended for long periods of time.

The WTO rules regarding waivers are tighter than those applicable under the former GATT. Under Article IX:3, the Ministerial Conference may waive an obligation, if consensus is reached. Otherwise an affirmative vote of three-quarters of all the WTO Members is required for the grant of a waiver. Moreover, waivers must now include a termination date and indicate the exceptional circumstances justifying the waiver. Waivers are intended for shorter-term use, rather than long-term application. While a waiver might be appropriate for transfers of bulk water in specific circumstances, in light of unusual circumstances, it would not be appropriate for a general exception to the GATT 1994 obligations.

c. Interpretation of the agreement

Under Article IX:2 of the Marrakesh Agreement, the WTO Ministerial Conference and the General Council have the exclusive authority to adopt interpretations of the WTO and its agreements, including the GATT 1994. After the relevant Council (in this case, the Council for Trade in Goods for the GATT 1994) recommends an Interpretation, three-fourths of all the Members must vote for it. The question could be raised as to whether the Chair of the Ministerial Conference and the General Council could propose a recommended Interpretation and have it adopted by consensus.[73]

An Interpretation is an attractive option, because it can be tailored to clarify the specific activities not subject to the GATT 1994. It could resemble the Statement that Canada, Mexico, and the United States issued regarding the application of the NAFTA to water, in which they declared that '[w]ater in its natural state . . . is not a good or product, is not traded, and therefore is not and never has been subject to the terms of any trade agreement'.[74] The Interpretation could cover not only water in its natural state, but bulk transfers of water, and the term 'bulk transfer of water' could be defined. Moreover, if trade in fresh water resources should develop in ways not foreseen, or the conditions surrounding bulk transfers of water change, an Interpretation might be adjusted accordingly.

Members may be reluctant to issue a formal Interpretation regarding fresh water, however, from concern that it would create a precedent for the treatment of environmental or other natural resource issues, or of multilateral environmental agreements. Members would also need to satisfy themselves that the Interpretation was not being used in lieu of an Amendment. Article IX:2 explicitly notes that Interpretations 'shall not be used in a manner that would undermine the amendment provisions in Article X'.[75]

[73] For example, when countries with limited drug manufacturing capabilities needed to obtain generic drugs produced under a compulsory license to serve public health needs, the General Council issued a Decision detailing the circumstances under which the obligations of a member under Art. 31(f) of the TRIPS Agreement could be waived for compulsory licensing with respect to pharmaceutical products. In conjunction with the Decision, the Chair of the General Council issued a Statement setting forth several understandings regarding the interpretation and implementation of the Decision. Some countries viewed this as an integral part of the Decision. *See* World Trade Organization, General Council, *Implementation of paragrah 6 of the Doha Declaration on the TRIPS Agreement and Public Health*, WTO Doc. W/T/540 (August 30, 2003), available at http://www.wto.org/english/tratop_e/trips_e/implem_para6_e.htm (last visited March 28, 2005); World Trade Organization, *General Council Chairperson's Statement*, WTO Doc. WT/GC/M/82 (August 30, 2003), available at http://www.wto.org/English/news_e/news03_e/trips_stat_28aug03_e.htm (last visited March 28, 2005); Agreement on Trade-Related Aspects of Intellectual Property Rights, April 15, 1994, Marrakesh Agreement Establishing the World Trade Organization, Annex 1C, LEGAL INSTRUMENTS – RESULTS OF THE URUGUAY ROUND, vol. 31, 33 I. L. M. 81 (1994).

[74] 1993 Statement by the Governments of Canada, Mexico, and the United States, available at http://www.scics.gc.ca/cinfo99/83067000_e.html#statement (last visited January 8, 2005).

[75] Marrakesh Agreement, *supra* note 71, Art. IX:2.

d. Ordinary Decision related to fresh water

The Marrakesh Agreement provides rules for the Ministerial Conference and the General Conference to make an 'Ordinary Decision'. Article IX:1 continues the GATT 1994 practice of taking such decisions by consensus; but if there is no consensus, of making the decision on the basis of a majority of those votes cast. For this procedure to be useful in the fresh water context, members would have to be willing to treat a decision relating to the application of the GATT 1994 to fresh water as an 'Ordinary Decision'. This seems doubtful on its face. But if the Chair of the Ministerial Conference or General Council were to read a Statement along the lines of the NAFTA statement outlined above, it might be regarded as least conceptually not as an Interpretation but rather as a separate declaration of intention by WTO Members. If it were possible, it might be adopted by consensus as an Ordinary Decision. A Statement would have the advantage of resolving the issue in the lowest profile manner, which may be appropriate since no conflicts have yet occurred.

A statement, declaration, or decision that fresh water in its natural state and bulk fresh water transfers are not intended to be subject to the obligations of the GATT 1994 may be the most appropriate way of clarifying the issue before it becomes a source of conflict.

7. Conclusions

The essential role of fresh water in ecosystems and human life requires a cautionary approach in considering the application of the trade disciplines. Products that contain water, such as bottled water or drinks, and products produced with water are subject to the trade disciplines. For the reasons outlined above, it seems clear that international waters flowing in their natural state should *not* be subject to international trade disciplines. They are already subject in most cases to an international agreement between geographically related countries. These regimes apply to the allocation, use, and conservation of the watercourses.

Bulk transfers of water across national borders raise more difficult issues in determining whether the trade disciplines, and in particular the GATT 1994, apply or should apply. Because water serves vital roles both for human life and for ecosystems, it is important to adopt an approach of anticipatory caution in subjecting bulk transfers of fresh water to international trade rules. It is especially important that the trade disciplines not apply to bulk transfers in such a way that they triumph over the need to ensure that fresh water can continue to serve its essential functions.

Members of the WTO should consider either developing an Interpretation clarifying the application of the WTO to fresh water resources, or a consensus Statement by the Chair of the WTO General Council. Alternatively, concerned countries could issue a clarifying Statement, as the three countries party to the

NAFTA did. The Statement accompanied but did not form part of the formal agreement. While that Statement referred to water in its natural state and did not explicitly mention bulk transfers, a Statement concerning the WTO/GATT 1994 could explicitly cover water in its natural state and bulk transfers of water. Such actions may be premature, given the fledgling international economy in water and the absence yet of serious international conflicts over water trade, but they could be considered for the future.

PART II

WATER SERVICES, THE GATS, AND RELATED ISSUES

4

The Human Right to Water

STEPHEN C. McCAFFREY

No one disputes that humans should have a right to water of sufficient quantity and quality to sustain life. Oddly, however, there is no explicit recognition of such a right in the basic human rights instruments. Pressure on the world's freshwater resources continues to grow and governments are increasingly forced to find ways to increase the efficiency of water supply systems. These phenomena have led to an increasing recognition of a human right to water, most recently by the UN Committee on Economic, Social, and Cultural Rights. But the precise contours of the right, and of the corresponding obligations of governments, are still coming into focus.[1] This chapter will review the support for a human right to water and explore some of the issues the right raises with regard to current conditions.[2]

Access to safe water is a fundamental human need and, therefore, a basic human right. Contaminated water jeopardizes both the physical and social health of all people. It is an affront to human dignity. (Kofi Annan, United Nations Secretary-General)[3]

1. Introduction

Humans need water. We are composed mostly of it and cannot live for more than a few days without it. It seems almost axiomatic, therefore, that there should be a human right to water—especially since some 1.1 billion people lack access to potable supplies, according to the World Health Organization.[4] Indeed, it is not uncommon to encounter references to '*the* human right to water', implying that such a right incontrovertibly exists.[5] But while a case can

[1] This chapter 'revisits' the human right to water, explored in an earlier article. *See* note 6, *infra*.

[2] The author is grateful to Dinah Shelton for her comments on an earlier draft of this chapter, and to Elisa Skibsrud and Amie McTavish for their helpful research assistance.

[3] Quoted in World Health Organization, The Right to Water 6 (2003), available at http://www.who.int/water_sanitation_health/rightowater/en/.

[4] WHO, The Global Water Supply and Sanitation Assessment 2000 1 (2000), also indicating that some 2.4 billion individuals lack adequate sanitation. *See also* WHO, The Right to Water, *supra* note 3, at 7.

[5] *See*, e.g., WHO, The Right to Water, *supra* note 3, at 7; Draft Principles on Human Rights and the Environment, Principle 8, in Fatma Zohra Ksentini, Special Rapporteur, Human Rights and the Environment, Final Report, U.N. ESCOR Commission on Human Rights, Sub-Commission on Prevention of Discrimination and Protection of Minorities, U.N. Doc. E/CN.4/Sub.2/1994/9, Annex I

certainly be made for such a right,[6] it is not explicitly recognized in any of the instruments comprising the International Bill of Human Rights—notably,[7] the Universal Declaration of Human Rights of 1948[8] and the two human rights treaties of 1966 that grew out of the Universal Declaration: the International Covenants on Civil and Political Rights (CP Covenant), and on Economic, Social, and Cultural Rights (ESC Covenant).[9] Whether this omission was an oversight, whether it is explainable on the ground that it goes without saying that, as with air, humans may not be deprived of water, or whether water simply had not yet become a pressing issue even by the mid-1960s, the failure of these instruments to enshrine a right to water seems today to be odd, at best.

Of course, the fact that water is not mentioned in the International Bill of Human Rights does not mean that humans do not have a right to it. In fact, the United Nations Committee on Economic, Social, and Cultural Rights, the body monitoring implementation of the corresponding Covenant, has recently declared in a General Comment that a right to water exists as an independent right, by necessary implication from Articles 11 and 12 of the Covenant.[10] Unfortunately, however, this does not end the matter. While no doubt a highly authoritative interpretation of the Covenant, the Committee's finding does not bind the 147 States that are parties to it,[11] let alone other States.[12] States would have to accept this interpretation through their practice for it to have binding effect upon them. While thus far States Parties to the Covenant have not objected to the interpretation contained in the General Comment, State practice occurs more through accretion than avulsion. Thus it may take some time for countries to react, one way or another, to the Committee's views, and thus for observers to have evidence on which to base a judgment as to whether an independent human right to water truly forms part of international law. In any

(1994); Eyal Benvenisti, *Collective Action in the Utilization of Shared Freshwater: The Challenges of International Water Resources Law*, 90 AJIL 384, 406–07 (1996); Neil A. F. Popovic, *In Pursuit of Environmental Human Rights: Commentary on the Draft Declaration of Principles on Human Rights and the Environment*, 27 COLUM. HUM. RTS. L.REV. 487, 528 (1996).

[6] *See*, e.g., Peter H. Gleick, *The Human Right to Water*, 1 WATER POL'Y 487 (1998) (there is strong and broad support for the human right to a basic water requirement); Stephen C. McCaffrey, *A Human Right to Water: Domestic and International Implications*, 5 GEORGETOWN INT'L ENVTL. L.REV. 1 (1992) (existing rights should be interpreted to include a right to sufficient water to sustain life); and Henri Smets, *The Right to Water as a Human Right*, 30 ENVTL. POL'Y & L. 248 (2000).

[7] In addition to the instruments mentioned in the text, the International Bill of Human Rights is generally thought to include the human rights provisions of the U.N. Charter and the Optional Protocol to the Covenant on Civil and Political Rights, 19 Dec. 1966, UNGA Res. 2200 (XXI), 21 U.N. GAOR, Supp. (No. 16) 59, U.N. Doc. A/6316 (1967), reprinted in 6 ILM 383 (1967).

[8] G.A. Res. 217, U.N. GAOR, 3d Sess., U.N. Doc. A/64 (1948).

[9] International Covenant on Economic, Social, and Cultural Rights, G.A. Res. 2200, 21 U.N. GAOR, 22nd Sess., Supp. 49, U.N. Doc. A/6316 (1967), reprinted in 6 ILM 360 (1967) [hereinafter ESC Covenant]; International Covenant on Civil and Political Rights, G.A. Res. 2200, 21 GAOR, 22nd Sess., Supp. 52, U.N. Doc. A/6316 (1967), *reprinted in* 6 ILM 368 (1967) [hereinafter CP Covenant].

[10] General Comment No. 15, The Right to Water (Articles 11 and 12 of the International Covenant on Economic, Social and Cultural Rights), U.N. Doc. E/C.12/2002/11, 26 November 2002.

[11] *See* Multilateral treaties deposited with the Secretary-General, available at http://www.untreaty.un.org, visited August 18, 2003.

[12] *See* text accompanying note 59, *infra*.

event, as discussed below, it is clear that without water, other human rights become meaningless; and that in particular, an adequate supply of potable water is necessary to human health, the right to which is guaranteed in Article 12 of the ESC Covenant. However, these considerations do not answer the question of what precisely States are required to do in order to fulfill their obligations in relation to a human right to water. That question is the subject of the new General Comment.

Another possibility, that a human right to water is already part of customary international law, independent of the Covenant, is not considered here. The following considerations may be noted in this regard, however. As already indicated, no such right is mentioned in the Universal Declaration, which is often said to be largely reflective of custom. In addition, it is difficult to identify evidence of State practice on which to base such a customary right to water. Yet it is entirely possible, perhaps even probable, that the action of the ESC Committee in adopting General Comment 15 will attract sufficient State practice over time that a customary norm will be formed on the basis of that practice. This kind of process is one that the International Court of Justice has said 'is a perfectly possible one and does from time to time occur ...'.[13]

In the meantime, it is perhaps worth considering the General Comment and what some of the implications of such a right might be. After noting the provisions of the basic human rights instruments from which a human right to water might be inferred (section 2, below), I will examine the new General Comment on the right to water and discuss the implications of such a right (section 3, below). I conclude that while there is growing support for a human right to water, as exemplified by the new General Comment, development of international human rights law is necessary to afford protection to individuals against deprivations of water by governments in other countries.

2. Background: Inferring a Human Right to Water from the Basic Human Rights Instruments

In an earlier assessment of the human right to water, I examined provisions of the Universal Declaration and the two Covenants from which such a right might be inferred.[14] This section will review briefly the findings of that study to provide background and context for the present discussion.

2.1 The Universal Declaration

As already indicated, none of the general human rights instruments provides expressly for a human right to water. The 1948 Universal Declaration of Human Rights proclaims in Article 25 that '[e]veryone has the right to a standard of

[13] North Sea Continental Shelf Cases (FRG v. Denmark; FRG v. Netherlands), 1969 I.C.J. Rep. 3, at para. 71.

[14] *See* McCaffrey, *supra* note 6, at 7–12.

living adequate for the health and well-being of himself and of his family, including food ...'.[15] The word 'including' indicates that the list of items in the article is not exhaustive. It is obvious that water, even more than food, is essential to 'health and well-being'; it should therefore be taken to be included by necessary implication, even though lack of adequate water received little attention until relatively recently. In addition, the word 'food' may itself be taken to refer more broadly to sustenance, which would clearly include water. Moreover, water is necessary, directly or indirectly, to produce much of the food we eat.

Although as a General Assembly resolution the Universal Declaration is not binding per se,[16] many of its provisions concerning basic rights are thought to have become part of customary international law, or at least to be authoritative interpretations of the U.N. Charter's provisions on human rights. This may be true principally of so-called 'liberty rights' set forth in the Declaration, however, rather than the 'welfare rights' it also contains. Since the right to an adequate standard of living falls into the latter category, it is uncertain whether it can be considered to be protected by a norm of customary international law.[17]

2.2 The Covenants

One searching for support for a human right to water in the two 1966 Covenants will encounter similar difficulties.[18] For these agreements elaborate, in treaty form, upon the provisions of the Universal Declaration, in some cases adding rights and in others not including rights mentioned in the Declaration.[19] A critical difference between the Covenants is that parties have an immediate obligation to 'respect and ensure'[20] the rights contained in the CP Covenant, while they need only 'take steps ... to the maximum of [their] available resources, with a view to achieving progressively the full realization of the rights recognized in' the ESC Covenant.[21] This difference in approach reflects the fact that the rights in the CP Covenant can in large measure be guaranteed through abstention (e.g., from arbitrary killing), while those contained in the ESC Covenant generally require positive measures and programs, often entailing substantial expense, for their implementation. Therefore, even if a human right to water could be inferred from Article 11 of the ESC Covenant,[22] its

[15] Universal Declaration, *supra* note 8, Art. 25.

[16] *See* U.N. Charter, Art. 10.

[17] These points are discussed in greater detail in McCaffrey, *supra* note 6, at 8.

[18] *See* McCaffrey, *supra* note 6, at 8–12.

[19] E.g., the CP Covenant adds cultural, religious, and linguistic protections for minorities (Art. 27), but does not include the right to own property proclaimed in Art. 17 of the Universal Declaration.

[20] CP Covenant, *supra* note 9, Art. 2(1). The actual language provides that each State party 'undertakes to respect and to ensure to all individuals within its territory and subject to its jurisdiction the rights recognized in the present Covenant ...'.

[21] ESC Covenant, *supra* note 9, Art. 2(1).

[22] Art. 11(1) of the ESC Covenant, *id.*, provides as follows: 'The states Parties to the present Covenant recognize the right of everyone to an adequate standard of living for himself and his family, including adequate food, clothing and housing, and to the continuous improvement of living

counterpart to Article 25 of the Universal Declaration, States would only have to implement such a right progressively, within the limits of their available resources. And it must be said that a lawyer for a State accused of breaching this obligation would find in the language of the ESC Covenant (e.g., 'take steps', 'individually and through international assistance and cooperation, especially economic and technical', 'to the maximum of its available resources', 'with a view to achieving progressively the full realization', 'by all appropriate means'[23]) ample bases for a defense.

One is therefore led to inquire whether a right to water may be inferred from the CP Covenant, since States would then be required to implement it immediately. The most obvious source of such a right is the right to life itself, enshrined in Article 6 of the CP Covenant. But whether this provision merely protects against arbitrary deprivation of life by the State, or also guarantees against death from such causes as lack of water or food, exposure to the elements, or lack of medical attention, is controversial.[24] General Comments adopted by the Human Rights Committee in 1989 urge a broad interpretation of the right to life, so that it would not only guarantee against arbitrary deprivation (right to life), but would also comprise 'the right of every human being to have the appropriate means of subsistence and a decent standard of life (preservation of life, *right of living*)'.[25] The Comments also state that 'the protection of this right [i.e., the right to life] requires that States adopt positive measures'.[26]

On its face, this interpretation would seem clearly to encompass the right to water. However, the General Comments themselves cast doubt on this conclusion. They state that safeguarding the right to life 'is an essential condition for the enjoyment of the entire range of civil and political, as well as economic, social and cultural rights'.[27] In other words, the Human Rights Committee leaves the impression that the right to life does not in fact encompass a right to subsistence, including a right to water, but must be respected in order to make possible the enjoyment of other rights—which must be established independently. This interpretation is supported by respected commentators, who reason that rights such as one to an appropriate means of subsistence belong within the category of economic, social, and cultural rights.[28] Indeed, while interpreting the right to life to include a right to water may be unassailable as a matter of pure logic, the question is not what is logical but what States have accepted. In this connection it must be asked whether they have indeed accepted an

conditions. The States Parties will take appropriate steps to ensure the realization of this right, recognizing to this effect the essential importance of international cooperation based on free consent.'

[23] All of the phrases quoted are from the ESC Covenant, *id.*, Art. 2(1).

[24] The different views are discussed in McCaffrey, *supra* note 6, at 9–11.

[25] Human Rights Committee, General Comments adopted under Article 40, paragraph 4 of the CP Covenant, U.N. Doc. CCPR/C/21/Rev.1 (19 May 1989), at 51–52 (emphasis in original).

[26] *Id.*, at 5. [27] *Id.*, at 53.

[28] *See*, e.g., Antonio A. Cancado Trindade, *The Parallel Evolutions of International Human Rights Protection and of Environmental Protection and the Absence of Restrictions on the Exercise of Recognized Human Rights*, 13 Revista IIDH 35, at 52 (1991).

immediate obligation—i.e., not one that may be implemented progressively—to take *positive* measures to guarantee their citizens appropriate subsistence (including water) and a decent standard of life. Given the many qualifications of the obligation of States to give effect to the 'welfare' rights recognized in the ESC Covenant,[29] including Article 11's right to an adequate standard of living, it seems doubtful that States have accepted such an immediate obligation. Why would they insist on so heavily qualifying their obligations in one case (the ESC Covenant, which expressly recognizes the right to an adequate standard of living) but not in the other (the CP Covenant, from which such a right would have to be inferred)?

Given these difficulties with inferring a right to water from the CP Covenant, one is left with the ESC Covenant, in particular its Article 11, from which the right flows more naturally. One could also point to Article 12 and its guarantee of the right to health as providing support for a right to water. In either case, the obligation of governments would be to achieve progressively the fulfillment of the right to water. While not an ideal outcome, since the right to water of many would not be realized immediately, it must be said that this result accords with reality. No government can immediately turn on the tap for each and every unserved person in the country. The infrastructure involved in making this possible is enormous and expensive.

2.3 Other instruments

While a human right to water must be inferred from the general human rights instruments, an obligation to provide an adequate domestic or drinking water supply is expressly provided for in several human rights and humanitarian treaties of a more specialized character. These include such agreements as the 1989 Convention on the Rights of the Child,[30] the 1979 Convention on the Elimination of All Forms of Discrimination Against Women,[31] and the 1949 Geneva Convention relative to the Treatment of Prisoners of War.[32] However, none of these agreements casts the corresponding entitlement in human rights terms. Instead, they place a duty on governments to ensure that water, among other things necessary to life and good health, is provided to members of groups that have been identified as requiring special protection.[33]

[29] *See* the discussion of Art. 2(1) of the ESC Covenant in text at notes 21–23, *supra*.

[30] G.A. Res. 25 (XLIV), U.N. GAOR, 44th Sess., Supp. No. 49 at 167, U.N. Doc. A/RES/44/25 (1989), *reprinted in* 28 ILM 1457 (1989).

[31] G.A. Res. 34/180 (XXXIV), U.N. GAOR, 34th Sess., Supp. No. 46 at 194, U.N. Doc. A/34/830 (1979), *reprinted in* 19 ILM 33 (1980).

[32] Arts 20, 26, 29, and 46, 12 August 1949, 6 U.S.T. 3316, T.I.A.S. No. 3364, 75 U.N.T.S. 135. *See also* the 1949 Geneva Convention relative to the Protection of Civilian Persons in Time of War, Arts 85, 89, and 127, 12 August 1949, 6 U.S.T. 3516, T.I.A.S. No. 3365, 75 U.N.T.S. 287, as well as provisions of the two 1977 additional protocols to this Convention, Arts 54 and 55 of Additional Protocol I, 8 June 1977, 1977 U.N. Jurid. Y.B. 95, *reprinted in* 16 ILM 1391 (1977), and Arts 5 and 14 of Additional Protocol II, 8 June 1977, 1977 U.N. Jurid. Y.B. 135, *reprinted in* 16 ILM 1442 (1977).

[33] This point is further discussed in text at notes 86–88, *infra*.

The idea that governments have an obligation to provide safe drinking water finds support in the practice of certain regional human rights and other systems. In 1995, the African Commission on Human and Peoples' Rights found that Zaire (presently the Democratic Republic of Congo) had violated the right to health under Article 16 of the African Charter by failing 'to provide basic services such as safe drinking water and electricity . . .'.[34] And the Inter-American Commission on Human Rights, in its 1997 report on Ecuador, recognized the intimate connection between potable water and human well-being. In discussing the right to life and the duty to protect the physical integrity of the individual under the 1969 American Convention on Human Rights,[35] the Commission referred to the 'considerable risk posed to human life and health by oil exploitation activities in the Oriente' region through, inter alia, contamination of water supplies.[36] These regional human rights organizations thus recognize that governments must take appropriate measures to provide safe drinking water in order to fulfill their obligations in relation to the right to health, and the right to life and physical security. A right to water was not recognized per se in the cases mentioned, however. Rather, the failure to meet basic water needs was found to constitute, or at least to contribute to, violations of other rights.

The European Parliament declared in September 2003 that 'access to drinking water is a basic human right', and the European Council on Environmental Law has adopted a Resolution on the Recognition of the Right to Drinking Water in the Member States of the European Union.[37] These are positive steps that bolster the human right to water in the context of Europe.

Meetings held under the auspices of the United Nations and other organizations have recognized the importance of access to water of adequate quality and quantity for drinking and other domestic uses.[38] But the fact that neither the Plan of Implementation adopted at the World Summit for Sustainable Development held in Johannesburg, 2–11 September 2002,[39] nor—perhaps more

[34] African Comm. Hum. & Peoples' Rights, Comm. No. 25/89, 47/90, 56/91, 100/93, decision taken at the 18th Ordinary Session, 1995, para. 47, available at www1.umn.edu/humanrts/africa/comcases/25-89_47-90_56-91_100-93.html.

[35] American Convention on Human Rights, November 22, 1969, 1144 U.N.T.S. 123, 9 ILM 673, 65 AJIL 679 (1971).

[36] Inter-American Comm. Hum. Rights, Report on the Situation of Human Rights in Ecuador, OEA/Ser.L/V/II.96, Doc. 10 rev. 1, 24 April 1997; available at http://www.cidh.org/countryrep/ecuador-eng/chaper-8.htm. The Report referred to a study which concluded that 'Oriente [interior] residents are exposed to levels of oil-related contaminants far in excess of internationally recognized guidelines, and that human ingestion of water or fish from the waters sampled poses a significantly increased risk of serious health effects including cancer, neurological and reproductive problems.' *Id.*

[37] Resolution adopted 17 January 2004, referring in its third preambular paragraph to the September 2003 declaration of the European Parliament.

[38] *See*, e.g., the documents referred to in the ESC Committee's General Comment 15 (2002), U.N. Doc. E/C.12/2002/11, 26 November 2002, n. 5 at 3, including the 1977 Mar Del Plata Action Plan, Agenda 21, adopted at the 1992 Earth Summit, the 1992 Dublin Statement on Water and Sustainable Development, and the Report of the 1994 Cairo Conference on Population and Development.

[39] Plan of Implementation, adopted 4 September 2003, available at http://www.johannesburgsummit.org./html/documents/summit_docs/2309_planfinal.htm. The Plan contains a commitment to 'halve, by the year 2015, the proportion of people who are unable to reach or to

importantly—the final Ministerial Declaration of the Third World Water Forum held in Kyoto, 16–23 March 2003,[40] included a reference to a right to water, has aroused controversy.[41] This failure was apparently due to political hesitation regarding the idea, which does not auger well for a general recognition of the right by States. This is so despite the ESC Committee's General Comment, as discussed below.

An ethical perspective on the question has been provided by the Holy See, in the form of a note prepared by the Pontifical Council on Justice and Peace as a contribution of the Holy See to the Third World Water Forum.[42] The Note, entitled 'Water, An Essential Element for Life', was presented on World Water Day by the President of the Pontifical Council, Archbishop Renato R. Martino. It recognizes that the fundamental problem is not so much absolute scarcity of water as maldistribution, and states that 'people and countries, including future generations, have the right to fundamental access to those goods which are necessary for their development. Water is such a common good of humankind.' The Note goes on to argue that access to '[s]ufficient and safe drinking water is a precondition for the realization of other human rights', and that water, like air, is such a fundamental resource that the right to it was 'understood as a given which the drafters [of the basic human rights instruments] implicitly included'. Because '[w]ater is an essential commodity for life', the Note concludes that 'The right to water is . . . an inalienable right.' While not a legal analysis per se, the Note provides an ethical and moral basis for a human right to water and represents a powerful endorsement of such a right.

Finally, in the setting of freshwater shared by two or more States, several agreements provide support for a human right to water. The first two, both concluded under United Nations auspices, address obligations of governments rather than being cast in terms of individual rights. The 1997 U.N. Convention on the Law of the Non-Navigational Uses of International Watercourses,[43] a general, framework agreement negotiated within the U.N. General Assembly on the basis of a draft prepared by the International Law Commission, provides that in reconciling any conflict between different uses, States must give 'special regard' to 'the requirements of vital human needs'.[44] While this language falls short of an explicit recognition of a human right to water, it expresses

afford safe drinking water . . . and the proportion of people who do not have access to basic sanitation . . .'. *Id.*, para. 7.

[40] Text *reprinted in* 33 ENVTL. POL'Y & L. 172 (2003).

[41] *See*, e.g., Amnesty International, Public Statement, Human Right to Water, 24 March 2003, available at http://web.amnesty.org/library/index/englor100022003?open&of=eng_398. The Statement refers to Amnesty International's 'deep disappointment at the failure of the international community to recognize the human right to water in the final Ministerial Declaration of the World Water Forum . . .'. *Id.*

[42] Pontifical Council for Justice and Peace, Note, Water, An Essential Element for Life, Vatican City, 14 March 2003, available at http://www.vatican.va/roman_curia/pontifical_councils/justpeace/documents/rc_pc_justpeace_doc_20030322_kyoto-water_en.html (hereinafter Pontifical Council Note).

[43] 21 May 1997, G.A. Res. 229, U.N. GAOR, 51st Sess., U.N. Doc. A/51/869 (1997), *reprinted in* 36 ILM 700 (1997).

[44] *Id.*, Art. 10(2).

a fundamental idea behind such a right, namely, that in making allocation decisions governments must not forget basic needs of humans for water.

The second United Nations treaty is a regional instrument, focusing in its provisions of present interest on drinking water. The 1999 Protocol on Water and Health to the 1992 ECE Convention on the Protection and Use of Transboundary Watercourses and International Lakes[45] requires the parties to take 'all appropriate measures for the purpose of ensuring . . . [a]dequate supplies of wholesome drinking water'[46] and provides that the parties 'shall pursue the aims of . . . [a]ccess to drinking water for everyone . . .'.[47]

The third agreement is a rare example of a treaty referring expressly to a human right to water. It is the new Water Charter of the Senegal River.[48] In establishing principles and mechanisms for distributing water between different sectors, or uses, the Water Charter provides that any distribution of the River's water will aim at guaranteeing to the populations of the riparian States the full enjoyment of the resource, respecting the safety of persons and works as well as 'the fundamental human right to healthful water', in the perspective of sustainable development.[49] Not only does this provision characterize the right as 'fundamental', it also specifies that it is not only water, but 'healthful' water to which humans have a right. Perhaps in the coming years more river basin treaties will follow the example of the three countries that concluded the Senegal River Water Charter. But at present, the Water Charter's reference to a fundamental human right to water remains in the vanguard.

3. The new General Comment and its implications

At its twenty-ninth session in 2002, the U.N. Committee on Economic, Social, and Cultural Rights (ESC Committee) adopted General Comment No. 15 (2002) on 'The right to water (Articles 11 and 12 of the International Covenant on Economic, Social and Cultural Rights)'.[50] This is the first recognition by a United Nations human rights body of an independent and generally applicable human right to water.[51] As such, it is deserving of attention and examination. First, some background regarding the ESC Committee will help to place General Comment 15 in context.

[45] 17 June 1999, available at http://untreaty.un.org/English/notpubl/27-5a-eng.htm, visited 16 June 2003.

[46] *Id.*, Art 4(2)(a).

[47] *Id.*, Art. 6(1)(a).

[48] 28 May 2002 (Mauritania, Mali, Senegal) (copy on file with author).

[49] *Id.*, Art. 4, para. 3 (transl.). The original French reads: 'Les principes directeurs de toute répartition des eaux du Fleuve visent à assurer aux populations des Etats riverains, la pleine jouissance de la ressource, dans le respect de la sécurité des personnes et des ouvrages, ainsi que du droit fondamental de l'Homme à une eau salubre, dans la perspective d'un développement durable.'

[50] U.N. Doc. E/C.12/2002/11, 26 November 2002, adopted at the ESC Committee's 29th session, held in Geneva from 11–29 November 2002 (hereinafter General Comment 15).

[51] An earlier general comment by the ESC Committee, General Comment No. 6 (1995) on the economic, social, and cultural rights of older persons, recognized in that context that the right to water is a human right contained in Art. 11(1) of the ESC Covenant.

3.1 Background: the ESC Committee

Unlike the Committee on Civil and Political Rights, which is established in the CP Covenant, the ESC Committee is not provided for in the ESC Covenant.[52] This may be because the rights recognized in the latter instrument are for the most part to be 'achieve[d] progressively',[53] to the extent permitted by a State's available resources. The Committee was established by a 1985 resolution of the Economic and Social Council (ECOSOC)[54] and began functioning in 1987.[55] It replaced a Working Group composed of government representatives which, due to its very representative character, had not enjoyed success in monitoring government implementation. The eighteen members of the Committee are elected by the ECOSOC, on nomination of States parties to the Covenant, for four year terms and serve in their individual, expert capacities, not as government representatives.[56] Like the Working Group, the Committee's main function is to monitor the implementation of the ESC Covenant by the States that are parties. It performs this function chiefly through receiving reports from the parties,[57] posing questions to them on the reports, and issuing 'concluding observations', stating the Committee's opinion concerning the status of the parties' implementation of the Covenant.

The ECOSOC authorized the ESC Committee to adopt general comments on the ESC Covenant to assist the parties in fulfilling their obligations and to indicate its interpretation of particular provisions.[58] The Committee was *not* authorized to adopt general comments that would be binding on the States parties to the ESC Covenant.[59] The ESC Committee's sister body, the Human

[52] *See* the Committee's website, http://www.unhchr.ch/html/menu6/2/fs16.htm, visited 22 August 2003.

[53] ESC Covenant, *supra* note 9, Art. 2(1).

[54] ECOSOC Res. 1985/17.

[55] *See generally*, Philip Alston and Bruno Simma, *The First Session of the UN Committee on Economic, Social and Cultural Rights*, 81 AJIL 747 (1987).

[56] *See* the Committee's website, http://www.unhchr.ch/html/menu6/2/fs16.htm, also indicating that the Committee meets twice a year in Geneva.

[57] 'Under articles 16 and 17 of the Covenant, States parties undertake to submit periodic reports to the Committee—within two years of the entry into force of the Covenant for a particular State party, and thereafter once every five years—outlining the legislative, judicial, policy and other measures which they have taken to ensure the enjoyment of the rights contained in the Covenant. States parties are also requested to provide detailed data on the degree to which the rights are implemented and areas where particular difficulties have been faced in this respect.' *Id.*

[58] ECOSOC Res. 1987/5; Rule 65, CESCR, Rules of procedure of the committee, 1 September 1993, U.N. Doc. E/C.12/1990/4/Rev.1. Rule 65: 'The Committee may prepare general comments based on the various articles and provisions of the Covenant with a view to assisting States parties in fulfilling their reporting obligations.' *Id.* According to the Committee's website, 'The Committee decided in 1988 to begin preparing "general comments" on the rights and provisions contained in the Covenant with a view to assisting States parties in fulfilling their reporting obligations and to provide greater interpretative clarity as to the intent, meaning and content of the Covenant.... General comments are a crucial means of generating jurisprudence, providing a method by which members of the Committee may come to an agreement by consensus regarding the interpretation of norms embodied in the Covenant.' http://www.unhchr.ch/html/menu6/2/fs16.htm, visited 22 August 2003. Thus the Committee does not claim the authority to adopt interpretations that are binding on the States Parties.

[59] *See* ECOSOC Res. 1987/5, containing no such authorization. This is not surprising, since the Committee's counterpart for Civil and Political Rights was also not so authorized. *See* the following notes and accompanying text.

Rights Committee under the CP Covenant, generated a storm of controversy when it purported to do just that in a general comment on the permissibility of reservations.[60] This experience counsels caution in attributing sweeping effect to pronouncements such as the ESC Committee's new General Comment on the human right to water. The General Comment reflects the Committee's interpretation of Articles 11 and 12 of the ESC Covenant. Eminently sensible though this interpretation may be, it must be accepted by the States parties to the Covenant in order to be binding upon them. This is also true, *a fortiori*, of States that are not parties to the Covenant. The fact that States have not yet accepted explicitly a general human right to water suggests that the ESC Committee's General Comment may be somewhat ahead of State practice and therefore may be more in the nature of a statement *de lege ferenda* rather than *lex lata*. Even so, the ESC Committee will expect States parties to the ESC Covenant, in reporting on their implementation of the Covenant, to indicate what progress they have made in achieving the full realization of the human right to water. At the very least, this will help to raise awareness of the urgent need to ensure availability of, and ready access to, clean drinking water in sufficient quantity to sustain health.

3.2 General Comment 15: overview and general features

Turning to General Comment 15 itself, it is a rather substantial document, comprised of six parts: I. Introduction; II. Normative Content of the Right to Water; III. States Parties' Obligations; IV. Violations; V. Implementation at the National Level; and VI. Obligations of Actors Other than States. A comprehensive analysis of the General Comment is beyond the scope of this chapter; it will be possible here only to note some of its main features.

[60] General Comment No. 24 (52) of 2 November 1994, U.N. Doc. CCPR/C/Rev.1/Add.6, 34 ILM 839 (1995), stating that the consequence of an unacceptable reservation will be that the 'reservation will generally be severable, in the sense that Covenant will be operative for the reserving party without benefit of the reservation'. *Id.*, para. 18. France, the United Kingdom, and the United States were all critical of the Committee's assumption of the power to make such a binding determination, on the ground that it was not authorized to do so in the CP Covenant. *See* Observations, [1996] Report of the Human Rights Committee, vol. 1, GAOR, 51st session, Supp. No. 40, U.N. Doc. A/51/40, 104 Annex VI (France); Observations, [1995] Report of the Human Rights Committee, vol. 1, GAOR, 50th session, Supp. No. 40, U.N. Doc. A/50/40, 130, Annex VI B (U.K.); and Observations, [1995] Report of the Human Rights Committee, vol. 1, GAOR, 50th session, Supp. No. 40, U.N. Doc. A/50/40, 126, Annex VI A (U.S.). *See* HUMAN RIGHTS AS GENERAL NORMS AND A STATE'S RIGHT TO OPT OUT 185–207 (J. Gardner ed., 1997). Some commentators have defended the ESC Committee's action. *See*, e.g., Rosalyn Higgins, *Introduction*, HUMAN RIGHTS AS GENERAL NORMS AND A STATE'S RIGHT TO OPT OUT xv, xxvi–xxviii (Christine Chinkin et al. eds, 1997); and C. J. Redgwell, *Reservations to Treaties and Human Rights Committee General Comment No. 24* (52), 46 ICLQ 390 (1997). *But see*, e.g., the reaction of the Special Rapporteur of the International Law Commission on the topic of Reservations to Treaties: Alain Pellet, Second Report on Reservations to Treaties, U.N. Doc. A/CN.4/447/Add.1, 13 June 1996, paras 226–230, arguing that the Human Rights Committee's General Comment No. 24 'takes no account whatsoever of the consensuality that is the very essence of any treaty commitment'. *Id.*, para. 228.

a. Water as a 'public good'

Interestingly, the Comment begins by characterizing water as a 'public good'.[61] It is not clear in what sense that expression is used. In view of the contemporary controversy over the privatization of water supply systems,[62] the ESC Committee may have intended by using this term to send the message that governments must ensure that the human right to water is safeguarded if they place management of water services in private hands. The General Comment does not offer an explicit explanation of the sense in which it is using the term, however, which leaves open other possible interpretations.

The most common use of the expression 'public good' is in the field of economics. Basic textbooks on the subject define the term as 'a good or service for which exclusion cannot be applied and for which the marginal cost of an additional user is zero'.[63] A 'private good', on the other hand, is 'one for which exclusion is possible and for which the marginal cost of an additional user is positive'.[64] These definitions suggest that in economic terms, water is a private good, not a public one. It is in fact possible to exclude others from the use of water: many legal systems allow private individuals to acquire rights in fresh water, rights that allow the owner to exclude others from their infringement. Moreover, the marginal cost of an additional user of water is not zero, whether the user withdraws or pollutes the water. The remaining water is lower in quantity or quality and thus higher in price.[65]

The ESC Committee therefore seems to have intended to use the expression 'public good' not the way an economist would, but more generally, perhaps to convey the notion that water belongs to the public at large. Indeed, Roman law considered perennial streams to be common or public, *rei publicae jure gentium*, things whose use is common to all, a doctrine carried over into Spain's thirteenth-century *Siete Partidas* and France's *Code Napoleon*.[66] But if this is the

[61] General Comment 15, *supra* note 10, para. 1, at 1. Elsewhere, when discussing the 'Normative Content of the Right to Water', the General Comment states: 'Water should be treated as a social and cultural good, and not primarily as an economic good.' *Id.*, para. 11, at 5.

[62] Privatization of water systems is part of the worldwide tendency to privatize public utilities, a policy supported by donor countries and international financial institutions. One of the best known cases is that of Cochabamba, Bolivia, where the Bolivian government placed the water system under the control of a private consortium led by the U.S.-based Bechtel Corporation, leading to violent civil unrest. *See*, e.g., William Finnegan, *Leasing the Rain*, THE NEW YORKER, 8 April 2002, p. 43. The protests led the company to flee Cochabamba, whereupon the government informed it that its contract was revoked since it had 'abandoned' its concession. *Id.* at 51. This led to a dispute which is currently before the International Center for the Settlement of Investment Disputes (ICSID). Aguas del Tunari S. A. v. Republic of Bolivia (Case No. ARB/02/3), registered 25 February 2002. For information on the case, *see* http://www.worldbank.org/icsid/cases/pending.htm. On privatization of the water sector generally, *see Priceless, A Survey of Water*, THE ECONOMIST, 19 July 2003, arguing that the application of economic principles, particularly pricing and markets, is important to the solution of the world's water problems.

The latter source points out that 'privatization' of water is in a sense a misnomer since the water itself remains under government regulatory authority and control. *Id.*, at 6.

[63] *See*, e.g., Timothy Tregarthen, ECONOMICS 106 (1996). [64] *Id.*

[65] A reduction in supply of a good results in a higher price. *See*, e.g., *id.* at 61.

[66] *See generally* Stephen McCaffrey, THE LAW OF INTERNATIONAL WATERCOURSES 152–53 (2001).

concept the Committee wished to convey, perhaps a more felicitous formulation would have been one more along the lines of the Holy See's which, as we have seen, refers to water as 'a common good of humankind'.[67] The 1999 ECE Protocol on Water and Health is more elaborate, avoiding the term 'good' entirely. It provides that 'water has social, economic and environmental values and should therefore be managed so as to realize the most acceptable and sustainable combination of those values...'.[68] While this formula does not emphasize the human right to water, it perhaps better captures the role of water in the biosphere and the importance of maintaining a proper balance among its various functions.

In any event, the General Comment addresses the relationship between a human right to water and privatization of water systems, although only in rather general terms. It states that as part of the obligation to 'protect',[69] States parties to the ESC Covenant must prevent any third parties that operate or control water services[70] from 'compromising equal, affordable, and physical access to sufficient, safe and acceptable water'.[71] According to the General Comment, this requires the establishment of an effective regulatory system, i.e., one that includes 'independent monitoring, genuine public participation and imposition of penalties for non-compliance'.[72] Further, the General Comment states that the obligation to 'fulfill'[73] requires the parties to ensure that water is affordable.[74] Among the measures that should be adopted to this end, the Comment mentions 'appropriate pricing policies such as free or low-cost water' and 'income supplements'.[75] It goes on to state: 'Any payment for water services has to be based on the principle of equity, ensuring that these services, whether privately or publicly provided, are affordable for all, including socially disadvantaged groups.'[76]

It is thus evident that the ESC Committee does not regard privatization of water services as constituting a per se violation of the human right to water. This position seems realistic in view of global trends in the direction of privatization, as well as the enormous investment that will be required to meet the Millennium Development Goal,[77] and that of the Johannesburg

[67] Pontifical Council Note, *supra* note 42.

[68] ECE Protocol, *supra* note 45, Art. 5(g). The Protocol also states that 'Efficient use of water should be promoted through economic instruments and awareness-building.' *Id.*, Art. 5(h).

[69] The General Comment states that as with all other human rights, the right to water entails obligations of States to respect, protect, and fulfill. General Comment 15, *supra* note 10, para. 20, at 9.

[70] There are, of course, different ways of privatizing water services, ranging from retaining public ownership of the assets and contracting with private companies for operation and maintenance, to privatizing the assets as well. The former system prevails in France, the latter in England. More countries follow the French model than the British. *See* THE ECONOMIST, *Survey of Water, supra* note 62, at 6.

[71] General Comment 15, *supra* note 10, para. 24, at 9.

[72] *Id.*, at 10.

[73] *See* note 69, *supra*.

[74] General Comment 15, *supra* note 10, paras 26 and 27, at 10.

[75] *Id.*, para. 27. Some developing countries evidently believe that users must be charged for water. *See*, e.g., Lindsay Dentlinger, 'No Free Water, Says Angula', The Namibian (Windhoek), 13 April 2004 (stating that the Namibian Minister of Agriculture, Water and Rural Development, Helmut Angula, 'ruled out the possibility of the precious resource [water] being supplied free').

[76] *Id.*

[77] Millennium Declaration, 2000, adopted at the Millennium Summit of the United Nations in September 2000 by 150 heads of State and government. The Millennium Development Goals (MDGs) are available at http://www.un.org/millenniumgoals/. This United Nations website states that all

Summit,[78] of halving the number of people without safe access to clean water and basic sanitation by 2015.[79] Nor does the Committee exclude charging for water supplied to households; it requires only that water be affordable—i.e., that the user in question be able to afford to pay for it. This can be accomplished through subsidies, 'income supplements', or a sliding tariff scale for water users, under which poor users would pay less for water (to the point of paying nothing) than wealthier users. Any of these methods would require detailed legislation and effective monitoring and enforcement mechanisms. When 'genuine public participation and imposition of penalties for non-compliance' are added to the mix, the result is a system of which any developed country would be proud (and which most have in place, at least in theory), but which could well overtax the capacities of many developing countries. As *The Economist* puts it, 'any privatization [of water] requires a strong and permanent public regulator'. Full implementation of the human right to water would require this as well. But good government has yet to flower fully in many of the countries whose water situation is the most desperate. According to the Global Water Partnership, 'Water is a problem of governance, above all.'[80] Fortunately, as discussed below, the ESC Covenant does not require that the human right to water and all of its ramifications spring immediately, full-blown, into existence.

b. The sources of the human right to water

As indicated by its title, the General Comment bases the human right to water principally upon Articles 11 and 12 of the ESC Covenant, from which it infers the existence of the right. It notes that Article 11(1) refers to a number of rights relating to the right to an adequate standard of living, 'including adequate food, clothing and housing', and reasons that 'The use of the word "including" indicates that this catalogue of rights was not intended to be exhaustive.'[81] The General Comment continues: 'The right to water clearly falls within the category of guarantees essential for securing an adequate standard of living, particularly since it is one of the most fundamental conditions for survival.'[82]

191 Member States of the U.N. have pledged to meet the goals by the year 2015. Doubts have been expressed, both at the IMF–World Bank meetings held in April 2004 and at the high-level meeting of the U.N. Commission on Sustainable Development in the same month, about whether the MDG on water can be met. *See* U.N. Wire, 26 April 2004, 29 April 2004, and 30 April 2004, available at http://www.unwire.org/.

[78] World Summit for Sustainable Development, Plan of Implementation, *supra* note 39.

[79] The Economist, *Survey of Water, supra* note 62, at 5, notes the range of estimates of the additional investment in developing countries that would be required to meet this goal as being from $35 billion to $100 billion per year. However, U.N. Secretary-General Kofi Annan is reported to be 'skeptical that privatization of the world's water supplies will help resolve the problems facing [those] who have little or no access to safe drinking water'. *See* Thalif Deen, *Privatisation No Answer to Water Scarcity*, UN Internet Press Service News Agency, 18 March 2004, available at http://www.ipsnews.net/interna.asp?idnews=22931.

[80] Quoted in The Economist, *Survey of Water*, *supra* note 62, at 5.

[81] General Comment 15, *supra* note 10, para. 3, at 2.

[82] *Id.*

These arguments are not new,[83] but had not previously come from an official source. As to Article 12, the General Comment states that the right to health under paragraph 2(*b*) of that article requires parties to take steps 'on a non-discriminatory basis to prevent threats to health from unsafe and toxic water conditions'.[84]

The General Comment goes on to state that, 'The right to water has been recognized in a wide range of international documents, including treaties, declarations and other standards.'[85] As indicated earlier,[86] however, examination of the language of these instruments reveals that they do not refer expressly to a 'human right to water' but rather mention access to water in relation to other rights, obligations, or principles, such as those regarding adequate living conditions[87] and combating disease and malnutrition.[88] There is no doubt that the need for access to sufficient and safe water supplies, particularly for groups in special need of protection, has been repeatedly recognized in international instruments. But this does not necessarily mean that States have recognized a human right to water, with all of its implications, either generally or in those specific instruments.

The Comment notes that the right to water 'has been consistently addressed by the Committee during its consideration of States parties' reports', despite its not being explicitly mentioned in the ESC Covenant. The suggestion is thus that the Committee's recognition of a right to water should not come as an unfair surprise to States parties; and that the practice of the Committee will not change fundamentally as a result of General Comment 15, since the right to water has always been implicit in the Covenant in any event. One could expect that the right to water will now receive more focused attention by the Committee in its treatment of parties' reports, however.

c. *Content of the human right to water: the obligations of states*

I. How soon must the right be implemented?

The General Comment encapsulates the content of the human right to water in the following terms: 'The human right to water entitles everyone to sufficient, safe, acceptable, physically accessible and affordable water for personal and domestic uses.'[89] If all of these aspects of the right had to be implemented immediately, many governments would undoubtedly find themselves in breach. According to the World Health Organization, the World Bank, and the U.S. Agency for International Development, a person needs a minimum of between 20 and 40 liters of water per day to meet basic drinking water and sanitation

[83] *See*, e.g., the sources cited in note 6, *supra*.

[84] General Comment 15, *supra* note 10, para. 8, at 4.

[85] *Id.*, para. 4, at 2.

[86] *See* text at note 33.

[87] Convention on the Elimination of All Forms of Discrimination Against Women, Art. 14(2), referred to in General Comment 15, *supra* note 10, para. 4, at 2–3.

[88] Convention on the Rights of the Child, Art. 24(2), referred to in *id.*

[89] General Comment 15, *supra* note 10, para. 2, at 2.

requirements.[90] Another 10 liters has been recommended for food preparation.[91] Taking the higher figure of 40 liters per person per day (lpd), this would mean a total basic water requirement of 50 lpd. It bears emphasis that these are minimum figures. The estimated domestic water use for the year 2000 was less than 40 lpd in 58 developing countries and less than 50 lpd in four more, for a total of 62.[92]

Experts have concluded that it is not water availability—in the sense of the total water supply of a country—but institutional and management failures that account for the low rates of water use in these countries.[93] This is precisely what a human right to water would address: it would require States to improve their institutions, management capabilities, and infrastructure to the point that the basic water requirements of their populations could be met. This cannot be done overnight. Fortunately for countries in which minimum water needs are not satisfied, the ESC Covenant itself indicates that such improvements need not be effected immediately. As we have seen, the rights recognized in the ESC Covenant are to be implemented progressively, according to available resources. This is to be contrasted with the CP Covenant, which requires States to implement immediately ('respect and ensure') the rights it recognizes. Thus it would appear from the terms of the ESC Covenant that there would be considerable flexibility with regard to implementation of a human right to water.

Even assuming full compliance with the ESC Covenant (including a right to water), therefore, how soon all of the aspects of the right listed by the ESC Committee would actually be enjoyed by every member of a country's population would depend on a variety of factors, such as the level of development of the country in question, the availability of water, endogenous technical capacity, existing infrastructure, and the availability of external assistance. It could therefore be argued that even if a human right to water were explicitly enshrined in the ESC Covenant, it would be largely of symbolic value. Such a right that is only implicitly recognized—as is the case with the right to water—would have even less impact. Symbols are important, however, and in this case the ESC Committee's finding will help to call attention to the global freshwater crisis and the need for governments to address it. Moreover, the Committee will expect States parties to the ESC Covenant to report on their implementation of the right to water, as articulated in General Comment 15. This will inevitably provide further impetus to efforts to improve the availability of freshwater and sanitation services. The wild card regarding implementation is, however, the ESC Committee's concept of 'core obligations', discussed in the following section.

[90] Gleick, *supra* note 6, at 496.

[91] *Id.*, Table 1. *See also* Peter H. Gleick, *Basic Water Requirements for Human Activities: Meeting Basic Needs*, 21 WATER INT'L 83, 88 (1996), suggesting as recommended minima 5 liters per person per day (lpd) for drinking, 20 lpd for sanitation services, 15 lpd for bathing, and 10 lpd for food preparation.

[92] *See* Gleick, *supra* note 6, Table 2, at 497–98.

[93] *Id.*, at 499.

II. Water for personal and domestic use

As indicated previously, the ESC Committee states in the General Comment: 'The human right to water entitles everyone to sufficient, safe, acceptable, physically accessible and affordable water for personal and domestic uses.'[94] Each individual should have access to a quantity of water corresponding to World Health Organization guidelines.[95] Significantly, the Committee further explains that, in addition to personal and domestic uses, 'Priority should also be given to the water resources required to prevent starvation and disease, as well as water required to meet the core obligations of each of the Covenant rights.'[96]

The concept of 'core obligations' is a crucial one because, in General Comment No. 3 of 1990, the Committee declared that it 'is of the view that a minimum core obligation to ensure the satisfaction of, at the very least, minimum essential levels of each of the rights [recognized in the ESC Covenant] is incumbent upon every State party'.[97] The Committee finds in General Comment No. 15 that there are 'a number of core obligations in relation to the right to water' and, crucially, that they 'are of immediate effect'[98]—despite the fact that parties to the Covenant are generally required only to 'achiev[e] progressively the full realization of the rights' it recognizes.[99] Indeed, the General Comment seems somewhat inconsistent as to precisely which obligations must be fulfilled immediately. Earlier, it had stated that while the ESC Covenant generally provides for progressive realization of the rights it enshrines, within the limits of available resources, it does impose certain obligations that are of immediate effect. As examples of the 'immediate obligations in relation to the right to water', the Committee cites that of guaranteeing that the right will be exercised without discrimination,[100] and that of taking steps towards the full realization of Articles 11, paragraph 1, and 12.[101] It says nothing at this point of the 'core obligations' discussed later in the General Comment. The reader is left wondering whether the Committee actually intends that what it describes as 'core obligations' relating to the right to water must in fact be implemented immediately. The following discussion will assume that it does.

[94] General Comment 15, *supra* note 10, para. 2, at 2. The General Comment states that 'personal and domestic uses' ordinarily include 'drinking, personal sanitation, washing of clothes, food preparation, personal and household hygiene'. *Id.*, para. 12(a).

[95] *Id.*, para. 12(a), at 5.

[96] *Id.*, para. 6, at 3.

[97] General Comment 3, The nature of States parties' obligations (Art. 2, para. 1 of the Covenant), U.N. Doc. E/1991/23, para. 10 (Fifth session, 1990).

[98] General Comment 15, *supra* note 10, para. 37, at 12.

[99] ESC Covenant, *supra* note 9, Art. 2(1).

[100] With regard to the obligation of non-discrimination, the General Comment states that water must be 'accessible to *everyone* without discrimination, within the jurisdiction of the State party': General Comment 15, *supra* note 10, para. 12(c), at 6 (emphasis in original). Specifically: 'Water and water facilities and services must be accessible to all, . . . in law and in fact, without discrimination on any of the prohibited grounds [i.e., as to race, color, sex, language, religion, political or other opinion, national or social origin, property, birth or other status—Article 2(2)]; . . .' *Id.*, subpara. (iii).

[101] General Comment 15, *supra* note 10, para. 17, at 8.

The Committee identifies the following nine core obligations in relation to the right to water:

(a) To ensure access to the minimum essential amount of water . . . ;
(b) To ensure the right of access to water and water facilities and services on a non-discriminatory basis . . . ;
(c) To ensure physical access to water facilities or services that provide sufficient, safe and regular water; that have a sufficient number of water outlets to avoid prohibitive waiting times; and that are at a reasonable distance from the household;
(d) To ensure personal security is not threatened when having to physically access to [*sic*] water;
(e) To ensure equitable distribution of all available water facilities and services;
(f) To adopt and implement [, on the basis of a participatory and transparent process,] a national water strategy and plan of action addressing the whole population; . . . ;
(g) To monitor the extent of the realization, or the non-realization, of the right to water;
(h) To adopt relatively low-cost targeted water programs to protect vulnerable and marginalized groups;
(i) To take measures to prevent, treat and control diseases linked to water, in particular ensuring access to adequate sanitation.[102]

The fact that the Committee identified so many of what it considers 'core' obligations may simply reflect the essential nature of water. But it is one thing to recognize this obvious fact, and quite another to require that all of these obligations must be fulfilled immediately. It seems inevitable that many States will be hard pressed to guarantee immediately even 'minimal essential levels' of the corresponding rights, given the cost involved and capacity required to do so. The obligations identified in paragraph (c) alone would be extremely difficult for many developing countries to meet in the near future, let alone immediately (they are not even met for all people in every developed country[103]). The fact that the United Nations Millennium Development Goals call only for 'reduc[ing] by half the proportion of people without sustainable access to safe drinking water' by 2015[104] attests to this reality. The Ministerial Declaration adopted at the Third World Water Forum recognizes that achieving even this goal, within twelve years, 'requires an enormous amount of investment in water supply . . .'.[105]

[102] General Comment 15, *supra* note 10, para. 37(a)–(i), at 12–13.

[103] E.g., some residents of Zanesville, Ohio, in the United States, first received piped water from the city water service in January, 2004. Before that they collected water in cisterns and rain barrels, or drew it from wells. They received city water service only after filing a complaint with the Ohio Civil Rights Commission, alleging racial discrimination (the people in question are white, black, and American Indian). *See* James Dao, *Ohio Town's Water at Last Runs Past a Color Line*, N.Y. TIMES, 17 February 2004, at A1.

[104] Millennium Declaration, 2000, *supra* note 77. As indicated in that footnote, concerned international organizations have expressed doubts about whether the goal for water will be reached.

[105] Third World Water Forum, Kyoto, Japan, 16–23 March 2003, Ministerial Declaration, adopted 23 March 2003, para. 16, *reprinted in* 33 ENVTL. POL'Y & L. 172 (2003).

The Committee addresses these problems by placing the responsibility for enabling developing countries to fulfill the core obligations upon the international donor community:

> For the avoidance of any doubt, the Committee wishes to emphasize that it is particularly incumbent on States parties, and other actors in a position to assist, to provide international assistance and cooperation, especially economic and technical which enables developing countries to fulfill their core obligations ...[106]

It seems safe to assume that the international donor community will continue to do its best to provide assistance to developing countries in the water sector.[107] It is therefore not clear that the Committee's approach of placing heavy obligations upon these countries and then, in effect, imposing at least moral responsibility upon developed States and international financial institutions to make it possible to fulfill them, is a sound one.

III. Water to produce food

In addition to water for personal and domestic use, the General Comment points to the 'importance of ensuring sustainable access to water resources for agriculture to realize the right [under Article 11] to adequate food ...'.[108] In particular, it states:

> Attention should be given to ensuring that disadvantaged and marginalized farmers, including women farmers, have equitable access to water and water management systems, including sustainable rain harvesting and irrigation technology. Taking note of the duty in article 1, paragraph 2, of the Covenant, which provides that a people may not 'be deprived of its [own—*sic*] means of subsistence', States parties should ensure that there is adequate access to water for subsistence farming and for securing the livelihoods of indigenous peoples.[109]

Whether or not the prohibition of depriving 'a people' of its own means of subsistence is technically apposite in this context,[110] the virtue of this requirement is undeniable. However, it may well be less expensive for some countries—especially those in arid regions—to import food than to use precious water

[106] General Comment 15, *supra* note 10, para. 38, at 13.

[107] Evidence of this is plentiful. *See*, e.g., John Mbaria, *Uganda, Kenya Sign Water, Sanitation Deal*, THE EAST AFRICAN (Nairobi), 12 April 2004 (stating that the two countries have 'committed themselves to improving poor people's access to water and sanitation by signing an alliance with the World Bank's Water and Sanitation Programme's Africa office (WSP-AF)'). However, six non-governmental organizations, including Water Aid, Green Cross International, and Oxfam, have warned that the situation is becoming worse, not better, and that 'industrialized countries have failed to provide more funding to improve water and sanitation systems around the world'. *See* 'U.N. Official Urges World to Double Sanitation, Water Spending', U.N. Wire, 20 April 2004, available at http://www.unwire.org/.

[108] General Comment 15, *supra* note 10, para. 7, at 3.

[109] *Id.*, at 4.

[110] The referenced provision of the ESC Covenant, Art. 1(2), should probably be seen in the context of the entirety of Art. 1, which deals with self-determination. Depriving an entire 'people' of its means of subsistence, presumably as part of an effort to deny it the right of self-determination, is quite different from failing to provide sufficient 'water and water management systems, including sustainable rain harvesting and irrigation technology'.

resources to grow it. The General Comment does not allow for the use of such 'virtual water'[111] when it would be more economical to do so than to develop potentially expensive infrastructure and management systems.

IV. Transboundary implications: the non-'extraterritoriality' of human rights law

Under the heading 'International Obligations', the General Comment refers to the obligation of States parties to take joint and separate action to achieve the full realization of the right to water. It declares that 'States parties have to respect the enjoyment of the right in other countries' and, in particular, 'to refrain from actions that interfere, directly or indirectly, with the enjoyment of the right to water in other countries'. This language might be thought to mean, among other things, that a State has an obligation to use an *international watercourse* flowing through its territory in such a way as to ensure that individuals in a co-riparian State are able to enjoy their right to water. Put another way, it could be taken to mean that upstream State A, through its use of an international watercourse, could violate the right to water of individuals in downstream State B.[112]

It is generally accepted that a State's human rights obligations extend only to individuals within its territory or subject to its jurisdiction.[113] However, this portion of the General Comment could be interpreted to mean that one State could not take actions that could violate the human right to water of individuals who were in another State, and therefore neither within the territory nor subject

[111] The concept of 'virtual water' was developed by Professor J. A. Allan of King's College, London. *See*, e.g., J. A. Allan, *Virtual Water—the Water, Food, and Trade Nexus: Useful Concept or Misleading Metaphor?*, 28 WATER INT'L 4 (2003). The concept has been described as follows: 'Professor J. A. Allan, a specialist from London's School of Oriental and African Studies who has done his sums, argues that water-short countries can best help themselves by importing cheap food grown with cheap water: instead of using their scarce and costly water to grow their own food, they can get "virtual" water through world trade. It costs them less, and their water resources can be better used: the water that provides the livelihood of one farming family can keep ten non-farming families going.' *As thick as blood. Water in the Middle East*, THE ECONOMIST, 23 December 1995.

[112] This issue is discussed in McCaffrey, *supra* note 6, at 19–23.

[113] *See*, e.g., CP Covenant, *supra* note 9, Art. 2(1), providing that each party 'undertakes to respect and to ensure to all individuals *within its territory and subject to its jurisdiction* the rights recognized in the Covenant' (emphasis added). Theodor Meron, *Extraterritoriality of Human Rights Treaties*, 89 AJIL 78 (1995), emphasizes that a State's human rights obligations apply to individuals 'subject to its jurisdiction' even if they are not within its territory. This is also the position taken in the leading commentary on the CP Covenant, Thomas Buergenthal, *To Respect and to Ensure: State Obligations and Permissible Derogations*, in THE INTERNATIONAL BILL OF RIGHTS: THE COVENANT ON CIVIL AND POLITICAL RIGHTS 72, 74 (Louis Henkin ed., 1981); and the interpretation followed by the CP Human Rights Committee. For a case construing the term 'jurisdiction' as used in the European Convention on the Protection of Human Rights and Fundamental Freedoms, *see* Banković v. Belgium (Admissibility), App. No. 52207/99, available at www.echr.coe.int/Eng/Judgments.htm, European Court of Human Rights, 12 December 2001 (claims of those injured and representing persons killed in a NATO aircraft attack during the military operation in Kosovo were not admissible as against Belgium and sixteen other parties to the European Convention because the acts in question were extraterritorial and the individuals injured and killed were not within the 'jurisdiction' of the respondent States as required by Art. 1 of the Convention).

to the jurisdiction of the first State. The individuals' rights could be violated through excessive withdrawals of water from a river flowing into that other country, resulting in insufficient water for the basic human needs of individuals living there. Indeed, the Comment states: 'Any activities undertaken within the State party's jurisdiction should not deprive another country of the ability to realize the right to water for persons in its jurisdiction.'[114] A footnote to this sentence cites the 1997 UN Convention on the Law of the Non-Navigational Uses of International Watercourses and various of its provisions.

But the General Comment goes on to declare that State parties should refrain from imposing measures such as embargoes that prevent the supply of water. This, together with the lack of an explicit reference to obligations regarding individuals in other countries, suggests that the General Comment does not in fact purport to extend the human right to water to individuals in one country vis-à-vis the government of another. Thus, while the obligations in question may be 'international', they do not appear to relate to the use of an international watercourse by one country that prevents individuals in another country from enjoying their human right to water. Indeed, given that a State's human rights obligations are generally understood to apply only to individuals within its territory or under its jurisdiction, it may well be that the Committee went as far as it could go toward 'internationalizing' the human right to water by interpreting the Covenant to mean that parties to it must 'respect the enjoyment of the right in other countries'.

The lack of 'extraterritoriality' of human rights law[115] is striking in today's interdependent world, a world in which powerful States extend their influence, and affect individuals, in many other countries. But the effect of this lacuna in the field of water is attenuated somewhat by two considerations, one legal and one practical. On the legal plane, Article 10 of the 1997 UN Convention requires, as mentioned above, that 'special regard' be given to 'the requirements of vital human needs' in resolving conflicts between uses of an international watercourse by different riparian States. This is an obligation owed by the States concerned toward each other, not toward individuals whose needs are in question. Thus it does not represent a human rights approach to the problem. Still, Article 10 would require, for example, that upstream State A not use an international watercourse shared with downstream State B in such a way as to deprive individuals in State B of sufficient water to satisfy their vital needs. On a more practical level, experts have concluded that lack of available water is typically caused not by other States but by poor management practices, and the like, of the State in which the individuals are located.[116] To the extent that this is and remains the case, the non-extraterritoriality of human rights law will be inconsequential in the case of water. Whether it will continue to be the case as

[114] General Comment 15, *supra* note 10, para. 31, at 11.

[115] As emphasized in Meron, *supra* note 113, human rights law *is* 'extraterritorial' to the extent that the individuals seeking protection may be said to be subject to the 'jurisdiction' of the non-territorial State.

[116] See Gleick, *supra* note 6, at 500.

demands on internationally-shared freshwater resources intensify, only time will tell.

4. Conclusions

In this International Year of Freshwater,[117] it is important to understand clearly the challenges facing humanity in respect of this vital resource. Once those issues are identified, it is also important to set goals that address them, yet which are reasonably achievable. One of the kinds of implements in the toolbox of methods for achieving the goals is legal instruments. The human right to water is one such instrument. Properly applied, it can work in coordination with other tools to help countries and civil society achieve the goals they have set.

No one disputes that every human being on the planet should have a right to 'sufficient, safe, acceptable, physically accessible and affordable water for personal and domestic uses'.[118] The action of the ESC Committee in adopting General Comment 15 on the right to water, is therefore an important step in the right direction. The status of the human right to water should be evaluated with some care, however. Taking the right for granted—either because it seems obvious that there should be such a right, or on the assumption that the Committee's action creates one—could in fact devalue it. This could occur either by raising unrealistic expectations that are then dashed when States fail to comply fully with their obligations, as elaborated by the Committee, or by fostering cynicism regarding the reality of the right in reaction to perceived non-compliance by a potentially large number of States.

The foregoing examination of General Comment 15 in its legal and political context leads to several conclusions. First, the ESC Committee's finding that a human right to water may be inferred from Articles 11 and 12 of the ESC Covenant is sound. It is virtually tautologous that access to water is necessary to the fulfillment of other Covenant rights, because water is necessary to life itself. Secondly, care should be taken in drawing conclusions about the nature and even the very existence of a human right to water solely on the basis of the Committee's General Comment 15. The Committee does not have law-making power; its interpretations will have to be accepted by the States parties to the Covenant, to say nothing of those States that are not parties. An indication of the attitudes of States toward the right came at the Third World Water Forum, held four months after the Committee adopted its General Comment: at the Forum, participating governments, rejecting the entreaties of leading representatives of civil society, did not include a reference to the human right to water in the meeting's final Ministerial Declaration. Thirdly, despite the fact that the ESC

[117] The UN General Assembly proclaimed 2003 the International Year of Freshwater in its resolution: G.A. Res. 196, U.N. GAOR, 55th Sess., U.N. Doc. A/RES/55/196 (2000).

[118] The quotation is from General Comment 15, *supra* note 10, para. 2, at 2.

Committee's action alone cannot create a right to water, its declaration of the right is nevertheless constructive overall, for several reasons: it draws attention to the gravity of the problem and the importance of actions by States to address it; it triggers reports by States parties to the ESC Covenant on steps they are taking toward the full realization of the right, thus encouraging States to make real progress in this field and raising the consciousness of the international community regarding the seriousness of problems of access to water; and it helps pave the way toward sustainable access by all people to safe drinking water. Fourthly, even if and to the extent that a human right to water does exist—and this author believes that one does—States are not obligated to implement it immediately in all of its detail, as developed by the Committee. It seems indisputable that the two 'immediate' obligations identified by the ESC Committee at one point in the General Comment, namely, non-discrimination and the duty to 'take steps' toward the progressive realization of the right, must indeed be implemented immediately. Whether all of those characterized as 'core obligations' must also be is less certain, however. Fifthly, the ESC Committee's solution to the problem created by its identification of a range of 'core obligations' that must be implemented immediately may do more harm than good, because it makes unrealistic demands and creates lofty expectations that many aspects of the right to water will be discharged immediately. The result may be that these components of the right, and possibly even the right itself, will not be taken seriously. Sixthly and lastly, the Committee is to be commended for addressing 'international' aspects of the right to water. The importance of these problems is bound to grow as countries become ever more interdependent. However, the 'extraterritorial' aspect of the problem remains unaddressed by the international community, with respect to this as well as all other human rights. Growing water shortages, coupled with the large portion of Earth's freshwater that is shared by two or more States,[119] suggest that attention should be devoted to this problem.

The human right to water is crucial to the welfare of people around the world. Regardless of its precise source and content, it should be treated by the international community as a living and growing, but still somewhat fragile, newborn thing, in need of nurture and careful development. This is one important way in which we who inhabit Earth today can discharge our obligations to succeeding generations.

[119] International drainage basins account for some 60% of global river flows. *See*, e.g., Food and Agriculture Organization et al., ATLAS OF INTERNATIONAL FRESHWATER AGREEMENTS 2 (2002).

5

Water Services at the WTO

MIREILLE COSSY

1. Introduction[1]

The figures are painfully familiar: according to WHO/UNICEF, about 1.1 billion people do not have access to clean water and about 2.4 billion lack access to sanitation facilities.[2] The same report identifies four major challenges facing the water supply and sanitation services in the coming years: (i) keeping pace with a net population growth of more than a billion people over the next 15 years; (ii) closing the coverage and service gap, with emphasis on sanitation which lags considerably behind water supply; (iii) ensuring sustainability of existing and new services; and (iv) improving the quality of the services. At the World Summit on Sustainable Development, governments agreed to halve, by 2015, the proportion of people who do not have access to safe drinking water or basic sanitation services.[3] Finally, a recent report indicates that

> using the most basic standards of service and technology, the 2015 goals could be attained at an extra annual investment cost of about $10 billion. But providing full water and sewerage connections and primary wastewater treatment to the urban populations would raise the annual cost of the 2015 goal to $17 billion for water and $32 billion for sanitation and sewerage.[4]

Traditionally, water supply and sanitation services have been provided by public authorities. However, shrinking public budgets, increasing needs for water and sanitation services, and want for more efficient technologies to respond to tighter environmental regulations are prompting governments to look for new financial resources, including private sector investments. The private sector currently supplies water services to about 5 per cent of the world's population (3 per cent in developing countries), but forecasts indicate that its share may rise between 20 and 25 per cent by 2015.[5]

[1] The views expressed in this article are the author's only and do not bind WTO Members or the WTO Secretariat. The author would like to thank Rolf Adlung, Pierre Latrille, Ana Novik, and Elisabeth Tuerk for valuable comments and challenging discussions.

[2] WHO/UNICEF, *Global Water Supply and Sanitation Assessment 2000 Report*, at 7 and 31.

[3] *Johannesburg Declaration on Sustainable Development*, adopted on 4 September 2002, para. 8.

[4] Report of the World Panel on Financing Water Infrastructure, *Financing Water For All* (World Water Council, 3rd World Water Forum, Global Water Partnership, 2003), at 3.

[5] Jeffrey Delmon, *Water Projects—A Commercial and Contractual Guide* (The Hague: Kluwer Law International, 2001), at 2.

Privatization[6] of water services is politically difficult because it touches two sensitive issues, namely, water and public service. A range of concerns have been raised, the main ones relating to price increases and fear that poor people will not be able to afford water, lack of incentive from private firms to manage natural resources in a sustainable manner, and loss of public ownership of water resources. Recent failures of privatization operations contributed to trouble public opinion and strengthened oppositions groups. Success stories (they exist) have drawn less attention. And problems encountered by public authorities, in both developed and developing countries, in providing adequate water services, are less publicized.[7]

In the water sector, consumers' dependence on a supplier is double. First, they do not have a choice to connect on another network because water services are natural monopolies.[8] Secondly, water is essential and has no substitutes for most of its uses. Appropriate regulation is therefore essential to ensure protection of consumers, and implementation of various social and environmental objectives. When privatizing water services, the State moves away from its traditional role as service provider and becomes a regulator.[9] This presupposes strong institutions and an efficient regulatory capacity to establish the respective tasks and responsibilities of governments and private suppliers.[10]

In the—sometimes emotional—discussions surrounding the privatization of water services, a controversy has erupted concerning the role of the General Agreement on Trade in Services (GATS), which entered into force in 1995 under the auspices of the World Trade Organization (WTO). In short, champions of public service often consider the GATS as a kind of Trojan horse used by multinational companies to impose water privatization *urbi et orbi*. Part of this agitation stems from a misunderstanding of the Agreement, which is indeed

[6] The on-line *Oxford English Dictionary* defines it as 'The policy or process of making private as opposed to public', available at http://dictionary.oed.com. *The Concise Oxford Dictionary* (1995, 9th edn) defines the word 'privatize' as follows: 'make private, esp. assign (a business etc.) to private as distinct from state control or ownership.' In this contribution, 'privatization' is understood as including the transfer of assets or operations, through subcontracting for instance, to the private sector.

[7] *See*, e.g., Elisabeth Brubaker, *Privatizing and Regulating Canada's Water Utilities* (Toronto: University of Toronto Press, 2002).

[8] 'A natural monopoly occurs where it is feasible for one supplier to supply the service in question, perhaps because the service is dependent upon an existing infrastructure which would be prohibitively expensive to duplicate. A natural monopoly makes it impossible for a competing supplier to provide the services desired at a lesser or equal cost.' Jeffrey Delmon, *supra* note 5, at 39 and 397. It seems, however, that methods for introducing some competition in the water sector, or at least in some segments of the market, are being developed. *See id.*, at 239 and *Toolkits for Private Participation in Water and Sanitation*, The World Bank, 1997 (http://www.worldbank.org/html/fpd/water/wstoolkits/index.html).

[9] *See* Terence Lee and Andrei Jouraviev, *Regulating the Private Provision of Drinking Water and Sanitation Services*, CEPAL Review 65, at 155 (1998).

[10] *See* Jeffrey Delmon, *supra* note 5; Peter Gleick et al., *The New Economy of Water—The Risks and Benefits of Globalization and Privatization of Fresh Water* (Pacific Institute for Studies in Development, Environment and Security, 2002); OECD, *Improving Water Management—Recent OECD Experience* (Paris: OECD, 2003).

complex. The GATS is also a relatively 'young' agreement, and the fact that certain provisions remain to be tested in practice generates some discomfort.

The purpose of this contribution is to provide initial thoughts on some legal aspects stemming from the application of GATS disciplines to water services. The characteristics of these services[11]—role of public services, existence of natural monopolies, preference for outsourcing activities when involving the private sector as opposed to transferring ownership of assets, responsibilities of decentralized authorities, access to natural resources, etc.—raise various interesting questions.

This contribution begins by discussing the scope of the GATS in relation to water services. In this context, it examines the classification of water services in the WTO and in relevant UN bodies, and its consequences under the GATS. Looking at the concepts of 'monopoly' and 'services provided in the exercise of governmental authority', it discusses the implications of the GATS for water management policy choices. Considering that the contractual relationship between a private investor and a public authority can take various forms, the chapter also attempts to determine when water contracts are to be considered as government procurement, in which case they would escape key GATS disciplines. The chapter then provides an overview of existing commitments on sewage services. It also discusses the basic consequences of specific commitments under the four modes of supply identified by the GATS, as well as the implications of such commitments for control over water resources, policy choices by local authorities, and possibility to revert to public management. Lastly, it gives a brief account of water services in the ongoing multilateral negotiations.

2. Main features of the GATS[12]

The GATS is based on traditional principles of international trade such as the national treatment and the most-favoured-nation clauses. But the specificities of services activities—in particular the fact that services are intangible and not storable—called for innovative solutions to regulate the 'import' of foreign services.

The GATS defines 'trade in services' by reference to four modes of supply (Article I). 'Cross-border supply' (mode 1) refers to the supply of a service from the territory of one Member into the territory of any other Member. 'Consumption abroad' (mode 2) entails the supply of a service in the territory of one

[11] Unless otherwise specified, the expression 'water services' in this contribution will refer to water distribution and sanitation services (collection and distribution of drinking water, and treatment of waste water) provided to the public.

[12] The text of the GATS is available at http://www.wto.org/english/docs_e/legal_e/26-gats.pdf. For an introduction to the GATS, *see*, e.g., Mitsuo Matsushita, Thomas Schoenbaum, & Petros Mavroidis, *The World Trade Organization—Law, Practice, and Policy* (Oxford: The Oxford International Law Library, Oxford University Press, 2003); and Michael Trebilcock & Robert Howse, *The Regulation of International Trade* (London: 2nd edn, Routledge, 1999).

Member to a service consumer of another Member. A service can also be supplied through the establishment of a 'commercial presence' (mode 3), or through the 'presence of a natural person' (mode 4) in the territory of the 'importing' Member.

The GATS applies in principle to all services, 'except those provided in the exercise of governmental authority' (Article I:3(b)). Market access (Article XVI) and national treatment (Article XVII) are not general obligations but are granted only in sectors which a Member lists in its national schedule of specific commitments. Specific commitments can be defined as legal guarantees enjoyed by foreign services suppliers; they govern access to a market and conditions of competition vis-à-vis domestic suppliers. In GATS terms, the concept of market access refers to an exhaustive list of six types of restrictions.[13] National treatment refers to the obligation not to discriminate *de facto* or *de jure* between foreign and national service suppliers. The undertaking of specific commitments also triggers the application of other GATS disciplines which apply only in scheduled sectors, such as Article III:3 (notification) or Article VI:5 (domestic regulation).

Specific commitments may have a wider impact on regulatory capacity than tariff bindings have in trade in goods, but this is compensated by the flexibility left to Members in scheduling them. First, Members can choose and define the sectors, and select the modes of supply for which they are ready to undertake specific commitments. Secondly, these commitments can be qualified with various types of limitations, thus allowing a Member to tailor them to specific national policy objectives. Moreover, since the GATS stipulates that developing countries can have the right to open fewer sectors, there is a clear correlation between the level of development of Members and the number of activities listed in their schedules: developing and least-developed countries have undertaken fewer commitments than developed countries.

Specific commitments are not time-limited. However, under certain conditions, a Member can derogate from its commitments, for instance when measures are needed to protect public health or morals (Article XIV). A Member may also come back on a commitment, but it will most likely have to offer compensation to affected trading partners by offering commitments in other sectors (Article XXI).

In the absence of specific commitment, the GATS imposes only limited general obligations. The most significant of these is the most-favoured-nation (MFN) treatment (Article II), which is a prohibition to discriminate among foreign suppliers providing the same service. The MFN obligation *per se* does not open a

[13] There are four numerical limitations: (a) on the number of service suppliers; (b) on the total value of services transactions or assets; (c) on the total number of service operations, or on the total quantity of service output; (d) on the total number of natural persons that may be employed in a particular service sector, or that a service supplier may employ, and who are necessary for, and directly related to, the supply of a specific service. These limitations may be expressed in the forms of numerical quotas or economic needs tests. The last two limitations concern: measures which restrict or require specific types of legal entity or joint venture, and limitations on the participation of foreign capital.

market to foreigners, but it obliges countries choosing to do so, whether *de facto* or by undertaking specific commitments, to treat all foreigners alike. Each Member had the opportunity to seek exemptions from the MFN obligation at the date of entry into force of the GATS.

The GATS explicitly recognizes 'the right of Members to regulate the supply of services within their territories in order to meet national policy objectives' (GATS Preamble). In sectors where specific commitments are undertaken, regulations should be applied in a non-discriminatory manner to national and foreign suppliers. This means, in particular, that Members must ensure that regulatory measures are administered in a reasonable, objective, and impartial manner (Article VI:1); moreover, licensing and qualification requirements, as well as technical standards, should, *inter alia*, be 'based on objective and transparent criteria' and should not be 'more burdensome than necessary to ensure the quality of the service' (Article VI:5). This is an obligation of means, essentially calling for proportionality, which does not prejudge the policy objectives that a Member may want to achieve.

3. Classification of water services

3.1 Current classification instruments and their reference to water services

Classification of services consists in the identification and definition of individual services activities, and is used as a basis for establishing national schedules of specific commitments. Compared to the Harmonized System which exists for goods, classification of services exhibits a high level of aggregation.

Two main instruments are used in the WTO: the Provisional Central Product Classification[14] (CPC Prov.) and the Services Sectoral Classification List.[15] The CPC Prov., established in 1991 by the Statistical Office of the United Nations, was the first effort to provide in a comprehensive and mutually exclusive manner an international description of goods and services. It was established for statistical purposes, but governments decided to use it because it was the only classification system available at the end of the Uruguay Round. The CPC has been revised twice since 1991. The Services Sectoral Classification List was established by the Secretariat of the GATT in 1991. The 'W/120', as it is commonly referred to, can be seen as a simplification of the CPC: it lists twelve services sectors, disaggregated in about 160 sub-sectors, indicating for each of them the corresponding CPC number.

The GATS does not oblige Members to use any specific classification instrument, which means that governments are free to choose the reference system

[14] *Provisional Central Product Classification*, Department of International Economic and Social Affairs, United Nations, 1991.

[15] *Services Sectoral Classification List*, Note by the Secretariat, MTN.GNS/W/120, World Trade Organization (hereinafter 'W/120').

they prefer, or to establish their own. However, when included in a schedule of commitments, normally through the CPC reference number, the corresponding definition becomes legally binding.

Neither the CPC nor the W/120 contains a distinct category for water-related services, but certain sectors include water-related activities. In the W/120, the most relevant is the so-called 'environmental services' sector, which includes a sub-sector for 'sewage services', closely related to waste water treatment.[16] The corresponding CPC definition, under 9401, defines sewage services as 'sewage removal, treatment and disposal services. Equipment used are waste pipes, sewers or drains, cesspools or septic tanks and processes utilised may be dilution, screening and filtering, sedimentation, chemical precipitation, etc.'

Nothing in the Secretariat's list, however, refers to water distribution, and the question does not appear to have been raised at the time it was established. The CPC Prov. only contains an entry for 'distribution services on a fee or contract basis of . . . steam and hot water to household, industrial, commercial and other users' in a section dealing with *Services incidental to energy distribution* (CPC 88700); this reference concerns activities related to heating systems, but does not cover drinking water. Moreover, the CPC Prov. explicitly excludes from the environmental services section (9401) the 'collection, purification and distribution services of water', and classifies it in the subclass 18000, entitled 'natural water'. This subclass is in the goods section, which means that, technically, distribution of drinking water does not appear to be included in the CPC Prov.[17]

3.2 Water services activities in the UN Central Product Classification

Recent revisions of the CPC show a clear tendency to spell out water-related activities, in particular those related to distribution. The first revision[18] introduced water distribution services in the chapter dealing with *Production services, on a fee or contract basis* (Division 86), sub-sector *Electricity, gas and water distribution (on a fee or contract basis)* (8622), which contains a section on *Water distribution services through mains (on a fee or contract basis)* (86223).[19] The activity is not further defined. However, it can be deduced, by reference to the explanatory note to sewage treatment services (9401), that the

[16] The other sub-sectors of environmental services in the Secretariat's list are: Refuse disposal services (CPC 9402); Sanitation and similar services (CPC 9403); and 'Other'. The 'Other' category does not refer to any CPC definition, but it can be presumed to include the remaining items of the CPC environmental services, i.e. cleaning of exhaust gases (CPC 9404), noise abatement services (CPC 9405), nature and landscape protection services (CPC 9406), and other environmental protection services not included elsewhere (CPC 9409).

[17] The Division of the CPC dealing with distribution services does not refer to distribution of water.

[18] *Central Product Classification (CPC)—Version 1.0* (hereinafter 'CPC 1.0'), Statistical Papers, Series M, No. 77, Ver. 1.0, United Nations, 1998.

[19] Note that water distribution is also referred to in Division 69 of the CPC 1.0, *Electricity distribution services; Gas and water distribution services through mains*. Subclass 6921, *Water, except*

activities covered under 86223 are meant to include 'collection, purification and distribution services' of water.

In the second revision of the CPC[20] the activities relevant to water distribution have been organized in a different manner, but without adding clarity. *Water distribution services through mains (on a fee or contract basis)* (86330) are found in Section 8, dealing with *Business and production services*, and Division 86, *Services incidental to agriculture, hunting, forestry, fishing, mining and utilities*. However, unlike CPC 1.0, 'collection and purification' of water are delinked from distribution and are put under 18000 ('natural water'), as indicated in the explanatory note under 94110 (sewage treatment services). It is hard to find the logic behind the organization of water-related entries in the second revision of the CPC. The modifications between CPC 1.0 and 1.1, the back and forth between the section dealing with goods and the one devoted to services, seem to indicate that the drafters had difficulties making up their minds on whether water-related activities are to be considered as a service *stricto sensu* or as the 'production' of a good.

The revised CPCs did not have any impact on existing commitments under the GATS and do not prejudge future negotiations. No decision has been taken in the WTO as to whether the W/120 list should be revised to reflect recent revisions of the CPC, or whether and how the revised CPCs should be used at all in the WTO.

3.3 Classification of water services in the WTO

The classification of water-related services is also an issue in the WTO. Some seven years ago, the Committee on Specific Commitments undertook to revise the Secretariat's list W/120, and identified environmental services as a candidate for update.

Among the various proposals which have been tabled by governments, the most ambitious came from the European Communities, which suggested the creation of seven environmental sub-sectors (instead of the current four), based on the environmental media, i.e. water, air, soil, waste, noise, and eco-systems.[21] With respect to water, it proposed to introduce a section on *Water for human use and wastewater management*, including two sub-sectors. The first one, *Water collection, purification and distribution services through mains, except steam*

steam and hot water, distribution services through mains, refers to distribution services of water, as well as reading and maintenance of meters. However, this Division appears to deal only with distribution services on own account. This can be inferred from subclass 86223, dealing with *Water distribution services through mains (on a fee or contract basis)*, which explicitly excludes 'water distribution services on own account'. Distribution of water on own account is not relevant for GATS, which deals only with services supplied for account of a third party.

[20] *Central Product Classification (CPC)—Version 1.1* (hereinafter 'CPC 1.1'), available at http://unstats.un.org/unsd/cr/registry/regcst.asp?Cl=16&Lg=1.

[21] *GATS 2000: Environmental Services*, Communication from the European Communities and Their Members States, S/CSS/W/38 (22 December 2000).

and hot water, is not included in the current WTO classification. The proposal describes it as including 'potable water treatment, purification and distribution, including monitoring'. The second sub-sector corresponds to the current 'sewage services' of the WTO classification: it is entitled *Waste water services* and would include activities such as 'removal, treatment and disposal of household, commercial and industrial sewage and other waste waters, including tank emptying & cleaning, monitoring, removal and treatment of solid wastes'.

The suggestion explicitly to include water distribution services into the WTO classification is the main and most controversial novelty in the EC submission. The European Communities are also the only WTO Member to propose it. Other Members are in favour of revising and updating the classification of environmental services, but none of them mentions water distribution.[22] Several Members are in fact rather sceptical. Adopting a technical stance, some of them argue that water distribution should not be considered as an 'environmental service' *stricto sensu*, because, in their view, it does not benefit the environment. Others strongly oppose any reference to water distribution, on the ground that 'bulk water, which relate[s] to the issue of exhaustible natural resources, should be excluded from a possible classification of water distribution services under the GATS'.[23] The issue is not yet settled.

3.4 Consequences of an explicit reference to water distribution in the WTO classification

What would be the consequences of explicitly including water distribution in the WTO classification? From a legal point of view, none. The coverage of the GATS is not determined by the Secretariat's list or any other classification system, but by its Article I:1, which states that '[T]he Agreement applies to measures affecting trade in services'. The term 'services' includes '*any service in any sector* except services supplied in the exercise of governmental authority' (Article I:3(b), emphasis added).[24] Nobody seems to deny that the various operations necessary to bring fresh water to the tap are services activities. Hence, water services, whether or not they are 'classified' in the W/120, do fall under the GATS, subject to the carve-out in Article I:3(b).[25] However, including an explicit reference to water distribution may have an impact on the dynamics of the multilateral services negotiations, because governments are inclined to follow classification instruments, in particular the WTO W/120. Hence,

[22] Work on a revised classification of environmental services is currently based on proposals by the United States (S/CSS/W/25), the European Communities (S/CSS/W/38), Switzerland (S/CSS/W/76), Australia (S/CSS/W/112), Colombia (S/CSS/W/121), and Canada (Job No. 5542, 22 September 1999).

[23] *See* WTO documents S/CSC/M/17, para 7 and S/CSC/M/18/rev.1, paras 14 and 15.

[24] The relevance of the governmental services carve-out for water-related services is addressed below.

[25] This means, in particular, that, in the absence of specific commitments, the 'general' disciplines of the GATS, such as the obligation of most-favoured treatment (Art. II) or publication requirements (Art. III), are already applicable to water distribution.

identifying water distribution may facilitate requests and prompt specific commitments.

The fact that there is no consensus on making reference to water distribution in the WTO classification does not exclude this activity from the ongoing negotiations. In particular, it did not prevent the EC from requesting a number of countries to undertake specific commitments on water distribution. The *Summary of the EC's Initial Requests to Third Countries* indicates that

> the EC's requests [on environmental services] are based on the EC's proposal for classification of environmental services and cover all environmental subsectors. This includes water collection, purification, and distribution services, sewage services, waste management services, services related to protection and clean-up of air and climate, soil and water, as well as services related to the protection of biodiversity, and other related services.[26]

Since the scope of the GATS is not determined by a classification instrument, the European Communities, and any other Member, are free to present requests on services activities not classified. Countries to which these requests are addressed are equally free to respond positively or not.

4. The GATS and policy choices

The EC Treaty postulates, in its Article 295, that it 'shall in no way prejudice the rules in Member States governing the system of property ownership'.[27] Similarly, the GATS does not seek to impose a particular policy regime and is neutral with respect to whether ownership of companies should be public or private.[28] What applies in the Single European Market should be even more relevant in an organization like the WTO, where the level of policy integration and liberalization among Members is far less ambitious. However, unlike the EC Treaty, the GATS does not contain a specific provision stating its neutrality. But the fact that it is based on the same assumption regarding policy choices can be inferred from two of its provisions, namely, Article 1:3(b) on governmental services and Article VIII on monopolies and exclusive suppliers.

4.1 Services 'provided in the exercise of governmental authority'

Services 'provided in the exercise of governmental authority' are not subject to any GATS discipline and remain outside trade negotiations (Article I:3(b)). This carve-out indicates that WTO Member governments wanted some activities to remain outside multilateral trade rules because they are governmental prerogatives.

[26] *Summary of the EC's Initial Requests to Third Countries in the GATS Negotiations*, Brussels, 1 July 2002, http://europa.eu.int/comm/trade/services/gats_sum.htm, consulted on 30 August 2002.

[27] The Treaty Establishing the European Community (consolidated version).

[28] It should be noted that the word 'privatization' does not appear in the GATS.

In practice, it is likely that the scope of this exemption will differ from one country to another, depending in particular on national policy choices, and constitutional and administrative organization. However, uncertainties remain as to its exact scope. The GATS does not contain a list of these services and Members are not required to notify them. The GATS Article I:3(c) contains a *sui generis* definition, whereby services supplied in the exercise of governmental authority are services supplied 'neither on a commercial basis nor in competition with one or more service suppliers'. This definition does not allow one clearly to determine whether and in what circumstances water services provided by public utilities would fall outside the scope of the GATS.

The first question in relation to this definition is whether and when public utilities can be considered to supply water services on a non-commercial basis. Water services provided free of charge would undoubtedly fulfil this condition. However, in most countries, users normally pay a fee, meant to cover, at least in part, the cost of water supply or treatment of waste water. Does the fact that a user-fee is charged amount to providing the service on a 'commercial basis'? Or could it be argued that a service is provided commercially only in situations in which a profit is sought by the supplier? Should the first interpretation prevail, the scope of the carve-out would be extremely limited and only services provided for free would be considered as non-commercial. If, on the other hand, it were understood that 'commercial' concerned only those services provided for profit (or '*à but lucratif*'), it could be argued that services provided below costs, or even at a price covering the costs but excluding profit, would not be considered as being supplied 'on a commercial basis'. According to one commentator, the second interpretation would be supported by an examination of the ordinary meaning of the word 'commercial' in the GATS, which appears to refer to 'profit-seeking activities'.[29] To the extent that the first approach would largely deprive Article 1:3(b) of any useful purpose, one could also invoke the principle of effective treaty interpretation to support the second approach.[30]

The second condition of Article I:3(c) requires that a service supplied 'in the exercise of governmental authority' should not be in competition with other services suppliers. In other words, a public entity must not be competing with one or more private suppliers for the supply of the same service. Applying this requirement to water services is particularly challenging. A prerequisite for

[29] *See* Markus Krajewski, *Public Services and Trade Liberalization—Mapping the Legal Framework*, 6 Journal of International Economic Law 341, 351 (2003), 341–67, at 351. *See also*, *WTO Secretariat Hits False Attacks Against GATS*, Speech by David Hartridge, (then) Director of the WTO Trade in Services Division, at the European Services Forum, on 27 November 2000, Brussels, available at http://www.wto.org/english/news_e/news00_e/gats2000neg_hartridge_e.htm.

[30] The principle of effective treaty interpretation has been invoked on various occasions by the WTO Appellate Body. In the *US—Gasoline* case, it stated, in particular, that: 'One of the corollaries of the "general rule of interpretation" in the *Vienna Convention* is that interpretation must give meaning and effect to all the terms of a treaty. An interpreter is not free to adopt a reading that would result in reducing whole clauses or paragraphs of a treaty to redundancy or inutility.' *See WTO Analytical Index—Guide to WTO Law and Practice*, 1st edn (2003), Vol. 2, WTO, at 1282.

determining whether there is competition between them would imply that the public and private supplier(s) coexist in the same market. However, because water services are still considered natural monopolies, there can be only one supplier in a given market. Competition may exist between private suppliers before accessing that market, in the bidding process for a concession contract for instance. But in this case, a public authority is not competing with private suppliers since it is in fact seeking to contract out certain activities. A competition test in a sector which is inherently non-competitive amounts to trying to square the circle.[31]

While the principle of exempting certain activities from the GATS has never been questioned by any WTO Member, the exact boundaries of the Article I:3(b) carve-out remain to be determined. This situation may have prompted some governments to include in their schedules various limitations and footnotes with the purpose of clarifying the respective role of public and private services suppliers (see below), or not to commit at all on relevant subsectors. Pending a clarification of Article I:3(b), these limitations should be maintained and governments contemplating specific commitments on water services should consider including similar restrictions, if necessary.

4.2 Monopolies and exclusive services suppliers

Under GATS Article VIII, governments can maintain monopolies and exclusive service suppliers, but must ensure that they do not abuse their position in a way inconsistent with relevant GATS provisions. Monopoly suppliers are defined as 'any person, *public or private*, which in the relevant market of the territory of a Member *is authorized or established formally or in effect by that Member* as the sole supplier of that service'.[32] This definition indicates, first, that, as a matter of principle, the ownership of an enterprise (private or public) is irrelevant under the GATS. Thus, a government can decide to maintain public ownership and control over a sector of economic activity. In such a case, it should, of course, abstain from undertaking GATS commitments, since these are meaningless in a sector dominated by a public monopoly. Secondly, this definition also implies

[31] Another related question is whether the mere coexistence of a public and a private service supplier on a given market entails 'competition' within the meaning of Art. I:3(c). Take the education sector, for instance. To the extent that both public and private schools target the same group of consumers, one could consider that there is competition between them. However, this competition is in fact often asymmetrical. The private supplier may be 'competing' with the public system to enrol pupils, but not vice versa. A public supplier providing services on a non-commercial basis (free public schools, for instance), does not, in practice, 'compete' with private schools. This could lead to the conclusion that a supplier operating on a non-commercial basis and co-existing with private suppliers does not effectively compete with other suppliers within the meaning of Art. I:3(c). Therefore, it seems difficult to reconcile a factual situation with the general principle of textual interpretation of treaties. This question is, however, not directly relevant for natural monopolies like water services where, most often, two suppliers do not co-exist on the same market.

[32] *See* GATS Art. XXVIII(h) (emphasis added). *See also* Art. XXVIII(l), which defines 'juridical person' as 'any legal entity... whether privately-owned or governmentally-owned...'.

that the existence of a monopoly depends on a government's action: either a positive decision to create such a monopoly, or acceptance of a *de facto* existing monopoly. It would thus exclude natural monopolies, such as water services, which exist outside governments' action.

Nevertheless, some of the disciplines contained in Article VIII may be useful for natural monopolies. The main idea underlying this provision is that, when supplying services within and outside its monopoly rights, a monopolistic enterprise must act in a manner consistent with the specific commitments undertaken by the government (Article VIII: 1 and 2), and with the MFN obligation (Article VIII:1). Article VIII appears to be concerned with the behaviour of monopolies having control over infrastructural facilities, such as telecommunication and energy, which could use their position to undermine specific commitments in other sectors of economic activity.[33] In theory at least, the same type of concern could arise with respect to water services. A supplier of water charging higher fees to foreign enterprises could be an example of an abuse within a monopoly right, contrary to paragraph 1.

But water services raise another range of difficulties. In a natural monopoly situation, privatization does not lead to a competitive market but to the replacement of a public monopoly with a private one. What may be at stake, then, is perhaps less the need to protect commercial operators than to ensure that the interests of consumers are defended against potential abuses from private enterprise operating in a non-competitive environment. The elaboration of adequate regulatory instruments, at the national and international levels, may well be one of the most significant challenges for the water sector for the years to come. But this issue is largely outside the GATS.

5. Water services and government procurement

5.1 Main GATS disciplines do not apply to government procurement (but what is government procurement?)

Traditionally, governments have been reluctant to submit their own purchases to multilateral trade rules. In 1947, drafters of the GATT decided to exclude government procurement from the national treatment obligation (GATT Article III:8(a)). Fifty years later, the drafters of the GATS followed a similar path in Article XIII. Services procurement, defined as the 'procurement by governmental agencies of services purchased for governmental purposes and not with a view to commercial resale or with a view to use in the supply of services for commercial sale', are exempted from the obligations of the most-favoured-nation, market access, and national treatment (GATS Article XIII:1). Since 1995, WTO Members are negotiating on services procurement disciplines (GATS Article XIII:2), but

[33] *See* Aaditya Mattoo, *Dealing with Monopolies and State Enterprises: WTO Rules for Goods and Services*, in State Trading in the Twenty-First Century (Cottier & Mavroidis eds, 1998) at 37–70.

these negotiations have not yet led to any concrete result. For the time being, the only comprehensive WTO disciplines in this area are contained in the plurilateral Agreement on Government Procurement (GPA), which covers the purchase of goods and services, and which has been signed by twenty-eight Members, mostly developed countries.

The term 'privatization', which is used to refer to various kinds of involvement of the private sector in water activities, may, in practice, apply to various forms of contractual relationships between a public authority and a private operator. Full-fledged privatization of a public utility, i.e. the sale of assets to a private company, is rare in the water sector. So far, it seems to have been resorted to on a large scale in two countries, namely, Chile and the United Kingdom. In general, governments prefer solutions allowing them to retain the ownership of the facility and contract out certain tasks to a private company. So-called 'public–private partnerships' (PPPs) make use of various instruments, such as management, Build-Operate-Transfer (BOT), and concessions contracts,[34] the main differences lying in the degree of responsibilities delegated by a public authority and in the financial arrangements agreed between the parties concerned.

Do management contracts, BOT, and concessions fall under the Article XIII definition of government procurement? Should the answer be positive, these instruments would escape key GATS disciplines, since they would not be covered by specific commitments, but might be subject to the disciplines of the GPA for those countries which have signed it.[35] Discussions in relevant WTO bodies show that governments do not share the same views on this matter, and that there is even some confusion on basic questions. For instance, the Working Party on GATS Rules discussed some time ago the need for clarifying the definition of services procurement, and, in this context, the question arose as to whether concessions and BOT contracts should be considered a form of government procurement. Many countries considered that the current GATS definition of government procurement appeared to exclude concessions, which would thus be subject to all GATS disciplines. However, this view was not shared by all. Accounts of the debate also show that the very concept of concession is different from one country to another. Similar uncertainties arose with respect to BOT contracts.[36]

[34] For a description and comparison of the various contractual instruments used in the water sector, *see*, e.g., Jeffrey Delmon, *supra* note 5; National Research Council, *Privatization of Water Services in the United States—An Assessment of Issues and Experience* (Washington DC: National Academy Press, 2002); *Bridging the Water Divide*, Suez, 2003, and *Vivendi Water, Partner to Major Cities*, Vivendi Environment, 2003.

[35] Ten Members (Canada; European Communities; Hong Kong, China; Israel; Japan; Korea; Liechtenstein; Norway; Switzerland; and the United States) included sewage services in their list of services covered by the GPA. Except for Hong Kong, China, all of them have also undertaken specific commitments on sewage services under the GATS.

[36] *See* the Reports of the meetings of the Working Party of GATS Rules, in particular S/WPGR/M/14 to 24. *See also* the Reports of the Working Group on Transparency in Government Procurement (WT/WGTGP/2 + 3 and WT/WGTGP/M/10 + 11).

The difficulties encountered by WTO Members in trying to differentiate among these instruments are not surprising, and stem mainly from the lack of internationally agreed definitions. As a consequence, the same word can be understood to cover different realities, or, conversely, the same type of arrangement can be described with different terms. For instance, the word 'concession' is used to describe a wide range of situations when there is a contract between a public entity and a private operator; BOT contracts are sometimes referred to as a form of concession. On the other hand, BOT contracts share similarities with what the EC law calls 'public work concessions'.[37] Moreover, the boundaries between these types of instruments are not always clear, and sometimes contracts between a public authority and a private company can combine elements pertaining to one or another form.

5.2 What about water contracts?

With a *concession* contract, a private company is granted a licence to operate a facility during a specified period of time, normally twenty to thirty years, and to obtain payment directly from the consumers. The company must maintain the facility and may be required to improve it. Under such an arrangement, there is no purchase of a service from the government; on the contrary, the authorities generally levy a fee on the concessionaire in exchange for the right granted by the concession. Moreover, the service provided (water supply or sewage) is not for the direct consumption of the government, but is supplied to individual consumers on behalf of public authorities. Such concession contracts can thus not be considered a form of government procurement and would be subject to core GATS disciplines.

The situation is more complex with BOT contracts, whereby a private company finances and builds a public facility, and operates it during a specified period. At the end of that period, the facility reverts to the authority, normally free of charge.[38] The company may be paid by the public authority for providing the services, but may also be allowed to bill customers directly. Such BOT contracts combine elements of procurement (construction of a public facility) with concessional regimes (granting of an exclusive right to operate a facility and provide a service to the public).

It could be argued that the main object—and primary purpose—of BOT contracts is the construction of an infrastructure. In such a scenario, BOT contracts can be seen as complementing 'normal' procurement methods and offering an avenue for governments which are short of cash to finance basic infrastructural facilities. The right to operate the infrastructure, i.e. to provide a service, would only be incidental since it would derive from the construction of the facility. Should this interpretation prevail, BOT would be considered as

[37] Council Directive 93/37/EEC, of 14 June 1993, OJ L 199/54, concerning the coordination of procedures for the award of public works contracts, Art. 1.

[38] Jeffrey Delmon, *supra* note 5, at 30.

procurement and, thus, escape GATS main disciplines. If, on the contrary, the primary purpose was to confer on a private investor the right to provide a service, GATS disciplines would apply. However, this involves second-guessing the intention of a government and making a potentially subjective determination of what the 'primary purpose' of a BOT contract is.

Lastly, public authorities may choose to conclude a *management contract*, whereby a private company is entrusted with more specific and limited tasks, such as fixing leaks, billing and meter reading, or laboratory services. The case for government procurement appears to be stronger here, since a governmental authority clearly purchases a service. Considering the definition in GATS Article XIII, two questions remain to be considered, however. First, would such a purchase be 'for governmental purposes'? An unadopted GATT panel report found that elements such as 'payment by government, government use of or benefit from the product, government possession and government control over the obtaining of the product' could provide guidance to determine whether a transaction should be regarded as a government procurement.[39] At first glance, management contracts appear to exhibit these characteristics: the service would be paid by the government, would be destined for an infrastructure owned by it, and the government would oversee the overall implementation of the contract.

Secondly, the services should be purchased 'not with a view to commercial resale or with a view to use in the supply of services for commercial resale'. While the first condition would be met—the services procured under management contracts are not resold—the second condition may be more ambiguous. If we consider that a public utility supplies water services on a commercial basis, the argument could be made that the purchase of a service in relation to a water network (fixing a pipe, for instance) is made 'with a view to use in the supply of services for commercial sale' (for example, water distribution). Again, the interpretation of the word 'commercial' may be crucial and could lead to considerations similar as those raised in relation to the discussion of Article I:3(b) (see above).

This brief discussion is only a first insight into a complex question. There is little doubt that concession contracts would be covered by specific commitments. Other forms of contractual arrangements between a public authority and a private operator, such as management contracts, could be considered as government procurement and would not be subject to market access and national treatment rules. The situation of BOT contracts remains to be clarified. One should also remember that, in practice, water contracts do not necessarily fall clearly under one of these three categories, but can combine various elements. In the absence of clear categories and agreed definitions, it is necessary to make a case-by-case determination based on the main elements of a contractual relationship between a public authority and a private contractor.

[39] Panel Report on *United States—Procurement of a Sonar Mapping System*, GPR.DS1/R, 23 April 1992 (unadopted), paras 4.5–4.13.

6. Existing commitments on sewage services[40]

So far, forty-two Members at various levels of development have undertaken specific commitments with respect to sewage services.[41] This number is rather modest as compared to other services sectors,[42] and it certainly reflects the prevailing role played in many countries by public entities in providing these services.

Commitments on market access and national treatment follow a similar pattern across schedules and contain relatively few restrictions. Cross-border supply is generally *Unbound*[43] for both market access and national treatment, sometimes because Members consider that this mode of supply is not technically feasible. 'Consumption abroad' is generally bound, although it is not clear what the relevance of this mode is for activities related to sewage services (see below). Establishing a commercial presence is the most important mode of delivery for sewage services and commitments under mode 3 are generally liberal. Few countries have listed market access restrictions,[44] although some horizontal limitations may apply.[45] Mode 4 follows the usual pattern found in most Members' schedules for all sectors: it is 'unbound, except for' certain categories of natural persons mentioned in the horizontal section (these are usually managerial positions, intra-corporate transferees, or persons possessing some kind of specialized knowledge).

Various Members have limited the type of activities which can be carried out by foreign suppliers. For instance, Lesotho and South Africa restricted their environmental services commitments to 'consultancy services', which means that the actual supply of waste water treatment services is not covered.[46] Commitments undertaken by Korea, Estonia, and the United States exclude public sewage systems, since they are explicitly limited to sewage services purchased by private industry.[47] Other countries achieve a similar objective by

[40] No commitment has been taken with respect to water distribution.

[41] These are: Albania, Armenia, Australia, Austria, Bulgaria, Canada, China, Croatia, Czech Republic, Ecuador, Estonia, European Communities, Gambia, Georgia, Guinea, Iceland, Israel, Japan, Republic of Korea, Kuwait, Kyrgyz Republic, Latvia, Lesotho, Liechtenstein, Lithuania, Macedonia, Moldova, Morocco, Norway, Oman, Qatar, Sierra Leone, Slovak Republic, Slovenia, South Africa, Sweden, Switzerland, Taiwan, Thailand, Turkey, United Arab Emirates, United States.

[42] For instance, more than 120 Members have undertaken commitments on tourism services.

[43] The term *Unbound* indicates that the Member remains free in a given sector and mode of supply to introduce or maintain measures inconsistent with market access or national treatment. *See Guidelines for the Scheduling of Specific Commitments under the General Agreement on Trade in Services (GATS)*, adopted by the Council for Trade in Services on 23 March 2001, S/L/92.

[44] Iceland, for instance, stipulates that 'Environmental operation license [is] required' (GATS/SC/41). Korea limits to 25 the number of foreign suppliers allowed to establish a commercial presence (GATS/SC/48). China obliges them to establish joint-ventures, but allow foreigners to own a majority ownership (GATS/SC/135).

[45] The so-called 'horizontal commitments' apply in all scheduled sectors unless specified otherwise. These commitments, which often take the form of restrictions, are entered in a separate section at the beginning of the schedule, with the objective of avoiding repetition.

[46] GATS/SC/114, GATS/SC/78.

[47] GATS/SC/48, GATS/SC/127, and GATS/SC/90.

excluding 'public service functions whether owned and operated or contracted out' by local, regional, or central government.[48]

Some schedules reflect the primary role of the public sector in supplying these services to the public, or the fact that policy decisions may be delegated to a decentralized level. For example, Croatia indicates, with respect to the establishment of commercial presence, that sewage services 'are legally considered as municipal activities, provided primarily by entities owned by local authorities. Private operators may be allowed to provide those services on the basis of a concession granted by local authorities.'[49] Another case in point is the horizontal limitation found in the schedule of the European Communities, which indicates that '[i]n all EC Member States services considered as public utilities at a national or local level may be subject to public monopolies or to exclusive rights granted to private operators'. This limitation is complemented by a footnote explaining that

> Public utilities exist in sectors such as related scientific and technical consulting services, R&D services on social sciences and humanities, technical testing and analysis services, environmental services, health services, transport services and services auxiliary to all modes of transport. Exclusive rights on such services are often granted to private operators, for instance operators with concessions from public authorities, subject to specific service obligations. Given that public utilities often also exist at the sub-central level, detailed and exhaustive sector-specific scheduling is not practical.[50]

The latter limitations reflect the fact that waste water treatment is decentralized; local authorities retain the possibility to choose whether or not to involve a private supplier. They leave a high level of discretion to the Member concerned and, consequently, grant only limited guarantees to foreign suppliers.

7. What does a specific commitment on water services mean?

This basic and somewhat provocative question arises because water services exhibit certain characteristics which make them 'different' from other sectors. Water distribution and waste water treatment services provided to the public are almost perfect natural monopolies, and, in most instances, a private operator will be operating publicly-owned infrastructures, for which it will need to obtain an authorization from the relevant authorities. Against this background, the question arises as to what type of guarantee specific commitments offer to private operators and, correlatively, what kind of obligations they put on competent authorities.

[48] *See also* the schedules of Liechtenstein (GATS/SC/83-A), Norway (GATS/SC/66), Slovenia (GATS/SC/99), Sweden (GATS/SC/82), and Switzerland (GATS/SC/83).

[49] GATS/SC/130.

[50] GATS/SC/31.

7.1 Cross-border supply (mode 1) and consumption abroad (mode 2)

Water supply and waste water treatment are typical local services, delivered through a network in a defined geographical area. Mode 1 does not appear to be feasible for water distribution and waste water treatment. It is important to clarify that commitments under mode 1 cannot serve as a basis to promote the export of raw water. A commitment on water distribution by country X gives the right to collect and distribute water in the territory of X; it cannot offer any guarantee to pump water in a neighbouring country Y and send it to X. From a WTO point of view, the export of bulk water would be analysed as trade in goods, falling under the General Agreement on Tariffs and Trade (GATT).[51] Mode 2 seems to be equally inapplicable for water distribution. Concerning sewage services, a possible mode 2 situation might involve a sewage plant established near a border, which would treat waste water coming from the neighbouring country; the country getting its waste water treated would be 'consuming abroad' sewage services. However, such a scenario is likely to remain very marginal in practice.

Hence, modes 1 and 2 appear to be largely irrelevant for water services, except perhaps for certain support activities such as consulting. This view seems to be shared by the Members which have undertaken commitments on sewage services: most of them scheduled an *Unbound* for mode 1, sometimes with the indication that they consider this mode not technically feasible. But it is difficult to understand why most Members which left mode 1 unbound have undertaken full commitments under mode 2: the same reasons which would make the supply of this service irrelevant or unfeasible under mode 1 would seem to be also relevant under mode 2.

7.2 Establishment of a commercial presence (mode 3)

Establishment of a commercial presence is no doubt the most crucial mode of supply for water services. But what are the practical and legal consequences of a mode 3 commitment[52] in this sector? In banking services, for instance, it will give a foreign bank the possibility to establish a branch, subject to possible qualification and prudential requirements, and start operating in the market. However, the same type of commitment in water services will not give a foreign operator an 'automatic' right to access and operate a public network. To date, the most common form of participation of private operators in the water sector is to manage publicly-owned infrastructures, based on a contract, normally a concession, with a public authority.[53] A specific commitment will not give an

[51] See chapter 3 by Brown Weiss in Part I of this book.

[52] For working purposes, we shall take the example of a commitment which fully binds market access and national treatment.

[53] This is what is sometimes referred to as the 'French model'. As indicated above, full divestiture of assets is rare in the water sector, and there is no indication that water companies are interested in owning water-networks and plants.

individual supplier the right to obtain a contract, but merely a right to bid when the competent authority issues a call for offers. A GATS commitment may mean that foreign enterprises have the right to participate and to see their offer considered and treated like that of other national suppliers, for instance. This situation raises similar problems to those encountered in bidding procedures in government procurement, but the GATS does not contain specific disciplines regarding the granting of concessions. For the time being, procedures for bidding would presumably be subject to the general transparency requirements in Article III and to the Article VI provisions on domestic regulation. These include in particular the obligation to ensure that the measures 'are administered in a reasonable, objective and impartial manner' (Article VI:1) and to allow unsuccessful candidates to have a decision reviewed by an independent body (Article VI:2). In a second instance, a specific commitment is also relevant once the foreign supplier is in the market. For instance, a government which has chosen to undertake a full market access commitment could not require some type of legal entity, nor that a joint venture be established with a local company (Article XVI:2(e)–(f)). A full national treatment commitment might prevent the authorities from requiring foreign investors to train local employees. However, governments envisaging to undertake commitments on water services can keep the right to implement such measures if they enter corresponding limitations in their schedules.

Regulatory measures applying equally to national and foreign enterprises can be maintained, without being scheduled, provided that they comply with the requirements of Article VI, in particular paragraphs 1 and 5. Examples of such measures in the water sector could be a requirement that companies, whether national or foreign, serve all areas, and not only the profitable ones, or that poor households be supplied with a minimum of water free of charge in order to cover their basic needs.

7.3 Presence of natural persons (mode 4)

With respect to water services, the movement of natural persons is pertinent mostly for transfer of personnel in relation to the establishment of a commercial presence. It may be useful for a firm setting up a plant to be able to bring key personnel, such as managers and specialized technicians. Independent workers in water services appear to be confined to some consultancy activities. On the other hand, water services appear to be less labour-intensive than other sectors, thus reducing the interest of mode 4 commitments for unskilled workers.

In practice, experience with mode 4 shows that commitments are not generally made on the basis of sectoral considerations (needs of the industry, share of independent vs. intra-corporate transferees, for instance). Since they are influenced by considerations and constraints related to immigration policies and protection of labour markets, they are usually taken at a horizontal level, which means that they apply equally to all listed sectors. Moreover, they are restricted to some defined categories of people such as executives, managers, and specialists, which explains why the overall level of these commitments across countries and sectors is very low.

8. Ownership and control of water resources

Water resources are generally considered to be owned by the State, from which derives governments' right to control and regulate their use. In the controversies surrounding the privatization of water services, some argue that the involvement of the private sector may threaten this right and force governments to transfer ownership of water resources to private investors. The Bonn Ministerial Declaration echoes these concerns when it states that 'privately managed service delivery should not imply private ownership of water resources'.[54] The uncertainty surrounding many national legal regimes regarding the status of water resources does not contribute to clarifying the situation.

The privatization of water services does not imply a transfer of ownership of water resources,[55] and water companies themselves claim that they do not seek it.[56] The question whether a concession for supplying water may involve a transfer of ownership of the resource will depend primarily on national law. Assuming that domestic law vests ownership of water resources in the government and excludes private appropriation, there are no grounds for a foreign supplier operating a distribution facility to invoke the GATS to claim ownership of water resources or a right to buy them.[57]

In fact, the question seems to relate more to the effects of the GATS and specific commitments on control over, and use of, water resources, as opposed to ownership. A private supplier operating distribution facilities will need reliable access to raw water, whose modalities and conditions are generally determined in a contract with the public authority. This access may be direct (through obtaining the right to extract raw water from rivers, dams, etc.), or indirect (through buying the water from a raw water provider, generally a public entity).[58] A measure limiting the volume of water which can be withdrawn

[54] Ministerial Declaration adopted on the occasion of the International Conference on Freshwater, Bonn, 4 December 2001.

[55] *See* Jeffrey Delmon, *supra* note 5.

[56] 'I think we should be able to agree that water is a common good, one of the basic public goods. At SUEZ, we are opposed to the private ownership of water resources precisely because, in our eyes, water is not a commodity. We do not trade water. We do not sell a product. We provide a service. The services of making clean water continuously available to all, and returning water to the natural habitat once it has been treated. It is the price of that services that is billed, not the price of water as a raw material.' *The 'Water Truce'—An Open Letter*, by Gérard Mestrallet, Suez, 2003.

[57] The question of ownership of water resources has not been discussed in the WTO. However, an indication of Members' opinion can be found in the discussions relating to energy services, which share similarities with the water sector. There, it was emphasized that the question of public ownership of natural resources remained outside the negotiations. *See* S/CSS/W/24 (US), -W/58 (Canada); -W/59 (Norway); -W/69 (Venezuela); -W/144 (Cuba); -W/142/Suppl.3 (Japan). *See also* the minutes of the Special Session of the Council for Trade in Services in S/CSS/M/9, -12, and -13.

[58] *See* Jeffrey Delmon, *supra* note 5, at 306.

(because of a drought, or to change the allocation of water among competitive users, for instance) will impact the amount of water sold to consumers and, hence, the profits expected by a private company. Could that measure be challenged under the GATS if specific commitments have been undertaken?

The GATS Article XVI:2(c) identifies as a market access restriction, which has to be removed unless specified otherwise in the schedule, 'limitations on the total number of service operations or on the total quantity of services output expressed in terms of designated numerical units in the form of quotas or the requirement of economic needs test'. Footnote 9 to sub-paragraph (c) stipulates that this provision 'does not cover measures of a Member which limit inputs for the supply of services'. While a limitation on the quantity of water which can be withdrawn could have the effect of a 'limitation on the total quantity of services output', it could be argued that water is an 'input for the supply of a service', in which case measures limiting the amount of water available to a supplier would not be considered a restriction within the meaning of Article XVI. However, footnote 9 relates only to sub-paragraph (c) of Article XVI:2, while limitations on the amount of water which can be withdrawn might also be considered as indirectly restricting the 'total value of services transactions' (Article XVI:2(b)). Indeed, it is not clear yet whether the 'limitations' referred to in Article XVI are confined to direct numerical limitations and quotas, or whether measures which take different forms but have an indirect effect of market access restriction would also be covered.

The wording of footnote 9 was used by the European Communities to define the scope of its proposal on environmental services (see above): '[I]t is understood that the GATS does not cover measures of a Member which limit inputs for the supply of services.' The EC added that '[A]s a consequence, any commitment undertaken in this sub-sector does not preclude a Member to regulate the supply and demand of natural resources.'[59] This text clarifies footnote 9 by explicitly stating that natural resources are to be considered an 'input' for the supply of a service. It would also expand the scope of application of footnote 9 to 'the GATS', instead of limiting it to a specific provision. This clarification is interesting, but has limited relevance in its current location. Pending an amendment to the GATS—which may be difficult to achieve any time soon—a practical solution would be for Members which consider undertaking a market access commitment on water distribution to include in their schedule a limitation reflecting in essence the EC text.

9. GATS AND LOCAL AUTHORITIES

The management of water services is often delegated to regional, or even local, authorities. As a result, different systems may coexist in the same country if

[59] WTO document S/CSS/W/38, page 2, footnote 5.

some authorities prefer to maintain a public management and others choose to involve the private sector. The question is whether the undertaking of a specific commitment would oblige all local authorities to contract out water services to private companies, or whether the latter could enter the market only to the extent that the former so decide.

According to Article I:3(a), the GATS applies to central, regional, and local governments and authorities, which means that they would be bound by a specific commitment. However, this principle should be qualified in two respects. First, the exemption contained in Article I:3(b)[60] should arguably be applicable to decentralized authorities. Hence, a local authority providing water services 'in the exercise of governmental authority' should be 'carved-out' from the specific commitment.

Secondly, under GATS Article XVI, a government can schedule specific commitments 'on the basis of a regional subdivision or on the basis of its entire territory'. The *Scheduling Guidelines* further indicate that '[w]here commitments do not cover the entire national territory, the entry should describe the geographical scope of measures taken according to Article I:3(a)(i)'.[61] Therefore, a government may specify the region(s) where access to foreign suppliers is allowed, or, conversely, indicate those regions where a given commitment does not apply. The concept of 'region' may refer to states, provinces, or cantons, but also to municipalities. Several Members, especially among those with a federal structure, have made use of this possibility in a variety of sectors. In the absence of any specification, the commitment would be presumed to apply to the whole territory.

In practice, however, it may prove difficult to list all public utilities, especially in sectors with a high level of decentralization. To circumvent both this problem and the ambiguity of the Article I:3(b) exemption, another option is to subject the commitment to a general limitation carving-out public utilities. The horizontal limitation found in the schedule of the European Communities may be a useful source of inspiration in this regard.[62]

10. GATS AND THE 'LOCK-IN EFFECT'

Various views are being held with respect to the long-term consequences of specific commitments on water services. Some have voiced the concern that specific commitments may make privatization 'irreversible' (the so-called 'lock-in effect' of the GATS).

Under the GATS, a government may modify its schedule and withdraw a commitment in whole or in part, subject to various procedural and substantive

[60] *See* Section 4.1 above.

[61] *Guidelines for the Scheduling of Specific Commitments under the General Agreement on Trade in Services*, adopted by the Council for Trade in Services on 23 March 2001, S/L/92, para 4.

[62] *See* Section 6 above.

obligations enumerated in Article XXI. The most burdensome of these is no doubt the requirement to grant compensation to other Members which are 'affected' by the proposed withdrawal of commitments. The compensation to be offered does not take the form of a financial transfer, but consists in offering specific commitments in other sectors or modes 'so as to maintain a general level of mutually advantageous commitments not less favourable to trade than that provided for in Schedules of specific commitments prior to such negotiations' (Article XXI:2(a)). Moreover, this compensation must be granted on an MFN basis.

The principle contained in Article XXI is not new. This provision is modelled on GATT Article XXVIII, which allows a government to withdraw a tariff concession, subject to compensation. This provision has been applied on seventeen occasions since 1995,[63] while Article XXI has been invoked only once.[64] The main difference between the two provisions is that GATT Article XXVIII defines three categories of Members entitled to seek compensation.[65] No such specification is included in GATS Article XXI, which contains only a general reference to 'affected' Members. As a consequence, it is difficult to predict how many requests for compensation will be made in any given case to the Member wishing to withdraw a specific commitment. The number of Members allowed to seek compensation under Article XXI, and hence the final 'cost' of a withdrawal of commitments, will depend on how broadly an interpretation of 'affected' Members will be applied.[66] The final decision may be made through binding arbitration if the Members concerned cannot find a mutually acceptable solution.

Cancelling a contract with a private operator may not necessarily amount to a withdrawal of commitments in any given case. For instance, should a supplier not respect its contractual terms, it would be subject to the sanctions provided for in the contract—or relevant national law—including termination of the contract, as the case may be. The existence of specific commitments would not matter. On the other hand, a government envisaging radical policy changes and wishing totally to exclude private operators from its market, where they had been previously allowed, would need to invoke Article XXI.

It is important to recall that the GATS does not foresee any obligation for a government to compensate financially private firms in case of cancellation of concession contracts or expropriation. This is simply not an issue for the GATS, which is concerned only with relationships between States. Relevant rules may

[63] Article XXVIII has been invoked some 300 times since the entry into force of the GATT in 1947.

[64] At the time of writing this contribution, the procedure had just been initiated. *See* document S/C/N/231, 10 July 2003.

[65] Under the GATT, a Member wishing to withdraw a tariff binding must negotiate with Members having (i) 'initial negotiating rights', (ii) 'principal supplying interest', and (iii) 'substantial interest'. There may be more than one Member per category, and experience shows that, on average, between 3 and 6 countries are eligible for compensation when a tariff concession is withdrawn.

[66] Given the high concentration in the water sector, and the small number of enterprises playing on the international scene, the number of 'affected' Members may be relatively low.

be found in bilateral investment agreements, or in other public international law instruments.

11. Water services in the new round of services negotiations

The new round of services negotiations started on 1 January 2000, as mandated in Article XIX of the GATS. During the initial phase, the most directly relevant issue for water services was the discussion of the classification of environmental services and, in particular, the proposal to include water distribution; these issues are still under consideration (see above).

The Doha Ministerial Declaration, adopted in November 2001 on the occasion of the Fourth WTO Ministerial Meeting, marked the start of a new phase by providing a framework for the so-called market access negotiations. The Declaration called upon Members to start exchanging initial requests and initial offers as of 30 June 2002 and 31 March 2003, respectively.[67] So far, the European Communities appear to be the only Member requesting specific commitments on distribution of water. These requests are based on the EC's proposals for classification of environmental services and include water collection, purification, and distribution services, as well as sewage services.[68] By March 2005, more than fifty Members (the European Communities counting as one) had tabled an initial offer to the WTO; none of them proposed commitments on water distribution.[69]

Moreover, a specific reference to environmental services appears in the Doha Ministerial Declaration, under paragraph 31, dealing with 'Trade and Environment'. Ministers agreed, 'with a view to enhancing the supportiveness of trade and environment', to negotiations on 'the reduction, or as appropriate, elimination of tariff and non-tariff barriers to environmental goods and services'.[70] It is the Special Session of the Committee on Trade and Environment (SSCTE) which has been tasked to conduct the negotiations mandated under paragraph 31.

From a legal and practical point of view, paragraph 31(iii) of the Doha Declaration has not had an immediate impact on the negotiations on environmental services. It did not trigger them, since the services negotiations had already

[67] Ministerial Declaration, adopted on 14 November 2001, WT/MIN (01)/DEC/1, para 15.

[68] *Summary of the EC's Initial Requests to Third Countries in the GATS Negotiations*, Brussels, 1 July 2002, available at http://europa.eu.int/comm/trade/services/gats_sum.htm, visited on 30 August 2002.

[69] Even the EC, which is the main *demandeur* in this field, indicated that it would rule out 'talks in the Doha world trade round on further liberalisation of its health, education, energy and water markets'. According to the press, the official explanation for excluding energy and water appeared to be that the WTO has still to complete technical work in these sectors (presumably referring to classification work). *See EU likely to bar talks at Doha on four sectors*, Financial Times, 5 February 2003, *Restricted Services: The EU has set a bad example in the Doha trade talks*, Financial Times, 11 February 2003, and *Pascal Lamy présente son offre d'ouverture des services à l'OMC*, Le Monde, 6 February 2003.

[70] Ministerial Declaration, *supra* note 67, para 31(iii).

started, nor did it confer a 'special status' to environmental services. With a view to avoiding duplication, the negotiations on environmental services have so far remained the responsibility of the Special Session of the Council for Trade in Services, as decided by the SSCTE. World Trade Organization Members are in favour of a monitoring role for the SSCTE in these negotiations, which remains to be defined.[71]

12. Conclusion

The GATS is only one piece in the complex puzzle of water services management. It does not hold the keys—and does not pretend to—to solve the access problem to water supply and sanitation. But, in water services as in other sectors, the GATS can play a role in complementing policy decisions where and when governments choose to seek participation of the private sector. By providing a predictable legal framework, it can contribute to sending positive signals to investors, fostering foreign direct investment, and facilitating the transfer of technology and know-how.

Like any international treaty, the GATS does not make anything 'irreversible', but does put regulatory constraints on Member governments. In the absence of specific commitments, GATS obligations remain minimal: they consist mainly in treating all foreigners equally. Specific commitments will trigger the application of market access and national treatment obligations, with possible limitations, but also of other disciplines which apply in scheduled sectors. As a 'young' agreement, the GATS has not been fully tested yet in practice, and uncertainties remain concerning the interpretation of some of its provisions. Pending amendment or clarification by the WTO membership, these problems can be addressed through the scheduling of adequate limitations, as did various Members when they undertook commitments on sewage services.

It is generally acknowledged that privatizing water services requires the establishment of a complex regulatory framework. Because specific commitments limit regulatory options, in the water sector as in any other sector, they should be undertaken only once adequate sectoral regulation is in place.

[71] *See Statement by the Chairperson of the Special Session of the Committee on Trade and Environment to the Trade Negotiations Committee*, TN/TE/1, 12 April 2002.

6

GATS and its Impact on Private Sector Participation in Water Services

ELISABETH TUERK, AARON OSTROVSKY, and ROBERT SPEED[1]

1. Introduction

The importance of water to all forms of life is undisputable, yet half a billion people suffer from severe water shortages and nearly one billion people do not have access to safe drinking water. The availability of water is also a limiting factor for many industries, in particular agriculture. Balancing ecological and human requirements for water with the requirements of economic development raises many difficult environmental, social, and legal issues.

To meet these challenges, many countries are undergoing systemic changes to the management of water resources and the provision of water services. These changes include the privatization of water services. While privatization can be a useful tool to make domestic water services more functional and efficient, it should take place as part of strategies for sustainable development and not be deemed an end in itself.

Despite concerns that privatization should not be approached as a one-size-fits-all solution, especially in the area of water services, international trade policy-making continues to expand, promoting private sector involvement through progressive liberalization of trade in services. These two disparate areas, water management on the one hand and trade liberalization on the other, create unique legal and policy conflicts. In particular, some[2] fear that the

[1] Elisabeth Tuerk, CIEL, etuerk@ciel.org, Aaron Ostrovsky, and Robert Speed. This is a paper contributing to the workshop on water and international economic law, 3 March 2003, in Geneva. We are grateful to Mary Footer, Markus Krajewski, Stephen Porter, Mahesh Sugatan, and Simon Walker for valuable comments on an earlier version of this draft. Special thanks to Mireille Cossy for the numerous challenging discussions surrounding the issues discussed in this paper, and to Jennifer Federico, Suzanne Garner, and Zachary Kamykowski for their editing assistance.

[2] Ellen Gould, *Water in the Current Round of WTO Negotiations on Services*, Briefing Paper Series: Investment and Trade at Vol. 4, No. 1 (Canadian Centre for Policy Alternatives, Ottawa) (visited Jan. 16, 2004) <http://www.policyalternatives.ca/publications/brief4-1.pdf> (Jan. 2003); John Hilary, *GATS and Water: The Threat of Services Negotiations at the WTO*, Briefing Paper (Save the Children, London) (2003); John Hilary, *The Wrong Model, GATS, trade liberalization and children's right to health* (Save the Children, London) (2001); Jessica Woodroffe & Clare Joy, *Out of service: The development dangers of the General Agreement on Trade in Services* (World Development Movement, London) (March 2002); Jessica Woodroffe, *GATS: A Disservice to the Poor* (World

application of the General Agreement on Trade in Services (GATS) to water services and trends towards the privatization of water services will infringe on governments' abilities to ensure the human right to water.[3]

This chapter explores linkages between the GATS and domestic water policies.[4] Section 2 discusses recent trends in water management, briefly describing the legal and administrative models that have been adopted for managing water resources and supplying water services. Section 3 sets a stage for analysis in the remaining sections by providing an overview of the GATS. Section 4 then looks at privatization, analyzing how the GATS and privatization intersect generally. Section 5 discusses problems and pitfalls with the GATS market access obligation when applied to water services. Lastly, Section 6 addresses how the GATS,

Development Movement, London) (January 2002); Mark Ellis-Jones & Pete Hardstaff, *Serving (up) the nation, A guide to the UK's commitments under the WTO General Agreement on Trade in Services* (World Development Movement, London) (November 2002); Scott Sinclair, *GATS—How the World Trade Organization's new 'services' negotiations threaten democracy* (Canadian Centre for Policy Alternatives, Ottawa) (2000). Note that these concerns are not only voiced by non-governmental organizations (NGOs), but also by inter-governmental organizations (IGOs), including the World Health Organization (WHO) and the United Nations High Commissioner for Human Rights. *See* UNHCHR (2002), *Economic, Social and Cultural Rights: Liberalisation of Trade in Services and Human Rights*, Report of the High Commissioner E/CN.4/Sub.2/2002, (June 2002).

Early civil society documents have given rise to a fierce response by the WTO Secretariat. See: WTO Secretariat, *GATS—Fact and Fiction*, The World Trade Organization (visited Jan. 16, 2004), <http://www.wto.org/english/tratop_e/serv_e/gats_factfiction_e.htm>. For a response, *see generally* Scott Sinclair & Jim Grieshaber-Otto, *Facing the Facts: A Guide to the GATS Debate* (Canadian Centre for Policy Alternatives, Ottawa) (visited Jan. 16, 2004) <http://www.policyalternatives.ca/publications/pub1.html> (March 2002); Ellen Gould, *Separating WTO Fact and Fiction* (The Council of Canadians, Ottawa) (visited Jan. 16, 2004), <http://canadians.inline.net/display_document.htm?COC_token=024OJ24&id=128&isdoc=1&catid=77> (June 2001); *The GATS Debate: A response to the common arguments used against the critics of the General Agreement on Trade in Services* (World Development Movement, London) (visited Jan. 16, 2004), <http://www.wdm.org.uk/cambriefs/wto/gatsdeb.pdf> (May 2001); Chakravarthi Ragavan, '*GATS—Fact and Fiction' at best a partial truth* (Third World Network, Penang, Malay.) (visited Jan. 16, 2004), <http://www.twnside.org.sg/title/fiction.htm> (March 2001); Vice Yu, V., III, *Technical Comments on the WTO's 'GATS—Fact and Fiction' Paper* (Friends of the Earth International, Amsterdam) (visited Jan. 16, 2004), <http://www.gatswatch.org/factfict.html> (April 2001).

[3] 'The human right to water entitles everyone to sufficient, safe, acceptable, physically accessible and affordable water for personal and domestic uses. An adequate amount of safe water is necessary to prevent death from dehydration, to reduce the risk of water-related disease and to provide for consumption, cooking, personal and domestic hygienic requirements.' Committee on Economic, Social, and Cultural Rights, 'The Right to Water: articles 11 and 12 of the International Covenant on Economic, Social and Cultural Rights', General Comment No. 15 E/C.12/2002/11 (2002).

[4] As part of a volume containing other, related contributions, this paper looks only at a limited set of issues. E.g., this paper does not address the classification of water services, nor does it discuss questions about government procurement (e.g., which sort of water management arrangement could be considered government procurement and therefore would fall out side the scope of the GATS), or how Art. I:3(b), the GATS public services exclusion, would apply to water services. For a comprehensive analysis of these and other aspects, *see* Mireille Cossy, chapter 5 of the present work. For a discussion about GATS and water from an environmental perspective, *see* Elisabeth Tuerk, Robert Speed, & Aaron Ostrovsky, *Water and the GATS*, a CIEL/WWF discussion paper (Center for International Environmental Law, Geneva, and World Wide Fund for Nature, Zeist) (October 2003).

particularly the national treatment obligation, may limit regulatory space for implementing universal service obligations (USOs) and providing subsidies.

2. Responsible water management and trends towards privatization

Historically, administrative responsibility for all aspects of water management has rested with public authorities at different levels of governance. This is because of the essential nature of water services, because they are often natural monopolies,[5] and because of the unique nature of water as a natural resource. Thus, the government has traditionally played multiple roles as natural resource manager, service provider, and regulator. This combined responsibility carries a number of inherent conflicts. The necessarily economic nature of providing services often conflicts with a regulator or resource manager's goal of protecting and preserving public goods such as water, or ensuring that services are delivered to the poor or marginalized.

Water management has often focused on meeting the immediate needs of industry and agriculture. Historically, this has resulted in over-allocation of water resources for consumptive use, neglecting the needs of the environment. In recent decades, due to water shortages as well as a heightened understanding of water management practices, governments have begun to manage water resources with an eye towards sustainability, both for ecological protection as well as to ensure that marginalized segments of a society have access to clean water.

However, despite trends towards sustainable water management, governments still face problems with inefficient management of public water services. As a response, many governments have made changes to their water policy to encourage private investment (including foreign), with the hopes of improving the efficiency of domestic water services. States have experimented with various models, including public–private partnerships (PPPs), outsourcing services but maintaining State ownership, or full privatization of all aspects of water services.

Central to many of these models is the introduction of a corporate structure to the water service provider, with the government maintaining both ultimate ownership and control. This approach can assist to overcome potential conflicts between the State's roles as resource manager/service provider and regulator, and can pave the way for greater competition and private sector involvement, eventually including full privatization.

Overall, governments have a variety of options and models for structuring the provision of water services besides the traditional State-owned and -operated

[5] A natural monopoly is a situation where for technical/economic reasons there cannot be more than one efficient provider of a good or service. Public utilities frequently exhibit natural monopoly characteristics. This is especially true in the case of water provision services, as it is hardly conceivable that, within one geographical market, there will be two competing water service providers, operating two sets of pipes in parallel.

utility.[6] While most water services, particularly the actual provision of water, will inevitably be supplied by monopoly providers, many aspects of services could be supplied by independent, competing entities. This would provide opportunities for foreign, as well as local, suppliers in a market traditionally dominated by government-owned and -operated monopolies. In theory, such outsourcing can extend to any severable part of water service provision, including management, infrastructure construction and maintenance, customer service, or billing. Another option for private sector involvement is financing arrangements through private equity participation. Lastly, there are arrangements such as build-operate-transfer (BOT) contracts that combine both financing and outsourcing aspects.

Private sector involvement in itself, however, is not the panacea it is widely thought to be. Since private companies are profit-driven, they may be reluctant to service the poorest (and least profitable) parts of a society. For water management to be effective in maintaining a balance between economic interests, human rights, and environmental considerations, it is essential that the State maintain control of the pace and conditions of increasing private sector involvement. States should particularly focus on maintaining the ability to not only regulate the price of water, but also to put in place universal service obligations (USOs)[7] and to subsidize water services.

The goal that States maintain regulatory capabilities, such as implementing USOs and subsidies, is not merely advisable from a policy point of view, but also essential from a legal perspective. Specifically, access to a reliable, clean water source for drinking and sanitation is a basic human right, which obligates States progressively to fulfill it.[8] This means that individuals are legally entitled to the provision of water, and that States must ensure this provision without allowing it to fall prey to the 'whims of the marketplace' or to become a matter of 'charity'.[9] Universal service obligations and subsidies are regulatory tools to that effect.

However, a State's ability to regulate privatized water services may be compromised by international trade rules, including those contained in the GATS.[10] The GATS can reduce a government's flexibility to implement water management policies—both in terms of the provision of water services to the poor and in terms of the management of water resources.

[6] For a discussion of various options, *see* OECD, *Environmental Goods and Services, The Benefits of Further Global Trade Liberalization* (Paris, 2001) at 54 ff.

[7] USOs differ globally, but common examples are providing water services free to impoverished areas, or providing phone systems or postal services to remote areas.

[8] The 1977 United Nations Water Conference in Mar del Plata, Argentina, established the concept of basic water requirements to meet fundamental human needs, which was reiterated at the Earth Summit in Rio de Janeiro, Brazil, in 1992. Source: The World Health Organization, *The Right to Water*, 3 Health and Human Rights Publication Services (Geneva, 2003); *see also*, Committee on Economic, Social, and Cultural Rights, 'The Right to Water: articles 11 and 12 of the International Covenant on Economic, Social and Cultural Rights', General Comment No. 15 E/C.12/2002/11 (2002).

[9] UNHCHR (2002), *supra* note 2, at para 6.

[10] General Agreement on Trade in Services, Apr. 15, 1994, Marrakesh Agreement Establishing the World Trade Organization [hereinafter the WTO], Annex 1B, Legal Instruments—Results of the Uruguay Round vol. 31, 33 ILM 81 (1994) [hereinafter GATS].

3. GATS—A BRIEF OVERVIEW

The GATS is an international agreement under the legal framework of the World Trade Organization (WTO),[11] and it is the only multilateral framework to prescribe rules for international trade in services. The GATS aims to increase such trade by providing transparency in, and the progressive liberalization of, services markets. It essentially establishes a framework for WTO Members' services providers to access services markets in other WTO Member States by setting certain limits on how services provision can be regulated. Once undertaken, GATS rules and commitments are enforceable through the WTO dispute settlement system, which means national decision-making prerogatives may be subject to WTO authority.

The GATS' coverage is broad, both in terms of the services covered and in what is considered 'trade' in services. As regards services covered, the GATS applies to trade in all services, including activities as diverse as financial services, telecommunications, health, water supply, and sewage services. The agreement does not apply to services supplied 'in the exercise of governmental authority'.[12] However, the definition of what is supplied in the 'exercise of governmental authority' is both narrow and ambiguous, and there are concerns that this exclusion may save only a limited number of governmental or other regulatory activities.[13]

As regards the concept of 'trade', the GATS covers four so-called modes of supplying services.[14] The GATS definition of 'trade' includes not only traditional cross-border trade of services (mode 1), but also the movement of foreigners consuming services (mode 2), the provision of services through foreign direct investment (mode 3),[15] and the movement of 'natural persons' providing services (mode 4).[16]

[11] For a comprehensive analysis of the GATS and its legal aspects, see Markus Krajewski, *National Regulation and Trade Liberalization in Services—The Impact of the General Agreement on Trade in Services (GATS) on National Regulatory Autonomy* (London, 2003).

[12] GATS, Art. I:3(b).

[13] For a legal analysis of this provision, see generally Markus Krajewski, *Public Services and the Scope of the GATS*, Research Paper (CIEL Washington, D.C.) (visited Jan. 16, 2004), <http://www.ciel.org/Publications/PublicServicesScope.pdf> (2001). See also Markus Krajewski, *Public Services and Trade Liberalization: Mapping the Legal Framework*, 2003 J. Int'l Econ. L. 341. It is interesting to note that by now, even proponents of the GATS have acknowledged the limited nature of Art. I. Consequently, Members are currently trying to change their existing commitments to include a broad horizontal limitation that effectively excludes public utilities or public services entirely from the scope of their commitments.

[14] GATS, Art. I:2.

[15] Specifically, the GATS refers to supply of a service by a supplier of one Member through commercial presence in the territory of any other Member: GATS, Art. I:2(c). Commercial presence in turn is defined as '. . . any type of business or professional establishment, including through (i) the constitution, acquisition or maintenance of a juridical person, or (ii) the creation or maintenance of a branch or a representative office, within the territory of a Member for the purpose of supplying a service': GATS, Art. XXVIII(d).

[16] 'Natural Person' is defined as 'a natural person who resides in the territory of [another] Member . . . and who . . . is a national of that other Member': GATS, Art. XXVIII(k).

The GATS aims to liberalize trade in services by posing certain limits on 'measures... affecting trade in services'.[17] These measures include regulatory measures taken by federal, state, and local administrations, as well as those taken by non-governmental bodies exercising delegated governmental authority.[18] Member States must ensure that any domestic measures that 'affect trade in services' are consistent with the rules (or 'disciplines') under the GATS. These rules include *general* as well as *specific obligations*.

The GATS general obligations apply to all WTO Members, all of their service sectors and sub-sectors in all four modes of supply. The GATS general obligations include most-favoured-nation (MFN) treatment[19] and transparency.[20] The GATS specific obligations consist of market access[21] and national treatment[22] obligations. The market access provision prohibits Members from implementing quantitative restrictions or domestic ownership requirements on services, aiming to ensure market access for foreign service providers. The national treatment obligation prohibits governments from favoring domestic over foreign services, in effect requiring that foreign service providers are treated—at least—similarly to domestic ones.[23]

As specific commitments, market access and national treatment apply only to those sectors, sub-sectors, and modes of supply in which Members, on an individual basis, decide to be bound. In theory, this 'bottom-up' approach grants flexibility to WTO Member States.[24] Each Member defines its own services trade regime through its specific commitments, set out in its schedule of commitments. When making specific commitments, a country may include conditions or limitations, which restrict the application of the specific GATS rule in question. For example, a WTO Member can enter into national treatment commitments for transport services, but still retain its ability to provide subsidies to domestic service suppliers only. However, it is crucial that this 'condition or limitation' is inscribed in the Member's schedule.

Once a country commits itself in a specific service sector, it is effectively prevented from rescinding that commitment. While technically the GATS includes provisions allowing a party to withdraw a commitment, there are compensation requirements (in terms of granting market access in another area)

[17] GATS, Art. I:1. [18] GATS, Art. I:3(a). [19] GATS, Art. II.
[20] GATS, Art. III. [21] GATS, Art. XVI. [22] GATS, Art. XVII.

[23] Note that the GATS national treatment provision explicitly covers both *de jure* and *de facto* discrimination.

[24] Recently, this theoretical flexibility has been increasingly questioned. E.g., *see* Peter Hardstaff, *The 'Flexibility' Myth: Why GATS is a Bad Model for a new WTO Investment Agreement*, Paper to Seminar on WTO Investment Agreement (World Development Movement, London) (visited Jan. 16, 2004), <http://www.wdm.org.uk/cambriefs/wto/flexmyth/flex5.htm> (March 2003); UNCTAD, *Trade in Services and Development Implications*, Note by the UNCTAD Secretariat, Document TD/B/COM.1/55 (2002). See also Mina Mashayekhi & Elisabeth Tuerk, *The WTO Services Negotiations: Some Strategic Considerations, Trade-Related Agenda, Development and Equity*, Occasional Papers 14 (South Centre, Geneva) (visited Jan. 16, 2004), <http://www.southcentre.org/publications/workingpapers/paper14/toc.htm> (January 2003).

attached to such a withdrawal, and in practice this mechanism is unlikely to be used.[25]

As part of the Doha Round of trade negotiations, WTO Members are currently negotiating to increase the number of their specific commitments. This will expand the application of the GATS-specific obligations to more sectors and modes of supply. In that context, Members are also negotiating the elimination of many of the above described conditions and limitations.[26]

By analyzing how such conditions can be used to preserve regulatory flexibility to ensure that water is provided to the poor and marginalized and preserved as a natural resource, this paper highlights the value of such conditions for current and future commitments. While it acknowledges the value of such conditions, it is important to bear in mind the limitations the GATS-type bottom-up approach exhibits. These limitations arise from both the high level of expertise and understanding (about the GATS and about the country's regulatory system for services) required, and from the political, liberalization-driven nature of the request/offer negotiating process. These limitations are particularly problematic for developing countries, as many lack both the technical information and the political clout.

4. Privatization and the GATS—a multi-faceted relationship

4.1 Introduction

As stated above, there are concerns that the GATS, while aiming to promote growth and development by liberalizing trade in services,[27] may have detrimental consequences for the provision of water to the poor. To a large extent, these concerns relate to the fear that the GATS may constrain a government's ability to regulate privatized water services. Due to the effective irreversibility of GATS commitments, there is concern that Members could be 'locked in' to any level of privatization they have undertaken, even if it was agreed to only on an experimental basis. Further, there is concern that changes in domestic policy-making, including increasing private sector involvement in a specific sector, may inadvertently subject service sectors or activities to GATS coverage, even though a Member originally intended to exclude such sectors or activities from GATS coverage by placing conditions on its specific commitment.

[25] While the WTO Secretariat points to the flexibility granted by this mechanism (see *GATS—Facts and Fiction*, *supra* note 2), note that civil society groups have pointed to the practical limitations of this system (see *supra* note 2). It remains to be seen how easy it will be for WTO Members successfully to use this process. Currently, the European Communities are considering various options to withdraw the existing commitments of its most recently acceded Members.

[26] In addition, WTO Members are negotiating new, possibly *general* rules on services trade.

[27] GATS, preamble.

To develop the content of these concerns and identify what is at stake, this chapter explores, first, how the GATS market access and national treatment provisions, as well as political and economic pressure, indirectly encourage privatization. Secondly, it examines how Members can add conditions and limitations to their specific commitments in order to carve out—and thereby retain—a certain role for the public sector. In that context, this chapter explores the nuances of such conditions by looking at the specific commitments of those Members that have added relevant conditions and limitations to their environmental services commitments. Lastly, again looking at these same examples, the chapter examines how changes in Members' domestic policies can in turn alter the range of services that are either covered by or excluded from these Members' GATS commitments.

4.2 The intersection between privatization and GATS—legal, political, and economic considerations

Proponents of the GATS point out that nothing in the legal text of the agreement explicitly requires governments to privatize essential services. However, concerns should not be so easily dismissed. Rather, any analysis of the linkages between GATS and privatization should bear in mind two things: the nature of privatization as a broader concept, and the political and economic realities of GATS negotiations which make the GATS more than just a legal framework.[28]

Privatization, in a narrow sense, involves a change in the control and ownership of services from the public to the private sector. However, in many cases, privatization is also linked to the elimination of public monopolies and the introduction of competition through various forms of private sector participation. It is therefore important to look at how the GATS intersects with aspects related to both *changes in ownership* of services as well as issues linked to the elimination of public *monopolies*, i.e. those linked to the *number of services suppliers* present in a given market.

At a first glance, the GATS appears to be neutral as to whether service providers are *privately or publicly owned*. The language of the general obligations does not make a distinction between public or private entities. When defining whether a service is 'owned' by a Member, the GATS explicitly says that a service supplier could be public or private, indicating no preference.[29] In addition, the GATS contains language that is commonly understood to allow 'public monopolies'.[30]

[28] Civil society's concerns about the GATS as more than a purely legal framework need to be addressed not only in terms of privatization, but in general as well.

[29] GATS, Art. XXVIII(n) states that 'a juridical person is: (i) "owned" by persons of a Member if more than 50 per cent of the equity interest in it is beneficially owned by persons of that Member'. 'Juridical Person' is defined in Art. XXVII(l) as 'privately-owned or governmentally-owned'.

[30] GATS, Art. VIII. For a discussion of these aspects, see also Cossy, chapter 5 of the present work.

However, the GATS does contain provisions—notably in its specific obligations—which appear to favor privatization, or at least increasing private sector participation and ownership in the relevant economic activities or entities. For example, in terms of ownership, Article XVI prohibits a Member from placing limits on foreign ownership or foreign investments in a service sector or sub-sector.[31] While this obligation does not exclude public service providers, it *does* prohibit a governmental regulation *requiring public ownership* (including setting up a public monopoly) for any mode in any service sector or sub-sector to which it applies, as this would clearly limit foreign ownership. This provision also appears to rule out regulations limiting the participation of foreign investment, including private investment in privatized companies which were previously public.[32]

Article XVI also prohibits governments from requiring specific types of legal entities or joint ventures for the supply of a service.[33] Again, this provision may limit a Member's ability either to require public ownership of services providers, or to take a staggered approach to privatizing its water market. Instead of a government being able to require a certain percentage of public ownership or joint ventures, or to limit foreign investment throughout the course of a privatization process, a Member may be forced simply to open up a sector to private interests.

In addition to constraining a government's ability to impose various legal and financial requirements as regards public ownership of service providers, the GATS also contains obligations concerning limitations on the *number of service suppliers in a sector*. In many instances, privatization, i.e. change of ownership, goes hand in hand with the elimination of a public monopoly. Along these lines, Article XVI restricts Members from adopting a 'limitation on the number of services suppliers whether in the form of numerical quotas, monopolies, exclusive services suppliers or the requirement of an economic needs test'.[34] This provision explicitly requires the elimination of monopolies, whether public or private.

Proponents of the GATS would argue that—despite these inter-linkages—the GATS does not encourage—or, much less, force—privatization because Members are free to select, reject, or condition specific commitments as they choose. However, the political realities of trade negotiations paint a different picture. In light of the heavy-handed politics involved in services negotiations, new concerns emerge about privatization of services. For example, it is widely acknowledged that the flexibility allegedly built into the adoption of specific commitments is merely theoretical and that Members, specifically developing countries, are pressured to accept commitments.[35]

[31] GATS, Art. XVI:2(f).

[32] *Id.* Frequently, however, governments may wish to resort to such regulations not because of economic rationale, but rather to respond to the general feeling of the public to not sell off State companies to foreigners.

[33] GATS, Art. XVI:2(e).

[34] GATS, Art. XVI:2(a).

[35] *See supra*, note 24.

In addition to the political climate, there are also economic realities that effectively limit the role of the public sector. For example, in many countries it is common practice to cross-subsidize public services.[36] Again, while the GATS does not, strictly speaking, rule out non-discriminatory cross-subsidization,[37] the economic implications of increasing private sector participation effectively limit a government's ability to cross-subsidize. Private entities are usually attracted to the most profitable segments of markets, leaving other segments unserved.[38] At the same time, since private rather than public entities are receiving the revenues, the public is left empty-handed and unable to ensure full coverage of essential services, particularly for the poor and marginalized.[39]

Since the GATS does not explicitly mention privatization, it is difficult to determine the legal relationship between privatization and GATS. Although in various sectors outside of water there is substantial evidence to suggest that the GATS encourages privatization, the debate is highly polarized and emotionally charged on both sides. At this point, the debate should move beyond this stage and embark upon a genuine exploration of the legal and practical relationship between GATS and privatization. It is hoped that this paper will provide a first step in that direction.

4.3 Specific commitments—how WTO Members carve out a role for the public sector

Despite the murkiness of the linkages between GATS and privatization, the GATS framework does leave Members a degree of freedom to determine public or private service provision, or otherwise to regulate private water services provision. While Members cannot opt out of GATS general obligations,[40]

[36] There are many definitions of cross-subsidies. For the purposes of this paper, a services pricing scheme has cross-subsidies if the price of the service for some consumers is above average and the price of the same service for other consumers is below average. *See* Paulina Beato, *Cross Subsidies in Public Services: Some Issues*, Sustainable Development Department Technical Papers Series IFM-122, Inter-American Development Bank (visited Jan. 16, 2004), <http://www.iadb.org/sds/doc/IFM-122-CrossSubsidies-E.pdf> (Jan. 2000) (for a more detailed discussion of cross-subsidies in public services).

[37] *See* GATS, Art. VIII. The GATS legal framework focuses mainly on anti-competitive aspects of cross-subsidies.

[38] This practice is often referred to as 'cream skimming' or 'cherry picking'.

[39] E.g., in 1993, Ghana began implementing a World Bank-backed policy to segregate water markets in and around the capital city of Accra. The policy was implemented to encourage privatization of profitable parts of the water market. These policies require a community to contribute financially to the installation, repair, and maintenance of water infrastructure. The poorest areas, where residents spend between 18–25% of their income on water, have not been able to meet the costs and, as a result of unsafe water, have experienced a dramatic increase in cases of guinea worm. Ghana now has the highest incidence of guinea worm in the world after Sudan, whose outbreaks are attributed to Sudan's civil war. *See* Rudolf Amenga-Etego, *Water Privatization in Ghana: Still born or deformed?* (Public Agenda, Accra-North, Ghana) (visited Jan. 16, 2004), <http://www.ghanaweb.com/public_agenda/article.php?ID=1548> (July 7, 2003).

[40] Note, however, that WTO Members, today, when joining the GATS as part of their accession negotiations, or previously, when joining the GATS as part of the Uruguay Round, are entitled to

a Member can still reserve certain regulatory capacity by limiting the scope of its specific commitments.[41] This is generally done by 'carving out' those service sectors and sub-sectors—or those types of regulatory measures—which Members want either to reserve for public or quasi-public management, or to retain the ability to undertake. While the following analysis is based on Members' existing environmental services commitments,[42] it may prove instructive for potential future commitments in water services.

The schedules examined in this analysis are from those Members that have added conditions and limitations to their environmental services commitments. The relevant questions are: 'What types of conditions have Members attached to their specific commitments in order to carve out all or part of public sector provision?' and 'How effective are these carve outs?'[43]

The US[44] and Estonia,[45] for example, two very different countries and economies, adopt a similar approach towards limiting the scope of their commitments. Both schedules contain a clarification in the first column of the services schedule (listing the sector in question), which states 'contracted by private industry'.[46] This suggests that the decisive aspect of whether a service is covered by a commitment is whether or not the *consumer* of the service is *private industry*, as opposed to the public sector or private individuals for personal consumption.[47]

The EC schedule,[48] in its horizontal limitations, specifically allows regulators to use certain tools for 'services considered as public utilities at a national or local level'. In an explanatory footnote it adds that '[p]ublic utilities exist in

exempt certain regulatory policies from the GATS' MFN obligation: GATS, Art. II:2. Currently MFN exemptions are subject to elimination through review and negotiations.

[41] While retaining regulatory flexibility in spite of GATS commitments is—in theory—possible, this should not encourage Members to rush into adopting commitments. In addition, current negotiating processes develop new rules under the GATS, which in turn might constrain regulatory flexibility—once they are in force.

[42] Specifically, 'Sanitation and Similar Services' (CPC 9403). For the purposes of this analysis, sanitation services provide a good close approximation of water services, since both are subject to natural monopolies and both are considered essential to human health.

[43] E.g., the various models differ in the *way the qualifications are introduced*. While the EC uses a horizontal limitation, applying to all services sectors, Switzerland and the Nordic countries specify limitations only for the environmental services sector.

[44] The United States of America, *Schedule of Specific Commitments*, GATS/SC/90 (Apr. 15, 1995).

[45] The Republic of Estonia, *Schedule of Specific Commitments*, GATS/SC/127 (Oct. 5, 1999).

[46] For both countries this clarification applies only to two of the four environmental services sub-sectors mentioned, namely, sewage services and refuse disposal services. Sanitation services and other (landscape protection) services do not contain such a clarification. In all sub-sectors, both market access and national treatment are fully committed, without conditions and limitations; only mode 4 is listed as 'unbound, except as indicated in the horizontal section'.

[47] The Korean schedule is somewhat different, but goes into a similar direction. In a footnote to the first column of the row including commitments for 'refuse water disposal services', the schedule specifies that Korean commitments cover '[O]nly collection and treatment services of *industrial* waste water under CPC 9401' (emphasis added). The Republic of Korea, *Schedule of Specific Commitments*, GATS/SC/48 (Apr. 15, 1995).

[48] European Communities and their Member States, *Schedule of Specific Commitments*, GATS/SC/31 (Apr. 15, 1994).

sectors such as related scientific and technical consulting services, R&D services on social sciences and humanities, technical testing and analysis services, environmental services, health services, transport services and services auxiliary to all modes of transport'. In contrast, the Nordic/Swiss approach excludes the 'public works function whether owned and operated by municipalities, State or federal governments or contracted out by these governments'.[49]

In assessing how effectively the EC and Nordic/Swiss approaches carve out space for regulatory activities, two key ambiguities must be addressed: what *types of services activities* are considered public service; and whether or not the notion of 'public services', 'public works function', or 'public utility', as used and defined by different Members in their specific commitments, differs from that of 'services provided in the exercise of governmental authority', as mentioned in GATS Article I:3(c).[50]

In terms of services activities, the EC schedule refers to 'services *considered* as public utilities' (emphasis added). An explanatory footnote contains a list of services sectors in which public utilities exist. The language of Europe's condition, 'services *considered* public utilities', indicates that it reserves the right to define, ad hoc, what services are *considered* public utilities. This 'self-defining' interpretation grants considerable flexibility to the EC to define and alter what services are considered public utilities according to its social priorities. The fact that the list in the footnote is 'indicative' means that services not currently listed could be 'considered' as public utilities in the future.

The situation is different in the Nordic/Swiss approach. While this approach also seems to grant flexibility, much depends on how the terms 'public service function' or 'public works functions' are interpreted. Since neither the Swiss nor the Nordic commitments contain a specific list of services, this approach could potentially be more easily constrained by an unfavorable interpretation than could the European approach.

What seems to be clear, however, is that the word 'public', as being used in connection with the notion 'public service/works function' in the Nordic/Swiss schedule, does not imply 'public' ownership. Rather, the word 'public' appears to indicate the essential nature the service in question has for the general public. The same appears to be the case for the EC schedule, when it uses the term 'public utility'.[51]

[49] Note that Sweden refers to 'the public works functions' in the plural (Sweden, *Schedule of Specific Commitments*, GATS/SC/82 (Apr. 15, 1994)), as does Norway, referring to the 'public service functions' (Norway, *Schedule of Specific Commitments*, GATS/SC/66 (Apr. 15, 1994)), while Switzerland refers to the concept in the singular, 'public work function' (Switzerland, *Schedule of Specific Commitments*, GATS/SC/83 (Apr. 15, 1994)). Strictly speaking, Liechtenstein also belongs to this category: Liechtenstein, *Schedule of Specific Commitments*, GATS/SC/83-A (Apr. 15, 1994).

[50] An analysis of this question is, however, outside the scope of this paper. For a detailed discussion of Art. I:3(b), *see generally*, Markus Krajewski, *Public Services and Trade Liberalization: Mapping the Legal Framework*, *supra* note 13.

[51] While today the notion of public utility is broader, covering more than merely publicly-owned entities, as stated above, what really matters in the European context is whether or not a service is *considered* a public utility.

Thus, this analysis suggests that Members have realized the highly ambiguous and therefore limited nature of the Article I 'public services exclusion'.[52] The above-mentioned conditions and limitations some Members have included in their schedules are clearly a response to this need to carve out parts of the public sector to preserve regulatory power. However, due to the ambiguous nature of the exercise, it is not clear that the schedules are wholly adequate.

4.4 Increasing private sector participation—how can Members set conditions up front to manage change over time?

The above section has described how Members—by adding conditions to their specific commitments—can carve out certain services areas for public provision and regulation. Yet Members still need to take into consideration how the scope of services activities that are carved out from GATS disciplines could be affected by increased private participation occurring after the country has entered into its specific commitment under the GATS.

To date, many economies experience increasing private sector participation in the provision of essential services. This trend originates from changes in domestic policy, induced either internally or through mandates from outside sources such as international financial institutions (IFIs).[53] Contracting out services or increasing private equity participation are two prominent ways in which private sector participation is increased. When defining their public sector carve outs, WTO Members should consider how the scope of these carve outs would be affected by increasing private sector participation in water services. This depends, among other things, on the content of the condition and on the way that private sector participation is introduced.

The previous section has described various ways that Members can carve out public sector involvement through their schedules. The US/Estonian approach singles out the nature of the service consumer. The Nordic/Swiss schedules explicitly exclude 'public services functions' and 'public works functions' from their GATS commitments. The EC schedule states that any service supplier, public or private, providing services 'considered as public utilities' may be

[52] The limited capacity of GATS, Art. I:3 to preserve regulatory autonomy particularly for 'essential basic services' originates from several factors. Most importantly, the Art. I:3 exclusion does not explicitly address essential or basic services, but rather 'services provided in the exercise of governmental authority'. Further, the definition of a 'service provided in the exercise of governmental authority' is ambiguous, and the provision's application to new economic circumstances, such as increasing private sector participation in essential services sectors, may have unintended side-effects. These factors are compounded by the lack of additional guidance on how to interpret the exclusion. Members have not adopted any interpretative notes, and information about the provision's drafting history is limited. Even proponents of the GATS acknowledge that this provision is 'a piece of clumsy drafting'.

[53] For policy inter-linkages between the World Bank, the GATS, and investment agreements affecting the provision of water, *see Going With the Flow: How International Trade, Finance and Investment Regimes Affect the Provision of Water to the Poor*, CIEL Issue Brief (CIEL, Geneva) (visited Jan. 16, 2004), <http://www.ciel.org/Publications/Waterbrief_3Sept03.pdf> (2003).

granted exclusive rights, GATS notwithstanding. In the following pages, this paper will discuss how these three scheduling approaches retain regulatory flexibility when faced with the two above-mentioned types of private sector involvement—contracting out the services and increasing foreign equity participation in the service supplier.

Contracting out can take various forms, covering either whole services or merely parts of a service, such as management or billing. The US/Estonian approach states that only those services 'contracted by private industry' are covered by the GATS. This means that only service provisions for consumption by private industrial users would be covered by the US/Estonian GATS commitment. In this case, it would be irrelevant how much of the service is contracted out to the private sector as long as the service is consumed by non-industrial or public consumers. The US/Estonian approach not only grants considerable flexibility to regulate public services, but also ensures that, in the future, when considering contracting out as a means to increase private participation, the government is free to tailor the level of private sector participation to meet its needs without having to acquiesce to GATS commitments.

The Nordic/Swiss schedules explicitly exclude 'public services/works functions' from the relevant GATS commitments—whether those services are State run '*or* contracted-out by these governments'. This system is as effective as the US/Estonian approach in ensuring that contracted-out services do not automatically fall under a country's GATS commitments. However, again, since neither the Swiss nor the Nordic schedules offers a definition of 'public services/works functions', some part of a service sector intended to be carved out may end up falling under GATS commitments.

Additionally, the language of the European schedule, namely, that 'services considered public utilities may be subject to exclusive rights granted to private operators', allows for flexibility to define which services are 'public utilities' and consequently benefit from more regulatory space. While this is not as effective a system as the US/Estonian or Nordic/Swiss schedules (see above), the European system—by stating that such 'public utilities' can be subject to exclusive rights—at least ensures that public services, even if contracted out to private providers, would not be subject to *full* market access and national treatment commitments.

In addition to contracting out, another way of increasing private sector participation is through (public or private) foreign equity participation in the service provider. In all of the schedules we have analyzed thus far, a key factor in determining whether a service provider is subject to GATS commitments is whether the service provider or the consumer of the service is the private sector. According to GATS, Article XXVIII, a service could be considered privately owned if 50% or more of the equity interest is privately owned.[54]

[54] GATS, Art. XXVIII(n)(i).

The US/Estonian schedules emphasize the nature of the service consumer, not the provider.[55] The only questions relevant to whether the service is covered by GATS commitments is whether the *consumer* is private and whether the *consumer* is industrial. There is nothing indicating that private investment in the service *provider* would subject the service to GATS. Change of ownership of a public company providing services to the poor does not seem to affect whether a certain arrangement falls under the scope of the commitment. This scheduling grants the Member substantial flexibility to use private sector investment in services.

The Nordic/Swiss schedules specifically exempt all 'public services/works functions', whether they are owned and operated by regional or national governments, or contracted out by these governments to the private sector. This condition allows a public service provider or the regulator to contract out parts of the service to the private sector without subjecting the sector to GATS commitments. While—as discussed above—the phrase 'public services/works function' quite clearly suggests that the word 'public' does not necessarily imply public ownership of the service provider (but rather the essential nature of the service in question for the general public), one could also argue that the exemption applies only if the service provider is owned by the public. In that case, if more than 50% of the service provider were to be acquired, through private foreign equity participation by the private sector, the condition would no longer apply and the service provider would be fully covered by GATS commitments. In that case, the decisive aspect would appear to be the 50% or majority ownership of shares.

Furthermore, the European schedule does not specifically mention public or private *ownership*. Europe reserves the right in its horizontal commitments to grant public monopolies or exclusive rights to services 'considered as public utilities'. As stated above, the word 'considered' indicates that Europe reserves the right to define 'public utility' for the purposes of its horizontal condition. As referred to in the European schedule, 'public utility' does not necessarily mean a utility that is owned publicly, but rather services traditionally considered important for the public good. Therefore, regardless of what percentage of the service provider is owned by the private sector, as long as the service is something that is *considered* a 'public utility', the regulator retains the right to grant public monopolies or exclusive rights—GATS commitments notwithstanding. In addition, if the service provider experienced an *increase* in private sector involvement, through mergers of stock sales for instance, it would still fall outside the GATS commitments as long as the service it provides continues to be regarded as a 'public utility'.

When Members are designing specific commitments, they should consider the dynamic aspects of private sector involvement. This is especially important for developing countries, which, to a large extent, will make choices about levels of

[55] Specifically, these schedules contain a clarification in the column of the schedule listing the sector in question, which adds 'contracted by private industry'.

privatization based not only upon internal policy but also IFI requirements. Lastly, the fact that GATS commitments are extremely difficult to change means it is critical that Members are careful in drafting them.[56]

4.5 Conclusions

Despite the fact that the legal text of the GATS does not specifically mention privatization, there is strong evidence that the agreement does encourage private sector involvement in traditionally public services. The GATS contains many obligations relating to policies that are relevant for privatization processes. However, the exact boundaries of this relationship, or the depths to which it goes, are still unclear.

A clear understanding of how GATS relates to privatization and the private sector is especially important in terms of drafting specific commitments. Members have attempted to carve out public services—and thereby preserve a role for the public—in various ways. The myriad of approaches, as well as the ambiguities and uncertainties associated with each one, indicate the complexity of doing that. At this point, it remains to be seen how WTO panels or the Appellate Body—in a dispute settlement proceeding—will address questions of defining the various concepts of 'public services' either as used in individual Member's schedules, or as used in Article I:3 more generally.

There are also important interdependencies between domestic policy choices and the scope of GATS commitments. It is important for negotiators and services trade policy-makers to realize that changes in the domestic economic environment may affect the scope of their country's GATS commitments. This is especially relevant considering that many countries will undergo domestic policy changes involving contracting out to the private sector, or increasing foreign equity participation in domestic public services.

For developing countries, the interdependencies between GATS and domestic water policies are vital because developing countries frequently do not undertake policy changes, such as increasing private sector involvement, in a truly autonomous manner. Instead, changes in developing countries' domestic policy regimes are usually conditions in a World Bank or International Monetary Fund (IMF) financial arrangement. Having implemented these policy changes, developing countries might suddenly find that new private sector involvement has broadened the scope of their GATS commitments. While civil society groups (and some developing country policy-makers) have frequently pointed to the interdependencies between GATS and privatization policies, unfortunately these interdependencies have not yet been given adequate consideration, in either the WTO negotiations or in the relevant academic discourse.

In any case, flexibility is important. Privatization has many pitfalls and is not a clear solution to every problem. In cases where privatization fails to solve

[56] For more on the GATS 'lock in effect', *see* Mireille Cossy, chapter 5 of the present work, and generally, *supra* note 2.

problems for which it was implemented, governments must revert to public sector provision of services. This could potentially put them at risk of violating their GATS market access or national treatment obligations. If a certain degree of private sector involvement automatically renders the GATS applicable to the service in question, it may deprive governments of the ability to put in place much needed regulations. GATS commitments—even if limited—may arguably make it more difficult for governments to revert back to public provision of the service for the sector in which privatization has failed.

Because changing GATS commitments is extremely difficult politically, economically, and administratively, it is imperative that trade policy-makers carefully develop their commitments, particularly in sectors that may be prone to domestic policy changes in the future.

5. Unfettered market access—promises and pitfalls of the GATS market access obligation

5.1 Introduction

Increases in private sector involvement in services (whether GATS-driven or not) are particularly problematic in areas where the poor or marginalized are geographically isolated. Given that private service providers are likely to neglect this segment of a society for better profits elsewhere, the progressive realization of the human right to water is at risk. In terms of GATS, there are fears that market access commitments may give unfettered access to water services to foreign private suppliers and constrain a government's ability to regulate once privatization has taken place. These concerns relate not only to a government's ability to set up monopolies in general, but also to a government's ability to determine the specific boundaries of a monopoly.

Even if one brackets this concern, there is a great deal of uncertainty as to what market access means in services sectors where the service is a natural monopoly. Because water services, such as sewage services, are often natural monopolies, the question of how the GATS rules, particularly its market access provision, apply to natural monopolies is highly relevant. Market access is laid out in GATS Article XVI:[57]

2. In sectors where market-access commitments are undertaken, the measures which a Member shall not maintain or adopt either on the basis of a regional subdivision or on the basis of its entire territory, unless otherwise specified in its Schedule, are defined as:
   (a) limitations on the number of service suppliers whether in the form of numerical quotas, monopolies, exclusive service suppliers or the requirements of an economic needs test;
   (c) limitations on the total number of service operations or on the total quantity of service output expressed in terms of designated numerical units in the form of quotas or the requirement of an economic needs test;

[57] GATS, Art. XVI:2(a), (c), (e), (f).

(e) measures which restrict or require specific types of legal entity or joint venture through which a service supplier may supply a service; and
(f) limitations on the participation of foreign capital in terms of maximum percentage limit on foreign shareholding or the total value of individual or aggregate foreign investment.

In the following sections this paper discusses potential problems in defining and enforcing market access in water service sectors that are prone to natural monopoly situations. It also looks at how well the GATS framework preserves a government's ability to define geographic or other boundaries for service providers.

5.2 Natural monopolies—what is the role of the GATS market access obligation?

The potential for, or existence of, natural monopolies can make negotiating market access a dubious and unreliable proposition. While there has been much controversy surrounding the EC's recent request for market access in the water provision sector,[58] how the GATS market access provision applies to natural monopolies has not yet been thoroughly defined. This question of definition is highly relevant, not only for those concerned about market access (private service providers), but also for those concerned about provision of water (civil society).

A natural monopoly occurs when the economic, technological, or other specificities of a particular sector impose a quantitative limitation on the number of service suppliers in a given market. This quantitative limitation arises from conditions other than governmental regulation. For example, natural monopolies frequently occur in 'network services', such as railroads or highway management, where geographic and practical limitations create situations where it is only economically feasible to have a limited number of service providers.[59] Because water services, much like railroads, depend on an expensive infrastructure (in this case, pipe systems), and because more than one infrastructure is usually not economically feasible to service a population, natural monopolies in water services are common.

An additional factor unique to water provision is that consumer choice and health concerns mandate that water for drinking and sanitation be clean and reliable. This demand requires high standards for reliability and accountability

[58] *See* Press Release, European Union, 'WTO services: Commission submits draft offer to Council and Parliament—public services fully defended' (Feb. 5, 2003), at http://europa.eu.int/comm/trade/services/pr050203_en.htm. *See also EU to block talks on more public services liberalization*, Financial Times (London), Feb. 5, 2003; *EC Suggests Financial Services, Telecom For Possible Liberalization, Excludes Others*, Int'l Trade Rep. (Feb. 6, 2003).

[59] Recently, there have been trends in railroad management to separate the entities providing track from those providing trains, suggesting that railroads are no true natural monopoly. However, this type of system has also shown that such developments give rise to even more careful and thorough intervention by the relevant regulatory authorities.

for service providers. In most situations, because mixing water from different sources in one pipe makes accountability and responsibility problematic, one service supplier is more desirable than many.[60]

Although water corporations are pushing for more market access commitments in water sectors, it remains largely unexplored how exactly the GATS market access provision relates to limits imposed not by governmental regulation but by economic conditions (i.e., natural monopolies). In essence, the GATS market access provision aims to eliminate certain quantitative and other barriers to trade in services. However, in the case of water services, there are factors limiting market access that go beyond governmental regulations, and which are targeted by the GATS market access mandates. Even if governments do not impose any limitations on market access to water provision, economic limitations may make market access difficult nonetheless. In effect, the high cost of building new piping systems may mean it is virtually impossible to enter a market that is served by an existing supplier. Therefore, exactly what benefits foreign service suppliers will receive from market access commitments remains a question.

One possible answer lies in the fact that, despite extenuating economic factors, a natural monopoly will most likely still involve governmental concessions or licenses. So, the GATS market access provision could influence the way service suppliers obtain concessions or licenses. For instance, a market access commitment could mandate that foreign service providers be allowed to participate in the bidding process for concession contracts.[61] Another way the GATS market access provision becomes relevant is through the sub-headings of Article XVI that were discussed in section 4.2 above. The obligation not to place limits on foreign equity participation,[62] or not to require specific legal entities, such as joint venture operations,[63] are cases in point. While neither grants new market access in the strict sense, both are relevant in terms of eliminating barriers to economic activities for service providers.

This illustrates that, while the GATS tries to give service providers—both foreign and domestic—guarantees to market access, extenuating circumstances such as natural monopolies still limit market access, with no remedy found in the text of the GATS. In light of the fact that the GATS market access provision not only fails to provide what it promises but also creates

[60] Again, it could be argued that the circumstances which necessitate natural monopolies could be mitigated with increased regulation—in this case, strict water purity standards enforced at the water service provider level.

[61] At the same time, such arrangements could possibly also be considered domestic regulations, falling under GATS, Art. VI, or government procurement, currently excluded by means of Art. XIII. *See* Mireille Cossy, chapter 5 of the present work, for an analysis of the latter aspect; an interesting question arising in that context is whether a commitment for the GATS national treatment provision already grants national treatment in the bidding process, or only once the services supplier is providing its services. The latter aspect, however, appears to be less relevant when dealing with a natural monopoly situation, which by its very nature excludes services provision by two competing suppliers.

[62] GATS, Art. XVI:2(f).

[63] GATS, Art. XVI:2(e).

unnecessary complications, negotiators may consider stepping back from the negotiating process and seriously examining whether applying GATS to a regulating regime as complex as water services is at all feasible, or desirable.

5.3 Governmentally regulated monopolies—does market access interfere with using monopolies as a regulatory tool?

There are several ways in which the GATS market access provision constrains domestic prerogatives and regulatory tools that governments may wish to resort to, including the tool of governmentally-regulated monopolies.[64] In addition, the GATS may affect a government's ability to define the geographical boundary in which to operate a monopoly. The ability to define geographical boundaries in monopolies is important for market differentiation purposes. It allows a government to define boundaries not just along political or administrative lines, but along social, economic, or need-based lines as well. For instance, in Accra, Ghana, there have been movements to segregate the more profitable urban parts of the city from the less profitable outlying parts of the city.[65] In other instances it may be useful to combine more and less profitable geographical areas in one concession, with the goal of allowing the private supplier to offset losses with revenues. However, it remains unclear how this kind of geographic segregation relates to two of the GATS' main obligations, Article I and Article XVII.

The GATS market access provision, Article XVII, states that 'a Member shall not maintain or adopt either *on the basis of a regional subdivision or on the basis of its entire territory*, unless otherwise specified in its Schedule . . . (a) limitations on the number of services suppliers whether in the form of numerical quotas, monopolies, exclusive service suppliers . . . ' (emphasis added).[66] This could be interpreted as confirmation that, should a Member choose, it could operate either a regionally based monopoly or a national monopoly, as long as it first named this condition in its schedule. The language used in Article XVI also suggests that the GATS allows a Member to define geographical boundaries along social, economic, or need-based lines.

However, when read in conjunction with Article I, Article XVI appears to grant less flexibility. Article I defines the 'scope and definition' of the services agreement by specifying that the measures it covers are those taken by 'central, regional or local governments . . . ' or 'non-governmental bodies in the exercise of powers delegated by central, regional, or local governments or authorities'.[67] This could be interpreted to suggest that a Member—when setting up a monopoly, i.e. utilizing a 'measure'—must define regional subdivisions along these central, regional, or local governmental lines, conforming, both as regards

[64] Among those, the best known is the fact that full market access commitment rules out limitations on the number of services suppliers, including monopolies. [65] *See supra* note 39.
[66] GATS, Art. XVI:2(a). [67] GATS, Art. I:2(a)(i) and (ii).

the deciding entity as well as the geographical region, with the administrative or political structure of the country in question. However, from an economic or social perspective, it may be useful to organize water management and water provision along market lines instead of administrative or political lines (either to join densely populated areas with dispersed populations, or to divide them). Each of these subdivisions could incorporate parts of multiple administrative or political regions. It is not clear whether these areas would be considered geographical subdivisions according to Article XVI, specifically because it is unclear whether or not the definition in Article XVI would have to correspond to central, regional, or local governments and authorities as mentioned in Article I.

Several items suggest adoption of a more flexible reading of the GATS in terms of geographical divisions. First, a possible disconnect between Article XVI and Article I can be resolved if one considers that they deal with two different issues and, therefore, may be interpreted in terms of one another only to a limited degree. Article I deals with the scope of the GATS and, in that context, lists the entities whose actions are considered 'measures affecting trade in services'.[68] Therefore, the list in Article I should apply only to those entities which can issue 'measures' as defined in the GATS:[69] measures that have to correspond to their regulatory prerogatives not only in terms of content, but also in terms of scope of application. On the other hand, the term 'regional subdivisions', as defined in Article XVII, deals with market segregation, the content of the market access obligation. While the measure of course will have to be legitimate in terms of falling—both in content and geographical scope—under the entity issuing it, it cannot be constrained to the geographical subdivisions set out in Article I. Rather, the types of geographical or other subdivisions are meant to be defined by a Member in its schedule.

Two other items that suggest a more flexible reading of the GATS relate to Article VIII on 'monopolies and exclusive services suppliers'. For example, this provision refers to 'the supply of a monopoly service in the *relevant* market'[70] (emphasis added). Given that markets can exist in terms of services sectors, consumers, and geography, it is likely that a condition allowing a government to maintain monopolies for a particular service will also allow monopolies at any chosen regional level or any other geographical subdivision, including those based upon economic, social, or needs-based considerations.

Lastly, and perhaps most compelling, paragraph 2 of Article VIII states that:

> Where a Member's monopoly supplier competes, either directly or through an affiliated company, in the supply of a service outside the scope of its monopoly rights and which is subject to that Member's specific commitments, the Member shall ensure that such a

[68] It could well be argued, however, that the scope of application of a market access restriction corresponds to the area of competence of the respective authority undertaking this measure. This would suggest a linkage between the concepts of GATS Arts I and XVI.

[69] 'Measures' are defined as 'any measure by a Member, whether in the form of a law, regulation, rule, procedure, decision, administrative action, or any other form': GATS, Art. XXVIII(a).

[70] GATS, Art. VIII:1.

supplier does not abuse its monopoly position to act in its territory in a manner inconsistent with such commitments.[71]

This part of Article VIII deals specifically with abuse of monopoly positions and presents a pragmatic approach to geographical boundaries for monopolies. Specifically, this provision could be read to suggest that as long as a Member does not allow a monopoly to reach beyond its defined boundary and to abuse its monopoly positions by interfering with other open markets elsewhere, then whatever boundary the Member defines for the monopoly is acceptable under the GATS. This interpretation protects those areas of the market which are open to competition, but also ensures that a Member can provide water services to the most needy members of a society by establishing monopolies.

The above analysis suggests that despite the relationship between Article I and Article XVI, it seems probable that Members can define geographic boundaries for monopolies beyond the limited scope of Article I. This interpretation is also promising because it is consistent with the GATS' dual goals of 'liberalization of trade in services'[72] and 'recognizing the right of Members to regulate'.[73] This is specifically evident for the reading of Article VIII, which seems to prohibit monopoly boundaries only in situations where abuse of monopolies hurts competition in areas where—according to the country's market access commitments—competition is supposed to take place.

However, it is important to remember that this reading does not eliminate all ambiguities and is far from broadly accepted. Thus, before WTO Members enter into further-reaching market access commitments, they should aim to achieve clarity about the content of the obligation, specifically about the constraints it may place upon their ability to design and regulate various monopoly markets.

5.4 Conclusions

There are concerns about the application of the GATS market access rules to water services, specifically in light of the fact that access to clean water for sanitation and drinking is considered a basic human right. However, applying the GATS market access provision to water services is also problematic for other reasons.

First, water services are frequently natural monopolies, which in turn raises the question of whether the GATS Article XVI commitments would really have any effect, since conditions other than governmental regulation create the monopolies. Applying the GATS market access provisions to natural monopolies may not have the same market opening effect as applying the market access provision to other services sectors—while creating considerable constraints for regulatory prerogatives.[74]

[71] GATS, Art. VIII:2. [72] GATS, Preamble. [73] *Id.*

[74] In network services, most of which have natural monopoly characteristics, WTO Members have responded by considering additional regulatory frameworks, for instance so-called reference

Secondly, the GATS market access provision is problematic not only for natural monopolies, but also for situations where Members choose to impose Artificial monopolies. Specifically, there are fears that an Article XVI commitment, when read in conjunction with Article I, may constrain a regulator's ability to define and segregate markets according to economic, social, or needs-based criteria. While some interpretations suggest that Members can define the geographical boundaries of those monopolies based on any considerations they deem appropriate, lack of legal security means that Members should proceed cautiously when negotiating further commitments.

6. Access to water for the poor—protecting regulatory prerogatives by conditioning specific commitments

6.1 Introduction

Among the many concerns civil society groups raise with respect to the GATS and the provision of water, are concerns that the GATS will constrain the very policies necessary to ensure that water is provided to the poor. Two of the regulatory tools governments can use to ensure water provision for the poor are imposing universal service obligations (USOs) on private providers, or directly subsidizing service providers.[75] This section explores how WTO Members have addressed similar concerns in their existing environmental services commitments.[76]

6.2 Imposing USOs—is there flexibility for defining the nature of universal services and of USOs?

The private sector is likely to be most interested in those service sectors and segments of markets that are profitable. Consequently, private sector participation may not improve access to water for all of society. In order to ensure that private service providers still service the poorest and least profitable parts of

papers. Such reference papers may constitute a complementary tool to market access commitments. Members should not proceed hastily, however, but rather should assess the implications and effects of their options.

[75] Subsidies are an important mechanism for compensating companies required to provide commercially-unviable universal services. Civil society has expressed concerns that the GATS may impede governments' abilities to subsidize the provision of services, including basic services. These concerns mainly relate to situations where public and private provision of services co-exists: the private provider serving the profitable market and the public provider serving the less profitable market. The government may provide subsidies to the public domestic company, while not providing any to private foreign companies. Providing subsidies to one company and not another could be inconsistent with the GATS national treatment provision.

[76] Subsidies given to individuals rather than to service suppliers fall outside the scope of this paper.

a society, a State may want to make USOs an integral part of its contractual arrangement with the private service providers. These are requirements imposed on the service provider by the State. They usually involve an agreement to expand service delivery to certain previously unserved areas, or to provide the service at an affordable price. In very impoverished or marginalized areas, 'affordable' can mean that the service provider has to provide the service below its cost.[77]

A State must define what it considers a 'universal service' and determine how it will design and implement obligations to perform these services. To use USOs effectively as a means of ensuring services to the poor, a State must have maximum freedom to do both.

There are concerns that WTO Members' ability to establish USOs could be constrained by the GATS if Members do not carefully formulate conditions and limitations before signing up to specific commitments.[78] For example, a Member may decide not to apply USOs to all service providers in a sector but only to new service providers. New entrants are most likely those that enter markets with the primary goal to make profits, rather than to pursue broad public policy objectives. Given that, in many cases, these new entrants would be foreign private providers, a USO targeting such new entrants could be found to be discriminatory and consequently prohibited under the GATS national treatment requirements.

Some WTO Members appear to have recognized these potential problems surrounding their ability to apply USOs once they have entered into full market access and national treatment commitments. In order to retain the ability to do so, they have placed conditions and limitations on their commitments, with varying degrees of apparent effectiveness.

The European schedule, for example, reserves the right to subject certain services considered as public utilities '. . . to exclusive rights granted to private operators'. An explanatory footnote specifies that '[e]xclusive rights on such services are often granted to private operators, for instance operators with concessions from public authorities, subject to specific service obligations'. This schedule seems to allow the use of USOs, yet it does not provide a definition for 'universal service', or for 'exclusive service contract'.[79] This shortcoming is not

[77] *See generally*, Omar Chisari, *The Needs of the Poor in Infrastructure Privatization: The Role of Universal Service Obligations*, Universidad Centroamericana (visited Jan. 16, 2004), <http://bjcu.uca.edu.ni/biblioteca/debates/Chisari.pdf> (Jan. 1999) (for a discussion of the relationship between USOs and the poor).

[78] The only place USOs are specifically mentioned in the context of the GATS is the Telecom Reference Paper, which states that USOs 'will not be regarded as anti competitive per se, provided that they are administered in a transparent, non-discriminatory and competitively neutral manner': Negotiating Group on Basic Telecommunications, *Telecommunications Services: Reference Paper*, S/L/20, Art. 3, World Trade Organization (Apr. 24, 1996), (visited Jan. 16, 2004), <http://www.wto.org/english/tratop_e/serv_e/telecom_e/tel23_e.htm>. The Telecom Reference Paper informs our discussion on water services and USOs since both telecom and water services are network services.

[79] Art. VIII provides some insight into how to define 'exclusive rights'. For a general discussion of defining exclusive services contracts under GATS, *see* Elisabeth Tuerk and Robert Speed, *GATS and Water, A Draft Discussion Paper for the Workshop on Trade and Water–Geneva* (March 3, 2003) (on file with author).

particularly problematic, however, because a lack of a uniform definition in the European schedule could also allow flexibility for Europe to adopt definitions on a case by case basis, depending on the sector and social situation in question. Such an interpretation suggesting flexibility to define a universal service also appears to be fully consistent with the GATS preamblular reference to the right to regulate[80] and references to universal service aspects in other texts of the GATS legal framework.[81]

The next question is how a Member may design and implement USOs within the framework of the GATS. In this context, the primary concern of this paper is the ability of governments to require private service providers to 'roll-out' service provision to previously unserved geographical areas, or to provide services to those unable to pay.

Most likely, the European condition, with its reference to 'specific service obligations', does not limit the nature of these obligations and would therefore allow all types of USOs. Europe's ability to impose USOs could be hindered, however, if the USOs or their implementation were to exhibit discriminatory effects. Privatization of public services usually involves a private foreign entity wanting access to the profitable part of a domestic market. If Europe were to impose a facially neutral USO on all new water service providers, it could amount to a *de facto* violation of national treatment obligations, since it would—in practice—affect only foreign service providers.[82] Again, however, the European schedule appears to grant leeway, as the condition it contains applies to both the market access and the national treatment obligations.

Unlike the European approach, the Nordic/Swiss approach does not explicitly state what type of regulatory action is allowed for public utilities. Instead, it excludes the 'public work function' aspects of services from the commitments as such, even if the services are contracted out.[83] This approach is simpler and overall appears to grant more flexibility for governmental regulatory prerogatives. Once the threshold question of what is included in the term 'public service/works function' is passed, none of the GATS specific commitments apply to regulatory action undertaken in that field. That suggests that any measures taken to require USOs are permitted, as long as they do not violate the GATS general obligations.[84]

The US/Estonian schedules explicitly limit the application of national treatment and market access to 'services contracted by private industry'. Assuming

[80] GATS, Preamble, fourth recital.

[81] The Telecom Reference Paper, *supra* note 78, explicitly recognized Members' 'right to define the universal service obligation they wish to maintain'. Specifically, Art. 3 of the Paper states that '[a]ny Member has the right to define the kind of universal service obligation it wishes to maintain'.

[82] Note that Art. 3 of the Telecom Reference Paper states that USOs are 'not ... regarded as anti-competitive per se, provided they are administered in a transparent, non-discriminatory and competitively neutral manner and are not more burdensome than necessary for the kind of universal service defined by the Member'.

[83] *See* above, section 4.3.

[84] It is important to note, however, that even if a measure falls outside the GATS' specific commitments, Art. VIII still applies if the measure relates to the 'public works function' of the service. This is subject to the assumption that Art. VIII would apply to natural monopolies.

that the US/Estonian commitment covers only private industry consumption of services, the US or Estonia would be able to put in place USOs, even if discriminatory, as long as the purpose of the USOs is not to facilitate private industry, but rather to facilitate private individual consumption of water services.[85]

Imposing USOs is a useful way for regulators to ensure that water is provided to even the poorest segments of a population while still allowing privatization in more lucrative segments. More significantly, the imposition of USOs could be a significant way for WTO Members to meet their obligations under international human rights law in relation to the principle of non-discrimination.[86] However, WTO Members must be sure to design their specific commitments so that they retain the ability to define universal services, as well as to determine how to apply USOs.

6.3 Providing subsidies—is carving out regulatory space through conditions on specific commitments enough?

Along with USOs, subsidies are an important tool for ensuring affordable water services to all segments of a community. For instance, a State may choose to subsidize water services to poor areas because that segment of the market is unprofitable and otherwise would not be serviced at all. However, providing subsidies can be difficult for governments, either because they lack the capital or revenue to do so, or because they are constrained by international legal obligations such as those of the GATS agreements. In terms of the GATS, certain subsidies could be found to constitute anti-competitive behavior or violations of national treatment provisions.

If a State subsidizes providers servicing poor areas which would otherwise have trouble attracting service providers (and indeed are only serviced by subsidized *public* service providers), anti-competitive behavior may not be a problem, since the very fact that there is no competition for the specific area necessitated the subsidies in the first place.[87] However, a State may still run afoul

[85] Non-discriminatory USOs would of course be permitted. In addition, if the US/Estonian schedule is read to cover only private industry consumption, this could lead to national treatment violations if foreign services are the only ones servicing industry and therefore responsible for following the USO.

[86] The human rights principle of non-discrimination is a basic principle of human rights law and the prohibition on discrimination in relation to at least several of the categories is considered part of customary international law—and thus of application to all WTO Members. *See*, e.g., United Nations General Assembly, 'Report of the International Law Commission 53rd Session, 23 April–1 June; 25 July–10 August 2001', p. 208 (A/56/10). In order to protect against discrimination, States should take steps to remove *de facto* discrimination on the basis of sex, race, ethnicity, social status, and several other categories, where individuals and groups are deprived of the means or entitlements necessary for achieving the right to water.

[87] Art. VIII could be read to allows cross-subsidies (using funds from one service sector or one part of a market in the same service sector to subsidize another sector or another part of a market) as long as the subsidy is not anti-competitive, abusing the provider's monopoly position (that is generating the funds) outside the scope of its monopoly rights. *See* GATS, Art. VIII:2.

of the Article XVII national treatment provisions, which require a Member to treat all foreign and national service providers equally within a specific sector, regardless of whether they are servicing only a profitable part of the market.[88] Thus, Members may wish to consider conditions or limitations for their national treatment commitments.

Many Members have done so, addressing subsidies in their horizontal conditions to the national treatment commitments.[89] Both the European and Bulgarian horizontal limitations, for example, state that '[t]he supply of a service, or its subsidization, within the public sector is not in breach of this commitment'.[90] Such a commitment would clearly allow a government to subsidize public provision of the service. However, would the subsidy still be allowed if, for instance, the public sector out-sources certain aspects of the services to the private sector, thereby removing the sector from being 'within the public sector'?

This question does not matter so much for the Nordic/Swiss approach, which excludes altogether the 'public service/works function' of certain services, even if contracted out to private providers.

Similarly, the US/Estonian schedule. Assuming the interpretation which implies that only private industry *consumption* is covered by the commitment, public provision of services to the general public or citizens for private consumption would be excluded from the commitment. Given that the market segment of private consumption for non-industrial use may be the segment most in need of subsidization, it appears that the US/Estonian approach preserves adequate regulatory freedom for subsidies in this area.[91]

Lastly, another question arises when a government provides investment incentives to attract investment in a poorly-developed water sector. Would such investment incentives be considered subsidies, and therefore—if more favorable to domestic investors—be considered a national treatment violation? Again, to date there are no clear answers to these questions.

In any case, many of these issues remain open and undetermined, and WTO Members may wish carefully to design and double check their commitments and limitations as regards subsidies. An issue underlying all subsidies issues in the GATS is that, to date, subsidies are prohibited only insofar as they constitute

[88] GATS, Art. XVII:1. Of course, any finding on that matter would depend on a series of issues, notably the exact nature and design of the subsidies regime and how the WTO panels or the Appellate Body would interpret GATS concepts such as like services, like service providers, or *de facto* discrimination.

[89] Some horizontal limitations include statements that eligibility for subsidies may be limited to juridical persons established within the territory of the Member in question, or even of a particular geographical sub-division thereof.

[90] It is interesting that the EC is currently in the process of renegotiating its commitments, aiming to expand this conditionality to all those current Members who, when negotiating GATS individually, before joining the EC, had failed to introduce this conditionality.

[91] Questions would arise, however, if the government were to subsidize water or energy for industrial consumption.

anti-competitive behavior or a national treatment violation. If they are trade distortive, but not discriminatory and not anti-competitive, they are not covered by any existing trade rules. Members are, however, negotiating rules for trade distortive subsidies.[92] It is crucial that any eventual rules will not further constrain governments' abilities to provide subsidies to ensure the provision of services to the poor and those in need.

6.4 Conclusions

The potential of the GATS to constrain governments' abilities effectively to impose USOs and provide subsidies is one of the key concerns civil society groups have voiced with respect to the GATS. This analysis describes the different ways in which WTO Members have designed—and thereby limited—their GATS commitments, with the view to preserving a degree of regulatory flexibility. The fact that some WTO Members have gone to great lengths to include such conditions and limitations in their commitments suggests that at least those WTO Members share some of the concerns of civil society in terms of how the GATS affects the provision and regulation of public services.

In addition, the conditions reviewed in this chapter may provide valuable models for Members when negotiating future commitments, especially in sensitive sectors such as the provision of water. In cases where a Member decides to proceed in accepting water commitments, examining how other countries have conditioned related commitments in the past could offer instruction on how effectively to protect regulatory flexibility, including the flexibility needed for current and future privatization in service sectors.

Nevertheless, conditioned and carefully designed GATS commitments are no guarantee that private sector water provision will result in progressive fulfillment of the human right to water. While carefully drafted GATS commitments may allow flexibility for regulatory flanking policies, they do not ensure that regulators take the right complementary action, necessary to ensure that water is provided to the poor.

Another key element is the nature and content of the legal relationship between the government/regulator and the private service provider. Clearly, governments need as much regulatory space as possible to negotiate the type of service contracts that best suit the needs of their particular social and economic situation. Careful scheduling of GATS commitments can help preserve that space. In the cases examined here, the EC schedule makes a specific reference to this contractual relationship (the 'exclusive service contract'), and thereby carves out a certain degree of flexibility for the negotiation of such arrangements. However, while there is increasing analysis of the effects of the GATS on the provision of water to the poor, to date there is only limited analysis of how the

[92] GATS, Art. XV.

nature of contractual arrangements with private service providers either contributes to or impedes progress toward this goal.

7. Final observations

Globally, governments are seeking new solutions to ever-mounting water problems; both in terms of threats to natural water reserves as well as the difficulties of providing safe, accessible, and affordable water services to growing populations. Governments are increasingly choosing to solve these problems through greater private sector involvement in the provision of water services. Because access to water for drinking and sanitation is considered a basic human right, now more than ever it is essential that governments maintain the appropriate regulatory powers to ensure continued provision of this essential service to all, most especially the poor.

The GATS increases the momentum towards the liberalization of water services. Some are concerned that the GATS in effect drives privatization processes. However, civil society is also concerned that the GATS may impair governments' abilities to provide the increased level of regulation necessary in an open, privatized market. Specifically, there are concerns that the GATS may constrain flexibility when implementing monopolies, or prevent the imposition of USOs and the subsidization of services.

The extent to which the GATS impacts a country's policy choices depends significantly upon the way the country phrases its specific GATS commitments. While no country has yet made commitments in terms of water services, reviews of specific commitments made to date in the environmental services sector show that WTO Members have taken a range of approaches to placing limitations on these commitments.

These approaches range from placing horizontal limitations on all services or all of a specific sector or sub-sector, to specifically conditioning access to particular sectors and sub-sectors. Many countries have included safeguards for continued public sector involvement by excluding 'public utilities', 'public services', or 'public works functions' from the scope of their GATS market access and national treatment commitments. Governments have included these conditions notwithstanding GATS, Article I:3(b), an express exemption for services supplied in the exercise of governmental authority. Many countries have also conditioned their commitments to ensure that they will continue to be able to subsidize services. This display of awareness suggests that similar conditions might be placed upon the opening of water service markets, if commitments will be undertaken in that sector at all.

Pro-GATS groups argue that the conditions placed on existing services commitments demonstrate that the bottom-up approach works, and that the framework provides adequate flexibility to address any concerns that an individual government may have. However, the need for limitations across the board, where public utilities are involved, suggests a fundamental flaw in the structure of the GATS as it applies to essential services and the types of obligations it places upon governments.

From this review, it seems clear that governments share many of the concerns of civil society in terms of how the GATS affects the provision and regulation of public services, including implementing USOs. The various approaches adopted by WTO Members to conditioning market access all aim (so it would seem) to achieve the same end, regulatory flexibility. However, the varying nature of these approaches creates ambiguity in terms of what exactly the parties intended, which in turn creates potential for disputes. In the case of a dispute, a WTO panel or Appellate Body ruling would ultimately interpret a commitment, rather than the Member that crafted the commitment. Even in the absence of ambiguity, a real risk remains that Members, particularly developing countries, will make commitments without knowing the long-term consequences, or simply as a result of political or economic pressure exerted in negotiations.[93] Injecting further speed into the negotiating process would provide additional challenges to developing countries.

As stated above, privatization of basic public services is a great concern to civil society. While negotiators have addressed issues that stem from privatization, such as the loss of regulatory flexibility, no one has yet addressed privatization and the GATS encouragement of privatization directly as such. The reason negotiators have not addressed privatization head-on in specific commitments may not have to do so much with the fact that they are out of tune with their constituencies, but rather with the fact that the GATS process in general is not conducive to attempts to reduce privatization of basic public services.

Ideally, water services should not be covered by either specific or general GATS disciplines. Governments should be free to involve the private sector in water services, secure in the knowledge that they have every possible regulatory tool at their disposal.

[93] Hardstaff, *supra* note 24.

7

Economics of Water Services and the Right to Water

HENRI SMETS

1. Introduction

Although the right to water is now generally recognized as a fundamental right, some States do not want to acknowledge its importance, as they are in favour of privatizing water utilities and/or wish to avoid any interference due to social concerns. The potential conflict between trade laws and the fundamental right to water should not be exaggerated and should be examined in the context of national practice. The majority of French water services is managed by the private sector and, at the same time, France acts in conformity with its obligations under international law concerning the right to water. This chapter shows that water services can be operated under public–private partnership or as a public service, without special difficulties concerning the right to access to water.

2. The right to water at the international level

In November 2002 the right to water was officially recognized at the international level as a fundamental right, like the right to food or the right to health. This ended a period of uncertainty regarding the legal status of the right to water in the field of human rights.[1] It was achieved when the Committee on Economic, Social, and Cultural Rights (UN), which was in charge of following up the implementation of the International Covenant on Economic, Social, and Cultural Rights (adopted in 1966), approved the General Comment No. 15.[2]

[1] For a description and analysis, *see* Carlos Villán Durán, *The Right to Adequate Food and Drinking Water in International Law: New Developments*, in Liber amicorum to Professor Antonio Augusto Cançado Trindade, 2003. *See also* WHO, The Right to Water, 2003, available at www.who.int/water_sanitation_health/Documents/righttowater/righttowater.htm.

[2] *See* General Comment No. 15, The Right to Water (Articles 11 and 12 of the International Covenant on Economic, Social and Cultural Rights), U.N. Doc. E/C.12/2002/11, 26 November, providing: 'Water is a limited natural resource and a public good fundamental for life and health. The human right to water is indispensable for leading a life in human dignity. It is a prerequisite for the realization of other human rights.'

The right to water is a fundamental right because it is a necessary component of the right to an adequate standard of living (Article 11.1 of the Covenant[3]) and the right to health (Article 12.1 of the Covenant[4]). The adoption of this interpretation will assist and influence the 146 States which ratified the Covenant in their understanding of the scope of Article 11.1.

The right to water can be found explicitly in the Convention on the Elimination of All Forms of Discrimination against Women[5] (1979, 170 ratifications) and in the Convention on the Rights of the Child (1989).[6] As explained by UNICEF:

> The last Convention reflects a global consensus and, in a very short period of time, it has become the most widely accepted human rights treaty ever. It has been ratified by 191 countries; only two countries have not ratified. The United States, which has signaled its intention to ratify by formally signing the Convention, now stands as the only industrialized country in the world and one of only two United Nations member States yet to make this legal commitment to children. The other country is Somalia, which is presently without a recognized government.

This formal recognition of the right to water by the competent body of the UN system[7] was preceded by many statements in favour of the right to water. The oldest one is the Declaration of the UN Conference on Water held at Mar del

[3] Art. 11.1 of the Covenant provides: 'The States Parties to the present Covenant recognize the right of everyone to an adequate standard of living for himself and his family, including adequate food, clothing and housing, and to the continuous improvement of living conditions.' (Note the word 'including', which opened the way to the addition of drinking water.)

[4] Art. 12.1 provides: 'The States Parties to the present Covenant recognize the right of everyone to the enjoyment of the highest attainable standard of physical and mental health.'

[5] Art. 14.2 states: 'Parties shall take all appropriate measures to eliminate discrimination against women in rural areas in order to ensure, on a basis of equality of men and women, that they participate in and benefit from rural development and, in particular, shall ensure to such women the right: ... (h) To enjoy adequate living conditions, particularly in relation to housing, sanitation, electricity and water supply, transport and communications.'

[6] Art. 24.1 states: 'Parties recognize the right of the child to the enjoyment of the highest attainable standard of health and to facilities for the treatment of illness and rehabilitation of health. States Parties shall strive to ensure that no child is deprived of his or her right of access to such health care services.' Art. 24.2 states: 'Parties shall pursue full implementation of this right and, in particular, shall take appropriate measures: ... (c) To combat disease and malnutrition, including within the framework of primary health care, through, inter alia, the application of readily available technology and through the provision of adequate nutritious foods and clean drinking water, taking into consideration the dangers and risks of environmental pollution.' (Note that this article is particularly important because of the large number of children dying due to unsafe water.)

[7] The issue of the right to water was reviewed by the UN Sub-Commission on the Promotion and Protection of Human Rights, which published a preliminary report on the right to water in July 2002 (E/CN.4/Sub.2/2002/10), endorsing the view of the rapporteur El Hadji Guissé that access to safe water and proper sanitation is a human right. *See* Sub-Commission on Human Rights Resolution 2002/6, entitled 'Promotion of the realization of the right to drinking water and sanitation', which reaffirms, *inter alia*, 'the fundamental principles of equality, human dignity and social justice, and the right to drinking water supply and sanitation for every woman, man and child', and which refers to 'the urgent and persistent need for increased attention and commitment by all decision makers to the right of everyone to drinking water supply and sanitation'. The UN Sub-Commission adopted in August 2003 another Resolution on the 'Promotion of the realization of the right to drinking water and sanitation' (E/CN.4/Sub.2/2003/L.17), which also refers to 'the right to drinking water supply

Plata in 1977.[8] In 1992, a UN International Conference on Water held in Dublin adopted a Statement which makes reference to the basic right to water.[9]

According to Kofi Annan, Secretary General of the United Nations, access to safe water is a 'basic human right'.[10] This is also the view of the WHO.[11] In 2003, the Holy See published a message, according to which, '[t]here is a growing movement to formally adopt a human right to water. The dignity of the human person mandates its acknowledgment. ... *The right to water is thus an inalienable right*'.[12]

Representatives of international financial institutions, banks, and businesses sitting on the Panel chaired by Michel Camdessus, agreed to a Report which states that access to water is a right.[13] Similarly the Vice President of the World Bank, Mr Peter Woicke, stated that 'access to safe water is and should be regarded as a human right'.[14] The two leading water multinationals, Suez[15] and

and sanitation for every woman, man and child'. The Sub-Commission's final report on this topic was issued in 2004 (E/CN.4/Sub.2/2004/20). *See also* the interim report 'Le droit à l'eau et à l'assainissement' by El Hadji Guissé (E/CN.4/Sub.2/2003/WP3) (French only).

[8] The Mar del Plata Action Plan, 1977, provides, *inter alia*, that 'all peoples, whatever their stage of development and their social and economic conditions, have the right to have access to drinking water in quantities and of a quality equal to their basic needs'. *See* G.A. Res. 158, U.N. GAOR, 32nd Sess. (1977), in which the Assembly approved the Mar del Plata Action Plan (Report of the United Nations Water Conference, Mar del Plata, 14–25 March 1977).

[9] The Dublin Statement (International Conference on Water and the Environment), 1992, provides: 'Water has an economic value in all its competing uses and should be recognized as an economic good. Within this principle, it is vital to recognize first the basic right of all human beings to have access to clean water and sanitation at an affordable price.' (Note that the reference to water as being an 'economic good' is often made by people who carefully ignore the following sentence: in most countries water is sold well below its true cost.)

[10] 'Access to safe water is a fundamental human need and therefore a basic human right', World Water Day Message of 22 March 2001, available at http://www.worldwaterday.org.

[11] On World Water Day, 22 March 2001, Gro Harlem Brundtland, Director-General, WHO, stated: 'Access to safe water is a universal need and indeed considered a basic human right. It constitutes a fundamental component of primary health care.' At the 7th Conference of European Health Ministers (Oslo, 12 June 2003), the Director General of WHO gave a keynote address on 'Health, dignity and human rights' in which she stated: 'In recent years, we have become clearer as to what the right to health should actually mean. First and foremost, it is an inclusive right: it is not just about health care services—it is also about the underlying determinants of ill health. These are much broader and include access to safe drinking water, adequate sanitation, a supply of safe and nutritious food, healthy occupational and environmental conditions and access to information.' For an analysis of legal obligations of States, *see* WHO note: 'World water day 2001' (prepared by Margret Vidar and Ali Mekouar of FAO Legal Service), available at http://www.worldwaterday.org/thematic/hmnrights.html.

[12] Pontifical Council for Justice and Peace, *Water, an essential element for life*, Note presented at the 3rd World Water Forum (16–23 March 2003) (emphasis added), available at http://www.zenit.org/english/visualizza.phtml?sid=33276.

[13] James Winpenny, *Financing Water for All*, Report of the World Panel on Financing Water Infrastructure chaired by Michel Camdessus, 2003. The Report provides, *inter alia*: 'First, access to water is a right and a basic need' and 'Everyone should have access to water and sanitation at an affordable price'. This Panel was convened by the UN Secretary General Mr K. Annan. It is being considered in many international organizations because it opens the road to meeting the targets set in the Millennium Declaration (Millennium Development Goals).

[14] *See* INT'L HERALD TRIBUNE, 17 March 2003.

[15] *See* 'The "Water Truce", An Open Letter by G. Mestrallet, CEO, Suez', in Suez, *Bridging the Water Divide*, 2001, in which Mestrellat states: 'I think we should be able to agree that the universal

Véolia,[16] both consider that water is a fundamental human right. All non-governmental organizations (NGOs) and charitable organizations have spoken for at least fifteen years in favour of the official recognition of the right to water.

3. The right to water at the Third World Water Forum

During the opening ceremony of the Third World Water Forum (Tokyo, March 2003), President J. Chirac, who was unable to attend because of the imminent war in Iraq, proposed that 'access to water be recognized as a fundamental right'. In Kyoto, some hundred ministers and high-ranking civil servants discussed whether to include in their Ministerial Declaration a reference to the General Comment No. 15 on the right to water adopted by the competent UN body in November 2002. The United Kingdom proposed that Ministers agree to discuss the implications of this Comment at a domestic level. This proposal was not accepted and the text adopted by Ministers just after the beginning of the war in Iraq did not make any reference to any right concerning water. This did not come as a surprise, in spite of last-minute efforts by European Ministers, because for some governments referring to the right to water and any other economic or social rights is not 'politically correct'.[17]

The Prince of Orange has described the current controversy on the right to water in the following terms:

> A position that is strongly held by many, particularly in the NGO community, is that access to water is a human right and should be enshrined as a value and shared globally by all governments. Many in government circles argue that current declarations on human rights include basic water needs sufficiently and additional declarations are unnecessary and too complicated politically.[18]

It is symptomatic that the Prince of Orange does not make reference to any relevant convention in force and refers only to non-binding declarations. He does not indicate where the majority opinion lies, or the fact that most governments do not agree with the views of the 'many in government circles'. In Kyoto, most people who spoke publicly were in favour of the right to water and the arguments against were rarely expressed. Quite clearly, if there had not been

right of access to water must be recognized and that we should get down to work now to turn that right into a reality every day.'; 'Water is not a commodity.' The report is available at http://www.suez.com/popups/english/bataille_old.htm.

[16] Générale des Eaux/Vivendi/Véolia recognizes 'the social imperative of the right to water for all'. See Vivendi-Générale des Eaux, *L'eau, C'est la Vie*, Paris, 2001. In *Le Monde* (31/5/203), Véolia's CEO H. Proglio writes: 'L'eau n'est pas une marchandise mais un bien durable que personne ne peut s'approprier'; and he adds: 'La propriété publique des infrastructures de traitement et de distribution d'eau est fondamentale.'

[17] Economic and social rights are not recognized rights for those countries which did not ratify the relevant agreements, in particular the International Covenant.

[18] *See 'No Water, No Future'*, Contribution of HRH the Prince of Orange to the Panel of the UN Secretary General, in preparation for the Johannesburg Summit, August 2002.

an overwhelming majority in favour of the right to water, the General Comment No. 15 would not have been adopted. However, while it is true that 'current declarations on human rights include basic water needs', it would have been preferable that the 'many in government circles' acknowledged it clearly and did not seek to escape the issue by referring only to basic needs.

The reason for the permanent silence on this important issue in recent Ministerial Declarations at world level, after a series of ministerial statements on the right to water from 1977 to 1992, is related to the process of adoption of Ministerial Declarations by consensus. Any State against mentioning economic or social rights can effectively veto any reference to the right to water without even having to give any explanation to the public.[19]

4. The opposition to the right to water and to liberalization of water utilities

4.1 Opposition to the right to water

The opposition to the right to water is not coming from all business circles. For instance, Mr G. Mestrallet, CEO of Suez, has stated that the 'universal right of access to water must be recognized and that we should get down to work now to turn this right into a reality every day'. And he added: 'I am particularly proud of the fact that our programmes have extended services to nine million customers living below the poverty line.'[20]

The main 'reasons' given for not supporting the right to water are as follows:

(1) it creates international liability;
(2) it prevents commodification of water;
(3) it implies free access to water;
(4) it hinders liberalization or privatization of water utilities;
(5) it creates obstacles to free trade; and
(6) it facilitates legal harassment of water utilities or public authorities.

These reasons are mostly due to misconceptions as to the meaning of economic and social rights, which, if they were valid, would also apply to the right to food, clothing, housing, and health. The latter rights have been in force for many years and have not led to such emotional reactions, in spite of the huge commercial markets for food, clothing, housing, and health, and in spite of the vast number of impoverished people who are still deprived of food and shelter. The rights to

[19] At the Bonn Conference (2001), the US proposed to delete the words 'human right' in order to limit the recommendation to 'access to safe drinking water is a basic need', www.water-2001.de/co_doc/proposals/usa.pdf. The United States have publicly taken a position against the recognition of the right to housing or to food in so far as these rights would create any legal entitlement or obligation at domestic level or at international level. At UN CSD 13 (April 2005), the United States obtained the deletion of any reference to rights-based approach in the final document.

[20] *See supra* note 15.

food and housing are fundamental rights, yet few court cases have been brought for breaches of these rights. Thus the harassment argument is without foundation. There are legal cases concerning drinking water, but they are mostly linked to pollution laws, not water supply.

The right to water is not a civil right, such as the right to vote, which any person can demand to exercise immediately. An economic right is a right that must be put into force progressively, for instance by connecting more people to water networks each year.[21] This is being done in most countries, but there are also cases where countries ignore the right to water without a valid reason. In South Africa, for example, a local government was ordered by the court to provide standposts to squatters, but was not required to connect every person to the water networks because economic or social rights are to be implemented progressively.

Some diplomats have suggested that a State which recognizes economic rights at an international level would be under an obligation to finance actions to protect such rights in another State. This approach is far from reality; many people die from hunger or are left without proper medical treatment without any State being found *internationally liable*. Neither France nor the UK bears any international liability on the basis of the Covenant for the lack of funds against starvation in Ethiopia, or for the lack of drugs against AIDS in Africa. They bring technical and financial assistance to developing countries, and they seek to make drugs less expensive so as to promote the right to health.

An alternative objection is based on the concept that a State would be *internationally liable* if economic rights were not enforced at the national level.[22] This could happen within the framework of the implementation mechanism of the convention which would have been violated, provided that the claim was justified and the mechanism effective. Countries which are party to the International Covenant on Economic, Social, and Cultural Rights have to report on progress made, but are not found liable for lack of food, shelter, or medical care.[23] In relation to water, the European Court of Human Rights might be called upon in cases of gross violations of human rights.[24] While this has

[21] Concerning water, there is an enforceable right to provide water to the thirsty, not water to a house. An unresolved issue is the possibility to disconnect poor customers who fail to pay their water bills.

[22] No State was found liable for failing to provide as much international aid as it announced it would, nor for failing to provide technical assistance. In spite of the International Covenant on Economic, Social, and Cultural Rights, there are over one billion people living in miserable conditions, and no court has yet made any State liable for poverty, hunger, or lack of shelter. If a case were to be built on the grounds that safe water was unavailable, it could probably be argued more successfully on the more precise commitments found in the Millennium Declaration or the Johannesburg targets.

[23] French administrative courts find it difficult to enforce the right to housing because the International Covenant on Economic, Social, and Cultural Rights ratified by France is vague and is only binding between States (no individual right derives directly from it). Thus they would not find it possible to implement the right to water in the case of an individual complaint.

[24] The right to water could become directly applicable on the basis of the European Convention on Human Rights if the European Court of Human Rights were to recognize that it is a necessary element of some protected general human rights (e.g., the right to dignity, or the right to life). This could potentially occur, as the European Court is already moving towards recognition of the right to a clean environment (which did not exist when the Convention was adopted).

not taken place in areas such as food or shelter, it cannot be excluded in the future.[25]

Some 'circles' are fundamentally against economic and social rights because they could constitute an obstacle to free trade or development in the private sector. Such types of objections are linked to the application of liberal economic approaches to an economic sector in which it is very difficult to introduce free competition because it is a natural monopoly.

For some people, recognizing water as a 'right' is incompatible with water being a 'commodity'. In particular, water utilities would not be allowed to set water tariffs freely. Here again there are misconceptions, because water can be a right and a commodity at the same time. For instance, in South Africa water is free for small users and expensive for other users. Water can be provided to the poor at a reduced price (covered by a subsidy in Chile and by a cross-subsidy in Belgium) and still be considered as both a right and a commodity.

It has been argued that if water were a right, utilities would be unable to run their business, as they would be prevented from cutting off water supply to those persons who failed to pay their water bills. The case of South Africa shows that water can be a right and be disconnected. In the UK, disconnecting people from water supply became illegal a few years ago, but this did not prevent private water utilities from generating profits. To reconcile the right to water with the right to cut off water supply, some countries provide a minimum allocation of water, or access to standposts nearby.

Some people express concern that creating a right to water amounts to creating a right to *free water*.[26] This argument is without basis; the right to food, for example, never implied that food would be free for all. However, it may imply that those who cannot pay for their water will receive free water from public authorities, water utilities, or charitable organizations.[27] This was implemented through free public fountains in France and the UK and did not obstruct privatization or liberalization of water utilities in those countries. If utilities have to provide free water to public administrations, public fountains, hydrants, or poor people, this would need to be specified and paid for (by subsidies, cross-subsidies, etc.).

Some would argue that the right to water places an obligation on States to ensure control, or to regulate water prices. While it is true that water prices are

[25] The African Commission of Human Rights found the Democratic Republic of Congo (former Zaire) guilty of violating the African Charter of Human Rights (Art. 16 on provision of basic services) (opinion 4/4/96 et 10/7/96-Communications 25/89, 47/90 et 56/91).

[26] There are people who advocate free water for basic needs for all and payment for large quantities. Such a policy has not been supported to date to any significant extent by municipalities in Europe, who provide large subsidies to bring down the cost of water but rarely go as far as to make water free. When municipalities operate their utility as a public–private partnership (PPP), they generally continue to subsidize water. If they stop subsidizing water, they will need to increase water prices and face social consequences.

[27] The right to water does not imply that every person is entitled to receive 40 liters per day for free (just the same as the right to food never implied that everyone should be provided with a free loaf of bread). In many developing countries, the right to water is implemented by setting up standposts, or by establishing a progressive tariff scheme, with a first tranche of water sold at a very reduced price.

controlled by public authorities, because water is a *natural monopoly* this State intervention is not in relation to the recognition of a right to water. State control over water existed well before any economic or social right was adopted in any international treaty or declaration. The experience of the full privatization of the water sector in the UK has shown that a regulator was needed, which should be very effective if the government wishes to prevent profit margins growing too fast. A major difficulty in setting up an efficient and independent regulator in developing countries is the general opposition to privatization of the water sector.

The right to water has no direct relation with the type of management of water utilities. In France, municipalities are free to choose the type of management—public or private—for their utilities, and a large majority of them have decided to move away from a purely public enterprise and to run a mixed public/private system (public investment for the long term, private management for the short term[28]). Recognizing the right to water has had no effect on the choice of the type of management in France because social constraints can always be included in the contract between a municipality and a private water company.

The refusal by a few Ministers in Kyoto to recognize even the mere existence of an official report from the competent UN body on the right to water has no significance from a legal point of view, as international law derives from treaties and not from political statements which do not have a binding effect. However, this is troublesome, because it may be an indication that a number of governments are not ready to provide the financial means which are needed to meet the Millennium Development Goals or the Johannesburg targets in the area of water supply and sanitation. At the G8 Evian Summit, Heads of State did not express any views (was it an embarrassed silence?) on the recommendation of the Camdessus Panel to double the flow of aid for water. A few billion dollars additional aid is at stake but may be absorbed by other competing needs, such as the 'war against terrorism' or its aftermath.

4.2 Opposition to water liberalization/privatization from a human rights perspective

In most countries privatization of the water sector is opposed because water is considered an essential good (vital good), distributed by a natural monopoly which has significant fixed costs and is managed by local authorities. Such opposition is supported by trade unions (of public servants in countries with public water utilities), by consumer unions, and by charities, who are afraid that water becomes more expensive with privatization.[29] This concern extends to the

[28] A number of French municipalities have decided to revert to public management after an experiment with PPP ('gestion déléguée'), but the overall trend is still in favour of PPP. In many cases, negotiations after the end of the contract have led to price reductions.

[29] Often governments have promoted privatization in order to remove a budgetary burden, while transferring the responsibility for the water price increase onto the private sector. The same price increase would have taken place if the utility were made financially autonomous while remaining in the public sector.

possible transfer of all public industrial operations to the private sector as a matter of policy. In addition, there is a risk that private operators may be tempted to raise water tariffs because of their monopolistic situation and will refuse to distribute water to unprofitable clients ('cherry picking'). In order to assess the true situation, it is worth looking at the outcome of privatization or liberalization of water utilities in countries such as France or the UK, rather than in countries where governance is very weak and public management very poor.

The opposition to privatization of the water sector is also linked to the attitude of governments or international lending institutions who think that a private water utility[30] should not receive subsidies and should be entirely funded by its customers (user pays principle, full cost recovery), notwithstanding that this was not done in most industrialized countries in the past. Thus public authorities would be obliged to raise water prices.

Within the European Union, subsidies for water utilities are not automatically seen as State subsidies and can be protected from the general policy of abolishing all subsidies. There is strong opposition to treating public water utilities as if they were commercial enterprises, and no offer was made by the EU to liberalize its own water supply sector under the Doha Agreement.[31] Discussions are under way to give greater legal recognition to 'services of general economic interest', which fall under different rules than those applicable to commercial enterprises. These services may be subsidized in view of their mission for the public interest (social and territorial cohesion).[32] Furthermore, both the EU, in issuing a directive,[33] and the European Parliament[34] have recognized that water is not 'a commercial product like any other'.

[30] The bias in favour of public private partnership or private sector participation has been assessed by the World Bank. In its report, *Efficient, Sustainable Service for All?*, Report 26443 of September 2003, the Bank refers to 'the unrealistically high expectations from clients and Bank staff' towards private management.

[31] Telecommunication, electricity, gas, and postal services have been liberalized within the EU, but not water, which is not traded internationally and is very much of local concern. The EU made an offer to liberalize sanitation services and kept open the possibility to subsidize its public services to enable them to meet their mission.

[32] Charter of Fundamental Rights of the European Union, Art. 36 provides, *inter alia*: 'The Union recognizes and respects access to services of general economic interest as provided for in national laws and practices, in accordance with the Treaty establishing the European Community, in order to promote the social and territorial cohesion of the Union.' The European Constitution also includes an article on public services aimed at protecting them from constraints linked to trade law.

[33] *See* Directive 2000/60/EC of the European Parliament and of the Council of 23 October 2000, which establishes a framework for Community action in the field of water policy, providing: 'Water is not a commercial product like any other but, rather, a heritage which must be protected, defended and treated as such.'

[34] *See* the European Parliament resolution on the Commission communication on water management in developing countries and priorities for EU development cooperation COM(2002), 4 September 2003, which '[s]tresses that the key issue is not whether water provision is organized by a public or private entity but rather the specific obligations provided by the policy framework'; '[c]onsiders that the public private partnership system, whereby the public authorities retain the ownership of the infrastructure and conclude a management contract with the private sector—securing access for all and ensuring publicly transparent pricing—should be viewed not as a panacea but as one of several ways of providing improved access to water'; and '[e]ncourages the Commission

Giving away water infrastructure to the private sector is seen negatively by French water multinationals (Suez, Véolia), who prefer to manage a water utility than to own it.[35] There is fear that public authorities would alter the applicable rules to the detriment of the private operator or investor (e.g., concerning price rises or additional social constraints). Similarly, a private operator may underinvest by the end of its contract and not make all necessary repairs.

In his Report on Liberalization of Trade in Services and Human Rights, the High Commissioner for Human Rights has stated that all people are entitled to a certain level of drinking water supply and has encouraged States to use affirmative action to ensure supply of water to the poor.[36] Such a position was taken because in many cases of liberalization/privatization, poor people have suffered from higher prices making water unaffordable to them and, in a few cases, have enjoyed less effective service. However, the negative side effects of privatization are generally linked to the content of the contract (which ignores the poor), to the constraints set on the private operator, and to the implicit decision of governments not to subsidize water any more.

The High Commissioner for Human Rights has also emphasized the risk that privatization can imply in terms of unbalance of rights.[37] He stated that: 'While investment liberalization reduces to some extent the field of State action and policy in relation to investors and investment, a human rights approach emphasizes that liberalization should not go so far as to compromise State action and policy to promote and protect human rights.' In a few cases the private

and the Member States to call on the World Bank and the IMF to demonstrate flexibility with regard to the type of water management and supply services required as a condition of grants and loans and to accept the right of a country to decide freely on its method of water supply, whether this be private, public or a mixture of both'.

[35] According to the World Bank Report, *Efficient, Sustainable Service for All?*, Report 26443 of September 2003, '[t]he water supply and wastewater sector's political importance and the fact that it is by far the most capital intensive in relation to annual revenue makes it the riskiest of all infrastructure sectors for prospective private operators. (The fixed assets to annual revenue ratio for various infrastructures are: Water supply and sanitation, 7; Toll roads, 4; Electrical power, 4 and Telecommunication, 3.)'

[36] *See* Report of the High Commissioner for Human Rights, *Liberalization of Trade in Services and Human Rights*, E/CN.4/Sub.2/2002/9, 25 June 2002, which 'emphasizes that all people are entitled without discrimination to certain levels of health care, education, drinking water supply and other basic services and that these entitlements should be protected in the processes of liberalization and privatization. In particular, the High Commissioner emphasizes that States, in spite of their diminishing role in service supply, should not rely solely on market forces to resolve problems concerning human welfare. While increasing investments from the local and overseas private sector can assist States in the provision of basic entitlements, the State has the responsibility of ensuring the delivery of services on a non-discriminatory basis, even where this might be unprofitable. Consequently, the High Commissioner encourages States to take action to ensure universal supply of essential services, including through the use of affirmative action to ensure provision of services to the poor, isolated and marginalized, taking into account national circumstances and capacities.'

[37] *See* Report of the High Commissioner for Human Rights, *Human Rights, Trade and Investment*, E/CN.4/Sub.2/2003/9, August 2003, providing: 'The promotion of the rule of law—popular participation, transparency, legality, equality and accountability—is a significant aspect of ensuring access to essential services for all.'

investor has obtained better legal guarantees than consumers, who have not been consulted and who have been required to pay the price set by the investor under a contract between the government and the investor.

The opposition to liberalization is largely due to the effect of ill-conceived, badly negotiated contracts,[38] which led to weak protection of human rights and, in some cases, bad management of water networks. Commercial interests often dominate all other interests, in particular the interest of the poor in developing countries. Large political, technical, and commercial risks have led to the setting of high prices for water, especially in countries with poor governance.

As will be seen in the case of France, private operators can act in line with the right to water provided there are adequate checks and balances in place, if the scope of the right to water is clearly defined, and if the economic conditions of the contract are not fundamentally changed. Private operators have to provide an adequate service and a fair price, or they will lose the contract when a renewal decision is made. The risk of corruption is quite significant in this field as with any other large public contract, and new laws have been adopted to reduce it.

5. The content of the right to water

Because the right to water has been misrepresented, it is necessary to clarify its precise scope. In doing so, it can be seen that the right to water represents an economic constraint which increases water price, but arguably to a very small extent in industrialized countries. The social benefits can be assumed to far exceed the economic cost for society at large, taking into account the economic consequences of water-related epidemics such as those occurring a century ago.

The right to water means that all individuals, without discrimination and independent of their income, should be able to obtain a limited quantity of safe drinking water for their essential needs.[39] In an industrialized country, it implies an obligation on public authorities to organize the provision of water supply and sanitation at an affordable price. Public authorities have to organize, monitor, and control the supply of drinking water, protect the resource, and take reasonable measures to prevent water from becoming unavailable or polluted. Public authorities must intervene without delay in serious cases and combat the worse abuses.

[38] According to H. Proglio (CEO, Véolia), 'La pratique prouve que, lorsque ces réalités (sociologiques, sociales et économiques) sont ignorées par négligence des autorités publiques ou parce que les bailleurs de fonds internationaux l'imposent, les expériences de gestion privée se terminent souvent mal.' Le Monde, 31 May 2003.

[39] According to the UN Committee on Economic, Social, and Cultural Rights, the human right to water 'entitles everyone to sufficient, safe, acceptable, physically accessible and affordable water for personal and domestic use' (E/C.12/2000/11, para. 2).

Implementing the right to water is of particular concern for those without access to water, either because they are far away from a water source or because they are not able to afford the price of safe water. Authorities have to build water supplies and sanitation networks to ensure people can obtain drinking water in their neighbourhood and live in decent housing; they also have to set up systems to enable the poor to get water without spending too large a fraction of their income on water (affordability). Whether carried out by public authorities or by the private sector, such activities have a cost which in the end must be paid for, either by users or by taxpayers.

From a practical point of view, the four main components of the right to water are:

(1) any person living near a source of drinking water (well, network, etc.) must have access to the water, irrespective of nationality, race, religion, legal status, earnings, etc. Access to drinking water would thus be similar to the universal access to medical treatment in France, or to primary education in the European Union (a natural right of the human person, freely available, even for illegal immigrants);[40]
(2) a person who has access to drinking water may not be deprived of it. In case of non-payment by a poor person, the utility or the municipality has to provide a minimal quantity of water, or access to standposts nearby;
(3) emergency measures must be taken if water becomes unavailable because of a natural disaster, drought, flood, accident, interruption of service for repairs, pollution, war,[41] etc.; and
(4) persons supported by public authorities (the very poor, homeless, prisoners, etc.) must receive water necessary for their life in dignity (drinking water, showers, cleaning, washing, etc.).

Because drinking water is becoming more expensive, measures should be taken to ensure that water expenses do not become too large within a household budget (affordability constraint). This may be done by well-designed water tariffs, subsidies, targeted social aid, etc., and implies solidarity between the rich and the poor and between urban and rural areas. Implementation of the right to water has a cost which is shown to be very small in countries such as France or Belgium (less than 1% of the turnover) and could be spread over other users by

[40] Providing access to water does not mean water must be transported to people anywhere and at any time. People may have to fetch water themselves.

[41] Deliberate destruction of the water supply of a civilian population, or of water tanks in private houses, is unacceptable even during civil war, and water supplies should be quickly reinstated after having been damaged by military operations. Many States did not ratify the 1977 Protocols to the Geneva Conventions (such as Iran, Iraq, Turkey, Syria, Israel, Morocco, Somalia, Eritrea, Sudan, Pakistan, India, Sri Lanka, United States, Afghanistan, Japan, Indonesia, and the Philippines). Recent events have shown that civilian targets are deliberately chosen. *See* Report by the Special Rapporteur, Jean Ziegler, *Mission the Occupied Palestinian Territories*, E/CN.4/2004/10, 9 February 2004. Concerning deliberate destruction of water tanks of Palestinian houses, destruction of wells, and obstruction of access to water brought by trucks into the Gaza strip, *see also* Jean Ziegler, *The right to food*, E/CN.4/2002/58, December 2001 at paras 102–103.

means of solidarity funds. In countries which lack access to safe water, the right to water could be implemented progressively, due to the cost involved. This is not a foreign concept; industrialized countries took over a hundred years, for example, to install their water networks.

In less developed countries, the main problem is the lack of investment in the water sector. As a result, people (usually women) have to spend hours every day fetching water and young girls miss the chance of attending school. In these countries the right to water is closely linked to the right to life (millions of people die each year from water-related diseases in developing countries) and the right to education (girls).

While the right to water is rarely spelled out in the legislation of industrialized countries,[42] it is found in the constitution or laws of many developing countries, because in these countries the right is not self-evident.[43]

6. The right to water in French practice

France is a party to all international conventions dealing with economic or social rights and has taken consistent official positions in support of the right to water. In France, all stakeholders agree that the right to water is a human right, even if there is no text in domestic law to this effect.[44] Future laws on

[42] In Belgium, Art. 23 of the Constitution regarding life in dignity and the right to health and to decent housing has been interpreted by the supreme court as including the right to water. In April 2005, the Belgian Parliament agreed to initiate work towards amending the Constitution by including in it an explicit reference to the right to water.

[43] *See*, e.g., Ethiopia—Constitution, 1995, Art. 90 providing: 'To the extent the country's resources permit, policies shall aim to provide all Ethiopians access to public health and education, clean water, housing, food and social security'; Gambia—Constitution, 1996, Art. 216(4) providing: 'The State shall endeavour to facilitate equal access to clean and safe water'; South Africa–Constitution, 1996, Section 27 providing: '(1) Everyone has the right to have access to (a) health care services, including reproductive health care; (b) sufficient food and water; and (c) social security, including, if they are unable to support themselves and their dependants, appropriate social assistance. (2) The state must take reasonable legislative and other measures, within its available resources, to achieve the progressive realization of each of these rights'; Uganda—Constitution, 1995, Art. 14 providing: 'The State shall endeavour to fulfill the fundamental rights of all Ugandans to social justice and economic development and shall, in particular, ensure that . . . all Ugandans enjoy rights and opportunities and access to education, health services, clean and safe water, decent shelter, adequate clothing, food, security and pension and retirements benefits'; Zambia—Constitution, as amended in 1996, Art. 112 providing: 'The State shall endeavour to provide clean and safe water'. In Burkina Faso, Art. 2 of the Law of 8 February 2001 concerning water management states that: 'The law recognizes to each person the right to water in a quantity necessary to its needs and to the fulfillment of fundamental requirements of life and dignity.' The Supreme Court of India considers that the right to water is a fundamental right (originating in Art. 21 of the Indian Constitution on the right to life).

[44] *See* Henri Smets, *Le droit à l'eau*, Académie de l'eau, Paris 2002, and *Pour un droit effectif à l'eau potable*, Academic de l'eau, Paris 2004 (site www.academie/eau.org). *See also id., Implementing the Right to Drinking Water in OECD Countries*, OECD Seminar on the Social and Environmental Interface, ENV/EPOC/GEP(99)13, available at http://www.olis.oecd.org/olis/1999doc.nsf/LinkTo/env-epoc-gep(99)13; *Observations on the Right to Water as a Human Right*, E/CN.4/Sub.2/2000/NGO/19 (52th Session of the Sub-Commission on the promotion and protection of human rights), available at http://www.unhchr.ch/Huridocda/Huridoca.nsf; *L'eau et les pauvres*, 30 Environmental

water, which are currently in preparation, could specifically recognize the right to water.

From a practical standpoint, water is available everywhere as a result of hundreds of years of continuous effort and large subsidies from the State and other official bodies. Three-quarters of the French population are supplied by three French water multinationals which operate over 16,000 management contracts auctioned on a periodic basis. Municipalities are entitled to choose between a water system under public–private partnership, or a purely public system, and some revert to public management after a period under public–private partnership. The law states that all costs are to be paid for (i.e., there is financial autonomy of the water utility; the communal budget should not support the water utility except in small communes, 'water pays for water'). In practice there are still subsidies to cover 10% of the cost. Laws have been adopted to enhance competition and avoid abuses. Courts have given stiff sentences in cases of corruption and municipal councils have been more careful in their decisions.[45] Comparisons of water prices are made, and it is generally found that water delivered by the private sector is more expensive than water from the public sector (such comparison can only be made between municipalities of similar size operating similar installations).[46]

In spite of continuous efforts to improve water supply and sanitation,[47] there are still people who are not fully enjoying their right to water in France. These are:

(1) people living in remote villages not yet equipped with water networks (about 140 villages, or approximately 300,000 people, are not connected to a public water network);
(2) people receiving permanently unhealthy drinking water from the public network because of biological contamination, pollution from nitrates or pesticides (a few million people);
(3) gypsies, Roma, travelers and other people living in caravans or mobile homes, and people living in barracks or in squats (about 150,000 people);

Policy and Law 125 (2000); Henri Smets, *Social Protection in Urban Water Sector in OECD Countries*, OECD, March 2002, CCNM/ENV/EAP(2003)18, available at http://www.unece.org/env/wgso/eaptf_tbilisi/eaptf.18.consumerprotection.e.pdf; *Le droit de chacun à l'eau*, 2 *Revue européenne de droit de l'environnement* 123 (2002); *Reconnaissance et mise en œuvre du droit à l'eau*, 52 Revue trimestrielle des droits de l'homme 837 (2002); Académie de l'eau, *La solidarité pour l'eau potable*, available at http://www.academie-eau.org 2003; Henri Smets, *Le droit à l'eau au Forum de Kyoto*, Revue h2o.net, Avril 2003, available at http://www.h2o.net/magazine/urgences/enjeux/politiques/2003_kyoto/cede/francais/smets.htm.

[45] *See*, e.g., the general inspectorate report for the City of Paris on the water services, which outlines many deficiencies in the initial contracts, available at http://www.paris.fr/FR/La_Mairie/inspection_generale/rapports/filiere_eau.ASP.

[46] It should be remembered that there are large variations in water prices across the country and that variation with the type of management is generally smaller than other variations.

[47] The cumulative value of French investment in water works is: €82 billion for water supply ducts (825,000 km); €28 billion for water treatment; €70 billion for sewerage (250,000 km, connecting 47 million inhabitants in 1998); and €13 billion for waste water treatment. Total: €193 billion or €3,300 per inhabitant. *See* Office International de l'eau, OIEAU Nouvelles, December 2002.

(4) people who have to spend an inordinate amount of their income on water (over one million people, unemployed, pensioners, illegal immigrants, students, etc.);
(5) people who cannot pay their water bills and have been cut off (2,000 poor families per year);
(6) people living in housing without proper water equipment, toilets, etc. (usually very poor persons and illegal immigrants; at least 50,000 people);
(7) people living in houses built without a permit, or in caravans permanently attached to the ground without the relevant permit (at least 20,000 people).

Legal and financial measures have been taken to solve, at least partly, these remaining issues. To improve access to piped water, a national fund financed by a tax on water has provided subsidies for the construction of water networks in rural areas. In addition, State subsidies are provided for wastewater treatment.

Water utilities are under obligation to provide water which meets strict health standards (especially EU standards). In cases of underground water pollution, they have to provide bottles of mineral water. (Courts now strictly enforce this legal obligation under the health code, and people forced to buy mineral water can be compensated by utilities.[48])

The issue of providing water to travelers (people moving from one village to another, gypsies, etc.) is being addressed. All municipalities with over 5,000 inhabitants are required to provide a temporary parking area with running water and toilets. To overcome objections from mayors or local communities who would prefer not to have such people near their town, generous State subsidies are provided.

In France, subsidies for water supply and sanitation are relatively small (10%) and VAT is at the lowest rate. Nevertheless water is expensive (about $3 per cubic meter for water supply, sanitation, and tax). A very small percentage of the population pays over 3% to 5% of total household expenses for water. A special system of targeted social aid has been set up to help poor people pay their water bills. It is used by some 20,000 households (this aid comes on top of general social aid which is provided to over 3,000,000 people).

Water tariffs are generally based on a fixed charge (proportional to potential water consumption) and a proportional charge (proportional to the actual water consumption, which must be metered). A minority of municipalities use a progressive tariff so as to lower the price paid for the first cubic meter consumed per month. No social tariff exists in France as in Belgium (Flanders), where each

[48] French courts take strict measures against pollution of drinking water caused by agricultural activities or products (pesticides, nitrates, etc.). The Administrative Tribunal of Rennes found that the State was liable when a water distributor provided drinking water with too many nitrates originating from excessive pig farming allowed by the State in Brittany (Guincamp). The damage was €142,382 (April 2001). For details, *see* www.laportedudroit.com/htm/juriflash/droit_public/responsabilite_prefet1.htm.

person receives 40 liters per day at half price (only the poor are supplied with water without charge). A similar system was introduced in Brussels.

Cutting people off from water supply is viewed badly by the population and by local officials. Social assistance offices managed by municipalities help people pay their water bills; but if they run out of money, they are not able to provide assistance and water may be cut off. Courts oppose such disconnections because they are a disproportionate means of pressure. Indeed, people can no longer live in dignity if they lack water for their kitchen, bath, shower, toilets, etc. Thus courts request utilities to reinstate water,[49] or to provide a water standpost in the street.

Disconnecting families with young children or invalids is now forbidden. Any disconnection must be done in such a way that water can be reinstated within twenty-four hours of payment.

Renting a place to live without running water (hot and cold), bath, shower, or toilet in a flat is now illegal. Furthermore, landlords have to fix water leaks before renting out a flat.

People living temporarily in caravans on their own land now have the right to be connected to the water network; the mayor is not authorized to prevent this from occurring as was the case before.[50] If a house is built on land legally owned but without a building permit (e.g., a summer house in a non-construction area), or if a caravan is parked for more than three months at the same place, the mayor is still in a position to prevent the utilities from providing water and electricity (the housing code prevails over the right to water).

Provision of water to squats and slums (illegal occupiers) is made possible in Paris by special arrangements entered into between the water company, occupiers, and the local NGO acting in favour of the squatters, pursuant to which the water company is guaranteed to be paid by the local NGO for water delivered. Six squats on the Left Bank in Paris (over 200 persons) benefit from this arrangement and have paid their water bills in full.

At present, the major unresolved issues in relation to the right to water in France are:

(1) providing drinking water with fewer pollutants (in line with EU directives);

[49] In a number of cases, the civil court (Tribunal de Grande Instance) ordered the water distributor to reinstate water because it is essential to life (TGI Avignon, Référé, 12 mai 1995, n° 1492/95, www.cartel.oieau.fr/guide/c035b.htm), or because the trouble caused by water disconnection exceeds the illegality of partial payment (TGI Privas, Référé 5.03.1998 CISE c/Association Consommateurs Fontauliere, http://cgl92.free.fr/etudeau2.htm) or is an excessive means of pressure (TGI Roanne, 11 mars 1996, Revue CLCV, n° 97, janvier 1997).

[50] In one case the mayor was opposing connection because constructions were prohibited on such land. However, the court held that a caravan is not a construction. See Decision 243333 of 22 août 2002, 'Commune de Marignane' by Conseil d'Etat. *See also* Décision of Tribunal Administratif of Marseille n° 022051 of 8 octobre 2002 'Commune de Saint-Victoret' and the 'Ordonnances de Référé' of Tribunal administratif of Nantes n° 023982 et 023962 of 10 janvier 2002 'Commune d'Olonne sur Mer'. *See also* J.O. Sénat, Questions n° 07506 (9 avril 1998), Rép. p.1719, 28 mai 1998.

(2) reducing the burden of water bills on the poor (strengthening social tariffs); and
(3) reducing the number of disconnections due to poverty with a view to moving towards their prohibition, as in the UK.

Progress on the first issue can be expected in France, but the draft water laws currently in preparation remain silent on the last two issues.

7. Conclusion

France is probably the country with the largest number of utilities managed under public–private partnership (PPP). It is able to implement the right to water and maintain competition for the management of water networks by the private sector. But further progress is needed because there are still people who do not enjoy fully their right to water.

French practice shows that water utilities, either public or in private–public partnership, operate without creating special problems with respect to the implementation of the right to water. Public authorities retain strong control over them and at the same time are setting up social systems to organize solidarity. Subsidies are provided, water tariffs are set through a bidding process, financial control is exercised, affordability issues are taken care of, and the water supply and sanitation networks are being improved in order to meet EU standards. There are still unresolved issues in the area of water supply and sanitation, but these occur with water utilities managed under a public–private partnership or under a purely public management.

Water is not 'a commercial product like any other'; it is an essential good that must be provided to everyone, poor people and the rural population included. The State is creating economic conditions and competitive systems so that no one is left without the goods necessary for a life in dignity. The examples of France and the UK can be transposed to many industrialized countries which efficiently manage their public services and have good governance. In other cases, proposals concerning the proper management of water utilities should take into account the precise legal, political, social, and economic contexts, because a natural monopoly is always a target for abuses through excessive prices, excessive costs, excessive profits, and corruption.

PART III

WATER, SUBSIDIES, AND AGRICULTURE

8

Ground Water Regulation and Water Crisis Rhetoric: Syria as a Case Study

RONALD JAUBERT and MOHAMED AL-DBIYAT

1. Introduction

Since the early 1990s and the Dublin Conference on water management, the importance and seriousness of the water problem has been increasingly recognized by international organizations and NGOs. Water scarcity has generally given place to water crisis in the international rhetoric. As a result, governments of developing countries are increasingly under pressure from international organizations to enforce water management policies aimed at reducing withdrawals and improving the efficiency of water use.

In the case of Syria, attention at the international and national level was until recently mainly, if not exclusively, focused on the utilization of surface water and the international dispute over the Euphrates' water. However, a World Bank review of the irrigation sector in Syria emphasized the importance of ground water and the deficit of the water balance. According to this report, 'groundwater is probably the single most important water management challenge facing Syria'.[1] Between 1980 and 2001, the irrigated area in Syria rose from 539,000 to 1,267,000 hectares and the percentage of land irrigated by ground water from 40% to 60%. Indeed, the number of wells has rapidly increased in the past two decades. Wells used for irrigation are privately operated, and it is estimated that about 50% of them are illegal.

Several laws and decrees regulating the drilling of wells and the extension of land irrigated by ground water have been promulgated since 1950. The enforcement of these laws was until recently undermined by the objective of increasing the production of strategic crops, in particular cotton and wheat which are the two most important irrigated crops in the country.

Several studies have highlighted the overdraft problem and the alarming lowering of water tables.[2] In 2000 and 2001 the government promulgated a new

[1] World Bank, Syrian Arab Republic Irrigation Sector Report, Rural Development, Water and Environment Group, Middle East and North Africa Region, Report No. 22602-SYR, Washington D.C. (2001) at 18.

[2] *See* Ibrahim Nahal, *L'homme et la désertification au Proche-Orient*, SECHERESSE, Vol 4 No 2. (1991).

set of measures aiming at controlling the use of ground water for irrigation. Particular attention is paid to the drier areas in which the situation is perceived as critical. In recent years, irrigation by ground water has substantially expanded in the drier areas, and several villages have been reported to have lost their supply of domestic fresh water as a result of overdrafting for irrigation.

The management of ground water is generally a complex issue due, in particular, to the scanty information available concerning both the consumption and the availability of renewable water. Furthermore, the availability and utilization of ground water are very much location specific and highly variable.[3] In this respect, Syria is no exception, as the utilization of ground water by individual farmers is poorly monitored. Furthermore, the potential regarding land that can be irrigated is often highly variable.

This contribution focuses on the efficiency of measures aimed at controlling overdrafting problems in the drier cultivated areas. The case study we refer to is part of a research program on the conflicts of interest related to the use of water. The program includes two other cases studies in southern Niger and the State of Gujarat in north-western India.[4] The study area is located in the province of Hama, east of the city of Salamieh (See Map 8.1). The analysis is based on a detailed spatial study of current and past irrigation practices.

2. The expansion of irrigation

Over 70% of the country's territory is subjected to an arid or semi arid climate, with a six-month dry season from May to October. Furthermore, the rainfall pattern is characterized by a high year to year variability. Under such circumstances, rain-fed agriculture is an uncertain activity, as shown by the annual fluctuations of barley yields (see Figure 8.1). Irrigation offers a double advantage as it allows a significant increase in yields and helps to stabilize crop production. At present, irrigated crops are grown on 18% of the cultivated area and provide 50% of the value of the national agricultural production.

The expansion of irrigation is the keystone of the Syrian agricultural policy since the adoption of a centralized development strategy in the early 1960s. The main objectives were to achieve self-sufficiency, in particular in wheat production, and increase the production of cotton, which is the main agricultural export commodity accounting for about 10% of Syria's total export value.

[3] *See* Stephen Foster, *Essential Concepts For Groundwater Regulators*, Groundwater Legal and Policy Perspectives, Salman Salman M. A. ed., World Bank Technical Paper No. 456, World Bank, Washington, D.C. (1999).

[4] This research program benefits from the financial support of the Geneva International Academic Network (GIAN) and is conducted by the Graduate Institute of Development Studies, Geneva, The Centre for Human Ecology of the University of Geneva, the Swiss Institute of Technology, Lausanne and the University of Lausanne, the Maison de l'Orient Méditerranéen, CNRS–University of Lyon 2, in collaboration, in the case of Syria, with the Aga Khan Development Network.

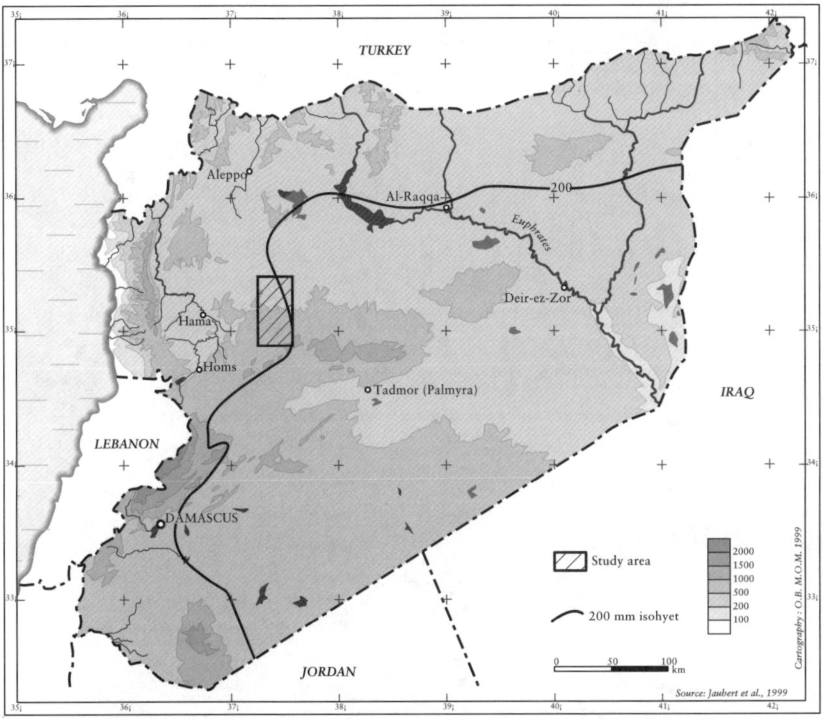

MAP 8.1: Location of the Study Area within Syria

SOURCE: Adapted from background map in Jaubert, R., Debaine, F., Besançon, J., Al-Dbiyat, M., Geyer, B., Gintzburger, G., Traboulsi, M., 1999, *Lana Use and Vegetation Cover, Semi Arid and Arid Areas of Aleppo and Hama Provinces, Syria*, Monde Arabe Contemporian, Maison de l'Orient Méditerranéen, Lyon.

As part of the import substitution policy, farmers growing strategic crops benefited from subsidized inputs (fertilizers and phytochemicals) distributed by governmental organizations. These subsidies were dismantled and replaced in 1996 by support prices. Between 1996 and 2002, wheat producer prices were on average 37% higher than world prices (see Figure 8.2).

Cotton producer prices are linked to world market prices. The price of seed cotton rose from 13 to 44 SL/Kg between 1991 and 1997. However, as a result of the recent fall in world prices, producer prices in Syria have dropped by 30% since 1997 (see Figure 8.3), the planted area was reduced by 25%, and cotton was replaced mainly by irrigated wheat.

Between 1988 and 2000, the production of wheat was increased by 130% (see Figure 8.4). The self-sufficiency ratio rose from 0.8 to 1.43. The expansion of irrigated areas played a major part in these achievements. In the 1960s, efforts were concentrated on small- and medium-scale irrigation projects in line with the agricultural development strategy proposed by the World Bank in the

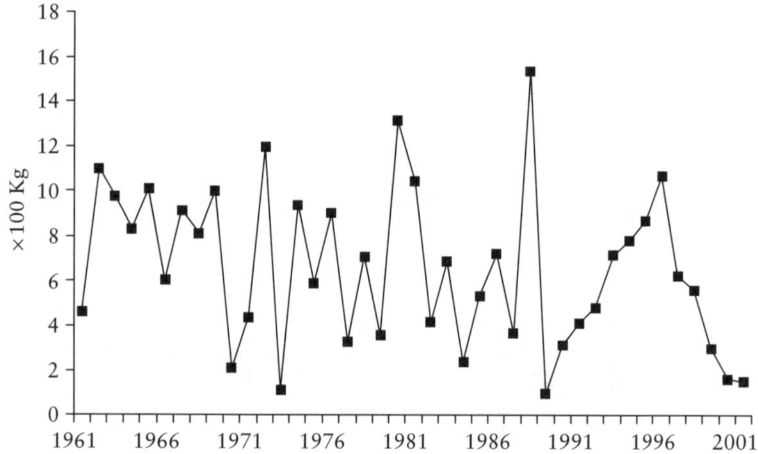

FIGURE 8.1: Barley Yields

SOURCE: FAOStat.

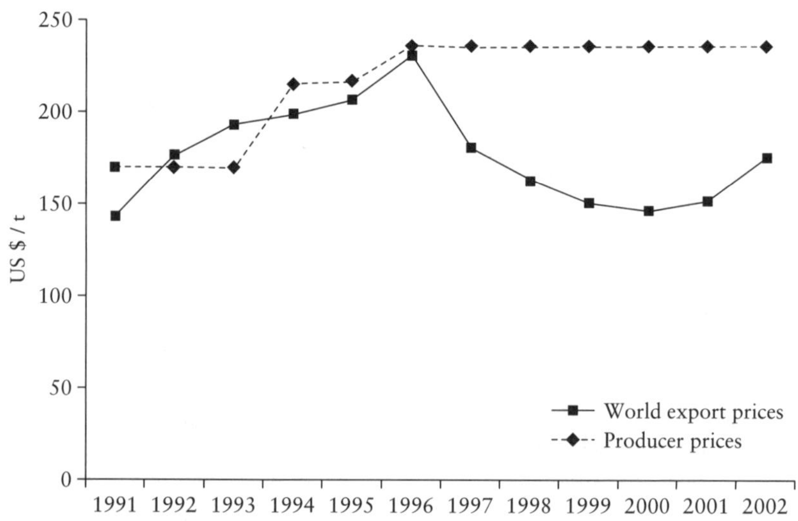

FIGURE 8.2: Wheat World Export and Producer Prices

SOURCE: World Bank and FAO.

mid-1950s.[5] Following the completion of the Tabka Dam in 1973, efforts have been largely concentrated on the Euphrates' valley project. The latter was designed with a dual goal, to bring 640,000 hectares under irrigation by the year 2000 and to produce a large share of the electricity requirement of the country.

[5] IBRD, THE ECONOMIC DEVELOPMENT OF SYRIA (John Hopkins Press, Baltimore, 1955).

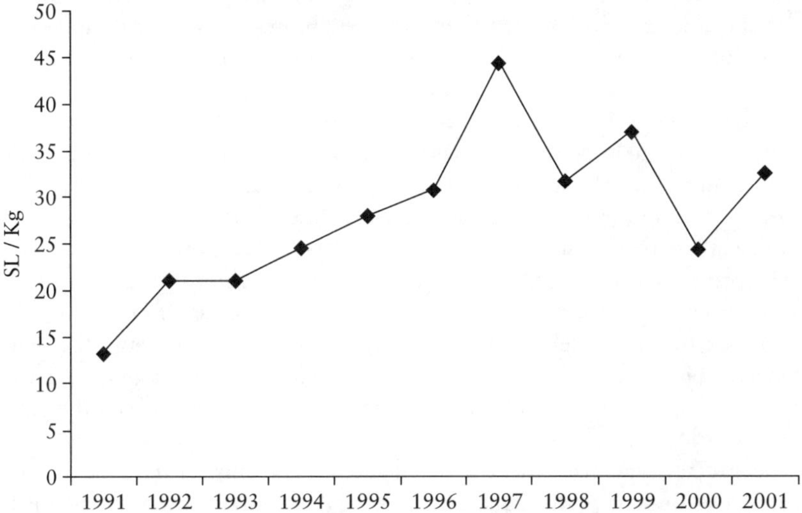

FIGURE 8.3: Producer Prices of Seed Cotton

SOURCE: FAOStat.

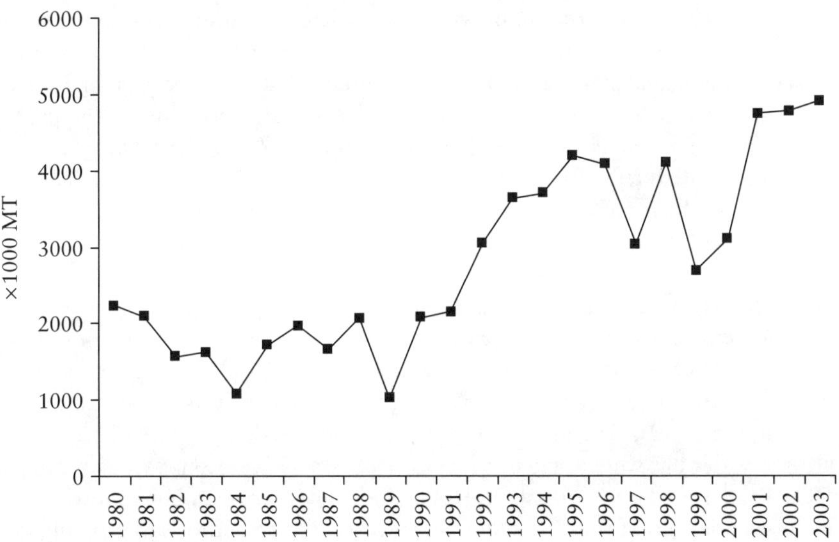

FIGURE 8.4: Wheat Production

SOURCE: FAOStat.

Furthermore, beyond these economic objectives, the project had indubitable symbolic and political dimensions. The Euphrates' project was indeed the symbol of the accession of the country to the era of modernity and a means to introduce a socialist mode of production in the agricultural sector.

Since the mid-1970s, the Euphrates program has absorbed about 70% of the funds allocated to agricultural development. In the last five years' plan, 76% of the agricultural development budget is allocated to surface irrigation. However, by the year 2000, less than 200,000 hectares were irrigated by the Euphrates' water, i.e. less than a third of the targeted 640,000 hectares.

The project has encountered several difficulties. Technical problems, such as the collapse of irrigation canals on gypsum soils and the salinization of soils in certain sectors, have delayed the fulfilling of objectives regarding the annual extension of irrigated areas. The conveyance efficiency of canals is relatively low, and on farm water use efficiency ranges from 40% to 60% according to the recent World Bank assessment.[6]

The project was also affected by financial problems. Several factors have limited its economic performance, such as the low land use intensity and the fact that farmers are charged only part of the operation and maintenance cost. However, the agro-industrial component of the project is probably one of the main factors limiting the economic return. This was the case, for example, with the paper pulp factory built in the valley as part of the program. The initial plan was to transform barley straw to be collected on rain-fed farms. While barley straw is generally considered as a low value by-product, this is not the case in Syria. Barley straw from local varieties has high nutritive value and is entirely fed to sheep flocks. In order to provide a substitute for barley straw to the paper pulp factory, 8,000 hectares of poplar trees were planted on the 28,000-hectare Masakana irrigated state farm. There is no doubt that the allocation of 28% of the cultivated area to the production of cellulose seriously reduces the profitability of the farm. Furthermore, the latter suffers from the usual problems affecting most state farms designed on the Kolkhoz model. The technical and economic problems affecting the program have reduced the investment capacity and increased the maintenance cost. In the last five years' plan, over 70% of the irrigation budget is allocated to operation and maintenance.

The control of the utilization of ground water was, until recently, of low priority, and the expansion of the area irrigated from individual wells made up for the low performance of the State-managed irrigation program. Indeed, two-thirds of the increase in the irrigated area originates from individual wells (see Figure 8.5).

From the 1950s, several laws and decrees were passed to regulate the use of ground water but were not generally enforced. As mentioned previously, almost 50% of the wells are illegal. In 2000 and 2001, presumably following the recommendations of the World Bank review team,[7] the authorities promulgated

[6] World Bank, *supra* note 1.

[7] The World Bank assessment of the irrigation sector in Syria began in 1999.

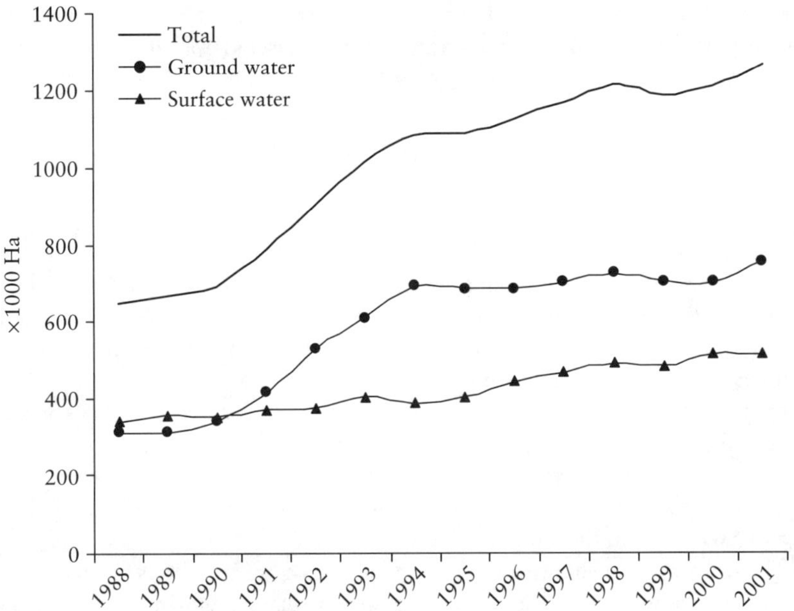

FIGURE 8.5: Irrigated Area by Ground and Surface Water

SOURCE: Statistical Abstracts, Central Bureau of Statistics, Damascus.

nine decrees aimed at combating the overdrafting of ground water and improving irrigation methods.

With regard to the drier areas, the decrees on water management:

—legalize existing wells and prohibit the drilling of new wells;
—ban cotton cultivation in the fourth agricultural zone (areas receiving less than 250 mm of annual rainfall);
—limit withdrawals to 7,000 m^3 per hectare to be controlled by volumetric meters;
—impose the mounting of volumetric meters on each well;
—prohibit the trade of water between farmers;
—define a maximum water withdrawal per basin according to the estimated mean annual recharge of ground water.[8]

The review team recommended a removal of support prices on strategic crops, which would have affected the self-sufficiency objective. Rather than modifying production plans and the current price policy, the measures taken by the Ministry of Agriculture address directly the consumption of water. They aim at reducing water drafting in order to maintain withdrawals within the estimated volume of renewable ground water. No actions are specified regarding the improvement of irrigation methods. It is assumed, as generally agreed, that

[8] Aljundi, H., LEGISLATIONS OF IRRIGATION WATER USE IN SALAMIEH, MIMEO (Ministry of Agriculture and Agrarian Reform, Agricultural Directorate of Hama, Salamieh, 2003).

limiting withdrawals will favour the adoption by farmers of water-saving techniques. In the following section, we will discuss the efficiency of these measures in relation to the specificities of the study area.

3. The efficiency of water management measures

We will analyze in our study area the use of ground water in the drier zones where average rainfall ranges from 200 to 250 mm per year. The 200 mm isohyet marks the limit between the cultivated areas to the west and the steppe to the east. Irrigated areas have been expanding since the early 1980s and irrigators use two sources of ground water: deep and superficial water tables. The two sources need to be clearly distinguished since they have different dynamics. The deep aquifer is replenished in the Bel As mountains located south of the study area and the superficial aquifers are replenished locally. The exploitation of the deep aquifer started in the early 1990s and is concentrated in the north of the study area (see Map 8.2). In this contribution we will focus on areas irrigated by ground water from the superficial aquifers.

The utilization of superficial ground water in the study area is not recent. The most well-known ancient infrastructures are the qanats, which are underground drainage galleries located at the bottom of temporary water streams (*wadi*). They collected superficial water flows and directed them towards agriculturally favourable zones, generally depressions with relatively good soils. Several qanats are found in the study area near the remains of the Byzantine city of Andarina. These qanats were dug most probably during the Byzantine period, and several were maintained until the beginning of the Islamic period.[9]

The Byzantine qanats were abandoned in the 13th century following the receding of sedentary populations. The restoration of the qanats began in the middle of the 19th century following the reoccupation of the area by sedentary farmers coming from the coastal mountains. Between 1849, the year of the resettlement of the city of Salamya, and 1900, villages of sedentary farmers expanded to the east and reached the 200 mm rainfall zone.[10] Villages were established in the more favourable areas where subsurface flows increase the availability of water. These first settlements were followed by the establishment of satellite villages, some of which are located beyond the 200 mm rainfall limit in zones benefiting from runoff water flows or easily accessible ground water. The interstitial least favourable areas were gradually settled by semi-nomads from Bedouin tribes for whom sheep breeding remained the main activity with rain-fed barley cultivation.

The qanats were restored, at least partly, in the first half of the 20th century. Their maximum reutilization was reached in the early 1950s. According to

[9] Geyer, B., Besançon, J., Calvet, Y., & Debaine, F., *Les marges arides de la Syrie du Nord: résultats préliminaires d'une prospection géo-archéologique*, B.A.G.F. 75/2 (1998).

[10] Norman N. Lewis, *Nomads and Settlers in Syria and Jordan 1800–1980* (Cambridge University Press, 1987).

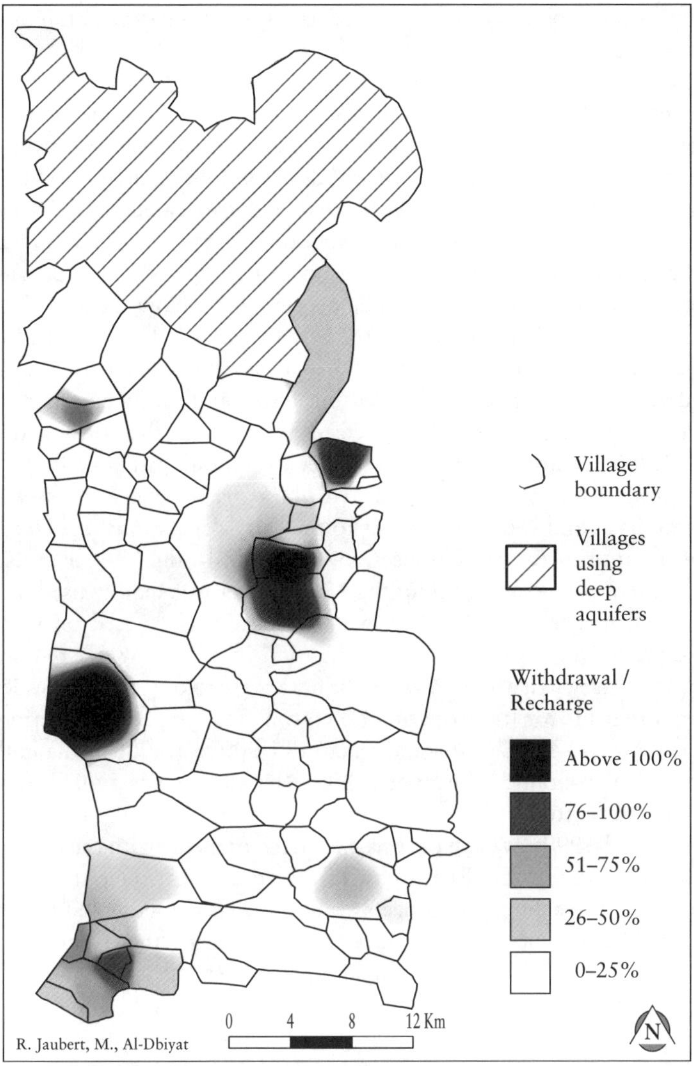

MAP 8.2: Irrigation by Deep and Superficial Groundwater and Withdrawal–Recharge Ratio

SOURCE: Field survey 2003 and village statistical data 2002.

farmers, the qanats in those days delivered water all year round. Aerial pictures from August 1958, which was a severe drought year, show that about half of the qanats located in the study area were functional in summer.

With very few exceptions, the qanats dried up in the 1960s and 1970s. The phenomenon is directly related to the lowering of the superficial water tables resulting from the drilling of wells and the generalization of motor pumps. The drying up of the qanats is often perceived as a sign of the exhaustion of ground water resources.

In the case of our study area, the analysis of changes which have taken place from the end of the 1950s at the watershed level provides a somewhat different interpretation. Changes were monitored using aerial pictures from 1958, satellite images from 1997, and statistical data for 1996 and 2002. The analysis of aerial and satellite pictures reveals that areas irrigated in 1958 near the ancient city of Andarina have been abandoned as a result of the lowering of water tables and the consequent drying up of the qanats which provided the water for irrigation. While wells can be deepened to follow the lowering water table, this is technically impossible in the case of qanats. However, the lowering of the water tables can be explained by the extension of irrigated areas upstream. Irrigated areas were not only displaced but also significantly enlarged. Indeed, following the drilling of wells, 700 hectares were lost in the north of the study area but 1,900 hectares were brought under irrigation upstream.[11]

Thus, ground water resources appear to be currently more intensively used than in the past, and less water is lost to the salty depressions (*sebkhas*) in the north of the study area where it loses all agricultural value. Water is also more efficiently used. While at the end of the 1950s water was mainly used on cotton requiring full irrigation in summer, water is now mainly used on wheat and barley in the form of complementary irrigation in winter. Water requirements for complementary irrigation on wheat or barley are two to three times less than water requirements for full irrigation on cotton. The supply of irrigation water on wheat is around 4,000 m^3/ha and reaches 11,000 to 13,000 m^3/ha in the case of cotton. The economic return per cubic meter of water is 5.60 SL for wheat and 3.90 SL for cotton.

Since the mid-1990s, we can observe new developments with the expansion of irrigated olive trees in the drier areas. In the study area, olive trees were first planted in 1993, reaching 1,670 hectares in 2002. It can be noted that there is evidence of the presence of large olive orchards during the Byzantine period. Olive trees require light irrigation in summer equivalent to 300 m^3/ha. Wheat and cotton irrigated fields need to be close to a well. In the case of olives, water can be brought to the plot by tanks moved by tractors or trucks. Trees are watered manually from the mobile tanks, or by drip irrigation systems. One-third of the farmers who have planted olive trees have drip irrigation systems. Farmers who do not own a well can purchase water from well owners trading water. The development of olive orchards takes place principally on shallow soils with a very low water storage capacity and a low potential for barley cultivation due to the presence of a calcareous crust close to the surface (and sometimes on the surface). The latter is disadvantageous for cereal production but an advantage for tree cultivation. The crust, generally between 20 cm and

[11] Ronald Jaubert, Bernard Geyer, Françoise Debaine, & Mohamed Al-Dbiyat, *L'exploitation des eaux de subsurface des marges arides de Syrie: dégradation ou transformation?*, SECHERESSE Vol. 13 No. 1 (2001).

40 cm thick, is broken to enable the trees to take advantage of a silt and marl horizon situated under the crust. The latter acts as a screen limiting water loss by evaporation. The presence of these calcareous crusts explains the spacing of the trees, which varies from 6 m to 8 m. In Tunisia, for example, in regions with comparable climatic conditions, the spacing between the olive trees varies from 16 m to 20 m.

Compared to wheat or cotton, olives offer a significantly higher economic return per unit of water; indeed, the net income per cubic meter is about 170 SL. It can be noted that olives do not benefit from support prices, and in the drier areas farmers do not have access to credit facilities or technical support to plant olive trees which are illegal. However, the land use regulation, with the recent exception of cotton, is not enforced and the uprooting of trees is illegal.

An important question is whether current water withdrawal exceeds or not the recharge of the superficial water tables. The estimated average annual recharge in the study area and the 2002 water consumption are respectively 20 million m^3 and 6.6 million m^3.[12] These results seem to be in sharp contradiction with the analysis of the ministry and the fact that overdrafting has been reported in several villages located in the study area. A more detailed analysis of the water balance reveals a large variability according to villages. In the majority of villages withdrawals are below the estimated recharge and in almost 50% of the villages, farmers do not irrigate. Nevertheless, there are also four villages where withdrawals exceed the estimated recharge (see Map 8.2). These 'black spots' correspond to villages with proportionally large areas of good soils suitable for the cultivation of irrigated wheat and cotton. Because of these favourable soil conditions and the availability of water, well owners can fully benefit from the combined effects of support prices and the subsidized energy mentioned previously.

The measure taken by the ministry with the aim of reducing withdrawals appears to be directed towards the 'black spots'. This bias can be attributed, at least partly, to the emphasis put on the water crisis at the international level. The World Bank report on the irrigation sector in Syria, for example, insists on the water deficit and the need for the Syrian authorities to adopt a water management policy.[13] It can be noted that the figures given in this report do not fully support the diagnosis since water deficit concerns two basins, Damascus and Aleppo. Indeed, the latter represent a large share of the population, but they are not representative of the situation in other basins, such as the coast or the steppe basin in which is located the study area.

The efficiency of the measures taken by the ministry to reduce withdrawals in the drier areas is questionable. Past experiences indicate that the limitation of the area under irrigation is difficult to control in the absence of cadastral surveys at the village level. So far, only total bans on cultivation of cotton, for example,

[12] The estimated recharge is of 200 m^3 per hectare corresponding to 10% of the average annual rainfall; the estimated total consumption is based on the following consumption per crop: wheat 4,000 m^3/ha, barley 3,500 m^3/ha, cotton 13,000 m^3/ha, olive trees 300 m^3/ha.

[13] World Bank, *supra* note 1.

in part of the drier areas, or of barley in the areas receiving less than 200 mm of annual rainfall, have been effectively enforced.[14] Trespassing in the case of illegal crops such as cotton is much easier to identify than in the case of area limitations when plots are planted with permitted crops such as wheat.

The ban on cotton had a limited effect due to the increase in wheat and barley. As mentioned previously, water is principally used in the study area on wheat and barley. The area planted to cotton was reduced from 297 hectares in 1996 to 169 hectares in 2002, but the area planted to wheat and barley was increased by 319 hectares. The water withdrawal was reduced by 460,000 m^3, representing 6.5% of the total estimated water withdrawal in 1996. Water quotas and volumetric meters are recognized as the most efficient means to control the consumption of water. However, the quota of 7,000 m^3 per hectare indicates that production objectives are still dominant. This volume is insufficient to grow cotton but is almost double the requirement for the production of wheat. Thus, the imposition of a water quota of 7,000 m^3, assuming it is actually monitored, will have a limited effect, if any, on water withdrawals.

Paradoxically, measures such as the restriction on the trade of water and the ban on new wells will affect much more severely the large majority of farmers who do not have access to water and those who use a small amount of water and have adopted water-saving techniques. These measures will indeed further restrict their access to water and opportunities in terms of irrigation for the large majority of farmers. Results from a survey of 1,320 farms in the study area indicate that irrigated lands are very unevenly distributed. Seventy four per cent of the farmers do not have irrigated land and 5% of the farmers cultivate 80% of the irrigated land in the study area.

4. Conclusion

The efficiency of the measures recently taken by the Syrian authorities to control the utilization of ground water in the drier areas is questionable. The measures will likely have a limited effect in reducing overdrafting where it occurs, but will certainly reduce the accessibility to water for farmers in villages where water is currently under-used or unused.

This situation results from the combined effects of the emphasis put on overdrafting, irrespective of the diversity characterizing the use of ground water, and the persistence of unsustainable production objectives.

The international water crisis rhetoric played an important part in making water professionals more aware of the challenges in terms of water management. However, as shown in our study area, the emphasis put on critical situations may induce strong biases in the perception of the water issue at the

[14] Ronald Jaubert & Françoise Debaine, *Spatial Division and Territorial Control in the Syrian Steppe*, Arab World Geographer, Toronto (2002).

local level. Measures such as the limitation of irrigated areas, the introduction of water quotas and volumetric meters, and the restriction of water trading may seem appropriate to prevent the over-use of ground water. In central Syria, however, the utilization of superficial ground water for irrigation ranges from over-pumping to no pumping. The challenge in terms of water management ranges from preventing overdrafting in certain villages to improving the access to water and increasing irrigation in the majority of villages.

Applied irrespective of the current withdrawal/recharge ratio, these measures will limit unnecessarily the access to water for farmers who are the most liable to use water on productions offering a high economic return per volume of water and who adopt water-saving irrigation techniques.

The likely counter-productive effect of the newly enforced water management measure is accentuated by the fact that production objectives still undermine water conservation objectives, as shown by current water quotas. The problem of overdrafting is related, at least partly, to the support prices and subsidies offered for strategic crops. The latter favoured the rapid increase in ground water withdrawals that took place in the past three decades. The non-removal of support prices on wheat and the large water quotas considerably reduce the capacity of the current water regulation to control overdrafting where it occurs in marginal areas.

9

Water, Agriculture, and Subsidies in the International Trading System

NATHALIE BERNASCONI-OSTERWALDER

1. Introduction

The world's fresh water resources are rapidly decreasing while per capita use of fresh water is increasing at an unprecedented rate.[*1] Large-scale farming and irrigation, the destruction of forests and wetlands, toxic dumping, and urban and industrial pollution are spoiling the Earth's surface water and forcing us to use our water reserves faster than they can be replenished.

Recent studies indicate that water-related subsidies can lead to the wasteful use of water for agricultural and other purposes.[2] Instead of encouraging the conservation of existing water supplies, subsidies can encourage wasteful practices such as excessive irrigation. Too much irrigation can often lead to additional environmental problems, including the waterlogging and salinization of irrigated croplands. Also, the intensive use of—often subsidized—fertilizers and pesticides in irrigated (and other) areas contributes to the pollution of soils and water resources.

While the problems related to water subsidies are numerous and cut across various policy areas, this chapter has a narrow legal scope: it examines whether international trade rules regarding subsidies apply to agricultural water-related subsidies, and whether they offer a framework that is useful for reducing and eliminating environmentally harmful agricultural water subsidies. The chapter only marginally addresses the very important social aspects of water subsidies.[3]

* The author would like to thank Jacques Berthelot, Sophia Murphy, Robert Speed, and Hiltone E. Zunckel for their useful insights and comments.

[1] *See*, e.g., UN Environment Programme (UNEP), *Vital Water Graphics 2003*, available at http://www.unep.org/dewa/water/default.asp (last visited 14 June 2004) and World Water Assessment Programme, The UN World Water Development Report, Water for People, Water for Life (2003).

[2] *See*, e.g., Sandra Postel, *Dividing the Waters: Food Security, Ecosystem Health and the New Politics of Scarcity*, Worldwatch Institute, Washington, D.C., 1996; Andre De Moor, *Key Issues in Subsidy Policies and Strategies for Reform*, paper prepared for the UN Fourth Expert Group Meeting on Financial Issues of Agenda 21, Santiago, Chile, 1997, available at http://www.ecocouncil.ac.cr/econ/keyissue (last visited 14 June 2004); Norman Myers, *Perverse Subsidies: Tax $s Undercutting Our Economies and Environments Alike*, 1998 (International Institute for Sustainable Development).

[3] On this topic, *see* Mona Sur, Dina Umali-Deininger, and Ariel Dinar, *Water-Related Subsidies in Agriculture: Environmental and Equity Consequences*, paper presented to the OECD Workshop on Environmentally Harmful Subsidies, Paris, 7–8 November 2002.

It begins with an overview of environmentally harmful subsidies in general and agricultural water subsidies in particular, focusing primarily on irrigation subsidies. It continues with a synopsis of the current legal framework regarding subsidies within the world trading system. It then examines how the framework addresses agricultural water subsidies and whether it supports their gradual elimination. Finally, the chapter concludes that the WTO's current system regarding subsidies, while marginally useful, is not the ideal approach for the international community to address the problems relating to the use of water subsidies. However, an enhanced notification regime within the WTO may be instrumental for increasing transparency in the use of water-related subsidies. Increased transparency and knowledge could contribute to a better understanding of ways in which the international community might address water-related problems arising from the use of subsidies in the agricultural sector.

2. Environmentally harmful subsidies

It has long been acknowledged that subsidies can have negative effects on the economy. More recent studies indicate that subsidies can also have harmful effects on the environment.[4] Such subsidies, which are harmful for both the economy and the environment, are often referred to as 'perverse subsidies'. However, it should be kept in mind that some subsidies, while affecting the economy, may have important environmental benefits. Thus, it is essential to distinguish between environmentally damaging subsidies and subsidies used to achieve environmental goals. As will be explained below, the international trading system focuses primarily on trade-distorting effects of subsidies, while largely ignoring their environmental effects. It does, however, provide for the special treatment of certain environmental subsidies, though some of these provisions have expired.

Many sectors host subsidies which have a particularly detrimental impact on the environment, including agriculture, fossil fuels and nuclear energy, forestry, road transportation, water, and fisheries. Subsidies for agriculture, for example, encourage overloading of croplands, which leads to erosion of topsoil, pollution from synthetic fertilizers and pesticides, and release of greenhouse gases. Subsidies for fossil fuels worsen acid rain, global warming, and smog. Subsidies for roads encourage pollution. Fisheries subsidies promote over-harvesting of depleted fish stocks. Lastly, subsidies for water foster overuse and misuse of an increasingly scarce natural resource.

Within these sectors, the types of subsidies come in many shapes and sizes. They can be direct or indirect, and can include budgetary transfers, market price support, subsidized and concessional credit, underpriced materials,

[4] *See*, e.g., OECD, *Improving the Environment Through Reducing Subsidies*, Part I, Summary and Conclusions, OECD Paris, 1998.

energy and water, foregone resource rents, and preferential tax treatment.[5] Besides these 'explicit' or 'conventional' subsidies, environmental economists in the past decade have also started to point to the importance of 'implicit subsidies'.[6] These include environmental externalities, that is, the (unpaid) damage caused to the environment and human health by the economic activity.

Given the large spectrum of subsidy types, the various approaches to define subsidies are accordingly numerous. Thus, economists, governments, and other entities can define subsidies in different ways. In some cases, subsidies are defined narrowly to include only certain forms of subsidies and not others. In the context of environmentally harmful subsidies, it would seem appropriate to include in the subsidy definition implicit subsidies or 'uninternalized externalities'. However, this is more easily said than done. Addressing the issue of including implicit subsidies in the subsidy definition, one subsidy expert at the OECD noted:

> It is an approach that is intuitively appealing to economists accustomed to thinking in terms of Pigouvian (i.e. corrective) taxes and subsidies. But for many reasons it is extremely difficult to reconcile with the way public finance and other practitioners—not to mention non-professional—understand the concept of subsidy.[7]

Given the differences in defining subsidies, it might not come as a surprise that only one internationally agreed-upon definition of subsidies exists to date: the definition included in the WTO Agreement on Subsidies and Countervailing Measures (hereinafter 'Subsidies Agreement'). Article 1 of the Subsidies Agreement provides that a subsidy exists if 'there is a financial contribution by a government or any public body within the territory of a Member', or if 'there is any form of income or price support . . .'. Thus, this subsidy definition includes a wide range of conventional subsidies. However, as will be explained in detail below, certain conventional subsidies are not covered by the definition. In addition, it is difficult to argue that the definition also covers implicit subsidies.

3. Water-related subsidies

3.1 In general

The three main uses of fresh water are: household/municipal, industrial, and agricultural. Worldwide, the household/municipal use of water taken from lakes,

[5] On the different types of environmentally harmful subsidies, see Gareth Porter, *Subsidies and the Environment: The State of Knowledge*, paper presented to the OECD Workshop on Environmentally Harmful Subsidies, 7–8 November 2002. *See also* OECD, *Subsidies and the Environment, Exploring the Linkages*, 1996. On the concept of a subsidy, see De Moor, *supra* note 2.

[6] On the evolution of subsidy definition and the consideration of environmental externalities, see Ronald Steenblick, *Subsidy Measurement and Classification: Developing a Common Framework*, paper presented to the OECD Workshop on Environmentally Harmful Subsidies, Paris, 7–8 November 2002.

[7] *Id.*, at para. 23.

rivers, and aquifers amounts to about 5 per cent, industrial use to 20 per cent, and agricultural use to 75 per cent.[8] Thus, the agricultural sector is clearly the largest user of fresh water. In the United States, for example, agriculture accounts for almost 50 per cent of the total fresh water used.[9] In Africa and Asia, the agricultural sector accounts for an estimated 85–90 per cent of all the fresh water used.[10]

This chapter will concentrate primarily on subsidies in the agricultural sector, which accounts for the highest use of water by far and is also heavily subsidized. The chapter does not address water-related subsidies for household and municipal or industrial use.[11]

3.2 Agricultural water-related subsidies

Most water-related subsidies are in the agricultural sector, which, as mentioned above, accounts for the largest use of water. Within this sector, water subsidies are primarily related to irrigation. Based simply on the massive use of irrigation, irrigation subsidies are arguably those which encourage waste, pollution, and contamination of fresh water on the largest scale. The world's irrigation areas amounted to approximately 253 million hectares in 1995. By 2010, they are expected to arrive at about 290 million hectares, and by 2025, about 330 million hectares. By the year 2000, an estimated 15 per cent of the world's cultivated lands were irrigated for food crops, accounting for almost half of the value of global crop production.[12]

Governments subsidize irrigation infrastructure, such as dams and piping, as well as the water delivery for irrigation, and the operation and maintenance of irrigation systems. Sometimes electricity costs and diesel for the irrigation pumps are also subsidized.

Irrigation subsidies can be defined in two ways. One method, often referred to as the 'cost-recovery' approach, defines the subsidy as the budgetary expenditures that benefit the irrigators, net of the revenues from water charges paid by the irrigators.[13] For small-scale irrigation, this calculation is straightforward, provided the data are available. However, for large-scale, surface-fed irrigation works, the calculation is more difficult for several reasons. First, the construction of the infrastructure takes several years and costs occur even before the irrigator has access to water. Secondly, infrastructure and reservoirs are often shared by the irrigators and other water users, or they are common with hydro-electric works. Lastly, governments generally levy charges partially to cover costs but, at the same time, often attribute significant portions of the project's cost to 'public' users, such

[8] *See* UNEP, *supra* note 1. [9] *Id.* [10] *Id.*

[11] On the topic of water pricing in these sectors, *see*, e.g., OECD, *Industrial Water Pricing in OECD Countries*, ENV/EPOC/GEEI(98)10/FINAL, OECD, Paris, 1999, and OECD, *Agricultural Water Pricing in OECD Countries*, ENV/EPOC/GEEI(98)11/FINAL, OECD, Paris, 1999. *See also* R. Andreas Kraemer, *Environmentally Harmful Subsidies in the Water Sector*, presented at the OECD Technical Experts Meeting on Environmentally Harmful Subsidies on 3 November 2003.

[12] UNEP, *supra* note 1. [13] Porter, *supra* note 5, at 46.

as recreational boaters, or other private users, such as electricity consumers.[14] In addition, the charge is often based on an interest rate in the amortization calculation that is below the market rate. Thus, to calculate the exact under-pricing to recover capital costs is an extremely complex and difficult task.

Besides subsidizing capital costs, many governments also cover costs relating to the operation and maintenance of irrigation systems. These include personnel costs, electricity, and diesel oil for pumping. Some economists also propose to take into account the foregone revenues that could have been generated if the irrigation water had been run through hydro-electric turbines.[15]

In addition to defining irrigation subsidies through the cost-recovery approach, some economists define irrigation subsidies based on the so-called 'resource-rent' definition. This definition is based on the 'actual value of the water to the irrigator rather than the amount of public expenditure'.[16] The subsidy is thus defined as the difference between the water's net economic benefit to the irrigator per unit and the charged price per unit.[17]

Little information is available on irrigation subsidies. No systematic data collection is currently underway. The OECD does produce estimates of agricultural support for all OECD countries in the form of aggregate data, which is largely available on the OECD website.[18] However, the OECD databases give only limited and incomprehensive insight into irrigation subsidies.

International financial institutions and independent researchers have also produced studies on irrigation water pricing and experiences in a number of countries, based either on the cost-recovery or on the resource-rent definition.[19]

While data relating to irrigation subsidies is sparse and not comprehensive or systematic, the studies that have been made indicates that irrigation is subsidized worldwide, in both developed and developing countries. Data gathered by the OECD for the years from 1995–1998 indicates that many OECD countries were recovering operations and maintenance, but that Greece, Italy, Mexico, and Turkey recovered only about 60–70 per cent of such costs.[20] With respect to capital costs, only a few OECD countries recovered fractions thereof. In some OECD countries, capital costs of irrigation projects were subsidized by up to 80 per cent.[21] In 1986, a study estimated that cost recovery in developing countries for irrigation was no higher than 10–20 per cent. Often, actual revenue did not even cover operating and maintenance costs.[22] More recent surveys show that

[14] *Id.* [15] *Id.*, at 47. [16] *Id.*

[17] For a good introduction to the resource-rent definition and references to economic studies, *see id.*, at 47–48.

[18] Data is available at http://www.oecd.org/document/23/0,2340,en_2825_293564_4348119_119656_1_1_1,00.html (last visited 14 June 2004).

[19] *See*, e.g., the bibliography in OECD, *Agricultural Water Pricing in OECD Countries, supra* note 11. [20] *Id.*

[21] Andre De Moor and Peter Calamai, *Subsidizing Unsustainable Development: Undermining the Earth with Public Funds*, 1997, at 14, available at www.ecocouncil.org (last visited 14 June 2004).

[22] Robert Repetto, *Skimming the Water: Rent-Seeking and the Performance of Public Irrigation Systems*, Research Report No. 4, Washington D.C., World Resources Institute, 1986, at 1.

much has stayed the same. Based on a cost-recovery rate of 20–25 per cent and total costs of about $25 billion, yearly subsidies to irrigation in developing countries can be tentatively calculated between $20 billion and $25 billion.[23]

In the United States, for example, the federal government is subsidizing irrigation systems in various ways. It incorporated a two-stage subsidy in the way it sets prices for irrigation water. First, the contractual water prices were based on an irrigator's ability to pay, rather than on the actual cost of supplying the water. Secondly, no interest was charged on the loans to fund construction costs. Researchers calculated a water subsidy of nearly $100 million for seventeen projects alone. The annual irrigation subsidies for the United States from such underpricing have been estimated at between $2 billion and $2.5 billion.[24]

Given the importance of irrigation subsidies, their impact on water resource management is obvious. Several studies show that irrigation subsidies can lead to excessive water use in both developed and developing countries.[25] Because water is inexpensive or free, farmers have no incentive to use water sparingly. Instead, they are encouraged to use inefficient technology, such as ineffective sprinklers, to irrigate croplands, or to water crops at the time of day when the temperatures are highest and much of the water is lost to evaporation. Moreover, by subsidizing irrigation water, governments sponsor the planting of water-demanding crops. For example, three of the main crops grown in California's Central Valley, with a desert-like climate, are water-intensive alfalfa, cotton, and rice, although these crops require a much moister climate. In some cases, crops are grown that are worth less than the water used for their cultivation.[26] Additionally, even in areas where fresh water is abundant, water pollution emanating from excessive irrigation remains problematic.

The argument that reducing or eliminating water subsidies promotes more sustainable agricultural practices is convincing: If farmers are charged the full or increased cost for their water deliveries, they are more likely adopt more water-efficient practices and grow less water-intensive crops. As a consequence, increasing water prices could lead to water conservation by farmers without increasing their water costs significantly. A theoretical study on the comparative costs of maintaining and dismantling large-scale water subsidies in Morocco predicted that a dramatic overhaul of agricultural water subsidies would reduce water use by about one third, while reducing GDP and real incomes by only 1 per cent.[27]

The subsidization of irrigation schemes leads not only to wasteful water use, but also to a series of additional environmental externalities related to excessive irrigation, affecting water bodies, soil, and fish. Examples are pests, disruptions of river hydrology, soil erosion, the draining of wetlands, and the depletion of fishstocks. Most importantly, excessive irrigation has led to the salinization and

[23] De Moor and Calamai, *supra* note 21, at 15.

[24] *Id.*, at 14. The authors also give other examples of irrigation subsidies in OECD countries, with a primary focus on the United States.

[25] For references, *see supra* note 2.

[26] De Moor and Calamai, *supra* note 21. *See also* Repetto, *supra* note 22.

[27] De Moor and Calamai, *supra* note 21, at 16.

waterlogging of croplands, with the consequence of decreasing crop yields. Such indirect costs to the environment remain unpaid and thus constitute additional (unconventional) subsidies which are ultimately paid by society at large.

In some regions, so much water is withdrawn from rivers for irrigation that the rivers begin to run dry, leading to a host of environmental and social problems. In Asia, for example, many rivers run dry during the driest season, when water for irrigation is needed most.[28] Across the globe, experience has shown that excessive irrigation also leads to declines in water tables. In the US, one-fifth of irrigated lands have displayed a lowering of water tables. In certain parts of China, water tables are dropping by 1–2 meters per year. In India, heavy water pumping for irrigation has even lead to the drying of the more shallow tube wells and the destruction of freshwater aquifers.[29] One of the most prominent examples is the shrinking of the Aral Sea in the former Soviet Union to less than half of its original size. The Aral Sea's fate was determined by Soviet planners in the 1960s, who wanted to make their country self-sufficient in cotton and to provide employment for a rapidly growing population. Irrigation water was diverted from the Amu Darya and the Syr Darya rivers flowing into the Aral Sea, leading to its shrinking. Disaster conditions also spread to large portions of the territories upstream of the Aral Sea, where productive wetlands in the deltas dried up and salinity in the rivers rose to very high levels, entailing serious threats to soil productivity. At the same time the lake's annual 44,000-ton fishing industry disappeared, taking with it 60,000 jobs.[30]

Other types of water-related agricultural subsidies include, for example, subsidies which encourage agriculture on marginal lands. Such subsidies are indirectly water-related because the cultivation of such lands requires excessive use of chemicals and thus can lead to the degradation of rivers and lakes, contamination of aquifers, destruction of wetlands, and toxic pollution of fish and wildlife. Similar effects can be caused by excessive fertilizer or pesticide use which is encouraged through the subsidization of fertilizers and pesticides. Average subsidy rates of almost 50 per cent for pesticide use in developing countries have been calculated.[31] Fertilizer use is also heavily subsidized at rates ranging from 50 to 90 per cent.[32]

4. Multilateral efforts to discipline the use of subsidies

While agricultural subsidies and their effects are being discussed in several intergovernmental fora, including the Organization for Economic Cooperation and

[28] *See* Postel, *supra* note 2.

[29] For all of these examples, see Myers, *supra* note 2, at 106–108.

[30] On the shrinking of the Aral Sea, *see* Laurence Boisson de Chazournes, *The Aral Sea Basin: Legal and Institutional Aspects of Governance*, in The Multi-governance of Water Through Four Cases (Matthias Finger & Ludivine Tamiotti eds, 2001); and Postel, *supra* note 2. *See* also UNEP, *supra* note 1, at paras 24 and 25, and *see also* Postel, *supra* note 2.

[31] De Moor and Calamai, *supra* note 21, at 25.

[32] *Id.*

Development (OECD) and the UN Food and Agriculture Organization (FAO),[33] it was only within the former General Agreement on Tariffs and Trade (GATT) and now within the World Trade Organization (WTO) that States have agreed on binding rules regarding subsidies. These rules, referred to as 'disciplines' in WTO parlance, aim mainly at the reduction and/or elimination of subsidies in order to promote international trade. Three major WTO agreements deal with agricultural subsidies: the Agreement on Agriculture, the Subsidies Agreement, and the GATT 1994.

It is not entirely clear how these agreements relate to each other and how the ongoing Doha Round of negotiations will shape the WTO's subsidies legal framework. The complex interrelationship between the various WTO agreements goes beyond the scope of this chapter and is not addressed here in detail.[34]

5. Agreement on agriculture

5.1 In general

The Agreement on Agriculture, which came into force on 1 January 1995, sets out specific commitments by WTO Members to reduce trade-distorting agricultural subsidies and improve market access. These commitments provide an implementation period of six years for developed and ten years for developing countries.[35] The Agreement on Agriculture also committed Members to start negotiations on continuing reform.[36] As a result, continued agricultural reform was addressed in the negotiating agenda set at the 2001 Ministerial Conference in Doha, Qatar. At the time of writing, the negotiations are still ongoing.

Agricultural products are defined in Annex 1 of the Agreement on Agriculture by reference to the harmonized system of product classification.[37] The definition covers basic agricultural products such as wheat, milk, and live animals; products derived from them such as bread, butter, and meat; and all processed agricultural products such as chocolate and sausages. The coverage also includes wines, spirits, and tobacco products, fibers such as cotton, wool, and silk, and raw animal skins destined for leather production. Fish and fish products, as well as forestry products, are explicitly excluded.

[33] The OECD organized two workshops on environmentally harmful subsidies in 2002 and 2003, which addressed, *inter alia*, agricultural subsidies and (separately) water-related subsidies. For an (older) overview of multilateral efforts on subsidies, *see* Ronald P. Steenblick, *Previous Multilateral Efforts to Discipline Subsidies to Natural Resource Based Industries*, OECD, Paris, 1999.

[34] For an elucidation of this relationship, see Didier Chambovey, *How the Expiry of the Peace Clause (Article 13 of the WTO Agreement on Agriculture) Might Alter Disciplines on Agricultural Subsidies in the WTO Framework*, 36 Journal of World Trade 305 (2002); and Hiltone E. Zunckel, *The Reform of Agricultural Subsidies Lights upon Pandora's Boxes*, South Africa, September 2001, at 56, on file with the author.

[35] Art. 1(f) of the Agreement on Agriculture defines the term 'implementation period' to mean a six-year period commencing in the year 1995.

[36] Agreement on Agriculture, Art. 20.

[37] Agreement on Agriculture, Annex 1 on 'Product Coverage'.

In the Uruguay Round a 'tariffication' package was negotiated, which required the replacement of agriculture-specific non-tariff measures with a tariff which allowed an equivalent level of protection. The Agreement on Agriculture prohibits all agriculture-specific non-tariff measures,[38] and the tariffs on virtually all agricultural products traded internationally are bound in the schedules of individual WTO Members. The schedules of tariff concessions cover all agricultural products and set out for each individual agricultural product, or, in some cases, agricultural products defined more generally, the maximum tariff that can be applied on imports into the territory of the Member concerned.[39]

While banning all export subsidies for non-agricultural products in the Subsidies Agreement, WTO Members agreed to bind and reduce the level of budgetary outlays for agricultural export subsidies and the quantities of exported agricultural products benefiting from export subsidies in the Agreement on Agriculture.[40] Under the Agreement on Agriculture, developed countries were generally required to make reductions of 36 per cent in budgetary outlays and 21 per cent in volumes over six years beginning in 1995, from a 1986-1990 base period. The precise commitments are specified in the WTO Members' Schedules of Concessions.[41] Under the so-called Peace Clause (discussed in further detail below), agricultural export subsidies were conditionally exempted from the general ban in the Subsidies Agreement until 31 December 2003. As of 1 January 2004, the Subsidies Agreement's ban on the use of export subsidies also applies to agricultural products because the WTO Members could not agree upon an extension to the exemption provided by the Peace Clause.

This chapter concentrates on domestic water-related subsidy schemes, such as, for example, subsidized irrigation. Thus, in this context, the most relevant aspect of the Agreement on Agriculture consists not in its market access and export subsidies rules, but in its rules on domestic support.

[38] Agreement on Agriculture, Art. 4.2 and footnote 1. Art. XI:2(c) of the GATT, which provides for exceptions to this prohibition, is now inoperative with respect to agricultural products because it is superseded by the Agreement on Agriculture. However, Art. 4.2 of the Agreement on Agriculture does not prevent the use of non-tariff import restrictions consistent with the provisions of the GATT or other WTO agreements. Such measures include those maintained under balance-of-payments provisions (Arts XII and XVIII of GATT), general safeguard provisions (Art. XIX of GATT and the related WTO agreement), general exceptions (Art. XX of GATT), the Agreement on the Application of Sanitary and Phytosanitary Measures, the Agreement on Technical Barriers to Trade, or other general, non-agriculture-specific WTO provisions.

[39] Developed country Members agreed to reduce their tariffs by 36 per cent on average for all agricultural products, with a minimum cut of 15 per cent for any specific product, over a six-year period beginning in 1995. Developing countries agreed to reductions of 24 and 10 per cent, respectively, to be implemented over ten years. Least-developed country Members agreed to bind all agricultural tariffs, but not to undertake tariff reductions.

[40] Agreement on Agriculture, Art. 9.

[41] The export subsidy commitments are on the basis of 18 standard commodity groups. Members may not shift subsidization from one group to another. Art. 9 of the Agreement on Agriculture lists non-exhaustively most of the export subsidy practices which are used in the agricultural sector. All listed export subsidies are subject to reduction commitments, expressed in terms of both the volume of subsidized exports and the budgetary outlays for these subsidies. For products not subject to export subsidy reduction commitments, no such subsidies can be granted in the future.

5.2 Domestic support

a. Reduction commitments

Generally, the Agreement on Agriculture requires the reduction of all domestic support that is considered trade-distorting (subject to some important exceptions). Trade-distorting support falls into the so-called Amber Box, which is defined in Article 6 of the Agreement on Agriculture as all domestic supports except those in the so-called Blue and Green Boxes (discussed further below). Commitments regarding the reduction of Amber Box measures are expressed in terms of a 'Total Aggregate Measurement of Support' (Total AMS), which includes all product-specific support and non-product-specific support in one single figure.[42] Thus, both budgetary and non-budgetary measures are included for the calculation of the AMS. Developed country Members with a Total AMS agreed to reduce base period support by 20 per cent over six years, and developing country Members by 13 per cent over ten years.[43]

b. Exemptions from domestic support reduction commitments

I. Green Box measures

Certain types of domestic support are exempt from reduction commitments and can be increased. Such measures are called 'Green Box' measures and are listed non-exhaustively in Annex 2 to the Agreement on Agriculture. For measures to be placed in this exempted category, they must have no, or at most minimal, trade-distorting effects or effects on production.[44] In addition, they must be provided through a publicly-funded government program not involving transfers from consumers by charging consumers higher prices, and must not have the effect of providing price support to producers.[45] Thus, Green Box measures are to be distinguished from the trade-distorting 'Amber Box' measures which are subject to reduction commitments as specified in the schedule of each WTO Member providing such support.

[42] Agreement on Agriculture, Arts 1(a) and 6. Article 1(a) of the Agreement on Agriculture defines the term 'AMS' as 'the annual level of support, expressed in monetary terms, provided for an agricultural product in favour of the producers of the basic agricultural product or non-specific-support provided in favour of agricultural producers in general, other than support provided under programmes that qualify as exempt from reduction under Annex 2 to this Agreement, which is: . . .'. Where it is not practicable to calculate a product-specific AMS as set out in the Agreement, provisions are made for an 'Equivalent Measurement of Support' (EMS) (see Art. 1(d) defining 'Equivalent Measurement of Support'). The EMS is generally calculated on the basis of budgetary outlays, which means the money spent by governments to support a product, for example, rather than market price support calculated with respect to a fixed external reference price. For more background on the calculation of the Total AMS, see Dale E. McNiel, *Furthering the Reforms of Agricultural Policies in the Millennium Round*, 9 Minn. J. Global Trade 41, 57 (2000).

[43] Pursuant to Art. 7.2(b) of the Agreement on Agriculture, Members with no scheduled reduction commitments must maintain any domestic support not covered by one of the exception categories outlined later in this chapter, within the relevant 'product-specific' and 'non-product-specific' *de minimis* levels.

[44] Agreement on Agriculture, Annex 2, para. 1.

[45] Agreement on Agriculture, Annex 2, para. 1(a) and (b).

The Green Box covers many government service programs, which are listed non-exhaustively in Annex 2 to the Agreement on Agriculture. The listed programs include 'general services' provided by governments,[46] public stockholding programs for food security purposes,[47] and domestic food aid.[48] They are exempt provided that the basic criteria described in the previous paragraph and the measure-specific criteria are met. The category of 'general services' lists programs such as:

—research, including, *inter alia*, research in connection with environmental programs;
—pest and disease control programs;
—agricultural training and advisory services;
—inspection services for health, safety, grading, or standardization purposes;
—marketing and promotion services;
—infrastructural services, including electricity reticulation, roads and other means of transport, market and port facilities, water supply facilities, etc.

The Green Box also allows certain direct payments to producers.[49] The conditions preclude any linkage between the amount of such payments, on the one hand, and production, prices, or factors of production in any year after a fixed base period. In addition, no production may be required in order to receive such payments.[50] Permitted measures include: decoupled income support measures; income insurance and safety-net program; natural disaster relief; a range of structural adjustment assistance programs; and certain payments under environmental programs and under regional assistance programs.[51]

The Agreement on Agriculture's Green Box provisions are of particular relevance in the context of water-related subsidies as they expressly include 'infrastructural services, . . . including water supply facilities'[52] (discussed below). The provisions on decoupling may also be relevant in so far as they apply to measures supporting small farmers in the context of a subsidies reform program, such as a program to reduce irrigation subsidies, for example.

II. Other exemptions from reduction commitments

In addition to Green Box measures, three further categories of domestic support measures are exempt from reduction commitments under the Agreement on Agriculture.[53] The first category consists of certain developmental measures in developing countries.[54] The second category consists of so-called 'Blue Box' measures. Blue Box measures would normally fall into the Amber Box but are

[46] Agreement on Agriculture, Annex 2, para. 2.
[47] Agreement on Agriculture, Annex 2, para. 3.
[48] Agreement on Agriculture, Annex 2, para. 4.
[49] Agreement on Agriculture, Annex 2, paras 5–13.
[50] Agreement on Agriculture, Annex 2, paras 5 and 6(b)–(e).
[51] Agreement on Agriculture, Annex 2, paras 6–13.
[52] Agreement on Agriculture, Annex 2, para. 2(g).
[53] Agreement on Agriculture, Art. 6.
[54] Developmental measures include measures of assistance, whether direct or indirect, designed to encourage agricultural and rural development, and that are an integral part of the development

treated differently if certain direct payments also require farmers to limit production. The Blue Box conditions are designed to reduce trade distortions.[55]

The Agreement on Agriculture sets out a third exemption in its *de minimis* provisions. These provisions allow for exemptions from reduction commitments where the annual aggregate value of the product-specific trade-distorting support does not exceed 5 per cent of the total value of production of the agricultural product in question.[56] In addition, non-product-specific support (such as generally available interest rate subsidies) is also exempt from reduction if it is less than 5 per cent of the value of total agricultural production.[57] For developing countries the *de minimis* ceiling is 10 per cent.[58]

c. The Peace Clause

Article 13 of the Agreement on Agriculture contains a 'due restraint' or 'Peace Clause', which was in effect until 31 December 2003. It regulated the application of other WTO agreements to agricultural subsidies. It provided that Green Box domestic support measures could not be the subject of countervailing duty action or other subsidy action under the Subsidies Agreement, nor could they be subject to actions based on non-violation nullification or impairment of tariff concessions under the GATT.

Other domestic support measures—even those conforming fully with the reduction commitments under the Agreement on Agriculture—could be subject to countervailing duties. However, Members were required to exercise due restraint in initiating such investigations. If the support provided to individual products did not exceed that provided in the 1992 marketing year, these measures were exempt from actions based on the GATT 1994, the Subsidies Agreement, or nullification or impairment action.[59]

5.3 Reducing water subsidies under the Agreement on Agriculture: Potential stumbling blocks

a. Reduction commitments—The Amber Box/Green Box/Blue Box classification

We have seen above that the Agreement on Agriculture requires the reduction of domestic support and that the reduction commitments are expressed in terms of a Total AMS. As explained earlier, some categories of support are exempt from the Total AMS calculation and, as a consequence, exempt from reduction

programs of developing countries. They include investment subsidies which are generally available to agriculture in developing country Members, agricultural input subsidies generally available to low-income or resource-poor producers in developing country Members, and domestic support to producers in developing country Members to encourage diversification from growing illicit narcotic crops.

[55] Agreement on Agriculture, Art. 6.5. [56] Agreement on Agriculture, Art. 6.4(a)(i).

[57] Agreement on Agriculture, Art. 6.4(a)(ii). [58] Agreement on Agriculture, Art. 6.4(b).

[59] On the Peace Clause, *see* David Morgan and Gavin Goh, *Peace in Our Time? An Analysis of Article 13 of the Agreement on Agriculture*, 37 Journal of World Trade 977 (2003).

commitments. Thus, for the purposes of this study, the relevant question is what type of water-related support is subject to reduction and what type of support is exempt. In order to answer that question, the first step is to determine whether domestic water-related subsidies fall into the Amber Box, the Green Box, or the Blue Box. Those water-related subsidies which qualify as Green Box or Blue Box measures are exempt from reduction commitments.

Amber Box subsidies are considered trade-distorting, while Green Box subsidies, on the other hand, are viewed as non-trade-distorting or—at most—minimally trade-distorting. If a water-related subsidy qualifies as an Amber Box subsidy, it is subject to reduction.

It is not always easy to know into which category a subsidy should fall. The system of notification under the Agreement on Agriculture suggests that it is mostly up to the notifying WTO Member to determine whether a subsidy is an Amber Box, Green Box, or Blue Box subsidy. No institutionalized body within the WTO reviews the accuracy of the classification notified by a given Member. Thus, although the classification chosen by the notifying State does not give the classification 'legal status', there is no remedy under the Agreement on Agriculture to challenge classification.[60]

Given the wide range of types of water-related subsidies generally, and irrigation subsidies in particular, the classification can vary from subsidy to subsidy. The United States' notification to the WTO Committee on Agriculture concerning domestic support commitments for the marketing year 1998, for example, lists irrigation subsidies as a domestic support measure, subject to reduction commitments (Amber Box).[61] In the notification, irrigation subsidies are listed under '*Non-Product-Specific AMS*' and average annual estimated irrigation subsidies levels[62] are indicated on the list.[63] Thus, in this case, the Agreement on Agriculture could help lead to a gradual reduction of irrigation and other water-related subsidies.[64]

But not all Members have listed their irrigation subsidies as Amber Box subsidies; some have instead listed them as Green Box subsidies, which are exempted from reduction commitments. For example, for the marketing year 1997/98, the European Communities listed '*Arterial drainage; collective*

[60] *See* Zunckel, *supra* note 34, at 56.

[61] The notification was submitted on 22 June 2001 and can be found at http://www.wto.org/english/tratop_e/agric_e/agric_e.htm.

[62] At another instance the table refers to 'water subsidies'. It is unclear whether this includes only irrigation.

[63] In its notification the U.S. notified figures for 1987, 1988, 1987-88, 1995, 1996, 1997, and 1998.

[64] However, according to a report by Grey, Clark, Shih and Associates dated 15 July 2003, the U.S. has failed to notify information relevant to other aspects of its agricultural production and agricultural support programs, including irrigation programs. The report notes (at p. 3): 'While the USA has notified monies to build infrastructure required for its irrigation programs to the WTO as non-product-specific support, the USA has failed to notify support in the form of water for irrigation provided to agricultural producers at below market rates'. The report is available at http://www.ong-omcmexico.org.mx/WebPage/web/doctos/AgricultoresCanada.pdf.

irrigation schemes; provision of electricity and water supply; farm roads; construction of reservoirs; flood protection' as a Green Box subsidy exempted from reduction commitments.[65] A notification from Korea for the marketing year of 2000 listed a subsidy for irrigation facilities as a Green Box measure not subject to reduction commitments, qualifying it as an Annex 2, paragraph 2(g) category support regarding infrastructure services (which includes the installation of infrastructure such as irrigation and drainage improvement).

Thus, the classification system of the Agreement on Agriculture may impede an efficient reduction of environmentally harmful water-related subisidies for various reasons. First, certain subsidies are seen and notified as Green Box subsidies and thus not subject to reduction commitments. Secondly, Members enjoy much liberty in classifying a subsidy as a Green Box subsidy, without any institutional organ supervising the accuracy of the notification. Thirdly, due to the lack of precision in the definition of Green Box exemptions, some notifications are not sufficiently precise, making it difficult to assess and compare the classifications of water-related subsidies. Some aspects relating to the interpretation of the Green Box exemptions are addressed in the following paragraph.

b. The 'general services' exemption

Green Box subsidies are listed non-exhaustively in Annex 2 to the Agreement on Agriculture and are exempted from reduction commitments. Paragraph 2 of Annex 2 on 'General Services' is one of the most relevant provisions in the context of irrigation and other water-related subsidies. It sets out a non-exhaustive list of exempted 'general services',[66] which contains the sub-category of 'infrastructural service' under paragraph 2(g). This sub-category includes 'electricity reticulation, roads and other means of transport, market and port facilities, *water supply facilities, dams and drainage schemes*, and infrastructural works associated with environmental programmes'.[67] The relevant paragraph limits the scope of infrastructural services by adding that:

> [i]n all cases the expenditure shall be directed to the provision or construction of capital works only, and shall exclude the subsidized provision of on-farm facilities other than for the reticulation of generally available public utilities. It shall not include subsidies to inputs or operating costs, or preferential user charges.[68]

As irrigation involves water supply facilities, dams, and drainage systems, many related subsidy schemes could potentially fall under this Green Box

[65] The notification can be found at http://www.wto.org/english/tratop_e/agric_e/agric_e.htm.

[66] Agreement on Agriculture, Annex 2, para. 2, 'General Services', reads: 'Policies in this category involve expenditures (or revenue foregone) in relation to programmes which provide services or benefits to agriculture or the rural community. They shall not involve direct payments to producers or processors . . .'

[67] Agreement on Agriculture, Annex 2, para. 2(g) (emphasis added).

[68] *Id.*, last two sentences.

category (provided the requirements set out under paragraph 1 of Annex 2[69] are also met) and thus be exempted from reduction commitments. However, given that 'subsidies to inputs or operating costs' are not exempted from reduction, an important portion of irrigation subsidies might nevertheless be subject to reduction commitments. This could be useful for encouraging the reduction of irrigation subsidies. Yet, due to the absence of a mechanism to determine the 'correct' classification, the Agreement seems to do little to seriously promote the reduction of water-related subsidies.

On the other hand, the Agreement seems helpful in that it obliges Members regularly to file notifications on the state of domestic support. Also, the regular meetings in the Committee on Agriculture give Members at least some insight into the practices of others and may allow Members to question notifications, in which case the notifying party is required to respond.[70] Additionally, if the notification requirements were more detailed, governments could more easily monitor the types of existing subsidies and their reduction.

c. *Calculation of Non-Product-Specific AMS and the Total AMS, the* de minimis *exemption, and decoupled support*

A further stumbling block to reducing water-related subsidies is that Members appear to retain much freedom regarding the manner of reducing different types of non-product-specific and product-specific subsidies for the calculation of Non-Product-Specific AMS and the Total AMS. A Member could avoid reducing irrigation or other water-related subsidies altogether by eliminating other subsidy types. Similarly, *de minimis* levels reduction exemptions might also limit effectiveness in reducing environmentally harmful water subsidies.

Lastly, the Agreement on Agriculture exempts from reduction certain socially and environmentally beneficial subsidies: Annex 2 to the Agreement permits decoupled support, such as structural adjustment assistance programs, as well as certain payments under environmental and regional assistance programs. It is unlikely that these exemptions hinder the reduction of water-related subsidies. Rather, domestic policy-makers attempting to reduce environmentally harmful water-related subsidies could consider using time-limited environmentally and socially beneficial subsidies to encourage a smoother and easier transition to a more conservation-oriented policy.

d. *The Peace Clause*

In addition to the considerations relating to the effectiveness of substantive rules of the Agreement on Agriculture in promoting the reduction of environmentally

[69] As discussed earlier, para. 1 provides that such domestic support may have no, or at most minimal, trade-distorting effects or effects on production, which means that the support must be provided through a publicly-funded government program, not involving transfers from consumers, and may not provide price support to producers.

[70] The Committee was established under Art. 17 of the Agreement on Agriculture.

harmful subsidies, one should recall that, while the Agreement covers reduction commitments, it does not provide remedial action. The agreements providing the remedies framework in the area of subsidies are the Subsidies Agreement and the GATT 1994. The Subsidies Agreement provides for withdrawal or countervailing remedies,[71] and GATT 1994 allows complaints in the case of serious prejudice or nullification.[72] As mentioned earlier, until 31 December 2003, the Peace Clause served as a partial shield against remedies available under the Subsidies Agreement and the 1994 GATT, in that Green Box measures were non-actionable and Amber Box subsidies were only partially actionable. While a new Peace Clause-type shield may be useful and necessary for certain types of agricultural support measures, it is important to note that—depending on how it is structured—a new Peace Clause might create a further hurdle to the reduction or elimination of certain water-related subsidies.

5.4 State of the negotiations

At the fourth WTO Ministerial Conference held in Doha, Qatar, in November 2001, Members issued a declaration launching new negotiations on a range of subjects, and including the negotiations already underway in agriculture. After the collapse of the negotiations at the fifth WTO Ministerial Conference held in Cancun, Mexico, in September 2003, WTO Members finally reached an agreement on 31 July 2004 on a framework package to keep the Doha Round trade negotiations alive. Agriculture is part of the single undertaking in which virtually all the linked negotiations are to end by a yet to be determined (postponed) deadline.

The framework package adopted in July 2004 includes concrete targets for overall domestic support reduction and a cap for permitted Blue Box levels. In the first year of implementing the agreement, the framework requires that Members reduce by 20 per cent their overall trade-distorting support, which comprises the final bound Total AMS plus the permitted *de minimis* levels, plus the permitted Blue Box levels. The framework also provides for capping product-specific AMS at average levels, based on a methodology to be agreed, in order to prevent circumvention of obligations through transfer of subsidies between different support categories. One contrast to the current rules thus is that the framework provides not only for capping, but also for reducing *de minimis* payments. However, the framework exempts from *de minimis* reduction commitments 'developing countries that allocate almost all de minimis programmes for subsistence and resource-poor farmers'.

The framework only marginally addresses the Green Box subsidies listed in Annex 2 of the Agreement on Agriculture, providing that 'Green Box criteria will be reviewed and clarified with a view to ensuring that Green Box measures have no, or at most minimal, trade-distorting effects or effects on production'. A provision

[71] *See* Subsidies Agreement, Parts II, III, and V.

[72] *See* GATT 1994, Arts 16 and 23.

similar to the expired Peace Clause was not adopted.[73] Overall, the framework does not substantially change the current structure of the Agreement on Agriculture, so that the stumbling blocks to a successful reduction or elimination of water-related subsidies referred to above largely remain the same.

6. Agreement on subsidies and countervailing measures

The Agreement on Subsidies and Countervailing Measures ('Subsidies Agreement') regulates the use of subsidies and of countervailing measures to offset injury caused by subsidized imports.

Part I of the Subsidies Agreement sets out the scope of the agreement by defining the term 'subsidy'[74] and laying out the concept of 'specificity'.[75] Only a measure which is a 'specific subsidy' within the meaning of Part I falls under the scope of the Agreement and can be subject to countervailing measures.

6.1 The definition of a subsidy

Pursuant to Article 1 of the Subsidies Agreement, a subsidy exists whenever (i) a financial contribution is made[76] (ii) by a government or any public body within the territory of a Member[77] (iii) which confers a benefit.[78] The Article distinguishes three categories of financial contributions:

(1) direct transfers of funds, potential direct transfers of funds or liabilities;
(2) foregone revenue; and
(3) the provision of goods or services other than general infrastructure.

Several examples are listed, including grants, loans, equity infusions, loan guarantees, fiscal incentives, the provision of goods or services, and the purchase of goods.[79] A financial contribution by a government is not a subsidy, however, unless it confers a 'benefit'. The WTO Appellate Body has ruled that the existence of a benefit is to be determined by comparison with the market place, that is, on the basis of what the recipient could have received in the market.[80]

The first step in determining whether water-related subsidies are covered by the Subsidies Agreement would be to determine whether the subsidy is a 'financial contribution'. This question is of particular significance in the context of implicit subsidies and environmental externalities, but also with respect to the other types of conventional water subsidies which are the subject of this study.

[73] Detailed information on the agriculture negotiations can be found on the WTO website at http://www.wto.org/english/tratop_e/agric_e/negoti_e.htm (last visited 4 August 2004).

[74] Subsidies Agreement, Art. 1.

[75] Subsidies Agreement, Art. 2.

[76] Subsidies Agreement, Art. 1.1(a)(1).

[77] *Id.*

[78] Subsidies Agreement, Art. 1.1(b).

[79] Subsidies Agreement, Art. 1.1(a)(1)(i)–(iii).

[80] WTO Appellate Body Report, *Canada—Measures Affecting the Export of Civilian Aircraft*, AB-1999-2, WT/DS70/AB/R (99-3221), adopted by Dispute Settlement Body, 20 August 1999.

6.2 Specificity

Once a measure qualifies as a subsidy as defined under the Subsidies Agreement, it is subject to the Subsidies Agreement only if it has been specifically provided to an enterprise or industry, or to a group of enterprises or industries.[81] The rationale behind this requirement is the presumption that subsidies that are widely available within an economy do not cause a distortion in the allocation of resources. As a result, only 'specific' subsidies are subject to the Subsidies Agreement disciplines. Article 2 of the Subsidies Agreement lists four types of 'specificity':

—Enterprise-specificity: a government targets a particular company or companies for subsidization;[82]
—Industry-specificity: a government targets a particular sector or sectors for subsidization;[83]
—Regional specificity: a government targets producers in specified parts of its territory for subsidization;[84] and
—Prohibited subsidies: a government targets export goods or goods using domestic inputs for subsidization.

The specificity element plays an important role in determining whether water-related subsidies fall under the scope of the Subsidies Agreement. As will be explained below, it is unclear whether water-related subsidies targeting the agricultural sector are 'specific' as required under the Subsidies Agreement.

6.3 Adverse effect

The Subsidies Agreement distinguishes between prohibited and actionable subsidies. Article 3 prohibits the use of export subsidies[85] and local content subsidies.[86] All other subsidies are actionable but not prohibited.[87] They are subject to challenge, either through multilateral dispute settlement or through countervailing action, provided they cause adverse effects to the interests of another Member. Article 5 of the Subsidies Agreement refers to three types of adverse effects:[88]

(1) Injury to a domestic industry caused by subsidized imports in the territory of the complaining Member—this is the only basis for countervailing action.

[81] Subsidies Agreement, Arts 1.2 and 2. [82] Subsidies Agreement, Art. 2.1(a). [83] *Id.*
[84] Subsidies Agreement, Art. 2.2.
[85] Subsidies Agreement, Art. 3.1(a). Export subsidies are subsidies contingent, in law or in fact, whether wholly or as one of several conditions, on export performance.
[86] Subsidies Agreement, Art. 3.1(b). Local content subsidies are subsidies that are contingent upon the use of domestic over imported goods.
[87] *See* Subsidies Agreement, Part III on Actionable Subsidies (Arts 5–7).
[88] A Member may not impose a countervailing measure unless it determines that there are subsidized imports, injury to a domestic industry, and a causal link between the subsidized imports and the injury. While the existence of a specific subsidy must be determined in accordance with the criteria in Part I of the Agreement, the criteria regarding injury and causation are found in Part V.

(2) Serious prejudice, for example caused by export displacement, in the market of the subsidizing Member or in a third country market—unlike injury, it can serve as the basis for a complaint related to harm caused to a Member's export interests.[89]

(3) Nullification or impairment of benefits accruing under the GATT 1994—nullification or impairment generally occurs where market access benefits from a bound tariff reduction are undercut by subsidization.

Practical problems could arise in applying existing provisions regarding adverse effects to water-related subsidies. It might be difficult to identify the sort of market distortions from which the Subsidies Agreement aspires to protect WTO Members.

6.4 Non-actionable subsidies

Until the end of 1999, the Subsidies Agreement also provided for a category of non-actionable subsidies. This category included subsidies for research activities conducted by firms subject to certain conditions; to adapt existing production facilities to new environmental requirements, provided that the subsidy was a one-time non-recurring measure and limited to 20 per cent of the cost of adaptation; and to assist in the development of industries in disadvantaged regions, provided that such assistance was not directed to specific enterprises or industries within the region.[90] Since the provision's expiration in 1999, no consensus has been reached for its continuation or re-introduction.

The absence of new rules regarding non-actionable subsidies may be problematic in the context of water-related subsidy policy reform. The transition from subsidized water-intensive techniques to water-saving techniques (such as drip irrigation), or the adoption of less water polluting technologies for industry, could be encouraged through targeted transitional subsidies. Under the current rules, however, such subsidies might be considered actionable. But, as discussed above, this would require that the subsidy caused adverse effects to the interests of other Members.

6.5 Reducing water subsidies under the Subsidies Agreement: Potential stumbling blocks

Since 1 January 2004, the Subsidies Agreement applies in full to the agricultural sector in terms of actionability. The Agreement is of particular importance as it

[89] The demonstration of adverse trade effects arising from subsidization requires extremely fact-intensive analysis. Until 31 December 1999, the Subsidies Agreement provided for a sub-category of actionable subsidies for which there was a rebuttable presumption of serious prejudice. The relevant provision has expired and has not been extended.

[90] Subsidies Agreement, Arts 8.2 and 31.

sets out the conditions for Members to bring claims against subsidizing WTO Members. The following section examines how the Agreement relates to agricultural water-related subsidies and whether it can serve as a useful tool to reduce environmentally harmful subsidization.

a. The definition of a subsidy

A major characteristic of the subsidy definition under the Subsidies Agreement is that a subsidy is 'a financial contribution by a government or any public body' by which a benefit is conferred.[91]

This definition resembles (at least in part) the cost-recovery approach, which, in the context of irrigation, defines the subsidy as the budgetary expenditures net of the revenues from water charges paid by the irrigators that benefit the irrigators. Such non-recovered expenditures or subsidies can include costs relating to irrigation infrastructure, such as dams and piping, as well as water delivery for irrigation, and the operation and maintenance of irrigation systems.

However, while the cost-recovery definition quite clearly covers costs relating to irrigation infrastructure, the Subsidies Agreement specifically exempts certain expenditures from cost recovery by providing that a subsidy is deemed to exist only where 'a government provides goods or services *other than general infrastructure*'[92] (emphasis added). What the phrase 'goods or services other than general infrastructure' covers is not entirely clear. Arguably, the term covers water delivery for irrigation, and the operation and maintenance of irrigation systems, while carving out from the scope of application of the Subsidies Agreement certain aspects of irrigation services, in particular the costs relating to large-scale irrigation infrastructure. Whether the carve-out covers all types of irrigation infrastructure, or whether it is limited to infrastructure serving specific additional (public or private) purposes, is unclear. The effectiveness of this provision for the reduction of irrigation subsidies therefore partly depends on the interpretation of 'general infrastructure'.

In order for the Subsidies Agreement's definitional scope to adequately cover water-related subsidies with environmentally harmful effects, the existing definition would have to be amended or clarified. Specifically, clarification is needed as to which government infrastructure programs in the agricultural sector are exempted from the scope of the definition, if at all. Moreover, a broader discussion of the definitional scope of a subsidy in the irrigation context might involve the question of whether the subsidy definition should leave sufficient room for the resource-rent approach described earlier. Under this approach, a subsidy is defined as the difference between the water's net economic benefit to the irrigator per unit and the charged price per unit. Arguably, this approach seems difficult to square with the current definition of a subsidy under the Subsidies Agreement.

[91] Subsidies Agreement, Art. 1.

[92] Subsidies Agreement, Art. 1.1(a)(1)(iii).

Finally, a subsidy definition that adequately addresses the problems raised with respect to water should arguably cover certain non-conventional subsidies, for example, those relating to low water quality standards or the lack of enforcement of pollution laws.[93]

b. Specificity

If a subsidy falls within the definition of Article 1 of the Subsidies Agreement, action can be brought only if the subsidy is specific in accordance with Article 2.[94] That is, it is actionable only if the subsidy is 'specific to an enterprise, industry or group of industries'. The Article lists situations in which subsidies are deemed to be specific or non-specific, and sets out certain factors to consider.[95] Pursuant to paragraph 1(a), a subsidy is specific if access to the subsidy is explicitly limited to 'certain enterprises' (meaning 'an enterprise or industry or group of enterprises or industries').[96] In addition, a subsidy is specific when it is 'limited to certain enterprises located within a designated geographical region'.[97]

The question raised in the context of agricultural subsidies is whether the specificity requirement is to be construed broadly or narrowly. Under a broad view, any agricultural subsidy would have to be considered specific by the mere fact that it is sector-specific.[98] Under a narrower approach, however, agricultural subsidies, such as irrigation subsidies, would not necessarily qualify as specific just because they concern one sector.[99] In the latter case, one could still argue that subsidized irrigation schemes are specific because they are limited to farmers within a designated geographical region. Clarification of the specificity requirement in the context of agricultural subsidies would be helpful to avoid future uncertainties.

c. Adverse effects

Subsidies that fall under the subsidy definition, and are specific, are actionable under the Subsidies Agreement. However, the Subsidies Agreement provides remedies (either through multilateral dispute settlement or through countervailing action) only in situations where a subsidy causes certain defined adverse effects to the interests of another Member. The disciplines under the Subsidies Agreement mainly address market distortions arising from subsidization. They do not address other negative economic, environmental, and developmental impacts of subsidies.

[93] For a discussion of the Subsidies Agreement's definition of a subsidy and potential problems in the context of fishing subsidies, *see* Gareth Porter, *Fisheries Subsidies and Overfishing: Towards a Structured Discussion*, Fisheries and Environment Series, UNEP, February 2002.

[94] Subsidies Agreement, Art. 2.

[95] Subsidies Agreement, Arts 2.1(a)–(c) and 2.2.

[96] Subsidies Agreement, Art. 2.1 introductory note.

[97] Subsidies Agreement, Art. 2.2.

[98] *See* Zunckel, *supra* note 34, at 55: 'Annex 2 subsidies are for the agricultural industry and hence would be specific (to an industry) under the ASCM Article 2.1', referring to S. Tangerman, *An Assessment of the Uruguay Round Agreement on Agriculture*, OECD, 1994.

[99] Porter, *supra* note 93, referring to J. Ragosta, *Natural Resource Subsidies and the Free Trade Agreement: Economic Justice and the Need for Subsidy Discipline*, 24 G. W. J. INT'L L. & ECON. 255 (1990), notes that in the past, a narrow approach has been taken with respect to agriculture.

In general, the imposition of a countervailing duty is the easier and more practical response to subsidized imports. However, countervailing duties may only be applied to imports entering the complaining Member's market and which have caused injury to the domestic industry.[100] This could be problematic for the goal of reducing environmentally harmful water subsidies: if the subsidizing Member is also a major consumer of crops the production of which benefits from subsidized irrigation or pesticides, and has relatively limited exports, the subsidies will affect primarily the subsidizing Member's market. While this would make it harder or impossible for other Members' exporters to compete within the subsidizing Member's market, the subsidies may not create a harmful impact in the market of another Member. The only dispute settlement remedy remaining for a harmed WTO Member in such a case would be under the WTO's dispute settlement mechanism.

Under the dispute settlement procedure,[101] the complaining Member must demonstrate that a subsidy has caused 'serious prejudice' to the interests of another Member by showing that, as a result of the subsidy:

(1) exports of a like product into the market of the subsidizing Member or into a third-country market have been displaced or impeded; or
(2) there has been significant price undercutting by the subsidized product as compared with the price of a like product in the same market; or
(3) that there has been significant price suppression, price depression, or lost sales in the same market.

It is difficult to know to what extent it is possible to establish the trade-distorting effects of water-related subsidies on market share or price of agricultural products. Difficulties could arise in quantifying the price effects of water-related subsidies. Additionally, there may be cases in which the unsubsidized reference price differs only minimally from the subsidized price. It might therefore be impossible to fulfill the 'serious prejudice' requirements provisions of the Subsidies Agreement needed to bring a claim at the WTO.

7. Transparency and notification requirements

Notification requirements to the WTO Committee on Agriculture and the Subsidies Committee ensure transparency with respect to Members' subsidy policies and countervailing duty laws, regulations, and actions. Various studies show that it has been difficult to estimate the use of water-related subsidies in the past.[102] The WTO's notification system has contributed, to some limited extent, to improving transparency in the use of irrigation subsidies and certain other water-related subsidies. Both the Agreement on Agriculture and the

[100] *See* Part V of the Subsidies Agreement.
[101] *See* Part III of the Subsidies Agreement.
[102] Porter, *supra* note 5.

Subsidies Agreement contain provisions which require Members to notify other Members of their agricultural subsidy programs through the WTO Secretariat.

Article 18 of the Agreement on Agriculture, on the 'Review of the Implementation of Commitments', requires that Members with scheduled domestic support reduction commitments notify the Current Total AMS.[103] Moreover, all Members are required to notify new or modified *exempted* domestic support measures.[104] These must reflect the criteria set out in the articles regarding exempted measures, including Green Box and Blue Box measures, developmental measures, and *de minimis* levels of support. The Committee on Agriculture adopted a document setting out the requirements and formats for notifications under Article 18.[105]

Article 25 of the Subsidies Agreement incorporates analogous notification obligations. It requires that Members notify any subsidy (as defined in the Subsidies Agreement) which is 'specific'.[106] The content should include: form; amounts; objectives; duration; and 'statistical data permitting an assessment of the trade effects of a subsidy'.[107] The Subsidies Committee adopted a Questionnaire Format for Subsidy Notifications under Article 25 of the Subsidies Agreement.[108] It lays out the notifications and information to be provided in the notifications. While Article 25 is binding, it is aimed at transparency and carries no legal effect with respect to the information provided.

The notification requirements under both the Agriculture and the Subsidies Agreements leave a fair amount of discretion to the notifying parties to determine which types of subsidies to notify and how. For example, if a Member regards an irrigation subsidy as non-specific, Article 25 of the Subsidies Agreement does not require notification. Problems also arise under the Agreement on Agriculture, the rules of which leave Members fairly free to categorize their agricultural subsidization schemes as Amber Box or Green Box. There is no mechanism to monitor the notification and subsequent classification. It is important to note, nevertheless, that even where subsidies are categorized as exempt, and thus not subject to reduction, their mere notification sheds light onto their existence and thus enhances transparency.

Notifications made pursuant to either of the agreements are publicly available on the WTO website.[109] Water-related notifications, however, are scattered and seem incomplete. A systematic overview of irrigation and other water-related subsidies notified under the Agriculture and the Subsidies Agreements would be useful to determine the extent to which Members respect their notification

[103] Agreement on Agriculture, Art. 18.2.

[104] Agreement on Agriculture, Art. 18.

[105] G/AG/2, adopted on 8 June 1995, available at http://www.wto.org.

[106] Subsidies Agreement, Art. 25. [107] *Id.*

[108] G/SCM/6, adopted 21 July 1995, available at http//www.wto.org.

[109] Information on notification on agriculture is available at http://www.wto.org/english/tratop_e/agric_e/agric_e.htm.

commitments in this context. A review of notifications in this particular field would also provide insight into patterns of water-related subsidy use.[110]

Transparency could be additionally furthered through a more detailed notification system. Currently, notifications can combine several types of subsidies in one category, such as 'infrastructure', making it more difficult to know to what extent roads, irrigation schemes, etc. were in fact subsidized. A more detailed reporting system, which, for example, would identify the various types of water-related subsidies and use uniform classification, could enhance transparency. It would help Members know what to report and make the reports more precise and transparent.

Under the present system, implicit subsidies, especially in the form of environmental externalities, are left unreported. Because the quantification of environmental externalities, such as, for example, the cost to clean up polluted water, is difficult and would possibly overburden some WTO Members, it might be preferable to consider the notification of environmental standards and laws, such as water quality standards. This would be a first step in getting a clearer picture of the differences in environmental standards and the resulting environmental and economic effects at the international level.

Lastly, a further avenue under the WTO that deserves mention is the system of WTO Trade Policy Reviews, which provides valuable information on subsidy policies of individual Member States. These reviews might provide a basis for further insight into the use of water-related subsidies across the globe.

8. Conclusion

International fora, including the FAO, UNEP, and the OECD, should continue to study and address the use and effects of agricultural water subsidies. Given the WTO's existing rules regarding subsidies, and given its elaborate and binding dispute settlement mechanism, one could argue that the organization should also play an important role in the effective reduction or elimination of harmful water subsidies in the agricultural sector. However, one must keep in mind that the WTO's principal goal is not the protection of water resources, but rather the elimination of trade distortions and adverse effects on WTO trading partners. As a consequence, the WTO's current system regarding subsidies, while marginally useful, is not the ideal approach for the international community to address the challenges to the protection of a natural resource.

The WTO's disciplines on subsidies, as they stand today, appear to contain too many trade-focused conditions to contribute effectively to the elimination of

[110] Such an overview was prepared in June 2001 by the WTO Secretariat regarding fishing subsidies in response to a request by the Committee on Trade and Environment. *See* Committee on Trade and Environment, GATT/WTO Rules on Subsidies and Aids Granted in the Fishing Industry, Update of Notifications under the SCM Agreement, Note by the Secretariat (WT/CTE/W/80), available at http://www.wto.org.

water-related agricultural subsidies. There are many ways for WTO Members to avoid the reduction of such subsidies under the Agreement on Agriculture. Moreover, even though the Subsidies Agreement has become fully applicable to agricultural subsidies since the expiration of the Peace Clause in December 2003, Members will likely be able to maintain environmentally harmful water subsidies without threat of action by other Members. Several reasons lead to this conclusion. Firstly, the scope of a subsidy as defined in the Subsidies Agreement does not clearly cover certain types of agricultural water subsidies, especially those relating to 'general infrastructure', which possibly include irrigation services. Moreover, many agricultural water subsidies might not be 'specific', a basic condition for the Subsidies Agreement to apply. Lastly, the Subsidies Agreement's requirements for adverse effects to interests of another Member may be difficult to fulfill, so that there may be no remedies available in the context of water subsidies.

Despite the inadequacy of the current WTO disciplines on subsidies to address the challenges regarding the protection and conservation of water resources, it might be useful to explore the possibility of addressing the issue of water-related subsidies within the WTO either as a separate issue, or in the context of other environmentally harmful subsidies. Both of these options would require a carve-out from existing rules of the Agreement on Agriculture and the Subsidies Agreement, and would have to focus not only on trade distortion but also on other economic, social, and environmental effects. The schemes under these two options could be subject to the WTO dispute settlement mechanism. A further option would be to deal with water subsidies in the context of a new subsidies framework covering all subsidies, similar to the Subsidies Agreement. In any event, experts other than trade and subsidies experts would have to be involved in discussions, in order adequately to address environmental and social aspects.

Another possibility would be to address the issue in a forum outside the WTO. Given the WTO's strong focus on the avoidance of trade distortion rather than environmental and natural resource protection, a separate forum—pre-existing or new—might be preferable. In this context, options for an effective dispute settlement and/or compliance mechanism would have to be explored.

All of these options require a clearer preliminary understanding of the use of water-related subsidies around the world. Only based on a better understanding can decision-makers clarify connections between the water-related and other subsidies and their effects on water resources. Although the usefulness of current WTO rules directly to reduce or eliminate water-related agricultural subsidies is limited, the WTO structure could nevertheless provide an excellent basis for collecting water subsidies-related data. Ways should be identified to enhance transparency and uniformity for notifying these types of subsidies. This could be the first important step towards more sustainable water-resource management through subsidy reforms.

PART IV
WATER AND INVESTMENT

10

Water-Related Investment: A European Perspective

ANDREAS R. ZIEGLER

1. Introduction

After the failure of the WTO Ministerial Conference in Cancun in late 2003, there is a continuous and increasing tendency for (newly) industrialized countries to conclude bilateral free trade agreements. They normally include bilateral concessions and rules on the liberalization of trade in services similar or comparable to the General Agreement on Trade in Services (GATS). Furthermore, they most often include important chapters on the liberalization and protection of foreign direct investment (FDI). Both areas can have important repercussions on national policies regarding water distribution and supply. This chapter examines the motives and basic structures regarding water-related services of the existing bilateral free trade agreements, taking as examples the agreements of the European Economic Community and its Member States, as well as of the European Free Trade Association (EFTA),[1] with numerous States since 1991. The objective is to identify similarities and differences to the current WTO negotiations on the one hand, and to bilateral investment treaties (BITs) on the other hand.

The most recent agreements of the EFTA States with Mexico, Singapore, and Chile go significantly further than the traditional agreements which mainly abolished customs duties and non-tariff barriers for industrial goods. The same is true for the European Economic Community's agreements with Mexico, Chile, and South Africa. They are typical so-called second or third generation agreements. In addition to the liberalization of trade in goods, these also carry on the liberalization of trade in services as achieved within the WTO framework (GATS), as well as the liberalization in areas such as public procurement or protection of intellectual property rights (IPRs). Furthermore, they partly include new areas such as FDI or competition law, areas on which so far no

[1] The European Free Trade Association was founded in 1960 by Denmark, the United Kingdom, Norway, Austria, Portugal, Sweden, and Switzerland. In 1970 Iceland joined EFTA, while Finland and Liechtenstein became members in 1986 and 1991 respectively. Over time, many members left EFTA and joined the far more integrated European Union. As of today, only Switzerland, Norway, Iceland, and Liechtenstein remain members of EFTA.

consensus exists within the WTO. The strong increase in very comprehensive bilateral agreements can lead to opportunities, but also to potential conflicts within the global trading system. With regard to water-related policies, the fact that these agreements sometimes combine a GATS-style liberalization of trade in services with a traditional BIT-style protection of investments in these industries may pose new challenges. This is also true for the alternative establishment approach sometimes used to mutually open the domestic markets for services with commercial presence.

2. Historical evolution of bilateral and multilateral trade negotiations

2.1 First generation agreements (1850–1910)

Bilateral trade agreements are significantly older than the global trading system. The General Agreement on Tariffs and Trade (GATT)[2] came into effect in 1947/8.[3] The first modern bilateral trade agreements were concluded in the middle of the 19th century. At that time, as a result of initiatives of the United Kingdom and the United States of America in particular, a large number of bilateral agreements, known as 'Commerce, Establishment and Friendship Treaties', were concluded. Between seafaring nations these agreements were usually concluded as 'Friendship, Navigation and Commerce Treaties'.[4] Switzerland concluded such a treaty with the United Kingdom in 1855. It remains—at least partly—in force today.[5] Because of the euphoria of that period relating to trade expansion and the liberal attitude of those States, these first general free trade agreements included an advanced framework not only for the free movement of goods,[6] but also for the free movement and establishment of persons in each Party. Towards the end of the 19th century, the necessity to finance wars (e.g., between France and Germany) and civil wars (e.g., in the United States of America) with income from customs duties, as well as the general movement

[2] *See* Swiss Official Collection of Laws and Treaties, SR 0.632.21, available at www.admin.ch.

[3] The GATT was only a provisional substitute for the failed project for the creation of an International Trade Organization (ITO); *see also* Odell, John, *The United States, the ITO, and the WTO* in Krueger, Anne O. (ed.), The WTO as an international organization (Chicago, 1998) 181–209, and Piquet, Howard S., The Havana Charter for an international trade organization (Washington, U.S. Government Pr. Office, 1950).

[4] For the United States, *see* The Avalon Project at Yale Law School, *American Diplomacy to the Present—Treaties, Agreements and Correspondence,* available at http://www.yale.edu/lawweb/avalon/amerdipl.htm.

[5] *Friendship Commerce, and Establishment Treaty*, between the Swiss Confederation and Her Majesty the Queen of the United Kingdom of Great Britain and Ireland, concluded on 6 September 1855, ratified by the Swiss Parliament on 7 February 1856; Exchange of Ratification Documents on 6 March 1856; entry into force on 6 March 1856, SR 0.142.113.67, *supra* note 2.

[6] *See also* Art. VIII/IX/X (Most-Favoured-Nation (MFN) Principle) and Art. VII/XI (National Treatment) in the *Friendship Commerce, and Establishment Treaty, supra* note 5.

towards 'protectionist nationalism', contributed to the turning away from free trade. Trade in water, or the use of establishment rights to provide water-related services, was not at issue at this time.

2.2 Second generation agreements (1950s to 1970s)

After the economic tensions of the 1920s and 1930s, and the creation of war economies during World War II, it was only in the 1940s that ideas for a liberal trade order (at least in basic terms) were also formulated internationally.[7] While the immediate post-war period was influenced by the idea of bringing about global economic liberalization, this ambitious project was quickly supplemented by, or partly replaced by, regional integration agreements. After failing to create the International Trade Organization (ITO) as conceived in the Havana Charter (1948), the legal basis for world trade remained solely the GATT (1947).[8] From the 1950s, several regional free trade area agreements came into force in parallel with the GATT. Actually, such regional preferential agreements were provided for through Article XXIV GATT, allowing for the deviation from the general most-favoured-nation (MFN) clause (Article III GATT). In Europe, these were the European Economic Community (EEC, now EC) on the basis of the Treaty of Rome (1957)[9] and the European Free Trade Area (EFTA)[10] on the basis of the Stockholm Convention (1960).[11] In the 1960s and 1970s, the EC and the EFTA began to integrate their trade in goods through agreements, and expanded such agreements to other European States.[12] In addition, the trade relations of the European Community in relation to the ACP (African, Caribbean, Pacific) States were also regulated on a preferential basis as a consequence of their status as former colonies.[13]

[7] They had been brought forward in the United States domestically already as from 1934; *see*, e.g., O'Rourke, Kevin and Williamson, Jeffrey, GLOBALISATION AND HISTORY: THE EVOLUTION OF A NINETEENTH-CENTURY ATLANTIC ECONOMY (MIT, Cambridge, MA, 2000).

[8] *See*, e.g., Lowenfeld, Andreas, INTERNATIONAL ECONOMIC LAW (OUP, Oxford, 2002) at 22–26.

[9] Hereafter EC; text and information *available at* http://www.europa.eu.int/.

[10] As of the time of writing, the Members of EFTA are Norway, Switzerland, Iceland, and Liechtenstein. Denmark and the United Kingdom were founding members of EFTA but joined the European Community (EC) as early as 1973. Portugal became an EC Member State in 1986. Sweden, Austria, and Finland left EFTA in 1995 to become Members of the European Union (EU).

[11] Agreement of 4 January 1960 for the creation of the European Free Trade Association (EFTA) for Switzerland, reprinted in SR 0.632.31 (*supra* note 2). About the Swiss considerations on this subject *see* Maurhofer, Roland, *The quest for the lesser evil: Great Britain, Switzerland and the decision to create EFTA*, Working Paper 286 (Institut für Politikwissenschaft, Universität St. Gallen, 2000).

[12] With the exception of Turkey, which had already received the status of an associated country in 1963, and Algeria (1976). *See also* the Free Trade Agreement of 22 July 1972 between the Swiss Confederation and the EEC (with Annexes and exchange of letters); for Switzerland see SR 0.632.401, *supra* note 2.

[13] *See*, e.g., the Agreement of Jaunde (1963 and 1969) and thereafter the Agreement of Lomé (1975); currently, the Lomé Agreement of 20 June 2000 applies to these countries, available at http://europa.eu.int/scadplus/leg/de/lvb/r12100.htm.

Outside Europe, besides a few isolated bilateral trade agreements, the most important initiatives were the Latin American Free Trade Area (LAFTA) of 1960,[14] the Caribbean Community (CARICOM) of 1973[15] in South America, as well as the Bangkok Agreement (1975)[16] and the Association of Southeast Asian Nations (ASEAN) of 1977[17] in Asia.

In general these agreements were limited to trade in goods, and trade in water was not normally discussed, although this was, in principle, possible under the GATT, and similarly construed bilateral or regional agreements did normally not exclude trade in water in general.

2.3 Third generation agreements (since the 1990s)

a. Regional integration

In the 1980s, less emphasis was placed on bilateral and regional free trade agreements. Priority focused on multilateral efforts in the Uruguay Round of trade negotiations from roughly 1986 until 1994, leading to the establishment of the World Trade Organization (WTO) on 1 January 1995.[18]

However, even whilst concluding the Uruguay Round, but in particular afterwards, there were substantial efforts from both industrialized countries and emerging nations to advance trade liberalization regionally or bilaterally. In the beginning, the achievement of the EC Internal Market Programme (1992) and the free trade agreement between the USA and Canada (CUSTA)[19] played an important role in this respect. The CUSTA was intended to serve as a model for the multilateral system, supported by the USA during the Uruguay Round.[20] Before the conclusion of the Uruguay Round, this agreement between the USA and Canada was expanded to include Mexico within the framework of the North American Free Trade Agreement (NAFTA).[21] It came into force on 1 January 1994. The enlarged Internal Market between the EC and the EFTA States creating the European Economic Area (EEA) also came into force on 1 January 1994.[22] As the third most important regional free trade area with at

[14] The Latin American Free Trade Association (LAFTA) became LAIA/ALADI in 1980. Texts *available at* http://www.aladi.org/.

[15] Texts *available at* http://www.caricom.org/expframes2.htm.

[16] *See also* the information available at http://www.unescap.org/itid/bkkagr.htm. The Member States are Bangladesh, India, the Republic of Korea, Laos, Sri Lanka, and (since 2000) China.

[17] Texts are *available at* http://www.aseansec.org/. The tariff abolishment was accomplished only in 2002/3.

[18] All the Agreements of the Uruguay Round can be found on the Internet, *available at* http://www.wto.org.

[19] *See* International Legal Materials, 1988, at 281.

[20] This is very obvious in the dispute settlement rules: *see*, e.g., Marceau, Gabrielle, *NAFTA and WTO Dispute Settlement Rules—A Thematic Comparison*, 31 Journal of World Trade (1997), at 25–81; and Kerr, William A., *Greener Multilateral Pastures for Canada and Mexico—Dispute Settlement in the North American Trade Agreements*, 35 Journal of World Trade 1169 (2001), at 1171.

[21] *See* the information available at http://www.nafta-sec-alena.org/english/index.htm.

[22] *See* the information available at http://secretariat.efta.int/euroeco/ECProg/. Meanwhile, the character of this Agreement has been strongly changed because of the absence of Switzerland (due to a negative referendum) and the entry of some important EFTA States into the EU.

least theoretically a great potential and with analogous political significance, mention should be made of the Mercosur/Mercosul Agreement between Brazil, Argentina, Uruguay, and Paraguay, which came into force on 29 November 1991.[23] In all these agreements not only liberalized trade in goods was at stake, but, more importantly, also investment and services supply, both particularly important for the supply of water-related services.

b. New Bilateral Agreements within a region

Besides the so-called regional integration agreements, another phenomenon strongly affirmed itself during this period and still does so today: purely bilateral free trade agreements. While this approach had been followed at a regional level by the EC and EFTA since their creation, it expanded after the end of the Cold War, first to Central and Eastern Europe[24] and later to the Mediterranean countries.[25] For the European Community these regional agreements were a direct step on the way to the integration of ten new Member States from these regions into the European Union (which is these days normally used to describe the comprehensive political integration model based on the EC). The accession of these new members to the European Union implies also their accession to the more extended arrangement of the European Economic Area (EEA), which is formed of the EU Member States and three of the four EFTA Member States.[26] Only Switzerland is not a member of the EEA despite its membership in the EFTA. For Switzerland, the relationship with current and future EU Member States is thus governed by the bilateral agreements between the EU and Switzerland and not by the EEA Agreement.

After the accession of ten candidate countries to the EU in Spring 2004, there remain three candidate countries (Romania, Bulgaria, and Turkey), as well as a number of countries in the Balkans and in the Mediterranean, which have specific bilateral trade agreements in place with the European Community[27] and the EFTA countries.[28] These agreements with European and Mediterranean partners normally address only trade in goods and some limited aspects of the

[23] The Treaty of Asunciòn (Spanish: Tratado de Asunciòn) of 26 March 1991, on the Internet in Spanish at http://www.mercosur-comisec.gub.uy/DOCUMENT/TRATADOA/Asuncion.htm.

[24] *See* the EU Association Agreements with these States and the efforts of some of these States to become full Members. On this point, *see* Nell, Philippe G., *Extension of the European Union/EFTA Regional Trading Bloc to Central and Eastern Europe*, 20 World Competition—Law and Economics Review 131 (1997).

[25] *See* the Agreements and negotiations with Morocco, Egypt, and Tunisia. So far, it has been necessary for all these EU trade partners to conclude free trade agreements amongst themselves, in order to create the Pan-European Cumulation System (for rules of origin). More information is *available at* http://www.osec.ch/osec/glossar-aw/paneurop-kumul;internal&action=buildframes.action. The expansion of this system to the Mediterranean States is under preparation (EUROMED cumulation system).

[26] Norway, Iceland, and Liechtenstein are members of the EEA Agreement.

[27] *See*, for detailed information, http://www.europa.eu.int/comm/trade/issues/bilateral/regions/index_en.htm.

[28] *See*, for details, the information available at http://secretariat.efta.int/Web/Agreements/.

access of foreign workers (such as in the case of the agreements with Turkey). Water is hence not really an issue at this stage.

c. New bilateral agreements among global trading partners

At the end of 1990s, extra-regional agreements, the existence of which could no longer be justified by purely regional integration efforts, became more prominent, such as the agreements negotiated between the EC and Mexico, or between Canada and the EFTA States. In fact, after the conclusion of the Uruguay Round, a certain vacuum appeared, which some countries attempted to overcome through bilateral agreements. Besides the EC and EFTA, most importantly Canada, Mexico, Chile, Singapore, New Zealand, Australia, South Korea, Japan, South Africa, Israel, Thailand, and (very recently) the US negotiated bilateral agreements. Mercosur/Mercosul is currently negotiating with the US and other South-American States for a Pan-American free trade area[29] and for an agreement with the EC, although the recent economic problems in Argentina have slowed down these efforts.

Meanwhile, a network of agreements has been created between all these States, similar to the network of bilateral friendship, navigation, and commerce treaties of the 19th century.[30] The failure to launch a new trade round at the WTO Ministerial Conference in Seattle (1999) had an important influence on the bilateral negotiation of free trade agreements, especially on the activities of Asian States in this respect. Among the treaties already concluded and in force, the following agreements are worth mentioning: United States–Israel (19 August 1985), Canada–Israel (1 January 1997), Canada–Chile (7 June 1997), Chile–Mexico (1 August 1999), Mexico–Israel (1st July 2000), New Zealand–Singapore (1 January 2001). An agreement has been signed between Japan and Singapore (13 January 2002). Korea and Chile agreed in principle on a free trade agreement on 24 October 2002. Finally, on 4 November 2002, Australia and Singapore announced that they had concluded free trade negotiations.[31] In 2003 and 2004 more agreements were concluded, such as, most recently, between the United States and Australia, as well as between Thailand and Japan.

With regard to Europe, the following agreements are important: the European Community and its Member States–South Africa (1 January 2000);[32] the European Community and its Member States–Mexico (1 July 2000);[33]

[29] Free Trade Area of the Americas (FTAA), text on the Internet *available at* www.ftaa-alca.org/.

[30] *See* on this point, *supra* section 2.1.

[31] *See* Neue Zürcher Zeitung, 5 November 2002, Nr. 257, at 21.

[32] *See* Agreement on Trade, Development, and Cooperation between the European Community and its Member States, of the one part, and the Republic of South Africa, of the other part, OJ 1999, L 311, pp. 3–297.

[33] Interestingly, the EC chose with Mexico a structure that is based on a framework agreement establishing organs that adopted the substantive agreements as decisions. *See*, on this subject, the information available at http://europa.eu.int/comm/trade/index_en.htm.

EFTA–Mexico (1 July 2001);[34] EFTA–Singapore (1 January 2003);[35] the European Community and its Member States–Chile (signed 18 November 2002);[36] and EFTA–Chile (1 February 2004).[37]

The EFTA States are currently also negotiating with South Africa to reach arrangements similar to those between the European Community and South Africa. The EFTA States have also started negotiations with SACU (South African Customs Union), while the EC has an agreement with South Africa only. The EC has been in negotiations with the Mercosur for some considerable time.

These new bilateral agreements are increasing not only in number and dynamism, but also in scope. Because of their broad coverage of trade in goods, services, and investment, these are often referred to as third generation agreements. The European Community started by including in its agreements with the Central and Eastern European candidate States rules relating to the other freedoms besides the free movement of goods, as it had done in the EEA Agreement. The inclusion of rules regarding trade in services, investment, competition, public procurement, etc. was considered a preparatory step to membership. It was in particular the NAFTA, and the expansion of the disciplines covered by the WTO in the Uruguay Round, which lead to the inclusion of trade in services, investment and public procurement in bilateral free trade agreements aiming purely at economic integration. Indeed, the provisions on intellectual property and competition law in most third generation agreements are as of today substantially more comprehensive than those included in classical trade agreements (even of the early 1990s).

3. Relationship between the global framework and regional integration

The relationship between bilateral preferential agreements and multilateral trade liberalization has always been the cause of intense controversy.[38]

[34] *See* the Free Trade Agreement between the EFTA States and Mexico (see Message of the Swiss Federal Council regarding the Free Trade Agreement with Mexico = Botschaft zum Freihandelsabkommen zwischen den EFTA-Staaten und Mexiko sowie zum Landwirtschaftsabkommen zwischen der Schweiz und Mexiko, of 14 February 2001, reprinted in BBl. 2001, pp. 1850 ff.).

[35] *See* Free Trade Agreement between the EFTA States and Singapore (see Message of the Swiss Federal Council regarding the Free Trade Agreement with Singapore = Botschaft zum Freihandelsabkommen zwischen den EFTA-Staaten und Singapur sowie zum Landwirtschaftsabkommen zwischen der Schweiz und Singapur, 4 September 2002, reprinted in BBl. 2002, pp. 6701 ff.).

[36] The negotiations were concluded in the summer of 2002. The agreement was accepted by the European Commission on 3 October 2002, *see* the information available at http://europa.eu.int/comm/trade/index_en.htm.

[37] The Agreement between the EFTA States and Chile is available at http://secretariat.efta.int/Web/ExternalRelations/PartnerCountries/Chile/CL/CL_FTA.pdf; *see also* Message of the Swiss Federal Council regarding the Free Trade Agreement with Chile = Botschaft zum Freihandelsabkommen zwischen den EFTA-Staaten und Chile sowie zum Landwirtschaftsabkommen zwischen der Schweiz und Chile, of 19 September 2003, reprinted in Bundesblatt (BBl.) 2003, pp. 7113 ff.

[38] *See* Imhoof, Rodolphe S., *Le GATT et les zones de libre échange* (thèse Genève, 1979); more recently, Cottier, Thomas und Panizzon, Marion, *Die sektoriellen Abkommen und das Recht der*

Basically, it can be said that the unconditional most-favoured-nation (MFN) principle, as contained in Article III GATT, is not compatible with regional or bilateral preferential treatment. Simultaneously, the GATT of 1947 already contained Article XXIV allowing for the possibility of further trade liberalization at a regional or bilateral level. At the time of its creation, Article XXIV applied most prominently to the BENELUX Cooperation Agreement between Belgium, the Netherlands, and Luxembourg. Generally speaking, Article XXIV GATT requires that the local welfare gains resulting from additional regional liberalization do not (excessively) affect the general welfare effects stemming from multilateral liberalization, or even outweigh the total welfare effects.

Finding the balance between safeguarding the multilateral approach and allowing for regional preferential treatment is not easy. The debate on how bilateral agreements should be drafted so as not to erode multilateral trade liberalization has always been vigorous. This became very obvious in recent years, first in the context of GATT and, since 1996, in the WTO Committee on Regional Trade Agreements (CRTA). A fundamental dispute has arisen around the question of whether under Article XXIV GATT, it is enough to liberalize a 'substantial part' of the actual trade between the 'free trade partners', or whether 'substantially all products' must be included. While in the first case it is sufficient to cover a 'substantial part of the actual trade volume', the second view usually refers to the 'sufficiently high number of tariff positions' under the harmonized system for the registration of customs positions (HS System) covered by the free trade rules of an agreement.[39] The background to this dispute is the fact that many bilateral agreements exempt agricultural products from free trade. This is especially the case for agreements concluded by European countries. The countries that are most critical of this approach are those disposing of very competitive and export-oriented agriculture. They are organized in the Cairns Group.[40]

Article XXIV GATT has never assumed the function it was originally assigned.[41] Its underlying criteria remain unclear and difficult to apply.[42] During the Uruguay Round, Article XXIV GATT was complemented by a more specific

WTO: Grundlagen und Spannungsfelder, in: ACCORDS BILATÉRAUX SUISSE—EU = BILATERALE ABKOMMEN SCHWEIZ—EU (COMMENTAIRES) (Felder, Daniel/Kaddous, Christine, eds, Basel, 2001) at 43–76, and Cottier, Thomas, *The challenge of regionalization and preferential relations in world trade law and policy*, 2 European Foreign Affairs Review 149 (1996).

[39] *See* the 'Harmonized Commodity Description and Coding System', available at http://www.wcoomd.org/ie/En/Conventions/conventions.html.

[40] The Cairns Group consists of important agricultural exporting countries: as of 2004 its members were Argentina, Australia, Bolivia, Brazil, Canada, Chile, Colombia, Costa Rica, Guatemala, Indonesia, Malaysia, New Zealand, Paraguay, Philippines, South Africa, Thailand, and Uruguay.

[41] *See* Cottier, Thomas, *Die Bedeutung des GATT im Prozess der europäischen Integration, in* EG-RECHT UND SCHWEIZERISCHE RECHTSORDNUNG (Jacot-Guillarmod, Olivier et al., eds, Basel, 1990) at 164.

[42] *See* John Jackson, WORLD TRADE AND THE LAW OF GATT (1969), at 621. See also the unclear result of the dispute in EC—Tariff treatment on Imports of Citrus Products from certain countries in the Mediterranean region, GATT Doc. L/5776, 7 February 1985, para. 5.1 section b, at p. 102.

'Understanding on the Interpretation of Article XXIV',[43] but this did not really clarify the situation. In the current Doha Round, this discussion continues in the WTO Negotiating Group on Rules. While this discussion already has a long tradition in the context of trade in goods, surprisingly, the discussion concerning the relationship between multilateral and bilateral liberalization in the area of services is so far not very developed, be it with regard to the academic discussion or to the political debates.[44] In principle, however, Article V GATS[45] foresees a similar solution as is contained in Article XXIV GATT. Maybe this difference can simply be explained by the modest degree of existing liberalization in international services trade. Another reason could be the limited experience with regional preferential trade in services (at least outside Europe).

4. Water-related policies in EFTA and EC third country agreements

4.1 Trade in goods

In principle, free trade agreements are concluded to achieve further liberalization of barriers to trade and investment flows through preferential treatment. As today's agreements normally also cover trade in services, investment, public procurement, competition policy, and rules related to intellectual property, they are no longer simple trade agreements but economic integration agreements. The Closer Economic Partnership Agreements between New Zealand and Australia, or between New Zealand and Singapore, are good examples of this development. Preferential treatment in bilateral agreements is normally chosen if a multilateral solution (in the WTO) seems unlikely to be achieved soon, or is economically or politically undesirable due to the application of the unconditional MFN treatment enshrined in the WTO (Article I GATT). Many industrialized countries could very easily abolish their remaining tariffs on industrial goods, as they do not rely on the income from this source and no longer have a strong protective interest for most industrial sectors.[46]

With regard to developing countries this is different. The fervent discussions regarding the liberalization of trade in textiles, clothing, and footwear are a

[43] Understanding on the Interpretation of Article XXIV of the General Agreement on Tariffs and Trade 1994, *supra* note 18.

[44] Art. V of the General Agreement on Trade in Services (GATS) corresponds systematically and substantially to Art. XXIV of the GATT, *supra* note 18. *See*, however, Sauvé, Pierre, *Regional versus Multilateral Approaches to Services and Investment Liberalization: Anything to Worry About?* in Regionalism and Multilateralism after the Uruguay Round (Demaret, Paul/Bellis, Jean-François/Jimenez, Gonzalo Garcia, eds, Brussels, 1997) at 429–55.

[45] GATS, *supra* note 18.

[46] In particular, one must note that among industrialized countries most tariffs on industrial goods are very low, especially after the conclusion of the Uruguay Round. The same holds true with regard to most imports of industrial goods from developing countries as a result of Part IV GATT (GSP = General System of Preferences).

telling example of this. There are also other isolated sectors like steel[47] and, partly related to this, shipbuilding[48] that remain difficult even among developed countries. The same developments are true for newly developed countries in South East Asia and Latin America, while most developing countries still rely heavily on tariffs for their revenue and fear foreign competition in many weak sectors. As a result, industrialized countries and certain emerging countries are able to agree on the complete dismantling of tariffs and the further elimination of existing non-tariff barriers to trade in bilateral agreements relatively easily. For the newly industrialized countries (and the former Communist countries of Central and Eastern Europe) this is especially the case if they have undertaken internal economic reforms (deregulation and liberalization).[49] Normally, as on the multilateral level, the issue of trade in water is not explicitly approached. Its special character is nowhere acknowledged and it therefore falls, generally, under the broad rules regarding trade liberalization, with the possibility to invoke exceptions for, say, environmental reasons.

4.2 Agriculture

In the area of agriculture the situation is much more difficult. The EFTA States are perfect examples of countries that have highly protected domestic agricultural sectors. Historically, this is partly due to their agricultural policy during the two world wars and the time between the wars when they relied on their increased domestic production to survive. At the same time the geographic and regional structure of countries such as Norway and Switzerland relies on the existence of small farmers in remote areas. In the WTO the term 'multifunctionality' has been coined to take into account these non-economic considerations.[50] In this situation these countries are only slowly liberalizing their agricultural sectors and are not able at this stage to make major concessions, let alone fully open their domestic markets to free trade in agricultural products.[51] As a result the scope of free trade agreements with these countries is limited in the area of agricultural goods, often including processed agricultural products. These problems at the global level also constitute constraints for the conclusion of bilateral agreements with countries that have a strong agricultural sector.[52]

[47] *See* the current debate on US safeguard measures for steel in the framework of the WTO. More information available at http://www.ustr.gov/sectors/industry/steel.shtml.

[48] *See* the current debate on EC countervailing measures in respect of South Korean shipbuilding. See Directive (EC) No. 1177/2002, Council, 27 June 2002, for the introduction of limited safeguard measures for the shipbuilding sector, OJ EC L 172/1 of 2 July 2002.

[49] *See*, for details, Ethier, Wilfred, J., *Unilateralism in a Multilateral World*, Tinbergen Institute Discussion Papers 01–033/2 (Tinbergen Institute, 2001).

[50] *See* OECD, MULTIFUNCTIONALITY: TOWARDS AN ANALYTICAL FRAMEWORK (OECD, Paris, 2001).

[51] This can also apply to specific products that can be used for animal feeding but are classified as industrial products.

[52] This simplifies the conclusion of agreements with countries like Singapore which do not have an important agricultural sector.

Among the latter are currently countries like Chile, South Africa, New Zealand, and, more recently, Australia, looking for free trade partners worldwide. For these countries, partners like Singapore, with no significant agricultural sector at all, are ideal, which explains the early conclusion of agreements between Singapore and New Zealand and Australia.

In the area of fish and other maritime products, however, the situation is fundamentally different for the EFTA States. Norway and Iceland are among the most competitive suppliers of fish and other maritime products globally. Although this sector is treated in the WTO under the heading of industrial products,[53] many countries have similar problems with their fishery sector as with agriculture. A prime example of this situation is the European Community with Member States such as Spain or Portugal. While all EFTA States have highly protected agricultural sectors, they are highly competitive in the area of fish and other maritime products.[54] With large natural resources they have a competitive advantage in this area without having to seek access to other waters outside their own exclusive economic zone. In contrast to the EC, for example, EFTA States thus do not ask for resource sharing when negotiating market access for fish and other marine products.[55] Hence EFTA free trade agreements normally include the principle of free trade in fish but have limitations in the area of agricultural products. With regard to water as a primary commodity which can be traded in bulk shipments or in bottled form as well as by pipelines, there have never been any particular rules integrated into these agreements.

4.3 Environmental cooperation

It is important to note that at least the EC's agreements with third states are much broader than pure economic integration (trade in goods, services, and investment). They also include political and development cooperation. A typical example is the Chapter on Environment in the Agreement between the EC and South Africa:

Article 84 Environment

1. The Parties will cooperate to pursue sustainable development through the rational use of non-renewable natural resources and the sustainable use of renewable natural resources, thus promoting protection of the environment, prevention of its deterioration and the control of pollution. The Parties will aim to improve the quality of the environment and work together to combat global environmental problems.

[53] *See supra* note 39.

[54] Iceland is an exception as it produces only a very limited number of agricultural products due to the existing climate. Some crops, however, are produced with geothermal heat in glasshouses. On the whole, Iceland imports most of its vegetables and fruit.

[55] See the recently concluded Agreement between Chile and the EC, which includes a protocol on access for European fishermen to Chilean waters. On this, *see* Riordan, Brian, in Samudra Report Online, July 2002, at p. 36 (available at icsf.net/jsp/samudra/english/issue_32/art8.pdf).

2. The Parties will give special consideration to the development of capacity in environmental management. There will be dialogue on the identification of environmental priorities. The impact of past South African policies on the state of the environment will be reviewed and addressed where possible.
3. The cooperative relationship will involve, inter alia, matters relating to urban development and land use for agricultural and non-agricultural purposes; desertification; management of waste, including hazardous and nuclear waste; management of dangerous chemicals; conservation and sustainable use of biological diversity; the sustainable management of forestry resources; water quality control; control of pollution from industrial and other sources; control of coastal and marine pollution and the management of marine resources; integrated water catchment management, including management of international river basins; water demand management and issues surrounding the reduction of greenhouse gas emissions.

Although this provision relates also to water, it is unclear how it could influence the interpretation of the services and establishment provision in the Agreement when it comes to water concessions or water-related policies in the services/investment context. The main focus of this provision with regard to drinking water lies on water quality control and integrated water catchment management, including management of international river basins as well as water demand management. This could obviously imply that both sides will make efforts to increase know-how transfer and promote common programs. In many cases this will involve private actors, i.e. specialized companies in the field of water treatment and distribution. At the same time the cooperation with regard to capacity-building shall be governed by the general objective of promoting protection of the environment, prevention of its deterioration, and the control of pollution. Therefore the involvement of private firms, at least when promoted by both sides, must be handled in a balanced way.

The same is true with regard to the EC's internal environmental policy regime and its implications for the common commercial policy.[56] Under the current EC founding treaties, the protection of the environment is a general objective of the Community that has to be taken into account in all common policies,[57] i.e. also the common commercial policy. A typical example is the support by the European Union of the increased acceptance of the precautionary principle in international agreements. Another example is the fact that the Community grants tariff reductions to countries which conform to international agreements regarding the protection of the environment.

It may also be worthwhile to recall the main features of the Community's internal environmental policy, as it may have an impact on the interpretation of

[56] *See* Ziegler, Andreas, TRADE AND ENVIRONMENTAL LAW IN THE EUROPEAN COMMUNITY (OUP, Oxford, 1996) 199–218. *See*, more recently, Klasing, Annette, *Ecologic Briefs: A Sustainable Constitution for Europe—The Common Commercial Policy in the Constitution for Europe—A Step Forward for the Environment?*, Discussion Paper, September 2003, available at http://www.ecofuturum.de/de/downloads/diskussionspapiere/EcoBriefs_Trade_EN.pdf

[57] Art. 6 EC Treaty.

some of the terms contained in the Community's external agreements. In the Preamble to the Treaty establishing the European Community, it is stated:

> The Community shall have as its task, by establishing a common market and an economic and monetary union and by implementing common policies . . . , to promote throughout the Community a harmonious, balanced and sustainable development of economic activities, a high level of employment and of social protection, equality between men and women, sustainable and non-inflationary growth, a high degree of competitiveness and convergence of economic performance, a high level of protection and improvement of the quality of the environment, the raising of the standard of living and quality of life, and economic and social cohesion and solidarity among Member States.

Article 6 of the EC Treaty reads:

> Environmental protection requirements must be integrated into the definition and implementation of the Community policies and activities referred to in Article 3, in particular with a view to promoting sustainable development.

The Community today has, internally, a very comprehensive environmental regime in place which complements, and often has fully replaced, the domestic environmental regulations, depending on the area concerned. When it comes to water, the Commission Communication of 21 February 1996 on Community water policy sets out the Commission's approach to water protection. It details the objectives of such a policy, namely: secure supply of drinking water; secure supply of drinking water or non-drinking water to meet economic requirements other than human consumption; protection and preservation of the aquatic environment; restriction of natural disasters (drought, floods). It also defines the various types of pollution which may affect water. The principles of this policy are as follows: high level of protection; precautionary principles; preventive action; damage to be rectified at source; principle of polluter pays; integration of this policy in other Community policies; use of available scientific and technical data; variability of environmental conditions in the regions of the Community; costs/benefits; economic and social development of the Community; international cooperation; and subsidiarity. In order to rationalize existing legislation on water management and pollution and step up controls on pollution at Community level, the Commission has put forward the idea of a Water Resources Framework Directive. Directive 2000/60/EC of the European Parliament and of the Council of 23 October 2000, establishing a framework for Community action in the field of water policy,[58] is based on the objectives and principles set out above and establishes common definitions; it repeals and replaces certain existing acts. Besides that, certain internal legal acts, such as the Drinking Water Directive, the Surface Water Directive, the Urban Waste Water Treatment Directive, and the Integrated Pollution Prevention and Control Directive, remain applicable.

[58] OJ L 327, 22 December 2001.

4.4 Developing new rules

a. WTO plus elements

Besides negotiating better market access through tariff dismantling and improved commitments in the areas not fully liberalized (services, public procurement, etc.), free trade agreements can serve to develop disciplines or improve existing WTO disciplines in areas where no global consensus can yet be reached. Especially in the 1960s and 1970s, when the GATT framework consisted in many areas only of rudimentary rules contained mostly in non-binding codes,[59] this objective of free trade agreements seemed worthwhile. The conclusion of a broad set of agreements under the umbrella of the WTO in the Uruguay Round, however, changed the situation considerably. The density, degree of concreteness, and level of detail achieved in the WTO regime is unprecedented. Many of the bilateral solutions found in agreements like the CUFTA or the NAFTA were adapted to the global framework and incorporated into the WTO regime.[60] There is certainly still room for improvement of the existing disciplines and for new disciplines to be integrated into the WTO framework, but the task is getting more difficult and politically sensitive. This often makes it difficult, even in bilateral agreements, to find WTO plus elements[61] for the covered disciplines.

A consequence is that in many of the recently concluded agreements, these WTO plus elements are relatively simple or mostly procedural. Examples are the elimination or limitation of anti-dumping measures[62] or general safeguard measures, and the introduction of additional consultations for time limits regarding the adoption of certain measures. Most often these agreements include a mere reference to the WTO in areas where satisfactory WTO disciplines exist, such as in the areas of subsidies, technical barriers to trade, sanitary and phytosanitary measures (SPS),[63] or exceptions.[64] In these areas the achievements of the Uruguay Round have sometimes even led to a harmonization of rules in

[59] See the competition rules or the rules on measures having equivalent effect as quantitative restrictions in the free trade agreement of the EC and the EFTA States, as contained, e.g., in the Free Trade Agreement between Switzerland and the EC, Arts 23 and 13. *See supra* note 11. On this, *see* also Borer, Jürg, *Massnahmen gleicher Wirkung wie mengenmässige Einfuhrbeschränkungen im Freihandelsabkommen Schweiz—EWG* (Diss. St. Gallen, 1988).

[60] *See*, for the area of dispute settlement, *supra* note 20.

[61] The term is often used in the context of specific trade concessions going beyond GATT or GATS commitments (*WTO plus commitments*). With regard to rules, the term is sometimes also applied to indicate that rules are more detailed and more liberal than the existing WTO rules.

[62] *See* the Agreement between New Zealand and Singapore, or the Agreement between Chile and Canada. This approach can, however, lead to additional problems at the multilateral level. In particular, it is very controversial whether WTO safeguard measures can be applied on a preferential basis under Art. XXIV, or whether this constitutes a violation of Art. III GATT. *See*, most recently, the decision of the Appellate Body in United States—Definitive Safeguard Measures on Imports of Circular Welded Quality Line Pipe from Korea, AB-2001-9, WT/DS202/AB/R of 15 February 2002.

[63] *See* the WTO Agreement on Sanitary and Phytosanitary Measures, *supra* note 18.

[64] *See* the Free Trade Agreement between the EFTA States and Mexico (see Message of the Swiss Federal Council regarding the Free Trade Agreement with Mexico = Botschaft zum Freihandelsabkommen zwischen den EFTA-Staaten und Mexiko sowie zum Landwirtschaftsabkommen

bilateral agreements where traditionally genuine solutions existed. A typical example is the fact that the concept of 'measures having equivalent effect as quantitative restrictions', found in many traditional EFTA agreements, has in more recent agreements been replaced by a reference to the WTO-based terminology of technical barriers to trade.[65]

b. Services (commercial presence)

Besides the liberalization of trade in goods, most recently concluded bilateral agreements in this area also include the liberalization of trade in services and access and/or protection for foreign investments and investors.[66] From an economic point of view the liberalization in this area is similar to that of trade in goods, but the legal and structural problems relating to liberalization of domestic service supply and investment/establishment are often very complex. They involve important issues related to highly regulated sectors of the economy, including such aspects as supervision and liberalization of existing State monopolies. Water treatment and distribution are typical examples of public utilities in the area of services which historically were governed by State or private monopolies. Only in recent times have privatization and competition among various suppliers taken place in certain countries, while in most countries the desirability of such developments is still subject to important controversies.

Apart from the European Community's Common Market (including its extension to the EEA) and the CER between New Zealand and Australia, the CUFTA/NAFTA Agreements were the first agreements to approach comprehensively the liberalization of trade in services. The services negotiations under the Uruguay Round led only to very modest results with regard to the liberalization of trade in services.[67] It was therefore no surprise that some countries with an important services sector would try to go further in bilateral agreements. As a matter of fact, the bilateral trade agreements concluded in recent years usually use the conceptual framework developed under the GATS and basically achieve better commitments among the bilateral trade partners. Despite this general development, it must be noted that the achievements so far are not very far-reaching. Many countries seem reluctant to open services sectors that have been protected from foreign competition for a very long time. They fear strong implications for their regulatory framework, e.g. on the price, quality, and availability of specific utilities such as drinking water or telephone services.

zwischen der Schweiz und Mexiko, of 14 February 2001, reprinted in BBl. 2001, 1850 ff.) and the Free Trade Agreement between the EFTA States and Singapore (see Message of the Swiss Federal Council regarding the Free Trade Agreement with Singapore = Botschaft zum Freihandelsabkommen zwischen den EFTA-Staaten und Singapur sowie zum Landwirtschaftsabkommen zwischen der Schweiz und Singapur, 4 September 2002, reprinted in BBl. 2002, pp. 6701 ff., at para. 4.1.1).

[65] See the current solution regarding subsidies in the EFTA Free Trade Agreements with the Central and Eastern European countries or the Mediterranean countries. The approach is now based on the WTO Agreement on Subsidies and Countervailing Duties, while the traditional approach was based on Art. 92 of the Treaty of Rome (now Art. 87).

[66] Public procurement rules are also relevant in this context.

[67] *See supra* note 44.

At the same time the economic theory advocating free trade in services seems less clear and stringent than the principles developed with regard to trade in goods. Furthermore, the strong connections between trade in services and investment, lead to a strong interdependence between the opening of services markets and investment rules.[68] In this area there exist so far no comprehensive rules in the framework of the WTO, besides the disciplines related to mode 3 of the GATS and the Agreement on Trade-related Investment Measures (TRIMs Agreement). The failure of the MAI (Multilateral Agreement on Investment) negotiations under the auspices of the OECD reminds us also of the myriad problems traditionally related to investment protection. The number of open questions and problems grows when market access in the form of a right to establishment is part of negotiations.[69] In the field of services and investment, the right of establishment corresponds to the classical market access concession in the field of trade in goods. If foreign suppliers are given the same right to establish themselves within an economy as the domestic suppliers of that economy, this basically leads to the opening up of the services market of that country. This will be illustrated further in the next section.

c. *Investment/establishment*

In the European context, recently negotiated trade agreements seldom include extensive rules on investment. Sometimes they are limited to the traditional rules concerning protection (post-establishment) already contained in many bilateral investment protection and promotion agreements (IPPAs). Since even rules concerning protection have become more controversial in recent years, due, amongst other things, to a growing number of controversial arbitral awards under the NAFTA (Chapter 11), negotiations for the inclusion of comprehensive investment rules into bilateral agreements are also getting more difficult.[70] Nevertheless, there is now a growing number of bilateral and regional agreements including market access for foreign investors (establishment).

The degree of openness of markets for foreign services differs considerably between these agreements if one looks at such agreements as the NAFTA, the Agreement between EFTA and Singapore,[71] or the recently concluded Agreement between Chile and the European Community. The relationship between the general right to establishment of investors and the specific market access commitments in the services sectors (mode 3) is interesting as, here, two different concepts of liberalizing investments apply. Traditionally, in investment negotiations, general rights are given to foreign investors, and certain exceptions are listed separately (negative list approach). Under the GATS, however, the rights of foreign services suppliers are listed in a positive way for each sector, i.e.

[68] *See*, e.g., Hauser, Heinz, *Kommentar: Ausbleibende Konvergenz von GATT und GATS, in*: WTO News 7 (St. Gallen, 2002), available at http://www.unisg.ch/org/siaw.

[69] *See* Multilateral Agreement on Investment: Documents Relating to the 1995–1998 Negotiations, available at http://www.oecd.org/EN/document/0,,EN-document-92-3-no-6-27308-92,00.html.

[70] *See supra* note 21. [71] *See infra*, section 5.

a sector not listed is fully closed. At the same time, it is also interesting to note that under the GATS a considerable part of all services commitments is made under mode 3 (establishment). Some observers actually claim that one of the main reasons for many countries to negotiate bilateral free trade agreements is to attract more foreign direct investment. In fact, the possibility to export from these countries under the preferential conditions negotiated in bilateral free trade agreements may be an important factor when choosing a location for a production plant abroad.[72]

In some of these agreements services- and investment-related aspects were approached through a right to establishment, the mechanism used in the European Community to establish the single market. Both the EC[73] and the EFTA States[74] have adopted this approach with Chile, and water-related investment is not, in principle, excluded.

With Mexico, both the EFTA States[75] and the EC[76] were only able to agree on standstill provisions, but an effective liberalization of services and investment—possibly including water-related services—is foreseen for the future. More recently the European Community has concluded a Trade, Development, and Cooperation Agreement (TDCA) with South Africa, in which most services liberalization is postponed to future negotiations. It is planned that this liberalization should take place through the exchange of commitments according to the model used in the GATS. Thus, in principle, similar problems as under the GATS will have to be tackled.[77]

The EFTA States have concluded an agreement with Singapore, in which investment protection and liberalization are included, including water-related services. However, the services liberalization is exclusively governed by a special GATS-type chapter based on a positive list of commitments not including, at least for now, any water-related services.[78]

5. Water-related investment issues in EFTA and EC third country agreements

5.1 Investment/establishment and water

Despite strong resistance by certain developing countries, the issues of investment, competition policy, transparency in government procurement, and trade

[72] *See* Ethier, *supra* note 49.

[73] The free trade agreement between the EU and Chile was signed on 18 November 2002.

[74] *See supra* note 37. [75] *See supra* note 34.

[76] For the EU, *see* Decision 2/2001 of the EU–Mexico Joint Council as established under the Economic Partnership, Political Coordination and Cooperation Agreement which entered into force on 1 October 2001.

[77] *See*, on this issue, the contribution by Elisabeth Tuerk in this volume, or Peter H. Gleick, Gary Wolff, Elizabeth L. Chalecki, & Rachel Reyes (The Pacific Institute), *The New Economy of Water: The Risks and Benefits of Globalization and Privatization of Fresh Water, 2002*, available at http://www.pacinst.org/reports/new_economy_of_water.pdf. [78] *See supra* note 35.

facilitation, were for the first time mentioned as possible future areas of WTO negotiations in the Declaration resulting from the Ministerial Meeting in Singapore in 1998.[79] Since then, these new items have normally been referred to as the 'Singapore Issues'. Specific working groups, *inter alia*, on trade and competition, as well as on trade and investment, have held meetings in Geneva. In accordance with the Doha Declaration of 2001, these issues were incorporated into the WTO post-Doha work programme for the following two years,[80] but three out of four issues (investment, competition, transparency in government procurement) were subsequently dropped from the negotiating agenda. The following remarks concentrate on how the issues of investment and competition have been dealt with in the EFTA free trade agreements.

With regard to investment rules, the Agreements that the EFTA States have concluded with Mexico, Singapore, and Chile, and that the EC and its Member States have concluded with Mexico, Chile, and South Africa, go considerably further than the traditional agreements with European and Mediterranean countries. Many of the EC Member States have for a long time been among the most active in negotiating bilateral investment treaties (BITs). It should also be noted that among the EFTA States, Norway and Switzerland especially have concluded an important number of bilateral investment protection treaties in the past.

The inclusion of investment protection rules, together with rules concerning the access of foreign investors and rules governing trade in goods and services, in the Agreements with Singapore and Mexico, was unprecedented for EFTA States. The WTO covers only some aspects of foreign direct investment: under the GATS with respect to establishment of foreign services providers; and in the TRIMs Agreement[81] with regard to performance requirements (host country measures).

The Agreement between the EFTA States and Mexico was the first EFTA Agreement to include substantive investment rules. Yet, this Agreement contains only very auxiliary disciplines on investment and an evolutionary clause for future negotiations. This is mostly due to the fact that the EFTA–Mexico Agreement had to follow the earlier agreement concluded between Mexico and the EC, which had led to only modest results in this field. With regard to substantive rules, the Agreement only contains a provision on the free transfer of payments (Article 46). At the same time both the EFTA States[82] and Mexico are members of the OECD, which allows for a reference to all the obligations the parties have accepted in the OECD investment framework (Article 48).

[79] *See* Ministerial Declaration adopted 13 December 1996 in Singapore, available at http://www.wto.org/english/thewto_e/minist_e/min96_e/wtodec_e.htm.

[80] *See* Ministerial Declaration adopted 14 November 2001 in Doha, available at http://www.wto.org/english/thewto_e/minist_e/min01_e/mindecl_e.htm.

[81] *See* Agreement on Trade-related Investment Measures, one of the multilateral agreements on trade in goods of the Final Act of the Uruguay Round, *supra* note 18.

[82] Except for Liechtenstein, which is not (yet) an OECD member.

These are traditionally the disciplines relating to transfers and capital movements.[83] Article 49 provides that the negotiations for a comprehensive liberalization of investment flows shall start no later than three years after the entry into force of the Agreement.[84] The Agreement between the European Community and South Africa similarly mostly contains transfer rules, while substantive protection rules for other investment-related areas are not included. The Agreement encourages, however, 'where appropriate', the negotiation of bilateral agreements between EC Member States and South Africa.

The Agreement between the EFTA States and Singapore is the first EFTA Agreement to include a comprehensive chapter on investment. It is important to recall that Singapore is not an OECD Member, and thus there was no common basis for the liberalization of investment flows between the Parties.[85] Singapore is Switzerland's primary location of investment in Asia, and the sixth most important host country for Swiss investments worldwide. Many of the rules contained in the EFTA Singapore Agreement resemble those already contained in the existing investment Agreements between Switzerland[86] and Singapore, and Norway and Singapore. At the same time, the EFTA–Singapore Agreement is the first agreement to contain a right to establishment for foreign firms from another Party. Article 40 provides for non-discriminatory access for investors. Investors from an EFTA State benefit from national or MFN treatment, whichever is better in a specific situation.[87] The MFN treatment, however, does not apply to those agreements of either Singapore or an EFTA State with third

[83] The OECD has long been at the forefront in efforts to develop international rules relating to capital movements, international investment, and trade in services. These instruments have been regularly reviewed and strengthened over the years to keep them up to date and effective. The 'Code of Liberalisation of Capital Movements' and the 'Code of Liberalisation of Current Invisible Operations' constitute legally binding rules, stipulating progressive, non-discriminatory liberalization of capital movements, the right of establishment, and current invisible transactions (mostly services). All non-conforming measures must be listed in country reservations against the Codes. The Codes are implemented through policy reviews and country examinations, relying on 'peer pressure' to encourage unilateral rather than negotiated liberalization. The Codes were initially adopted in 1961, but have since been revised and expanded in scope. Important recent additions were the right of establishment (1986) and cross-border financial services (1992). New work to promote liberalization of insurance services and professional services has been launched. For most Member countries, remaining reservations against the Code obligations relate to foreign direct investment, the purchase of real estate by non-residents, and the prohibitions of certain types of securities operations.

[84] The first meeting of the Joint Committee Mexico–EFTA that is in charge of overseeing the administration of the Agreement, on 22 October 2002, has not led to the initiation of negotiations yet. *See* EFTA Press Release of 22 October 2002, available at http://secretariat.efta.int/library/Library/dbafile24602.html.

[85] *See* Message by the Swiss Federal Council on the Free Trade Agreement between the EFTA States and Singapore, *supra* note 64, at 4.3. Singapore is currently looking at the option of adhering to the OECD Investment Declaration.

[86] *See* Bilateral Investment Promotion and Protection Agreement between Switzerland and Singapore of 6 March 1978, reprinted in the Swiss Systematic Treaty Collection as SR 0.975.268.9, *see supra* note 2.

[87] *See* Message by the Swiss Federal Council on the FTA EFTA–Singapore, *supra* note 64, at para. 4.3.

States that provide for a substantial liberalization of investment flows. Nevertheless, the conclusion of such agreements with third States entitles the Parties to the EFTA–Singapore Agreement to re-negotiate their market access if desired.

The establishment right for investors and investments is limited to the goods sector. With regard to investments in the field of services supply, the specific commitments undertaken under the services chapter of this Agreement prevail (Article 38). The Agreement thus combines a top-down liberalization in the area of investments in the goods sector with a bottom-up approach in the area of services, as is already contained in the GATS (mode 3, establishment). This means that the investment disciplines apply to all areas but list some exceptions (top-down), while services liberalization is subject to a negotiated opening sector-by-sector (bottom-up). For investments in goods sectors, exceptions are listed in a specific annex. This corresponds to the method used in the OECD investment instruments. In view of the sensitivities regarding access for foreign investors, these exceptions can be altered and new areas can be added at any time. It is very important to note that this Agreement also includes protection disciplines, just as can be found in traditional BITs. In particular, the Agreement provides for investor–State dispute settlement (Article 48). Therefore, the Agreement could also become the source of investment disputes relating to expropriation and/or fair and equitable treatment as generally discussed under the Agreement's title on 'regulatory measures'.[88]

Article 39 of the EFTA–Singapore Agreement provides, under the title 'Promotion and Protection' in its paragraph 2, for a fair and equitable treatment guarantee:

1. Each Party shall, in accordance with the provisions of this Chapter, create and maintain stable, equitable, favourable and transparent conditions for investors of the other Parties to make investments in its territory.
2. Such conditions shall include a commitment to accord at all times to investments of investors of another Party fair and equitable treatment. Such investments shall also enjoy the most constant protection and security.

Article 42 of the EFTA–Singapore Agreement provides, under the title 'Dispossession, Compensation':

1. None of the Parties shall take, either de jure or de facto, measures of expropriation or nationalisation against investments of investors of another Party, unless such measures are in the public interest; non-discriminatory; carried out under due process of law; and accompanied by the payment of compensation. The amount of compensation shall be settled in a freely convertible currency and paid without delay to the person entitled thereto without regard to its residence or domicile.

[88] *See*, e.g., Peterson, Luke Eric, *Research Note: Emerging Bilateral Investment Treaty Arbitration and Sustainable Development*, available at www.iisd.org/pdf/2003/trade_bits_disputes.pdf; or Feldman, Mark B., *State Responsibility for Regulatory Measures under International Law: Recent NAFTA Arbitrations*, available at http://www.gsblaw.com/resource/pub_result.asp?ID=1524251242003.

2. Investors of a Party whose investments in the territory of another Party have suffered losses due to armed conflict or civil strife in the territory of the latter Party, shall benefit from treatment in accordance with Article 40 as regards restitution, indemnification, compensation or any other settlement it adopts or maintains relating to such losses.

In addition, Article 43 provides, under the title 'Domestic Regulation':

Nothing in this Chapter shall be construed to prevent a Party from adopting, maintaining or enforcing any measure consistent with this Chapter that is in the public interest, such as measures to meet health, safety or environmental concerns.[89]

Lastly, investor–State arbitration (although somewhat limited) is provided for in Article 48 of the EFTA–Singapore Agreement:

Disputes Between an Investor and a Party

1. If an investor of a Party considers that a measure applied by another Party is inconsistent with an obligation of this Chapter, thus causing loss or damage to him or his investment, he may request consultations with a view to solving the matter amicably.
2. Any such matter which has not been settled within a period of six months from the date of request for consultations may be referred to the courts or administrative tribunals of the Party concerned or, if both parties to the dispute agree, be submitted to one of the following:
   a) arbitration under the Convention on the Settlement of Investment Disputes between States and Nationals of other States (the 'ICSID Convention'), if this Convention is available;
   b) conciliation or arbitration under the Additional Facility Rules of the International Centre for the Settlement of Investment Disputes;
   c) arbitration under the Arbitration Rules of the United Nations Commission on International Trade Law.
3. A Party may conclude contractual agreements with investors of another Party giving its unconditional and irrevocable consent to the submission of all or certain types of disputes to international conciliation or arbitration in accordance with paragraph 2 above. Such agreements may be notified to the Depositary of this Agreement.

In the Agreement between the EFTA States and Chile, an identical approach was used as in the previously negotiated agreement between the EC and Chile. Instead of referring to investment as such, a section on establishment has been included which does not relate to classical protection disciplines and contains no investor–State arbitration. The objective of the Section on establishment (Articles 32–37) in the Agreement between Chile and the EFTA States, for example, is the improvement of the investment environment and, in particular, the conditions of establishment of companies between the Parties. The EFTA States and Chile grant each other national treatment for the establishment of investors,

[89] This approach reminds us of the approach used in NAFTA and suggested in the MAI negotiations. However, it remains unclear how an arbitral tribunal would apply this provision. It should be noted that under the EFTA–Singapore Agreement, an investor–State arbitration is not automatic, and is possible only with the prior consent of the State involved (Art. 48.2).

except for a few cases where the Parties have lodged reservations based on restrictions in their national legislation. The EFTA States maintain certain reservations, which correspond to their reservations maintained with regard to the relevant OECD instruments in this field.[90]

Article 34 of the EFTA–Chile Agreement reads:

National treatment

With respect to establishment, and subject to the reservations set out in Annex X, each Party shall grant to juridical and natural persons of the other Party treatment no less favourable than that it accords to its own juridical and natural persons performing a like economic activity.

It must be noted, however, that all EFTA States and most EC Member States have previously negotiated bilateral investment treaties with Chile. Iceland negotiated such an agreement with Chile immediately following the negotiations of the EFTA–Chile Agreement, to be at a similar level of protection as the other EFTA and EC Member States.

Taking the BITs and the trade agreements between the EC, the EFTA, and their Member States with Chile together, a fully-fledged investment liberalization and protection regime is in place. The same is true for the BITs in place between EC and EFTA Member States with Mexico or South Africa. Several EFTA Member States also have separate BITs in force with Singapore, in addition to the new chapter in the EFTA–Singapore trade agreement. Wherever investment-related provisions are included in the trade agreements, their interplay with existing BITs may pose additional problems.

In the existing BITs and in the Agreement between the EFTA States and Singapore, we find rules on fair and equitable treatment and expropriation that resemble each other and are all based on the classical type of rules also used in Chapter 11 of NAFTA.[91] It is therefore in principle possible that similar disputes relating to water policies may arise as under NAFTA. The Cochabamba/Aguas del Tunari dispute[92] between Bolivia and a US–Dutch investor is based on the BIT between the Netherlands and Bolivia, although observers claim the

[90] *See supra* note 83. *See also*, with regard to the reservations, the information on the Internet, available at http://secretariat.efta.int/Web/ExternalRelations/PartnerCountries/Chile/CL/CL_ Summary.doc.

[91] *See* the contribution by Nathalie Bernasconi-Osterwalder in this volume.

[92] *See* ICSID, Aguas del Tunari S.A. [Bechtel] v. Republic of Bolivia, Case No. ARB/02/3. The Bolivian government put up for private lease the water system of its third largest city, Cochabamba. In 1999, following a process with just one bidder, a 40-year concession was granted to Aguas del Tunari, a majority-owned subsidiary of Bechtel Enterprises of California set up for that sole purpose. Within weeks of taking over control of the water system, the company raised water rates by an average of more than 50%, and in some cases far higher. Massive and widespread public protests took place. To protect the company's contract the Bolivian government took extraordinary measures against its people, including a declaration of a state of emergency, the suspension of constitutional rights, and the violent repression of the protests, resulting in more than 100 injuries and the death of one 17-year-old boy, Victor Hugo Daza. In April 2000, with the government unable to stop the protests, the company abandoned its management of the water system and left the country, and sued the Bolivian government under the BIT between Bolivia and the Netherlands.

nationality has been assumed frivolously. The Aguas del Aconquija S.A. dispute[93] between Argentina and a French investor which operated water and sewage systems in the Argentinian province of Tucumán, is based on the BIT between France and Argentina. Disputes like these two, or the Azurix dispute[94] (which involves a US investor and the Argentinian government under the 1991 USA–Argentina BIT), are therefore just as likely under some of the bilateral agreements (trade agreements and/or bilateral investment agreements) of the EFTA States and the EC and its Member States as under existing BITs or the GATS. Observers still have to realize this additional way for liberalization regarding water-related services, and the risks and opportunities of such an approach.

5.2 Services (commercial presence) and water

In the EFTA Agreements with Mexico, Singapore, and Chile, as well as in the EC Agreements with Mexico, South Africa, and Chile, the services chapters are all based on the GATS approach. That is, the disciplines are framed along the lines of the GATS and the benefit of the Agreements mostly lies in the extension of commitments by both sides. While in the Agreements with Chile and Singapore such an extension of existing agreements was possible, respective negotiations with Mexico and South Africa in the future are built into the Agreements.[95] Therefore all the issues treated with regard to the interaction of the GATS and water-related services also apply to these Agreements.[96] Some observers are afraid that WTO Members may be forced in negotiations to open up their water treatment and distribution sectors to private companies from other WTO Member States. Such private investors are often considered as harmful for the

[93] *See* ICSID, Compañía de Aguas del Aconquija S.A. & Vivendi Universal v. Argentine Republic, Case No. ARB/97/3. A French company and its Argentine affiliate operated water and sewage systems in the Argentinian province of Tucumán under a 1995 Concession Contract between the Argentine affiliate and Tucumán. After renegotiation efforts failed in 1997, the Claimants and Tucumán respectively rescinded and terminated the Contract, with each party accusing the other of default.

[94] *See* ICSID, Azurix Corp v. The Argentine Republic, Case No. ARB/01/12. Azurix Corp ('Azurix'), a U.S. company incorporated in Delaware, brought a claim concerning its investment in a utility that distributes drinking water and treats sewage in the province of Buenos Aires, Argentina. Azurix's subsidiary, Azurix AGOSBA S.R.L. ('AAS'), incorporated Azurix Buenos Aires ('ABA') in Argentina to act as its concessionaire and to enter into a concession agreement for the distribution of potable water in the province of Buenos Aires. Azurix claimed that Argentina breached the BIT through measures tantamount to expropriation, by failing to accord it fair and equitable treatment, full protection and security, and treatment required by international law, by failing to observe obligations Argentina entered into with regard to Azurix's investment and by failing to provide transparency concerning the regulations, administrative practices, procedures, and adjudicatory decisions that affect Azurix's investment.

[95] *See*, e.g., Art. 30 of the Agreement between the EU and South Africa.

[96] *See*, e.g., Gould, Ellen, *Water in the Current Round of WTO Negotiations on Services*, Canadian Centre for Policy Alternatives Briefing Paper Series: Trade and Investment 4 of 1 January 2003, available at http://www.policyalternatives.ca/.

general policies applied by governments in water distribution and treatment, which are normally linked to social and environmental goals. Especially in countries where governments may not be strong enough to impose and control these public interests, it is feared, privatization and foreign investors, rights may be detrimental to the general welfare and deprive especially the poorest layers of society in developing countries of basic utilities previously guaranteed by the State.[97]

A typical example is the Agreement between the EFTA States and Chile. Chapter IV, Articles 22 to 31, covers trade in services, including a separate Annex on telecommunication services (Annex IX). The Agreement covers all four modes of delivery (supply) of a service, as defined under GATS: cross-border trade, consumption abroad, commercial presence, and presence of natural persons. The Agreement addresses all services sectors.[98] As in the GATS, positive lists of specific commitments of each Party are an integral part of the Agreement. These lists will be reviewed every three years, or more frequently, with a view to providing for the reduction or elimination of substantially all remaining discrimination between the Parties for trade in services covered by the present section on services.[99]

Due to the similarity of this approach to the GATS approach, all the concerns often raised regarding the threat of GATS services negotiations at the multilateral level apply also to the bilateral negotiations. Several NGOs have raised concerns over the possibility of major water companies pressuring smaller and less developed countries to commit their water sectors under the GATS and under bilateral negotiations. In particular, the European Community was criticized for pressing partners in GATS negotiations for 'real and meaningful market access' in this sector.[100]

The issue generally raised under the GATS is particularly relevant from a European perspective, as especially French companies dominate the world's water industry. In France, private companies have provided water since more than 150 years. The two biggest companies are the French Générale des Eaux, now owned by Veolia, and Lyonnaise des Eaux, now owned by Suéz. Another important service provider in the field is RWE/Thames of the United Kingdom, also an EC company. A third French company active in the field is Saur. The US provider Azurix has lost market share due to its connections to the collapsed US energy giant Enron.

[97] *See*, e.g., Tuckwiller, Tara, *Will state have a say about its own water?* in: Sunday Gazette Mail online of 8 December 2002, available at http://sundaygazettemail.com/display_story.php3?sid=2002120726&format=prn.

[98] However, it has been agreed that with regard to financial services, the possible coverage and the extent of liberalization will be reconsidered two years after the entry into force of the Agreement.

[99] The text of the Agreement is on the Internet, available at http://secretariat.efta.int/Web/ExternalRelations/PartnerCountries/Chile/CL/CL_FTA.pdf.

[100] For details of such criticism, *see* Save the Children UK, *GATS and Water: The Threat of Services Negotiations at the WTO*, 8 April 2003, on the Internet, available at http://www.savethechildren.org.uk/temp/scuk/cache/cmsattach/21_GATS%20and%20water.pdf.

Nevertheless, the official EC policy regarding water services in both bilateral and multilateral negotiations is that 'EU requests do not touch on the issue of access to (water) resources and in no way undermine or reduce governments' ability to regulate pricing, availability and affordability of water supplies as they choose'.[101] So far, the bilateral commitments in the European Community's agreements do not include water-related services. The EFTA States have never committed themselves in this respect, and hence do no require commitments from their trading partners in this area either.

6. Conclusions

During the consolidation phase of the global trading system from the conclusion of the Uruguay Round until the Doha Ministerial Declaration in November 2001, many countries concluded bilateral and regional free trade agreements and arrangements. This is certainly not only due to the fact that many trade diplomats and lawyers had to be kept busy, but related to a genuine desire of certain States to continue their liberalization processes and use the results of domestic reforms undertaken for increased participation in world trade and investment.[102] Whether these bilateral attempts will ultimately harm multilateral solutions is by no means certain. A recent OECD report claims that multilateral and bilateral initiatives can be mutually supportive.[103]

With regard to the substantive issues dealt with in bilateral second or third generation trade agreements, in the European context only very few non-WTO areas are contained in these agreements. Often, they merely refer to existing WTO disciplines. Thus, these agreements normally achieve substantial WTO plus commitments in the areas of trade in services and trade in goods, but contain few WTO plus elements with regard to rules. WTO plus commitments would be additional sector openings that some WTO Members may not want to open on an MFN basis, but may be prepared to open to selected bilateral partners. WTO plus elements consist in more or different disciplines that can sometimes be agreed upon between regional or bilateral partners despite resistance at the multilateral level. Often such new bilateral disciplines are later, important reference models for multilateral negotiations at the WTO.

The fact that achieving such WTO plus elements is so difficult even at the bilateral level, has the positive effect of not leading to a situation where a great number of existing bilateral trade agreements would contain an even

[101] *See* the statement on the Internet, available at http://www.europa.eu.int/comm/trade/issues/sectoral/services/index_en.htm.

[102] *See* Ethier, *supra* note 49.

[103] *See* OECD, *Regional Trade Agreement and the Multilateral Trading System: Consolidated Report*, TD/TC(2002)8/FINAL, on the Internet, available at www.oecd.org.

bigger number of divergent disciplines applicable in a given field. Such a development could lead to a so-called 'spaghetti bowl-effect', i.e. an obscure and unmanageable number of different rules and preference systems that could easily lead to incompatibilities with the WTO system.

Overall, most agreements contain WTO commitments allowing use of the existing trade regime for further liberalization of market access for foreign suppliers. Such preferential treatment of specific trading partners often leads to a domino effect, as competing trading partners will try to engage in negotiations giving them equal treatment and avoiding disadvantageous market distortions. As different countries compete in very different sectors, this may lead to interesting multiplier effects. The recently concluded agreement between South Korea and Chile[104] has important implications for Norwegian fish exports and car exports from many nations.

At the same time, there is a limited number of trade-related areas where multilateral coordination and harmonization seem desirable to certain States but not to others. Amongst these are issues such as competition and investment. With regard to these areas, bilateral agreements can serve as laboratories where new approaches are tested and different regional or national approaches can be melted down, refined, and recast. At the same time, one should not forget that at the bilateral level the difference in negotiating power between the partners has a much higher impact than at the multilateral level, where strategic alliances are possible.

The issue of water-related services and investments has so far played a minor role in the European Community's and EFTA's bilateral negotiations with trading partners. The approach of integrating GATS-type services chapters and (sometimes) additional BIT-like investment chapters, or alternatively establishment provisions, into bilateral agreements leaves, however, the possibility of addressing water-related services and investment at a later stage through the negotiations of explicit commitments.

In addition, one must read these agreements together with existing BITs by individual Member States of the EC and EFTA. Cases like the Cochabamba/Aguas del Tunari dispute, the Azurix dispute, or the Aguas del Aconquija S.A. dispute are therefore just as likely under some of the bilateral agreements (trade agreements and/or bilateral investment agreements) of the EFTA States and the EC and its Member States as under existing BITs or the GATS. It is interesting that the EC's agreements do not provide for investor–State arbitration as they do not directly approach the issue of treatment of foreign investments. Most other bilateral agreements which include investment chapters, however, contain such a possibility, even if sometimes subject to conditions.[105] An important exception is certainly the recently negotiated

[104] As announced in the international press; *see*, e.g., Dow Jones, 24 October 2002.
[105] *See*, e.g., the EFTA–Singapore Agreement, *supra* note 35.

Agreement between Australia and the United States of February 2004, which does contain an impressive chapter on investment without providing for investor–State dispute settlement. The two Parties argued that between two OECD countries with very similar legal and economic conditions, such a mechanism was not necessary.

11

International Investment Rules and Water: Learning from the NAFTA Experience

NATHALIE BERNASCONI-OSTERWALDER and EDITH BROWN WEISS

1. Introduction

In the ten years since its entry into force in 1994, the North American Free Trade Agreement (NAFTA)[1] between the Governments of Canada, the United Mexican States, and the United States of America has drawn much attention from environmentalists, academics, politicians, and media. To the surprise of many, it has not been the trade rules that have raised concern, but rather the rules on investment contained in NAFTA's Chapter 11. Over half of the disputes between investors and host States initiated under Chapter 11 to date have involved challenges by investors of measures relating to environmental and health protection, including the protection of water resources. Decisions in many of the disputes are still pending, but both those decided as well as those initiated have reinforced fears that Chapter 11's set of investor guarantees (and corresponding host State obligations) may inhibit host governments from adopting environmental and health measures. On the issue of water, investors can sue host States to pay monetary damages for setting standards to ensure safe drinking water, to support aquatic life, or to sustain the recreational use of water. This calls for an analysis of how Chapter 11 can put limits on a government's ability to manage its water resources and control water pollution from industrial, agricultural, and municipal sources.

This chapter looks at the relationship between the investment rules under Chapter 11 and domestic environmental regulation, with a particular focus on the protection of water resources. It first sets the stage by briefly introducing Chapter 11 and its provisions on investor guarantees. It then notes the absence of a general exception or carve-out for domestic environmental or public interest regulation, and identifies the implications that this lack entails. It moves on to

[1] North American Free Trade Agreement, December 17, 1992, Can.-Mex.-U.S., Pub. L. No. 103-182, 107 Stat. 2047 (NAFTA), reprinted in 32 ILM 289; text is also available at http://www.nafta-sec-alena.org.

look at the more specific question of whether water-related measures are covered under Chapter 11 obligations and concludes that water-related measures are treated no differently from other measures of the host State. In this context, the chapter provides some examples of specific disputes involving water initiated under Chapter 11 to date. The following section of the chapter analyzes the arbitral tribunals' interpretations of the investor guarantees and considers their implications for a host State's ability to protect its water resources. Specifically, it concentrates on the national treatment clause, the provisions on performance requirements, and on the protection against expropriation. Special attention is paid to the fact that the compensation rights granted to foreign investors under Article 1110 may go further than expropriation protection available under domestic laws for domestic investors. The chapter then provides a short overview of the procedural aspects of the investor-to-State process and points to the lack of transparency in processes involving public interests as vital as those relating to water. It concludes with a short summary and conclusions.

2. An introduction to Chapter 11

Chapter 11 of NAFTA aims at protecting foreign investments in host countries. It does not include protections or guarantees for the host State or its citizens. Chapter 11's investment rules, also referred to as 'investor guarantees', include protection against expropriation and nationalization of property, as well as non-discrimination standards, which ensure that the foreign investor is not treated less favorably than national investors or other foreign investors. Also included in Chapter 11 are provisions guaranteeing a minimum standard of treatment, protecting the investor against arbitrary actions of the host State, and rules setting out restrictions on the use of so-called 'performance requirements'.[2]

In addition to these substantive obligations, Chapter 11 contains procedural provisions on the settlement of disputes. Under these rules, an investor of a NAFTA Party can claim against a host State for the violation of certain treaty provisions. As of 1 October 2004, Chapter 11's investor-to-State process had led to ten final arbitral reports and several more cases were pending. A total of at least thirty-seven intents to arbitrate had been filed. Several disputes have involved challenges to domestic environmental and health regulations of host States, such as the creation of protected areas or restrictions on the use of certain substances that pollute ground water. In all of the cases, the investor sought compensation for alleged violations of the investor guarantees, claiming, for example, that the investor was treated less favorably than domestic investors, or that the environmental regulation amounted to indirect expropriation.

[2] For an excellent introduction to NAFTA Chapter 11, *see* Institute for Sustainable Development (IISD) and World Wildlife Fund (WWF), *Private Rights, Public Problems—A guide to NAFTA's controversial chapter on investor rights* (2001) (written by Howard Mann).

Chapter 11 arbitral rulings seem to concentrate mainly on the economic and investor-focused objectives of NAFTA, rather than on balancing economic and environmental goals. For example, in *Metalclad v. Mexico* (which was an environmental case involving the construction of a hazardous waste facility), the arbitral tribunal based its interpretation of Chapter 11 on three objectives, namely, transparency, the increase in investment opportunities, and a predictable framework for investors. This interpretative approach neglected to consider other elements, such as environmental protection or sustainable development.

3. Chapter 11 contains no general exception for environmental or other public interest measures

Many commentators are concerned that Chapter 11 constrains host States' actions to protect their environment or other public interests if they may affect foreign investment. Although NAFTA's preamble declares, *inter alia*, that the Parties resolve to preserve their flexibility to safeguard the public welfare, to promote sustainable development, and to strengthen the development and enforcement of environmental laws and regulations, these matters are notably omitted from NAFTA's list of objectives in Article 102 of the text. The NAFTA does include a general exceptions clause for the protection of the natural resources and public health in relation to international trade in goods and technical barriers to trade.[3] Significantly, however, there is no such general exception for Chapter 11 on investment.

Chapter 11's Article 1114 specifically addresses environmental measures.[4] However, the article falls far short of creating an environmental exception. Negotiators included Article 1114 to ensure that the new investment rules would not lead to a race to the bottom by countries hoping to attract foreign investment through lax environmental regulation and enforcement. Its relevance, however, is negligible. The provision is divided into two paragraphs. The first paragraph simply stipulates that nothing in Chapter 11 prevents a Party from adopting an environmental measure that is otherwise consistent with Chapter 11. The second

[3] Art. 2101 (which refers to GATT Art. XX and its interpretative notes).

[4] Art. 1114 on Environmental Measures provides:

1. Nothing in this Chapter shall be construed to prevent a Party from adopting, maintaining or enforcing any measure otherwise consistent with this Chapter that it considers appropriate to ensure that investment activity in its territory is undertaken in a manner sensitive to environmental concerns.
2. The Parties recognize that it is inappropriate to encourage investment by relaxing domestic health, safety or environmental measures. Accordingly, a Party should not waive or otherwise derogate from, or offer to waive or otherwise derogate from, such measures as an encouragement for the establishment, acquisition, expansion or retention in its territory of an investment of an investor. If a Party considers that another Party has offered such an encouragement, it may request consultations with the other Party and the two Parties shall consult with a view to avoiding any such encouragement.

paragraph consists of a commitment to avoid relaxing health, safety, or environmental measures to attract foreign investment. However, the language used is not mandatory (the word 'should' not 'shall' is used) and, in contrast to obligations relating to investor protection, a derogation cannot be brought to binding arbitration. Rather, where a Party considers another Party has offered to derogate from its existing health or environmental measures in order to encourage investment, it may request a 'consultation' with that Party. To date, Article 1114 has not been used to request consultations, nor has it influenced the outcome of arbitral decisions involving environmental measures.

In the absence of a general exception for environmental measures, host States can only rely on the very limited exceptions contained in Article 1106, regarding performance requirements (discussed further below), and Article 1108, allowing Parties to annex certain non-conforming measures.

Pursuant to Article 1108, a Party is entitled to annex schedules of activities to which the national treatment (Article 1102), most-favored-nation treatment (Article 1103), and performance requirements (Article 1106) do not apply. Canada's schedule includes, *inter alia*, the energy (oil and gas, uranium) and the fisheries (harvesting and processing and related services) sectors. No provision in Annex I relates to water in particular. However, the schedules also include general exceptions. Canada's schedule to Annex I, for instance, lists certain measures that apply to all sectors of the economy. One measure listed in Canada's schedule which is applicable to all sectors is the Investment Canada Act, providing exceptions to Chapter 11's national treatment obligation (Article 1102), performance requirements (Article 1106), and obligations relating to senior management and boards of directors (Article 1107). The description of the Act included in Canada's schedule provides that Canada retains the right to screen investments from the U.S. or Mexico in Canada above a specified threshold. Moreover, in the review process an applicant for an investment has to demonstrate the net benefit of such an acquisition to Canada. Lastly, Canada has the right to impose requirements 'in connection with the establishment, acquisition, expansion, conduct or operation of an investment of an investor of another Party . . .'.

Pursuant to Canada's schedule to Annex I, and the reference to the Investment Canada Act in particular, Canada retains substantial control over its water resources. However, whether this control is politically feasible is questionable.[5] To the authors' knowledge, as of May 2005, neither Canada nor another NAFTA party has invoked Article 1108. In addition, it is notable that the provision, while allowing Parties to list exemptions to national treatment, most-favored-nation treatment, and performance requirements, does not allow such exemptions with respect to expropriation.

[5] Annex I Schedule of Canada is available at http://www.dfait-maeci.gc.ca/nafta-alen/chap25a-en.asp (last visited 20 April 2004). On the relevance of the Investment Canada Act, *see* Scott Philip Little, *Canada's Capacity to Control the Flow: Water Export and the North American Free Trade Agreement*, 8 Pace Int'l L. Rev. 127, at p. 153.

The absence of a general exception or carve-out means that a host State's environmental and other public interest measure must be consistent with all Chapter 11's provisions to protect foreign investment, or else fit within the narrow and untested exceptions in Articles 1106 and 1108. Failing these, a host State may be required to compensate an investor for measures it takes to protect its environment or its citizens.

4. No exemption for measures to protect water resources

As with environmental and health measures generally, Chapter 11 does not provide a shield for measures to protect water resources from investor challenges. Although water was a major subject of concern during the negotiations between Canada, the U.S., and Mexico (given that 20% of the world's freshwater supply is in Canada), water-related measures are not explicitly excluded from the scope of the agreement, nor are they subject to different rules. At the time, skeptics already feared that Canada could lose control over its water resources and be barred from using export restrictions on such resources. Fears arose from the definition of 'goods' in Chapter 3 of NAFTA on the international trade in goods. The NAFTA bases its definition of 'goods' on the term 'product' as defined in the GATT, which includes 'waters, including natural or artificial waters and aerated waters'. An explanatory note adds that 'ordinary natural waters of all kinds (other than sea water)' are included.[6] Many perceived this definition as a clear risk to water resource management, and some argued that Canada should specifically exempt water from NAFTA. However, this was not done, as the Canadian government believed such an exemption unnecessary. It argued that NAFTA did not apply to Canada's waters, provided that water was not being traded for commercial purposes. This view was later incorporated in the 1993 Joint Public Statement of the Parties clarifying NAFTA rules. The Statement asserts that NAFTA creates no rights to the natural water resources and that '[u]nless water, in any form, has entered into commerce and become a good or product, it is not covered by the provisions of any trade agreement including the NAFTA. And nothing in the NAFTA would oblige any NAFTA Party to either exploit its water for commercial use, or to begin exporting water in any form'.[7] Although the Statement considers the link between water and free trade in goods, it neglects the question of how the investment rules in Chapter 11 might affect the ability of a State to protect its water resources.

This implies that, unlike Chapter 3, Chapter 11 does not hinge upon the definition of water and the point at which water becomes a tradable good. As a

[6] Trade in goods and water export restrictions (both in the context of the GATT and NAFTA) are discussed in more detail in the chapter by Edith Brown Weiss in Part I of this book.

[7] Statement is available at http://www.scics.gc.ca/cinfo99/83067000_e.html.

consequence, any domestic water-related measure affecting an investment could be immediately challenged under the investor-to-State dispute mechanism.

If water-related measures are not generally excluded from the scope of Chapter 11, one may still ask whether Chapter 11 also covers water-related *trade* measures. Clearly, trade measures, such as import and export restrictions imposed on goods, fall under the scope of Chapter 3 on trade in goods. At the same time, Chapter 11 does not explicitly exclude trade measures from its scope. This situation raises the question of whether trade measures can fall under Chapters 3 and 11 simultaneously.[8]

Several Chapter 11 cases indicate that not only Chapter 3 on the trade in goods covers export restrictions but also Chapter 11 on investment. None of the tribunals examining the legality of export restrictions found inconsistencies between Chapters 11 and 3, and thus proceeded with an analysis under Chapter 11 rather than rejecting the case and referring to the State-to-State proceedings required to examine violations of Chapter 3. In *S.D. Myers*,[9] for example, a tribunal examined a Canadian measure banning the export of PCB waste from Canada into the United States for disposal. Another case, *Pope & Talbot*,[10] involved an export restriction on lumber exported from Canada to the U.S. Although that measure did not consist of an actual export ban, the case is of particular relevance for the present analysis on water because the NAFTA tribunal examined export restrictions on a natural resource. Neither of the two tribunals hesitated to examine the export restrictions described above under Chapter 11 in an investor-to-State process. In both cases they found that they were covered by Chapter 11 and that the right to export is a protected right of the investor as part of a business operation under Chapter 11. Although no decision has specifically addressed export restrictions on water resources, there is no reason to believe that NAFTA tribunals would not also extend their jurisdiction to trade measures involving water. And there is no reason to believe that such a case will never occur. In 1998, Sun Belt Water Inc. of Santa Barbara, California, initiated Chapter 11 proceedings to challenge measures restricting the export of water. At issue was a refusal by the Canadian province of British Columbia to expand a water export license for the bulk export of freshwater, and the subsequent suspension of a pre-existing water export license. The case has apparently been abandoned but offers a good example of the types of water-related cases that can be initiated under Chapter 11. Water export restrictions that may be allowed under the general exceptions of trade rules might be disallowed under investment rules.

[8] Art. 1112 of Chapter 11 addresses the relation of Chapter 11 to other chapters. Paragraph 1 provides that '[i]n the event of any inconsistency between [Chapter 11] and another Chapter, the other Chapter shall prevail to the extent of the inconsistency'. Thus, Chapter 11 applies as long as a measure relates to a foreign investor or investment *and* is not inconsistent with another NAFTA Chapter, such as, e.g., Chapter 3 dealing with trade in goods. This, in turn, raises the question of what is to be considered 'inconsistent'.

[9] *S.D. Myers, Inc. v. Canada*, Partial Award (Decision on the Merits), November 13, 2000.

[10] *Pope & Talbot v. Canada*, Interim Award, June 26, 2000. Final Merits Award, April 10, 2001.

5. NAFTA DISPUTES AND THE PROTECTION OF WATER RESOURCES

Investors have challenged a wide array of measures adopted by host States, including measures aimed specifically at protecting water resources. In the *Methanex v. United States* case, which was pending as of May 2005, a Canadian investor has challenged a Californian measure aimed at protecting ground water from contamination through the phasing out of a gasoline additive. In the case of *Sunbelt*, discussed above, a U.S. investor challenged measures taken by British Columbia restricting the export of water.

More recently, a group of Texan irrigation districts, water rights holders, and a water supply company launched a notice of intent to submit a claim against Mexico over the alleged expropriation of water from the Rio Grande.[11] The claimants allege that under a 1944 Treaty between Mexico and the United States, they are entitled to one-third of the Rio Grande's natural flow. They claim that between 1992 and 2002, Mexico operated dams and reservoirs to artificially manipulate tributaries into the Rio Grande for its own irrigation purposes, and in doing so expropriated approximately 1,000,000 acre-feet of water in which the claimants had rights of use. While this case deals less with natural resource protection, it indicates that investors can initiate Chapter 11 proceedings in disputes involving water rights of different users. Whether jurisdiction will be granted remains unclear at this stage.

The investors in these and other environment-related disputes generally allege violations of a number of Chapter 11 provisions, including Articles 1102 on national treatment, 1105 on minimal standard of treatment, and 1110 on expropriation. Some investors also allege breaches of Article 1106 on performance requirements. An analysis of how the tribunals have interpreted some of the most relevant investor guarantees and the implications for a host State's ability to protect and manage its water resources follows.

6. NATIONAL TREATMENT[12]

Investors have repeatedly invoked Chapter 11's national treatment clause under Article 1102. Article 1102 provides that each NAFTA Party must accord to investors and investments of another Party treatment no less favorable than that it accords, in like circumstances, to its own investors and investments with

[11] Notice of intent to submit a claim to arbitration under Section B, Chapter 11 of the North American Free Trade Agreement, 27 August 2004. *See* http://www.naftaclaims.com.

[12] This chapter does not specifically analyze Chapter 11's most-favored-nation provision (Art. 1103), which provides that host countries must accord to investors or investments of a NAFTA Party 'treatment no less favorable than it accords, in like circumstances' to investors or investments of any other Party or non-Party. Interpretational complexities arising under Art. 1103 are similar to those discussed in the analysis of the national treatment clause.

respect to the establishment, acquisition, expansion, management, conduct, operation, and sale or other disposition of investments.

In the context of Article 1102 three issues relevant to our discussion on water resource management and water delivery are discussed here. First, Article 1102 raises the question of whether the foreign and the domestic investments are 'in like circumstances'. If a tribunal concludes that they are, the domestic investment may not be treated more favorably than a foreign investor. Secondly, cases have raised the question of whether Article 1102 requires that a measure be the least inconsistent with trade rules among all reasonably available measures. Thirdly, Article 1102 raises questions relating to market access.

6.1 'In like circumstances'

The question as to whether a measure is discriminatory in the sense of Article 1102 hinges in large part on the interpretation of the term 'in like circumstances'. Four cases are particularly relevant for the interpretation of the term in the context of water resources. These are *S.D. Myers v. Canada*; *Pope & Talbot v. Canada*; *Methanex v. U.S.*; and *Sun Belt v. Canada.*

S.D. Myers was the first Chapter 11 decision dealing with the national treatment question. The tribunal took a broad approach to interpreting the term 'like circumstances'. It compared the U.S. investment in Canada (which consisted of acquiring clients for their waste disposal facility in the U.S.) with the Canadian investments (which consisted in actual waste disposal in Canada). The decision compared these two circumstances and determined that they were 'like'. In reaching that conclusion, the tribunal pointed out that the interpretation of 'like circumstances' required the taking into account of the general principles of NAFTA, 'including both its concern with the environment and the need to avoid trade distortions that are not justified by environmental concerns'.[13] However, the reference to environmental concerns remained merely hortatory. In its analysis the tribunal relied exclusively on business considerations. The tribunal focused on the question whether the foreign investor was in the same 'sector' as the national investor, and took the view 'that the word "sector" has a wide connotation that includes the concepts of "economic sector" and "business sector".'[14] It concluded that

> [f]rom the business perspective, it is clear that SDMI and Myers Canada were in 'like circumstances' with Canadian operators such as Chem-Security and Cintec. They all were engaged in providing PCB waste remediation services. SDMI was in a position to attract customers that might otherwise have gone to the Canadian operators because it could offer more favorable prices and because it had extensive experience and credibility.[15]

[13] *S.D. Myers, Inc. v. Canada*, Partial Award (Decision on the Merits), November 13, 2000, para. 250.
[14] *Id.*, para. 250.
[15] *Id.*, para. 251.

The tribunal's focus on the business sector leaves little room for distinctions based on environmental grounds as it excludes a comparison of the actual activities of the domestic and the foreign investors in the host State, and does not include an evaluation of the environmental circumstances of the operation.

In *Pope & Talbot*, the investor contended that the manner in which Canada implemented the Softwood Lumber Agreement constituted a breach of Chapter 11's national treatment provision. In determining whether Canadian softwood lumber exporters were in 'like circumstances' as the investor, the *Pope & Talbot* tribunal was somewhat more nuanced than the *S.D. Myers* tribunal.[16] In *Pope & Talbot* the tribunal pointed out that determining whether producers should be considered in 'like circumstances' depended largely on the facts, but that 'an important element surrounding the facts was the character of the measures under challenge'.[17] To determine the character of the measure, the tribunal found that it had to keep in mind the trade and investment-liberalizing objectives of NAFTA on the one hand, and the background of disputes between the U.S. and Canada regarding softwood lumber trade on the other.[18] It noted that it would first have to determine whether there was a difference in treatment between foreign and domestic investments in the same business or economic sector, and then, if a difference in treatment was found, it would address the question of whether they were in 'like circumstances'. It would be in that context that the issue of discrimination would arise. The tribunals found that a difference in treatment would be presumed to violate the national treatment clause, unless the measures at issue had 'a reasonable nexus to rational government policies that (1) do not distinguish, on their face or *de facto*, between foreign-owned and domestic companies, and (2) do not otherwise unduly undermine the investment liberalizing objectives of NAFTA'.[19]

In comparing the investor's treatment with the manner in which various groups of other domestically-owned softwood lumber producers were treated, the tribunal found that, in each case, Canada's implementing legislation of the Softwood Lumber Agreement was reasonably related to rational government policy, namely the Agreement itself, and that it could not be reasonably said that the policy was motivated by discrimination against foreign-owned producers. It found that as a consequence the producers accorded more favorable treatment were not 'in like circumstances' with those less favorably treated.[20]

The meaning of the term 'in like circumstances' according to the *Pope & Talbot* tribunal remains somewhat murky. One could imply from the tribunal's reasoning that it adopted the so-called 'aims and effects' test, a test developed in the 'like product' analysis in trade law. Under the aim and effects test the question of whether a regulation has a protective aim or effect is part of the

[16] *Pope & Talbot v. Canada*, Award on the Merits of Phase II, April 10, 2001, paras 73 to 104.

[17] *Id.*, para. 76. [18] *Id.*, para. 77. [19] *Id.*, para. 78.

[20] *Id.*, paras 87 and 88 (discussing the treatment of softwood lumber producers in the non-covered provinces); para. 93 (discussing treatment of softwood lumber in the covered provinces); and para. 102 (discussing treatment of softwood lumber producers in British Columbia).

'likeness' analysis: if the conclusion is that the aim and effect of a measure is not protective, products could be considered not 'like'. Thus measures rationally related to an environmental policy would lead to the conclusion that circumstances are not 'like' and thus not in violation of the national treatment clause. Arguably, the WTO Appellate Body rejected the test in the WTO *Japan—Taxes on Alcoholic Beverages* case.[21] However, one must recall that in the trade context the defending State can justify environmental measures under a general exceptions clause, a defense that is not available under Chapter 11.

In the currently pending *Methanex* case, the investor alleges that the ban discriminates against methyl tertiary butyl ether (MTBE) in favor of a U.S.-produced gasoline additive, ethanol. In that case the investor submitted a second amended statement of claim[22] based primarily on the violation of Article 1102. Taking a very narrow business-oriented approach, the investor claims that 'if two or more investors or their investments compete for the same business, they are in like circumstances.'[23]

To justify further its view that its investment was 'in like circumstances' with other U.S. investors, the investor compares the self-produced methanol and the U.S.-produced ethanol and concludes that they are 'like products'. The investor rejects a distinction between the products for environmental reasons, namely, because MTBE contaminates drinking water. It bases much of its reasoning on WTO jurisprudence on like products, although it neglects the WTO Appellate Body decision in *EC-Asbestos*,[24] which agreed to take the health factor into account when comparing highly carcinogenic products with other products.[25]

The *Methanex* case demonstrates the tendency for investors and tribunals to use WTO law and jurisprudence on national treatment as an important reference to interpret Article 1102. However, the GATT analysis on 'likeness' can serve as a reference only up to a certain point, if it can be used at all. Article XX of the GATT provides exceptions for measures relating to the conservation of natural resources and measures necessary for the protection of human, animal, and plant life or health. This means that, under the GATT, a broad interpretation of 'likeness', which excludes distinctions based on environmental

[21] Report of the Appellate Body, *Japan—Taxes on Alcoholic Beverages*, WT/DS8/AB/R, adopted on 1 November 1996. Robert Hudec provided an excellent overview of the aims and effects test in *GATT/WTO Constraints on National Regulation: Requiem for an 'Aim And Effects' Test*, 32 Int'l Law 619 (1998).

[22] Investor's Re-Submitted Amended Statement of Claim (Claimant's Second Amended Statement of Claim), November 5, 2002.

[23] *Id.*, para. 303.

[24] Report of the Appellate Body, *European Communities—Measures Affecting Asbestos and Products Containing Asbestos*, WT/DS135/AB/R, adopted on April 5, 2001. In that WTO dispute, Canada challenged a French measure banning the import of highly carcinogenic asbestos fibers and asbestos-containing products, alleging that the ban was inconsistent with, among other provisions, Art. III of the GATT (which deals with national treatment). The EC defended the measure by arguing, in part, that carcinogenic asbestos fibers are not 'like' non-carcinogenic fibers. After conducting an examination of various well-established criteria, the Appellate Body agreed with the EC.

[25] The WTO Panel in *EC-Asbestos* had previously held that the products were 'like'. This conclusion was rejected by the Appellate Body. However, it should be noted that the Panel had upheld the EC measure under Art. XX of the GATT, which provides exceptions, *inter alia*, for measures aimed at protecting human health.

and health reasons, can be balanced out to a certain extent by Article XX. However, as Chapter 11 provides no such exceptions, the interpretative approach must be a different one. In *Methanex*, for example, California's measure to protect its natural resources (water) and human health (protection from drinking contaminated water) would be the type of measure qualifying under the exceptions of Article XX of the GATT. In absence of such exceptions, interpretations of 'like circumstances' should allow distinctions for environmental and health reasons. To base the interpretation of likeness primarily on business considerations (as did the *S.D. Myers* tribunal) would stand in stark contrast to the overall NAFTA goal of sustainable development.[26]

In sum, NAFTA Chapter 11 decisions indicate that tribunals tend to give more weight to business considerations and less to environmental elements in determining whether or not a host State has violated the national treatment obligation. Under this approach, differential treatment between investors for environmental reasons, including for the protection of water resources, will more likely be considered in violation of the national or most-favored-nation treatment obligation. On the other hand, the *Pope & Talbot* case indicates that tribunals could conclude that measures 'rationally related to' natural resource protection policies are not in like circumstances, a conclusion which could generally sanctify environmental measures. The outcome in the *Methanex* case will be of primary importance for future cases involving the protection of water resources and the environment and human health in general.

6.2 The 'least-trade restrictive' approach?

In addition to the discussion of 'like circumstances', another surprising issue has arisen in the context of Article 1102. In *S.D. Myers*, the tribunal imported the so-called necessity test established under WTO jurisprudence into Article 1102. It requires that a measure be the least inconsistent with trade rules among all reasonably available measures (often referred to as the 'least-trade-restrictive approach').[27] Concluding that Canada had other alternatives available to obtain its objectives, the *S.D. Myers* tribunal found that Canada was in violation of its national treatment obligation.[28] In doing so, the tribunal read a 'least restrictive obligation' into Article 1102 for which there is no basis in NAFTA's text. This approach has had impacts on later case developments. In the ongoing *Methanex* case, the Canadian investor claimed—referring to the *S.D. Myers* decision—that

[26] *See* NAFTA Preamble.

[27] It is worthwhile noting that the test was elaborated in the context of WTO provisions other than those relating to national treatment provisions. For an analysis of the necessity test under WTO Agreements, *see* e.g., Jan Neumann and Elisabeth Tuerk, *Necessity Revisited—Proportionality in WTO Law after Korea-Beef; EC-Asbestos and EC-Sardines*, 37 J. World Trade (2003), or Alan O. Sykes, *The Least Trade Restrictive Means*, 70 U. Chi. L. Rev. 403 (2003).

[28] *S.D. Myers, Inc. v. Canada*, Partial Award (Decision on the Merits), November 13, 2000, para. 255. The tribunal listed two examples of legitimate alternative measures: Canada's right to source all government requirements and to grant subsidies to the Canadian industry.

the Californian MTBE ban was not the least trade-restrictive method of solving the water contamination problem, and thus was in violation of Article 1102.[29] The investor suggested that California could solve the drinking water problem by stopping the leakage of underground storage tanks instead of banning MTBE. Should the *Methanex* tribunal follow the *S.D. Myers* approach and require the least-trade-restrictive alternative, then Chapter 11 would effectively dictate the types of water-related policies that can or cannot be adopted.

6.3 Market Access

Since Article 1102 is applicable to investors and investments not only once established in the host State's territory but also with respect to the establishment, acquisition, and expansion of investments, Article 1102 provides the prospective investor with right of access. This means, for example, that if a host State privatizes its water delivery services and opens the sector to public companies, Article 1102 comes into effect, requiring that foreign companies be treated no less favorably than domestic ones. Similarly, if a permit for water exports is granted to a domestic investor, a foreign investor may claim to have the right to do the same. Thus, without formally opening the water services sector under services negotiations, NAFTA Parties liberalized the water sector through Chapter 11.

7. Protection against performance requirements

Article 1106 , which prohibits the use of a number of 'performance requirements', is relevant for the discussion of the protection of natural resources for at least two reasons. First, Article 1106 could inhibit a State from banning or restricting the export of its natural resources. This concern has been exemplified in the *Pope & Talbot* case, in which the tribunal held that export restrictions on lumber could qualify as a requirement to export a given level or percentage of goods, in violation of Article 1106. Secondly, Article 1106 could circumscribe a host State's ability to control the use of environmentally harmful substances. For example, in the (settled) *Ethyl v. Canada* case, the investor argued that the import ban on methylcyclopentadienyl manganese tricarbonyl (MMT) from the U.S. into Canada for environmental reasons, was in effect a requirement to use domestic substitute products, contrary to Article 1106. These cases are discussed further below.

Prohibited performance requirements are exhaustively listed in Article 1106. One of the listed prohibited requirements relevant in the context of water export restrictions is the requirement 'to export a given level or percentage of goods or services' under paragraph 1(a). The economic logic behind the provision is that many countries, in trying to increase exports, condition foreign investors to export as much of their production as possible in order to increase the inflow of

[29] Methanex Draft Amended Claim, February 12, 2001.

capital. The prohibition was likely adopted to avoid having such conditions placed upon the foreign investors.

The *Pope & Talbot* case, however, was not about Canada's attempt to *increase* exports. Rather, Canada, in implementing the Softwood Lumber Agreement, was trying to *curb* export of softwood lumber. The U.S. investor contended that this violated Article 1106(1)(a). Under the Softwood Lumber Agreement, Canada was required in four provinces to place softwood lumber on an Export Control List and require a federal export permit for each exportation to the U.S. Under this regime, Canada was bound to collect an export permit fee for quantities of lumber over an established yearly base.[30] The investor alleged that Canada's implementing legislation violated Article 1106, which disallows a host State from requiring that a given level or percentage of goods or services be exported, because the Export Control Regime required the investor to export a given level of lumber that was lower than that which the investor would export if it did not have to pay export fees on exports above its fee-free allocation.[31]

Following the economic logic of Article 1106(1)(a) described above, Canada took the position that paragraph (a) is directed only at requirements to export, not restrictions on exports. The tribunal did not agree. It observed that the language of Article 1106 was not expressly limited to the imposition or enforcement of a *higher* level or percentage of exports, but could also include the imposition or enforcement of any given level or percentage of those exports.[32] Although the tribunal found no valid claim *in casu* because the export regime did not 'impose or enforce requirements', the tribunal adopted a particularly broad scope of that article by extending Article 1106(1)(a) to export restrictions.[33] This interpretation would make it illegal for a host State to adopt export import bans or restrictions to protect its water resources. While providing environmental exceptions to some prohibitions of performance requirements, Article 1106 provides no such environmental exception with respect to paragraph (1)(a). It is unclear how Article 1106(1)(a) relates to the 1993 Joint Public Statement (that provides that water is not covered by the provisions of NAFTA until it enters into commerce and becomes a good or product).

Other prohibited requirements under Article 1106 relevant to the discussion on water are the requirements to use a given level of domestic content in Article 1106(1)(b), or to give other preferences for domestic goods and services under Article 1106(1)(c). In the (settled) *Ethyl* case, for example, the investor argued that the import ban on methylcyclopentadienyl manganese tricarbonyl (MMT)

[30] Exports up to the established base were free of charge. Exports above the base could be exported for a 'Lower Fee Base' up to a certain quantity and 'Upper Fee Base' for higher quantities. Canada was bound to allocate the established yearly base and the Lower Fee Base among the Canadian softwood lumber exporters.

[31] *Pope & Talbot v. Canada*, Interim Award, June 26, 2000, para. 47.

[32] *Id.*, para. 74.

[33] *Id.*, para. 75. The tribunal found that the export regime was rather a tariff-rate export restraint regime, and concluded: 'While the Regime undoubtedly deters increased exports to the U.S., that deterrence is not a "requirement" for establishing, acquiring, expanding, managing, conducting or operating a foreign owned business in Canada.'

from the U.S. into Canada for environmental reasons, was in effect a requirement to use domestic substitute products, and thus in violation of Article 1106. An investor could invoke the same article to challenge the import or sales ban of a substance which is considered to pollute drinking water.

It should be noted, however, that Article 1106 provides an exception in connection with domestic content requirements and local purchase requirements.[34] This stands in contrast with the previously discussed export quota requirement for which no exception is provided. For domestic content and local purchase requirements to qualify as legitimate exceptions to the prohibition, they must:

(1) not be applied in an arbitrary or unjustifiable manner;
(2) not constitute a disguised restriction on international trade and investment; and
(3) 'be necessary to protect human, animal or plant life or health', or 'be necessary for the conservation of living or non-living exhaustible natural resources'.[35]

The language used here is based on GATT Article XX, which provides exceptions with respect to the conservation of natural resources[36] and the protection of human, animal, and plant life health.[37] However, the Article 1106 exception differs from Article XX in that it uses the word 'necessary' for both the 'protection of human, animal or plant life or health' *and* 'the conservation of living and non-living natural resources'. GATT Article XX, on the other hand, allows exceptions for measures that are '*necessary*' for the protection of human, animal, and plant life,[38] or that are '*related to*' the protection of natural resources.[39] GATT and WTO Panels have clearly distinguished between the terms 'necessary' and 'relating to', and have set a higher standard in respect of the word 'necessary'. Interpretations of the term 'necessary' in trade law are generally linked to the condition that a measure be the least trade restrictive amongst all reasonably available alternatives available. To date, no tribunal has addressed the exceptions under Article 1106. However, one could expect that arbitral tribunals will follow the approach taken by trade panels, and thus read the exceptions under Article 1106 on the protection of natural resources (including water resources) narrowly due to the use of the term 'necessary'.

8. Expropriation without compensation

Pursuant to Article 1110, no Party may directly or indirectly nationalize or expropriate an investment, or take a measure tantamount to nationalization or

[34] *See* NAFTA Art. 1106(6).

[35] NAFTA Art. 1106(6)(a) also provides an exception for measures 'necessary to secure compliance with laws and regulations that are not inconsistent with the provisions of [NAFTA]'.

[36] *See* Art. XX(g) of the GATT.

[37] *See* Art. XX(b) of the GATT.

[38] *Id.*

[39] *See* Art. XX(g) of the GATT.

expropriation, except for a public purpose, on a non-discriminatory basis, and on payment of compensation.[40] This provision has proven to be one of the most controversial investor guarantees in Chapter 11. Public interest groups, as well as government officials and legislators, have expressed concerns about the potential chilling effect of the provision on the ability and willingness of governments to adopt and implement environmental and other public welfare regulations. Many also fear that foreign investors will be treated more favorably under Article 1110 than domestic investors to whom domestic laws on expropriations (referred to in the U.S. as 'takings') apply. Article 1110 is directly relevant in the context of measures taken to protect water resources. Both measures taken to restrict or prohibit the extraction or export of water resources, as well as standards set to control the pollution of lakes, rivers, and groundwater, could be challenged under Article 1110 where an investor conceives the impact of the measure as 'tantamount to expropriation'.

The scope of the expropriation clause hinges partly on the term 'investment', which is defined very broadly in NAFTA[41] and interpreted broadly by arbitral tribunals. The definition of investment covers not only hard investments, such as real estate and equipment, but also financial assets, such as stocks and bonds and contractual rights and rights conferred by law. Chapter 11 tribunals have found that access to markets and market shares also constitute an investment as defined in Chapter 11.[42] As a consequence, the range of rights that can be subject to 'expropriation', for which the host State must compensate, is extremely broad.

In addition to the expansive definition of 'investment', the scope of the types of expropriations covered is also broad. Early (usually bilateral) instruments dealing with foreign investment usually contained provisions regarding 'nationalization' and/or 'expropriation'. These terms were understood to cover direct

[40] NAFTA Art. 1110 reads:
Expropriation and Compensation

1. No Party may directly or indirectly nationalize or expropriate an investment of an investor of another Party in its territory or take a measure tantamount to nationalization or expropriation of such an investment ('expropriation'), except:
   (a) for a public purpose;
   (b) on a non-discriminatory basis;
   (c) in accordance with due process of law and Article 1105(1); and
   (d) on payment of compensation in accordance with paragraphs 2 through 6.
2. Compensation shall be equivalent to the fair market value of the expropriated investment immediately before the expropriation took place ('date of expropriation'), and shall not reflect any change in value occurring because the intended expropriation had become known earlier. Valuation criteria shall include going concern value, asset value including declared tax value of tangible property, and other criteria, as appropriate, to determine fair market value.

...

[41] NAFTA Art. 1139 defines the 'investment of an investor of a Party' as 'an investment owned or controlled directly or indirectly by an investor of such Party'.

[42] *See S.D. Myers, Inc. v. Canada*, Partial Award (Decision on the Merits), November 13, 2000, para. 232, and *Pope & Talbot v. Canada*, Interim Award, June 26, 2000, para. 96.

expropriations of property by the host State through legislative or administrative measures, which resulted in a compulsory transfer of property rights. Article 1110, in line with more recent bilateral investment treaties, expanded the definitional scope of expropriation to include indirect expropriation, which is also referred to as disguised or creeping expropriation and is the equivalent of a 'regulatory taking' under U.S. law.[43] Moreover, Article 1110 refers to a third category of expropriation: 'measures tantamount to expropriation'. Investors have argued that this third category of expropriation exceeded the generally internationally accepted coverage of indirect expropriation. However, both the *Pope & Talbot* and the *S.D. Myers* tribunals refused to accept the investors' point of view. In *Pope & Talbot*, the tribunal noted that it did 'not believe that the phrase "measure tantamount to nationalization or expropriation" in Article 1110 broadens the ordinary concept of expropriation under international law to require compensation for measures affecting property interests without regard to the magnitude or severity of that effect'.[44] Rather, it observed that '[t]antamount' meant 'nothing more than equivalent' and that '[s]omething that is equivalent to something cannot logically encompass more'.[45]

The scope of measures considered compensable under Article 1110 remains broad nevertheless. As of this writing, four Chapter 11 arbitral tribunals have examined in detail the question whether a measure taken by a host State amounted to a compensable expropriation, and several more cases involving allegations of Article 1110 violations are pending.[46] The decisions interpreting the expropriation clause all involved regulatory takings, i.e. indirect expropriations. Except for *Metalclad*, the cases all involved personal, not real, property rights. To date, the *Metalclad* decision is the only Chapter 11 ruling to find that a disputed measure amounted to a compensable taking. Nevertheless, while not finding Article 1110 violations in the specific cases, other tribunals also adopted very broad interpretations of Article 1110.

The measures at issue in *Metalclad* were a permit denial for the construction and operation of a hazardous waste disposal landfill and, later, the issuance of an ecological decree for the creation of a protected area. In interpreting Article 1110, the *Metalclad* tribunal applied a standard which did not require the total loss of value of property, or even that interference be substantial. It stated that

[43] For an analysis of indirect expropriation, *see* Rudolf Dolzer, *Indirect Expropriation of Alien Property*, 1 ICSID Rev. Foreign Investment L.J. 41 (1986). On the evolution of expropriation clauses in international agreements, *see* UNCTAD, *Taking of Property*, UNCTAD Series on issues in international investment agreements, 2000. *See also* Howard Mann, *Assessing the Impact of NAFTA on Environmental Law and Management Processes*, Working Paper, presented at the First North American Symposium on Understanding the Linkages Between Trade and Environment, October 2000, at p. 32.

[44] *Pope & Talbot v. Canada*, Interim Award, June 26, 2000, para. 96.

[45] *Id.*, para. 104 (footnotes omitted).

[46] Decisions on Art. 1110 include: *Metalclad Corp. v. Mexico*, Final Award, August 30, 2000; *S.D. Myers, Inc. v. Canada*, Partial Award (Decision of the Merits), November 13, 2000; *Pope and Talbot v. Canada*, Interim Award, June 26, 2000; and *Marvin Ray Feldman Karpa v. Mexico*, Final Award, December 16, 2002.

expropriation under NAFTA included 'covert or incidental interference with the use of property which has the effect of depriving the owner, in whole or in significant part, of the use or reasonably-to-be-expected economic benefit of property even if not necessarily to the obvious benefit of the host State'.[47] Applying this very broad standard, the tribunal came to the conclusion that both the denial of the permit as well as the ecological decree amounted to expropriation as defined under Article 1110.[48] The tribunal did not take into account the environmental public purpose of the measures.

The *S.D. Myers* tribunal examined a measure banning the export of PCB waste from Canada to the U.S. It acknowledged that the 'general body of precedent usually does not treat regulatory action as amounting to expropriation'. It noted that '[r]egulatory conduct by public authorities is unlikely to be subject of legitimate complaint under article 1110 of the NAFTA, although the Tribunal does not rule out that possibility'.[49] In deciding whether or not the measure at issue amounted to a compensable taking under Chapter 11, the tribunals focused mainly on the severity and the scale of the impact of the measure at issue rather than on the regulatory character of the measure (i.e., that the measure was an environmental measure in accordance with the 1989 Basel Convention on the Control of Transboundary Movements of Hazardous Wastes and their Disposal).

The *Pope & Talbot* tribunal did not require that the interference result in total loss of value either, but—in contrast to the Metalclad approach—it held that the interference had to be substantial.[50]

In the more recent case of *Marvin Feldman v. Mexico*, the tribunal also looked at the scale of the impact at issue in deciding, on balance, that denying tax rebates to a cigarette exporter was not an expropriation.[51] *Feldman* concerned a U.S. national who ran an international trading enterprise in Mexico, which exported to the United States a range of goods that included bargain brand cigarettes. Feldman claimed, *inter alia*, that the Mexican authorities' refusal to grant his enterprise excise tax rebates on cigarette exports resulted in an indirect or 'creeping' expropriation of his investment and was tantamount to expropriation under Article 1110.

The arbitral tribunal held, on balance, that there was no violation of Article 1110. Amongst its reasons for finding there was no expropriation, it said that the

[47] *Metalclad Corp. v. Mexico*, Final Award, August 30, 2000, para. 103.

[48] *Id.*, paras 107 and 109.

[49] *S.D. Myers Inc. v. Canada*, Partial Award (Decision on the Merits), November 13, 2000, para. 281.

[50] To determine whether Canada's interference with Pope & Talbot's investment amounted to a taking, the tribunal applied standards used in the Draft Convention on the International Responsibility of States for Injuries to Aliens (Harvard Draft) and the Third Restatement. The Harvard Draft provides that there is a taking when the owner will no longer be able to use, enjoy, or dispose of the property. The Third Restatement provides that a regulation may be considered expropriation when action is confiscatory, or prevents, unreasonably interferes with, or unduly delays effective enjoyment of an alien's property (*Pope & Talbot v. Canada*, Interim Award, June 26, 2000, para. 102).

[51] *Marvin Feldman v. Mexico*, Final Award, December 16, 2002, paras 110–12.

Claimant's 'investment', his exporting business, remained under his control with a right to engage in the export of a range of other goods for which he would be entitled to claim rebates. It also said that not every business problem experienced by a foreign investor is an expropriation under Article 1110, and at no relevant time had the specific tax invoice requirements of the Mexican law given non-taxpayers a 'right' to the tax rebates. The tribunal expressed its reluctance, in the absence of a finding of expropriation, to give excessive weight to the public purpose of Mexico's measures, but indicated that it considered that there was a rational public purpose for the policy, including combating illegal cigarette smuggling and excessive tax rebate claims.

In sum, the tribunals, in determining whether a measure amounted to a compensable expropriation, set a standard that focuses primarily on the degree of interference of the regulatory measure. However, none of the tribunals required that the loss of value of the taken investment be total, nor did they require that the environmental or other public interest nature of the measure be taken into account. Moreover, tribunals neglected to distinguish between real or personal property rights when assessing measures under Article 1110 on expropriation. The tribunals' interpretations have led many scholars, environmentalists, and legislators to argue that foreign investors under Article 1110 have greater rights to compensation than domestic companies under the laws of Canada, Mexico, and even the United States.[52]

9. Domestic expropriation and takings law

A comparison of Article 1110 and the domestic expropriation and takings laws in the NAFTA States indicates that Article 1110 may be more advantageous for foreign investors seeking compensation than the domestic laws on expropriation and takings. In Canada, for example, property rights are not even enshrined in the Constitution. Canadian courts have preferred expansive definitions of police powers and have generally refrained from subjecting regulatory expropriation to compensation unless expressly stipulated in the law.[53] Under the Mexican Constitution of 1917,[54] the government also has broad authority to expropriate and regulate private

[52] *See*, e.g., John Eccheverria, *The Real Contract On America*, in The Environmental Forum, July/August 2003.

[53] Julie A. Soloway, *Environmental Regulation as Expropriation: The Case of NAFTA's Chapter 11*, 33 Canadian Business Law Journal, 92 (2000), at 104, referring to Eric C.E. Todd, *The Law of Expropriation in Canada*, 2nd edn (Toronto, Carswell, 1992).

[54] 1917 Constitution of Mexico, as amended, available at http://www.ilstu.edu/class/hist263/docs/1917const.html#N_6_ (last viewed March 19, 2005) and at http://historicaltextarchive.com/sections.php?op=viewarticle&artid=123 (last viewed March 19, 2005). Article 27 provides, *inter alia*: 'The Nation shall at all times have the right to impose on private property such limitations as the public interest may demand, as well as the right to regulate the utilization of natural resources which are susceptible of appropriation, in order to conserve them and to ensure a more equitable distribution of public wealth.'

property in the public interest. It requires compensation for 'expropriation' (which consists in 'legally taking a thing from its owner, for reasons of public utility'), but does not require compensation for other 'limitations' (which are generally applicable and consist in the partial extinction of the rights of the owner).[55]

Not only Canadians and Mexicans have fears regarding the interpretation of Article 1110. Many Americans are claiming that NAFTA is also going further than U.S. domestic law regarding taking of private property.[56] They claim that Article 1110 is providing extensive rights to foreign investors, which are not available to the domestic investors under domestic laws. In addition, some have argued that Chapter 11 rulings may influence U.S. domestic jurisprudence and encourage a shift towards the greater protection of individual property rights to the detriment of the environment and public welfare in general.[57] In contrast to Canadian law, U.S. law gives constitutional protection to property rights,[58] but does not distinguish between compensable 'expropriation' (or 'taking' in U.S. legal parlance) and non-compensable 'limitations', as does the Mexican Constitution. While it is difficult to summarize U.S. jurisprudence, one can safely say that U.S. jurisprudence is not as clear on regulatory takings as Canadian and, possibly, Mexican jurisprudence. Foremost, in the U.S., compensation can also be required in absence of an explicit requirement in the law, contrary to the Canadian common law. In contrast to Mexican law, U.S. law may in very limited cases require compensation for only partial extinction of the owner's rights, although *Lingle v. Chevron* has surely narrowed this universe of cases.[59]

The fear that under Article 1110 foreign investors might be compensated in situations in which U.S. domestic investors would not, is understandable.[60] As

[55] Martin Wagner, *Nature Beyond the Nation State Symposium: International Investment, Expropriation and Environmental Protection*, 29 Golden Gate U. L. Rev 465, at 514–16.

[56] This later led to the adoption of the 'no greater substantive rights requirement' of the U.S. Trade Act of 2002, discussed further below.

[57] *See* William Greider, *The Right and US Trade Law: Invalidating the 20th Century*, in The Nation, October 15, 2001.

[58] The Fifth Amendment to the U.S. Constitution provides, '[N]or shall private property be taken for public use, without just compensation.'

[59] *Lingle v. Chevron*, U.S. Sup. Ct., May 23, 2005. *See* Gregory M. Starner, *Taking a Constitutional Look: NAFTA Chapter 11 As An Extension of Member States' Constitutional Protection of Property*, 33 Law and Policy in Int'l Bus 405 (2002), at 408, and Edward M. Graham, *Regulatory Takings, Supernational Treatment and the Multilateral Agreement on Investment: Issues Raised By Nongovernmental Organizations*, 31 Cornell Int. L.J. 3 (1999). Starner suggests that Art. 1110 of NAFTA was crafted and interpreted in a way which most closely resembles U.S. takings law, and that NAFTA tribunals interpreting Art. 1110 have incorporated relevant provisions of U.S. takings jurisprudence into NAFTA case law. This development, Starner argues, could lead to the imposition of U.S. principles abroad through the investor-to-State process (see Starner, at 427).

[60] Francisco Orrego Vicuna argues that the support for maintaining the supremacy of national standards for treatment of both domestic and foreign investors appears to be the modern version of the Calvo Clause. *See* Francisco Orrego Vicuna, *Carlos Calvo, Honorary NAFTA Citizen*, 11 N.Y.U. Envtl. L. J. 19 (2002). The Calvo doctrine, named after Carlos Calvo, 1824–1906, an Argentine diplomat and historian, attempts to give local courts final jurisdiction and to obviate any appeal to diplomatic intervention. The doctrine is based on Calvo's argument in favor of national treatment as opposed to international standards.

shown above, Chapter 11 protection of the foreign investor's property is extensive, and covers both personal and real property equally. In contrast, U.S. jurisprudence clearly distinguishes between personal and real property. The U.S. Supreme Court, examining a measure affecting the use of personal property, found that to find a taking, the statutes at issue had to deprive the owner of all value.[61] In another case, Justice Scalia, one of the most property rights-oriented Supreme Court Justices, even went a step further, observing that personal property could be deprived of all its economic value and still not be subject to compensation.[62] He stated that

> in the case of personal property, by reason of the State's traditionally high degree of control over commercial dealings, [the owner] ought to be aware of the possibility that new regulation might even render his property economically worthless (at least if the property's only economically productive use is sale or manufacture for sale).[63]

As mentioned above, the majority of NAFTA investor claims alleging breach of the expropriation provision involved personal and not real property. However, in the three decisions involving personal property, none of the tribunals specifically distinguished between personal and real property in deciding whether or not an investor should be compensated. This stands in clear contrast with U.S. jurisprudence on compensable takings, which sets the bar much higher for the loss of value of personal property.

In addition to the distinction between real and personal property, the U.S. Supreme Court has identified factors of 'particular significance' in determining whether a governmental action is compensable.[64] One of the factors to consider on a case-by-case basis has been the character of the governmental action: if it is in the public interest, such as for the protection of the environment and public health, it is generally considered as legitimate and not subject to compensation.[65] This rule was subject to a narrow exception in the 1992 *Lucas* case.[66] There, the U.S. Supreme Court identified two categories of regulatory action that are subject to compensation 'without case-specific inquiry into the public interest advanced in support of the restraint'.[67] These include, first,

[61] *Andrus v. Allard*, 444 U.S. 51 (1979). In this case the Supreme Court rejected a claim that prohibitions on the sale of bird parts under the federal Eagle Protection Act and the Migratory Bird Protection Act resulted in a taking. In that case, the plaintiff had lawfully acquired eagle feathers before the statutes were enacted. The prohibition to sell the feathers barred the plaintiff from the most profitable use of personal property. However, the Supreme Court refused to find a taking because the statutes did not deprive the owner of all value.

[62] *Lucas v. South Carolina Coastal Council*, 505 U.S. 1003 (1992).

[63] Lower courts have followed the approach distinguishing personal from real property. *See* Glenn P. Sugameli, *Lucas v. South Carolina Coastal Council: The Categorical and Other 'Exceptions' to Liability for Fifth Amendment Takings of Private Property Far Outweigh the 'Rule'*, 29 Environmental Law 939 (1999), at 986.

[64] *Palazollo v. Rhode Island*, 121 S. Ct. 2448 at 2465, citing *Penn Central Transp. Co. v. New York City*, 438 U.S. 104, 124 (1978). *Lingle v. Chevron*, U.S. Sup. Ct., May 23, 2005 (listing four accepted takings theories).

[65] *Concrete Pipe & Prods. of Calif. v. Construction Laborers Pension Trust*, 508 U.S. 602, 643 (1993).

[66] *Lucas, supra* note 62, at 1003.

[67] *Id.*, at 1015.

compelled permanent physical invasions of land and, secondly, actions that essentially are the equivalent of a physical appropriation, denying all economically beneficial or productive use of the property.[68] Under *Lucas*, a taking is compensable independent of the public interest of the governmental action only where (1) it pertains to real property, and (2) all economic value is denied. The later *Tahoe Sierra Preservation Council v. Tahoe Regional Planning Agency*[69] case involved a thirty-two month moratorium on the development of a substantial portion of property in order to address the serious pollution problems of Lake Tahoe. The Court stated that a taking must be evaluated in relation to the claimant's entire property, and the evaluation should include temporal, spatial, and functional dimensions. It required the permanent obliteration of property value, and indicated that even a 95% loss of value was not enough to trigger a *Lucas* taking. In May 2005 the Supreme Court in the landmark *Lingle v. Chevron* case decided that whether a regulation 'substantially advances' a legitimate state interest is no longer a valid method for determining a Regulatory taking.

Chapter 11 tribunals, on the other hand, did not seriously examine the nature and purpose of the measures at issue to determine whether the expropriation was compensable. Instead, they focused almost exclusively on the economic impact of the measures. In contrast to U.S. courts, they did not require that the investor be deprived of the total value of its property, but rather that interference had to be 'substantial', in order for an expropriation to be compensable. The *Metalclad* tribunal even went so far as to state that 'incidental interference' was sufficient. Moreover, both the *S.D. Myers* and the *Pope & Talbot* tribunals indicated that in some cases temporary measures or partial deprivations could amount to a compensable taking. The NAFTA tribunals thus have expanded the notion of compensable expropriation beyond that generally adopted by U.S. courts.

Additionally, U.S. courts have established further limitations to takings claims, including the inquiry of whether the regulation has interfered with distinct investment-backed expectations.[70] In the context of Chapter 11, tribunals have not consistently applied this concept.[71] In the *Metalclad* ruling, for example, the tribunal found that the permit denial for the development and operation of a hazardous landfill[72] at issue in that case, required Mexico to

[68] *Id.* Based on such economic considerations, courts have rejected takings claims involving regulations affecting less than an entire parcel of land. *See* Sugameli, *supra* note 63, at 948–53. Furthermore, courts have found that prohibitions limited in time did not amount to a compensable taking. *See* Sugameli, *supra* note 63, at 953–5.

[69] *Tahoe Sierra Preservation Council v. Tahoe Regional Planning Agency*, 122 S. Ct. 1465 U.S. (2002).

[70] *Concrete Pipe, supra* note 65, at 645. *See also Palazzolo, supra* note 64, at 2466.

[71] More recent free trade agreements increasingly refer to this requirement.

[72] Metalclad, a U.S. company, had obtained federal construction and operating permits for the landfill. The question arose whether an additional municipal permit for the construction was also required. Allegedly, Mexican federal officials had assured that no further permits were required. Notwithstanding Mexico's contention and the testimony of Mexican constitutional experts, including a former Supreme Court justice, the arbitrators found that the municipality did not have the authority to deny the permits.

compensate for expropriation under Article 1110.[73] The tribunal ignored the fact that a municipal construction permit had already been denied to Metalclad's predecessor, indicating that a municipal permit system on hazardous waste was already in place and that the investor must have known about it. Thus, the tribunal did not examine whether the investor actually had distinct investment-backed expectations.[74]

In the U.S., a further limitation to the government's obligation to compensate consists in the notion of 'background principles of the State's law of property or nuisance'. Under this concept the government is under no obligation to compensate if it prohibits activities that were not permitted under the laws of property and nuisance. The Supreme Court has defined nuisances as harms 'to public lands and resources, or adjacent private property, posed by the claimant's proposed activities'.[75] Chapter 11 tribunals have never applied this concept to their interpretation of Article 1110. Its significance in the context of water resource protection is apparent. A limitation to property in order to protect public water resources could be justified under the nuisance concept, thus protecting the government from compensation.

An overview of domestic laws on expropriation show that NAFTA tribunals have not taken public interest concerns sufficiently into account for their analysis of Article 1110. While domestic courts are constantly in search of a balance between public interests and property rights, NAFTA tribunals have tended to take a fairly one-sided approach in favor of investors. This has direct implications on host States' ability to protect the environment and manage natural resources, and has led to a situation in which domestic investors are potentially treated less favorably than foreign investors. U.S. legislators have attempted to address these issues in the U.S. Trade Act of 2002.[76] Section 2102 on Negotiating Objectives provides, in a subsection on investment:

> Recognizing that United States law on the whole provides a high level of protection for investment, consistent with or greater than the level required by international law, the principal negotiating objectives of the United States regarding foreign investment are to reduce or eliminate artificial or trade-distorting barriers to foreign investment, *while ensuring that foreign investors in the United States are not accorded greater substantive rights with respect to investment protections than United States investors in the United States*, and to secure for investors important rights comparable to those that would be available under United States legal principles and practice, by
>
> ...

[73] This holding was subsequently reversed under a Canadian decision reviewing the case: the British Columbia Supreme Court did uphold the finding of a violation of Art. 1110 but only with respect to the Ecological Decree creating a protected area in the location of the landfill, not the permit denial (see *The United Mexican States v. Metalclad Corporation*, 2001 BCSC 664, May 2, 2001).

[74] In *Palazollo v. Rhode Island*, *supra* note 64, the Supreme Court appeared to acknowledge that the *Lucas* background principles include preexisting state and federal statutes that were in effect when the claimant acquired the property at issue.

[75] *Lucas*, *supra* note 62, at 1030–1031 (citing Restatement (Second) of Torts Sections 826–827 (1979)).

[76] The text is available at http://www.tpa.gov/pl107_210.pdf.

(D) *seeking to establish standards for expropriation and compensation for expropriation, consistent with United States legal principles and practice;*[77]

...

The specifications on the negotiation objectives for future investment treaties between the U.S. and other countries reflect the concern of the U.S. public regarding the investor-to-State dispute settlement in general and expropriation in particular. They reflect the fear that longstanding takings jurisprudence could be undermined by a parallel process that is primarily focused on investor protection. The sometimes expansive reading of the expropriation clause under NAFTA seems to already have influenced subsequent bilateral and regional trade agreements negotiated by the U.S. These clarify that, 'except in rare circumstances, nondiscriminatory regulatory actions by a Party that are designed and applied to protect legitimate public welfare objectives, such as public health, safety, and the environment, do not constitute indirect expropriations'. This language has found its way into agreements between the U.S. and Australia (Annex 11-B (4)(b)), the U.S. and five central American states and the Dominican Republic (Annex 10 (4)(b)), the U.S. and Chile (Annex 10-D (4)(b)) and the U.S. and Singapore (Article 15.26 on expropriation referring to the exchange of letters on expropriation).

After *Lingle v. Chevron*, however, whether the regulatory action substantially 'advances' a legitimate state objective would not be an independent factor for finding a taking in U.S. law.

10. Transparency and public participation

A further criticism levelled at NAFTA's Chapter 11 has been the lack of transparency and absence of public participation in its investor-to-State dispute settlement mechanism. The investor-to-State dispute settlement mechanism takes its rules of procedure from a number of international commercial arbitral bodies. Under NAFTA, investors may submit a claim under the rules of the Convention on the Settlement of Investment Disputes between States and Nationals of Other States (the ICSID Convention),[78] the Additional Facility Rules of ICSID (for disputes where only one party is an ICSID Member),[79] or the United Nations Commission on International Trade Law (UNCITRAL) Arbitration Rules. These bodies and their rules were designed for disputes over commercial contracts involving two private parties, or an investor and a host

[77] U.S. Trade Act of 2002, Section 2102(b)(3)(D), emphasis added.

[78] *See* Convention on the Settlement of Investment Disputes Between States and Nationals of Other States, March 18, 1965, 4 I.L.M. 532 (1965), available at http://www.worldbank.org/icsid/basicdoc [ICSID Convention]. *See generally*, Ibrahim F.I. Shihata, Towards a Greater Depoliticization of Investment Disputes: The Roles of ICSID and MIGA (ICSID 1993).

[79] Rules Governing the Additional Facility for the Administration of Proceedings by the Secretariat of the ICSID, Sept. 27, 1978, Artice 4(3), 21 I.L.M. 1446 (1979), available at www.worldbank.org/icsid/facility [hereinafter ICSID Additional Facility Rules].

State, and accordingly are based on principles of confidentiality and secrecy. While such considerations may arguably be appropriate for purely commercial cases, they are inappropriate for cases involving public welfare issues such as the management and protection of water resources.

Although there is nothing in NAFTA to prevent the public release of documents filed in Chapter 11 arbitration proceedings, Parties and investors, until recently, generally did not do so. The NAFTA's critics considered that such a lack of transparency put private investors in a strong bargaining and lobbying position, whilst inhibiting civil society's ability to learn about issues of public concern. Ongoing controversy over this issue culminated in an attempt by the Parties in July 2001 to clarify questions regarding access to documents in Chapter 11 proceedings by way of an interpretative note.[80] The interpretative note, which is binding on all Chapter 11 tribunals, specifies that nothing in Chapter 11 precludes a NAFTA Party from providing public access to relevant documents submitted to or issued by Chapter 11 tribunals. Furthermore, documents are to be made available on a timely basis, subject to limited specific exceptions, including confidential business information, information protected under a Party's domestic law, and information to be withheld under applicable arbitral rules. The interpretative note does not specify what confidential business information might be exempted from the transparency obligation.

Subsequent to the July 2001 interpretative note, all three Parties have made documents filed in cases to which they are a party available on the internet.[81] This has made a significant contribution to the transparency of Chapter 11 dispute settlement proceedings. However, further transparency and public participation are still required. First, while the NAFTA Secretariat is required to maintain a public register of all Notices of Arbitration filed,[82] there is no requirement for the Secretariat to update the register in a timely manner. As at 1 October 2004, no such register was available on the NAFTA Secretariat's website.[83] Secondly, Chapter 11 is silent on the issue of public access to arbitration hearings. In the absence of a NAFTA provision, ICSID, ICSID Additional Facility, or UNCITRAL Rules apply. Under these rules, hearings are generally closed to the public unless all disputing parties agree to the contrary.[84] Thirdly, neither NAFTA Chapter 11 nor applicable arbitration rules discuss the

[80] Notes of Interpretation of Certain NAFTA Provisions, issued July 31, 2001 available at http://www.dfait-maeci.gc.ca/tna-nac/NAFTA-Interpr-en.asp. The interpretation is binding on an arbitral tribunal (NAFTA Art. 1131).

[81] *See* Canada's Department of Foreign Affairs and International Trade Canada (http://www.dfait-maeci.gc.ca/tna-nac/nafta-en.asp); Mexico's Secretaría de Economía (http://www.economia-snci.gob.m/ls23al.php?s=18&p=1&l=2); and the U.S. Secretary of State (http://www.state.gov/s/1/c3439x.htm).

[82] Art. 1126(13) NAFTA.

[83] *See* http://www.nafta-sec-alena.org.

[84] *See* the ICSID Convention's Rules of Procedure for Arbitration Proceedings, *supra* note 78, Rule 32(2) (on oral procedure); ICSID Additional Facility Rules, *supra* note 79, at Art. 4.4(2) (on publication of minutes of hearings) and Art. 39 (on persons permitted to attend hearings); UNCITRAL Arbitration Rules, Art. 25(4) (on hearings), available at http://www.uncitral.org/english/texts/arbitration/arb-rules.htm.

possibility of the submission of amicus curiae briefs to the tribunals, and the July 2001 clarification did not address this issue. Significantly, however, the tribunal in the pending *Methanex* arbitration issued a decision holding that it had the ability to accept amicus briefs.[85]

Lastly, the rules governing the publication of final awards are somewhat confusing. Pursuant to the interpretative note, the U.S. and Canada are obliged to make awards public. However, in the case of Mexico, the three sets of arbitral rules (ICSID, Additional Facility, or UNCITRAL) apply.[86] Under these rules, the publication of awards is regulated and restricted in varying ways. Under the ICSID Convention, the International Centre for Settlement of Investment Disputes is barred from publicizing an award without the consent of both parties to the dispute;[87] and under both the ICSID Additional Facility and the UNCITRAL arbitration rules, the final award may be made public only if all parties to the dispute agree.[88]

In sum, the binding July 2001 interpretative note was a step in the right direction in many ways, but greater transparency and public participation remain to be achieved.

11. Summary and Conclusion

Chapter 11 provides investor guarantees and requires host States to compensate in case of violations of these guarantees, without providing exceptions for measures taken in order to conserve water resources or protect public health. It allows foreign investors to sue the host State directly in opaque arbitral proceedings to which the public has only limited access, if any at all. Investors have initiated numerous proceedings to challenge environmental and health measures, including measures to protect water resources. This chapter has focused on three investor guarantees which appear of particular concern for host governments wishing to protect their water resources. These are provisions on national treatment, performance requirements, and expropriation. The common concern with respect to all of these guarantees is the absence of an exception or a carve-out for measures adopted to protect the environment and natural resources. In absence of such an exception, the legitimacy of an environmental measure remains in jeopardy.

So far, tribunals have adopted expansive interpretations of the investor guarantees: they have taken a business-oriented approach in analyzing the national

[85] Methanex Corporation and the United States of America, Decision of the Tribunal on Petitions from Third Persons to Intervene as '*Amici Curiae*' (January 15, 2001), available at www.state.gov/s/l/c5821.htm.

[86] NAFTA Art. 1137.4 (Publication of an Award) referring to Annex 1137.4.

[87] ICSID Convention, *supra* note 78, at Art. 48(5) (on publication of the award). Mexico has not signed the ICSID Convention, however.

[88] ICSID Additional Facility Rules, *supra* note 79, at Art. 53(3), and UNCITRAL Arbitration Rules, *supra* note 84, at Art. 32(5) (on publication of the award).

treatment clause and have largely ignored environmental considerations to determine whether domestic and foreign investors were 'in like circumstances'. They have expanded the prohibition to use export quotas to include export restrictions, potentially prohibiting host governments to restrict water exports. And lastly, they have interpreted the expropriation clause in a manner that exceeds property rights protection under the domestic laws of each of the NAFTA States, thus circumventing domestic laws and jurisprudence which are in constant search of an appropriate balance between private and public interests.

Proponents of the current framework will argue that the concerns are misplaced because in many of the disputes the host State prevailed, not the investor. This disregards the fact that expansive readings of investor guarantees—even if resulting in a rejection of the investor claims in individual cases—can have a chilling effect on legislators wishing to comply with NAFTA rules. Additionally, the costs of the dispute settlement procedures on host States are significant and must be considered for the evaluation of the status quo.

Negotiators of ongoing and future international investment rules might contemplate excluding certain measures to protect water resources from the scope of measures covered by investment treaties. If not, investment rules should at least allow for exceptions for measures taken to conserve natural resources, the environment, and public health. Such exceptions should be formulated in a way that would unambiguously cover the protection of water resources from over-exploitation and pollution. In any case, disputes involving environment and health, including the protection of a resource as important to life as fresh water, should be transparent and participatory.

12

Water Concessions and Protection of Foreign Investments under International Law

SERGE PANNATIER and OLIVIER DUCREY

1. Introduction

Water is life. The multiple uses of water contribute to the satisfaction of many human basic needs: consumption, sanitation, irrigation, source of energy, means of communication, etc. This explains why the poisoning and spoilage of water have always been feared.

Fresh water is a rather abundant natural resource. A rough estimation shows that there are approximately 7,000 m^3 of water per person living on planet Earth. Its distribution, however, is extremely uneven. Today, forty countries do not have enough stocks to satisfy the basic needs of their population.[1]

Due to its characteristics, water cannot be considered as an ordinary commodity. The economic, environmental, and social roles played by water resources explain why it is difficult to develop a regulatory system that is able to cope with all these realities.

In most countries, water belongs to the public domain. Consequently, rights to use water resources can either be exercised by the State itself (or a local authority), or be granted to private individuals or corporations pursuant to the applicable national—or local—legislation. Corporations, however, will be interested in investing in water projects only if they receive guarantees that they will be able to develop their business and have sufficient return on their investments.

Because water is essential for life, everybody should have access to it. This means that management of water resources should not be fully privatized. If this were the case, only people with sufficient income to pay would have access to water services. Unregulated privatization would also result in depriving people located in remote areas from access to water distribution services, as it would turn out to be extremely expensive to build the infrastructure necessary to reach those regions.

[1] Mostafa K. Tolba and Osama A. El-Kholy (eds), The World Environment 1972–1992, at 83–103 (London, 1992).

Many arguments, however, plead in favour of partial privatization of public utilities networks. The main advantage lies in the neo-liberal theory according to which private ownership is more efficient than public ownership. On the basis of this theory, governmental management cannot be efficient due to the fact that publicly-owned entities are not driven by cost-effective considerations. Such argument finds its root in the famous 'tragedy of the commons' developed by Hardin[2] and according to which 'the more attenuated the property rights of a person in an asset which the person managed, the less incentive that person has to manage it efficiently'.[3] In other words, as it is driven by market forces, private management would inevitably be more efficient than public management and thus have positive consequences on social welfare.

Such theory, however, fails to take into account the fact that most public utility industries have either monopolistic structures, or are natural monopolies where competition is absent.[4] In such a market, a private operator has no real incentives to improve the quality of the services it provides and nothing prevents it from imposing the price of its services.

Due to the peculiar characteristics of public utilities, privatization cannot be left only to market forces but must be subject to some regulatory limits which impose the terms and conditions under which a private company operates in order to prevent a reduction in social welfare. Traditionally, such limits have been included in the concession contracts that national or provincial authorities grant to private corporations to operate a specific public utility network. Concession contracts are lengthy legal documents in which the parties agree to the scope of the services to be provided. They embody the requirements that the granting authority imposed on all bidding companies, and describe in detail the rights and obligations of the private operator.

Investments in the sector of public utilities are often significant. In fact, development of infrastructures necessitates large amounts of financial resources that can only be provided by public funding or large multinational corporations. For private investors, the political instability that prevails in many developing countries adds to the risks of their investment. In such markets, private companies will engage in big projects only if they receive guarantees of sufficient return on their investment and if they are provided with sufficient legal protection to secure their interests in case of political changes that would affect their investment.

Some of these guarantees are included in the concession contracts concluded with a local or a national authority. In such contracts, investors generally require a guarantee of profitability by the public authority, or the right to abandon the

[2] *See* Garrett Hardin, *The Tragedy of the Commons*, Science 162 (1968) at 1243–48, and Garrett Hardin and John Baden, (eds), MANAGING THE COMMONS (San Francisco, 1977).

[3] Michael Whincop and Stuart Rowland, *Markets and Corporate Law*, in WHO BENEFITS FROM PRIVATISATION? (London, 1998).

[4] On this issue, *see* Jenny Piaget, *Limits in Water Concession Contracts: the case of Aguas del Aconquija (Argentina)*, Master of International Management, University of Lausanne, 11–25 (2003).

project if the rate of return is not sufficient.[5] They also require the authority to set up the prices of the services they provide. Other guarantees are found in bilateral investment treaties entered into between the State that is granting the concession (the host State) and the State of the investor. Such instruments aim at protecting the investors against the risks linked to the political instability that still prevails in many countries (expropriation, breach of commitments taken by previous governments, etc.).

The present chapter looks at how water concessions are granted and regulated under national and international law. As such concessions are often attributed to private corporations that rely on bilateral investment treaties to protect their investments, the chapter focuses in particular on the interrelationship between water concession contracts and bilateral or regional investment treaties. This relationship is well illustrated in the case that the Compañía de Aguas del Aconquija, S.A. and Compagnie Générale des Eaux brought against the Argentine Republic before the International Centre for the Settlement of Investment Disputes (ICSID)[6] regarding the violation of the bilateral investment agreement between France and Argentina.

2. International protection of foreign investment

The legal framework developed to protect foreign investments essentially consists in bilateral treaties entered into between capital-exporting and capital-importing countries. The main purpose of these instruments is to protect foreign investors against risks associated with nationalization, expropriation, and the political instability that prevails in many countries. So far, no multilateral agreement on the protection of investments has been adopted. Recently, however, provisions relating to the protection of foreign investments have been included in the text of regional trade agreements.[7] Despite these latest developments, there are still no multilateral agreed standards governing this matter, thus leading Sornarajah to state that:

> The absence of any significant multilateral treaty on foreign investment protection and the increasing number of bilateral investment treaties themselves are indications of an absence of sufficient community of interests to make any customary international law in this area.[8]

[5] In December 1999, UK Water Company Biwater pulled out of a major water supply project in Zimbabwe because the project could not yield the rate of return expected by the private sector; *see* Jenny Piaget, *supra* note 4, at 26.

[6] ICSID, Case No. ARB/97/3.

[7] *See*, e.g., Chapter 11 of the North American Free Trade Agreement; *see also* the Protocol of Colonia of 17 January 1994 on the Mutual Promotion and Protection of Investments under the MERCOSUR.

[8] Muthucumaraswamy Sornarajah, The International Law on Foreign Investment, 232 (Cambridge, 1994).

However, bilateral and regional investment treaties have today become a familiar feature of inter-State relations. The first modern bilateral investment treaty (BIT) was concluded between Germany and Pakistan in 1959 and came into force in 1962.[9] Since the late 1980s, BITs have come to be universally accepted instruments for the promotion and legal protection of foreign investments. The reason for this situation is quite simple: 'Bilateral solutions became necessary simply because of an absence of a consensus to create multilaterally acceptable norms.'[10]

At the end of 2002, the total number of BITs concluded amounted to some 2,181.[11] If the great majority of such treaties has been entered into between developed and developing countries, recent practice shows that an increasing number of BITs are now concluded between developing countries themselves.[12]

The aim of BITs is to promote foreign investments and improve the legal protection offered to foreign investors. Many of these instruments therefore share common provisions concerning, *inter alia*: the definition of investments; corporate nationality and protection of shareholders; the treatment of foreign investment; the repatriation of profits; expropriation and compensation; and the settlement of disputes.[13]

The most significant contribution of BITs to the protection of foreign investments is probably found in the area of dispute resolution. By enabling a foreign investor to have direct access to an international arbitration forum to settle the disputes that could arise between the investor and the host State, BITs have removed the lack of confidence that such foreign investor may vest in the impartiality of local courts. Today, the majority of BITs submit disputes to the ICSID (see further below).

3. The concession agreement

Rules protecting foreign investments are also found in the text of the concession contract entered into between the investor and the authority that requests a private operator to manage a public utility service, and to rehabilitate an existing infrastructure and expand services. As already mentioned, water concessions often require huge investments from the concessionaire, especially in

[9] *See* ICSID, *List of Parties to Bilateral Investment Treaties*, available at http://www.worldbank.org/icsid/treaties/i-1.htm.

[10] Sornarajah, *supra* note 8, at 232.

[11] United Conference on Trade and Development, *World Investment Report 2003*. In a recent publication, the Secretariat of the International Centre for the Settlement of Investment Disputes between States and National of Other States has listed over 1,100 BITs.

[12] In 1996, e.g., BITs were concluded between Chile and Cuba (10 January 1996), Egypt and Sri Lanka (11 March 1996), Argentina and El Salvador (9 May 1996), El Salvador and Peru (13 June 1996), Chile and Guatemala (8 November 1996).

[13] The typical content of investment treaties is discussed in more detail in chapters 10 and 11 of this book.

countries where the infrastructure maintenance has been neglected for years. In such contracts, the compensation received by the concessionaire is traditionally linked to the prices it can levy for the services it provides and should cover the investment over the concession period. Therefore, the parties to such contracts will carefully draft the provisions governing the prices that the concessionaire will be allowed to charge for its services, the possibility to raise such prices, and the ways to recover the money from those beneficiaries that do not pay the price.

Governments normally wish to keep the property over their water distribution network. This is the reason why they generally choose to enter into concession agreements in which they entrust a private operator with the tasks to manage, rehabilitate, and expand an existing infrastructure over a specific period of time. In view of the significant investment required from the private operator, concession contracts are often granted for free. Any other solution would not be attractive for foreign investors, as the latter would not be interested in purchasing assets which are in rather poor condition. For governments, a concession contract can be a good solution for ensuring future investments and improvements while keeping a certain control over the infrastructure. However, the Aguas del Aconquija case demonstrates the types of problems that can occur under such agreements.

4. The International Convention on the Settlement of Investment Disputes

The International Centre on the Settlement of Investment Disputes (ICSID) was established in 1966 under the auspices of the World Bank to facilitate the settlement of investment disputes between foreign investors and host States, and thus increases the legal protection offered to foreign investors.[14]

The Centre has been entrusted with legal personality and has its seat in Washington D.C. Its purpose is to offer States and foreign private investors a forum to conciliate or to arbitrate their dispute relating to investments. The procedure is entirely governed by the provisions of the Convention. The Centre also maintains a list of conciliators and arbitrators which is at the disposal of the parties.

The jurisdiction of ICSID is subject to the provisions of Article 25 of the Convention. This jurisdiction is subject to the fulfilment of three conditions:

(1) the consent of the parties;
(2) the status of the parties (the parties must be the States parties to the ICSID Convention, or a private investor located in one of those States and the host State); and

[14] Convention of 18 March 1965 on the Settlement of Investment Disputes between States and Nationals of Other States, 575 *UNTS* 161.

(3) the nature of the dispute (the dispute must be related to an investment project).

The consent of the parties must be provided in writing (Article 25.1). It can be given on a case-by-case basis, or be included in previous acts such as an investment contract, a local statute of the host State, or a BIT.

Article 25.3 of the ICSID Convention provides that 'consent by a constituent subdivision or agency of a Contracting State shall require the approval of that State unless that State notifies the Centre that no such approval is required'. This provision establishes, with the consent of the central government, the right of such agencies or subdivisions to be parties in their own right to an ICSID proceeding.

The jurisdiction of the ICSID extends to any legal dispute directly related to an investment (Article 25.1 of the ICSID Convention). Such wording is broad enough to cover any disputes concerning either the existence and the scope of a specific right or obligation, or the nature and the amount of the compensation due as a result of a violation of a BIT. Contracting Parties are entitled, however, to notify the Centre of the categories of disputes which they would not consider submitting to the jurisdiction of the Centre (Article 25.4 of the ICSID Convention).

5. The case of Aguas Del Aconquija[15]

5.1 Factual situation

At the beginning of the 1990s, the Argentine economy was undergoing deep reforms. After a period of political instability and huge inflation, the election of Carlos Menem as President in 1989 resulted in a significant liberalization of the Argentinian economy, which was at the root of the good performance achieved by said economy throughout the 1990s. Through the enactment of the 'convertibility law', which pegged the Argentinian peso to the dollar, and a series of reforms aimed at privatizing the economy, inflation was brought under control and the economy achieved an impressive recovery.

Tucumán is the smallest province of Argentina and one of the poorest. In 1991, 83.6% of the urban population of Tucumán had access to drinking water, while only 38% was connected to the sewage network.[16] In 1993, in the middle of the process of economic reform outlined above, the provincial government

[15] Water and sewer services concession agreements are currently subject to five cases pending before ICSID Arbitration Tribunals: Azurix Corp. v. Argentine Republic (Case No. ARB/01/12); Aguas Provinciales de Santa Fe, S.A., Suez, Sociedad General de Aguas de Barcelona, S.A. and Intergua Servicios Integrales de Agua, S.A. v. Argentine Republic (Case No. ARB/03/17); Aguas Cordobesesas, S.A., Suez, and Sociedad General de Aguas de Barcelona, S.A. v. Argentine Republic (Case No. ARB/03/18); Aguas Argentinas, S. A., Suez, Sociedad General de Aguas de Barcelona, S.A. and Vivendi Universal S.A. v. Argentine Republic (Case No. ARB/03/19); and Azurix Corp. v. Argentine Republic (Case No. ARB/03/30).

[16] CETI, *Análisis de la situación actual*, Dirección Provincial de Obras Sanitarias (DIPOS), Provincia de Tucumán. Versión Final, Octubre 1993a.

decided to privatize all its water and sewage facilities, which were then being operated by a provincial authority. This was considered to be the best solution to modernize a water distribution network which was in extremely poor condition.[17] The contemplated investment project linked to the grant of a concession was to generate significant costs, which would eventually be charged to the consumers. As a noticeable portion of the population already experienced difficulties in paying the price of their water consumption, the privatization was going to have an important social impact.

The authorities of the Tucumán province took the concession of the Buenos Aires water system as a model for the privatization process of their own water network. The Buenos Aires water concession was ten times larger than the concession of the water supply services contemplated by the Tucumán province. The Buenos Aires concession, which became one of the world's largest water concessions, brought an initial reduction in water tariffs and offered good return on investment for the beneficiary of the concession.[18]

At first, five corporations showed interest in investing in the water concession of Tucumán. Following the publication of a study detailing all the technical aspects of the water project,[19] only one consortium, lead by the Compagnie Générale des Eaux (CGE), a French corporation which later became Vivendi Universal, made a bid. This offer, however, did not correspond to the requirements set up by the provincial authorities, as it included a reduced amount of investments and was based on a higher price to be charged to the consumers than the price suggested by the provincial authorities. As there was no other offer, the provincial government accepted the conditions included in the bid of CGE and awarded a thirty-year water concession to Compañía de Aguas del Aconquija, S.A., the Argentine affiliate set up by the Compagnie Générale des Eaux.

Under the concession contract signed on 18 May 1995, Compañía de Aguas del Aconquija S. A. committed to invest US$ 384.5 million throughout the entire period of the concession. As a result of this commitment, the company did not have to pay any royalties to the authorities of Tucumán.

Soon after the concession contract entered into force, a radical political change occurred in the province of Tucumán.[20] At the time of this change, the economy of the province was in an alarming situation. The new elected governor

[17] At that time, 45% of the drinking water network and 60% of the sewerage network were over forty years old. Moreover, the Dirección Provincial de Obras Sanitarias provided no systematic annual maintenance programme. *See* Inter American Development Bank, *El proceso de transformación del sector de agua potable y saneamiento en Argentina*, July 1996.

[18] However, this initial enthusiasm progressively disappeared. The company had to increase its tariffs and accumulated a large debt. According to the company, this increase was necessary as it did not have enough income for anything more than paying wages and keeping up basic investment, while the population accused the private investor of not respecting its commitment concerning water treatment and environmental conservation.

[19] Plan de Mantenimiento, Mejoras y Expansión del Servicio, mentioned in Jenny Piaget, *supra* note 4, at 36.

[20] A new governor opposed to the concession was elected.

undertook to renegotiate the concession contract, as promised during his election campaign. At the beginning of 1996, the government requested a reduction of the price that Compañía de Aguas del Aconquija S.A. was charging for its services, a re-dimensioning of the perimeter of the concession, and an adaptation of the projected investments to the economical reality of Tucumán.

The first attempts to amend the initial concession contract failed, notably because of contradictory opinions about incorporation of taxes in the price of the services performed by Compañía de Aguas del Aconquija S.A. In May 1996, the Argentine Republic and the authorities of Tucumán entered into an agreement pursuant to which the national government would provide assistance and expertise for the successful renegotiation of the concession contract.[21] Following long negotiations, Tucumán and Compañía de Aguas del Aconquija S.A. agreed on a final draft of a new concession contract. Surprisingly, the provincial governor submitted to the legislative power a draft contract which included substantive modifications when compared with the draft agreed with Compañía de Aguas del Aconquija S.A. For the investor, this act of the governor was just another example of the numerous attempts made by various branches of the provincial authorities to undermine the concession contract and to prevent the company from fulfilling its obligations.[22] The company therefore refused to sign the amended concession agreement and, after the failure of a last round of negotiations in 1997, Compagnie Générale des Eaux and Compañía de Aguas del Aconquija S.A. notified the provincial governor of Tucumán that the company was rescinding the concession contract because of the alleged default of Tucumán. Tucumán rejected the rescission of the contract and terminated the concession contract, alleging a default in the performance of its obligation by Compañía de Aguas del Aconquija S.A.

5.2 Legal proceedings

On 26 December 1996, Compagnie Générale des Eaux and Compañía de Aguas del Aconquija S.A. filed a claim with the ICSID against the Argentine Republic, alleging, *inter alia*, Argentina's liabilities for Tucumán's actions under Article 8 of the 1991 Argentine–French Agreement for the Promotion and Reciprocal Protection of Investments.[23] The investor also based its claims on the ICSID Convention, to which both France and Argentine Republic were parties and which came into force before the conclusion of the concession contract.

In its statement of claims, the investor alleged that the Argentine Republic did not respect its commitments, by failing to protect its interests in not

[21] ICSID, Case No ARB/97/3, Compañía de Aguas del Aconquija, S.A. and Compagnie Générale des Eaux v. the Argentine Republic, Award, para. 35.

[22] *See* Jenny Piaget, *supra* note 4, at 39–41; and Emmanuel Gaillard, *Centre International pour le règlement des différends relatifs aux investissements: chronique des sentences arbitrales*, JDI, 2003, at 230–40.

[23] Signed on 3 July 1991, approved by Argentine Law No. 24.100, *Boletin Oficial*, 14 July 1992.

obliging the province of Tucumán to act for the successful performance of the concession contract. More specifically, the claimant raised four categories of 'acts of the province attributable to the Argentine Republic that violated its rights under the BIT':

(1) 'Acts that resulted in a fall in the recovery rate under the Concession Contract';
(2) 'Acts that unilaterally reduced the tariff rate';
(3) 'Abuses of regulatory authority'; and
(4) 'Dealings in bad faith'.[24]

On the basis of these alleged violations, the French multinational claimed damages of over US$ 300 million.

Not surprisingly, the Argentine Republic responded that it had not consented to the submission of the dispute for resolution to the ICSID Arbitral Tribunal. The government challenged the jurisdiction of the ICSID Arbitral Tribunal, arguing that the concession contract included a clause of jurisdiction submitting any dispute to the local courts of Tucumán.[25] The Argentine Republic added that it was a party neither to the concession contract nor to the negotiations that led to its conclusion and, as the facts disputed by claimants arose under and were exclusively related to the concession contract, the ICSID Arbitral Tribunal lacked jurisdiction.

The Argentinian government further explained that it only intervened to assist the local authorities in the renegotiation of the concession contract. On this basis, the Argentine Republic submitted that, as it was not a party to the concession contract, it owed no legal duty to the claimants and that there was no basis in international law to attribute the actions of the provincial authorities of Tucumán to the Argentine Republic.[26]

Last but not least, the Argentine Republic argued that the provincial authorities did not violate any provision or obligation arising out of the concession contract. Finally, the concession contract itself made no reference to either the BIT or the ICSID Convention, or to remedies that were available to a French foreign investor in Argentina under these treaties.[27]

5.3 Award

The Arbitral Tribunal issued its award on 21 November 2000. This award is divided into two parts. The first part deals with the question of jurisdiction,

[24] ICSID, Case No. ARB/97/3, Compañía de Aguas del Aconquija, S.A. and Compagnie Générale des Eaux v. the Argentine Republic, Award, para. 63.

[25] Art. 16.4 of the Concession Contract provides: 'For the purposes of interpretation and application of this contract the parties submit themselves to the exclusive jurisdiction of the Contentious Administrative Tribunal of Tucumán.'

[26] ICSID, Case No. ARB/97/3, Compañía de Aguas del Aconquija, S.A. and Compagnie Générale des Eaux v. the Argentine Republic, Award, para. 44.

[27] *Id.*, Introduction and Summary.

while the second part examines the merits of the claims put forward by Compañía de Aguas del Aconquija S.A. and Compagnie Générale des Eaux.

a. Jurisdiction

In a first stage, the ICSID Tribunal examined whether it had jurisdiction under the ICSID Convention to rule on the Tucumán water concession case.

The Tribunal noted that Article 16.4 of the concession contract between the Compagnie Générale des Eaux, Compañía de Aguas del Aconquija S.A., and Tucumán submitted the resolution of disputes, concerning both its interpretation and application, to the exclusive jurisdiction of the contentious administrative courts of Tucumán. The Tribunal noted, however, that, under Article 25 of the ICSID Convention, its jurisdiction extended to 'any legal dispute arising directly out of an investment', provided that the parties had given their formal consent. In this respect, Article 8 of the French–Argentinian BIT entitles any French investor in the Republic of Argentina to submit any 'dispute relating to investments, within the meaning of this [the BIT] agreement' to the ICSID. According to Article 1(1) of the BIT, investments include '[c]oncessions granted by law or by virtue of an agreement',[28] such as the Tucumán concession contract. On this basis, the Tribunal rejected the arguments raised by the Argentine Republic to challenge the jurisdiction of the Tribunal, according to which it was not party to the concession contract and that under its 1994 Constitution, the acts of officials of the province of Tucumán could not be attributed to the federal government.

The Tribunal relied on the well-established principle of international law according to which actions of a federal State's administrative subdivisions are attributable to the central government and that the internal constitutional structure of a country cannot alter these obligations,[29] to come to the conclusion that actions of the officials of Tucumán were legally attributable to the Argentine Republic and that it had jurisdiction in this case.[30] The Tribunal added that the contract's forum selection provision 'did not and could not' divest the Tribunal of jurisdiction, as the cause of action fell under the BIT rather than the concession contract.[31]

b. Merits

In a second stage, the Tribunal considered the question of the responsibility of the Argentine Republic for the alleged violations of the concession contract on the basis of the claims put forward by the investor.

[28] ICSID, Case No. ARB/97/3, Compañía de Aguas del Aconquija, S.A. and Compagnie Générale des Eaux v. the Argentine Republic, Award, para. 45.

[29] 'A federal state is responsible for the conduct of its political sub-divisions and cannot evade that responsibility by alleging that its constitutional powers of control over them are insufficient for it to enforce compliance with international obligations.' Max Sorensen, MANUAL OF PUBLIC INTERNATIONAL LAW, 1968, p. 557.

[30] ICSID, Case No. ARB/97/3, Compañía de Aguas del Aconquija, S.A. and Compagnie Générale des Eaux v. the Argentine Republic, Award, paras 49–50.

[31] *Id.*, para. 53.

The Tribunal noted that the parties had different views of a number of contractual obligations, such as 'the method for measuring water consumption, the level of tariffs for customers, the timing and percentage of any increase in tariffs, the remedy in case of non-payment of tariffs, the rights of CGE to pass-through to customers certain taxes and the quality of the water delivered'.[32]

The Tribunal held that the Argentine Republic could not be held liable *unless and until* the claimants had asserted their rights before Tucumán's 'contentious administrative courts' and had been procedurally or substantively denied their rights. The Tribunal further held that it could not make any determinations as to whether the acts of the provincial authorities performed under its sovereign authority (*iure imperiis*) or as a party to the concession contract (*iure iestionis*), as this would require a 'detailed interpretation and application' of the concession contract. The Tribunal recalled that the parties allocated this task to the exclusive jurisdiction of the Tucumán administrative courts, and came to the conclusion that, since the French investor had failed to seek remedies in the administrative courts of Tucumán, there was no basis to hold the Argentine Republic liable under the BIT.[33]

Lastly, the Tribunal dismissed the claims according to which the Argentine Republic had failed to respond to actions of Tucumán Officials, thus violating its obligation to grant fair and equitable treatment to investments made by investors of the other Party, and to do it in such a way that the exercise of such right is not obstructed de iure or de facto under Articles 3 and 5 of the BIT.[34] In order to accept such claims, the Tribunal stressed that the investors should have demonstrated that the actions of the Tucumán officials amounted to a breach of the BIT and that such breach was reported to the Argentine government, together with a request to do everything in its power, including the initiation of legal proceedings, to convince the Tucumán officials to comply with their obligations under the BIT. Yet the Tribunal found nothing in the record of the proceedings that would provide a basis for holding that the Argentine Republic did not respond to the situation in Tucumán and to the requests of the claimants in accordance with its obligations under the BIT.[35]

Therefore, the ICSID Tribunal dismissed the claims of US$ 300 million for damages and insisted on the point that the claimants should have first pursued their case before the local tribunal of the Tucumán province.

5.4 Annulment of the award

Further to the criticisms that followed the publication of the arbitral award,[36] the claimants sought partial annulment of the award pursuant to Article 52(1) of

[32] *Id.*, para. 32. [33] *Id.*, paras 78–80. [34] *Id.*, paras 83–92. [35] *Id.*, para. 92.

[36] *See*, e.g., Thomas W. Wälde/Todd Weiler, *Investment Arbitration under the Energy Charter Treaty in the Light of the New NAFTA Precedents: Towards a Global Code of Conduct for Economic Regulation*, in INVESTMENT TREATIES AND ARBITRATION (Gabrielle Kaufmann-Kohler/Blaise Stucki, eds), ASA Special Series No. 19, 2002, at 159–221.

the ICSID Convention, arguing that the Tribunal had manifestly exceeded its powers, that there had been a serious departure from a fundamental rule of procedure, and that the award failed to state the reasons on which it was based.

In its Decision, the Annulment Committee recalled that 'a state may breach a treaty without breaching a contract, and vice versa'. On the basis of this general principle, it explained that

> whether there has been a breach of the BIT and whether there has been a breach of contract are different questions. Each of these claims will be determined by reference to its own proper or applicable law—in the case of the BIT, by international law; in the case of the Concession Contract, by the proper laws of the contracts.[37]

The Annulment Committee underlined that it

> is settled, and neither party disputes, that an ICSID tribunal commits an excess of powers not only if it exercises a jurisdiction which it does not have under the relevant agreement or treaty and the ICSID Convention, read together, but also if it fails to exercise a jurisdiction which it possesses under those instruments.[38]

The Committee noted that the dispute not only related to the conformity of the actions of the Tucumán provincial authorities with the concession contract, but also to the consistency of such actions with the BIT entered into between Argentina and France. More specifically, the Arbitral Tribunal should have checked whether the Tucumán provincial authorities complied with their obligation to grant 'fair and equitable' treatment to the investment made by Compañía de Aguas del Aconquija S.A./Compagnie Générale des Eaux, under Article 3 of the BIT.

The Annulment Committee added that, if the analysis of the claims based on the BIT required an interpretation of the concession contract, the Tribunal should have carried out that task. The Annulment Committee explained that

> under Article 8(4) of the BIT the Tribunal had jurisdiction to base its decision upon the concession contract, at least so far as necessary in order to determine whether there had been a breach of the substantive standards of the BIT.[39]

Eventually, the Annulment Committee criticized the assumption made by the Tribunal, according to which the conduct of Tucumán in the exercise of its rights as a party to the concession contract could not, *a priori*, have breached the BIT. According to the Annulment Committee, 'there is no basis for such an assumption: whether a particular conduct involves a breach of a treaty is not determined by asking whether the conduct purportedly involves an exercise of contractual rights'.[40] Consequently, by denying jurisdiction over the conduct of the provincial authorities even if this required 'detailed interpretation and application of the Concession Contract',[41] the Arbitral Tribunal committed a

[37] ICSID, Case No ARB/97/3, Compañía de Aguas del Aconquija, S.A. and Compagnie Générale des Eaux v. the Argentine Republic, Decision on Annulment, July 3, 2002, in 41 *ILM* 1135 (2002) 1354.

[38] *Id.*, para. 1352. [39] *Id.*, para. 1357. [40] *Id.*

[41] ICSID, Case No. ARB/97/3, Compañía de Aguas del Aconquija, S.A. and Compagnie Générale des Eaux v. the Argentine Republic, Award, para. 79.

'manifest excess of jurisdiction' in dismissing the claim and failing to decide whether or not there was a breach of the BIT.[42]

6. Conclusion

Several lessons can be drawn from the case of Aguas del Aconquija. The first and most important one is that, despite the presence of a jurisdiction provision in a concession contract, an investor can still validly submit a dispute to a foreign tribunal on the basis of a BIT. The *ad hoc* Annulment Committee reached this conclusion by reminding that breaches of a contract and breaches of a treaty are independent issues. On the basis of this premise, it was not possible to dismiss the treaty-based claim because this would have left the investor with the obligation to exhaust local remedies, with the risk of having its case decided by a local court the impartiality of which was questionable.

In the future, central government will have to pay more attention to make local authorities aware of the country's international obligations and of the consequences resulting from a violation of said obligations. This will contribute to the improvement of the legal security which is the prerequisite of any decision regarding an investment abroad.

As clearly pointed out by Thomas Wälde, 'Foreign investors tend to be successful in international arbitration, mainly because the law (BIT; contract) is largely on their side'.[43] This opinion is undoubtedly reinforced by the decision of the Annulment Committee in the case of Aguas del Aconquija. This does not mean, however, that a successful litigation is the end of the story. Enforcement of a compensation award may turn out to be difficult, thus leaving the investor in a rather uncomfortable situation. Eventually, parties may have to return to the negotiating table to discuss the most reasonable ways to put an end to their dispute.

The second lesson that can be learned from this case is that, nearly ten years after the water concession was granted to Aguas del Aconquija, the situation has not improved for the population of the province of Tucumán. To the contrary, the price of water services has increased and no investment has been made to modernize the obsolete water distribution network of the province. The public authority that took over the management of the water distribution network when the concession contract was terminated is now heavily indebted, partly due to the difficulties experienced in trying to recover payment for the services provided.

[42] For an analysis of the Annulment Award, see Emmanuel Gaillard, *supra* note 22, at 230–40. The request for resubmission of the dispute was filed and registered on October 24, 2003. The proceeding is pending.

[43] Thomas W. Wälde, *'ICSID Annulment Committee'* in Oil, Gas & Energy Law Intelligence, Vol. I, Issue 02, March 2003.

The modernization and maintenance of a water distribution network is extremely expensive. For developing countries such as Argentina, where the water distribution network is old and not fully developed, it is crucial to find the funds necessary to modernize and manage the distribution network effectively in order to make sure that the population can have access to this essential resource under acceptable conditions. Such funds can be raised either through public borrowings, or through private investments. Private investors, however, will be interested in such projects only if they can secure a sufficient return on their investment. This will inevitably result in an increase of the price the population will have to pay to benefit from these services. Such increase will, however, be extremely difficult to impose in areas where the population already live under precarious conditions.

The political instability that often prevails in developing countries increases the risks faced by private investors. This will prompt them to condition their investment decision to even higher requirements concerning the return they expect on their investment. As a result of this situation, and under the present circumstances, it might be more interesting for a developing country to raise the funds it needs to develop and manage its water distribution system effectively through public borrowing.

The fact that the cost of private capital is onerous should not lead to the conclusion that the private sector has no role to play in the modernization and effective management of public utility networks. However, in order to mitigate negative reactions from the population and the political authorities in relation to the social consequences resulting from the involvement of the private sector in the modernization and management of public utility networks, it is important that concession contracts are carefully drafted and are in line with the general development policy of the host State. If the concession contract is generally perceived to be fair, and the rights and obligations of the parties are clearly defined, then the risks of disputes will be reduced.

13

Local Communities and Water Investments

PHILIPPE CULLET and ALIX GOWLLAND-GUALTIERI

1. Introduction

Water investments in developing countries have until recently been undertaken primarily by governments themselves. Thus, most projects relating to hydropower, irrigation and drainage, water supply and sanitation, fisheries, and water services have been financed either by governments, or by outside funding agencies through governments. In recent times, there has been a rapid shift towards the involvement of national and international private sector actors to make up for declining public sectors resources. This ongoing shift is of tremendous importance in that individuals and communities often bear the negative consequences of major water investments. This chapter focuses on the procedural rights in international law of local communities that are adversely affected by water investments.[1] It examines in particular issues concerning the extent to which local communities have rights to be informed and consulted in the context of proposed legislative changes, programmes, and specific projects before they are adopted and implemented. It also looks at the extent to which local communities have been given rights to participate in, and ultimately accept or refuse, specific water investments affecting them. In practice, there has been relatively little by way of international and regional decisions focusing expressly on water investments. As a result, wherever water-related practice is not available, this chapter looks at decisions and standards that concern the broader field of natural resources as a proxy.[2]

This chapter is divided into four sections. The first section looks at the legal framework for procedural rights in the field of sustainable development. It examines in particular the evolving rights to environmental information, participation in decision-making processes, and access to justice for local

[1] The term 'local communities' is used here as a shortcut for reference to local communities, indigenous peoples, tribal peoples, and other groups of people affected by water investments or more generally natural resource investments. Specific reference to indigenous or tribal peoples is made wherever instruments or decisions directly refer to one or the other.

[2] This chapter does not purport to provide an exhaustive survey of existing norms and practice concerning participation of local communities. It examines some of the most salient norms and decisions in chosen contexts, with a view to provide a basis for further developments in the specific field of water investments.

communities. It then moves on to the specific notion of prior informed consent (PIC), which goes one step further in giving local communities an input into decisions concerning water investments. Given the paucity of practice concerning participatory rights in the environmental field, the second section moves on to examine how similar issues have been treated in the case law of international and regional human rights bodies. The third section then analyses the practice of two international organizations, the World Bank and the International Labour Organization (ILO), whose internal policies and complaint mechanisms have significantly contributed to the development of participatory standards for local communities. The last section brings together the different fields examined in previous sections and seeks to provide guidelines for the development of a stronger model for participatory principles for local communities, in the context of the shift towards private water investments and the increased need to ensure that the rights of affected local communities are respected by all parties involved.

2. The sustainable development framework for the participation of local communities

It is with respect to the relationship between environment and development that there has been the most significant development of norms for greater participation of local communities in decision-making processes affecting them. The concept of participation in international environmental law is generally recognized as subsuming three components, namely, access to environmental information, participation in decision-making, and recourse before administrative and judicial bodies. The notion of PIC has also emerged in specific areas. Participatory rights in environmental matters have been given substantial support in sustainable development documents adopted in the wake of the 1992 United Nations Conference on Environment and Development (UNCED). This section gives an overview of the way in which the concepts of information disclosure, participation, access to justice, and PIC are treated in some major international instruments, both generally and specifically with respect to water-related issues.

2.1 Information disclosure, participation, and access to justice

The rights of individuals and groups to have access to environmental information, participate in decision-making processes, and have access to administrative and judicial proceedings in the realization of sustainable development on the national and international levels have been broadly endorsed.[3] This includes the effective participation of indigenous people and other local communities.[4]

[3] *See* Principle 10 of the Rio Declaration on Environment and Development, Rio de Janeiro, 13 June 1992, 31 *ILM* 874 (1992).

[4] *Id.*, Principle 22.

Participatory standards in the field of sustainable development have in particular been given expression in Agenda 21, which sets standards not only for States but also for international organizations, including the multilateral development banks (MDBs).[5] Agenda 21 confirms that civil society should have access to timely and relevant information on environmental and related matters, and adds that access to information encompasses a more 'proactive' dimension, reflected in the necessity for promoting public awareness and education in environmental matters.[6] It underscores generally that broad public participation in decision-making is one of the fundamental prerequisites for the achievement of sustainable development, and calls for the establishment of judicial and administrative procedures for legal redress accessible *inter alia* to groups and organizations with a recognized legal interest.[7] Chapter 26 explicitly designates indigenous peoples and their communities as the beneficiaries of participatory processes.[8] Agenda 21 also acknowledges public participation as forming an integral part of the undertaking of environmental impact assessment (EIA),[9] thereby allowing local communities likely to be affected by a decision to be fully informed of its implications and given an opportunity to respond. This is of particular relevance when water projects are concerned.[10] The importance of involving local communities in a number of Agenda 21's programme areas is further highlighted.[11] Most significantly for the present chapter, Chapter 18 sets forth standards regarding the participation of local communities in water resources management. For instance, it mandates States to design, implement, and evaluate projects and programmes based on the full participation of local communities and indigenous peoples in water management policy-making and decision-making.[12]

Support for participatory rights for local communities can also be found in instruments that address problems specifically related to water and sustainable development. For instance, a general participatory approach to water

[5] Agenda 21, Rio de Janeiro, 13 June 1992, UN Doc. A/CONF.151/26 (Vols. I, II, & III) (1992).

[6] *Id.*, at paras 8.4(f), 23.2, and Chapter 40.

[7] *Id.*, at paras 1.3 and 23.2 and 8.18, respectively.

[8] Other beneficiaries include women (Chapter 24) and children and youth (Chapter 25).

[9] Detailed provisions on public participation in the context of EIA are found at Arts 2(2) and (6), 3(8), and 4(2) of the Convention on Environmental Impact Assessment in a Transboundary Context, Espoo, 25 February 1991, 30 *ILM* 800 (1991) and in several provisions of its Protocol on Strategic Environmental Assessment, Kiev, 21 May 2003, available at http://www.unece.org/env/eia/documents/protocolenglish.pdf.

[10] For instance, Agenda 21 recommends mandatory EIA of all major water resource development projects potentially impairing water quality and aquatic ecosystems, as well as of new irrigation schemes in case significant negative environmental impacts are expected.

[11] Agenda 21, n. 5 above, at para. 28.1.

[12] *See further*, UN General Assembly, Resolution S-19/2, Programme for the Further Implementation of Agenda 21, 28 June 1997, UN Doc. A/RES/S-19/2 (1997), at paras 34(c), 108, 112, and 150. *See also* the Report of the Secretary-General, Commission on Sustainable Development, Organizational Session, Water: a key resource for sustainable development, E/CN.17/2001/PC/17 (2001), at para. 11, and Report of the Secretary-General, Commission on Sustainable Development, Implementing Agenda 21, UN Doc. E/CN.17/2002/PC.2/7 (2001), at para. 132, entrenching the need for stakeholder participation in freshwater resources management (with particular emphasis on indigenous peoples and women).

development and management is promoted in the 1992 Dublin Statement on Water and Sustainable Development, which provides that decisions should be taken at the lowest appropriate level, with full public consultation and involvement of users, including women, in the planning and implementation of water projects.[13] The Bonn Recommendations for Action issued at the 2001 International Conference on Freshwater further underline the importance of the participation of local communities when water resources are concerned, for instance in the construction of large infrastructure projects.[14] Participation in water resources management and project implementation is also mentioned in the Plan of Implementation adopted during the 2002 World Summit on Sustainable Development.[15] Specific guidance can be found in the World Commission on Dams (WCD) Report, which sets forth strategic priorities and guidelines to define a participatory decision-making process for both water and energy policy-making and project design. The Report includes a process for identifying stakeholders in each decision, policy, or project, with particular reference to indigenous and tribal peoples, women, and other vulnerable groups.[16] It provides that stakeholders must share in the benefits of the project, requiring the government or others sponsoring a dam to identify those whose rights are affected by the proposed project and to ensure that they are able to participate in the planning, design, construction, and operation of the dam. Of further interest are the guidelines adopted by the Conference of the Parties to a multilateral environmental treaty, the Ramsar Convention on Wetlands, regarding greater transparency and full participation of local communities and indigenous peoples in wetlands management, restoration, and rehabilitation.[17] The guidelines call for, amongst other things, the establishment by States Parties of a legal and policy context to facilitate the direct involvement of local communities and indigenous peoples in national and local decision-making for the sustainable use of wetlands, and target the bilateral and multilateral donor agencies supporting wetland conservation and integrated water resource management projects in general to take into consideration the priorities for action identified by the Conference of the Parties.[18] Such decisions adopted by

[13] *See* Principles 2 and 3 of the Dublin Statement on Water and Sustainable Development, International Conference on Water and the Environment (ICWE), Dublin, 26–31 January 1992, UN Doc. A/CONF.151/PC/112.

[14] Bonn Recommendations for Action, International Conference on Freshwater, Bonn, 3–7 December 2001.

[15] World Summit on Sustainable Development—Plan of Implementation, 4 September 2002, UN Doc. A/CONF.199/20, at para. 24(b).

[16] World Commission on Dams, *Dams and Development—A New Framework for Decision-Making* (London: Earthscan, 2000), at 215. *See also* text at nn. 33–34 below.

[17] Convention on Wetlands of International Importance, Ramsar, 2 February 1971, 11 *ILM* 963 (1972).

[18] As provided in Res. VII.8, Local communities and indigenous peoples, Guidelines for establishing and strengthening local communities' and indigenous peoples' participation in the management of wetlands, *Seventh Meeting of the Conference of the Contracting Parties to the Ramsar Convention*, San José, Costa Rica, 10–18 May 1999. *See also*, The Ramsar Strategic Plan

the governing bodies of multilateral environmental treaties can significantly contribute to the development of a framework of international participatory norms in specific water-related areas.[19]

While the above instruments are generally considered soft law, States have gone much further through the adoption of the Aarhus Convention.[20] The Convention comprehensively addresses procedural rights in environmental matters, including water issues. Its detailed treatment of the way in which information disclosure, public participation, and access to justice must be carried out by States will no doubt contribute to fleshing out existing international participatory standards for local communities. Importantly, the Convention binds States Parties to promote the application of principles thereunder not only in a domestic context, but also 'in international environmental decision-making processes and within the framework of international organizations in matters relating to the environment'.[21] This implies that Contracting Parties must, for instance, apply the Convention's participatory standards when they act in the context of MDBs. This is particularly relevant when States undertake water investments in the framework of international organizations.

With respect to information disclosure, first, the Aarhus Convention provides that States Parties are bound to make environmental information available to the public upon request, without the requester having to show an interest in the information.[22] The scope of information covered is quite broad, encompassing a non-exhaustive list of environmental elements, including water, and factors likely to affect the environment. Access to environmental information is based on a presumption in favour of disclosure subject to explicit—and restricted—exceptions such as confidentiality. The Convention also makes clear that the information disclosed or disseminated must be relevant, adequate, and understandable, and must be made available in a transparent way and be effectively accessible. Time constraints are likewise significant, as information must be provided in a timely manner if it is to be the basis for effective public participation. Secondly, the implementation of measures allowing for public participation in decisions on specific development activities when they have a significant effect on the environment or are listed in Annex I, is required under the Convention.[23] The Convention provides that effective participation involves the actual incorporation of the results of consultations in the final

2003–2008, *Eighth Meeting of the Conference of the Contracting Parties*, Valencia, Spain, 18–26 November 2002.

[19] As seen in the next section, guidelines adopted under the Convention on Biodiversity and its Protocol on Biosafety have in fact been instrumental in the emergence of the notion of PIC.

[20] Convention on Access to Information, Public Participation in Decision-Making and Access to Justice in Environmental Matters, Aarhus, 25 June 998, 38 *ILM* 517 (1999). The Convention, whilst a regional treaty, has potential for universal application since it is open for signature not only by States Members of the United Nations Economic Commission for Europe (UNECE) but also by UN Members, subject to the approval of the Convention's Meeting of the Parties.

[21] *Id.*, at Art. 3(7). [22] *Id.*, at Arts 4 and 5.

[23] *Id.*, at Arts 6, 7, and 8. Dams, large water projects, and pipelines are listed in Annex I.

decision-making process, so that changes can be made in development operations that are more reflective of the variety of potentially affected interests.[24] As in the case of information disclosure, time constraints are important in that participation must occur before the adoption of final decisions so that alternatives can be envisaged and adopted if necessary. Thirdly, the principle of access to justice is well entrenched in the Convention. It concerns, on the one hand, the right to legal remedies to enforce the participatory rights granted to the public under it. On the other hand, it reflects the availability of suits by citizens in environmental matters (*actio popularis*) by requiring States to ensure that members of the public have access to administrative or judicial procedures to challenge acts and omissions by private persons and public authorities in order to enforce national environmental laws.[25]

2.2 Prior informed consent

The question of local communities' right to environmental information and their participation in decision-making concerning natural resource management has been the object of increasing attention in international law and policy, as highlighted above. It is generally understood that the possibility to have access to information, or to participate in the planning, preparation, and implementation of a development project, can result in the possibility to have an impact on the way in which the project is carried out.

The notion of PIC seeks to go beyond existing concepts and provides a framework for allowing States or other actors the right to determine whether they want a specific activity to take place or not. In international environmental law, PIC is in particular reflected in the Convention on Biological Diversity.[26] The Convention specifically provides at Article 15(5) that access to genetic resources is subject to the PIC of the State providing access. This implies that the State providing access can determine the conditions under which access is to be provided. Further elaboration of the content of the PIC requirement is found in the Bonn Guidelines adopted in 2002.[27] The Guidelines first recognize that in addition to the consent of the relevant competent national authorities, the consent of indigenous and local communities must also be obtained in situations where this is appropriate. The Guidelines go beyond most existing international

[24] *Note* that under Art. 2(5) to the Convention, environmental NGOs are deemed to have an automatic interest in any environmental decision-making.

[25] *See also* the establishment under the Aarhus Convention of a non-compliance procedure in the form of a Compliance Committee competent to receive communications from one or two members of the public concerning a Party's compliance with the Convention, unless that Party has notified that it is unable to accept the consideration of such communications, in Draft Dec. I/7, Review of Compliance, *First Meeting of the Parties to the Aarhus Convention*, Lucca, Italy, 21–23 October 2002, Doc. MP.PP/2002/9.

[26] Convention on Biological Diversity, Rio de Janeiro, 5 June 1992, 31 *ILM* 818 (1992).

[27] Bonn Guidelines on Access to Genetic Resources and Fair and Equitable Sharing of the Benefits Arising out of their Utilization, UN Doc. UNEP/CBD/COP/6/20 (2002).

instruments in this field by giving an outline of the specific ways in which a PIC system may be established. They also give a number of interesting pointers concerning the substantive requirements that should be followed. This includes the need to seek PIC adequately in advance to make it meaningful for both the party seeking access and the party granting access, the need for PIC to be specific and indicate the specific uses for which consent is being given, and the need for PIC to be based on mutually agreed terms, implying that no party can impose its terms on the other.[28]

The concept of PIC has been further developed in the context of inter-State relations in recent years. Thus, the central mechanism put in place in the context of the Biosafety Protocol is a so-called Advance Informed Agreement (AIA) procedure.[29] The AIA procedure gives States importing living modified organisms (LMOs) a legal framework within which they can base their decision to accept or refuse a specific shipment of LMOs covered under the Protocol. The Biosafety Protocol is significant because it is one among few international treaties that gives importing States the right not only to assess the risk posed by a specific shipment, but also to reject it on the basis of a precautionary approach that does not require clear scientific evidence. It thus gives importing States some leeway in determining the appropriateness of specific shipments. Similarly, the 1998 Rotterdam Convention seeks to limit the harm caused by certain hazardous pesticides and chemicals by encouraging better sharing of information between countries and promoting reliance on PIC as the principle on which States can rely to deny consent or attach conditions to the shipment of certain pesticides and chemicals.[30]

While PIC has been progressively accepted as a regulatory tool in the context of inter-State relations, its application to local communities has proved much more difficult to achieve. Some documents seek to promote the use of PIC in the context of natural resources use. The Draft Declaration on the Rights of Indigenous Peoples provides, for instance, that where indigenous peoples' lands have been occupied, confiscated, or damaged without their 'free and informed consent', indigenous peoples have the right to the restitution of these lands.[31] The Draft

[28] *Note* that while the Bonn Guidelines do not focus specifically on the rights of local communities, the Recommendations for the Conduct of Cultural, Environmental and Social Impact Assessments Regarding Developments Proposed to Take Place on, or which are Likely to Impact on, Sacred Sites and on Lands and Waters Traditionally Occupied or Used by Indigenous and Local Communities are not more specific since they only provide that PIC must be obtained if the national legal regime provides it (in Annex II, Decision VI/10. Art. 8(j) and related provisions, UN Doc. UNEP/CBD/COP/6/20, 2002).

[29] Cartagena Protocol on Biosafety to the Convention on Biological Diversity, Montreal, 20 January 2000, 39 *ILM* 1027 (2000), at Arts 7 ff.

[30] Convention on the Prior Informed Consent Procedure for Certain Hazardous Chemicals and Pesticides in International Trade, Rotterdam, 11 September 1998, 38 *ILM* 1 (1999).

[31] *See* Art. 27 of the Draft United Nations Declaration on the Rights of Indigenous Peoples, 26 August 1994, in Report of the Sub-Commission on Prevention of Discrimination and Protection of Minorities on its Forty-Sixth Session, Geneva, 1–26 August 1994, UN Doc. E/CN.4/1995/2—E/CN.4/Sub.2/1994/56.

Declaration further affirms that indigenous peoples have the right to require from States that they obtain their free and informed consent before approving projects that affect their land or resources.[32]

Another non-binding document, the report of the World Commission on Dams, adopts similar principles in its recommendations to influence future decision-making concerning dams. It first recommends that decisions on projects affecting indigenous and tribal peoples should be 'guided by their free, prior and informed consent achieved through formal and informal representative bodies'.[33] The Commission then goes on specifically to acknowledge that PIC gives in practice indigenous and tribal peoples the right to consent to proposed projects and the power to negotiate the conditions under which they can proceed.[34]

The preceding review indicates that while PIC has become acceptable in certain circumstances at the level of inter-State relations, its application at the non-governmental level remains confined to the realm of policy documents and non-binding instruments in the context of natural resources. There is, however, one related area where interesting developments have taken place concerning PIC. In the context of the increasing interest for biodiversity-related traditional knowledge, there have been calls for the development of new requirements in patent law that would force the patent applicant to disclose the source of the knowledge and biological resources used in the invention. This would directly contribute to the better implementation of the PIC requirement included in the Biodiversity Convention.[35] While the inclusion of a disclosure requirement at the international level remains controversial, some developing countries have already incorporated requirements of PIC and disclosure. The Costa Rican Biodiversity Law provides, for instance, that intellectual property rights on inventions using biological resources can only be granted if the certificate of origin and a statement on prior informed consent are provided to the organs instituted under this Law.[36] The Philippines have adopted an even stricter framework in their Indigenous Peoples Rights Act.[37] This Act provides that access to biological resources or associated knowledge is only allowed with prior and free consent from the communities. The Act specifically indicates that free and prior consent involves a consensus of the indigenous peoples concerned, which must be 'free from any external manipulation, interference coercion, and

[32] Art. 30 of the Draft United Nations Declaration, n. 31 above, singling out water as one of the specific areas where this is required. *Note also* that the Permanent Forum on Indigenous Issues has attempted to raise the profile of PIC by recommending at both its first and second session the creation of a three-year working group on free, prior informed consent. *See* Permanent Forum on Indigenous Issues, Report on the Second Session, UN Doc. E/2003/43—E/C.19/2003/22 (2003).

[33] World Commission on Dams, n. 16 above, at 218.

[34] *Id.*, at 219. *Note* that following this description of PIC, the Commission immediately qualifies its own statement by stating that where PIC cannot be achieved, decisions should be made following a process of good faith negotiations.

[35] As acknowledged in Dec. VI/24, Access and Benefit-Sharing as Related to Genetic Resources, *Report of the Sixth Meeting of the Conference of the Parties to the Convention on Biological Diversity*, The Hague, 7–19 April 2002, UN Doc. UNEP/CBD/COP/6/20.

[36] Biodiversity Law, 1998.

[37] The Indigenous Peoples Rights Act of 1997.

obtained after fully disclosing the intent and scope of the activity, in a language and process understandable to the community'.[38] Further, the Act also recognizes the rights of indigenous peoples to the restitution of their intellectual property in case it has been acquired without PIC, or in violation of local laws or customs.[39]

3. Participatory rights in human rights case law

While there have been significant efforts towards the development of participatory principles in sustainable development instruments, relevant practice related to these instruments remains limited. In the human rights field, there has been extensive emphasis on the development of substantive individual rights, while group rights, including the rights of local communities, and procedural rights are still developing.[40] There are, however, a number of decisions by various human rights adjudicative bodies that are of relevance in this context, either directly or indirectly. This section examines the practice under some of the main human rights treaties, the International Covenants on Human Rights, the African Charter on Human and Peoples' Rights, the American Convention on Human Rights, and the European Convention on Human Rights.

3.1 International covenants on human rights

The two International Covenants are relevant in the context of water and participatory rights for independent reasons. The International Covenant on Economic, Social, and Cultural Rights (CESCR) indirectly recognizes a human right to water, while the International Covenant on Civil and Political Rights (CCPR) includes limited protection for minorities.[41] While the former is more relevant from a substantive point of view, the lack of a formal mechanism for bringing individual or collective communications to the Committee on Economic, Social, and Cultural Rights (ESCR Committee) implies that most of the relevant practice is found in the context of the CCPR.

The ESCR Committee, which oversees the implementation of the CESCR, has recently given interesting guidance concerning participatory rights in the context of the human right to water. In the context of its General Comment on the right to water, the ESCR Committee has acknowledged that individuals and groups have the right to participate in decision-making processes that may affect their exercise of the right to water. Further, the ESCR Committee also states that

[38] *Id.*, at Section 3(g). [39] *Id.*, at Section 32.

[40] *See* the Draft Principles on Human Rights and the Environment, in Report of the Special Rapporteur on Human Rights and the Environment, UN Commission on Human Rights, 6 July 1994, UN Doc. E/CN.4/Sub.2/1994/9.

[41] *See* respectively, Art. 11 of the International Covenant on Economic, Social, and Cultural Rights, New York, 16 December 1966, 6 *ILM* 360 (1967), and Art. 27 of the International Covenant on Civil and Political Rights, 16 December 1966, 6 *ILM* 368 (1967).

individuals and groups should be provided full access to information concerning water and water services held both by public authorities and third parties. Of special relevance in the context of this chapter, the ESCR Committee highlights that to ensure the realization of the right to water, States must make sure that the private sector and civil society consider the importance of the right to water in the pursuit of their activities.[42] These pronouncements are significant from a general perspective and indicate the direction in which participatory rights should be seen in the context of human rights treaties. As long as no procedure exists for bringing specific cases to the attention of the ESCR Committee, more specific elaboration on participatory rights cannot be expected in this context.

Unlike the first Covenant, the CCPR includes an Optional Protocol which provides that the Human Rights Committee is competent to hear individual communications alleging violations of the CCPR.[43] Of particular interest is a series of communications that have focused on Article 27, which provides a limited framework for the protection of the rights of ethnic, religious, or linguistic minorities. In *Lubicon Lake*, it was recognized that the rights protected by Article 27 include the right of persons, in community with others, to engage in economic and social activities which are part of the culture of the community to which they belong, thereby confirming that Article 27 can be applied in the context of the exploitation of natural resources.[44]

With regard to participatory rights, the Human Rights Committee has specifically indicated in its General Comment on Article 27 that the enjoyment of the rights protected under Article 27 may require measures to ensure the effective participation of members of minority communities in decisions which affect them.[45] Several communications have dealt with the issue of lack of consultation before the carrying out of measures for the exploitation of natural resources. In *Länsman*, the Finnish State authorized quarrying activities in a small portion of the region where reindeer herding was carried out by certain herdsmen of Sami origin. The Committee found, first, that only economic activity which amounts to a denial of the right to enjoy one's own culture can constitute a violation of Article 27. Further, the Committee, while agreeing that effective participation was required under Article 27, found that Finland had fulfilled its obligations through the consultations held with the minority community before the delivery of the quarrying permits.[46] In another similar

[42] Committee on Economic, Social, and Cultural Rights, General Comment No. 15 (The Right to Water), UN Doc. E/C.12/2002/11 (2002), at paras 48–49.

[43] Optional Protocol to the International Covenant on Civil and Political Rights, 999 *UNTS* 302 (1976).

[44] Communication No. 167/1984, Bernard Ominayak, Chief of the Lubicon Lake Band v. Canada, 26 March 1990, UN Doc. CCPR/C/38/D/167/1984. *See also* Communication No. 197/1985, Ivan Kitok v. Sweden, 27 July 1988, UN Doc. CCPR/C/33/D/197/1985.

[45] Human Rights Committee, General Comment No. 23, Art. 27 (Fiftieth Session, 1994), UN Doc. E/C.12/2000/4 (2000).

[46] Communication No. 511/1992, Ilmari Länsman et al. v. Finland, 26 October 1994, UN Doc. CCPR/C/52/D/511/1992.

communication brought by Sami reindeer breeders concerning logging and road construction, the Committee further elaborated its views on the question of consultation. It found that while the authors of the communication may have found the process unsatisfactory, the fact was that the Finnish State had consulted the Muotkatunturi Herdsmen's Committee to which the authors belonged, and that body had not objected to the logging plans.[47] In another communication against New Zealand, the Committee had to examine the consultation process within the context of legislative measures. It found that the State had carried out significant consultations, had specifically consulted Maori communities and national Maori organizations, and that their proposals had made an impact on the final result. Further, the Committee noted that in situations where the rights of certain individuals within a minority affect the exercise of parallel rights by other members of the same group, it is necessary to consider whether the limitation is in the interests of all members of the minority, and whether there is reasonable and objective justification for its application to the individuals who claim to be adversely affected. In this case, the Committee regretted that the measures had given rise to divisions among the Maori but concluded that the broad process of consultation and the attention paid by the State to the sustainability of Maori fishing activities constituted sufficient steps within the context of Article 27.[48]

3.2 African Charter on Human and Peoples' Rights

The African Charter on Human and Peoples' Rights includes among the basic rights it recognizes Article 24, which acknowledges all peoples' right to a generally satisfactory environment.[49] It is in the context of the right to environment that the most relevant communication for this chapter is found. In the *Ogoni* case, it was contended that the Nigerian government had withheld information from Ogoni communities on the dangers created by oil activities and had failed to involve them in decisions affecting the development of Ogoniland.[50] The African Commission on Human Rights, while dealing with the specific claims of the Ogoni people, also gave broader directions on the scope of Article 24. Interestingly, it indicated that compliance with the spirit of Article 24 must include a requirement to undertake and publicize environmental and social impact studies prior to any major industrial development, as well as the appropriate monitoring of environmental conditions, the provision of information to communities exposed to hazardous materials and activities, and the

[47] Communication No. 671/1995, Jouni E. Länsman et al. v. Finland, 30 October 1996, UN Doc. CCPR/C/58/D/671/1995.

[48] Communication No. 547/1993, Apirana Mahuika et al. v. New Zealand, 27 October 2000, UN Doc. CCPR/C/70/D/547/1993.

[49] African Charter on Human and Peoples' Rights, Banjul, 19 January 1982, 21 *ILM* 58 (1982).

[50] Communication No. 155/96, The Social and Economic Rights Action Center and the Center for Economic and Social Rights v. Nigeria, African Commission on Human & Peoples' Rights, 30th Ordinary Session, 13–27 October 2001.

provision of meaningful opportunities for individuals to be heard and to participate in the development decisions affecting their communities.[51] In the specific case of the Ogoni, the Commission concluded that the Government was obliged to take measures to ensure the protection of the environment, health, and livelihood of the Ogoni people, including appropriate environmental and social impact assessment for any future oil developments. Interestingly, the Commission has thus recognized that the substantive right to environment found at Article 24 includes specific procedural guarantees concerning the carrying out of environmental and social impact assessment. Further, it has clearly indicated that Member States have specific duties to make environmental information available and that they should promote people's participation in the development of activities affecting them.

3.3 American Convention on Human Rights

Like the African Charter, the American Convention on Human Rights[52] recognizes a number of basic rights, including, under Article 11 to its Additional Protocol, the right to a healthy environment.[53] The question of local communities' participatory rights has arisen primarily with respect to the rights of indigenous peoples to receive information on and participate in the development of activities affecting them and their traditional lands and resources.[54] Of particular interest is a series of reports elaborated by the Inter-American Commission on Human Rights regarding the human rights conditions of particular Organization of American States (OAS) Member countries, which deal with the issue of consultation of indigenous communities before the undertaking of measures for the exploitation of natural resources. In the case of Peru, the Commission has recognized that large-scale exploitation of natural resources and raw materials in indigenous territories, undertaken without consulting or obtaining the consent of the communities affected, led in many cases to environmental degradation and endangered the survival of these peoples, and recommended the enactment of a domestic indigenous law guaranteeing participatory mechanisms for indigenous peoples in the adoption of political, economic, and social decisions that affect their interests.[55] A report on Ecuador

[51] Communication No. 155/96, The Social and Economic Rights Action Center and the Center for Economic and Social Rights v. Nigeria, African Commission on Human & Peoples' Rights, 30th Ordinary Session, 13–27 October 2001, at para. 53.

[52] American Convention on Human Rights, San José, 22 November 1969, 9 *ILM* 673 (1970).

[53] Additional Protocol to the American Convention on Human Rights in the Area of Economic, Social, and Cultural Rights, San José, 17 November 1988, 28 *ILM* 156 (1989), 28 *ILM* 573 and 1341 (1989).

[54] *Note also* that Art. XIII(2) and (4) of the Proposed American Declaration on the Rights of Indigenous Peoples (Approved by the Inter-American Commission on Human Rights on February 26, 1997, at its 1333rd session, 95th Regular Session), OEA/Ser/L/V/.II.95 doc.6 (1997), expressly acknowledges the participatory rights of indigenous peoples.

[55] *See* Chapter X to the Second Report on the Situation of Human Rights in Peru, Inter-Am. C. H.R., OEA/Ser.L/V/II.106, doc.59 rev., 2 June 2000, at paras 26 and 39(1) respectively.

has further recommended that the protection of the rights of indigenous communities affected by oil and other development activities requires that States take the measures necessary to ensure the meaningful and effective participation of these communities in the decision-making processes about development and other issues that affect them.[56] On several occasions, the Commission has also specified that appropriate consultation in the context of projects to build infrastructure or exploit natural resources on indigenous lands should include prior consent from the affected indigenous communities.[57]

The Inter-American Commission is authorized to examine complaints or petitions regarding specific cases of human rights violations. In the *Yanomami* case, the Commission, in considering the adverse environmental and social effects for the Yanomami of the construction of a highway in their territory, gave passing recognition to the importance of consulting affected indigenous groups in the context of decisions affecting natural resources on their territories.[58] In the *Awas Tingni Mayagna (Sumo) Indigenous Community* case brought by the Inter-American Commission before the Inter-American Court of Human Rights, the Court had the opportunity to examine the scope of the right to property protected under Article 21 of the American Convention on Human Rights, including corollary participatory rights for indigenous peoples in activities relating to the exploitation of natural resources.[59] It was contended that Nicaragua had approved destructive logging concessions on lands traditionally owned by the Awas Tingni without consultation with or agreement of the affected communities, and that it had failed to carry out its legal obligation to demarcate and legally secure indigenous lands. In examining the contention that Nicaragua had violated Article 21 of the Convention, the Court determined that under this provision the State is required to adopt all necessary means to create effective surveying, demarcating, and title mechanisms for the properties of indigenous communities, in accordance with customary laws and indigenous values, uses, and customs.[60] The Court concluded that Nicaragua had violated the rights of the Mayagna Awas Tingni Community to the use and enjoyment of

[56] *See* Chapter IX to the Report on the Situation of Human Rights in Ecuador, Inter-Am. C. H.R., OEA/Ser.L/V/II.96, doc.10 rev.1, 24 April 1997 (Recommendations). The Commission added that 'meaningful' in this sense necessarily implies that indigenous representatives have full access to the information that will facilitate their participation. In Chapter VIII to this Report, the Commission addressed the rights of all persons under the American Convention to have access to environmental information (Art. 13), to participate in decisions affecting them, including in the conduct of EIA (Art. 23), and to effective judicial recourse (Art. 25). *See also* Chapter VI to the Report on the Situation of Human Rights in Brazil, Inter-Am. C. H.R., OEA/Ser.L/V/II.97, doc.29 rev.1, 29 September 1997, at para. 82.

[57] *See* Chapter X to the Third Report on the Human Rights Situation in Colombia, Inter-Am. C. H.R., OEA/Ser.L/V/II.102, doc.9 rev.1, 26 February 1999, at para. J(4) and Chapter X to the Second Report on the Situation of Human Rights in Peru, n. 55 above, at para. 39(5).

[58] Case 7615 (Brazil), Inter-Am. C. H.R., 1984–1985 Annual Report 24, OEA/Ser.L/V/II.66, doc.10, rev.1 (1985).

[59] Awas Tingni Mayagna (Sumo) Indigenous Community v. Nicaragua, Judgment of 31 August 2001, Inter-Am. Ct. H.R. (Ser. C) No. 79 (2001).

[60] The applicants also alleged the violation of Arts 1 and 25 of the American Convention, n. 52 above.

their property, in particular by granting concessions to third parties to utilize the property and resources located in an area which could correspond to the lands which must be delimitated, demarcated, and titled.[61] Significantly, the Court found that the State's obligation under Article 21 to delimitate, demarcate, and title the property of indigenous communities implies a corollary duty to ensure 'full participation' of the indigenous community in the process, thereby recognizing that the substantive right of indigenous peoples to their traditional lands protected under Article 21 includes specific procedural guarantees for the populations concerned.[62] This judgment will likely establish an important precedent on indigenous land rights under international and regional human rights law, by recognizing that the human rights norms that protect indigenous peoples' interests in land and natural resources obligate States to consult with the groups concerned when decisions on the exploitation of natural resources on their lands are taken, and adequately to integrate those interests in the decision-making process.

3.4 European Convention on Human Rights

While the case law under the European Convention on Human Rights[63] has not as such addressed the participatory rights of local communities, it is relevant from a general perspective by showing the way in which information disclosure and participation in an environmental context are addressed in the human rights system. The most interesting claims for present purposes have invoked two types of rights. On the one hand, the question of a right of access to environmental information has arisen under both Articles 8 and 10 of the European Convention. In the *Guerra* case, the applicants asserted that the government's failure to inform the public of the risks and the measures to be taken in case of a major accident violated their right to freedom of information as guaranteed by Article 10 of the Convention. The European Court of Human Rights found that this provision prohibits a government from restricting a person from receiving information that others wish, or may be willing, to impart to him, but does not confer a *positive* duty on the part of the State to collect and disseminate specific environmental information to the public.[64] The European Court concluded, however, that Article 8 of the European Convention, which safeguards the right to respect for private and family life, confers a positive duty on the State to impart information, the argument being that the right protected is infringed unless the subject can obtain information about the health risks to which she or he is exposed.[65]

[61] Awas Tingni Judgement, n. 59 above, at para. 153. [62] *Id.*, at para. 164.

[63] European Convention for the Protection of Human Rights and Fundamental Freedoms, Rome, 4 November 1950, 213 UNTS 221.

[64] Guerra and Others v. Italy (1998) 26 *Eur. H.R. Rep.* 357, at para. 53. This interpretation reversed the prior broader interpretation given by the European Commission on Human Rights.

[65] *Id.*, at para. 60. The right to respect for private life has been used also as the basis for several substantive environmental claims. In Lopez Ostra v. Spain (1994) 20 *Eur. H.R. Rep.* 277, where the

On the other hand, the question of the right of recourse to administrative or other bodies for the purposes of participating in decision-making processes relating to activities impacting on the environment is also of relevance in the context of this chapter. This question has been addressed by the European Court under Article 6 of the European Convention, which stipulates the right to a fair and public hearing. In particular, the Court has examined the reach of the right of access to a court in regard to water pollution in the *Zander* case.[66] The applicants alleged that their rights under Article 6 had been violated because they had been unable to challenge in legal proceedings the decision of a licensing authority to allow a company to dump waste on a tip without requiring the company concerned to take precautionary measures to avoid pollution of the applicants' drinking water. The Court concluded that the unreviewability of the rejected appeal by a court was a breach of Article 6.[67]

4. Participation in the Practice of International Organizations

The development and application of participatory standards for local communities and indigenous peoples have also taken place within the internal practice of international organizations. Two prominent institutions in this regard are the World Bank[68] and the ILO, which have both adopted standards and developed internal mechanisms for reviewing their implementation. This section examines in turn the contribution of these two organizations to the development of participatory rights in the context of natural resources and water investments.

4.1 World Bank

Significantly for this chapter, the World Bank has since the mid-1980s progressively adopted a series of operational policies and procedures that contain both mandatory and non-mandatory standards on information disclosure and

applicant alleged that the fumes of a tannery waste treatment plant operating close to her home had caused important health problems, the European Court found a breach of Art. 8, noting that 'severe environmental pollution may affect individuals' well-being and prevent them from enjoying their homes in such a way as to affect their private and family life adversely, without, however, seriously endangering their health' (para. 51). The European Commission on Human Rights has held that the traditional way of life of an indigenous group can amount to 'private and family life' and 'the home' under Article 8, in a case brought by two members of the Sami People contending that a proposed hydroelectric project would flood part of their traditional reindeer grazing grounds. *See* G & E v. Norway, Joined Applications Nos. 9278/81 and 9415/81, 35 *D&R* 30 (1983).

[66] Zander v. Sweden (1993) 18 *Eur. H.R. Rep.* 175. [67] *Id.*, at para. 29.

[68] The term 'World Bank' (or 'Bank') is used here to encompass the International Bank for Reconstruction and Development (IBRD) and the International Development Association (IDA). 'World Bank Group' usually covers, in addition, the International Finance Corporation (IFC), Multilateral Investment Guarantee Agency (MIGA), and International Centre for Settlement of Investment Disputes (ICSID).

participation of local communities and indigenous peoples during the preparation and implementation of all Bank-funded projects, including those involving water resources.[69] Participatory standards found in World Bank policies and procedures can be binding not only upon the Bank, but also on the borrowing country when they are incorporated in the terms of loan or credit agreements entered into between these two parties. The private branches of the World Bank Group, the IFC and MIGA,[70] which provide financial support to private sector projects in all developing countries or countries in transition, have also adopted policies and procedures addressing information disclosure and public participation in the context of private sector financing.[71] In addition to project-based lending, the Bank provides adjustment lending, primarily in the form of structural adjustment loans and credits and sectoral adjustment loans and credits.[72] The conditions attached to adjustment lending can require policy reforms such as privatization in various sectors, including the water sector. In spite of the adverse environmental and social impacts that can result from the privatization of water service systems,[73] Bank policy-based loans are in general subject at the most to very limited information participatory requirements.

The Bank has created an Inspection Panel competent to receive, and if necessary investigate, requests by local communities adversely affected by development funding operations and claiming the violation by the Bank of its own operational policies.[74] The Panel has been increasingly active in dealing with claims concerning Bank funding of water-related projects such as large-scale dams, urban drainage/sanitation, river infrastructure, and lake management projects. Significantly, most claims brought to the Panel have alleged Bank non-compliance with information disclosure and public participation requirements. The Panel's jurisdiction is considered to apply both to project-based lending and to adjustment lending by the Bank,[75] although the Panel has to date

[69] Since the early 1990s, Bank policies are embodied in 'Operational Policies' (OPs), 'Bank Procedures' (BPs), and 'Good Practices' (GPs): OPs and BPs contain strict, mandatory rules for Bank staff, while GPs set out advisory guidance.

[70] *See* IFC, Policy on Disclosure of Information (1998) and OP 4.01 on Environmental Assessment (1998), and MIGA, Disclosure Policy (1999) and Environmental Assessment Policy (1999).

[71] The IFC has also been instrumental in the adoption of the recently adopted voluntary 'Equator Principles' by private project financiers who have committed to adopting IFC social and environmental guidelines for their financing. *See* The Equator Principles—An Industry Approach for Financial Institutions in Determining, Assessing and Managing Environmental & Social Risk in Project Financing, 2003.

[72] *See* Operational Directive (OD) 8.60 on Adjustment Lending Policy (1992).

[73] *Note*, for instance, the case currently before the ICSID concerning the privatization of the water system in Cochabamba, Bolivia.

[74] World Bank Board of Executive Directors, Resolutions No. 93-10 and 93-6, 22 September 1993, 34 *ILM* 520 (1995). The Resolution has been interpreted and amended by two sets of Clarifications adopted by the Executive Directors in 1996 and 1999. *Note also* the independent investigation mechanisms set up at the Inter-American Development Bank (IADB) in 1994 and Asian Development Bank (ADB) in 1996, as well as the independent recourse mechanism at the European Bank for Reconstruction and Development (EBRD) established in 2003.

[75] *See* Report and Recommendation on Request for Inspection—Bangladesh: Jute Sector Adjustment Credit (INSP/R97-3), 20 March 1997; Report and Recommendation on Request for

not dealt with a case involving the privatization of water services. While the Panel's jurisdiction covers only IBRD and IDA projects, the Compliance Advisor/Ombudsman (CAO) can respond to requests by private parties alleging non-compliance of the IFC and MIGA with their environmental and social policies, including those on information disclosure and participation.[76]

The following discussion examines some instances of the treatment in Inspection Panel reports on water resources projects of the standards for information disclosure and participation of local communities and indigenous peoples couched in World Bank operational policies and procedures.

a. *Information disclosure*

The information disclosure standards found in World Bank policies and procedures provide for the public availability of certain project and environment-related documents subject to explicit exceptions. Disclosure requirements are found in an overarching Bank policy on the disclosure of information,[77] as well as in the policies and procedures regulating the EIA of Bank-funded projects.[78]

The disclosure of information to the public by the Bank is in principle based on a presumption in favour of disclosure. Exceptions to disclosure can reflect concerns related, for instance, to the functioning of the Bank and the integrity of its decision-making processes, and to the protection of confidential or proprietary information received by third parties. The Bank's policies on information disclosure adopt a 'passive' approach, in that usually the available information is accessible to those who request it; they set forth real measures neither for more active and local dissemination of information to local communities, nor for facilitating practical access to released information.[79] They contain, moreover, only very limited requirements for the release of information about the Bank's structural adjustment operations.

The implementation of the World Bank's information disclosure requirements has been examined in several Inspection Panel reports, and most significantly in the investigation report on the China Western Poverty Reduction Project.[80] The Panel report reiterated the importance for the improvement of projects of the timely disclosure of information and the opportunity for public

Inspection—Argentina: Special Structural Adjustment Loan (Loan 4405-AR), 16 December 1999; Report and Recommendation on Request for Inspection Papua New Guinea: Governance Promotion Adjustment Loan (Loan No. 7021-PNG), 30 April 2002.

[76] *See* Terms of Reference of the Compliance Advisor/Ombudsman (2000). The functions of the CAO are not limited to investigating complaints from affected parties ('Ombudsman role'), like the Inspection Panel, but include also the undertaking of compliance audits of the IFC and MIGA's social and environmental performance ('Compliance role'), as well the provision of advice and assistance to both institutions on controversial projects or on specific policies and procedures ('Advisory role').

[77] *See* BP 17.50 on Disclosure of Information (2003) and the 2002 Policy on Disclosure of Information.

[78] *See* OP 4.01 on Environmental Assessment (1999).

[79] For instance, by allowing for better on-site dissemination of information or making available translations of documents in local languages.

[80] The Qinghai component of the project involved the renovation of an existing dam and the construction of a new one, as well as the construction of two canals to supply water for irrigation.

comment.[81] It also provided specifications on the types of documents that are to be disclosed under Bank policy. In particular, project information documents, which represent the main source of information available to the public while a project is still under preparation, are to be made publicly available at the project concept stage, with the initial document updated and expanded periodically as project preparation proceeds. Documents relating to the EIA should be publicly available in the borrowing country before the start of project appraisal.[82] Although the Panel in this case found the Bank to be in violation of these disclosure standards, it considered that overall the Bank has tried to move beyond the minimum requirements.[83] Other Panel reports have, however, pointed to inadequate information disclosure to local communities in the course of Bank-funded projects involving water resources.[84] Moreover, a CAO report has notably highlighted the deficiencies in the implementation of IFC disclosure and participatory policies in the context of a water-related project financed by the IFC in Chile.[85]

b. Participation of local communities and indigenous peoples

On the basis of preliminary, adequate disclosure of relevant information, a number of World Bank policies and procedures provide for the participation of local communities in the preparation and implementation of all Bank-funded projects. These documents acknowledge that the sustainability of Bank-funded projects can only be ensured with adequate public involvement. In particular, the Bank's policy on environmental assessment requires the undertaking during EIA of 'meaningful consultation' of potentially interested and/or affected parties in order for them to express their concerns regarding the environmental impacts of projects and for their interests to be taken into account.[86] It specifies that consultation must be undertaken as early as possible and throughout project implementation. Indigenous peoples and involuntary resettled persons are two

[81] Investigation Report—The Qinghai Project: A Component of the China:Western Poverty Reduction Project (Credit No. 3255-CHA and Loan No. 4501-CHA), 28 April 2000, at para. 421.

[82] *Id.*, at paras 411–13 and 416–18, respectively. [83] *Id.*, at para. 420.

[84] *See* Report and Recommendation—Bangladesh: Jamuna Bridge Project (Credit 2569-BD), 26 November 1996, at paras 47–48, and Investigation Report—Uganda: Third Power Project (Credit No. 2268-UG), Fourth Power Project (Credit No. 3545-UG), and Bujagali Hydropower Project (PRG No. B003-UG), 30 May 2002, at para. 332.

[85] *See* Assessment by the Office of the Compliance Advisor/Ombudsman in relation to a complaint filed against IFC's investment in ENDESA Pangue S.A., May 2003. *Also* of interest is the Final Report on the Independent Assessment of Water Quantity and Quality near the Yanacocha Mining District, Cajamarca, Peru, prepared for the IFC/MIGA CAO, November 2003, commissioned by a group of stakeholders, including urban and rural communities, with an interest in the environmental, social, and economic consequences of the operation of the Yanacocha mine.

[86] *Note that* Bank-funded projects are categorized according to their environmental impacts. Under OP 4.01, a full EIA is only required for Category 'A' projects which are likely to have 'significant adverse environmental impacts that are sensitive, diverse, or unprecedented', while a less exhaustive form of assessment is required for Category 'B' projects whose potential adverse environmental impacts are 'less adverse' than Category A projects. Category 'C' relates to projects that are likely to have 'minimal or no adverse environmental impacts', where no EIA is required.

particular groups that benefit from specific participatory standards in Bank policy during project design and implementation.[87] In addition, the commitments of the Bank in regard to participatory requirements for local communities in the course of water-related operations are highlighted in its 1993 Policy on Water Resources Management and 2004 Water Resources Sector Strategy.[88]

In contrast to water infrastructure projects, Bank investments in water services are generally not subject to participatory requirements.[89] In particular, Bank policy does not give affected communities consultation or participation rights with respect to particular sectoral or structural adjustment loans requiring the privatization of water services.[90] On the other hand, the Bank involves civil society organizations in the review of its structural adjustment strategies.

Of special relevance in the context of this chapter, the scope and level of implementation of existing Bank participatory requirements have been the object of close scrutiny in several Inspection Panel reports involving water projects.[91] Early on in the Panel's existence, two controversial dam projects, the Arun III Hydroeletric Project (Nepal)[92] and Yacyretá Hydroelectric (Argentina/Paraguay) Project,[93] were the object of requests to the Panel concerned with the adverse impacts of the dams on indigenous peoples and other displaced local communities. The Panel has also examined problems stemming from the inadequate participation and consultation of resettled minorities (here the char people) in the development of mitigation measures relating to a project financing the construction of a multipurpose bridge over the Jamuna River in Bangladesh.[94]

More recently, the Panel's investigation report into the China Western Poverty Reduction Project contained a number of interesting findings on the interpretation and implementation of public participation standards in Bank policies on indigenous peoples and involuntary resettled persons. These first

[87] *See* OP/BP 4.10 on Indigenous Peoples (2001) and OP/BP 4.12 on Involuntary Resettlement (2001).

[88] *See also* the specific policies applying to water-related projects, namely, OP 4.07 on Water Resources Management (2000), OP/BP 4.37 on Safety of Dams (2001), and OP/BP 7.50 on International Waterways (2001).

[89] Para. 13 of OD 8.60 merely recommends that Bank staff should review the environmental policies and practices in the country concerned, and that the design of adjustment programs should take into account the findings and recommendations of such reviews.

[90] Notwithstanding the problem of identifying affected parties when measures deriving from privatization often affect population at large rather than a circumscribed circle of parties.

[91] The importance of the participation of local communities in development water-related projects has been underscored in a regional context also, in particular by the ADB investigation mechanism in Final Report of Inspection Panel on Samut Prakarn Wastewater Management Project, 14 December 2001, at paras 117, 152–153, and 165–166.

[92] Request for Inspection: Panel Investigation Report—Nepal Arun III Proposed Hydroelectric Project (INSP/SecM95-3), 22 June 1995.

[93] Request for Inspection—Argentina/Paraguay: Yacyretá Hydroelectric Project, Panel Recommendation (INSP/R96-2), 26 December 1996. *See also* Report and Recommendation—Paraguay: Reform Project for the Water and Telecommunications Sectors (Loan No. 3842—PA), Argentina: Segba v. Power Distribution Project (Loan No. 2854-AR), August 2002.

[94] *See* Jamuna Report, n. 84 above, at paras 46 and 54.

concerned the methodology of consultation and survey methods used for the affected populations in the preparation of the project, and the importance of correctly determining the scope of those being consulted in order to ensure adequate representation in the survey sample of affected minority groups.[95] In this context, the Panel noted that when a particular domestic context is conducive to reluctance on the part of local communities to impart their opinion freely, the Bank has the responsibility to guarantee the confidentiality of those being consulted.[96] Panel findings secondly related to the application of the Bank policy on indigenous peoples. They indicated that separate, free-standing indigenous peoples development plans have to be developed for the different minority groups affected by the project in order to preserve their cultural uniqueness, and that the elaboration of these plans has to be accompanied by adequate participation of the relevant local groups.[97] Overall, the Panel's findings concluded that the level of consultation of affected populations during the project had been inadequate. The report moreover addressed the question of the implementation of Bank policies generally, underscoring that they cannot be taken to authorize a level of interpretation and flexibility that would enable to override those standards that are clearly binding.[98] These statements, and the problems that they raise regarding the status of the Bank's internal operational policies, will no doubt impact on the way in which participatory standards are to be implemented in future Bank water-related projects.

Other water projects that are illustrative of the way in which the Panel has dealt with participatory requirements for local communities include the Lake Victoria Environment Management Project[99] and three IDA-financed hydropower projects in Uganda.[100] In regard to the former, the Panel's investigation report found poor levels of participation of affected communities, due to the fact that stakeholders were not fully consulted during the scoping of the environmental analysis, the issues raised were not fully taken account of, and that the EIA was not made available to them for discussion or review before or after finalization.[101] The absence of adequate consultation of local groups in the decision-making process led in this case to a lack of clear understanding as to the purpose and scope of the operation.[102] The Panel investigation report on the Uganda hydropower projects set forth useful guidelines regarding participatory techniques applicable during EIAs. According to the Panel, particularly effective techniques include making available environmental documents in local public libraries, placing notices in national and local newspapers, translating issues statements in local languages, diffusing public hearings, considering public submissions, and organizing forums to consult with civil society.[103]

[95] *See* China Report, n. 81 above, at paras 94–95. [96] *Id.*, at para. 116.
[97] *Id.*, at paras 275–76 and 336–37. [98] *Id.*, at para. 37.
[99] Investigation Report—Kenya: Lake Victoria Environmental Management Project (IDA Credit 2907-KE) (GEF TF 23819), 15 December 2000. [100] *See* Uganda Report, n. 84 above.
[101] *See* Kenya Report, n. 99 above, at para. 50. [102] *Id.*, at para. 167.
[103] *See* Uganda Report, n. 84 above, at paras 343–46.

4.2 International Labour Organization

The ILO has adopted a significant number of conventions in the past few decades. Conventions 107 and 169, which focus on the rights of indigenous peoples, are of particular importance in the context of this chapter.[104] Both Convention 107 and its successor Convention 169 seek to protect indigenous and tribal peoples' rights and help their integration in mainstream society. Convention 107 provides, for instance, some minimal rights, like the right of indigenous and tribal peoples not to be removed from their habitual territories without their free consent.[105] Convention 169 goes much further and includes the obligation for Member States to 'consult the peoples concerned, through appropriate procedures and in particular through their representative institutions, whenever consideration is being given to legislative or administrative measures which may affect them directly'.[106] The implementation of Convention 169, which is yet to be widely ratified, has attracted a fair number of complaints in recent years, a number of which relate to consultation and participation.

In the context of legislative instruments, the Committee of Experts on the Application of Conventions and Recommendations has had the opportunity to reaffirm the importance of consultation procedures in the case of a Columbian Decree that was adopted by the government without consultations.[107] The Committee emphasized that it was not enough to propose the establishment of a process of consultation in the Decree but that the procedure leading to the adoption of the Decree should also have involved consultations.[108] The Committee also reiterated that Article 6 should be seen in light of other provisions of the Convention, in particular Article 7, which provides a right of indigenous peoples to participate in the development of policies and programmes affecting them, and Article 15, which reminds Member States that even where they retain ownership of minerals, they must consult indigenous peoples before undertaking any exploitation of the same. On the whole, the Committee clearly indicated that while Article 6 does not require consensus, it requires, alongside other relevant articles, that people should have an opportunity to participate freely at all levels in the formulation, application, and evaluation of measures that directly

[104] Convention concerning the Protection and Integration of Indigenous and Other Tribal and Semi-Tribal Populations in Independent Countries, 26 June 1957 [hereinafter Convention 107], and Convention concerning Indigenous and Tribal Peoples in Independent Countries, 27 June 1989 [hereinafter Convention 169], 28 *ILM* 1382 (1989).

[105] Convention 107, n. 104 above, at Art. 12. *Note* that removal is authorized under Art. 12 as long as it is 'in accordance with national laws and regulations for reasons relating to national security, or in the interest of national economic development or of the health of the said populations'.

[106] Convention 169, n. 104 above, at Art. 6.

[107] Representation alleging non-observance by Colombia of the Indigenous and Tribal Peoples Convention, 1989 (No. 169), made under Article 24 of the ILO Constitution by the Central Unitary Workers' Union (CUT), Document GB.276/17/1—GB.282/14/3.

[108] *See* the Report of the Committee set up to examine the representation alleging non-observance by Peru of the Indigenous and Tribal People's Convention, 1989 (No. 169), made under Article 24 of the ILO Constitution by the General Confederation of Workers of Peru (CGTP), Document GB.270/16/4—GB.273/14/4.

affect them. It also specifically indicated that while speedy decisions could be welcome under some circumstances, the speed should not be to the detriment of effective consultation.[109]

A number of representations have been made concerning consultation in the context of specific activities or projects. In a case from Ecuador, it was claimed that the government had failed to consult indigenous peoples before entering into an agreement with the Arco company. This case provided the Committee an opportunity to discuss the temporal requirement of consultation since the Convention came into force after the agreement with Arco. It indicated that the obligation to consult does not apply only to the conclusion of agreements, but 'also arises on a general level in connection with the application of the provisions of the Convention'.[110] The Committee emphasized the central importance of participation by stating that the spirit of consultation and participation constitutes the cornerstone of Convention 169. It also took this opportunity to provide a general interpretation of consultation. It indicated that consultation should include a genuine dialogue between concerned parties, characterized by communication, understanding, mutual respect, good faith, and the sincere wish to reach a common accord. An information meeting is not enough for compliance with the terms of the Convention. Further, consultation should always take place beforehand. In this regard, the Committee specifically indicated that communities should participate early on in the process, including in the preparation of EIA studies. The Committee finally stressed the importance of representative participation, which implies at least the duty not to exclude a representative organization.[111] In another case concerning mining and logging activities in the Tarahumara range in Mexico, the Committee found that, in the specific case of Article 15 concerning peoples' rights to natural resources, peoples should not only have the right to participate in their use, management, and conservation, but that the government was required to establish and maintain procedures for consulting the peoples concerned with a view to ascertaining whether and to what degree their interests would be prejudiced, before undertaking or permitting any programmes for the exploration or exploitation of resources pertaining to their lands.[112]

5. Towards the Development of Participatory Principles in the Context of Water Investments

Most of the material examined above tends to refer to natural resources management generally rather than water investments, with the exception of the

[109] Document GB.276/17/1—GB.282/14/3, n. 107 above, at para. 79.

[110] Representation alleging non-observance by Ecuador of the Indigenous and Tribal Peoples Convention, 1989 (No. 169), made under article 24 of the ILO Constitution by the Confederación Ecuatoriana de Organizaciones Sindicales Libres (CEOSL), Document GB.277/18/4—GB.282/14/2, at para. 30.

[111] *Id.*, at para. 44.

[112] Mexico, Individual observation, C169, Labour representatives: FAT (1999).

World Bank where significant practice in the field of water already exists. This can be explained in part by the lack of a comprehensive treatment of water issues in international law. Further, existing practice often concerns situations where the rights holders are not necessarily local communities. Accordingly, this section first seeks to provide an understanding of the law as it stands today on the basis of the evidence examined, and then moves on to outline some of the principles that should inform the future development of participatory rights in the context of private water investments.

5.1 Existing participatory norms and principles

The practice examined above allows a number of general observations on the status of participatory norms and principles at present. First, international sustainable development instruments provide a general legal framework recognizing a number of basic participatory rights for local communities, which are considered crucial to the sustainability of development projects and the representation of different interests in decision-making processes. There is in particular a growing recognition of the need for participatory mechanisms when water issues are at stake, for instance in the case of dams. One of the main characteristics of these standards is that the rights are either framed at a high level of generality, or included in non-binding instruments. They typically include the right of access to environmental information, the right to participate, and the right to have access to administrative or judicial mechanisms. They are granted to a wide range of beneficiaries that can be quite diffuse, but there is often express reference to local communities and indigenous peoples as well as a growing emphasis on the role of women in the context of water. The instruments examined, especially the binding Aarhus Convention, are important in fleshing out the content and scope of these concepts as they are crystallizing in international law. A particular application of these rights, the right to consent or refuse consent to specific water investments, does not yet seem to be included in any widely accepted legal instrument, even though PIC is developing rapidly at the level of inter-State relations and some policy documents like the World Commission on Dams report argue in favour in the recognition of such a right.

The field of sustainable development law, while relatively developed at the level of principles and norms, does not yet provide significant practice, partly because participatory rights are still emerging and partly because compliance with international environmental law does not significantly rely on traditional dispute settlement mechanisms. As a result, the human rights foundation for participatory rights is important as it rests on universally accepted international human rights concepts and norms, and can also provide for individual complaint mechanisms of a judicial and quasi-judicial character. The human rights case law is noteworthy because it shows that human rights supervisory bodies have often striven to recognize participatory rights in the context of existing substantive human rights which do not specify participation through an evolutionary interpretation of the treaties. Since none of the main human rights treaties specifically provide for consultation or participation in the context of development activities, the rights recognized are not tailored for application in an environmental context, with the consequence that they remain fairly general in their formulation and may not be directly applicable in water investments. There is no doubt, however, that today basic human rights include the right of local communities in groups or as individuals, including of indigenous peoples, to participate in decisions directly affecting their fundamental rights, such as where displacement is involved or where the realization of their right to a clean environment, right to health, right to life, or right to land is at risk. Therefore, more attention should be focused on developing existing rights to make them more specific.

Besides human rights, the contribution of the World Bank and the ILO to the development of international participatory norms and principles has been significant. The practice of these two organizations is more relevant than human rights instruments because the standards applied are much more specific with regard to the need for consultation and participation. The first striking feature in the case of the World Bank is that the Bank has developed a detailed body of operational policies requiring information disclosure and participation from the preparation to the implementation of projects that adversely affect local communities, including indigenous peoples. Given the level of specificity encountered in Bank policies, these could provide a model for the development of more comprehensive standards at the international level. There remains, however, a lack of participatory procedures applicable to the Bank's adjustment lending operations. A further significant feature in the World Bank context is the contribution of the Inspection Panel to the strengthening of participatory rights for local communities. It provides one of the few existing forums at the international level allowing local communities to bring grievances directly in the context of water investments carried out by an international organization. The findings of the Panel have provided guidelines on the way in which Bank policies should be interpreted and implemented when water-related projects funded by the Bank have impacts on local communities. They also highlight that, despite the significant body of standards adopted by the Bank, implementation of participatory standards remains inadequate. Given the prominence of the role of the World Bank and other MDBs in development assistance, and particularly in water investments, the systematic application of information disclosure and public participation requirements should be ensured through formalized procedures with respect to all lending operations, including adjustment lending, and compliance with participatory policies reviewed by specific, independent mechanisms.

The various representations in the ILO under Convention 169 have provided relevant bodies an opportunity to shed light on the particular meaning of participation in the context of indigenous peoples' rights. Some of their main contributions include the recognition that participation should take place from the formulation to the implementation of a given activity, and the recognition that while it may slow down proceedings, speed cannot be an excuse for compromising the level of participation. Further, it has been clearly indicated that information is not the same as consultation, which necessitates a sustained engagement between parties genuinely seeking to reach a common accord, and that the duty to consult cannot be deemed to be fulfilled by hand-picking representatives of a given community.

On the whole, the practice examined in this chapter establishes a clear consensus in principle in favour of strong participatory principles. There is, however, a significant discrepancy between the principles that have been and are being established and the reality observed on the ground. This is due in part to the fact that the principles developed in institutions like the ILO and the World Bank apply only in specific contexts. Further, the contribution of supervisory organs can, for instance, be limited by their own terms of reference. Thus, the Inspection Panel can investigate the World Bank's compliance in the context of a particular project, but can neither assess the adequacy of Bank policies and procedures themselves nor review the range of applicable international standards. The relevance of some of the norms and principles examined is also limited by the fact that they apply only to specific groups of people, such as indigenous and tribal peoples in the case of the Convention 169 of the ILO. From the perspective of water investments, there is no justification for limiting participatory principles to particular groups. In other words, the right to be consulted, the right to participate, or the right to consent to a project should be provided to all communities adversely affected by water investments, whether or not they are part of a specific sub-group.

5.2 Principles for participation in private water investments

As noted above, while there already exists a significant body of practice on participatory rights in international law and policy, it is often not applicable specifically to water investments, or is relevant only in some particular context. Most importantly, most of the standards have evolved until now in contexts where the main proponents of water investments were States or international organizations and they therefore do not purport to bind private parties. The growing importance and impacts of private water investments necessitate the development of participatory principles applicable to all relevant situations.

When water investments in project infrastructure or in services are concerned, it appears important to go beyond existing principles to strengthen local communities' opportunities not only to participate but to have a final say in investment decisions that directly and significantly affect their livelihoods and human rights, including the right to affordable and clean water, as well as the sustainability of water resources management. The basis for further development should be the guarantees already recognized in existing international legal frameworks and institutions. In more specific terms, some of the basic minimum principles that should be guaranteed in the case both of public and private water investments include the following:

—Participation can be meaningful only if potentially affected local communities are fully informed by investors in a timely manner of all the risks and impacts involved in specific water investments. This includes, for instance, providing comprehensive information on displacement and rehabilitation, such as in the case of dam projects which require the acquisition of inhabited lands.
—The information disclosed or disseminated must be relevant, adequate, and understandable by affected communities. Sufficient information must include the prior notification of consultation procedures.
—There should be a presumption in favour of information disclosure. While there is no absolute right to all existing information and a balance must be struck between the interests of different actors, affected communities have a right to receive all information which is directly or indirectly linked to the realization of their human rights.
—Information and participation must not be selective but must be continuous and iterative processes. This includes the provision of information from the stage of planning to the stage of implementation, the active dissemination of information especially in remote areas, and translation in local languages.
—Participation should take into account the existence of different interest groups within a given local community. In other words, participation should not be limited to specific individuals or groups within a community handpicked by investors. It should on the contrary include broad-based representative participation, giving all opinions within a community a chance to be heard. This is of great importance in a context where some sub-groups of affected communities, such as women, which might be the most directly affected by water investments, are often excluded from decision-making procedures. Participation must thus not only target appropriate communities, but also identify each individually affected group within a given community.
—Participation should constitute a process which takes place from the time of project planning to the adoption of final decisions and the implementation of the project itself. This is the only way to ensure that alternatives are considered and adopted if necessary. Participation can easily become meaningless in situations where people are consulted only at the implementation stage. Thus, in the context of adjustment lending, disclosing adjustment-related information prior to loan approval would enable communities and civil society as a whole to be aware of the commitments entered into by their governments and to make proposals regarding alternative water management options.

—Participation often has limited impacts because it is conceived in an ad hoc manner. Where specific fora for participation do not exist, there is a risk that the results of consultations depend to an extent on the goodwill of the actors involved. The creation of specific institutions through which participation is routed would significantly strengthen the whole process. This need not involve the creation of new institutions, for instance, in cases where local self-governance bodies already exist. Thus, in a country like India, which has constitutionally recognized democratically elected bodies at the local level (panchayats), strengthening participation could be achieved by using panchayats as the consultative forum rather than the legally amorphous concept of local communities. The latter should be kept for situations where other representative bodies at the local level do not exist.

—The inputs provided through participatory procedures must be used in taking final decisions. This should crucially also involve the need to factor in the possibility not to go ahead with the project. In other words, participation can be fully meaningful only if it includes a 'no-project' option. On a substantive level, this implies giving local communities the right to negotiate under what conditions specific water investments can be carried out. In its strongest form, this form of PIC authorizes affected communities to decide whether they want to accept or reject specific water investments.

—Participation in itself does not provide any guarantees concerning the type of decisions that are taken. The most important element here is the need to take decisions at the lowest possible level, or, in other words, the need to let the communities that are directly affected by water investments decide their own future in order to promote a more efficient and productive use of water resources.

—Participatory principles outlined should apply similarly to all water investment actors. While there is an increasing recognition in the field of human rights, as noted by the ESCR Committee, that private actors should also respect human rights, this should be generally extended to all participatory procedures and rights.

—Following on strict participatory rights, there must be mechanisms for determining the accountability of all actors involved. In other words, local communities must benefit from the establishment of administrative, quasi-judicial, and judicial mechanisms, both on the international and domestic levels, to adjudicate their participatory rights.

The adoption of these basic procedural criteria that need to be fulfilled to improve the outcomes of decision-making in private water investments would significantly contribute to enhance the situation for adversely affected local communities. It must be noted, however, that procedural rights can be meaningful only if they are considered within the broader context of substantive rights. In other words, the fulfilment of procedural guarantees is required not as an aim in itself but as a tool to guarantee the realization of substantive rights. This implies, for instance, that all actors involved in water investments must work towards procedures that ensure that the fundamental rights of local communities, and each person within these communities, are not violated because of proposed water investments.

PART V

RESOLUTION OF WATER DISPUTES, WITH SPECIAL EMPHASIS ON ECONOMIC ISSUES

14

Water and Economics: Trends in Dispute Settlement Procedures and Practice

LAURENCE BOISSON DE CHAZOURNES

1. INTRODUCTION

Competing demands over freshwater resources may result in tensions. In some instances, there are outright disputes between users of freshwater whose requirements and uses conflict with those of other users. Water disputes are notably compounded by the steady increase in the world's population and the pressures arising therefrom. Every region of the world today is afflicted with international water disputes.

Water disputes concern both quantity and quality and are triggered by various factors, including economic ones. To date, dams, diversions, water-quality issues, and, more recently, investment matters have been major causes of disputes. The case law of the Permanent Court of International Justice (PCIJ), the International Court of Justice (ICJ), and the Permanent Court of Arbitration (PCA) is illustrative of this situation. To cite two examples, the *Gabčìkovo-Nagymaros* case adjudicated by the ICJ in 1997 involving the building of a system of locks,[1] and the case concerning the application of the *Convention on the Protection of the Rhine against Pollution by Chlorides* (1976 Rhine Convention), submitted by the Netherlands and France to the PCA,[2] addressed water-quality issues. Concession agreements regarding water and sewage services are core questions in several recent cases referred to arbitral tribunals constituted under the aegis of the International Centre for Settlement of Investment Disputes (ICSID).[3] Moreover, several requests brought to the Word Bank

[1] Case concerning the *Gabčìkovo-Nagymaros* Project (Hungary/Slovakia), ICJ (25 September 1997), available at www.icj-cij.org.

[2] Case concerning the application of the *Convention on the Protection of the Rhine against Pollution by Chlorides* (3 December 1976) and its *Additional Protocol* (25 September 1991), Netherlands/France Final Award (12 March 2004), www.pca-cpa.org (only French text available). For the text of the Convention see *UNTS*, 1404 (1985), at 91. For the text of the Protocol, see *UNTS*, 1840 (1994), at 423.

[3] *See*, among others, *Compañía de Aguas del Aconquija, S. A. and Compagnie Générale des Eaux v. Argentine Republic* (ICSID Case No. ARB/97/3), Award (21 November 2001), *ICSID Review—FILJ* 16 (2001); *Aguas del Tunari S.A. v. Republic of Bolivia* (Case No. ARB/02/3) still pending. *See infra.*

Inspection Panel are related to projects involving the construction of large-scale water infrastructure.[4] These examples illustrate both the importance and the extent of the relationship between water and economics. In the present contribution, these relationships, including trade and investment issues, will be broadly construed.

The progressive erosion of the traditional reluctance on the part of States to commit themselves, in advance, to judicial and quasi-judicial dispute settlement mechanisms[5] has coincided with the considerable progress made towards the institutionalization of dispute settlement facilities. In the last decade new permanent courts and institutionalized arbitration bodies,[6] vested with broad subject-matter jurisdiction, have begun operating. In addition to courts and other permanent adjudication mechanisms, several investigatory procedures have also recently emerged. These mechanisms include the World Bank Inspection Panel, as well as the parallel investigation procedures adopted by the Inter-American Bank, the Asian Development Bank, and the European Bank for Reconstruction and Development.[7] Other mechanisms to add to this list include those established in the environmental and human rights areas, such as UN treaty bodies, regional human rights courts, and the newly established compliance mechanism under the *Aarhus Convention on Access to Information, Public Participation in Decision-Making and Access to Justice in Environmental Matters* (Aarhus Convention).[8]

The multiplication of dispute settlement mechanisms and procedures has an impact on the resolution of water disputes. On the one hand, the existence of various dispute settlement mechanisms and procedures gives States and other actors the opportunity to bring their complaints before these bodies. On the other hand, it raises the issue of potential conflicts between different interpretations of specialized fields of law (for example, environmental and

[4] *See* Mbengue & Tignino and Cullet & Gowlland-Gualtieri's chapters in this book.

[5] *See*, e.g., *United Nations Convention on the Law of the Sea*, 12 December 1982, 21 *ILM* (1982) 1261; *WTO Understanding on Rules and Procedures governing the Settlement of Disputes* 15 April 1994, 33 *ILM* (1994); *Protocol No. 11 to the Convention for the Protection of Human Rights and Fundamental Freedoms*, 11 May 1994, *ETS* 155; Treaty of Amsterdam, 2 October 1997, *OJ* (C 340) 173.

[6] As an example, in Africa five new courts have been established, namely: the African Court of Human Rights, the Court of Justice of the Common Market of Eastern and Southern Africa, the Court of Justice of the Economic Community of West Africa, the Southern African Development Community Tribunal, and the Court of Justice of the Union économique et monétaire Ouest Africaine. One should also note the establishment of: the Court of the European Economic Area, the Economic Court of the Commonwealth of Independent States, the Central American Court of Justice, the Caribbean Court of Justice, the International Criminal Court, the International Tribunal on the Law of the Sea, and the WTO Appellate Body. One can also refer to the institutionalized bodies introduced in the North American Free Trade Agreement (NAFTA) and in the MERCOSUR.

[7] The Compliance Advisor and Ombudsman (CAO) Office created by the International Finance Corporation/Multilateral Investment Guarantee Agency (1999) and the citizen submission procedure established by the *North American Agreement on Environmental Cooperation* (NAAEC) are also part of this category.

[8] *Aarhus Convention on Access to Information, Public Participation in Decision-Making and Access to Justice in Environmental Matters*, Decision I/7, Meeting of the Parties, 31 October 2002, www.unece.org/env/pp/mop1/decision.1.7.e.doc.

trade law). It is interesting to note that water disputes have been brought to courts and tribunals since the very establishment of the latter in the early part of the twentieth century. Since then, they have been brought before almost all of the new dispute settlement bodies established over the last decades.

The aim of this chapter is to provide an overview of the mechanisms and procedures which have jurisdiction over water and economic disputes. It will focus on the actors entitled to bring a water dispute before international mechanisms. The chapter will be divided into two main sections. In the first section, State-to-State dispute resolution mechanisms will be considered. In this context, special emphasis will be placed on judicial (such as the ICJ and inter-State arbitration mechanisms) and quasi-judicial means (such as the WTO Dispute Settlement Body and regional economic and trade procedures).[9] The chapter will then turn to the settlement mechanisms that are accessible to non-State actors. Both sections will highlight that water disputes are, in most cases, embedded in wider disputes dealing with other issues.

2. Inter-State dispute settlement mechanisms, with particular emphasis on judicial means

International law provides several mechanisms and procedures to States to avoid or settle water disputes. Several conventions and agreements dealing with water issues involving economic features, as well as codification endeavors, foresee the need to resort to dispute settlement mechanisms—be they of a diplomatic or a judicial nature.[10] There have been a number of disputes which have been brought before the various judicial and quasi-judicial bodies established over time.

2.1 Treaty practice and codification endeavors

The *Convention Relating to the Development of Hydraulic Forces Affecting More Than One State*, adopted in Geneva in 1923 under the auspices of the League of Nations, is currently the only water-related convention in force with universal scope.[11] Its Article 12 states that:

> If a dispute arises between contracting States as to the application or interpretation of the present Statute, and if such dispute cannot be settled either directly between the Parties or

[9] For a presentation of diplomatic means, see L. Boisson de Chazournes, *The Role of Diplomatic Means of Solving Water Disputes: A Special Emphasis on Institutional Mechanisms*, Resolution of International Water Disputes (Peace Palace Papers, Kluwer Law International, 2003) at 91–110.

[10] *See* L. Caflisch, *Règles générales du droit des cours d'eau internationaux*, 219 *RCADI*, at 9 (1989-VII); S. C. McCaffrey, *The Law of International Watercourses: Non-Navigational Uses* (Oxford University Press, Oxford/New York, 2001).

[11] *Convention Relating to the Development of Hydraulic Forces Affecting More Than One State* Geneva, 9 December, 1923, 36 *LNTS* 76. However, this Convention has not been implemented because only two of the signatory States are riparian to an international watercourse.

by some other amicable method of procedure, the Parties to the dispute may submit it for an advisory opinion to the body established by the League of Nations as the advisory and technical organization of the Members of the League in matters of communications and transit, unless they have decided or shall decide by mutual agreement to have recourse to some other advisory, arbitral or judicial procedure.

The 1997 *United Nations Convention on the Law of the Non-Navigational Uses of International Watercourses* (UN Watercourses Convention), although not yet in force, expressly provides for dispute settlement mechanisms under the terms of Article 33.[12] According to this provision, when parties to a dispute cannot reach agreement by negotiation,

they may jointly seek the good offices of, or request mediation or conciliation by, a third party, or make use, as appropriate, of any joint watercourse institutions that may have been established by them or agree to submit the dispute to arbitration or to the International Court of Justice.

After six months, where negotiations or any other means of dispute settlement provided for in the Convention have failed, 'the dispute shall be submitted, at the request of any of the parties to the dispute, to impartial fact-finding'. In the latter case, the procedure can be invoked by any of the parties.

Numerous regional water-related agreements provide for inter-State dispute settlement mechanisms. In this context, mention should be made of the 1992 *Southern African Development Community Treaty* (SADC Treaty) and its Protocols.[13] The 1992 SADC Treaty obliges its parties to resolve disputes amicably through negotiations as a first resort.[14] Where negotiations fail, the matter can be brought before the SADC tribunal, created to 'ensure adherence to and the proper interpretation of the provisions of the treaty and the subsidiary instruments, and to adjudicate upon such disputes as may be referred to it'.[15] The tribunal has jurisdiction over all disputes related to the interpretation, application, and validity of the SADC Treaty and its Protocols.[16] The scope of jurisdiction of the tribunal includes 'disputes between States and between natural or legal persons and States'[17] and between 'States and the Community'.[18]

At the European level, besides the 1992 Helsinki *Convention on the Protection and Use of Transboundary Watercourses and International*

[12] *Convention on the Law of the Non-Navigational Uses of International Watercourses*, UN Doc. A/RES/51/869, 21 May 1997, 36 *ILM* (1997) at 70.

[13] *Treaty of the Southern African Development Community*, 17 August 1992, 32 *ILM* (1993), at 120. *SADC Revised Protocol on Shared Watercourses in the Southern Africa Development Community*, Windhoek, 7 August 2000, 40 *ILM* (2001), at 317 (in particular, see Art. 7.2, which reads as follows: 'Disputes between State Parties regarding the interpretation or application of the provisions of this Protocol which are not settled amicably, shall be referred to the Tribunal'). *Protocol on Tribunal and the Rules of Procedures Thereof*, Windhoek, 7 August 2000, www.sadc.int.

[14] SADC Treaty, *supra* note 13, Art. 4.

[15] *Ibid.*, Art. 16(1).

[16] Tribunal Protocol, *supra* note 13, Art. 14.

[17] *Ibid.*, Art. 16.

[18] *Ibid.*, Art. 17.

Lakes,[19] several water-related agreements provide for resort to arbitral and judicial mechanisms in water disputes. Many of these agreements establish compulsory rather than optional arbitration or adjudication, in the event that negotiations fail.[20] It is interesting to note that recourse to the ICJ has been avoided in the most recent watercourse conventions. In this area, even when resort to the ICJ is anticipated, such provisions do not *per se* constitute an authorization to take a dispute before the ICJ. On the contrary, the jurisdictional avenue is only open by way of specific agreement rather than unilateral recourse. These provisions have the effect of encouraging recourse to the ICJ but they do not provide for it.

The Institut de droit international (IDI) and the International Law Association (ILA)[21] have both addressed the topic of dispute settlement in case of water disputes. The Madrid Declaration adopted by the IDI in 1911 recommended the appointment of permanent joint commissions to give opinions when works or utilizations by a State might result in serious consequences in the territory of another State.[22] Several Articles of the 1966 ILA *Helsinki Rules on the Uses of the Waters of International Rivers* are devoted to dispute settlement mechanisms.[23] The Helsinki Rules envisage both diplomatic and judicial means, stating that 'if the States concerned have not been able to resolve their dispute through

[19] *UN/ECE Convention on the Protection and Use of Transboundary Watercourses and International Lakes*, Helsinki, 17 March 1992, www.unece.org. In particular, *see* Art. 22 of this instrument providing that: '1. If a dispute arises between two or more Parties about the interpretation or application of this Convention, they shall seek a solution by negotiation or by any other means of dispute settlement acceptable to the parties to the dispute. 2. When signing, ratifying, accepting, approving or acceding to this Convention, or at any time thereafter, a Party may declare in writing to the Depositary that, for a dispute not resolved in accordance with paragraph 1 of this Article, it accepts one or both of the following means of dispute settlement as compulsory in relation to any Party accepting the same obligation: (a) Submission of the dispute to the International Court of Justice; (b) Arbitration in accordance with the procedure set out in Annex IV. 3. If the parties to the dispute have accepted both means of dispute settlement referred to in paragraph 2 of this Article, the dispute may be submitted only to the International Court of Justice, unless the parties agree otherwise.'

[20] *Convention on the Protection of the Rhine*, Rotterdam, 22 January 1998, 1404 *UNTS* at 59 (Art. 16); *Danube Convention on Cooperation for the Protection and Sustainable Use of the Danube River*, Sofia, 29 June 1994, 34 *ILM* (1995) at 851 (Art. 24); *Convention on the Protection of the Rhine against Pollution by Chlorides, supra* note 2 (Art. 13).

[21] On the work of the ILA in water issues, *see* S. Bogdanovic, *International Law of Water Resources—Contribution of the International Law Association* (Kluwer Law International, 2001).

[22] Institut de droit international, *International Regulations Regarding the Use of International Watercourses for Purposes Other than Navigation, Annuaire de l'Institut de droit international*, 24, (1911) at 265–7. Other relevant resolutions of the IDI are: the Salzburg Resolution of 1961, *Resolution on the Utilization of Non-Maritime International Waters (Except for Navigation)*, Salzburg, *Annuaire de l'Institut de droit international*, 49, (1961) at 381–94; the Athens Resolutions of 1979, *The Pollution of Rivers and Lakes and International Law, Annuaire de l'Institut de droit international*, 58 (1979) at 169; and the three resolutions adopted in Salzburg in 1997, the *Environment, Responsibility and Liability for Environmental Damage under International Law, and Procedures, Annuaire de l'Institut de droit international*, 67 (1997) at 217.

[23] International Law Association, *The Helsinki Rules on the Uses of the Waters of International Rivers, Report of the Fifty-Second Conference Held at Helsinki* (Arts XXX–XXXVII), 1966 (London, 1967), at 486.

negotiation', or they have been unable to agree through joint institutional mechanisms, good offices, or resort to a conciliation commission,[24] 'it is recommended that the States concerned agree to submit their legal disputes to an ad hoc arbitral tribunal, to a permanent arbitral tribunal or to the International Court of Justice'.[25]

2.2 Resort to the PCIJ and ICJ

The first case brought before the PCIJ to deal with water issues was in relation to the principle of freedom of navigation. At stake was the identification of the sections of the River Oder to which the international regime established by the Treaty of Versailles was to apply so as to allow for international navigation.[26] It thus had a strong economic component as it dealt with the scope of freedom of passage within the context of a specific watercourse. According to Articles 341 and 343 of the Treaty of Versailles, the Oder was placed under the administration of an International Commission composed of representatives of Poland, Prussia, Czechoslovakia, Great Britain, France, Denmark, and Sweden. The Commission was charged, *inter alia*, 'to define the sections of the river or its tributaries to which the international regime shall be applied'.[27] In the course of discussion, differences of opinion arose with respect to the extent of the jurisdiction of the Commission, as well as to the interpretation of Article 331 of the Versailles Treaty. That Article provides that the Oder 'and all navigable parts' thereof 'which naturally provide more than one State with access to sea' are 'international'.

The Polish government contended that two tributaries of the Oder (the Netze and the Wartha), located in Poland, provided only Poland with access to the sea, and that therefore they did not fall within the terms of Article 331. On the other hand, the six other States of the International Commission maintained that the condition prescribed by Article 331 was fulfilled. In their view, the two tributaries were thus submitted to the jurisdiction of the International Commission.

The PCIJ was asked to determine whether the jurisdiction of the Commission extended to the tributaries of the Oder situated in Poland. In holding that the jurisdiction of the Commission extended to those tributaries, the Court stated that a solution 'has been sought not in the idea of a right of passage in favor of upstream States, but in that of community of interest of riparian States'.[28] Moreover, it held that this community of interest in a navigable river 'becomes the basis of a common legal right, the essential features of which are the perfect

[24] International Law Association, *The Helsinki Rules on the Uses of the Waters of International Rivers, Report of the Fifty-Second Conference Held at Helsinki* (Arts XXX–XXXVII), 1966 (London, 1967), at 486, Art. XXXIII.

[25] *Ibid.*, Art. XXXIV.

[26] *Territorial Jurisdiction of the River Oder Commission* (Czech., Den., Fr., Ger., Gr. Brit., and Swed., v. Pol.), PCIJ ser. A No. 23 (10 September 1929).

[27] Treaty of Versailles, Art. 343.

[28] *Territorial Jurisdiction of the River Oder Commission, supra* note 26, at 27.

equality of all riparian States in the user of the whole course of the river and the exclusion of any preferential privilege of any one riparian State in relation to the other'.[29]

Another case brought to the PCIJ dealt with the use of the waters of the Meuse River by Belgium and the Netherlands.[30] This river, although for a large part unsuitable for navigation, served as a water reservoir for several artificial canals used for the transportation of goods.[31] Indeed, the Meuse River crosses one of the earliest and most highly industrialized areas of Europe. In order to meet their growing economic needs, Belgium and the Netherlands started the construction of a series of canals, fed by the waters of the Meuse, which would have allowed the expansion of commercial traffic.

In 1863, the two countries signed a treaty that regulated the withdrawal of water from the Meuse.[32] Yet, during the 1920s, it became clear that other canals needed to be built and a larger supply of water had to be drawn from the Meuse. In particular, the development of the coal-fields in the Dutch and Belgian Limburg called for an improvement in the waterways communications with the ports of the North Sea. Thus, because of the building of new canals fed by the waters of the Meuse, the Netherlands and Belgium began competing over a limited amount of water drawn from this river. In this context, the Dutch government instituted proceedings against Belgium before the PCIJ.

Belgium and the Netherlands advanced parallel claims during the proceedings before the PCIJ. In brief, the Netherlands asked the Court to decide that the diversion works carried out by Belgium were in violation of the treaty concluded in 1863 between both countries. At the same time, the Belgian government, rejecting the Dutch claim, filed a counterclaim inviting the Court to find that the works performed by the Netherlands were in breach of the same treaty. Thus, both parties cited the same instrument as a source of rights and duties, but differed in their interpretation of its scope.

The PCIJ, taking a narrow approach, stated that the 1863 Treaty did not prevent parties from constructing, modifying, or enlarging canals wholly situated in the national territory, provided that the diversion of water at the Maastricht intake and the volume of water discharged therefrom was not affected.[33] Thus, the Court confined its reasoning to issues related to the law of treaties. Its judgment gave priority to the principle of *pacta sunt servanda*, without taking into account the underlying reasons for the dispute, namely,

[29] *Ibid.*

[30] *Diversion of Water from the Meuse* (Netherlands v. Belgium), PCIJ ser. A/B No. 70 (28 June 1937).

[31] C. Romano, *The Peaceful Settlement of International Environmental Disputes: A Pragmatic Approach* (Kluwer Law, 2000) at 234.

[32] *Treaty between Belgium and the Netherlands for the Regulation of Drawings of Water from the Meuse*, The Hague, 12 May 1863, Consolidated Treaty Series, vol. 127, at 438–43. *See* C. Romano, *supra* note 31, at 234–5.

[33] *Diversion of Water from the Meuse* (Netherlands v. Belgium), *supra* note 30, at 26.

the commercial rivalry between Belgium and the Netherlands.[34] In the view of the Court, the parties could build as many canals as they wanted, even if they were entering into stiff competition for a limited amount of water, provided the principles of the 1863 Treaty were maintained. However, in adopting this approach, the PCIJ was unable to settle the question concerning the amount of water which parties had the right to draw from the Meuse. In addition, the judgment did not assist the parties to engage in further negotiations on this issue. It was only some fifty years after the judgment had been rendered that the parties were finally able, through negotiations, to establish a legal regime that was satisfactory to both sides, on the drawings from the Meuse.[35]

The dispute over the *Gabčikovo-Nagymaros* project settled by the ICJ in 1997 centered on the 1977 Treaty between Hungary and Czechoslovakia (from 1993 Slovakia).[36] It provided for the construction of two series of locks, one at Gabčikovo, in the territory of Czechoslovakia, and the other at Nagymaros in Hungary. The two constituted 'a single and indivisible operational system of works'. Yet, as a result of intense criticism generated by the project in Hungary, in 1989 the Hungarian government decided to suspend and then to abandon the project. Czechoslovakia worked out various alternative solutions, but Hungary maintained that further environmental studies were required before construction could be pursued. The failure of negotiations paved the road to the undertaking of unilateral actions: Czechoslovakia started to work on Variant C, which entailed, among other things, a unilateral diversion of the Danube by Czechoslovakia on its territory and the construction of a dam and two hydroelectric plants. During this phase, Hungary notified Czechoslovakia of the termination of the 1977 Treaty.

In 1993, Hungary and Slovakia signed a special agreement submitting their dispute to the ICJ. In the special agreement, the parties asked the Court to decide, *inter alia*, whether Slovakia was entitled to proceed to Variant C and to determine the legal effects of the notification of the termination of the 1977 Treaty by Hungary. In 1997, the ICJ decided that the 1977 Treaty remained in force and that Slovakia was not entitled to put Variant C in operation. While for the purposes of the present chapter, considerations on how the Court came to

[34] In this regard the Court stated: 'From the history of the dispute given above, it will be seen that one of the difficulties in achieving a settlement of the differences between the two States has been the Belgian desire to obtain The Netherlands' consent to the construction of a new canal connecting Antwerp and the Rhine, a point upon which one may infer that the Netherlands Government [has felt itself] unable to accede to the wishes of the Belgian Government because of the commercial rivalry between Antwerp and Rotterdam. With this aspect of the question the Court is in no way concerned. Its task is limited to a decision on the legal points submitted to it as to whether . . . certain work constructed by the Belgian Government . . . infringe[s on] the Treaty of 1863 and [regarding] the Belgian counterclaim, as to whether . . . certain work constructed by The Netherlands Government . . . constitute(s) an infringement of the Treaty of 1863.' *Ibid.*, at 16.

[35] See *Agreement on the Protection of the Rivers Meuse and Schedt*, Charleville Mezieres, 26 April 1994, 34 *ILM* (1995), at 851.

[36] Case concerning the *Gabčikovo-Nagymaros* Project, *supra* note 1.

these conclusions can be left aside,[37] it should be noted that the Court (as the PCIJ did in the *Diversion of the Meuse* dispute) left the parties to negotiate an agreement that would put an end to their dispute on the basis of the Court's decision.

In the words of the Court:

> It is not for the Court to determine what shall be the final result of these negotiations to be conducted by the Parties. It is for the Parties themselves to find an agreed solution that takes account of the objectives of the Treaty, which must be pursued in a joint and integrated way, as well as the norms of international environmental law and the principles of the law of international watercourses . . . What is required in the present case by the rule pacta sunt servanda, as reflected in Article 26 of the Vienna Convention of 1969 on the Law of Treaties, is that the Parties find an agreed solution within the cooperative context of the Treaty.[38]

Since the *Gabčikovo-Nagymaros* case, the ICJ has adjudicated two other cases involving water issues: the *Kasikili/Sedudu* case in 1999,[39] and the *Cameroon v. Nigeria* dispute in 2002.[40] Both cases concerned boundary issues. In addition, there were underlying economic and trade aspects to the disputes. Lastly, Niger and Benin have taken their dispute over the Niger River to the ICJ,[41] which deals with demarcation of borders across boundary rivers and the attribution of the islands in the Niger River.

It should be noted that in the *Kasikili/Sedudu* case the ICJ had the opportunity explicitly to bring an economic perspective to the issues concerning the

[37] On the case, *see* C. Bourne, *The Case concerning the Gabčikovo-Nagymaros Project: An Important Milestone in International Water Law*, YEARBOOK OF INTERNATIONAL ENVIRONMENTAL LAW, vol. 8 (1997), at 6–12; A. Boyle, *The Gabcikovo-Nagymaros Case: New Law in Old Bottles*, *ibid*, at 13–20; J. Sohnle, *L'irruption du droit de l'environnement dans la jurisprudence de la CIJ: l'affaire Gabčikovo-Nagymaros*, REVUE GÉNÉRALE DE DROIT INTERNATIONAL PUBLIC, vol. 102 (1998) at 85–121.

[38] Case concerning the *Gabčikovo-Nagymaros* Project (Hungary/Slovakia), *supra* note 1, at 141 and 142. At the beginning of March 1998, representatives of the two countries initialled a draft framework agreement which was approved by Slovakia but not by Hungary. Frustrated by the failure of the framework agreement, Slovakia requested the ICJ to render an additional judgement. *See* ICJ Press Communiqué 98/28 of September 1998.

[39] Case concerning *Kasikili/Sedudu Island* (Botswana/Namibia), ICJ (13 December 1999), www.icj-cij.org.

[40] Case concerning the *Land and Maritime Boundary* between Cameroon and Nigeria (Cameroon v. Nigeria: Eq. Guinea intervening) (10 October 2002), www.icj-cij.org. It should be noted that in this case the ICJ, dealing with the delimitation of the frontier in Lake Chad, refers to the works of the Lake Chad Basin Commission. This Commission was established by the Convention and Statutes relating to the Development of Chad Basin on May 22, 1964 (Cameroon, Chad, Nigeria, and Niger). For the text of the Convention, *see Treaties concerning the Non-Navigations Uses of International Watercourses*, Africa, FAO, Legislative Study, 61, at 10. Art. 8 of the Statutes establishes the Chad Basin Commission and Art. 9(g) endows the Commission with authority to examine complaints and to promote the settlement of disputes. The ICJ noted that in 1983 the riparian States gave the Commission the task of dealing with certain boundary and security issues, and the Commission has since met regularly to discuss those issues. *See* Case concerning the *Land and Maritime Boundary* between Cameroon and Nigeria, *ibid.*, paras 36 and 53.

[41] *Benin and Niger jointly submit a Boundary Dispute to the International Court of Justice*, ICJ, Information Office (2002), www.icj-cij.org.

delimitation of boundary rivers. The ICJ, recognizing the economic importance of navigation (mainly due to tourist activities and fishing) in the Chobe River,[42] held that

> the Parties have undertaken to one another that there shall be unimpeded navigation for craft of their nationals and flags in the channels of Kasikili/Sedudu Island. As a result, in the southern channel of Kasikili/Sedudu Island, the nationals of Namibia, and vessels flying its flag, are entitled to, and shall enjoy, a treatment equal to that accorded by Botswana to its own nationals and to vessels flying its own flag. Nationals of the two States, and vessels, whether flying the flag of Botswana or of Namibia, shall be subject to the same conditions as regards navigation and environmental protection. In the northern channel, each Party shall likewise accord the nationals of, and vessels flying the flag of, the other, equal national treatment.[43]

The Court reminded the parties of their commitment to cooperate with each other. In highlighting this, the ICJ thus gave a modern perspective to the issues concerning the delimitation of rivers. It recognized that social and economic interactions between the people living in the two co-riparian States must be preserved and encouraged.

2.3 Inter-State arbitration

Water disputes may also be brought before inter-State arbitration tribunals. The *Lake Lanoux case* and the dispute related to the interpretation of the 1976 Rhine Convention and its 1991 Protocol provide examples of a resort to arbitration in water-related disputes.

In the *Lake Lanoux case*, a French diversion project of the waters of Lake Lanoux, located in the Pyrenean region, was at the center of the dispute. The use of transboundary waters in that region had long been the subject of disputes: since the middle of the nineteenth century, water diversion projects had resulted in tensions between France and Spain. In this context, in 1866, the two parties concluded a treaty that regulated certain transboundary issues, including the apportionment of water.[44]

In 1950, the French government presented a plan aiming to exploit the hydroelectric potential of the waters of Lake Lanoux by diverting its waters towards the River Ariège, thereby affecting the course of waters which naturally drained into Spanish territory via the Carol River.[45] Although the French project also ensured the full restoration of flow to the Carol River, it met with opposition from the Spanish government. In particular, Spain argued that, under the provisions of the 1866 Treaty, the works affecting transboundary waters could be executed only with its consent.

[42] Case concerning *Kasikili/Sedudu Island* (Botswana/Namibia), *supra* note 39, para. 40.

[43] *Ibid.*, para. 103.

[44] *See The Treaty of Bayonne and its Additional Act*, 26 May 1866, *Consolidated Treaty Series*, vol. 132, at 359–74.

[45] C. Romano, *supra* note 31, at 219–32.

Due to these divergent positions, Spain and France brought the dispute before an *ad hoc* arbitration tribunal. In its award, the tribunal, developing well-established principles of international law such as the principle of good faith, concluded that the French project did not violate the 1866 Treaty.[46]

The arbitral tribunal affirmed that consultations and negotiations between the two States relating to the dispute must comply with the rules of good faith and must not be mere formalities.[47] Sanctions could also be applied in the event, for example, of an unjustified breaking off of discussions, abnormal delay, disregard of agreed procedures, systematic refusals to take adverse proposals or interests into consideration, and, more generally, in cases of violation of the rules of good faith.[48] In case of projected works, riparian States have a duty to inform and consult in good faith, as well as to take into account the interests of other riparian States.[49]

The case relating to the 1976 Rhine Convention and its 1991 Protocol, in which the Netherlands was matched with France, provides another example of a resort to arbitration.[50] In that case too, water protection and economic factors were closely entangled. The objective of the 1976 Rhine Convention and its 1991 Protocol is the improvement of water quality through the adoption of measures against pollution by chlorides. In order to realize the aim of the Convention, Germany, France, Luxembourg, the Netherlands, and Switzerland adopted a Protocol in 1991 which set out a system of allocation of payment that participating countries would make in furtherance of this aim. A dispute arose between the Netherlands and France with respect to the interpretation and application of the 1991 Protocol. An arbitral tribunal was asked to clarify the modalities of payment as provided in the 1991 Protocol. In order to determine the amount that France was expected to pay to the Netherlands, the tribunal analyzed the relevant provisions of the 1991 Protocol in light of the rules of interpretation established by the *Vienna Convention on the Law of Treaties*.[51] In particular, the tribunal paid attention to the principle of good faith and to the purpose and object of the Rhine Convention. During the pleadings before the tribunal, the parties adopted divergent positions with regard to the purpose of the Rhine Convention. While France argued that the aim of the 1976 Rhine Convention is to establish solidarity between riparians, taking into account the fact that pollution sources are multiple and not only located in France, the Netherlands considered that its purpose is the improvement of water quality and ensuring the supply of drinking-water. The tribunal found that both interpretations were compatible, since solidarity between riparians

[46] *Lake Lanoux* arbitration (Spain/France), (16 November 1957) *Report of International Arbitral Awards*, vol. 12, (1957), 281–317, at 306–307. English text: *International Law Reports*, vol. 24 (1957), at 101–42.

[47] *Ibid.*, para. 11.

[48] *Ibid.*

[49] *Ibid.*

[50] Case concerning the application of the *Convention on the Protection of the Rhine against Pollution by Chlorides* (3 December 1976) and its *Additional Protocol* (25 September 1991), *supra* note 2.

[51] *Vienna Convention on the Law of Treaties*, United Nations, 22 May 1969, *Treaty Series*, vol. 1155, at 331, Arts 31 and 32.

was the basis for the measures adopted by parties aiming to improve Rhine water quality.

For several years the Netherlands had made payments so that France could adopt measures against the pollution caused by chlorides. It argued that France had only partially fulfilled its responsibilities according to the 1991 Protocol. The tribunal decided that France was obliged to reimburse the Netherlands for payments made and not used, and at the same time the tribunal determined the accrued interest owing to the Netherlands.

The tribunal, recalling the holding of the PCIJ in the dispute over the *Territorial Jurisdiction of the River Oder Commission*,[52] considered that the 1976 Rhine Convention aims at safeguarding water quality as well as creating a 'community of interest' between riparians.[53] When riparians establish a common legal regime dealing with the utilization of their shared watercourse, they highlight the relevance of the notion of community of interest. Thus, the solidarity between riparians is an element of their 'community of interest'.

2.4 Trade dispute settlement mechanisms: specialized procedures for water-trade disputes

Depending on the status of water in relation to issues of interpretation and application of the relevant agreements, disputes could arise under WTO as well as regional economic agreements.[54]

The compulsory jurisdiction of the WTO dispute settlement mechanism encompasses all disputes between Members arising under the so-called 'covered agreements'.[55] Therefore, if water-related issues fall under one or more of the WTO agreements, water-trade disputes could be referred to the WTO dispute settlement mechanism.

Within the WTO, besides the 'mainstream procedures' resting on consultations, the establishment of a panel, and recourse to the Appellate Body, there also exists the possibility of resorting to arbitration in application of Article 25 of the DSU. This Article reads as follows:

> Expeditious arbitration within the WTO as an alternative means of dispute settlement can facilitate the solution of certain disputes that concern issues that are clearly defined by both parties.[56]

[52] *Territorial Jurisdiction of the River Oder Commission, supra* note 26, at 27. *See also* Case concerning the *Gabčíkovo-Nagymaros* Project (Hungary/Slovakia), *supra* note 1, para. 85.

[53] Case concerning the application of the *Convention on the Protection of the Rhine against Pollution by Chlorides* (3 December 1976) and its *Additional Protocol* (25 September 1991), *supra* note 2, paras 97–98.

[54] *See* Edith Brown Weiss and Mireille Cossy's chapters in this book.

[55] *See* Appendix I to the Dispute Settlement Understanding [hereinafter DSU].

[56] The idea behind this arrangement was that some simple disputes would be more amenable to arbitration rather than to the more cumbersome panel proceedings. *See* L. Boisson de Chazournes, *L'arbitrage à l'OMC*, REVUE DE L'ARBITRAGE, n° 3 (2003) at 949–89.

States can also agree to resort to other means of dispute settlement of a more diplomatic nature, such as good offices, conciliation, and mediation.[57] The language used in the DSU appears to provide for an inflexible exclusive jurisdiction regime, barring referral of cases coming under the WTO legal system to any outside dispute settlement forum.

With respect to the exclusiveness of the DSU provisions, one should also note that according to Article 1(2) of the DSU, the specific dispute settlement rules included in some of the covered agreements override the provisions of the DSU. In such context, it would seem that specific jurisdiction-regulating clauses providing for non-exclusive jurisdiction of the WTO dispute settlement should prevail.[58] Furthermore, the language used in Article 23(1)[59] only bars Members from seeking the redress of a violation of the WTO agreements before another forum than a WTO Panel and the Appellate Body, but it does not explicitly bar other outside courts or tribunals from interpreting WTO provisions. [60]

Inter-State trade disputes may also fall under the jurisdiction of a regional dispute settlement procedure such as the *North American Free Trade Agreement* (NAFTA), or under the jurisdiction of the European Court of Justice (ECJ). Chapter 20 of the NAFTA provides the main inter-State dispute settlement provisions.[61] It establishes a Free Trade Commission, on which each Member State has a cabinet-level representative, to oversee the implementation of the Agreement and resolve disputes concerning its interpretation or application.[62] According to Article 2003, Member States are obliged to overcome difficulties wherever possible through cooperation and consultation, but a comprehensive dispute settlement procedure is provided in case they should not succeed in doing so.

[57] *See* Art. 5.6 of the DSU. Thus far there has been only one case of mediation through the Director-General of the WTO. In this single case, however, the requesting Members specified that the mediator 'could be provided by procedures similar to those envisaged for mediation under Article 5 of the DSU'. *See* General Council, *Request for Mediation by the Philippines, Thailand and the European Communities—Joint Communication from the European Communities, Thailand and the Philippines*, 16 October 2002, doc. WT/GC//66.

[58] *See Agreement on the Application of Sanitary and Phytosanitary Measures* (15 April 1994), Art. 11(3), Annex 1A to *WTO Agreement and Agreement on Trade-Related Aspects of Intellectual Property Rights*, 15 April 1994, Article 64, 33 *ILM* (1994), at 1197.

[59] Article 23(1) reads as follows: '1. When Members seek the redress of a violation of obligations or other nullification or impairment of benefits under the covered agreements or an impediment to the attainment of any objective of the covered agreements, they shall have recourse to, and abide by, the rules and procedures of this Understanding.'

[60] Obviously WTO provisions are interpreted from time to time by national courts of the Members, including the European Court of Justice. *See* Y. Shany, *The Competing Jurisdictions of International Courts and Tribunals* (Oxford University Press, Oxford, 2003), at 184.

[61] *North American Free Trade Agreement between the governments of Canada, Mexico and United States*, 1 January 1994, 32 *ILM* (1994), at 289. Special provisions are made for the settlement of disputes concerning antidumping and countervailing duty obligations (Chapter 19, NAFTA). In addition to the inter-State procedure, Chapter 11 provides for the settlement of disputes between a party and an investor of another party (*see infra*).

[62] NAFTA, Art. 2001.

First, consultation and good offices, mediation, and conciliation by the Free Trade Commission are available to the States parties.[63] Should those steps fail, the parties may request the establishment by the Commission of a five-person arbitral Panel.[64] The Panel may seek technical information and advice from experts, and may establish a Scientific Review Board to give a written report on any factual issue concerning environmental, health, safety, or other scientific matters raised by a disputing party in the proceedings.[65] The Panel renders an Initial Report, where it sets out its findings of fact and its determination as to whether the measure at issue is or would be inconsistent with the obligations of the NAFTA.[66] It then presents its Final Report to the Free Trade Commission. On receipt of the Final Report the parties may agree upon the resolution of the dispute, in conformity with the determinations and recommendations of the Panel.[67]

To the extent that the subject matter of a dispute falls within both the NAFTA and the WTO dispute settlement mechanisms, the dispute may be settled in either forum at the discretion of the complaining party. In this regard, under the terms of Article 2005, the NAFTA provides that in disputes falling under the jurisdiction of both NAFTA and the WTO, the applicant party can choose where to litigate. Upon selection, the chosen forum has exclusive jurisdiction. It should be noted that certain disputes between NAFTA Members concerning the environment, conservation, or health and safety are subject to a special arrangement. In these cases the respondent State may insist that the dispute will be adjudicated before NAFTA dispute settlement bodies. The applicant is then prevented from seizing the WTO procedure and must withdraw from WTO proceedings, if already initiated.[68]

At the European level, the ECJ has jurisdiction over a wide range of disputes. In particular, it has jurisdiction over disputes brought by the Community institutions against Member States, alleging non-compliance with EC law.[69] The Court may also rule upon challenges to the legality of acts of the Community, and of refusals of Community institutions to act in circumstances where they are obliged to act.[70] A third kind of jurisdiction derives from Article 177 of the EC Treaty. The Court may receive requests from the national courts of the Member States for an authoritative interpretation of Community law.

[63] NAFTA, Art. 2007. [64] NAFTA, Art. 2008. [65] NAFTA, Arts 2014, 2015.

[66] NAFTA, Art. 2016.

[67] NAFTA, Art. 2018. Unless the parties agree otherwise, the Initial Report is to be presented within ninety days of the appointment of the last panellist, and the Final Report within a further thirty days. [68] NAFTA, Art. 2005(3)–(5).

[69] Claims may be brought by one or more States, or by Community institutions. *See* Consolidated Version of the Treaty establishing the European Community (EC Treaty), 2001 *OJ* (C80/1), at 84. EC Treaty, Arts 169–70.

[70] In this case, claims can be brought by any Member State, or by a Community institution. In addition, the ECJ may be seized by natural or legal persons having a direct interest in the matter. *See* EC Treaty, Arts 173, 174, and 175.

With respect to water disputes, it is to be noted that the ECJ has rendered decisions dealing with the failure of a Member State to comply with EC water legislation. As an example, on 14 November 2002, the ECJ ruled against Ireland on account of its failure to ensure compliance with the microbiological standards set out in Annex I to Council Directive 80/778/EEC of 1980, relating to the quality of water for human consumption.[71]

The analysis of case law practice relating to water disputes shows that disputes have been brought before inter-State dispute settlement mechanisms, be it the PCIJ, the ICJ, or through arbitration. This could also be the case on the basis of the WTO DSU as well as various regional procedures. The latter are additional mechanisms to which States may have recourse in case the water issue at stake falls within the scope of jurisdiction of these procedures. Other dispute settlement procedures allow non-State actors to be parties to them. Such is the case, for example, in the areas of investment and human rights.

3. Non-State actors and water disputes

Water disputes may also emerge when individuals and groups of individuals allege that their interests are affected.[72] International procedures to which these non-State actors can have access are still rather an exception. The limited number of procedures in which non-State actors are entitled to participate can be found mainly in the fields of investment law and human rights law. Under international investment law, in particular multilateral and regional treaties such as the ICSID Convention and Chapter 11 of the NAFTA dealing with investment protection, private parties are entitled to challenge a State in an international forum. Human rights instruments can also provide avenues for settling water disputes. Lastly, other international procedures, such as the World Bank and multilateral development banks' inspection panels, the PCA Environmental Rules, or the SADC tribunal, grant a right of access to non-State actors. One must also add to this list the new compliance mechanism established under Aarhus Convention, entitling members of the public to make communications concerning a Party's compliance with the Convention.

[71] Case C-316/00 *Commission v. Ireland*, 14 November 2002. *See also* Case C-63/02 *Commission v. UK*, 15 October 2002 (Directive 98/83/EC—Quality of water intended for human consumption); *see also* Case C-396/00 *Commission v. Italy*, 25 April 2002 (Directive 91/271/EEC—Urban waste-water treatment); Case C-161/00 *Commission v. Germany*, 14 March 2002 (Directive 91/676/EEC—Pollution by Nitrates); Case C-384/97 *Commission v. Greece*, 25 May 2000 (Directive 2000/60/EC—Dangerous Substances); Case C-20027122 *Commission v. Belgium*, 16 January 2003 (Directive 80/778/EEC—Quality of water intended for human consumption).

[72] *See* A. Tanzi and C. Pitea, *Emerging Trends of Non-State Actors in International Water Disputes*, Resolution of International Water Disputes (Peace Palace Papers, Kluwer Law International, 2003) at 259–97; E. Hey, *Non-State Actors and International Water Disputes: A Search for the Nexus between the Local and the Global, ibid.*, at 299–318.

3.1 Investor-to-State dispute resolution mechanisms: the ICSID and the NAFTA experiences

The ICSID is the oldest institutionalized arbitration procedure granting non-State actors access to international arbitration tribunals.[73] This instrument entitles a private party to proceed directly against a State in an international forum. In so doing, it is important that the consent of both States concerned by the dispute is obtained (namely, the host State and the investor's State of nationality). Article 25(1) of the ICSID Convention provides that:

> The jurisdiction of the Centre shall extend to any legal dispute arising directly out of an investment, between a Contracting State (or any constituent subdivision or agency of a Contracting State designated to the Centre by that State) and a national of another Contracting State, which the parties to the dispute consent in writing to submit to the Centre. When the parties have given their consent, no party may withdraw its consent unilaterally.[74]

Arbitration before ICSID arbitration tribunals depends not only on accession to the Convention by the relevant States, but also on a specific agreement to arbitrate a dispute before ICSID, entered into by the investor's State of nationality and the host State. This agreement may be expressed in several ways. The most common form is a direct agreement between the two parties recorded in a single instrument, such as a bilateral investment treaty (BIT). Alternatively, the parties may submit a dispute that has already arisen by way of a *compromis*. Moreover, national legislation and multilateral and regional agreements may also establish the jurisdiction of ICSID tribunals to settle State-investor disputes.[75]

Article 26 of the ICSID Convention states:

> Consent of the parties to arbitration under this Convention shall, unless otherwise stated, be deemed consent to such arbitration to the exclusion of any other remedy. . . .

This provision establishes a typical exclusive jurisdiction clause. Indeed, the arbitration clause or agreement establishing the ICSID jurisdiction is normally *lex specialis* and overrides any general dispute settlement arrangement entered into by the contracting States. Thus, if the parties to a dispute have chosen to refer it to the ICSID, the Centre will normally have exclusive jurisdiction.

[73] *Convention on the Settlement of Investment Disputes between States and Nationals of Other States*, Washington, 18 March 1965, 4 *ILM* 524 (1966).

[74] Under the so-called Additional Facility Rules, the ICSID offers a second set of arbitration rules in order to accommodate disputes which involve a State (or an investor's home State) which has not already acceded to the ICSID Convention. ICSID *Additional Facility Rules*, 21 *ILM* 1443 (1982).

[75] Over the last ten years, several multilateral agreements have been concluded granting the jurisdiction of ICSID Tribunals to settle investor-State disputes. These include: the NAFTA (Art. 1120); the *Colonia Protocol on the Reciprocal Promotion and Protection of Investments within Mercosur*, signed on 17 January 1994 (Art. 9), and the *Buenos Aires Protocol on the Promotion and Protection of Investments Made by Countries that are not Parties to Mercosur*, signed on 8 August 1994 (Art. 2(h)) (both protocols concluded under the *Asunción Treaty Establishing a Common Market Between Argentina, Brazil, Paraguay and Uruguay* (Mercosur), signed on 26 March 1991); and the *Energy Charter Treaty, 34 ILM* 381 (Art. 26).

Another important characteristic of the ICSID Convention deals with diplomatic protection. Article 27 provides that:

> No Contracting State shall give diplomatic protection, or bring an international claim in respect of a dispute which one of its nationals and another Contracting State shall have consented to submit or shall have submitted to arbitration under this Convention, unless such other Contracting State shall have failed to abide by and comply with the award rendered in such a dispute.

Through this provision, the ICSID Convention bars inter-State adjudication over disputes that the parties have agreed to submit to ICSID dispute settlement procedure. The aim of this Article is to strengthen the exclusivity of the ICSID regime as the only forum for settling investment disputes, and thereby to prevent the rendering of conflicting judgments.[76]

Because of the increased number of bilateral, regional, and multilateral treaties providing for ICSID jurisdiction, this mechanism is likely to play a growing role in the settlement of disputes over water issues. Indeed, several cases concerning water services concession agreements have already been submitted to ICSID tribunals.[77] To date, two awards have been rendered in this area: the *Zhinvali Development project*[78] and the *Compañía de Aguas del Aconquija S.A. and Vivendi Universal* [formerly Compagnie Générale des Eaux] *v. Argentina.*[79] However, this last award (rendered in 2000) has been annulled by an *ad hoc* Committee and the case is currently pending before a new ICSID tribunal.[80] Concerning matters of jurisdiction, a decision has been handed down in another dispute, the *Azurix v. Argentina* case.[81]

In the case concerning the *Zhinvali Development project*, the investor reclaimed the reimbursement of the costs incurred in the course of its negotiations with the Georgian government for the rehabilitation of a hydro-electric

[76] *See* C. Schreuer, *The ICSID Convention. A Commentary* (Cambridge University Press, Cambridge, 2001).

[77] ICSID pending cases on water issues: *Azurix Corp. v. Argentine Republic* (Case No. ARB/01/12); *Aguas del Tunari S.A. v. Republic of Bolivia* (Case No. ARB/02/3); *Jacobs Gibb Limited v. Hashemite Kingdom of Jordan* (Case No. ARB/02/12); *Salini Costruttori S.p.A. and Italstrade S.p.A. v. The Hashemite Kingdom of Jordan* (Case No. ARB/02/13) (Dam construction project); *Impregilo S.p.A. v. Islamic Republic of Pakistan* (Case No. ARB/03/3) (Hydropower project); *Aguas Provinciales de Santa Fe, S.A., Suez, Sociedad General de Aguas de Barcelona, S.A. and Interagua Servicios Integrales de Agua, S.A. v. Argentine Republic* (Case No. ARB/03/17); *Aguas Cordobesas, S.A., Suez, and Sociedad General de Aguas de Barcelona, S.A. v. Argentine Republic* (Case No. ARB/03/18) (Water services concession); *Aguas Argentinas, S.A., Suez, Sociedad General de Aguas de Barcelona, S.A. and Vivendi Universal, S.A. v. Argentine Republic* (Case No. ARB/03/19).

[78] *Zhinvali Development Ltd v. Republic of Georgia* (Case No. ARB/00/1) (Rehabilitation of a hydropower plant), Award (24 January 2003). Award not yet published.

[79] *Compañía de Aguas del Aconquija S.A. and Vivendi Universal v. Argentine Republic* (Case No. ARB/97/3), Award (21 November 2000), 16 *ICSID Rev.—FILJ* 641 (2001); 40 *ILM* 426 (2001); 26 *Y.B. Com. Arb.* 61 (2002).

[80] *Compañía de Aguas del Aconquija S.A. and Vivendi Universal v. Argentine Republic*, Decision on application for annulment (3 July 2002), 41 *ILM* 1135 (2002).

[81] *Azurix Corp. v. The Argentine Republic* (Case No. ARB/01/12), Decision of the Tribunal on Jurisdiction (8 December 2003), at 78–80, 85, http://www.asil.org/.

power plant,[82] while the dispute between Vivendi and Argentina deals with the interpretation of a concession agreement and its relation with a BIT concluded between France (the investor's State) and Argentina. This latter dispute (which started in 1996) illustrates the juridical complexities of investment-water disputes. As stated by the ICSID tribunal, the dispute raised 'a set of novel and complex issues not previously addressed in international arbitral precedent relating to the interplay of a bilateral investment treaty, a concession contract with a forum-selection clause and the ICSID Convention'.[83] The ICSID tribunal, despite holding that it had jurisdiction to hear the Vivendi and Argentina dispute, dismissed the claims on the grounds that the investors ought first to pursue their case before national courts. After the dismissal on the merits of the case, Vivendi requested the annulment of the award pursuant to Article 52 of the ICSID Convention.[84] The *ad hoc* Committee established in accordance with this provision found that the tribunal had 'manifestly exceeded its powers'.[85] A new ICSID tribunal was constituted on April 2004 to render an award in the dispute between Vivendi and Argentina.[86]

Other cases pending before ICSID dispute settlement mechanisms present many similarities with the *Compañía de Aguas del Aconquija S.A. and Vivendi Universal v. Argentina* dispute. The *Azurix*[87] and the *Aguas del Tunari*[88] cases also deal with the relation between a BIT and a concession agreement. In the *Azurix* case, an ICSID tribunal, in its recent decision on jurisdiction, affirmed that

> the waiver of jurisdiction in forum selection clauses did not exclude ICSID jurisdiction because the subject-matter of any proceedings before the domestic courts under the contractual arrangements and the dispute before the ICSID tribunal are different.[89]

Therefore, even when the investors agree in the concession contract to the jurisdiction of national courts over all disputes and to the waiver of all other fora, the jurisdiction of ICSID tribunals is not excluded.

[82] Although the award has not yet been published, the *Investment Law and Policy Weekly News Bulletin* of the International Institute of Sustainable Development reported that the ICSID tribunal ruled that up-front costs do not fall under the definition of investment as set out in the ICSID Convention. *Investment Law and Policy Weekly News Bulletin*, 11 April 2003, www.iisd.ca. The Zhinvali case echoes an earlier ruling of an ICSID tribunal, where it affirmed that expenditures made in furtherance of a prospective investment could not be qualified as an investment under the ICSID Convention. (See *Mihaly International Corporation v. Democratic Socialist Republic of Sri Lanka* (ICSID Case No. ARB/00/2), *ICSID Review—FILJ*, 17, 2002.)

[83] *Compañía de Aguas del Aconquija S. A. and Vivendi Universal v. Argentine Republic, supra* note 79, at 95.

[84] In their application, the claimants sought the partial annulment of the award on three grounds: (1) that the Tribunal has manifestly exceeded its powers; (2) that there has been a serious departure from a fundamental rule of procedure; and (3) that the award has failed to state the reasons on which it is based. *Compañía de Aguas del Aconquija S. A. and Vivendi Universal v. Argentine Republic*, Decision on application for annulment rendered, *supra* note 80.

[85] *Ibid.*

[86] *See* Pannatier & Ducrey's chapter in this book.

[87] *Azurix Corp. v. The Argentine Republic, supra* note 81.

[88] *Aguas del Tunari, S. A. v. Bolivia* (Case No. ARB/02/3).

[89] *Azurix Corp. v. The Argentine Republic, supra* note 81.

In the dispute *Aguas del Tunari v. Bolivia*, the private investor is attempting to enforce the concession agreement through a BIT. The case arises from a dispute associated with a concession contract that Bechtel (an American private corporation) and its Bolivian affiliate made with Cochabamba (the third largest city in Bolivia). The measures adopted by the private company, such as higher water rates, provoked public anger: protests and a general strike brought the city to a halt for four days. In this context, the government of Bolivia declared a state of emergency and deployed soldiers and police. More than 100 people were injured and a 17-year-old boy was killed. The company claimed that factors other than increased water rates were responsible for the civil unrest and it reaffirmed its commitment to meeting the area's water service needs. However, in April 2000, as anti-Bechtel protests continued to grow, the company's managers abandoned the project. In November 2001, Aguas del Tunari filed a legal action with the ICSID under a BIT between the Netherlands and Bolivia. Although Aguas del Tunari is a subsidiary of the American corporation Bechtel, it had established a P.O. box presence in the Netherlands in order to make use of the BIT. This case is now pending before an ICSID tribunal which was constituted in July 2002 and held its first session in December 2002. The *Aguas del Tunari v. Bolivia* dispute raises issues of public concern. In particular, the tribunal will have to address the relationship between a concession agreement and the government's authority to guarantee public order and access to water. Given the broad public impact of this case, some NGOs requested permission to intervene as parties in the arbitration, or, in the alternative, to participate as *amici curiae.*[90] The petitioners also requested public disclosure of the submissions made to the tribunal, the opening of the hearings to the public, and that the tribunal visit Bolivia to conduct public hearings concerning the facts of this claim. In January 2003 the ICSID tribunal dismissed the request of the petitioners to participate as *amici curiae.*[91]

A number of regional agreements have also set up mechanisms that allow private investors to have access to arbitration against the host State. Among the regional agreements, Chapter 11 of the NAFTA, in its Article 1120, provides that private investors from one of the NAFTA Member States investing in another NAFTA State may unilaterally bring their investment dispute with the host State either to the ICSID (or the ICSID Additional Facility Rules), or to arbitration in accordance with the UNCITRAL Rules. In doing so, they waive their rights to pursue the same matter before any other dispute settlement procedure operating under domestic law.[92]

[90] Petition of La Coordinadora para la Defensa del Agua y Vida, la Federaciòn Departamental Cochabambina de Organizaciones Regantes, Semapa Sur, Friends of the Earth-Netherlands, Father Luis Sànchez and Congressional Jorge Alvarado, 29 August 2002, www.earthjustice.com.

[91] Decision of the ICSID Tribunal on Petition from Third Persons to Intervene as 'Amicus Curiae', 29 January 2003 (on file with the author). *See* Mbengue & Tignino's chapter in this book.

[92] NAFTA, Art. 1121. *See* Edith Brown Weiss and Nathalie Bernasconi-Osterwalder's chapters in this book.

During the negotiations of the NAFTA some consideration was given to the link between the water and free trade;[93] however, it appears that almost no attention was given to the question of how international investment rules would affect the ability of a State to protect its natural resources. In this context, it is interesting to note that in 1998 a case on water issues was initiated by Sun Belt (an American company) against Canada. In the 1980s, Sun Belt, Inc. of California and a Canadian company, Snow Cap, saw an opportunity to capitalize on the water shortage in northern California by shipping water from British Columbia in retrofitted oil supertankers. In 1991, the government of British Columbia, concerned about the environmental implications of this new venture market, passed a temporary ban on bulk water exports and refused to award new or expanded licenses on water export. This was codified by a permanent ban in 1995. Both Snow Cap and Sun Belt sued British Columbia for damages for contracts lost due to the initial moratorium. Although the government of British Columbia settled the dispute with the Canadian company, Snow Cap, in 1996, it did not reach an agreement with Sun Belt. The American company brought an arbitration claim under the Chapter 11 of the NAFTA against Canada. In particular, it claimed loss of profits, market access, and access to resources.[94]

Although not dealing directly with water issues, an ICSID tribunal constituted under Chapter 11 of the NAFTA in the case *Metalclad v. Mexico* considered national environmental measures aimed, *inter alia*, at the protection of water resources. This case deals with the construction of a hazardous waste landfill in Mexico by a private company, Metalclad. Given the denial by the municipality of a local construction permit and the issuance of an ecological decree, Metalclad was prevented from operating the landfill. In particular, the town council of Guadalcazar, where the landfill was located, denied the permit 'for reasons which included, but may not have been limited to, the opposition of the local population, the fact that construction had already begun when the application was submitted, . . . and the ecological concerns regarding the environmental effect and impact on the site and surrounding communities'.[95] In this respect, the ICSID tribunal affirmed that 'the Municipality denied the local construction permit in part because of the Municipality's perception of the adverse environmental effects of the hazardous waste landfill and the geological unsuitability of the landfill site. In so doing, the Municipality acted outside its authority'.[96]

[93] *See* the 1993 *Joint Statement of Canada, United States, and Mexico*, which declares 'unless water, in any form, has entered into commerce and becomes a good or product, it is not covered by the provisions of any trade agreement, including the NAFTA . . . Water in its natural state in lakes, rivers, reservoirs, aquifers and the like is not a good or product . . .'. *See* Appendix D of this book.

[94] *Sun Belt Inc. v. Canada*, Notice of intent to submit a claim to arbitration, 27 November 1998, Notice of claim and demand for arbitration, 12 October 1999, www.naftaclaims.org. This case has not proceed to arbitration at this time according to available information.

[95] *Metalclad Corp. v. The United Mexican States* (Case No. ARB(AF)/97/1), Award of 30 August 2000, at 111; *ICSID Review—FILJ*, vol. 16 (2001), at 92.

[96] *Ibid.*, at 106.

For the ICSID tribunal, the denial of the municipal permit amount to an indirect expropriation.[97]

Moreover, the ICSID tribunal also identified the ecological decree as a further ground for a finding of expropriation. Some provisions of this decree deal with water protection. In particular, Article 14 forbids 'any conduct that might involve the discharge of polluting agents on the reserve soil, subsoil, running water or water deposits and prohibits the undertaking of any potentially polluting activities'.[98] In relation to the ecological decree, the *Metalclad* tribunal stated that

> [it] need not decide or consider the motivation or intent of the adoption of the Ecological Decree. Indeed, a finding of expropriation on the basis of the Ecological Decree is not essential to the tribunal's finding of a violation of NAFTA Article 1110. However, the tribunal considers that the implementation of the Ecological Decree would, in and of itself, constitute an act tantamount to expropriation.[99]

Therefore, in the light of the tribunal's interpretation of Article 1110,[100] measures taken to protect a State's water resources might, in certain circumstances, constitute an act tantamount to expropriation and thus not be exempt from compensation. In the tribunal's view, expropriation under the NAFTA

> includes not only open, deliberate and acknowledged takings of property, such as outright seizure or formal or obligatory transfer of title in favour of the host State, but also covert or incidental interference with the use of property which has the effect of depriving the owner, in whole or in significant part, of the use or reasonably-to-be-expected economic benefit of property even if not necessarily to the obvious benefit of the host State.[101]

In the context of the NAFTA, another case still pending concerning water issues has been submitted under UNICTRAL rules.[102] The Methanex corporation, a Canadian marketer and distributor of methanol (a key component of MTBE[103]), has submitted a claim for arbitration for alleged injuries resulting from a Californian ban on the use or sale in California of the gasoline additive MTBE. In particular, when gasoline containing MTBE is discharged into the environment some of the MTBE may dissolve in the surrounding groundwater rendering it unfit for human consumption. In 1999, as a result of these environmental concerns, the Governor of California issued an executive order calling

[97] *Ibid.*, at 107. [98] *Ibid.*, at 109–10. [99] *Ibid.*, at 111.

[100] Article 1110 reads as follows: 'A Contracting Party shall not expropriate or nationalize directly or indirectly expropriate an investment in its territory of an investor of another Contracting Party or take any measure or measures having equivalent effect... except... accompanied by payment of prompt, adequate and effective compensation... equivalent to the fair market value of the expropriated investment.'

[101] *Metalclad Corp. v. The United Mexican States, supra* note 95, at 103.

[102] *Mehanex Corp. v. United States of America*, Notice of Intent to Submit a Claim to Arbitration, 2 July 1999. The tribunal issued a first partial award on issues of jurisdiction and admissibility. *See* First Partial Award (7 August 2002) and Methanex Submission on Its Application for Reconsideration of the First Partial Award (8 March 2004), www.naftaclaims.org.

[103] Methyl tertiary-butyl ether.

for the removal of the MTBE from gasoline. Following this order, the Methanex corporation initiated an arbitration proceeding against the US.

3.2 Human rights procedures and water-related disputes

Although most human rights treaties were drafted and adopted before water protection became a matter of international concern,[104] UN treaty bodies and regional human rights courts have dealt with water issues. Indeed, they have addressed water issues in relation to the protection of natural resources taking into account various economic aspects.

a. United Nations treaty bodies

Concerning the practice of the Human Rights Committee (HRC) established by the *Optional Protocol to the International Covenant on Civil and Political Rights* (ICCPR),[105] one can note the communication brought by the Lubicon Lake Band and its chief B. Ominayak.[106] In this case, the author of the communication alleged the violation of the right to self-determination as protected by Article 1, which includes the right freely to dispose of natural resources. In particular, the communication regarded the expropriation of part of the Band's territories in favor of private gas and oil corporations. However, under the Optional Protocol to the ICCPR, an individual communication may not be brought by or on behalf of groups of individuals. As a result, the communication was considered inadmissible with regard to the alleged violation of Article 1. However, the HRC found that the communication was admissible to the extent that it raised issues under Article 27, which deals with the question of the right of persons belonging to communities,[107] as well as under other Articles of the Covenant. The Committee accepted many arguments of the author of the communication, saying that '[h]istorical inequities, to which the State party refers, and certain more recent developments threaten the way of life and culture of the Lubicon Lake Band, and constitute a violation of Article 27 as long as they continue'.[108] Therefore, the HRC, through Article 27, ensured the safeguard of natural resources.

Moreover, in the communication *Ilmari Lansman et al. v. Finland*, the HRC, dealing with alleged violations brought by the Sami population, observed that a

[104] Three human rights instruments explicitly refer to water: *Convention on the Elimination of All Forms of Discrimination Against Women*, U.N. Doc. A/34/46 (1979) (Art. 14(2)(h)); *Convention on the Rights of the Child*, U.N. Doc. A/44/49 (1989) (Art. 24(1), (2)(c); *African Charter on the Rights and Welfare of the Child*, OAU Doc. CAB/LEG/24.9/49 (1990) (Art. 14).

[105] *Optional Protocol to the International Covenant on Civil and Political Rights*, G.A. res. 2200A (XXI), 21 UN GAOR Supp. (No. 16) at 59, U.N. Doc. A/6316 (1966), 999 *UNTS* at 302.

[106] Communication No. 167/1984, *Ominayak, Chief of the Lubicon Lake Band v. Canada*, Human Rights Committee, CCPR/C/38/D/167/1984.

[107] Art. 27 of the ICCPR reads as follows: 'In those States in which ethnic, religious or linguistic minorities exist, persons belonging to such minorities shall not be denied the right, in community with the other members of their group, to enjoy their own culture, to profess and practice their own religion, or to use their own language.'

[108] Communication No. 167/1984, *Ominayak, Chief of the Lubicon Lake Band v. Canada, supra* note 106, at 33.

State may wish to encourage economic development, but that nevertheless this freedom must be tested by reference to the obligations established under Article 27.[109] The communication *Apirana Mahuika et al. v. New Zealand* arose as a result of New Zealand's violations of Maoris' minority rights because of New Zealand's efforts to regulate commercial and non-commercial fishing. In this case the Committee emphasized that

> the acceptability of measures that affect or interfere with the culturally significant economic activities of a minority depends on whether the members of the minority in question have had the opportunity to participate in the decision-making process in relation to these measures and whether they will continue to benefit from their traditional economy.[110]

The *General Comment No. 15 on the Right to Water* adopted by the United Nations Committee on Economic, Social, and Cultural Rights recognized that States must demonstrate that 'they have taken the necessary and feasible steps towards the realization of the right to water'.[111] Moreover, States have to prevent third parties, including 'individuals, groups, corporations and other entities', from interfering 'in any way with the enjoyment of the right to water'.[112] States also have to adopt the 'necessary and effective legislative and other measures to restrain third parties from denying equal access to adequate water; and polluting and inequitably extracting from water resources, including natural sources, wells and other water distribution systems'.[113] The *International Covenant on Economic, Social, and Cultural Rights* (ICESCR)[114] does not establish the right of individuals or groups to submit communications concerning non-compliance.[115] However, under Article 16, States Parties have an obligation to submit reports on the measures which they have adopted in order to comply with the rights recognized by the Covenant.

b. Regional human rights bodies

At the regional level, the European Court of Human Rights,[116] the Inter-American Commission on Human Rights,[117] and the African Commission on

[109] Communication No. 511/1992, *Ilmari Lansman et al. v. Finland*, Human Rights Committee, CCPR/C/52/D/511/1992, at 74.

[110] Communication No. 547/1992, *Apirana Mahuika et al. v. New Zealand*, Human Rights Committee, CCPR/C/70/D/547/1993.

[111] UN Committee on Economic, Social, and Cultural Rights, *General Comment No. 15 on the Right to Water. See* Appendix A of this book.

[112] *Ibid.*, at 23.

[113] *Ibid.*

[114] *International Covenant on Economic, Social, and Cultural Rights*, GA res. 2200A (XXI), 21 UN GAOR Supp. (No. 16) at 49, UN Doc. A/6316 (1966), 993 *UNTS* 3.

[115] *See Draft Protocol for the Consideration of Communications concerning Non-Compliance with the International Covenant on Economic, Social, and Cultural Rights, Commission on Human Rights*; E/CN.4/1997/105, 18 December 1996, www.unhchr.ch.

[116] Established by the *European Convention for the Protection of Human Rights and Fundamental Freedoms*, 4 November 1950 (*ETS* 5), 213 *UNTS* 222.

[117] Established by the *American Convention on Human Rights*, 22 November 1969, OASTS 36, 9 *ILM* 673 (1970).

Human and Peoples' Rights[118] have also dealt with water issues. This has been done by means of a teleological interpretation of the constitutive instruments of these bodies.

The European Court has dealt with several cases raising environmental and water concerns, notwithstanding the fact that there is no explicit provision in its mandate dealing with these issues. Most cases that have come to the Court have involved either the right to respect for private life and family life (Article 8), or the right to information (Article 10). Article 6, which provides judicial guarantees of a fair trial, has also been invoked in order to protect the right of access to justice in relation to environmental issues.

In the *Zander v. Sweden*[119] case, the European Court found a violation of Article 6.1, which provides that: 'In the determination of his civil rights and obligations or of any criminal charge against him, everyone is entitled to a fair and public hearing within a reasonable time by an independent and impartial tribunal established by law.' This protection was applied to persons who had been denied judicial review for threatened environmental harm resulting from contamination of their well water by cyanide from a neighboring dump site. In particular, following the discovery of high levels of cyanide in water wells, the municipality established temporary water supplies. However, subsequently, the municipality raised the permissible level of cyanide and halted the city supply. When the company maintaining the dump site sought a renewed and expanded permit, the applicants argued that the threat to their water supply would be sufficiently high that the company should be obliged to provide free drinking water if pollution occurred. However, the government granted the permit and denied the applicants' request. The claimants had sought but could not obtain judicial review of the national decision. It was thus considered that Article 6.1 of the European Convention applied in granting the right of judicial review where civil rights had been violated by national decisions.[120]

At the level of the *Inter-American Convention on Human Rights*, it is interesting to note that the Inter-American Commission on Human Rights has recently published several country reports where it devoted particular attention to the relationship between the environment, water, health, and human rights.[121]

[118] Established by the *African Charter on Human and Peoples' Rights*, 27 June 1981, OAU Doc. CAB/LEG/67/3 rev. 5, 21 *ILM* 58 (1982).

[119] European Court of Human Rights, *Zander v. Sweden*, (14282/88), 1993, ECHR, 59 (25 November 1993).

[120] In this regard, the Court notes that 'the applicants' claim was directly concerned with their ability to use the water in their well for drinking purposes. This ability was one facet of their right as owners of the land on which it was situated. The right of property is clearly a "civil right" within the meaning of Article 6.1.' *Zander v. Sweden, supra* note 119, at 27.

[121] Inter-American Court of Human Rights, *Report on the Situation of Human Rights in Brazil*, OEA/Ser.L/V/II.97, doc. 29, rev. 1 (1997). In particular, the Report on Brazil discusses problems of environmental destruction leading to severe consequences on the rights to health and culture. Indigenous cultural and physical integrity are said to be under constant threat and attack. State protection is called 'irregular and feeble', leading to constant danger and environmental deterioration.

In its country report concerning the situation in Ecuador, the Commission responded to claims that oil exploitation activities were contaminating the water, air, and soil, thereby causing the people of the region to become sick and to have a greatly increased risk of serious illness.[122] After an on-site visit, it found that both the government and inhabitants agreed that the environment was contaminated, with inhabitants exposed to toxic byproducts of oil exploitation in their drinking and bathing water, in the air, and in the soil. The inhabitants were unanimous in claiming that oil operations, especially the disposal of toxic wastes, jeopardized their health and their lives. In addition, many claimed that pollution of local waters contaminated fish and drove away wildlife, threatening food supplies. The Commission emphasized the right to life and physical security, stating that

> [t]he realization of the right to life, and to physical security and integrity is necessarily related to and in some ways dependent upon one's physical environment. Accordingly, where environmental contamination and degradation pose a persistent threat to human life and health, the foregoing rights are implicated.[123]

In the country report on Paraguay, the Inter-American Commission directly addressed concerns on economic development, noting that the Convention neither prevents nor discourages it, but rather requires that it take place under conditions of respect for the rights of affected individuals.[124] Thus, while the right to development implies that each State may exploit its natural resources, 'the absence of regulation, inappropriate regulation, or a lack of supervision in the application of norms may create serious problems with respect to the environment which translate into violations of human rights protected by the American Convention'.[125] The Commission concluded that

> [c]onditions of severe environmental pollution, which may cause serious physical illness, impairment and suffering on the part of the local populace, are inconsistent with the right to be respected as a human being ... The quest to guard against environmental conditions which threaten human health requires that individuals have access to: information, participation in relevant decision-making processes, and judicial recourse.[126]

The Inter-American Commission thus recommended that the State adopt the necessary measures to protect indigenous communities from environmental degradation, with special emphasis on protecting the forests and waters, which are fundamental for their health and survival as communities.

With respect to African practice following several communications against Zaire, the African Commission held that failure by the government to provide basic services such as safe drinking water constituted a violation of Article 16 of the *African Charter on Human and Peoples' Rights* providing for the recognition

[122] Inter-American Court of Human Rights, *Report on the Situation of Human Rights in Ecuador*, OEA/Ser.L/V/II.96, doc. 10 rev. 1 (1997).
[123] *Ibid.*, at 88.
[124] Inter-American Court of Human Rights, *Report on the Situation of Human Rights in Paraguay*, OEA/Ser.L/V/II.110, Doc. 52 (2001).
[125] *Ibid.*, at 89.
[126] *Ibid.*, at 92, 93.

of a human right to health.[127] In 2002, the African Commission found the former military government of Nigeria guilty of economic, social, and cultural rights violations against the Ogoni people concerning an oil development project in the Niger Delta. In particular, the Commission affirmed the violation of Articles 16 and 24[128] of the *African Charter on Human and Peoples' Rights*. The Commission stated that the right to a general satisfactory environment, as guaranteed under Article 24 of the Charter, 'imposes clear obligations upon a government'. It required the 'State to take reasonable and other measures to prevent pollution and ecological degradation, to promote conservation, and to secure an ecologically sustainable development and use of natural resources'.[129]

As this brief survey illustrates, most of the global and regional human rights bodies have considered the link between water resource degradation and internationally-guaranteed human rights. This practice demonstrates the benefits of using human rights-based approaches to water-related problems.

3.3 New trends in dispute settlement procedures

Newly established dispute settlement procedures, whilst not all addressing water issues in a specific manner, do cover a wide range of water-related issues. Procedures such as the Environmental Rules adopted by the PCA, the tribunal established by the SADC, the inspection panels established by multilateral development banks, and the compliance mechanism adopted under the aegis of the Aarhus Convention allow non-State actors to have access to them.

a. PCA Environmental Rules

In 2001, the *Optional Rules for Arbitration of Disputes relating to Natural Resources and/or the Environment* (PCA Environmental Rules) were adopted under the aegis of the PCA.[130] They enable States, international organizations, and private entities such as NGOs and multinational corporations to submit disputes to arbitration.[131] The peculiar characteristic of this mechanism is its flexibility: the Rules are available for the use of all parties who have agreed to

[127] The finding followed the consolidation of several communications asserting torture, killings, arbitrary detention, unfair trials, restrictions on the right to association and peaceful assembly, suppression of freedom of the press, denial of the right to education and the right to health. With respect to the last, the Commission said that the failure of the government to provide 'basic services such as safe drinking water and electricity and the shortage of medicine as alleged in communication 100/93 constitutes a violation of Article 16'. African Commission on Human and People's Rights, Communications 25/89, 47/90, 56/91, 100/93 *World Organization against Torture et al./Zaire*, 2 October 1995, at 8, http://www1.umn.edu/humanrts/africa.

[128] Art. 24 reads as follows: 'All peoples shall have the right to a general satisfactory environment favourable to their development.'

[129] Communication 155/96, *The Social and Economic Rights Action Center and the Center for Economic and Social Rights / Nigeria*, 27 May 2002, at 52, available at www.cesr.org.

[130] PCA Environmental Rules, adopted 19 June 2001, reprinted in *Yearbook of International Law Arbitration* (2001) at 425, www.pca-cpa.org/EDR/ENRrules.htm.

[131] PCA Environmental Rules, *ibid.*

use them and they can be used for a wide range of disputes.[132] Under Article 1.1 of the PCA Environmental Rules, 'the characterization of the dispute as relating to the environment or natural resources is not necessary for jurisdiction, where all the parties have agreed to settle a specific dispute under these rules'. Thus, the Rules permit great flexibility not only in the number and nature of the parties, but also in the characterization of the dispute. Therefore, the scope *ratione materiae* of the PCA Environmental Rules is broader than the ICSID Convention which is limited to investment disputes. Parties to a dispute have to agree to submit it to the PCA Environmental Rules. In particular, Article 1.1 provides that 'all parties have to agree in writing that a dispute that may arise or that has arisen between them shall be referred to arbitration'. This provision specifies that the expression 'agree in writing' includes provisions in agreements, contracts, conventions, treaties, the constituent instrument of an international organization or agency, or reference upon consent of the parties by a court.

The 2003 *Protocol on Civil Liability and Compensation for Damage caused by the Transboundary Effects of Industrial Accidents on Transboundary Waters to the 1992 Convention on the Protection and Use of Transboundary Watercourses and International Lakes and to the 1992 Convention on the Transboundary Effects of Industrial Effects* defines the grounds for resorting to the PCA Environmental Rules.[133] It applies to damage caused by the transboundary effects of an industrial accident on transboundary waters. Under Article 13, claims for compensation may be brought before the courts of a Party where the damage was suffered, where the industrial accident occurred, or where the defendant 'has his or her habitual residence . . . or if the defendant is a company where it has its principal place of business'. According to Article 14, victims and harm-causing operators may also have recourse to international arbitration under the aegis of the PCA.[134]

b. Southern African Development Community (SADC) regime

The regional SADC regime offers another avenue for non-State actors to bring their claims before an international tribunal. Indeed, the scope of jurisdiction of the SADC tribunal is not limited to State-to-State disputes but includes disputes between natural or legal persons and States, between States and the Community, as well as between natural or legal persons and the Community.[135] Insofar as natural or legal persons are concerned, they must first exhaust all available remedies or be unable to proceed under the relevant domestic jurisdiction before they can submit a dispute against a State party to the tribunal.[136] It is important

[132] *Ibid.*

[133] The Protocol was adopted and signed by 22 countries, at the Ministerial Conference held in Kiev, on 21 May 2003, www.unece.org.

[134] Art. 14 reads as follows: 'In the event of a dispute between persons claiming for damage pursuant to the Protocol and persons liable under the Protocol, and where agreed by both or all parties, the dispute may be submitted to final and binding arbitration in accordance with the Permanent Court of Arbitration Optional Rules for Arbitration of Disputes Relating to Natural Resources and/or the Environment.'

[135] Tribunal Protocol, *supra* note 13, Arts 15, 17, 18.

[136] *Ibid.*, Art. 15(2).

to note that while this rule entails the obligation for non-State actors to exhaust local remedies, it also establishes that claimants may bring a claim before the tribunal if such remedies are not available. Therefore, a non-State actor prevented from having access to administrative or judicial bodies in a country could bring a dispute between itself and that other State before the tribunal.

Moreover, SADC Community water policies and laws can also be challenged before the SADC tribunal. Indeed, under the tribunal Protocol, non-State actors are entitled to bring a claim against the SADC Community before the tribunal.[137] As can be seen, the SADC instruments provide for innovative opportunities for non-State actors to participate in international water disputes.

c. Investigatory procedures

International financial institutions, such as the World Bank, the Inter-American Development Bank (IDB), and the Asian Development Bank (AsDB), have established dispute settlement mechanisms to which non-State actors can bring requests in relation to violations of their respective policies and procedures. The World Bank Inspection Panel, created in 1993, was the first international forum whereby non-State actors were granted the possibility of bringing complaints against an international organization in order to hold it accountable for non-compliance with its policies and procedures.[138] Its creation led two other multilateral development banks to create inspection mechanisms of their own shortly after.[139] In 2003, the European Bank for Reconstruction and Development (EBRD) created in like fashion its own mechanism.[140] Such investigatory procedures constitute a response to the requests to see the multilateral development banks becoming more accessible to non-State actors.

The World Bank Inspection Panel procedure enables groups of persons affected by a Bank-financed project to seize the Panel in order to request that the organization assess, and even correct, its own behavior.[141] The Panel decides on the complaint's eligibility, as well as on the merits of asking the Board to

[137] According to Art. 18: 'The Tribunal shall have exclusive jurisdiction over all disputes between natural or legal persons and the Community. Such disputes may be referred to the Tribunal either by the natural or legal person concerned or by the competent institution or organ of the Community.'

[138] *See* Resolution Establishing the Inspection Panel, Resolution No. IBRD 93–10, Resolution No. IDA 93–6 (22 September 1993), *reprinted* in 34 *ILM* (1995) at 503. Operating Procedures of the Inspection Panel (19 August 1994, *reprinted* in 34 *ILM* (1995) at 510.

[139] The IDB created an Independent Investigation Mechanism in 1994, which was reviewed in 2001. Pursuant to a decision taken in May 2003, the AsDB replaced in December 2003 its Inspection Function (itself created in 1995) with a mechanism modeled on the Investigation Mechanism of the IDB. *See* www.iadb.org and www.adb.org.

[140] EBRD, 'Independent Recourse Mechanism as Approved by the Board of Directors on 29 April 2003', www.ebrd.com.

[141] On this issue, *see* L. Boisson de Chazournes, *Public Participation in Decision-Making: The World Bank Inspection Panel*, in The World Bank, International Financial Institutions and the Development of International Law (E. B. Weiss, A. Rigo Sureda, L. Boisson de Chazournes, Studies in Transnational Legal Policy, No. 31, The American Society of International Law, 1999) at 91. On the procedure, *see* Mbengue & Tignino's, chapter in this book. *See also* The Inspection Panel, *Accountability at the World Bank, The Inspection Panel 10 Years On* (Washington D.C., 2003).

authorize an investigation into the Bank's action with regard to the application of its operational policies and procedures. In the event of an investigation, the Bank may adopt an action plan in order to correct the litigious situation. This process is innovative, if not original, since it gives civil society a place at the core of the international decision-making system within the organization, and paves the way for ensuring greater accountability of the organization.

On a number of occasions, the Inspection Panel has received requests relating to water issues; for example, the Arun III,[142] the Bujagali,[143] and the Yacyretà dam projects. In this last case, the Inspection Panel found that the management of the Bank had failed to comply with the policies on environmental assessment (OD 4.01) and on involuntary resettlement (OD 4.30).[144]

The Chad-Cameroon Oil Pipeline Project is the largest energy infrastructure development on the African continent. Among the claims of the request was the fact that the project would affect access to safe and clean water for people living in the project area. With respect to this issue, the Investigation Report considered that

> although the consortium of financial institutions has incorporated a number of mitigation measures in the Project design to avoid contamination of regional water supplies, the institutional mechanism for regional water management has not been developed to a similar extent.

In particular, the Panel's view was that

> it is imperative that Management ensures that the Regional Development Plan, and those responsible for its implementation, gives priority to the provision of safe and clean water

[142] The Arun III dam project was the first case brought before the World Bank Inspection Panel. The requesters claimed that the World Bank did not comply with its own operational policies and procedures (such as Operational Directive (OD) 4.01 and OD 4.30) in designing and financing a hydroelectric dam in the Arun Valley. The Panel recommended further investigation and the World Bank Board of Directors approved the investigation. In August 1995, the World Bank announced that it would not approve funds for the dam and would instead study energy conservation and small-scale hydro power. The Inspection Panel Investigation Report Nepal: Arun III Proposed Hydroelectric Project and Restructuring of IDA Cre-it-20 9-NEP (21 June 1995).

[143] In July 2001, the Panel received a request for inspection concerning the Bujagali Hydroelectric Project in Uganda. The requesters claimed violations of several Bank policies and procedures, including: environmental assessment, involuntary resettlement, natural habitat, as well as indigenous people's policies. The Inspection Panel found that the World Bank was not in compliance with the policy on environmental assessment. It also expressed concerns that a cumulative impact assessment of hydroelectric projects on the Nile was not properly completed. The Bank's management responded to the Panel's findings and proposed in its report specific actions that would remedy any cases of non-compliance. The most important outcome was the Bank's commitment to amend the agreement between Uganda and the Bank regarding the protection of the Kalagala falls. The Ugandan government also affirmed its commitment not to develop the Kalagala falls for hydropower but to set it aside exclusively as a natural habitat and for tourism. *See* Inspection Panel's Report and Findings on the Uganda Third Power Project, the Power IV Project and the Bujagali Hydropower Project (17 June 2002). For other cases *see* The Inspection Panel Report and Recommendation on Request for Inspection Lesotho/South Africa: Proposed Loan for Phase 1B of Lesotho Highlands Water Project (15 May 1998); The Inspection Panel Report and Recommendation on Request for Inspection Lesotho/South Africa: Lesotho Highlands Water Project (Loan No. 4339-LSO) (26 April 1999).

[144] The Inspection Panel Report, Investigation Report, Paraguay—Reform Project for the Water and Telecommunications Sector (Loan No. 3842-PA); Argentina—SEGBA V Power Distribution Project (Loan 2854-AR), at 148–57.

to those living in the Project area. It is also imperative that such Area Specific Oil Spill Plans contain a review of the response to a spill to watercourses that form part of the watershed of Lake Chad.[145]

In its investigation report into the Western Poverty Reduction Project in China, the Inspection Panel noted that the environmental impact assessment relating to the project dealing with the improvement and the building of dams, as well as the construction of irrigation and drainage systems, was inadequate for predicting either possible environmental or social impacts. In particular, it did not adequately assess the impact of the dam on water resources and on the region's ecology, including salt marsh wetlands. Moreover, it stated that the environmental impact assessment 'is uninformative about the layout of the new towns and villages, their infrastructure, and the facilities such as water, heat and light that will be provided for the settlers'.[146] The Inspection Panel concluded that Bank Management had violated the Environmental Assessment policy, the Indigenous Peoples policy, and the Involuntary Resettlement policy.[147]

In April 2004, the World Bank Inspection Panel registered a request for an inspection of a water supply project in Cartagena. According to the request, the project involves an upgrading and expansion of Cartagena's water and sewerage system, which includes the construction of a pipeline and submarine outfall that will carry the city's essentially untreated wastewater 20 kilometres north of the city and discharge it into the Caribbean Sea. The requesters claim that the project affects some coastal fishing villages close to the proposed outfall discharge site. The residents of these villages are indigenous people who maintain a subsistence living from fishing and farming in this area. In the view of the requesters, this project will also have major health implications for fishermen, residents, and others exposed to the polluted waters.[148]

d. Aarhus compliance mechanism

Apart from the mechanisms already mentioned, compliance mechanisms such as those provided under Multilateral Environmental Agreements (MEAs) may be new fora for non-State actors. Although in most MEAs non-State actors are not entitled to make communications claiming that a State Party to the agreement is

[145] The Inspection Panel Investigation Report Chad-Cameroon Petroleum and Pipeline Project (Loan No. 4558-CD); Petroleum Sector Management Capacity Building Project (Credit No. 3373-CD); and Management of the Petroleum Economy (Credit No. 3316-CD) (17 September 2002) at 99.

[146] The Inspection Panel Report and Recommendation on Request for Inspection Re: Request for Inspection China: Western Poverty Reduction Project (Credit No. 3255-CHA and Loan No. 4501-CHA) (28 April 2000), at 229.

[147] In relation to this case it may be noted that, on 7 July 2000, before the Executive Directors were able to reach a conclusion on the Inspection Panel Investigation Report, China withdrew its application for one of the loan components on the grounds that new conditions were unacceptable as the loan conditions had already been agreed upon, and noted that it would pay for the project itself.

[148] Notice of Registration Re: Request for Inspection Colombia: Cartagena Water Supply, Sewerage and Environmental Management Project (Loan No. 4507-CO) (22 April 2004). On July 13, 2004, the World Bank's Board of Executive Directors approved the Panel's recommendation to conduct an investigation, http://wbln0018.worldbank.org/.

not fulfilling its obligations under an agreement,[149] an innovative procedure has been adopted under the Aarhus Convention. Under this new mechanism, members of the public may make communications concerning a Party's compliance with the Convention.[150] The right of the public to make communications[151] to the Aarhus compliance committee, as well as the entitlement for NGOs officially to submit candidatures for the committee's membership,[152] are the most innovative features of this compliance mechanism. The new characteristics of the Aarhus compliance mechanism reflect the principles of public participation, transparency, and access to justice that are endorsed by the Aarhus Convention itself.

While focusing on public participation and access to justice, the Aarhus compliance mechanism also encompasses water-related issues. In particular, the failure to allow for public participation in water-related decision-making processes may be challenged before the Aarhus compliance committee. This was the case in a communication submitted by an NGO, Ecopravo Lviv, concerning the Ukrainian project of building a navigable ship canal to the Black Sea through the Danube Delta.[153] The communication by the NGO raises important water-related issues such as the protection of the Danube Delta, which is a Wetland of International Importance under the Ramsar Convention on Wetlands as well as a Biosphere Reserve protected by the UNESCO 'Man and the Biosphere' Program.

Ecopravo-Lviv alleged non-compliance by Ukraine with Article 6 of the Aarhus Convention. This provision provides, *inter alia*, that 'the public concerned shall be informed, either by public notice or individually as appropriate, early in an environmental decision-making procedure, and in an adequate, timely and effective manner...'. According to the Ecopravo-Lviv communication: 'The fact that [the] Ministry of Environment did not inform EPL (Ecopravo-Lviv], either by a public notice or individually, and even not upon our written request, of the commencement of the state environmental expertiza and

[149] *See, inter alia*, the compliance procedures under: the Montreal Protocol to the 1985 Vienna Convention on Substances that Deplete the Ozone Layer (Decision IV/5); Geneva Protocol concerning the Control of Emissions of Volatile Organic Compounds (VOCs) and Oslo Protocol on Further Reduction of Sulphur Emissions to the 1979 Convention on Long-Range Transboundary Air Pollution (Decision 1997/2); Convention on Environmental Impact Assessment in a Transboundary Context (Decision III/2); Basel Convention on the Transboundary Movement of Hazardous Wastes and Their Disposal (Decision VI/12).

[150] Decision I/7, Meeting of the Parties, 2002, ECE/MP.PP/2/Add.8, 2004, paras 18–24, www.unece.org.

[151] According to para. 20 of Decision I/7, the compliance committee 'shall consider any such communication unless it determines that the communication is: (a) Anonymous; (b) An abuse of the right to make such communications; (c) Manifestly unreasonable; (d) Incompatible with the provisions of this decision or with the Convention'. When determining the admissibility of the communication, the compliance committee should also take into account 'any available domestic remedy unless the application of the remedy is unreasonably prolonged or obviously does not provide an effective and sufficient means of redress'. Decision I/7, *ibid.*, paras 20–21.

[152] *Ibid.*, para. 4.

[153] Communication ACCC/C/2004/03-Ukraine, 6 May 2004. For the text of the communication submitted to the Compliance Committee, *see* http://www.ecopravo.lviv.ua/files/Danube/Aarhus%20Complaint.doc.

its procedure leads to breach of the obligations set by paragraph 2 of the Article 6 [of the Aarhus Convention],'[154] In particular, Ecopravo-Lviv's communication to the Aarhus compliance committee was motivated by the lack of information on the commencement of the State environmental impact assessment (environmental expertiza) and the short timeframe between the publication of the State environmental expertiza and the approval of the project by the Ukrainian Ministry of the Environment.[155]

Although most agreements on transboundary waters, including the 1997 UN Watercourses Convention, do not provide for compliance mechanisms, some instruments, such as the 1999 *Protocol on Water and Health to the Convention on the Protection and Use of Transboundary Watercourses and International Lakes*,[156] foresee the elaboration of a compliance procedure. In this regard, the draft decision on the compliance mechanism to be adopted at the first meeting of the Parties to the Protocol on Water and Health is interesting, as it will entitle non-State actors to make communications concerning a Party's compliance with the Protocol.[157] This compliance mechanism will certainly have a great impact on the settlement of water-related disputes.

[154] Communication ACCC/C/2004/03-Ukraine, 6 May 2004. For the text of the communication submitted to the Compliance Committee, *see* http://www.ecopravo.lviv.ua/files/Danube/Aarhus%20 Complaint.doc., para. 85.

[155] In relation to this case, it should be noted that, in 2003, Ecopravo-Lviv filed a lawsuit before national courts against the Ministry of Environment challenging the conclusions of the State environmental expertiza. However, while the first instance national court ruled that the Ministry of Environment violated the right of the public to participate in the State environmental expertiza, the Appeal Court annulled the court of first instance's decision and dismissed Ecopravo-Lviv's suit. The court ruled, in particular, that 'the Ministry of Environment might involve [the] public into the state environmental expertiza, but had no obligation to do so' (*see* Communication from Ecopravo-Lviv, *ibid.*, paras 112–114). Moreover, before filing a complaint with the Aarhus compliance committee, Ecopravo-Lviv attempted to bring a communication before the implementation committee of the Convention on Environmental Impact Assessment in a Transboundary Context (Espoo Convention), claiming that Ukraine violated this Convention by not carrying out an environmental impact assessment in a transboundary context. However, at its Fifth Meeting, the Espoo Implementation Committee dismissed the claim on procedural grounds. According to the Report on the Fifth Meeting of the Implementation Committee, 'the majority [of the Implementation Committee] agreed not to consider the information, because considering unsolicited information from NGOs and the public relating to specific cases of non-compliance was not within the Committee's existing mandate. A minority disagreed, interpreting the present mandate to mean that there were no restrictions on how the Committee became aware of a case of possible non-compliance, preferring to examine the information further'. Report of the Fifth Meeting of the Implementation Committee, MP.EIA/WG.1/2004/4, 8 April 2004, para. 7.

[156] Protocol on Water and Health to the 1992 UN/ECE Watercourse Convention, London, 17 June 1999, www.unece.org.

[157] Draft Decision, Review of Compliance to be adopted at the first meeting of the Parties to the Protocol on Water and Health, MP.WAT/AC.4/2004/8, 23 July 2004, www.unece.org. *See also* the *Geneva Strategy and Framework for Monitoring Compliance with Agreements on Transboundary Waters*, setting out the principles and guidelines meant to provide guidance for the establishment of compliance review procedures for any legal instruments negotiated under, or in connection with, the UN/ECE Watercourse Convention. In particular, the Geneva Strategy invites Parties to focus on 'whether it is appropriate for the Compliance Review Committee to consider communications from the public' (para. 23.a). *Geneva Strategy and Framework for Monitoring Compliance with Agreements on Transboundary Waters*, Meeting of the Parties to the Convention on the Protection and Use of Transboundary Watercourses and International Lakes, MP.WAT/2000/5, 23–25 March 2000, www.thewaterpage.com.

4. Conclusions

Water protection and management issues are playing a growing role in the context of dispute settlement mechanisms and procedures at the inter-State level, as well as in relation to procedures involving non-State actors. Almost all international dispute settlement bodies have dealt with water issues. This trend can be explained by the complex nature of water disputes, which may involve multiple factors. Indeed, in almost all cases, water disputes are embedded in wider disputes involving issues of pollution abatement, investment protection, human rights, or trade policies.

Moreover, dispute settlement mechanisms and procedures nowadays are characterized by their openness to a wide array of actors, be they States, international organizations, or non-State actors. Non-State actors, such as individuals, NGOs, and private firms, have gained *locus standi* before various dispute settlement mechanisms. At the same time, the existence of the various sets of rules allows water disputes to be tackled in new ways. The opening of dispute settlement mechanisms to several actors and the emergence of specialized universal and regional dispute settlement bodies represent a key element in the development of a corpus of norms and principles with respect to water disputes. This situation contributes to greater legal normalcy in the operation of international law in the water area.

15

Transparency, Public Participation, and Amicus Curiae *in Water Disputes*

MAKANE MOÏSE MBENGUE and MARA TIGNINO

1. Introduction

Public participation confers a new standing to the rights and duties of individuals in international law.[1] It challenges established boundaries and concepts of law by cutting across distinctions and dichotomies, such as national versus international law, private versus public law, and private versus public interests.[2] Public participation itself

> reflects the increased concern of international law with issues once thought to be part of a state's *domaine réservé*, such as public participation, transparency, legal procedure, public administration, secrecy, and the very notion of democracy itself—that is, issues the regulation of which usually is considered to be one of the essential attributes of state sovereignty.[3]

A deep analysis of the notion of public participation shows its polymorphous and hybrid nature. From one point of view, public participation can be interpreted as a general category. In this sense, public participation should be considered, *lato sensu*, as a philosophy, an approach in the management of natural resources, shared or not, as well as an archetype in international, national, and local decision-making. Consequently it can also be regarded as a model of

[1] A. Cassese, International Law (2001), at 81 ('[T]hat, strictly speaking, there is nothing to prevent States from providing in international rules for international obligations incumbent upon individuals and corresponding rights accruing to them, in the international field. What matters is the intention of the lawmakers.')

[2] *See* J. Ebbesson, *The Notion of Public Participation in International Environmental Law*, Yearbook of International Environmental Law, 8 (1997), at 55. *See also*, B. Conforti, International Law and the Role of Domestic Legal Systems (1993), at 125–6. The Convention on Access to Information, Public Participation in Decision-Making and Access to Justice in Environmental Matters, 25 June 1998, 38 *I.L.M.* 517 (1999) (hereinafter the Aarhus Convention), e.g., more or less precisely, defines the 'legal position' of private persons—their rights, duties, and competences that are to be provided for in national law. Thus, while formally addressed to States, these international norms are ultimately directed at individuals through the intermediary of national institutions.

[3] J. Ebbesson, *supra* note 2, at 55.

international governance. In this context, public participation is an operative and interactive notion, which includes the concepts of transparency, access to justice, and public participation *stricto sensu*. Public participation *stricto sensu* or *per se* should be regarded as a procedural issue which affords non-State actors, to participate actively in decision-making processes concerning natural resources. Whereas public participation *lato sensu* involves States[4] and non-State actors through the framework of transnational participation,[5] public participation *stricto sensu* is limited to the involvement of non-State actors.[6] This chapter focuses mainly on this last issue.

Before analysing the relationship between public participation and water issues, it seems interesting to point out some cornerstones of its history in international environmental law. The road to transparency and public participation in international and regional instruments has been long, and it is still under construction. While public participation and 'access to justice' in environmental matters became an issue in domestic discourse and law in the 1970s,[7] it took another fifteen to twenty years for the topic to attain equal attention in international law and policy. This is not to say that the issue was entirely neglected in the international context until the 1990s;[8] in 1972, this topic was addressed by

[4] In international law procedures such as notification, prior informed consent and advance informed agreement are based on access to information and participation between States. *See*, e.g., Convention for the Protection of the Marine Environment of the North-East Atlantic (OSPAR Convention), Paris, 22 September 1992, available at http://www.ospar.org/; Prior Informed Consent Procedure (Rotterdam Convention), 10 September 1998, 38 *I.L.M.* (1999), at 1; Cartagena Protocol on Biosafety to the Convention on Biological Diversity, 29 January 2000, entered into force on 11 September 2003, 39 *I.L.M.* (2000), at 1027; United Nations Convention on the Non-Navigational Uses of International Watercourses, 21 May 1997, U.N. Doc. A/RES/51/869, 36 *I.L.M.* (1997), at 700. On the question of public participation between States, *see Dispute Concerning Access to Information Under Article 9 of the OSPAR Convention (Ireland versus United Kingdom of Great Britain and Northern Ireland)*, Permanent Court of Arbitration, Award of 2 July 2003.

[5] On the question *see* E. Benvenisti, CAMBRIDGE STUDIES IN INTERNATIONAL AND COMPARATIVE LAW, SHARING TRANSBOUNDARY RESOURCES: INTERNATIONAL LAW AND OPTIMAL RESOURCE USE, 43–63 (2002).

[6] The Rio Declaration specifically mentions women (Principle 20), youth (Principle 21), and indigenous people and other local communities (Principle 22). Agenda 21, in its section 3 (Strengthening the role of major groups), goes further to include workers, trade unions, business and industry, the scientific community, and farmers among the enumerated groups, and included among the activities aimed at strengthening their role, promoting freedom of association and strengthening participation and consultation. *See also infra*, the definition of the term 'public' in many public participation-related conventions.

[7] N. Wengert, *Citizen Participation: Practice in Search of a Theory*, 16 NAT. RESOURCES J. 23 (1976); K. Raustiala, *The Participatory Revolution in International Environmental Law*, 21 HARVARD ENVIRONMENTAL LAW REVIEW, 1997, at 537; L. P. Breckenridge, *Nonprofit Environmental Organizations and the Restructuring of Institutions for Ecosystem Management*, 25 ECOLOGY L.Q., at 692.

[8] *See*, e.g., 1966 International Covenant on Civil and Political Rights, adopted by the United Nations General Assembly in New York on 16 December 1996. Its Art. 19 deals with the 'freedom to seek, receive and impart information.' *See also* 1980 Salzburg Declaration on the Protection of the Right of Information and of Participation, adopted at the Second European Conference on the Environment and Human Rights at Salzburg (Austria) on 3 December 1980; 1981 Council of Europe Recommendation N°(81) 19 of the Committee of Ministers to member States on the access to information held by public authorities, adopted at Strasbourg (France) on 25 November 1981.

the international community at the Stockholm Conference on the Human Environment.[9]

Three main international documents can be seen as the landmark texts in relation to what could be defined *proprio motu* as the international law of public participation: two of them are 'soft law' instruments and one is a conventional text. The starting point of the international law of public participation is the 1982 World Charter for Nature adopted by the UN General Assembly.[10]

The Rio Declaration on Environment and Development can be considered as the 'catalyseur' text concerning the international law of public participation. Indeed, in 1992, more than 150 States agreed at the Rio Conference on Environment and Development (UNCED) that '[e]nvironmental issues are best handled with the *participation of all concerned citizens*, at the relevant level'. Principle 10 was significant as a clear global expression of the developing concept of public participation in relation to the environment.[11] More specifically, Chapter 18 of Agenda 21 of the UNCED calls for active public participation in shared freshwater management,[12] which includes not only the provision of a right of hearing to oppose plans that could be detrimental to certain individuals or groups, but, more generally, requires States to aim for 'an approach of full public participation, including that of women, youth, indigenous people and local communities in water management policy-making and decision-making'[13] and suggests the 'development of public participatory techniques and their implementation in decision-making'.[14]

Although the States' practice in public participation issues is not yet well established, the Aarhus Convention[15] 'crystallizes' the materialization of a branch of international law devoted to public participation through the consolidation of an emerging *opinio juris*.[16] An *opinio juris* constituting the

[9] The 1972 Action Plan for the Human Environment, Recommendation 7(a). In different respects, public participation is also referred to in Recommendations 39(a) and 97. In addition to that, Principle 19 of the 1972 Stockholm Declaration recognizes the need for improving education and public awareness in the field of the environment. *Report of the United Nations Conference on the Human Environment*, UN doc. A/CONF/48/14/Rev. 1, 11 *I.L.M.*, (1972) at 1416.

[10] *See* the World Charter for Nature, UN/GA 37/7 (1982), paras 16, 23, and 24.

[11] Within Principle 10, three pillars are addressed internationally: access to information, public participation, and access to judicial and administrative proceedings.

[12] *See* E. Hey, *Sustainable Use of Shared Water Resources: The Need for a Paradigmatic Shift in International Watercourses Law*, in THE PEACEFUL MANAGEMENT OF TRANSBOUNDARY RESOURCES, 133 (Gerald H. Blake et al. eds, 1995).

[13] Agenda 21, Principle 18.9(c).

[14] Agenda 21, Principle 18.12(n).

[15] *Supra* note 2.

[16] According to Kofi Annan, 'Although regional in scope, the significance of the Aarhus Convention is global. It is by far the most impressive elaboration of principle 10 of the Rio Declaration, which stresses the need for citizen's participation in environmental issues and for access to information on the environment held by public authorities. As such it is the most ambitious venture in the area of "environmental democracy" so far undertaken under the auspices of the United Nations' (available at http://www.unece.org/env/pp/). The idea of an emerging *opinio juris* is exemplified, after the adoption of the Aarhus Convention, by several texts which recognize the right of public participation. *See*, e.g., 1999 Water and Health Protocol to the UN/ECE Convention on the Protection and Use of International Watercourses and Transboundary Lakes; 2003 Protocol on Pollutant Release and Transfer Registers to the Aarhus Convention; 2003 Protocol on Strategic Environmental Assessment

foundation of the international law of public participation and characterized—*ex ante*—by the access to information and—*ex post*—by the access to justice is not a utopia. In order to prove this, it is sufficient to decipher and analyse the panoply of environmental treaties which set out norms on information, participation, and access to court at the domestic level.[17] Public participation is at the crossroads of the protection and the management of the environment. Water issues are intrinsically and extrinsically linked to the protection of the environment.[18] As a result, water issues fall under the *ratione* and the problematics of public participation. Several reasons explain why water issues request a public participation approach. Given the often transboundary nature of water resources and their diverse uses, several actors, such as governments, intergovernmental organizations, and non-governmental organizations (NGOs), are involved in water-related activities and in any disputes that arise. Decisions involving natural resources in general, and water in particular, increasingly have an international dimension. Often several States, international organizations, and/or multinational corporations are involved in the decision-making process and, consequently, also in any disputes that arise. In particular, the involvement of multilateral organizations has led to water management attaining global dimensions, especially in developing countries, where organizations such as the World Bank and regional development banks are involved in water-related projects. Specific activities, plans, or policies regarding water issues are likely to cause transboundary effects, which give rise to a public interest in both States

to the Convention on Environmental Impact Assessment in a Transboundary Context, available at http://www.unece.org/. *See Dissenting Opinion of Gavan Griffith in the Dispute Concerning Article 9 of the OSPAR Convention (Ireland\UK)*, Final Award, Permanent Court of Arbitration, The Hague, 2 July 2003, at 70, para. 12: '. . . certain provisions of the Aarhus Convention may be recognized as reflecting or codifying customary practice and general principles of international law that are binding on the Parties [to the OSPAR Convention] . . .'

[17] Several conventions on civil liability, relating to nuclear accidents, marine pollution from ships, and other dangerous activities, provide rules on standing and jurisdiction that are to be implemented in domestic laws. Other treaties foresee the establishment of procedures for public participation, either in general terms or in more specific terms related to environmental impact assessment, to measures for the prevention of, and preparedness for, industrial accidents, and to the formulation of certain programs and policies. *See*, e.g., Convention on Third Party Liability in the Field of Nuclear Energy, 29 July 1969, 956 *U.N.T.S.*, at 251, as amended 28 January 1964, 956 *U.N.T.S.*, at 325; Vienna Convention on Civil Liability for Nuclear Damage, 21 May 1963, 2 *I.L.M.* (1963), at 727; International Convention on Civil Liability for Oil Pollution Damage, 29 November 1969, 9 *I.L.M.* (1970), at 46; International Convention on Liability and Compensation for Damage in Connection with the Carriage of Hazardous and Noxious Substances by Sea, 6 May 1996, 35 *I.L.M.* (1996), at 1406; 1991 UN/ECE Convention on Environmental Impact Assessment in a Transboundary Context [hereinafter the Espoo Convention], 25 February 1991, 30 *I.L.M.* (1991), at 800; Protocol to the 1979 Convention on Long-Range Transboundary Air Pollution concerning the Control of Emission of Volatile Organic Compounds or their Transboundary Fluxes, 18 November 1991, 31 *I.L.M.* (1992), at 568; United Nations Framework Convention on Climate Change (UNFCC), 31 *I.L.M.* (1992), at 1330.

[18] Several definitions of the meaning of 'environment' include water resources. The Aarhus Convention lists examples to illustrate what is meant by 'elements of the environment'. These elements in this non-exhaustive list include 'air and atmosphere', 'water', 'soil, land, landscape and natural sites', and 'biological diversity and its components, including genetically modified organisms'.

involved.[19] This means that whenever individuals or NGOs in the State where the activity takes place can pursue public environmental interests, the same options must be available to individuals and NGOs based in neighboring States that wish to pursue public interests in regard to the activity.

Public participation and access to information (as specific tools for transparency) are matrix vectors for the avoidance of water disputes. In particular, they ensure consensus between multiple stakeholders in relation to water-related projects, avoiding—and even annihilating—emerging water disputes. As such, they operate in *a priori* logic to prevent the arising of water disputes. In case of water disputes, public participation and transparency must still be provided for.

Water law disputes have been singled out as a category in which non-State intervention representing a public interest concern is most needed. In order to explain the role of non-State actors in designing and implementing international water law, two factors have to be considered: the development of the concept of 'community interest', and the recognition of individual, group, and collective rights. In this regard, policy-makers increasingly recognized the 'global dimension' in the use, management, protection, and conservation of freshwater resources. Moreover, it should be observed that water-related problems primarily affect individuals and group of individuals at the local level.[20]

In recent years, many NGOs have claimed that the rights of citizens and civil society have been infringed by GATT/WTO rules and regional trade agreements such as NAFTA.[21] Indeed, the increasing ramifications of international trade are not concerned primarily with tariff reduction and the like, but extend more deeply into the inner workings of the State. Consequently, groups have been demanding increased access to and participation in WTO and NAFTA functions to ensure the representation of all interests. The skepticism of many is arguably heightened by the confidentiality of the WTO's and NAFTA's dispute settlement mechanisms. In this context, NGOs of many types have requested the right to submit *amicus curiae* briefs to WTO[22] and NAFTA dispute settlement bodies.

The issue of whether the WTO and regional trade agreements are open and transparent is not limited to NGOs and public participation in the dispute settlement mechanisms. The issue of transparency is also about increased access to documents and greater public participation in WTO or NAFTA meetings. One

[19] M. T. Ponte Iglesias, *Les accords conclus par les autorités locales de différents Etats sur l'utilisation des eaux transfrontalières dans le cadre de la coopération transfrontalière*, 2 Schweizerische Zeitschrift fuer Internationales und Europaeisches Recht 103 (1995).

[20] A. Tanzi & C. Pitea, 'Emerging Trends in the Role of Non-State Actors in International Water Disputes', in *Resolution of International Water Disputes* (Peace Palace Papers, Kluwer Law International, 2003) at 259–60.

[21] North American Free Trade Agreement between the governments of Canada, Mexico, and United States, 1 January 1994, reprinted in 32 *I.L.M* (1993), at 289, also available at: http://www.worldtradelaw.net/nafta/index.htm.

[22] *See* L. Boisson de Chazournes & M. M. Mbengue, *The* Amici Curiae *and the WTO Dispute Settlement System: The Doors are Open*, 2 The Law and Practice of International Courts and Tribunals 205–48 (2003).

central argument supporting NGOs' participation in WTO and NAFTA matters is the role that NGOs can play in disseminating information at the national level.

Leaving aside considerations about the legitimacy of NGOs' claims for greater transparency and further public participation in the WTO and NAFTA, our purpose is to discuss the actions that these institutions have taken to increase transparency and openness. The paper draws attention to the practice of WTO panels and other international fora, such as the NAFTA and ICSID, in relation to involvement of non-parties through the use of witnesses and experts as well as of *amici* briefs. In this context, it is important to observe that when NGOs are allowed to act as witnesses or as an *amicus curiae*, they do not gain standing *per se* but may participate at the discretion of the tribunal. Under the Permanent Court of Arbitration Optional Rules for Arbitration of Disputes relating to Natural Resources and/or the Environment (hereinafter PCA Environmental Rules)[23] and the 2000 Southern African Development Community Protocol on Tribunal and Rules of Procedures Thereof[24] (2000 SADC Protocol on the Tribunal), non-State actors have a *locus standi* before international tribunals. Thus, private parties have an access to justice and they may take advantage of the PCA Environmental Rules and of the SADC Tribunal as parties to a dispute. When private parties have no *locus standi* before dispute settlement bodies, tribunals may accept the submission of *amici* briefs. Although not parties to a dispute, through the submission of *amici* briefs, non-State actors may express their concerns on the issues submitted to the tribunals. Therefore, the receipt of *amici* briefs strengthens the notions of public participation and transparency in dispute settlement mechanisms.

This chapter will focus first on issues of transparency and public participation as means of water-disputes avoidance. Public participation and access to information play an essential role in the avoidance of water disputes. This role is recognized in several conventional texts, such as the Aarhus Convention and the Senegal Water Charter.[25] The aim of the first section will be to show that the concept of public participation is dynamic. Effective public participation in the taking of decisions enables the public to express, and the decision-maker to take account of, opinions and concerns which may be relevant to those decisions. Thus, contributing to public awareness of environmental issues, it increases the accountability and the transparency of the decision-making process.

In its second section, this chapter will turn to the settlement of water disputes with special focus on international trade law. This section will point out the

[23] PCA Environmental Rules, adopted 19 June 2001, reprinted in YEARBOOK OF INTERNATIONAL LAW ARBITRATION, p. 425 (2001), also available at www.pca-cpa.org/EDR/ENRrules.htm.

[24] Southern African Development Community Protocol on Tribunal and Rules of Procedures Thereof, Windhoek, 7 August 2000, Arts 15(1),(3) and 18. SADC documents available at www.sadc.int.

[25] Organisation pour la Mise en Valeur du Fleuve Sénégal, OMVS, Charte des Eaux du Fleuve Sénégal, 18 May 2002. Text available at www.lexana.org (only French version available).

actions that the WTO and the NAFTA have taken with the aim to increase their transparency and openness. Two issues will be particularly addressed: the role of *amici* briefs as means of public participation before dispute settlement bodies; and the issue of transparency in arbitration proceedings. *Amici* briefs and access to information on the tribunal proceedings are essential in order to ensure public participation and transparency in the settlement of water disputes.

Lastly, the chapter will highlight the role of compliance mechanisms established by international financial organizations such as the World Bank, the Asian Development Bank, and the Inter-American Development Bank. These mechanisms constitute a new vehicle of public participation in water disputes. Indeed, they provide the intended beneficiaries of banks' projects with a new tool of participation. Under these mechanisms, non-State actors can file requests against projects financed by these financial institutions.[26] Thus, non-State actors have the opportunity to participate in the formulation and implementation of banks' projects.

2. Water-disputes avoidance: issues of transparency and public participation

> One of the fundamental prerequisites for the achievement of sustainable development is broad public participation in decision-making. Furthermore, in the more specific context of environment and development, the need for new forms of participation has emerged. This includes the need of individuals, groups and organizations to participate in environmental impact assessment procedures and to know about and participate in decisions, particularly those that potentially affect the communities in which they live and work. Individuals, groups and organizations should have access to information relevant to environment and development held by national authorities, including information on products and activities that have or are likely to have significant impact on the environment, and information on environmental protection measures.[27]

This profession of faith, expressed by the Agenda 21, underscores the importance of public participation and access to information in the field of the management of natural resources such as water. It also affirms the interaction and the inter-changeability between these two notions.

A practical benefit of public participation and access to information in water issues is the enhancement of the quality and implementation of decisions.[28] The quality of decisions can be improved by the public's provision of additional information, as well as through the influence that advocacy of alternative

[26] *See also*, P. Cullet & A. Gowlland-Gualtieri's chapter in this book.

[27] Agenda 21, Chapter 23, 23.2.

[28] *See* Economic Commission for Europe, *The Aarhus Convention: An Implementation Guide*, United Nations, New York and Geneva, 2000. In the preamble to the Aarhus Convention, the Parties recognize that, in the field of the environment, access to information and public participation in decision-making 'enhances the quality and the implementation of decisions'.

solutions can have on the careful consideration of possible solutions. Members of the public will often have a special knowledge of local conditions and of the practical implications of proposed activities. The implementation of decisions can be improved when the members of the public who are most interested in the result have been included in the process and have had their concerns considered. In such cases, their support can be expected to increase,[29] restricting the probability of possible disputes. The public and authorities often have a common interest in achieving an optimal result for the good of society, although there might be disagreement as to the means or as to the balancing of interests. The active involvement of the public in a transparent decision-making process confirms the accountability[30] of the public authorities, and increases respect for them and for their decisions, even among those members of the public who have had to suffer a loss as a result of the final decision. In the absence of such accountability, members of the public who may be adversely affected by a decision will think the worst, and assume that the public authority has been corrupted by special interests. In this context, disputes can be expected.[31]

Public participation and access to information play an essential role in the avoidance of water disputes. This role is recognized in several conventional texts, such as the Senegal Water Charter.[32] In particular, its Article 2 states that one of the objectives of the Charter is to specify how private parties will be able to participate in the management of the river. Through the Permanent Water Commission (Commission Permanente des Eaux, PWC), NGOs, representatives of local communities, and private users are involved in decision-making concerning the allocation of water to various use sectors, as well as in the decisions regarding projects and measures planned in Member States[33]. Therefore, the PWC increases the involvement of representatives of various stakeholders in the resource management decision-making process.

With the aim to avoid water disputes, access to information on water-related activities and effective participation in the taking of decisions are indispensable. Both means are necessary for the avoidance of water disputes.

[29] Ninth preambular paragraph of the Aarhus Convention, *supra* note 2.

[30] *See*, on the concept of 'accountability', I. F. I. Shihata, The World Bank Inspection Panel: In Practice, 2nd edn (2000) at 237–40.

[31] Tenth preambular paragraph of the Aarhus Convention, *supra* note 2.

[32] *Supra* note 25.

[33] Under Art. 23 of the Charter, NGOs and representatives of local communities (also at district level), as well as as private users, attend the meetings of the PWC as observers. According to this provision, the decisions concerning the status of observer are taken by the Council of Ministers. In light of Art. 19, the most important task of the PWC is to establish principles and modalities in the allocation of water to various use sectors. In accordance with Art. 26, the PWC is entitled to advise the Council of Ministers whether projects and measures planned in Member States are consistent with the organization's objectives. In particular, whether they may have an adverse effect upon, *inter alia*, human health or water quality (Art. 10 of the Charter specifies the projects submitted to the regime of prior authorization). Several articles of the Charter refer to the rights of the individuals in relation to the Senegal water: Art. 4 establishes the rights of the riparian States, as well as those of the individuals over the utilization of the Senegal.

2.1 Access to information on water-related activities

Access to information and transparency are closely linked. Transparency means that the public can clearly follow the path of environmental information, understanding its origin, the criteria that govern its collection, holding, and dissemination, and how it can be obtained.[34] Water issues fall under the scope of environmental information.[35] Indeed, environmental information[36] includes any information relating to the state of the elements of the environment.[37] Environmental information may be in any material form, which specifically includes written, visual, aural, and electronic form.[38] Thus, paper documents, photographs, illustrations, video and audio recordings, as well as computer files, are all examples of the form the information can take.[39] Access to information for specific water issues can be expressly provided for in certain instruments.[40] By analogy, referring to the definition of environmental information mentioned in the European Directive on public access to environmental information,[41] one may consider, in short, that 'water-related environmental information' could be defined as

> any information in written, visual, aural, electronic or any other material form on:
> (a) the state of water and the interaction among water and other elements of the environment such as air and atmosphere, soil, land, landscape;
> (b) factors, such as substances, energy, noise, radiation or waste, including radioactive waste, emissions, discharges and other releases into the water, affecting or likely to affect water;

[34] *The Aarhus Convention: An Implementation Guide, supra* note 28, at 5–6.

[35] The definition of environmental information is of central importance to Art. 4 on access to environmental information and Art. 5 on the collection and dissemination of environmental information of the Aarhus Convention. *See*, e.g., *Dispute Concerning Article 9 of the OSPAR Convention (Ireland/UK), supra* note 4.

[36] Some environmental treaties prescribe the use of environmental information as 'best environmental practice'. *See*, e.g., Convention on the Protection of the Marine Environment of the Baltic Sea Area, Arts 3 and 6 and Annex II; OSPAR Convention, Art. 3, Annex I and Appendix 1; UN/ECE Convention on the Protection and Use of International Watercourses and Transboundary Lakes, Helsinki, 17 March 1992, Art. 3 and Annex II.

[37] *See*, e.g., Directive 2003/4/EC of the European Parliament and of the Council of 28 January 2003 on public access to environmental information and repealing Council Directive 90/313/EEC, *Official Journal of the European Union*, L 41/26 (14 February 2003), para. 10. *See also* the Aarhus Convention.

[38] The Aarhus Convention makes reference to information technology in Art. 2(3) (information in electronic form) and in Art. 5(3) (accessible electronic databases) and (9) (structured, computerized, and publicly accessible database), *supra* note 2.

[39] It is also important to distinguish between documents and information. E.g., the Aarhus Convention guarantees access to *information*. The 'material form' language is not meant to restrict the definition of environmental information to finished products or other documentation as that may be formally understood. Information in raw and unprocessed form is obtainable as well as documents, *see The Aarhus Convention: An Implementation Guide, supra* note 28, at 54.

[40] *See*, e.g., Protocol on Pollutant Release and Transfer Registers, which provides for access to information in the field of specific water issues, *supra* note 16.

[41] Directive 2003/4/EC of the European Parliament and of the Council of 28 January 2003 on public access to environmental information and repealing Council Directive 90/313/EEC, *supra* note 37, Art. 2(1).

(c) measures (including administrative measures), such as policies, legislation, plans, programs, water (or environmental) agreements, and activities affecting or likely to affect water and factors referred to in (b) as well as measures or activities designed to protect water;
(d) reports on the implementation of water (or environmental) legislation;
(e) cost-benefit and other economic analyses and assumptions used within the framework of the measures and activities referred to in (c).

While the States enjoy discretion in choosing the means of distributing the information, the Aarhus Convention specifies certain elements that must be part of the information provided.[42] These elements include, for example, the names of the companies involved in the activity, comprehensible explanations of the hazardous activities concerned, descriptions of the substances used and their properties, precautionary measures taken, and contingency plans adopted. The Aarhus Convention does not establish any minimum or mandatory elements to be included in the system; it provides only that such a system 'may' include information on inputs, releases, and transfers of substances and products from a specific range of activities to environmental media and so on.[43]

Access to information in this context grants a right to know which is extensible.[44] This right to know, or this right of access to information, implies a double-faceted obligation: on the one hand it is characterized by a vertical relation State/non-State actors; on the other hand it also establishes a horizontal relation non-State actor/non-State actor. Concerning the first relation, there is an obligation on the part of the State to collect and make available the information,[45] and also an obligation on the part of the operators of potentially harmful activities to transmit relevant information about their activities to the competent authorities.[46] With the relation non-State actor/non-State actor, operators have the obligation to make information available to the public regarding their activities.[47]

[42] *See*, e.g., Convention on Transboundary Effects of Industrial Accidents, Helsinki, 17 March 1992, 31 *I.L.M.* (1992) 1330, Annex VIII.

[43] Art. 5(9) of the Aarhus Convention, *supra* note 2.

[44] P. H. Sands, *Information Disclosure as an Instrument of Environmental Governance*, 63 Zeitschrift für ausländisches öffentliches Recht und Völkerrecht 487 (2003). *See also*, J. Ebbesson, *supra* note 2, at 89: 'From states, international obligations with respect to environmental information may include the collection of information and its dissemination either to other states or to non-state actors... From the perspective of individuals and other non-state actors, access to relevant information is a concern not only when new harmful operations are examined or when existing permits are reviewed; it also comprises continuous access for citizens to accurate information on the state of the environment.'

[45] A comprehensive right-to-know implies an obligation for each State to provide user-friendly systems whereby individuals may seek specified environmental information. *See*, e.g., Protocol on pollutant release and transfer registers, *supra* note 40, Art. 4.

[46] *See* Protocol on pollutant release and transfer registers, Art. 7. States may encourage operators to disseminate information on the environmental impacts of their activities and products through voluntary systems like eco-labelling and eco-auditing (see, Art. 5(6) of the Aarhus Convention).

[47] It concerns the flow of information from an 'operator' directly to the public. An 'operator' can be a private enterprise or a governmental body that conducts activities with a significant impact on the environment.

One fundamental problem in the field of environmental information about water issues is that it can challenge the confidentiality characterizing trade and commercial activities.[48] Especially from the side of private companies, several issues can be often raised, such as, *inter alia*, that the information required may allow or assist competitors to build market share or to benchmark their own operations, or allow customers or competitors to understand the specific economics and processes of the fabrication of an item. Still more complex is the topic of the distinction between the issues pertaining *ex facie* to the environmental information and the questions which are *stricto sensu* related to the trade information. The recent dispute concerning Article 9 of the OSPAR Convention exemplifies this complexity.[49]

This being said, public authorities are not allowed in general to impose any condition for supplying information that requires the applicant to state the reason why he or she wants the information, or how he or she intends to use it. Requests cannot be rejected because the applicant does not have an interest in the information. Public authorities may refuse a request for information that they do not 'hold'[50] or that is 'manifestly unreasonable'. They may also refuse to disclose materials 'in the course of completion', or materials 'concerning internal communications', but only when national law or customary practice exempts such materials.[51] If access to information is denied, the authority in question must make its decision within a short period of time, stating the reasons for the refusal. Of importance then, although it does not necessarily ensure access to the information, is the right to legal review and appeal to a court.[52] As already pointed out:

> . . . the right to information means that the disclosure of information should be the general rule and that public authorities should be permitted to refuse a request for environmental information in specific and clearly defined cases. Grounds for refusal should be interpreted in a restrictive way, whereby the public interest served by disclosure should be weighed against the interest served by the refusal.[53]

In order to avoid water disputes, access to information must be complemented by effective public participation in the taking of decisions. The concept of public

[48] *See*, e.g., *Ecopravo-Lviv v. Brodyvodocanal* (case n°4/2436–31/97), cited in *Handbook on Access to Justice under the Aarhus Convention*, edited by Stephen Stec, Hungary, March 2003, at 205–206.

[49] *Dispute Concerning Access to Information under Article 9 of the OSPAR Convention (Ireland/UK), supra* note 4.

[50] One could distinguish between 'information held *by* a public authority' (environmental information in its possession which has been produced or received by that authority) and 'information held *for* a public authority' (environmental information which is physically held by a natural or legal person on behalf of a public authority). Directive 2003/4/EC of the European Parliament and of the Council of 28 January 2003 on public access to environmental information and repealing Council Directive 90/313/EEC, Art. 2(3) and (4).

[51] Quoted from *The Aarhus Convention: An Implementation Guide, supra* note 28, at 56–9. Other exceptions to access to information are provided for in Art. 4(4) of the Aarhus Convention.

[52] See Art. 9(1) of the Aarhus Convention.

[53] Directive 2003/4/EC of the European Parliament and of the Council of 28 January 2003 on public access to environmental information and repealing Council Directive 90/313/EEC, para. 16.

participation is dynamic.[54] Effective public participation in the taking of decisions enables the public to express, and the decision-maker to take account of, opinions and concerns which may be relevant to those decisions. Thus, contributing to public awareness of environmental issues, it increases the accountability and the transparency of the decision-making process.[55]

2.2 Public participation per se in water-related decisions

In light of the Aarhus Convention and other international instruments on public participation and environmental impact assessments (EIAs), some preliminary elements can be identified as the traits of participatory processes. According to Jonas Ebbesson:

> ...first, the process should provide a true opportunity for the public to take part in decision-making, offering it a possibility to influence the outcome. Second, it should reflect a broad understanding of who may act to protect the 'public interests'—the premise being that not only governmental and administrative institutions should do so. Third, the decision-making process, as well as the follow-up monitoring of any implementation measures, should be transparent and open. Fourth, the public at large should have access to environmental information. Fifth, it should allow for legal review and the right to appeal.[56]

How to ensure that a participatory process is not merely '*pro forma*'?[57] In other words, how can it be ensured that public participation influences *de facto* and *in abstracto* decision-making in water issues? The Aarhus Convention, for example, sets out several means for enhancing the impact of participation as '*early* public participation', and the right to have the decision reviewed by a court.[58]

In particular, reasonable time-frames for the different phases of the participatory process in water issues should be provided. They should allow sufficient time for informing the public, and for the public concerned to prepare and participate effectively in environmental decision-making. The Aarhus Convention highlights two methods of informing the public: public notice and individual notice. Therefore, notification has a different meaning in international law. Notification goes beyond the narrow perspective of States, as came out in

[54] It is essential to note the substantial link between environmental education and participation. This link has been made in several international instruments. *See*, e.g., the 1997 Thessaloniki Declaration of the UNESCO Conference on Environment and Society: Education and Public Awareness for Sustainability, which built upon declarations made at the Belgrade Conference on Environmental Education (1975); the Tbilisi Intergovernmental Conference on Environmental Education (1977); the Moscow Conference on Environmental Education (1987); and the Toronto World Congress for Education and Communication on Environment and Development (1992). *See also* Chapter 36 of Agenda 21 on the promotion of education, public awareness, and training.

[55] *See* Directive 2003/35/EC of the European Parliament and of the Council of 26 May 2003 providing for public participation in respect of the drawing up of certain plans and programmes relating to the environment and amending with regard to public participation and access to justice, Council Directives 85/337/EEC and 96/61/EC, *Official Journal of the European Union*, L 156/17, 25 June 2003.

[56] J. Ebbesson, *supra* note 2, at 59.

[57] *See id.*, at 86.

[58] Art. 9, Aarhus Convention.

the Lake Lanoux case[59] and in the United Nations Convention on the Non-Navigational Uses of International Watercourses (hereinafter the UN Watercourses Convention).[60] Public notice means the dissemination of particular information to as many members of the public as possible, making use of the usual means for general and widespread transmission of information. Public notice would be considered adequate so long as it targets the public concerned early enough in the procedure to render effective public participation. Means of notification may include publication in a newspaper or other generally available printed media, dissemination through electronic mass media (TV, radio, Internet), or posting of notices in areas with heavy traffic.[61] Individual notice—that is, dissemination of particular information to certain classes of persons individually—is possible in appropriate situations. Individual notice is especially important where individual interests might be affected by the decision. This illustrates the interchangeability and the systemic interaction between access to information and public participation *per se*.

Regarding water-related decisions, international conventions can ensure *expressis verbis* a mandatory involvement of the public in decision-making processes referring to 'water specific activities',[62] as well as establishing, implicitly the obligation on the States to provide for public participation in a general context, such as concerning 'plans, programs, and policies' and for 'executive regulations and generally applicable rules'. The right to participate in decision-making procedures that do not relate to a specific activity is more generally defined and provides a wider margin of discretion for the State Parties.[63]

A particular technique of international law allows implementation of the notion of public participation in water issues: EIA.[64] The concept of the EIA has developed based upon the assumption that the quality of decisions would be enhanced by public participation.[65] The Espoo Convention, which is to date the most advanced treaty on EIA, indicates that an EIA consists of a participatory

[59] Lake Lanoux Arbitration (Spain/France), 1957 (Nov. 16), Report of International Arbitral Awards, vol. 12 (1957), 281–317, at 306–307. English text: International Law Reports, vol. 24 (1957), at 101–42, para. 11.

[60] *See*, e.g., Part III of the 1997 UN Watercourses Convention (Arts 11–19), which, sets out a number of procedural provisions aimed at enhancing cooperation between co-riparians concerning 'planned measures'.

[61] Quoted from *The Aarhus Convention: An Implementation Guide, supra* note 28, at 96–7.

[62] Annexes to the conventions contain usually references to water specific activities. *See*, e.g., Annex I of the Aarhus Convention, *supra* note 2, and Appendix I of the Espoo Convention, *supra* note 17.

[63] *See*, e.g. Arts 7 and 8 of the Aarhus Convention.

[64] *See* 1992 Rio Declaration, Principle 17: 'Environmental impact assessment, as a national instrument, shall be undertaken for proposed activities that are likely to have a significant adverse impact on the environment and are subject to a decision by competent national authority.' A large number of treaties and other international instruments—in more or less precise language—require EIAs for activities likely to cause some environmental impairment.

[65] According to J. Ebbesson, *supra* note 2, at 68–9: 'In addition to contributing information, the involvement of non-state actors secures critical reviews of the information presented by the project proponent . . . the information contributed by the public is not limited to environmental "facts" but also

procedure, as well as of documentation of the proposed activity's likely impacts.[66] The Espoo Convention prescribes non-discrimination with respect to transboundary participation. It therefore reflects the notion that public participation is conceptually linked to such assessments.[67] Moreover, the adoption of the Protocol on Strategic Environmental Assessment to the Espoo Convention strengthens the participatory approach of the EIAs. Strategic environmental assessment[68] means

> the evaluation of the likely environmental, including health, effects, which comprises the determination of the scope of an environmental report and its preparation, the carrying-out of public participation and consultations, and the taking into account of the environmental report and the results of the public participation and consultations in a plan or programme.

Strategic environmental assessment is *expressis verbis* provided for water-related activities.[69]

Public participation has a double aspect concerning the *ratione personae* issues. In this regard, it is relevant to define the notion of 'public' in general and of the 'public concerned' in particular.[70] The definition of 'public' applies the 'any person' principle. The definition of 'public' in Article 1(x) of the Espoo Convention, is 'one or more natural or legal persons'. The same definition can be

includes more subjective perceptions of environmental concerns. In a transboundary setting, the participation of non-state actors may point public institutions towards transboundary effects that they might otherwise not have considered. In this area too, EIA procedures provide a means for improving the quality of decisions, e.g. by shedding light on the sensitivity of the environment in the neighboring state.' *See also* Protocol on Strategic Environmental Assessment, *supra* note 16. Its Art. 10, entitled 'Transboundary Consultations', states: '1.Where a Party of origin considers that the implementation of a plan or programme is likely to have significant transboundary environmental, including health, effects or where a Party likely to be significantly affected so requests, the Party of origin shall as early as possible before the adoption of the plan or programme notify the affected Party.... 4. *Where such consultations take place, the Parties concerned shall agree on detailed arrangements to ensure that the public concerned and the authorities..., in the affected Party are informed and given an opportunity to forward their opinion on the draft plan or programme and the environmental report within a reasonable time frame.*' (emphasis added)

[66] The parties to the Convention are obliged to 'ensure that in accordance with the provisions of [the Espoo Convention] an environmental impact assessment is undertaken prior to a decision to authorize or undertake a proposed activity listed...that is likely to cause a significant adverse transboundary impact'. Espoo Convention, *supra* note 17, Art. 3.

[67] This linkage is also reflected, among others, in the 1987 UNEP Goals and Principles of Environmental Impact Assessment (UNEP Goals, Principle 7), the World Bank Operational Directive on EIA, Operational Directive 4.01 (para. 19: 'The Bank expects the borrower to take the views of affected groups and local NGOs fully into account in project design and implementation, and in particular in the preparation of EIAS'.)

[68] *See*, e.g., Art. 4(2) of the Protocol: 'A strategic environmental assessment shall be carried out for plans and programmes which are prepared for agriculture, forestry, fisheries, energy, industry including mining, transport, regional development, waste management, *water management*, telecommunications, tourism, town and country planning or land use...' (emphasis added).

[69] Protocol on Strategic Environmental Assessment, Water-related activities in Annex I and Water-related activities in Annex II.

[70] The following ideas are quoted from *The Aarhus Convention: An Implementation Guide*, *supra* note 28, at 39–41.

found in Article 1(j) of the Industrial Accidents Convention.[71] The Aarhus Convention also explicitly mentions associations and groups. These definitions imply that no person can be excluded from the definition on the grounds of nationality, domicile, citizenship, or place of registered seat.[72]

The Aarhus Convention's definition of 'public' differs from that of other conventions since it also refers to associations, organizations, or groups of natural or legal persons. In most cases, an association, organization, or group of natural or legal persons will itself have legal personality, and therefore will already fall under the definition. The language can only be interpreted, therefore, to provide that associations, organizations, or groups *without legal personality* may also be considered to be members of the public. This addition is qualified, however, in the Aarhus Convention by the reference to national legislation or practice. Thus, *ad hoc* formations can be considered to be members of the public only where the requirements, if any, established by national legislation or practice are met.

The term 'public concerned'[73] refers to a subset of the public at large with a special relationship to a particular environmental decision-making procedure, like one including water issues. To be a member of the 'public concerned' in a particular case, the member of the public must be likely to be affected by the environmental decision-making, or the member of the public must have an interest in the environmental decision-making. This definition includes members of the public whose legal rights guaranteed under law might be impaired by the proposed activity. It also applies, however, to a category of the public that has an unspecified interest in the decision-making procedure. A person does not need to show a *legal* interest to be a member of the public concerned.[74] Thus, the term may encompass both 'legal interest' and 'factual interest'.[75]

Access to justice is one of the most important means for essentially protecting transparency and public participation in water issues.[76] Judicial mechanisms should be effective to ensure transparency and public participation in water

[71] Convention on Transboudary Effects of Industrial Accidents, *supra* note 42.

[72] *See*, e.g., Arts 3(9) and 4 of the Aarhus Convention.

[73] The term can be found in Art. 6 on public participation in decisions on specific activities of the Aarhus Convention. This concept of 'public concerned' has impact on *locus standi* in dispute-settlement fora. *See*, e.g., in order to have standing before the European Court of Justice in a case against a decision of one of the EC institutions, it is not sufficient that the person concerned shows that he or she is affected; the person must also prove that he or she is affected in a different manner than the public at large. This is the logic of the interpretation of the European Court of Justice (ECJ) with regard to Art. 173 of the 1957 EC Treaty as amended. See Case T-585/93, *Greenpeace and Others v. Commission of the European Communities*, para. 51; The order of the Court of First Instance in this case was later confirmed by the ECJ, Case C-321/95P; *see also*, Case T-219/95, *Danielsson et al v. the Commission*, paras 66–76.

[74] Art. 2(5), Aarhus Convention.

[75] Arts 6 and 9, Aarhus Convention.

[76] *See*, e.g., Commission of the European Communities, *Proposal for a Directive of the European Parliament and of the Council on Access to Justice in Environmental Matters*, Brussels, 24 October 2003, COM (2003) 624 final, available at http://europa.eu.int/eur-lex/en/com/pdf/2003/com2003_0624en01.pdf.

disputes. If there are technical barriers to access to the courts, such as unreasonable standing requirements, justice may not be accessible.[77] Several international legal texts emphasize the right of a natural and judicial person to have recourse to court without any discrimination. The UN Watercourses Convention, for example, provides as follows:

> Watercourse States shall not discriminate on the basis of nationality or residence in granting access to judicial and other procedures, in accordance with their legal system, to any natural or judicial person who has suffered appreciable harm as a result of an activity related to an international watercourse or is exposed to a threat thereof.[78]

The Aarhus Convention, too, prohibits discrimination on the basis of the person's citizenship, nationality, domicile, and, in case of a legal person, the place of its registered seat or effective centre. Unlike the 1974 Nordic Convention, the Aarhus Convention does not restrict access to court to subjects of the Parties to the Convention.[79]

Having examined public participation and access to information as matrix vectors for the avoidance of water disputes, this paper now focuses on the settlement of water disputes. The purpose of the next section will be to point out the actions that the WTO and the NAFTA have taken with the aim to increase their transparency and openness. Two issues will be particularly addressed: the role of *amici* briefs as means of public participation before dispute settlement bodies; and the issue of transparency in arbitration proceedings.

3. Water-dispute settlement: issues of public participation and transparency in disputes fora

At the international level, non-State actors have limited rights of participation before dispute settlement bodies. When non-State actors have not the right to be parties to international disputes before settlement bodies, the submission of *amici* briefs is an essential means of public participation. Indeed, through the submission of *amici* briefs, non-State actors, not parties to a dispute, may express their concerns on the issues submitted to the tribunals. *Amicus curiae* is defined in *Black's Law Dictionary* to mean 'literally, friend of the Court. A person with a strong interest in or views on the subject-matter of an action, but not a party to the action, may petition the Court for permission to file a brief...

[77] Aarhus Convention, Art. 2(5) and Art. 9(2).

[78] Art. 32 of the UN Watercourses Convention. For a critical analysis of this provision, *see*, e.g., E. Hey, *supra* note 12, at 133. For Ellen Hey: 'The article clearly does not impose upon states a duty to develop adequate administrative and judicial procedures to secure public participation in the formulation and implementation of policy and for obtaining redress of damages suffered. Instead, the object of the article is to avoid discrimination between persons residing in the state where the source of harm is located. Thus, if a watercourse state does not provide adequate procedures to protect the interests of its own nationals, that same inadequate level of protection will be accorded to nationals and residents of other watercourse states as well as to its residents.'

[79] Art. 3(9) of the Aarhus Convention.

Such *amicus curiae* briefs are commonly filed in appeals concerning matters of broad public interest'.[80] *Amici* briefs have a long history. They evolved under Roman Law and they were developed within Common Law.

As friends of the court, a primary purpose of *amici* should be to assist the courts to fulfill their obligations by providing additional sources of objective information. It may be noted that the aim of *amicus curiae* intervention has evolved from supporting a party's claim to the representation of a public interest in the proceedings.[81] *Amici* briefs are a new vehicle for public participation in dispute settlement mechanisms. Indeed, they allow the participation of non-State actors in the settlement of water disputes. Many international fora exclude the participation of non-State actors before their dispute bodies. Nevertheless, through the receipt of *amici* briefs, tribunals may allow private parties to express their concerns on the issues submitted to the courts.

In light of the fragmentation of the law of procedure of international courts, the admissibility of *amici curiae* varies greatly depending on the forum concerned. In some international fora, such as the human rights bodies[82] or the International Criminal Court,[83] non-State actors have significant rights of participation; in others, opportunities to be involved are minimal, or non-existent (for instance, the International Court of Justice).

In addition to deciding *whom* to permit to participate as an *amicus,* any procedures should address the *degree to which amici* may participate. In NAFTA cases, as well as in WTO and ICSID dispute settlement mechanisms, *amici* are likely to seek varying levels of access to the tribunals and to information about the proceedings.[84] It is essential to enhance transparency in order

[80] *Black's Law Dictionary*, 6th edn., West Publishing Co., St. Paul, Minn., 1990, at 82.

[81] A. Tanzi & C. Pitea, *supra* note 20, at 287.

[82] The *European Convention for the Protection of Human Rights and Fundamental Freedoms*, as amended by Protocol 11, authorizes the participation of individuals and NGOs before the European Court of Human Rights (Art. 34). Protocol 11 also formalized the acceptance of *amicus* briefs (Art. 36.2). The Inter-American Court of Human Rights has developed an extensive practice of accepting *amicus* briefs. Art. 44(1) of its rules of procedure allows the acceptance of third-party information. However, the Court has generally referred to *amicus* briefs in its opinion without reference to this provision. Furthermore, Art. 25(2) of the *Protocol establishing the African Court of Human and Peoples' Rights* empowers the Court to accept *amicus* briefs on a case-by-case basis. However, according to the Protocol, the Court cannot accept cases submitted by individuals unless 'exceptional grounds' can be demonstrated and the NGOs comply with the admissibility criteria contained in Art. 56 of the African Charter on Human and People's Rights. *See* D. Shelton, *The Participation of Non-Governmental Organizations in International Judicial Proceedings*, 88 American Journal of International Law 611 (1994) at 638.

[83] Rule 103 of the Rules of Evidence and Procedure of the International Criminal Court, entitled '*Amicus Curiae* and other forms of submissions', states that 'at any stage of the proceedings, a Chamber may, if considers it desirable for the proper determination of the case, invite or grant leave to a State, organization or person to submit, in writing or orally, any observation on any issue that the Chamber deems appropriate'.

[84] *See Methanex v. United States of America*, Decision of the Tribunal on Petition from Third Persons to Intervene as 'Amicus Curiae', 15 January 2001, para. 5. Arbitral tribunal established under the UNCITRAL Rules. *United Parcel Service of America Inc. v. Government of Canada*, Decision of the Tribunal on Petitions for Intervention and Participation as 'Amici Curiae', 17 October 2001, para. 1. Arbitral Tribunal established under the UNCITRAL Rules.

to ensure a greater participation of third parties who could be affected, directly or indirectly, by the tribunals' decisions.

The submission of *amici* briefs before WTO dispute settlement bodies and NAFTA Chapter 11 investor–State tribunals allows non-State actors, and even States not directly involved in a dispute, to express their concerns on issues submitted to the tribunals.

The WTO Dispute Settlement Understanding (DSU), the NAFTA, and the UNCITRAL arbitration rules do not set out express provisions on *amici* briefs. Yet the WTO Appellate Body and NAFTA Chapter 11 tribunals have considered having the full discretion to accept *amici* briefs. Their decision is based on the assumption that accepting *amici* briefs does not affect the substantive rights of the parties since this decision concerns only procedural issues.

In the context of the WTO, there is a consolidated Appellate Body's jurisprudence which considers that Panels and the Appellate Body itself have full discretion to accept submissions in the form of *amici* briefs from individuals, NGOs, and even States.

3.1 The Practice of the *amicus curiae* briefs before the WTO dispute settlement mechanism

Following previous GATT practice, WTO panels did not grant permission to submit non-solicited *amici* briefs in the US-Gasoline and US-Hormones cases.[85] Nevertheless, in *United States-Import Prohibition of Certain Shrimp and Shrimp Products* (hereinafter the US-Shrimp case), the Appellate Body, reversing the findings of the Panel on this point, granted permission to file *amicus* briefs.[86] It considered that, in contrast with the duty to accept and give appropriate consideration to the submissions by the disputing parties and intervening third parties, panels have the authority to ascertain the acceptability and relevancy of information or advice received by an NGO or an expert.[87]

In *United States—Imposition of Countervailing Duties on Certain Hot Rolled Lead and Bismuth Carbon Steel Products Originated in the United Kingdom* (hereinafter the US-British Steel case), the Appellate Body clarified its approach to *amicus* briefs.[88] In this case, it found that it had discretionary authority to accept and consider *amicus* submissions in an appeal when it is 'pertinent and useful to do so'.[89] The decisions of the Appellate Body in US-Shrimp and

[85] *United States—Standards for Reformulated and Conventional Gasoline* (hereinafter US-Gasoline), WT/DS4, Panel Report, adopted 7 August 1995; *United States—Measures Affecting Meat and Meat Products* (hereinafter US-Hormones), WT/DS26&48, Panel Report, adopted 13 February 1998.

[86] *United States—Import Prohibition of Certain Shrimp and Shrimp Products* (hereinafter US-Shrimp), Appellate Body Report, 12 October 1998, WT/DS58/AB/R, at paras 102–110.

[87] US-Shrimp, Appellate Body Report, para. 104.

[88] *United States—Imposition of Countervailing Duties on Certain Hot Rolled Lead and Bismuth Carbon Steel Products Originated in the United Kingdom* (hereinafter US-British Steel), Appellate Body Report, 10 May 2000, WT/DS138/AB/R, paras 39–42.

[89] US-British Steel, Appellate Body Report, para. 42.

US-British Steel have sparked controversy among WTO Members. Some States argued that recognizing the Appellate Body's authority to accept *amicus* submissions would grant *amici* greater rights than those accorded to the WTO Members. However, in the US-British Steel case, the Appellate Body specified that only WTO Parties have the right to participate in dispute settlement proceedings as third parties. Conversely, it has 'no legal duty to accept or consider unsolicited *amicus curiae* briefs submitted by individuals or organizations, not members of the WTO'.[90]

In the context of the *Asbestos* litigation, the Appellate Body decided, for the first time, publicly to invite briefs from all interested sources.[91] Nevertheless, it subsequently rejected all the requests for leave to file *amicus* briefs, 'for failure to comply sufficiently with all the requirements' set out in the Appellate Body's procedures, without giving a precise reasoning for such refusal.[92] This decision caused concerns and criticism from the NGO community.[93]

The acceptance and consideration of *amicus* briefs raises some important practical issues: on one hand, WTO adjudicating bodies have not pointed out circumstances under which they may consider the information 'pertinent and useful'; on the other hand, they have not provided criteria as to the appropriate source and nature of information. Consequently, WTO Members have little guidance as to what practice to expect in future cases.[94] Nevertheless, the WTO practice, in particular in the US-Shrimp and in the US-British Steel litigations, demonstrates that the scope of a procedural power can extend to the receipt of written submissions from a non-party third person, even in a juridical procedure affecting the rights and obligations of State Parties. Lastly, it also shows that the receipt of such submissions confers no rights, procedural or substantive, on non-party third persons. Such analysis of the *amicus* question by tribunals is not limited to the WTO; investor–State arbitral tribunals set up by Chapter 11 of the NAFTA have followed a similar approach.

[90] US-British Steel, Appellate Body Report, paras 40–41. *See also European Communities—Trade Description of Sardines*, Appellate Body Report, 26 September 2002 WT/DS231/AB/R, para. 166.

[91] *See Procedures in European Communities—Measures Affecting Asbestos and Asbestos Containing Products*, Communication of the Appellate Body, 8 November 2000, WT/DS135/9.

[92] *European Communities—Measures Affecting Asbestos and Asbestos Containing Products*, Appellate Body Report, 12 March 2001, WT/DS 135/AB/R. In its last decision concerning *amici curiae*, the Appellate Body refused again to consider *amicus curiae* submissions. However, in this case, the Appellate Body explained its refusal, considering that the *amici* brief submitted by Morocco provided mainly factual information and was not of assistance in the appeal. *European Communities—Trade Description of Sardines*, Appellate Body Report, 26 September 2002, WT/DS231/AB/R, paras 169–170.

[93] In this regard, *see A Court Without Friends. One Year after Seattle, the WTO slams the door on NGOs, available at* www.ciel.org ; *see also* the Joint Statement by the Foundation for International Environmental Law and Development (FIELD), Greenpeace International, International Ban Asbestos Secretariat, and WWF International, 'NGOs Welcome WTO Green Light to French Ban on Asbestos but Remain Skeptical about the WTO Dispute Settlement Process', 14 March 2001, available at www.field.org.uk.

[94] G. Marceau & M. Stilwell, *Practical Suggestions For Amicus Curiae Briefs Before WTO Adjudicating Bodies*, 1 4 Journal of International Economic Law 155 (2001).

3.2 The practice of *amicus curiae* briefs before NAFTA Chapter 11 Tribunals and the ICSID

The most common type of water-related disputes is arbitration of foreign investment disputes. Chapter 11 of the NAFTA requires that Canada, the United States, and Mexico meet certain standards in relation to foreign investment. If a State fails to meet its obligations under Chapter 11, a foreign investor protected under the agreement may seek monetary compensation from the State in binding arbitration for any injury suffered. This mechanism is known as an investor–State dispute mechanism.

Chapter 11 has attracted virulent criticism on the basis that it imposes severe constraints on national sovereignty through a dispute settlement mechanism that is lacking in transparency. In particular, Chapter 11 provides little in the way of guidance on transparency issues. However, the investor-State process has proven itself to be a flexible mechanism, permitting a surprising degree of openness, and even possible third-party participation as an *amicus curiae*. In *Methanex Corporation v. United States of America*[95] (hereinafter the Methanex Decision) and in *United Parcel Service v. Canada*[96] (hereinafter the UPS Decision), NAFTA Tribunals considered that they had the power but not the duty to accept written briefs by *amici*. However, the receipt of such briefs does not confer on tribunals the authority to add parties to the arbitration.[97] The NAFTA Tribunals and the WTO Appellate Body decisions permitting the submission of *amicus* briefs were predicated on the assumption that the decision was procedural only and did not affect the substantive rights of the parties.

Neither the Methanex Tribunal nor the UPS Tribunal grounded its authority to accept *amici* briefs in Article 1133 of the NAFTA. This provision allows a Tribunal, in certain circumstances, to appoint 'one or more experts to report to it in writing on any factual issue concerning environmental, health, safety or other scientific matters raised by a disputing party'. *Amici* do not serve the same function as tribunal-appointed experts. The NAFTA Article 1133 permits the Tribunal to appoint experts in only two circumstances: at the request of a disputing party; or on its own initiative, 'unless the disputing parties disapprove'.[98] Accordingly, pursuant to the express terms of Article 1133, the Tribunal cannot

[95] Methanex Decision, *supra* note 84, paras 31–33.

[96] UPS Decision, *supra* note 84, paras 61 and 64.

[97] *See* Amicus Petition by the Canadian Union of Postal Workers and the Council of Canadians, 10 May 2001. Text available at www.naftaclaims.com. For NAFTA Chapter 11 Tribunals, the request to stand as parties to the proceeding is a substantive question. The Tribunal determined that neither the claimant investor nor the State had consented to arbitrating with anyone except each other. *See* UPS Decision, paras 35–36, and Methanex Decision, para. 30.

[98] Article 1133 reads as follows: 'Without prejudice to the appointment of other kinds of experts where authorized by the applicable arbitration rules, a Tribunal, at the request of a disputing party or, unless the disputing parties disapprove, on its own initiative, may appoint one or more experts to report to it in writing on any factual issue concerning environmental, health, safety or other scientific matters raised by a disputing party in a proceeding, subject to such terms and conditions as the disputing parties may agree.'

appoint experts without the consent of the disputing parties. In the Methanex Decision, the Tribunal concluded that '*Amici* are not experts'.[99] This is consistent with the Tribunal's determination that *amicus* submissions 'could not adduce the evidence of any factual or expert witness'.[100]

The NAFTA Tribunals refer to Article 15.1 of the UNCITRAL's arbitration rules, which establishes that the 'arbitral tribunal may conduct the arbitration in such manner as it considers appropriate', provided that the 'parties are treated with equality and that at any stage in the proceedings each party is given a full opportunity of presenting its case'. In the Methanex Decision, the Tribunal affirmed that this Article is intended to provide the 'broadest procedural flexibility within fundamental safeguards'.[101]

The NAFTA Tribunals have recognized that arbitration claims with broad public impacts require public participation. In particular, the *amici* participation would promote the openness of the NAFTA proceedings. In the case of Methanex, NGOs strongly argued that the case would have significant implications for the NAFTA States' ability to enact environmental protection legislation. Thus, the NAFTA Tribunal determined that it had the authority to permit participation by an *amicus curiae* because 'there is undoubtedly a public interest in this arbitration' and 'the substantive issues extend far beyond those raised by the usual transnational arbitration between commercial parties'.[102] According to the Tribunals, there is also a broader argument:

> ...the NAFTA Chapter 11 arbitral process could benefit from being perceived as more open or transparent; or conversely be harmed if seen as unduly secretive. In this regard, the Tribunal's willingness to receive *amicus* submissions might support the process in general and this arbitration in particular, whereas a blanket refusal could do positive harm.[103]

Therefore, the grant of permission to submit *amicus* briefs would considerably allay such public concerns.

In this context, one should mention the recent statement of the Free Trade Commission, which could be considered as a kind of codification of an emerging *lex arbitri* on the participation of *amici curiae* before NAFTA Tribunals.[104] The Commission recognizes that 'no provision of the North American Free Trade Agreement ("NAFTA") limits a Tribunal's discretion to accept written submissions from a person or entity that is not a disputing party (a "non-disputing party")'. However, the Commission clarifies that 'nothing in this statement by the Commission prejudices the rights of NAFTA Parties under Article 1128 of the NAFTA'. According to this provision, a 'Party may make submissions to a Tribunal on a question of interpretation of the NAFTA Agreement'. Therefore,

[99] Methanex Decision, para. 38. [100] Methanex Decision, para. 36.
[101] Methanex Decision, para. 27. *See also* UPS Decision, para. 69.
[102] Methanex Decision, para. 49; UPS Decision, para. 65.
[103] Methanex Decision, para. 49.
[104] Statement of the Free Trade Commission on non-disputing party participation, available at http://www.ustr.gov/regions/whemisphere/nafta2003/statement-nondisputingparties.pdf.

'non-disputing Parties may, pursuant to Article 1128, address any issues of interpretation of the Agreement presented in the non-disputing party submission'. The Free Trade Commission also recommends that Chapter 11 Tribunals adopt particular procedures with respect to *amicus* briefs. Moreover, it specifies some of the factors which could be considered by NAFTA Tribunals in determining whether to grant leave to file a non-disputing party submission. The NAFTA Tribunals will consider, among other things, the extent to which:

(1) the non-disputing party submission would assist the Tribunal in the determination of a factual or legal issue related to the arbitration by bringing a perspective, particular knowledge, or insight that is different from that of the disputing parties;
(2) the non-disputing party submission would address matters within the scope of the dispute;
(3) the non-disputing party has a significant interest in the arbitration; and
(4) there is a public interest in the subject-matter of the arbitration.

The last factor mentioned by the Free Trade Commission is of particular interest since it acknowledges that many of the issues submitted before the NAFTA Tribunals can extend far beyond those raised by the usual arbitration between commercial parties. Arbitration claims with broad public impacts therefore require processes that afford opportunities for public awareness and participation.

For the first time, in the case of *Aguas del Tunari v. Bolivia*, an ICSID Tribunal[105] dealt with the issue of the acceptance of *amicus briefs*. In January 2003, with a brief reply, the Tribunal dismissed the request of the petitioners to participate as *amici curiae*.[106] The *Aguas del Tunari v. Bolivia* arbitration was being conducted according to the rules of the ICSID Convention. The question of *amicus curiae* participation is not addressed by the ICSID Convention, nor by the investment agreement between the Netherlands and Bolivia. This being said, nothing in these texts precludes participation as *amicus curiae*. In light of Article 44 of the ICSID Convention, the Tribunal has the authority to decide any questions of procedure not explicitly covered by ICSID's rules or by a rule agreed to by the parties. Moreover, the power of the Tribunal to regulate the arbitration process, in the absence of explicit regulation, has been recognized by NAFTA Tribunals and by the WTO dispute settlement system. In this context it should be noted that Article 44 of the ICSID Convention is virtually identical to Article 15(1) of the UNCITRAL Rules to support the same interpretation. Nevertheless, in January 2003, the ICSID Tribunal in its reply to the NGOs submitting the *amici* brief, considered that the interplay of the ICSID Convention and the *1992 Bilateral Agreement on Encouragement and Reciprocal*

[105] *Aguas del Tunari S.A. v. Republic of Bolivia* (Case No. ARB/02/3) (Water and sewer services concession agreement).

[106] Letter sent by the President of the Tribunal in the matter of Aguas del Tunari v. The Republic of Bolivia to Earthjustice, 29 January 2003. It should be noted that the Tribunal answered to the petitioners by letter, without giving a formal decision concerning its refusal to accept *amicus* briefs.

Protection of Investment between the Kingdom of the Netherlands and Bolivia, as well as the consensual nature of arbitration, 'places the control of the issues' raised by the NGOs 'with the parties, not the Tribunal. In particular the Tribunal cannot, absent the agreement of the Parties, join a non-Party to the proceedings'. However, the receipt of *amici* briefs has never been interpreted by tribunals as a means to join non-parties to the proceedings. As specified by the Chapter 11 Tribunals and by the WTO Appellate Body, decisions permitting the submission of *amici* briefs are exclusively procedural and they do not affect the substantive rights of the parties. The acceptance of such briefs confers no rights, procedural or substantive, on non-party third persons.

With the aim to ensure greater participation of non-State actors that could be affected by the tribunals' decisions, it is essential to guarantee an enhanced transparency in the tribunal proceedings. Yet confidentiality remains one of the distinctive traits of all arbitration proceedings.[107] In a NAFTA dispute brought to an ICSID tribunal, the arbitral tribunal considered 'whether there exists any general principle of confidentiality that would operate to prohibit public discussion of the arbitration proceedings by either party'.[108] The tribunal specified:

> Neither the NAFTA nor the ICSID (Additional Facility) Rules contain any express restriction on the freedom of the parties in this respect. Though it is frequently said that one of the reasons for recourse to arbitration is to avoid publicity, unless the agreement between the parties incorporates such a limitation, each of them is still free to speak publicly of the arbitration. It may be observed that no such limitation is written into such major arbitral texts as the UNCITRAL Rules or the draft Articles on Arbitration adopted by the International Law Commission . . . [109]

It also affirmed that

> it would be of advantage to the orderly unfolding of the arbitral process and conducive to the maintenance of working relations between the Parties if during the proceedings they were both to limit public discussion of the case to a minimum, subject only to any externally imposed obligation of disclosure by which either of them may be legally bound.[110]

3.3 Transparency before dispute settlement bodies

In NAFTA cases, as well as in WTO and ICSID dispute settlement mechanisms, *amici* are likely to seek varying levels of access to the tribunals and to information about the proceedings. For instance, before NAFTA Tribunals, the parties seeking *amicus* status sought permission to read the parties' written pleadings, to make oral submissions, and to have observer status at oral hearings.[111]

[107] *See*, e.g., *Award on Confidentiality in the NAFTA/UNCITRAL Case Ethyl Corporation v. Government of Canada* (2 July 1998), which contains a 'Confidentiality Agreement' opposable to the Tribunal, available at http://www.appletonlaw.com/cases/ECONFID.PDF.

[108] Metalclad v. Mexico, *Yearbook of International Commercial Arbitration*, XXVI, (2001), at 103–104.

[109] *Id.*

[110] *Id.*

[111] Methanex Decision, para. 5; UPS Decision, para. 1, *supra* note 84.

The NAFTA Tribunals held that third-party participation must be limited to submitting written *amici* briefs. Article 25(4) of the UNCITRAL Rules provides that all hearings must be *in camera* unless the parties consent to a more open process. *Amici* in Methanex and UPS requested permission to attend the hearings in those cases. However, in light of Article 25, both Tribunals rejected those requests, given that there was no agreement between parties to open the process to non-parties.[112]

An inescapable corollary to the participation of *amici* is the extent to which they have access to documents generated in the course of the proceedings. The NAFTA Tribunals have not authorized any special access to information for *amici*. The Methanex Tribunal acknowledged that the question of whether Article 25(4), or some obligation of confidentiality implicit in arbitration, required documents to be held *in camera,* was a difficult one. However, it did not have to address this question given the consent order on confidentiality agreed to by the parties in that case.[113] In particular, the Tribunal held that the *amici* would have no right to receive any materials generated in the arbitration, except insofar as a member of the public might gain access according to the consent order regarding disclosure and confidentiality.[114] The UPS Tribunal also declined to address the issue, although it acknowledged that a distinction might be drawn between the privacy of the hearings and 'the confidentiality or availability of documents'.[115]

It may be noted that the emerging trend in arbitration practice is that no inherent obligation of confidentiality exists.[116] Tribunals have recognized that arbitration claims with broad public impacts require processes that afford opportunities for public awareness and participation.[117] In particular, several arbitral tribunals have recognized the benefits of transparency. The High Court of Australia noted that an arbitration concerning efforts to raise the price of natural gas sold to public utilities had a clear public impact that mandated

[112] Methanex Decision, para. 42; UPS Decision, para. 67, *supra* note 84.

[113] Methanex Decision, paras 43–46, *supra* note 84.

[114] Minutes of Order of the First Procedural Meeting where the parties agreed to the disclosure of orders, awards, and pleadings (available at www.state.gov/s/1/c3757.htm).

[115] UPS Decision, para. 68.

[116] O. Oakley-White, 'Confidentiality Revisited: Is International Arbitration Losing one of its Major Benefits?', *International Arbitration Law Review* 6 (2003), at 29.

[117] *See Esso/BHP v. Plowman*, C.L.R. 10, 183 (1995); *Commonwealth of Australia v. Cockatoo Dockyard Pty. Ltd.*, N.S.W.L.R. 36, 662 (1995). Moreover, on 27 October 2000, the Swedish Supreme Court determined that international commercial arbitrations are not subject to an implied duty of confidentiality. This case concerned an appeal of an award in an arbitration where, aside from an *in camera* rule for hearing, no governing rule explicitly addressed the issue of a general duty of confidentiality (Case No. T 1881–99 Sweden Supreme Court, 27 October 2000). An opposite view has been expressed by the decision of the English Court of Appeal, in the case of *Dolling-Baker v. Merrett*, where the Court restrained a party to arbitration from disclosing documents relating to the arbitration. *See also Dolling-Baker v. Merrett* [1990] 1 WLR 1205. Cited in the Statement of Respondent USA in Response to Canada's and Mexico's Submissions Concerning Petitions for *Amicus Curiae* Status, 22 November 2000. Text available at: http://www.state.gov/documents/organization/3965.pdf.

public access to the arbitration processes.[118] The Australian Court also commented that a rule that made proceedings and documents confidential simply by virtue of being part of an arbitration proceeding would be 'unduly narrow' and would 'not recognize that there may be circumstances, in which third parties and the public have a legitimate interest in knowing what has transpired in an arbitration, which would give rise to a "public interest" exception'.[119] In light of the public character of water, as well as of the diverse interests that may be adversely affected in a water dispute, it may be affirmed, without doubt, that water disputes are characterized by such a 'public interest' exception.

The need to ensure a greater transparency in NAFTA processes has been recognized by the Free Trade Commission. In July 2001, the Commission adopted an Interpretive Note[120] that provides, in part, as follows:

1. Nothing in the NAFTA imposes a general duty of confidentiality on the disputing parties to a Chapter 11 arbitration, and, subject to the application of Article 1137(4), nothing in the NAFTA precludes the Parties from providing public access to documents submitted to, or issued by, a Chapter 11 tribunal.
2. In application of the foregoing:
   a. ... The NAFTA Parties agree that nothing in the relevant arbitral rules imposes a general duty of confidentiality or precludes the Parties from providing public access to documents submitted to, or issued by, Chapter 11 tribunals, apart from the limited specific exceptions set forth expressly in those rules.
   b. Each Party agrees to make available to the public in a timely manner all documents submitted to, or issued by, a Chapter 11 tribunal subject to redaction of:
      i. confidential business information;
      ii. information that is privileged or otherwise protected from disclosure under the Party's domestic law; and
      iii. information that the Party must withhold pursuant to the relevant arbitral rules, as applied.

Enhanced transparency is essential in order to ensure greater participation of private parties that could be affected, directly or indirectly, by the tribunals' decisions. The Interpretive Note commits the NAFTA Party States to disclose all documents submitted to or issued by an arbitral tribunal, but acknowledges 'limited specific exceptions' in the applicable arbitral rules. Thus, the commitment to openness expressed by the Free Trade Commission faces an impediment to implementation in the arbitral rules that govern the Chapter 11 process.[121]

[118] Australian High Court, *Esso/BHP v. Plowman*, *supra* note 117, para. 46. In particular, the Court held (3:2, the leading judgment being given by the Chief Justice) that confidentiality is not an essential attribute of private arbitration. It considered that a party in arbitration proceedings cannot be deemed to be bound by a duty of confidentiality, unless the parties have concluded an agreement concerning this matter.

[119] *Id.*, para. 38.

[120] Notes of Interpretation of Certain NAFTA Provisions, issued 31 July 2001, texts available at www.dfait.maeci.gc.ca/ma-nac/NAFTA-Interpr-e.asp.

[121] Both the UNCITRAL Rules and the Additional Facility Rules provide that procedural matters are to be addressed by the Tribunal (*see*, e.g., UNCITRAL Rules, Art. 15, and Additional Facility Rules, Arts 28 and 29). Under the Additional Facility Rules, the Tribunal is obliged to seek the views of the parties on how disclosure and any other procedural matters are to be dealt with, and must apply any agreement of the parties.

The Interpretive Note does not deal with the issue of transparency in a comprehensive way.[122] However, in light of this document, it may be expected that the governments and NAFTA Secretariat will 'make available to the public in a timely manner all documents submitted, or issued by, a Chapter 11 Tribunal'.[123]

Amici briefs and access to information on the tribunal proceedings are essential in order to ensure public participation and transparency in the settlement of water disputes. Compliance mechanisms are a new vehicle for public participation and transparency in water issues.

As already considered, international financial institutions, such as the World Bank, the Inter-American Development Bank (IDB), and the Asian Development Bank (ADB), have established compliance mechanisms to which non-State actors may bring complaints on the violations of the banks' policies. Many of the projects financed by multilateral development banks are in relation to water issues, e.g. hydroelectric dams. Through the World Bank Inspection Panel, as well as through other mechanisms set up by several international financial institutions, the intended beneficiaries of banks' financed projects may express their concerns on the formulation and implementation of such projects.

4. Compliance mechanisms as new means of public participation in water disputes

The World Bank (WB) Inspection Panel was the first international forum to which non-State actors could bring complaints against an international organization in order to hold it accountable for non-compliance with its stated policies. Its creation led two other multilateral development banks, the IDB and the ADB, to implement inspection mechanisms of their own. The International Finance Corporation/Multilateral Investment Guarantee Agency have also created their own mechanism, the Compliance Advisor and Ombudsman (CAO)

[122] It should be noted that the recent Statement of the Free Trade Commission on non-disputing party participation confirms that 'access to documents by non-disputing parties . . . will be governed by the Free Trade Commission's Note of 31 July 2001'.

[123] Interpretive Note, *supra* note 120, para. 2.b. It should be observed that access to NAFTA documents is ensured by the websites of the Canadian Department of Foreign and International Trade and the US State Department. *See* Department of Foreign and International Trade (http://www.dfait-maeci.gc.ca/tna-nac/NAFTA-en.asp, accessed July 2003); US Department of State (http://www.state.gov/s/l/c3741.htm, accessed July 2003). Moreover, Art. 1126(13) of the NAFTA contemplates that notices of arbitration will be made available in a publicly accessible register maintained by the NAFTA Secretariat. Currently the Secretariat does maintain such a register, but it can be accessed only by visiting the Secretariat office. The websites of the NAFTA Secretariat and of the national sections are very poor sources of information about Chapter 11 claims. Conversely, various private websites maintained by the investors, their counsel, and others are very rich in documents and texts on Chapter 11 proceedings. In this regard, several private websites provide excellent sources of information about NAFTA Chapter 11 claims, in particular http://www.appletonlaw.com/4acases.htm; www.naftaclaims.com.

Office. With the creation of these new mechanisms, multilateral development banks established a new vehicle for public participation.

Furthermore, in April 2003, the Board of Directors of the European Bank for Reconstruction and Development (EBRD) approved the creation of its Independent Recourse Mechanism. The African Development Bank (AfDB) is also developing a proposal for the establishment of a compliance mechanism.[124]

These mechanisms place the promotion of public participation in an institutional context, that of international organizations. Among the reasons for the establishment of compliance mechanisms by financial institutions, there was the need to enhance the quality of their activities.[125] They also aim to ensure transparency and to increase accountability of the banks' management and staff vis-à-vis their boards. Through these mechanisms, public participation was conceived as a new way of placing under scrutiny the organization's compliance with its own policies. Moreover, for their part, individuals participate in a compliance process by bringing claims, and in so doing they instigate scrutiny of a bank's actions.

Among the compliance mechanisms established by multilateral development banks, the example of the WB Inspection Panel should be highlighted.[126] Its purpose is to provide 'people directly and adversely affected by a Bank-financed project with an independent forum through which they can request the Bank to act in accordance with its own policies and procedures'.[127]

4.1 Compliance mechanisms established by Multilateral Development Banks

Before the WB Inspection Panel, requests may be brought by any group of persons who share common concerns or interests in the country where the project is located, and who can demonstrate that 'its rights or interests have been or are likely to be directly affected by any action or omission of the Bank'.[128] As underscored by Ellen Hey, the Inspection Panel recognizes that 'there exists a link between projects supported by the World Bank and the individuals and

[124] *See* http://www.adb.org/Documents/Policies/ADB_Accountability_Mechanism/default.asp.

[125] L. Boisson de Chazournes, *Public Participation in Decision-Making: The World Bank Inspection Panel*, in THE WORLD BANK, INTERNATIONAL FINANCIAL INSTITUTIONS, AND THE DEVELOPMENT OF INTERNATIONAL LAW (E. Brown Weiss, A. Rigo Sureda, & L. Boisson de Chazournes, Studies in Transnational Legal Policy, No. 31, The American Society of International Law) at 91.

[126] The Panel procedure consists of two phases: an admissibility phase and an investigatory phase. In each phase, the Panel submits its findings to the Executive Directors of the Bank. If the Board of Executive Directors decides that 'a request shall be investigated, the Panel will collect information and provide its findings, independent assessment and conclusions to the Board'. On the basis of the Panel's findings the Board establishes what consequences are to be drawn from an investigation. *See* Resolution Establishing the Inspection Panel, Resolution No. IBRD 93–10, Resolution No. IDA 93–6; *reprinted at* 34 *I.L.M.*, (1995) 503, 22 September 1993 (in particular paras 16–20, 20–25). Operating Procedures of the Inspection Panel as Adopted by the Panel on 19 August 1994 *reprinted* in 34 *I.L.M.* (1995), at 510.

[127] World Bank, Operating Procedures, *supra* note 126, Purpose.

[128] Resolution Establishing the Inspection Panel, *supra* note 126, para. 12. The Resolution allows for representation of an affected party by a local representative, or, in exceptional cases where local representation is not available and the Executive Directors agree to this, by another representative.

groups that may be affected by such projects';[129] thus, this procedure is an attempt to integrate local concerns into a global institution.

Non-State actors may not only trigger the procedure before the WB Inspection Panel, they can also provide additional information to the Panel. Thus, other forms of public participation can take place during an investigation undertaken by the Inspection Panel. The Operating Procedures specify that 'during the course of the investigation, in addition to any information requested by the Inspector(s), any member of the public may provide the Inspector(s), either directly or through the Executive Secretary, with supplemental information that they believe is relevant to evaluating the Request'. They continue, saying that 'information should not exceed ten pages' and inspectors 'may request more details if necessary'.[130] Therefore, representatives of the public-at-large may provide the Panel with information if they believe that it is relevant to a request.[131]

Yet reactions of the Bank management to the findings of the Panel are not open to comment by those submitting the request for investigation. Furthermore, the Panel's recommendations and the reactions of the Bank management are made available to the requester and the public only after the Executive Directors have taken a decision in the matter.[132]

The establishment of the Inspection Panel allows individuals to file requests against the World Bank if they believe that it has failed to comply with its operational policies.[133] The Panel's mandate extends to projects financed by the International Bank for Reconstruction and Development (IBRD) and the International Development Association (IDA).[134] The WB Panel does not apply to the International Finance Corporation (IFC) or Multilateral Investment Guarantee Agency (MIGA), which provide loans, insurance guarantees, and other support to private sector projects. In 1999, the IFC and MIGA created the office of the Compliance Advisor/Ombudsman (CAO). The CAO Office has three distinct but related roles: responding to complaints by persons who are

In this context it may be noted that in the case of *China/Western Poverty Reduction Project*, the procedure before the WB Inspection Panel was triggered by a US-based NGO, the International Campaign for Tibet, which acted for and on behalf of 'Tibetan and Mongolian ethnic people' living in the project area. *See* International Campaign for Tibet, Request for Inspection: China Western Poverty Reduction Project, 18 June 1999.

[129] E. Hey, *Non-State Actors and International Water Disputes: A Search for the Nexus Between the Local and the Global*, in RESOLUTION OF INTERNATIONAL WATER DISPUTES (Peace Palace Papers, Kluwer Law International, 2003), at 314.

[130] Operating Procedures of the Inspection Panel, *supra* note 126, paras 50–51.

[131] On this basis, NGOs in Switzerland and in the United States submitted memoranda in the Indian NTPC Power Generation Project. *See*, e.g., R.E. Bissell, *Recent Practice of the Inspection Panel of the World Bank*, 91 AMERICAN JOURNAL OF INTERNATIONAL LAW 741 (1997), at 743.

[132] Inspection Panel's Resolution, 1993, *supra* note 126, para. 25; Inspection Panel Operating Procedures, 1994, *supra* note 126, paras 40, 48, and 56.

[133] For a general assessment on the activities of the WB Inspection Panel, *see The World Bank Inspection Panel, Accountability at the World Bank, The Inspection Panel 10 Years On* (Washington D.C., 2003).

[134] Resolution establishing the Panel, *supra* note 126, para. 28.

affected by projects and attempting to resolve the issues raised using a flexible, problem-solving approach (the ombudsman role); providing advice to the management of the IFC and MIGA in relation to particular projects, and in relation to broader environmental and social policies (the advisory role); and ensuring compliance with the IFC and MIGA's policies and procedures (the compliance role). Concerning the ombudsman role, according to the CAO Operational Guidelines, the aim of the ombudsman 'is to identify problems, recommend practical remedial action and address systemic issues that have contributed to the problems, rather than to find fault'. When a complaint is accepted for assessment, the CAO undertakes a preliminary investigation in order to assess the complaint and determine how it should be handled.[135]

In this context should be mentioned the CAO Assessment Report on the IFC's involvement in the Pangue/Ralco hydroelectric project in Chile. While this request was considered ineligible by the WB Inspection Panel because the project was financed by the IFC, the CAO accepted the complaint. The main issue raised before the CAO was the question of transparency. In particular, the complainants asked for the disclosure of a number of documents and information which, they argued, were pertinent to the present day development of Pangue. In the Assessment Report, the Ombudsman affirmed that

> the IFC should ensure that in future projects that the present information disclosure policy is interpreted in such a way to ensure the release of technical reports and supporting or additional reports that contextualize environmental assessment documents, environmental management plans and/or shed light on environmental and social impacts during implementation. The CAO recommends that IFC press Pangue S.A. to disclose the results of monitoring and supervision in relation to the downstream impacts and that IFC, despite its exit from the project, request that Pangue disclose the original report.[136]

Therefore, in its report the CAO underscores the importance ensuring transparency in the IFC's projects.

The majority of the requests submitted to the WB Inspection Panel cite violations of the Bank's safeguard policies, in particular the policies on environmental assessment (OD 4.01),[137] indigenous peoples (OD 4.20),[138] and involuntary resettlement (OD 4.30).[139]

Several claims concern large-scale water infrastructures financed by the World Bank. In the request concerning the Lesotho Water Project, petitioners invoked

[135] International Finance Corporation/Multilateral Investment Guarantee Agency, 2000, *CAO Operational Guidelines*, April 2000, Washington, D.C., at 13.

[136] Assessment by the Office of the Compliance Advisor/Ombudsman in relation to a complaint filed against IFC's investment in ENDESA Pangue S.A., May 2003, at 26–7.

[137] The OD 4.01 includes consultation of concerned populations and local NGOs in the environmental assessment of a project. *See* OD/OP 4.01 on Environmental Assessment, para. 15.

[138] The OD 4.20 underscores the necessity of an informed participation of indigenous populations in projects in which they have interests at stake. *See* OD 4.20 on Indigenous people, para. 8.

[139] The OD 4.30 affirms the community participation and consultations with people affected by a resettlement as a result of a project financed by the Bank. *See* OD 4.30 on Involuntary Resettlement, paras 7–10.

the violation of the directive on environmental policy on dams and reservoirs projects, and of the policies on water resources management, as well as on poverty reduction. Concerning this case, two claims were brought before the Inspection Panel (in 1998 and in 1999). In both cases the Panel found the requests ineligible for inspection. In particular, in the second complaint, the requesters claimed that World Bank financing of this project could deter South Africa's water conservation efforts. They affirmed that proceeding with the project would divert funds needed to provide the poor with access to water. The Panel's preliminary assessment noted that for reasons of historical neglect, poor communities suffer widespread inequities in terms of lack of, or limited access to, water. Moreover, leakages within the water systems were causing severe wastage and health problems. However, the Panel found no evidence linking this situation to the project. The Panel therefore found the request ineligible for inspection. Rather, it concluded that the conditions appeared to be the direct result of historical neglect of these communities during South Africa's period of apartheid.[140]

It should be noted that the requesters did not only receive benefits if the request resulted in the Panel recommending an investigation.[141] In the case regarding a project to build a bridge over the Jamuna River in Bangladesh, the Bank Management did not recognize violations and the Inspection Panel refrained from recommending an investigation. The claim nevertheless resulted in the development of an action plan to remedy problems in the project: *inter alia*, approximately 70,000 people who were originally excluded from the resettlement plan were included.[142] In the case of the Itaparica dam in Brazil, the Board decided that no investigation was needed. However, the Panel proceeding led to additional financing to address adverse social and environmental impacts of the Bank-funded project.

In July 2001, the Panel received a request for inspection concerning the Bujagali Hydroelectric Project in Uganda.[143] The requesters claimed violations

[140] *See* Request for Inspection Lesotho/South Africa: Phase 1B of Lesotho Highlands Water Project Panel Report and Recommendation 18 August 1998; The Inspection Panel Report and Recommendation on Request of Inspection Re: Request for Inspection from Swissbourgh Diamond Mines (Pty) Ltd. & Others-Lesotho: Lesotho Highlands Water Project (Loan No: 4339-LSO).

[141] The Inspection Panel recommended investigation in all the claims concerning the projects of dams (except for the Lesotho and Pangue projects): Arun III in Nepal, Yacyretà dam on the Argentina/Paraguay border, Bujagali project in Uganda, Itaparica dam in Brazil, China Western Poverty Reduction Project. However, the Board approved investigation only in the following cases: the Arun III project, the Bujagali Hydroelectric Project, and the Yacyretà dam. In the case of China: Western Poverty Reduction Project, the Board met to consider the Panel's Investigation Report and Management's Response, but during the meeting the borrower informed the Bank that it withdrew one of the components of its loan application.

[142] D.D Bradlow, *Precedent-Setting NGO Campaign Saves the World Bank's Inspection Panel, Human Rights Brief* 6 Brief No. 3 (1999), available at www.wcl.american.edu.

[143] The Bujagali project should be financed not only by the World Bank but also by the IFC. In 2001, a complaint was also filed before the CAO Office. The CAO concluded that several issues fell under the ombudsman role, and other issues would be better dealt with under the advisory role. In its recommendations, the CAO affirmed that it 'is aware that there is a request to the Inspection Panel' and

of several of the Bank's safeguard policies, including: environmental assessment, involuntary resettlement, natural habitat, and indigenous peoples policies. In 2002, the Board of Executive Directors approved the Management's response to the Panel's Investigation Report. In particular, the Board affirmed the necessity to amend the Indemnity Agreement between Uganda and the World Bank in order to reaffirm the government's commitment not to develop the Kalagala Falls for hydropower. It also stated the need to have expanded multi-stakeholder consultations and its engagement to provide support to the Nile Basin Initiative. Indeed, it considered that 'the Nile Basin Initiative for a Strategic/Sectoral Social and Environmental Assessment will be a prerequisite to any future World Bank-financing of investments in power generation facilities under the Nile Equatorial Lakes Subsidiary Action Program'.

The Yacyretà Dam Project, on the Argentina/Paraguay border is co-financed by two financial institutions: the World Bank and the IDB. The WB Inspection Panel received two requests, in 1996 and in 2002. In both cases the complaint was also filed with the IDB mechanism. In reviewing the eligibility of the second request on the Yacyretà dam, the WB Inspection Panel examined the content of allegations made in both requests for inspection. In particular, the Panel considered the provisions of paragraph 14(d) of the Resolution establishing the Inspection Panel, which provides:

> ... the following requests shall not be heard by the Panel: Requests related to a particular matter or matters over which the Panel has already made its recommendation upon having received a prior request, unless justified by new evidence or circumstances not known at the time of the prior request.

Based on the foregoing and the findings of the Panel's visit to the project area, the Panel found that the second request met the eligibility criteria. Therefore the Panel concluded that 'although generally of a similar nature, most of the particular matters or claims on both Requests are substantially different'. The Panel continued: 'In the light of the foregoing, the Panel recommends an investigation into the matters alleged in the Request.'[144] As to the IDB compliance mechanism, in the case of the first request, the IDB Board agreed to an independent review of the situation in the project area rather than authorizing an investigation. Thus, in 1997, the IDB Board took note of the Panel report and

that it 'now needs the Complainant to consider the assessment of the Ombudsman and comments by IFC management [under the CAO's Advisory role] and request further intervention, if necessary'. In its report, the CAO concluded that it 'does not see a role for facilitation or mediation at this stage because the IFC has not made a final decision to participate in the project'. Assesment Report, Complaint filed before the CAO regarding the Uganda Bujagali Hydropower Project, September 2001, *available at* http://nilebasin.com/documents/annex.htm.

[144] Report and Recommendation on Request for Inspection Paraguay—Reform Project for the Water and Telecommunications Sectors (Loan No. 3842—PA), Argentina—SEGBA V Power Distribution Project (Loan No. 2854—AR), para. 42. In May 2004, the World Bank Board discussed the findings of the Inspection Panel review of the Yacyretà Hydroelectric Project, and also Management's official response to the review.

management's comments, without taking a final decision on the recommendations of the Panel. Regarding the second complaint, an investigation has been authorized by the IDB board.

Last should be mentioned the proposed hydroelectric project in Nepal (the Arun III project) and the Western Poverty Reduction Project in China. The Arun III project was the first case brought before the WB Inspection Panel. The requesters claimed that the World Bank did not comply with its own operational policies and procedures in designing and financing a hydroelectric dam in the Arun Valley, to the east of Kathmandu. The Panel recommended further investigation and the WB Board of Directors approved the investigation.[145] In August 1995, the World Bank announced that it would not approve funds for the dam and would instead study energy conservation and small-scale hydro power.

The Western Poverty Reduction Project in China is one of the World Bank's most controversial projects because of its serious social and environmental effects. In particular, its aim is to alleviate poverty through the resettlement of about 57,000 farmers in an area where the renovation of an existing dam will supply water. The requesters' main claim was that 'the resettlement of the new migrants ... [would] directly and adversely impact on the entire country, including a serious risk of escalation of ethnic tension and conflicts over resources'. The Inspection Panel Investigation Report concluded that Bank Management had violated, *inter alia*, operational directives regarding indigenous peoples, involuntary resettlement, and environmental assessment. On 7 July 2000, before the Executive Directors were able to reach a conclusion, China withdrew its application for one of the loan components on the grounds that new conditions were unacceptable as the loan conditions had already been agreed upon, and noted that it would pay for the projects itself.[146] As a consequence, the government in charge of the project will complete the project on its own, with the probable support of private investors who do not, or do only to a much lesser extent, adhere to social and environmental standards as enshrined in the Bank's safeguard policies.

Although a means of last resort, the recommendations of the compliance mechanisms established by the World Bank and other regional banks have increased both staff and management awareness of the need for the institutions to comply with their operational policies so as to prevent requests from being brought before the Panel. Indeed, the recommendations and findings of these accountability mechanisms have underscored the need to pay greater attention to compliance with operational policies. They have also contributed to the

[145] *See* Nepal: Arun III Hydroelectric Project (25 October 1994), http://wbln0018.worldbank.org/IPN/ipnweb.nsf/WReport/89813D438233F87B85256DBB0068E792.

[146] *See* The Inspection Panel Report and Recommendation on Request for Inspection, Re: Request for Inspection China: Western Poverty Reduction Project, 24 August 1999, para. 6. In this regard, *see* S.R. Roos, *The World Bank Inspection Panel in its Seventh Year: An Analysis of its Process, Mandate, and Desirability with special reference to the China (Tibet) case*, Max Planck Yearbook of United Nations Law, 5, 2001, at 473–521.

establishment of various mechanisms, such as internal review processes during the preparation of a project.[147]

The mechanisms established by the IDB[148] and the ADB[149] mirror the World Bank Panel in many features. Nevertheless they differ in one important respect. In place of a standing Panel, the IDB and the ADB have a roster of ten individuals from which the Board selects panels of three or more to investigate particular complaints. Moreover, whereas the WB Inspection Panel initially screens each request for inspection and makes a recommendation to the Executive Directors as to whether an inspection is warranted, the IDB[150] and ADB[151] Board of Directors first decide whether an investigation is warranted and convene an investigation panel only after making such a finding.

However, in May 2003 the ADB approved a new accountability mechanism. This new mechanism consists of two complementary functions: a consultation phase and a compliance review phase. On one hand, the aim of the consultation phase is to assist project-affected people through a number of informal, consensus-based methods such as consultative dialogue, good offices, or mediation; on the other hand, the compliance review phase strengthens the ADB's accountability.[152]

[147] L. Boisson de Chazournes, *supra* note 125, at 93.

[148] Only four claims have been brought before the IDB's Independent Investigation Mechanism: the Yacyretá Hydroelectric Project (Argentina–Paraguay—brought twice before the Mechanism), the Termoeléctrica del Golfo Project (Mexico), and the Cana Brava Hydroelectric Project (Brazil). Regarding the Termoeléctrica del Golfo project, the IDB Board authorized an investigation. The Panel completed its investigation and submitted its findings in February 2003. For the fourth claim, the 2002 annual report affirms that the complaint was filed in accordance with the requirements for application of the Mechanism and, as a result, the President of the Bank will appoint a member of the roster (see below) in order to make a recommendation to the Board whether an investigation should be authorized. *See*, e.g., Independent Investigation Mechanism 2002 Annual Report, available at: http://www.iadb.org/cont/poli/investig/iimar02eng.pdf.

[149] As of July 2003 the ADB had received eight requests for inspection: only one request—the Samut Prakarn Wastewater Management Project in Thailand—has gone through a full inspection process. In November 2002, the ADB received a request for inspection regarding the Chashma Right Bank Irrigation Project (Stage III) in Pakistan from six NGOs representing local persons affected by this project. The request alleged violations of the ADB's policies and guidelines. In particular, requesters assert that the implementation of this project has caused several problems, including displacement. Moreover, they claim a severe lack of transparency for the planning and implementation of the project, and various other social and environmental impacts such as flooding, land degradation, and deforestation. In April 2003, the Board authorized an inspection which started in December 2003. Report of the Board Inspection Committee to the Board of Directors on the Request for Inspection on Chashma Right Bank Irrigation Project (Stage III) (ADB Loan No. 1146-PAK [SF]) in the Islamic Republic of Pakistan. *See* http://www.adb.org/Inspection/projects/chashma_right.asp#inspection.

[150] It may be noted that in 2000, after a brief review of its policy, the IDB Board created a staff 'coordinator' position that reviews the initial complaint along with the legal department to determine whether the request meets the initial eligibility requirements. *See* http://www.adb.org/Documents/Policies/ADB_Accountability_Mechanism/default.asp.

[151] In the context of the ADB, the six-member committee of the Board of Directors takes the decision as to whether an investigation is warranted.

[152] The ADB emphasizes that operations at all stages of the consultation and compliance phase will be as transparent as possible. For a review of this new mechanism, *see* http://www.adb.org/Documents/Policies/ADB_Accountability_Mechanism/default.asp.

It should be observed that there is also a need of accountability mechanisms at institutions other than multilateral development banks. For instance, in 2001, the executive board of the International Monetary Fund (IMF) established the Independent Evaluation Office (IEO) to provide evaluations of IMF policies. Its aim is to improve the IMF's effectiveness through increased transparency, and also to promote greater understanding of IMF work.[153]

Compliance mechanisms are not only established under the aegis of international organizations, they are also increasingly being provided under multilateral[154] and regional environmental agreements. Among the regional agreements should be mentioned the mechanism set up by the North American Agreement on Environmental Cooperation (NAAEC).

4.2 The North American Agreement on Environmental Cooperation

In its preamble, the NAAEC emphasizes 'the importance of public participation in conserving, protecting and enhancing the environment'. One of the objectives of the NAEEC is to promote 'transparency and public participation in the development of environmental laws, regulations and policies'. In order to ensure public participation, the NAAEC established a citizen submission process and the fifteen-member Joint Public Advisory Committee (JPC), which advises the Council of the Commission for Environmental Cooperation (CEC) on a broad range of issues.

According to Article 16.4 of the NAEEC:

> The Joint Public Advisory Committee may provide advice to the Council on any matter within the scope of this Agreement, including on any documents provided to it under paragraph 6 (namely the draft annual report, and any report the Secretariat prepares pursuant to Article 13), and on the implementation and further elaboration of this Agreement, and may perform such other functions as the Council may direct.

In accordance with this provision, in 2002 the JPC provided advice to the Council on how the CEC can engage in the complex issue of freshwater management in North America. In its advice, the JPC underscores the role of public awareness concerning the problems associated with freshwater. The JPC affirms that 'the CEC has gathered valuable contributions to what is already known at the institutional level about the status of freshwater in North America. However, this information is not widely known by the general public, and therefore fails to influence behaviour'.[155]

[153] Two leading bilateral export credit agencies (Export Development Canada and Japan Bank for International Cooperation) also announced their intention to create accountability mechanisms. *See* http://www.adb.org/Documents/Policies/ADB_Accountability_Mechanism/default.asp.

[154] *See*, e.g., Montreal Protocol on Substances that Deplete the Ozone Layer, Non-Compliance Procedure, Annex IV (UNEP/OzL.Pro4/15, 1992) at 44; Basel Convention on the Control of Transboundary Movements of Hazardous Wastes and their Disposal, Decision VI/12, Establishment of a Mechanism for Promoting Implementation and Compliance (2002), Appendix, available at www.basel.int.

[155] Advice to Council, No. 02–10, Re: The CEC and the Management of Freshwater in North America, 4 October 2002, available at http://www.cec.org/files/pdf/JPAC/02-10e1-fin.pdf.

In March 2003, the JPC, in its advice regarding the 'Balance between the Interests of the Public and Investors in the Application of Chapter 11 of the North American Free Trade Agreement', affirmed the necessity to ensure transparency and public participation before NAFTA Chapter 11 Tribunals. It considered that the CEC should support 'the establishment of a structured public process, including such elements as the ability to attend tribunal hearings, enshrining the principle of *amicus* briefs, and access to information, as appropriate to and necessary for informed participation in the process'.[156] With this advice, the JPC aims to promote transparency and public participation in the dispute settlement mechanism set up by the NAFTA Chapter 11.

According to Article 14 of the NAEEC: 'The Secretariat may consider a submission from any non-governmental organization or person asserting that a Party is failing to effectively enforce its environmental law.' It should be noted that submissions can also be filed by for-profit entities. For instance, in October 1999, a submission was filed by the Methanex Corporation, a Canadian private company. In its submission, Methanex alleged that the US government was failing effectively to enforce various environmental laws relating to water resource protection and the regulation of underground storage tanks. However, the NAEEC Secretariat dismissed the submission since Methanex had already filed a claim under Chapter 11 of the NAFTA. Under Article 14(3)(a) of the NAAEC, the Secretariat 'shall proceed no further' if a submission 'is the subject of a pending judicial or administrative proceeding'.[157]

As explained by the *Guidelines for Submissions on Enforcement Matters under Articles 14 and 15 of the North American Agreement on Environmental Cooperation*: 'A "submission on enforcement matters" is a documented assertion that a Party to the NAAEC is failing to effectively enforce its environmental law'.[158] The Secretariat may consider a submission on enforcement matters only if that submission meets the criteria set forth in Article 14(1) of the Agreement.[159] Therefore, through this mechanism non-State actors can contribute to the enforcement of environmental law in NAFTA Party States.

[156] Advice to Council No. 03–01, Re: Seeking Balance between the Interests of the Public and Investors in the Application of Chapter 11 of the North American Free Trade Agreement (NAFTA), 27 March 2003, available at http://www.cec.org/files/pdf/JPAC/Advice-03-01_en.pdf.

[157] *See*, e.g., Secretariat of the Commission for Environmental Cooperation Determination pursuant to Article 14(3) of the North American Agreement on Environmental Cooperation, 30 June 2000, available at http://www.cec.org/citizen/submissions/details/index.cfm?varlan=english&ID=66.

[158] Guidelines for Submissions on Enforcement Matters under Articles 14 and 15 of the North American Agreement on Environmental Cooperation, adopted in Oaxaca on 13 October 1995, amended by Council Resolution 99–06, Banff, 28 June 1995 and by Council Resolution 01–06 adopted on 29 June 2001. In particular, the 2001 Council Resolution commits the Council to provide 'a public statement of its reasons whenever it votes not to instruct the Secretariat to prepare a factual record'. Text available at http://www.cec.org/citizen/guide_submit/index.cfm?varlan=english.

[159] Under the criteria set forth in Art. 14.1 of the NAEEC, the submission has to be written in a language designated by that Party in a notification to the Secretariat; it has to identify clearly the person or organization making the submission. The submission must provide sufficient information to allow the Secretariat to review the submission, including any documentary evidence on which the submission may be based. The aim of the petition must be to promote the enforcement of

Article 15 delineates the rest of the procedure that can lead to the publication of a factual record on the case. Following a review of the submission, the CEC may investigate the matter and publish a factual record of its findings, subject to approval by the CEC Council.[160] The factual record ensures a transparency and publicity function. In particular, its aim is to draw attention to the non-enforcement of environmental law by a Party.

It should be noted that since 1995, the CEC Council has approved the publication of factual records for only ten cases out of fifty-one.[161] Among these cases, the *BC Hydro, Aquanova*, and *Rio Magdalena* cases should be mentioned. In the submission concerning the *BC Hydro* case, the submitters alleged that the Canadian government failed to ensure the protection of fish and fish habitat in British Columbia's rivers from ongoing and repeated environmental damage caused by hydro-electric dams. Moreover, in the *Aquanova* and *Rio Magdalena* cases, petitioners alleged, *inter alia*, that the authorities failed effectively to enforce legal provisions regarding the prevention of water pollution. In these cases, the publication of the factual records has led to increased public awareness of a lack of enforcement of environmental law. Thus, the public places increased pressure on the government to enforce the environmental laws in question.

Several provisions of the NAEEC aim to ensure transparency and public participation in environmental matters. In this context should be mentioned Article 1, which obliges the Parties to 'periodically prepare and make publicly available reports on the state of the environment'. Article 4 also aims to promote access to information; in particular it provides that 'Each Party shall ensure that

environmental law and not to harass an industry. The submission must indicate that the matter has been communicated in writing to the relevant authorities of the Party and indicate the Party's response, if any; and finally, it must be filed by a person or organization residing or established in the territory of a Party. Moreover, Art. 14 provides that the Party then has 30 days (or 60 days in special circumstances) to respond to the allegations, especially regarding whether the subject of the submission is undergoing any other legal proceedings.

[160] Art. 15 of the NAAEC. In particular, Art. 15.2 reads as follows: 'The Secretariat shall prepare a factual record if the Council, by a two-thirds vote, instructs it to do so.' Once the final record is completed, by a 2:3 vote, the Council can decide whether to make the factual record publicly available (Art. 15.7), otherwise it remains confidential. The Council, the governing body of the CEC, is composed of the environment ministers (or the equivalent) of each country. It meets at least once a year to discuss CEC programs and activities.

[161] *See*, e.g.: *Aquanova* (SEM-98-006), Date filed: 20/10/98, Party concerned: Mexico (the final factual record was publicly released on 23/06/2003); *BC Hydro* (SEM-97-001), Date filed: 2/04/1997, Party concerned: Canada (the final factual record was publicly released on 11/06/2000); *Cozumel* (SEM-96-001), Date filed: 17/01/1996, Party concerned: Mexico (the final factual record was publicly released on 24/10/1997); *Metales y Derivados* (SEM-98-007) Date filed: 23/10/1998, Party concerned: Mexico (the final factual record was publicly released on 11/02/2002); *Migratory Birds* (SEM-89-002), Date filed: 19/11/1999, Party concerned: United States (the final factual record was publicly released on 24/04/2003); *Oldam River II* (SEM-97-006), Date filed: 4/10/1997, Party concerned: Canada (the final factual record was publicly released on 11/08/2003); *Rio Magdalena* (SEM-97-002), Date filed: 15/03/1997, Party concerned: Mexico (the final factual record was publicly released on 11/12/2003) visited August 2004. Status of the submissions available at: http://www.cec.org/citizen/status/index.cfm?varlan=english.

its laws, regulations, procedures and administrative rulings of general application respecting any matter covered by this Agreement are promptly published or otherwise made available...' Through these rules, State Members of the NAEEC affirm their commitment to guarantee effective transparency in environmental issues. Indeed, effective transparency in decision-making depends on full, accurate, up-to-date information.

Moreover, Article 6.2 reads as follows:

> Each Party shall ensure that persons with a legally recognized interest under its law in a particular matter have appropriate access to administrative, quasi-judicial or judicial proceedings for the enforcement of the Party's environmental laws and regulations.

This provision strengthens the enforcement of domestic environmental law. Access to justice is one of the most important means for essentially protecting transparency and public participation. Judicial mechanisms should be effective to ensure transparency and public participation in water disputes.

5. General conclusions: transparency, public participation, and non-compliance mechanisms

Water-related decisions and disputes have an impact on issues of public interest. At the local level, decisions may affect the interests of peoples and individuals. At the international level, disputes may have transboundary effects that engage issues of public interest in both States. Given their public interest character, there are calls for decision-making processes to be 'transparent'. Transparency in water-related decisions can be ensured through access to information and public participation. This approach is indispensable in order to avoid water disputes at local, national, and international level.

After the proclamation of a need for 'participation of all concerned citizens' in environmental decisions made by the Rio Declaration, the Aarhus Convention 'crystallizes', although at the European level, an emerging *opinio juris* in relation to the involvement of the public in environmental decisions. In another region of the world, the Senegal Water Charter also highlights the need to involve local communities and private users in decision-making concerning water issues. Public participation, access to documents, and EIAs are essential tools for the avoidance of water disputes, allowing the involvement of non-State actors and States, which could be affected by decisions taken by another State, in water-related decisions.

Water disputes have been singled out as a category in which non-State participation is most needed, since they involve public interest issues. In the settlement of water disputes, through the submission of *amici* briefs, non-parties may express their concerns on the issues submitted to a tribunal. The analysis of the WTO and NAFTA jurisprudence shows the role of *amici* briefs as means of public participation in the settlement of disputes.

Compliance mechanisms are a new tool to ensure public participation and transparency in water disputes. Institutional procedural arrangements for facilitating and promoting compliance, on a multilateral and cooperative basis, are not only established under the aegis of international organizations, they are also increasingly being provided under MEAs.

Most agreements on transboundary waters, including the 1997 UN Watercourses Convention, do not provide for compliance review. However, certain instruments, such as the 1999 Protocol on Water and Health to the 1992 UN/ECE Watercourse Convention[162] (hereinafter the 1999 London Protocol), envisage the setting up of a compliance review procedure. Article 15 to the 1999 London Protocol provides that

> Parties shall review the compliance of the Parties with the provisions of this Protocol on the basis of the reviews and assessments referred to in article 7. Multilateral arrangements of a non-confrontational, non-judicial and consultative nature for reviewing compliance shall be established by the Parties at their first meeting. These arrangements shall allow for appropriate public involvement.

In light of this provision, the signatories to the 1999 London Protocol entrusted a group of experts with the task of creating a compliance review mechanism. This group drafted in 1999 the *Geneva Strategy and Framework for Monitoring Compliance with Agreements on Transboundary Waters*,[163] setting out the principles and guidelines meant to provide guidance for the establishment of compliance review procedures for any legal instruments negotiated under, or in connection with, the UN/ECE Watercourse Convention.

The Geneva Strategy illustrates that compliance is increasingly recognized as a key issue for international water treaties. This recognition strengthens the role of compliance mechanisms as means for the promotion of issues of public participation and transparency in conventional texts.

The development of an innovative compliance mechanism under the Aarhus Convention will also affect water issues, ensuring public participation and transparency in water-related decisions. This mechanism reflects the principles of transparency and participation that are hallmarks of the Aarhus Convention itself. For example, NGOs are entitled to nominate candidates for the Compliance Committee.[164] Information held by the Committee is generally public and may be kept confidential only in limited and clearly defined circumstances, for example, where a person making a complaint does not want his or her identity to be revealed, or where the Committee needs to examine information claimed by a Party to be confidential under the Aarhus Convention to decide whether the claim is justified.[165]

[162] Text available at www.unece.org.

[163] United Nations Economic and Social Council, UN DOC. MP.WAT/2000/5, 17 December 1999.

[164] Decision I/7, Meeting of the Parties, 31 October 2002, para. 4. Available at www.unece.org/env/pp/mop1/decision.1.7.e.doc.

[165] *Id.*, section VIII.

The Aarhus compliance mechanism provides for members of the public to make communications to the Committee in cases of alleged non-compliance with the Convention, which the Committee is then required to review.[166] In international environmental agreements, it is unusual that the public has the right to make communications claiming that a State Party to the agreement is not fulfilling its obligations under that agreement. However, this could be seen as a logical consequence of the fact that the Aarhus Convention seeks to guarantee the rights of the public, not only the rights of Parties vis-à-vis one another. In other fields of international law, in particular human rights law, this is a well-established and much-used mechanism to ensure that States respect the basic human rights as set out in various treaties.

Human rights law can play an important role in the development of the notion of public participation and transparency in international environmental law in general and water law in particular.[167] The norms of this branch of international law have already influenced the conceptualization of rules established by the Aarhus Convention and water-related conventions. At the same time, the notions developed by international environmental law can strengthen and give new models for human rights law. Whether such legal texts succeed in finally enhancing public participation depends not only on their formal implementation but also on the extent to which implementation is scrutinized. In particular, compliance mechanisms play an important role. In this field, the activities and involvement of non-State actors are the most needed in the future.

[166] Para. 18 of Decision I/7 provides: 'On the expiry of twelve months from either the date of adoption of this decision or from the date of the entry into force of the Convention with respect to a Party, whichever is the later, communications may be brought before the Committee by one or more members of the public concerning that Party's compliance with the Convention, unless that Party has notified the Depositary in writing by the end of the applicable period that it is unable to accept, for a period of not more than four years, the consideration of such communications by the Committee.'

[167] *See, inter alia*, G. Palmer, *New Ways to Make International Environmental Law*, 86 American Journal of International Law, 259 (1992); T. M. Franck, *The Emerging Right to Democratic Governance, id.* 46; A. Boyle, *The Role of International Human Rights Law in the Protection of the Environment*, in Human Rights Approaches to Environmental Protection (A. Boyle and M. R. Anderson, 1996), at 59; J. Cameron & R. Mackenzie, *Access to Environmental Justice and Procedural Rights in International Institutions*, in id., at 134–5.

Appendix A

Committee on Economic, Social and Cultural Rights

General Comment No. 15, The Right to Water (Articles 11 and 12 of the International Covenant on Economic, Social and Cultural Rights), U.N. DOC. E/C.12/2002/11, 26 November 2002*

I. Introduction

1. Water is a limited natural resource and a public good fundamental for life and health. The human right to water is indispensable for leading a life in human dignity. It is a prerequisite for the realization of other human rights. The Committee has been confronted continually with the widespread denial of the right to water in developing as well as developed countries. Over one billion persons lack access to a basic water supply, while several billion do not have access to adequate sanitation, which is the primary cause of water contamination and diseases linked to water.[1] The continuing contamination, depletion and unequal distribution of water is exacerbating existing poverty. States parties have to adopt effective measures to realize, without discrimination, the right to water, as set out in this general comment.

The legal bases of the right to water

2. The human right to water entitles everyone to sufficient, safe, acceptable, physically accessible and affordable water for personal and domestic uses. An adequate amount of safe water is necessary to prevent death from dehydration, to reduce the risk of water-related disease and to provide for consumption, cooking, personal and domestic hygienic requirements.

3. Article 11, paragraph 1, of the Covenant specifies a number of rights emanating from, and indispensable for, the realization of the right to an adequate standard of living 'including adequate food, clothing and housing'. The use of the word 'including' indicates that this catalogue of rights was not intended to be exhaustive. The right to water clearly falls within the category of guarantees essential for

* Text available at: http://www.unchr.ch/html/menu2/6/gc15.doc. The original text does not have a footnote 27.

[1] In 2000, the World Health Organization estimated that 1.1 billion persons did not have access to an improved water supply (80 per cent of them rural dwellers) able to provide at least 20 litres of safe water per person a day; 2.4 billion persons were estimated to be without sanitation. (See WHO, *The Global Water Supply and Sanitation Assessment 2000*, Geneva, 2000, p. 1.) Further, 2.3 billion persons each year suffer from diseases linked to water: see United Nations, Commission on Sustainable Development, *Comprehensive Assessment of the Freshwater Resources of the World*, New York, 1997, p. 39.

securing an adequate standard of living, particularly since it is one of the most fundamental conditions for survival. Moreover, the Committee has previously recognized that water is a human right contained in article 11, paragraph 1 (see General Comment No. 6 (1995)).[2] The right to water is also inextricably related to the right to the highest attainable standard of health (art. 12, para. 1)[3] and the rights to adequate housing and adequate food (art. 11, para. 1).[4] The right should also be seen in conjunction with other rights enshrined in the International Bill of Human Rights, foremost amongst them the right to life and human dignity.

4. The right to water has been recognized in a wide range of international documents, including treaties, declarations and other standards.[5] For instance, Article 14, paragraph 2, of the Convention on the Elimination of All Forms of Discrimination Against Women stipulates that States parties shall ensure to women the right to 'enjoy adequate living conditions, particularly in relation to [...] water supply'. Article 24, paragraph 2, of the Convention on the Rights of the Child requires States parties to combat disease and malnutrition 'through the provision of adequate nutritious foods and clean drinking-water'.

5. The right to water has been consistently addressed by the Committee during its consideration of States parties' reports, in accordance with its revised general guidelines regarding the form and content of reports to be submitted by States parties under articles 16 and 17 of the International Covenant on Economic, Social and Cultural Rights, and its general comments.

[2] See paras 5 and 32 of the Committee's General Comment No. 6 (1995) on the economic, social and cultural rights of older persons.

[3] See General Comment No. 14 (2000) on the right to the highest attainable standard of health, paragraphs 11, 12 (*a*), (*b*) and (*d*), 15, 34, 36, 40, 43 and 51.

[4] See para. 8 (*b*) of General Comment No. 4 (1991). See also the report by Commission on Human Rights' Special Rapporteur on adequate housing as a component of the right to an adequate standard of living, Mr. Miloon Kothari (E.CN.4/2002/59), submitted in accordance with Commission resolution 2001/28 of 20 April 2001. In relation to the right to adequate food, see the report by the Special Rapporteur of the Commission on the right to food, Mr. Jean Ziegler (E/CN.4/2002/58), submitted in accordance with Commission resolution 2001/25 of 20 April 2001.

[5] See art. 14, para. 2 (*h*), Convention on the Elimination of All Forms of Discrimination Against Women; art. 24, para. 2 (*c*), Convention on the Rights of the Child; arts 20, 26, 29 and 46 of the Geneva Convention relative to the Treatment of Prisoners of War, of 1949; arts 85, 89 and 127 of the Geneva Convention relative to the Treatment of Civilian Persons in Time of War, of 1949; arts 54 and 55 of Additional Protocol I thereto of 1977; arts 5 and 14 Additional Protocol II of 1977; preamble, Mar Del Plata Action Plan of the United Nations Water Conference; see para. 18.47 of Agenda 21, *Report of the United Nations Conference on Environment and Development, Rio de Janeiro, 3–14 June 1992* (A/CONF.151/26/Rev.1 (Vol. I and Vol. I/Corr.1, Vol. II, Vol. III and Vol. III/Corr.1) (United Nations publication, Sales No. E.93.I.8), vol I: *Resolutions adopted by the Conference*, resolution 1, annex II; Principle No. 3, The Dublin Statement on Water and Sustainable Development, International Conference on Water and the Environment (A/CONF.151/PC/112); Principle No. 2, Programme of Action, *Report of the United Nations International Conference on Population and Development, Cairo, 5–13 September 1994* (United Nations publication, Sales No. E.95.XIII.18), chap. I, resolution 1, annex; paras 5 and 19, Recommendation (2001) 14 of the Committee of Ministers to Member States on the European Charter on Water Resources; resolution 2002/6 of the United Nations Sub-Commission on the Promotion and Protection of Human Rights on the promotion of the realization of the right to drinking water. See also the report on the relationship between the enjoyment of economic, social and cultural rights and the promotion of the realization of the right to drinking water supply and sanitation (E/CN.4/Sub.2/2002/10) submitted by the Special Rapporteur of the Sub-Commission on the right to drinking water supply and sanitation, Mr. El Hadji Guissé.

6. Water is required for a range of different purposes, besides personal and domestic uses, to realize many of the Covenant rights. For instance, water is necessary to produce food (right to adequate food) and ensure environmental hygiene (right to health). Water is essential for securing livelihoods (right to gain a living by work) and enjoying certain cultural practices (right to take part in cultural life). Nevertheless, priority in the allocation of water must be given to the right to water for personal and domestic uses. Priority should also be given to the water resources required to prevent starvation and disease, as well as water required to meet the core obligations of each of the Covenant rights.[6]

Water and Covenant rights

7. The Committee notes the importance of ensuring sustainable access to water resources for agriculture to realize the right to adequate food (see General Comment No. 12 (1999)).[7] Attention should be given to ensuring that disadvantaged and marginalized farmers, including women farmers, have equitable access to water and water management systems, including sustainable rain harvesting and irrigation technology. Taking note of the duty in article 1, paragraph 2, of the Covenant, which provides that a people may not 'be deprived of its means of subsistence', States parties should ensure that there is adequate access to water for subsistence farming and for securing the livelihoods of indigenous peoples.[8]

8. Environmental hygiene, as an aspect of the right to health under article 12, paragraph 2 (*b*), of the Covenant, encompasses taking steps on a non-discriminatory basis to prevent threats to health from unsafe and toxic water conditions.[9] For example, States parties should ensure that natural water resources are protected from contamination by harmful substances and pathogenic microbes. Likewise, States parties should monitor and combat situations where aquatic eco-systems serve as a habitat for vectors of diseases wherever they pose a risk to human living environments.[10]

9. With a view to assisting States parties' implementation of the Covenant and the fulfilment of their reporting obligations, this General Comment focuses in Part II on the normative content of the right to water in articles 11, paragraph 1, and 12, on States parties' obligations (Part III), on violations (Part IV) and on implementation at the national level (Part V), while the obligations of actors other than States parties are addressed in Part VI.

[6] See also World Summit on Sustainable Development, Plan of Implementation 2002, paragraph 25 (c).

[7] This relates to both *availability* and to *accessibility* of the right to adequate food (see General Comment No. 12 (1999), paras 12 and 13).

[8] See also the Statement of Understanding accompanying the United Nations Convention on the Law of Non-Navigational Uses of Watercourses (A/51/869 of 11 April 1997), which declared that, in determining vital human needs in the event of conflicts over the use of watercourses 'special attention is to be paid to providing sufficient water to sustain human life, including both drinking water and water required for production of food in order to prevent starvation'.

[9] See also para. 15, General Comment No. 14.

[10] According to the WHO definition, vector-borne diseases include diseases transmitted by insects (malaria, filariasis, dengue, Japanese encephalitis and yellow fever), diseases for which aquatic snails serve as intermediate hosts (schistosomiasis) and zoonoses with vertebrates as reservoir hosts.

II. Normative content of the right to water

10. The right to water contains both freedoms and entitlements. The freedoms include the right to maintain access to existing water supplies necessary for the right to water, and the right to be free from interference, such as the right to be free from arbitrary disconnections or contamination of water supplies. By contrast, the entitlements include the right to a system of water supply and management that provides equality of opportunity for people to enjoy the right to water.
11. The elements of the right to water must be *adequate* for human dignity, life and health, in accordance with articles 11, paragraph 1, and 12. The adequacy of water should not be interpreted narrowly, by mere reference to volumetric quantities and technologies. Water should be treated as a social and cultural good, and not primarily as an economic good. The manner of the realization of the right to water must also be sustainable, ensuring that the right can be realized for present and future generations.[11]
12. While the adequacy of water required for the right to water may vary according to different conditions, the following factors apply in all circumstances:

(a) *Availability*. The water supply for each person must be sufficient and continuous for personal and domestic uses.[12] These uses ordinarily include drinking, personal sanitation, washing of clothes, food preparation, personal and household hygiene.[13] The quantity of water available for each person should correspond to World Health Organization (WHO) guidelines.[14] Some individuals and groups may also require additional water due to health, climate, and work conditions;
(b) *Quality*. The water required for each personal or domestic use must be safe, therefore free from micro-organisms, chemical substances and radiological *hazards* that constitute a threat to a person's health.[15] Furthermore, water should be of an acceptable colour, odour and taste for each personal or domestic use.

[11] For a definition of sustainability, see the *Report of the United Nations Conference on Environment and Development, Rio de Janeiro, 3–14 1992*, Declaration on Environment and Development Principles 1, 8, 9, 10, 12 and 15; and Agenda 21, in particular principles 5.3, 7.27, 7.28, 7.35, 7.39, 7.41, 18.3, 18.8, 18.35, 18.40, 18.48, 18.50, 18.59 and 18.68.

[12] 'Continuous' means that the regularity of the water supply is sufficient for personal and domestic uses.

[13] In this context, 'drinking' means water for consumption through beverages and foodstuffs. 'Personal sanitation' means disposal of human excreta. Water is necessary for personal sanitation where water-based means are adopted. 'Food preparation' includes food hygiene and preparation of food stuffs, whether water is incorporated into, or comes into contact with, food. 'Personal and household hygiene' means personal cleanliness and hygiene of the household environment.

[14] See J. Bartram and G. Howard, 'Domestic water quantity, service level and health: what should be the goal for water and health sectors', WHO, 2002. See also P. H. Gleick, (1996) 'Basic water requirements for human activities: meeting basic needs', *Water International*, 21, pp. 83–92.

[15] The Committee refers States parties to WHO, *Guidelines for drinking-water quality*, 2nd edition, vols. 1–3 (Geneva, 1993) that are 'intended to be used as a basis for the development of national standards that, if properly implemented, will ensure the safety of drinking water supplies through the elimination of, or reduction to a minimum concentration, of constituents of water that are known to be hazardous to health.'

(c) *Accessibility*. Water and water facilities and services have to be accessible to *everyone* without discrimination, within the jurisdiction of the State party. Accessibility has four overlapping dimensions:
  (i) *Physical accessibility*: water, and adequate water facilities and services, must be within safe physical reach for all sections of the population. Sufficient, safe and acceptable water must be accessible within, or in the immediate vicinity, of each household, educational institution and workplace.[16] All water facilities and services must be of sufficient quality, culturally appropriate and sensitive to gender, life-cycle and privacy requirements. Physical security should not be threatened during access to water facilities and services;
  (ii) *Economic accessibility*: Water, and water facilities and services, must be affordable for all. The direct and indirect costs and charges associated with securing water must be affordable, and must not compromise or threaten the realization of other Covenant rights;
  (iii) *Non-discrimination*: Water and water facilities and services must be accessible to all, including the most vulnerable or marginalized sections of the population, in law and in fact, without discrimination on any of the prohibited grounds; and
  (iv) *Information accessibility*: accessibility includes the right to seek, receive and impart information concerning water issues.[17]

Special Topics of Broad Application

Non-discrimination and equality

13. The obligation of States parties to guarantee that the right to water is enjoyed without discrimination (art. 2, para. 2), and equally between men and women (art. 3), pervades all of the Covenant obligations. The Covenant thus proscribes any discrimination on the grounds of race, colour, sex, age, language, religion, political or other opinion, national or social origin, property, birth, physical or mental disability, health status (including HIV/AIDS), sexual orientation and civil, political, social or other status, which has the intention or effect of nullifying or impairing the equal enjoyment or exercise of the right to water. The Committee recalls paragraph 12 of General Comment No. 3 (1990), which states that even in times of severe resource constraints, the vulnerable members of society must be protected by the adoption of relatively low-cost targeted programmes.

14. States parties should take steps to remove de facto discrimination on prohibited grounds, where individuals and groups are deprived of the means or entitlements necessary for achieving the right to water. States parties should ensure that the allocation of water resources, and investments in water, facilitate access to water for all members of society. Inappropriate resource allocation can lead to discrimination that may not be overt. For example, investments should not disproportionately favour

[16] See also General Comment No. 4 (1991) para. 8(*b*), General Comment No. 13 (1999) para. 6(*a*) and General Comment No. 14 (2000) paras 8(*a*) and (*b*). Household includes a permanent or semi-permanent dwelling, or a temporary halting site.

[17] See para. 48 of this General Comment.

expensive water supply services and facilities that are often accessible only to a small, privileged fraction of the population, rather than investing in services and facilities that benefit a far larger part of the population.

15. With respect to the right to water, States parties have a special obligation to provide those who do not have sufficient means with the necessary water and water facilities and to prevent any discrimination on internationally prohibited grounds in the provision of water and water services.

16. Whereas the right to water applies to everyone, States parties should give special attention to those individuals and groups who have traditionally faced difficulties in exercising this right, including women, children, minority groups, indigenous peoples, refugees, asylum seekers, internally displaced persons, migrant workers, prisoners and detainees. In particular, States parties should take steps to ensure that:

(a) Women are not excluded from decision-making processes concerning water resources and entitlements. The disproportionate burden women bear in the collection of water should be alleviated;
(b) Children are not prevented from enjoying their human rights due to the lack of adequate water in educational institutions and households or through the burden of collecting water. Provision of adequate water to educational institutions currently without adequate drinking water should be addressed as a matter of urgency;
(c) Rural and deprived urban areas have access to properly maintained water facilities. Access to traditional water sources in rural areas should be protected from unlawful encroachment and pollution. Deprived urban areas, including informal human settlements, and homeless persons, should have access to properly maintained water facilities. No household should be denied the right to water on the grounds of their housing or land status;
(d) Indigenous peoples' access to water resources on their ancestral lands is protected from encroachment and unlawful pollution. States should provide resources for indigenous peoples to design, deliver and control their access to water;
(e) Nomadic and traveller communities have access to adequate water at traditional and designated halting sites;
(f) Refugees, asylum-seekers, internally displaced persons and returnees have access to adequate water whether they stay in camps or in urban and rural areas. Refugees and asylum-seekers should be granted the right to water on the same conditions as granted to nationals;
(g) Prisoners and detainees are provided with sufficient and safe water for their daily individual requirements, taking note of the requirements of international humanitarian law and the United Nations Standard Minimum Rules for the Treatment of Prisoners;[18]
(h) Groups facing difficulties with physical access to water, such as older persons, persons with disabilities, victims of natural disasters, persons living in disaster-prone

[18] See arts 20, 26, 29 and 46 of the third Geneva Convention of 12 August 1949; arts 85, 89 and 127 of the fourth Geneva Convention of 12 August 1949; arts 15 and 20, para. 2, United Nations Standard Minimum Rules for the Treatment of Prisoners, in *Human Rights: A Compilation of International Instruments* (United Nations publication, Sales No. E.88.XIV.1).

areas, and those living in arid and semi-arid areas, or on small islands are provided with safe and sufficient water.

III. States parties' obligations

General legal obligations

17. While the Covenant provides for progressive realization and acknowledges the constraints due to the limits of available resources, it also imposes on States parties various obligations which are of immediate effect. States parties have immediate obligations in relation to the right to water, such as the guarantee that the right will be exercised without discrimination of any kind (art. 2, para. 2) and the obligation to take steps (art. 2, para. 1) towards the full realization of articles 11, paragraph 1, and 12. Such steps must be deliberate, concrete and targeted towards the full realization of the right to water.

18. States parties have a constant and continuing duty under the Covenant to move as expeditiously and effectively as possible towards the full realization of the right to water. Realization of the right should be feasible and practicable, since all States parties exercise control over a broad range of resources, including water, technology, financial resources and international assistance, as with all other rights in the Covenant.

19. There is a strong presumption that retrogressive measures taken in relation to the right to water are prohibited under the Covenant.[19] If any deliberately retrogressive measures are taken, the State party has the burden of proving that they have been introduced after the most careful consideration of all alternatives and that they are duly justified by reference to the totality of the rights provided for in the Covenant in the context of the full use of the State party's maximum available resources.

Specific legal obligations

20. The right to water, like any human right, imposes three types of obligations on States parties: obligations to *respect*, obligations to *protect* and obligations to *fulfil*.

(a) Obligations to respect

21. The obligation to *respect* requires that States parties refrain from interfering directly or indirectly with the enjoyment of the right to water. The obligation includes, inter alia, refraining from engaging in any practice or activity that denies or limits equal access to adequate water; arbitrarily interfering with customary or traditional arrangements for water allocation; unlawfully diminishing or polluting water, for example through waste from State-owned facilities or through use and testing of weapons; and limiting access to, or destroying, water services and infrastructure as a punitive measure, for example, during armed conflicts in violation of international humanitarian law.

22. The Committee notes that during armed conflicts, emergency situations and natural disasters, the right to water embraces those obligations by which States

[19] See General Comment No. 3 (1990), para. 9.

parties are bound under international humanitarian law.[20] This includes protection of objects indispensable for survival of the civilian population, including drinking water installations and supplies and irrigation works, protection of the natural environment against widespread, long-term and severe damage and ensuring that civilians, internees and prisoners have access to adequate water.[21]

(b) Obligations to protect

23. The obligation to *protect* requires State parties to prevent third parties from interfering in any way with the enjoyment of the right to water. Third parties include individuals, groups, corporations and other entities as well as agents acting under their authority. The obligation includes, inter alia, adopting the necessary and effective legislative and other measures to restrain, for example, third parties from denying equal access to adequate water; and polluting and inequitably extracting from water resources, including natural sources, wells and other water distribution systems.

24. Where water services (such as piped water networks, water tankers, access to rivers and wells) are operated or controlled by third parties, States parties must prevent them from compromising equal, affordable, and physical access to sufficient, safe and acceptable water. To prevent such abuses an effective regulatory system must be established, in conformity with the Covenant and this General Comment, which includes independent monitoring, genuine public participation and imposition of penalties for non-compliance.

(c) Obligations to fulfil

25. The obligation to *fulfil* can be disaggregated into the obligations to facilitate, promote and provide. The obligation to facilitate requires the State to take positive measures to assist individuals and communities to enjoy the right. The obligation to promote obliges the State party to take steps to ensure that there is appropriate education concerning the hygienic use of water, protection of water sources and methods to minimize water wastage. States parties are also obliged to fulfil (provide) the right when individuals or a group are unable, for reasons beyond their control, to realize that right themselves by the means at their disposal.

26. The obligation to fulfil requires States parties to adopt the necessary measures directed towards the full realization of the right to water. The obligation includes, inter alia, according sufficient recognition of this right within the national political and legal systems, preferably by way of legislative implementation; adopting a national water strategy and plan of action to realize this right; ensuring that water is affordable for everyone; and facilitating improved and sustainable access to water, particularly in rural and deprived urban areas.

27. To ensure that water is affordable, States parties must adopt the necessary measures that may include, inter alia: (*a*) use of a range of appropriate low-cost

[20] For the interrelationship of human rights law and humanitarian law, the Committee notes the conclusions of the International Court of Justice in *Legality of the Threat or Use of Nuclear Weapons (Request by the General Assembly), ICJ Reports (1996)* p. 226, para. 25.

[21] See arts 54 and 56, Additional Protocol I to the Geneva Conventions (1977), art. 54, Additional Protocol II (1977), arts 20 and 46 of the third Geneva Convention of 12 August 1949, and common article 3 of the Geneva Conventions of 12 August 1949.

techniques and technologies; (*b*) appropriate pricing policies such as free or low-cost water; and (*c*) income supplements. Any payment for water services has to be based on the principle of equity, ensuring that these services, whether privately or publicly provided, are affordable for all, including socially disadvantaged groups. Equity demands that poorer households should not be disproportionately burdened with water expenses as compared to richer households.

28. States parties should adopt comprehensive and integrated strategies and programmes to ensure that there is sufficient and safe water for present and future generations.[22] Such strategies and programmes may include: (*a*) reducing depletion of water resources through unsustainable extraction, diversion and damming; (*b*) reducing and eliminating contamination of watersheds and water-related ecosystems by substances such as radiation, harmful chemicals and human excreta; (*c*) monitoring water reserves; (*d*) ensuring that proposed developments do not interfere with access to adequate water; (*e*) assessing the impacts of actions that may impinge upon water availability and natural-ecosystems watersheds, such as climate changes, desertification and increased soil salinity, deforestation and loss of biodiversity;[23] (*f*) increasing the efficient use of water by end-users; (*g*) reducing water wastage in its distribution; (*h*) response mechanisms for emergency situations; (*i*) and establishing competent institutions and appropriate institutional arrangements to carry out the strategies and programmes.

29. Ensuring that everyone has access to adequate sanitation is not only fundamental for human dignity and privacy, but is one of the principal mechanisms for protecting the quality of drinking water supplies and resources.[24] In accordance with the rights to health and adequate housing (see General Comments No. 4 (1991) and 14 (2000)) States parties have an obligation to progressively extend safe sanitation services, particularly to rural and deprived urban areas, taking into account the needs of women and children.

International obligations

30. Article 2, paragraph 1, and articles 11, paragraph 1, and 23 of the Covenant require that States parties recognize the essential role of international cooperation and assistance and take joint and separate action to achieve the full realization of the right to water.

31. To comply with their international obligations in relation to the right to water, States parties have to respect the enjoyment of the right in other countries. International cooperation requires States parties to refrain from actions that interfere, directly or indirectly, with the enjoyment of the right to water in other countries.

[22] See footnote 5 above, Agenda 21, chaps. 5, 7 and 18; and the World Summit on Sustainable Development, Plan of Implementation (2002), paras. 6(*a*), (*l*) and (*m*), 7, 36 and 38.

[23] See the Convention on Biological Diversity, the Convention to Combat Desertification, the United Nations Framework Convention on Climate Change, and subsequent protocols.

[24] Article 14, para. 2, of the Convention on the Elimination of All Forms of Discrimination Against Women stipulates States parties shall ensure to women the right to 'adequate living conditions, particularly in relation to [. . .] sanitation'. Article 24, para. 2, of the Convention on the Rights of the Child requires States parties to 'To ensure that all segments of society [. . .] have access to education and are supported in the use of basic knowledge of [. . .] the advantages of [. . .] hygiene and environmental sanitation.'

Any activities undertaken within the State party's jurisdiction should not deprive another country of the ability to realize the right to water for persons in its jurisdiction.[25]

32. States parties should refrain at all times from imposing embargoes or similar measures, that prevent the supply of water, as well as goods and services essential for securing the right to water.[26] Water should never be used as an instrument of political and economic pressure. In this regard, the Committee recalls its position, stated in its General Comment No. 8 (1997), on the relationship between economic sanctions and respect for economic, social and cultural rights.

33. Steps should be taken by States parties to prevent their own citizens and companies from violating the right to water of individuals and communities in other countries. Where States parties can take steps to influence other third parties to respect the right, through legal or political means, such steps should be taken in accordance with the Charter of the United Nations and applicable international law.

34. Depending on the availability of resources, States should facilitate realization of the right to water in other countries, for example through provision of water resources, financial and technical assistance, and provide the necessary aid when required. In disaster relief and emergency assistance, including assistance to refugees and displaced persons, priority should be given to Covenant rights, including the provision of adequate water. International assistance should be provided in a manner that is consistent with the Covenant and other human rights standards, and sustainable and culturally appropriate. The economically developed States parties have a special responsibility and interest to assist the poorer developing States in this regard.

35. States parties should ensure that the right to water is given due attention in international agreements and, to that end, should consider the development of further legal instruments. With regard to the conclusion and implementation of other international and regional agreements, States parties should take steps to ensure that these instruments do not adversely impact upon the right to water. Agreements concerning trade liberalization should not curtail or inhibit a country's capacity to ensure the full realization of the right to water.

36. States parties should ensure that their actions as members of international organizations take due account of the right to water. Accordingly, States parties that are members of international financial institutions, notably the International Monetary Fund, the World Bank, and regional development banks, should take steps to ensure that the right to water is taken into account in their lending policies, credit agreements and other international measures.

Core obligations

37. In General Comment No. 3 (1990), the Committee confirms that States parties have a core obligation to ensure the satisfaction of, at the very least, minimum

[25] The Committee notes that the United Nations Convention on the Law of Non-Navigational Uses of Watercourses requires that social and human needs be taken into account in determining the equitable utilization of watercourses, that States parties take measures to prevent significant harm being caused, and, in the event of conflict, special regard must be given to the requirements of vital human needs: see arts 5, 7 and 10 of the Convention.

[26] In General Comment No. 8 (1997), the Committee noted the disruptive effect of sanctions upon sanitation supplies and clean drinking water, and that sanctions regimes should provide for repairs to infrastructure essential to provide clean water.

essential levels of each of the rights enunciated in the Covenant. In the Committee's view, at least a number of core obligations in relation to the right to water can be identified, which are of immediate effect:

(a) To ensure access to the minimum essential amount of water, that is sufficient and safe for personal and domestic uses to prevent disease;
(b) To ensure the right of access to water and water facilities and services on a non-discriminatory basis, especially for disadvantaged or marginalized groups;
(c) To ensure physical access to water facilities or services that provide sufficient, safe and regular water; that have a sufficient number of water outlets to avoid prohibitive waiting times; and that are at a reasonable distance from the household;
(d) To ensure personal security is not threatened when having to physically access to water;
(e) To ensure equitable distribution of all available water facilities and services;
(f) To adopt and implement a national water strategy and plan of action addressing the whole population; the strategy and plan of action should be devised, and periodically reviewed, on the basis of a participatory and transparent process; it should include methods, such as right to water indicators and benchmarks, by which progress can be closely monitored; the process by which the strategy and plan of action are devised, as well as their content, shall give particular attention to all disadvantaged or marginalized groups;
(g) To monitor the extent of the realization, or the non-realization, of the right to water;
(h) To adopt relatively low-cost targeted water programmes to protect vulnerable and marginalized groups;
(i) To take measures to prevent, treat and control diseases linked to water, in particular ensuring access to adequate sanitation;

38. For the avoidance of any doubt, the Committee wishes to emphasize that it is particularly incumbent on States parties, and other actors in a position to assist, to provide international assistance and cooperation, especially economic and technical which enables developing countries to fulfil their core obligations indicated in paragraph 37 above.

IV. Violations

39. When the normative content of the right to water (see Part II) is applied to the obligations of States parties (Part III), a process is set in motion, which facilitates identification of violations of the right to water. The following paragraphs provide illustrations of violations of the right to water.

40. To demonstrate compliance with their general and specific obligations, States parties must establish that they have taken the necessary and feasible steps towards the realization of the right to water. In accordance with international law, a failure to act in good faith to take such steps amounts to a violation of the right. It should be stressed that a State party cannot justify its non-compliance with the core obligations set out in paragraph 37 above, which are non-derogable.

41. In determining which actions or omissions amount to a violation of the right to water, it is important to distinguish the inability from the unwillingness of a State

party to comply with its obligations in relation to the right to water. This follows from articles 11, paragraph 1, and 12, which speak of the right to an adequate standard of living and the right to health, as well as from article 2, paragraph 1, of the Covenant, which obliges each State party to take the necessary steps to the maximum of its available resources. A State which is unwilling to use the maximum of its available resources for the realization of the right to water is in violation of its obligations under the Covenant. If resource constraints render it impossible for a State party to comply fully with its Covenant obligations, it has the burden of justifying that every effort has nevertheless been made to use all available resources at its disposal in order to satisfy, as a matter of priority, the obligations outlined above.

42. Violations of the right to water can occur through *acts of commission*, the direct actions of States parties or other entities insufficiently regulated by States. Violations include, for example, the adoption of retrogressive measures incompatible with the core obligations (outlined in para. 37 above), the formal repeal or suspension of legislation necessary for the continued enjoyment of the right to water, or the adoption of legislation or policies which are manifestly incompatible with pre-existing domestic or international legal obligations in relation to the right to water.

43. Violations through *acts of omission* include the failure to take appropriate steps towards the full realization of everyone's right to water, the failure to have a national policy on water, and the failure to enforce relevant laws.

44. While it is not possible to specify a complete list of violations in advance, a number of typical examples relating to the levels of obligations, emanating from the Committee's work, may be identified:

(a) Violations of the obligation to respect follow from the State party's interference with the right to water. This includes, inter alia: (i) arbitrary or unjustified disconnection or exclusion from water services or facilities; (ii) discriminatory or unaffordable increases in the price of water; and (iii) pollution and diminution of water resources affecting human health;

(b) Violations of the obligation to protect follow from the failure of a State to take all necessary measures to safeguard persons within their jurisdiction from infringements of the right to water by third parties.[27, 28] This includes, inter alia: (i) failure to enact or enforce laws to prevent the contamination and inequitable extraction of water; (ii) failure to effectively regulate and control water services providers; (iv) failure to protect water distribution systems (e.g., piped networks and wells) from interference, damage and destruction; and

(c) Violations of the obligation to fulfil occur through the failure of States parties to take all necessary steps to ensure the realization of the right to water. Examples includes, inter alia: (i) failure to adopt or implement a national water policy designed to ensure the right to water for everyone; (ii) insufficient expenditure or misallocation of public resources which results in the non-enjoyment of the right to water by individuals or groups, particularly the vulnerable or marginalized; (iii) failure to monitor the realization of the right to water at the national level, for example by identifying right-to-water indicators and benchmarks; (iv) failure to take measures to reduce the inequitable distribution of water facilities and services; (v) failure to adopt mechanisms for emergency relief; (vi) failure to

[27] (*Note to reader*: there is no footnote 27 in the original text.)

[28] See para. 23 for a definition of 'third parties'.

ensure that the minimum essential level of the right is enjoyed by everyone (vii) failure of a State to take into account its international legal obligations regarding the right to water when entering into agreements with other States or with international organizations.

V. Implementation at the national level

45. In accordance with article 2, paragraph 1, of the Covenant, States parties are required to utilize 'all appropriate means, including particularly the adoption of legislative measures' in the implementation of their Covenant obligations. Every State party has a margin of discretion in assessing which measures are most suitable to meet its specific circumstances. The Covenant, however, clearly imposes a duty on each State party to take whatever steps are necessary to ensure that everyone enjoys the right to water, as soon as possible. Any national measures designed to realize the right to water should not interfere with the enjoyment of other human rights.

Legislation, strategies and policies

46. Existing legislation, strategies and policies should be reviewed to ensure that they are compatible with obligations arising from the right to water, and should be repealed, amended or changed if inconsistent with Covenant requirements.

47. The duty to take steps clearly imposes on States parties an obligation to adopt a national strategy or plan of action to realize the right to water. The strategy must: (*a*) be based upon human rights law and principles; (*b*) cover all aspects of the right to water and the corresponding obligations of States parties; (*c*) define clear objectives; (*d*) set targets or goals to be achieved and the time-frame for their achievement; (*e*) formulate adequate policies and corresponding benchmarks and indicators. The strategy should also establish institutional responsibility for the process; identify resources available to attain the objectives, targets and goals; allocate resources appropriately according to institutional responsibility; and establish accountability mechanisms to ensure the implementation of the strategy. When formulating and implementing their right to water national strategies, States parties should avail themselves of technical assistance and cooperation of the United Nations specialized agencies (see Part VI below).

48. The formulation and implementation of national water strategies and plans of action should respect, inter alia, the principles of non-discrimination and people's participation. The right of individuals and groups to participate in decision-making processes that may affect their exercise of the right to water must be an integral part of any policy, programme or strategy concerning water. Individuals and groups should be given full and equal access to information concerning water, water services and the environment, held by public authorities or third parties.

49. The national water strategy and plan of action should also be based on the principles of accountability, transparency and independence of the judiciary, since good governance is essential to the effective implementation of all human rights, including the realization of the right to water. In order to create a favourable climate for the realization of the right, States parties should take appropriate steps to ensure that the private business sector and civil society are aware of, and consider the importance of, the right to water in pursuing their activities.

50. States parties may find it advantageous to adopt framework legislation to operationalize their right to water strategy. Such legislation should include: (*a*) targets or goals to be attained and the time-frame for their achievement; (*b*) the means by which the purpose could be achieved; (*c*) the intended collaboration with civil society, private sector and international organizations; (*d*) institutional responsibility for the process; (*e*) national mechanisms for its monitoring; and (*f*) remedies and recourse procedures.

51. Steps should be taken to ensure there is sufficient coordination between the national ministries, regional and local authorities in order to reconcile water-related policies. Where implementation of the right to water has been delegated to regional or local authorities, the State party still retains the responsibility to comply with its Covenant obligations, and therefore should ensure that these authorities have at their disposal sufficient resources to maintain and extend the necessary water services and facilities. The States parties must further ensure that such authorities do not deny access to services on a discriminatory basis.

52. States parties are obliged to monitor effectively the realization of the right to water. In monitoring progress towards the realization of the right to water, States parties should identify the factors and difficulties affecting implementation of their obligations.

Indicators and benchmarks

53. To assist the monitoring process, right to water indicators should be identified in the national water strategies or plans of action. The indicators should be designed to monitor, at the national and international levels, the State party's obligations under articles 11, paragraph 1, and 12. Indicators should address the different components of adequate water (such as sufficiency, safety and acceptability, affordability and physical accessibility), be disaggregated by the prohibited grounds of discrimination, and cover all persons residing in the State party's territorial jurisdiction or under their control. States parties may obtain guidance on appropriate indicators from the ongoing work of WHO, the Food and Agriculture Organization of the United Nations (FAO), the United Nations Centre for Human Settlements (Habitat), the International Labour Organization (ILO), the United Nations Children's Fund (UNICEF), the United Nations Environment Programme (UNEP), the United Nations Development Programme (UNDP) and the United Nations Commission on Human Rights.

54. Having identified appropriate right to water indicators, States parties are invited to set appropriate national benchmarks in relation to each indicator.[29] During the periodic reporting procedure, the Committee will engage in a process of 'scoping' with the State party. Scoping involves the joint consideration by the State party and the Committee of the indicators and national benchmarks which will then

[29] See E. Riedel, 'New bearings to the State reporting procedure: practical ways to operationalize economic, social and cultural rights—The example of the right to health', in S. von Schorlemer (ed.), *Praxishandbuch UNO*, 2002, pp. 345–358. The Committee notes, for example, the commitment in the 2002 World Summit on Sustainable Development Plan of Implementation to halve, by the year 2015, the proportion of people who are unable to reach or to afford safe drinking water (as outlined in the Millennium Declaration) and the proportion of people who do not have access to basic sanitation.

provide the targets to be achieved during the next reporting period. In the following five years, the State party will use these national benchmarks to help monitor its implementation of the right to water. Thereafter, in the subsequent reporting process, the State party and the Committee will consider whether or not the benchmarks have been achieved, and the reasons for any difficulties that may have been encountered (see General Comment No.14 (2000), para. 58). Further, when setting benchmarks and preparing their reports, States parties should utilize the extensive information and advisory services of specialized agencies with regard to data collection and disaggregation.

Remedies and accountability

55. Any persons or groups who have been denied their right to water should have access to effective judicial or other appropriate remedies at both national and international levels (see General Comment No. 9 (1998), para. 4, and Principle 10 of the Rio Declaration on Environment and Development).[30] The Committee notes that the right has been constitutionally entrenched by a number of States and has been subject to litigation before national courts. All victims of violations of the right to water should be entitled to adequate reparation, including restitution, compensation, satisfaction or guarantees of non-repetition. National ombudsmen, human rights commissions, and similar institutions should be permitted to address violations of the right.

56. Before any action that interferes with an individual's right to water is carried out by the State party, or by any other third party, the relevant authorities must ensure that such actions are performed in a manner warranted by law, compatible with the Covenant, and that comprises: (*a*) opportunity for genuine consultation with those affected; (*b*) timely and full disclosure of information on the proposed measures; (*c*) reasonable notice of proposed actions; (*d*) legal recourse and remedies for those affected; and (*e*) legal assistance for obtaining legal remedies (see also General Comments No. 4 (1991) and No. 7 (1997)). Where such action is based on a person's failure to pay for water their capacity to pay must be taken into account. Under no circumstances shall an individual be deprived of the minimum essential level of water.

57. The incorporation in the domestic legal order of international instruments recognizing the right to water can significantly enhance the scope and effectiveness of remedial measures and should be encouraged in all cases. Incorporation enables courts to adjudicate violations of the right to water, or at least the core obligations, by direct reference to the Covenant.

58. Judges, adjudicators and members of the legal profession should be encouraged by States parties to pay greater attention to violations of the right to water in the exercise of their functions.

59. States parties should respect, protect, facilitate and promote the work of human rights advocates and other members of civil society with a view to assisting vulnerable or marginalized groups in the realization of their right to water.

[30] Principle 10 of the Rio Declaration on Environment and Development (*Report of the United Nations Conference on Environment and Development*, see footnote 5 above), states with respect to environmental issues that 'effective access to judicial and administrative proceedings, including remedy and redress, shall be provided'.

VI. Obligations of actors other than States

60. United Nations agencies and other international organizations concerned with water, such as WHO, FAO, UNICEF, UNEP, UN-Habitat, ILO, UNDP, the International Fund for Agricultural Development (IFAD), as well as international organizations concerned with trade such as the World Trade Organization (WTO), should cooperate effectively with States parties, building on their respective expertise, in relation to the implementation of the right to water at the national level. The international financial institutions, notably the International Monetary Fund and the World Bank, should take into account the right to water in their lending policies, credit agreements, structural adjustment programmes and other development projects (see General Comment No. 2 (1990)), so that the enjoyment of the right to water is promoted. When examining the reports of States parties and their ability to meet the obligations to realize the right to water, the Committee will consider the effects of the assistance provided by all other actors. The incorporation of human rights law and principles in the programmes and policies by international organizations will greatly facilitate implementation of the right to water. The role of the International Federation of the Red Cross and Red Crescent Societies, International Committee of the Red Cross, the Office of the United Nations High Commissioner for Refugees (UNHCR), WHO and UNICEF, as well as non-governmental organizations and other associations, is of particular importance in relation to disaster relief and humanitarian assistance in times of emergencies. Priority in the provision of aid, distribution and management of water and water facilities should be given to the most vulnerable or marginalized groups of the population.

Appendix B

General Agreement on Tariffs and Trade 1994*

(Extracts)

[For the convenience of the reader, **asterisks** mark the portions of the text that should be read in conjunction with notes and supplementary provisions in Annex I to the Agreement. In accordance with Article XXXIV, Annexes A to I are an integral part of the Agreement.]

Article I

General Most-Favoured-Nation Treatment

1. With respect to customs duties and charges of any kind imposed on or in connection with importation or exportation or imposed on the international transfer of payments for imports or exports, and with respect to the method of levying such duties and charges, and with respect to all rules and formalities in connection with importation and exportation, and with respect to all matters referred to in paragraphs 2 and 4 of Article III,* any advantage, favour, privilege or immunity granted by any contracting party to any product originating in or destined for any other country shall be accorded immediately and unconditionally to the like product originating in or destined for the territories of all other contracting parties.

Article III*

National Treatment on Internal Taxation and Regulation

1. The contracting parties recognize that internal taxes and other internal charges, and laws, regulations and requirements affecting the internal sale, offering for sale, purchase, transportation, distribution or use of products, and internal quantitative regulations requiring the mixture, processing or use of products in specified amounts or proportions, should not be applied to imported or domestic products so as to afford protection to domestic production.*
2. The products of the territory of any contracting party imported into the territory of any other contracting party shall not be subject, directly or indirectly, to internal taxes or other internal charges of any kind in excess of those applied, directly or indirectly, to like domestic products. Moreover, no contracting party shall otherwise apply internal taxes or other internal charges to imported or domestic products in a manner contrary to the principles set forth in paragraph 1.*
3. With respect to any existing internal tax which is inconsistent with the provisions of paragraph 2, but which is specifically authorized under a trade agreement, in force on April 10, 1947, in which the import duty on the taxed product is bound against increase, the contracting party imposing the tax shall be free to postpone the application of the provisions of paragraph 2 to such tax until such time as it can obtain release from the obligations of such trade agreement in order to permit the

* Text available at: http://www.wto.org.

increase of such duty to the extent necessary to compensate for the elimination of the protective element of the tax.

4. The products of the territory of any contracting party imported into the territory of any other contracting party shall be accorded treatment no less favourable than that accorded to like products of national origin in respect of all laws, regulations and requirements affecting their internal sale, offering for sale, purchase, transportation, distribution or use. The provisions of this paragraph shall not prevent the application of differential internal transportation charges which are based exclusively on the economic operation of the means of transport and not on the nationality of the product.

Annex I
Notes and Supplementary Provisions
Ad *Article III*

Any internal tax or other internal charge, or any law, regulation or requirement of the kind referred to in paragraph 1 which applies to an imported product and to the like domestic product and is collected or enforced in the case of the imported product at the time or point of importation, is nevertheless to be regarded as an internal tax or other internal charge, or a law, regulation or requirement of the kind referred to in paragraph 1, and is accordingly subject to the provisions of Article III.

Paragraph 1

The application of paragraph 1 to internal taxes imposed by local governments and authorities with the territory of a contracting party is subject to the provisions of the final paragraph of Article XXIV. The term 'reasonable measures' in the last-mentioned paragraph would not require, for example, the repeal of existing national legislation authorizing local governments to impose internal taxes which, although technically inconsistent with the letter of Article III, are not in fact inconsistent with its spirit, if such repeal would result in a serious financial hardship for the local governments or authorities concerned. With regard to taxation by local governments or authorities which is inconsistent with both the letter and spirit of Article III, the term 'reasonable measures' would permit a contracting party to eliminate the inconsistent taxation gradually over a transition period, if abrupt action would create serious administrative and financial difficulties.

Paragraph 2

A tax conforming to the requirements of the first sentence of paragraph 2 would be considered to be inconsistent with the provisions of the second sentence only in cases where competition was involved between, on the one hand, the taxed product and, on the other hand, a directly competitive or substitutable product which was not similarly taxed.

Article VI
Anti-dumping and Countervailing Duties

1. The contracting parties recognize that dumping, by which products of one country are introduced into the commerce of another country at less than the normal

value of the products, is to be condemned if it causes or threatens material injury to an established industry in the territory of a contracting party or materially retards the establishment of a domestic industry. For the purposes of this Article, a product is to be considered as being introduced into the commerce of an importing country at less than its normal value, if the price of the product exported from one country to another

(a) is less than the comparable price, in the ordinary course of trade, for the like product when destined for consumption in the exporting country, or,
(b) in the absence of such domestic price, is less than either
  (i) the highest comparable price for the like product for export to any third country in the ordinary course of trade, or
  (ii) the cost of production of the product in the country of origin plus a reasonable addition for selling cost and profit.

Due allowance shall be made in each case for differences in conditions and terms of sale, for differences in taxation, and for other differences affecting price comparability.*

2. In order to offset or prevent dumping, a contracting party may levy on any dumped product an anti-dumping duty not greater in amount than the margin of dumping in respect of such product. For the purposes of this Article, the margin of dumping is the price difference determined in accordance with the provisions of paragraph 1.*

3. No countervailing duty shall be levied on any product of the territory of any contracting party imported into the territory of another contracting party in excess of an amount equal to the estimated bounty or subsidy determined to have been granted, directly or indirectly, on the manufacture, production or export of such product in the country of origin or exportation, including any special subsidy to the transportation of a particular product. The term 'countervailing duty' shall be understood to mean a special duty levied for the purpose of offsetting any bounty or subsidy bestowed, directly, or indirectly, upon the manufacture, production or export of any merchandise.*

4. No product of the territory of any contracting party imported into the territory of any other contracting party shall be subject to anti-dumping or countervailing duty by reason of the exemption of such product from duties or taxes borne by the like product when destined for consumption in the country of origin or exportation, or by reason of the refund of such duties or taxes.

5. No product of the territory of any contracting party imported into the territory of any other contracting party shall be subject to both anti-dumping and countervailing duties to compensate for the same situation of dumping or export subsidization.

6. (a) No contracting party shall levy any anti-dumping or countervailing duty on the importation of any product of the territory of another contracting party unless it determines that the effect of the dumping or subsidization, as the case may be, is such as to cause or threaten material injury to an established domestic industry, or is such as to retard materially the establishment of a domestic industry.
  (b) The Contracting Parties may waive the requirement of sub-paragraph (a) of this paragraph so as to permit a contracting party to levy an anti-dumping or countervailing duty on the importation of any product for the purpose of offsetting dumping or subsidization which causes or threatens material injury to an industry in the territory of another contracting party exporting the

product concerned to the territory of the importing contracting party. The Contracting Parties shall waive the requirements of sub-paragraph (a) of this paragraph, so as to permit the levying of a countervailing duty, in cases in which they find that a subsidy is causing or threatening material injury to an industry in the territory of another contracting party exporting the product concerned to the territory of the importing contracting party.*

(c) In exceptional circumstances, however, where delay might cause damage which would be difficult to repair, a contracting party may levy a countervailing duty for the purpose referred to in sub-paragraph (b) of this paragraph without the prior approval of the Contracting Parties; Provided that such action shall be reported immediately to the Contracting Parties and that the countervailing duty shall be withdrawn promptly if the Contracting Parties disapprove.

7. A system for the stabilization of the domestic price or of the return to domestic producers of a primary commodity, independently of the movements of export prices, which results at times in the sale of the commodity for export at a price lower than the comparable price charged for the like commodity to buyers in the domestic market, shall be presumed not to result in material injury within the meaning of paragraph 6 if it is determined by consultation among the contracting parties substantially interested in the commodity concerned that:

(a) the system has also resulted in the sale of the commodity for export at a price higher than the comparable price charged for the like commodity to buyers in the domestic market, and
(b) the system is so operated, either because of the effective regulation of production, or otherwise, as not to stimulate exports unduly or otherwise seriously prejudice the interests of other contracting parties.

Annex I
Notes and Supplementary Provisions
Ad *Article VI*

Paragraph 1

1. Hidden dumping by associated houses (that is, the sale by an importer at a price below that corresponding to the price invoiced by an exporter with whom the importer is associated, and also below the price in the exporting country) constitutes a form of price dumping with respect to which the margin of dumping may be calculated on the basis of the price at which the goods are resold by the importer.
2. It is recognized that, in the case of imports from a country which has a complete or substantially complete monopoly of its trade and where all domestic prices are fixed by the State, special difficulties may exist in determining price comparability for the purposes of paragraph 1, and in such cases importing contracting parties may find it necessary to take into account the possibility that a strict comparison with domestic prices in such a country may not always be appropriate.

Paragraphs 2 and 3

1. As in many other cases in customs administration, a contracting party may require reasonable security (bond or cash deposit) for the payment of anti-dumping

or countervailing duty pending final determination of the facts in any case of suspected dumping or subsidization.

2. Multiple currency practices can in certain circumstances constitute a subsidy to exports which may be met by countervailing duties under paragraph 3 or can constitute a form of dumping by means of a partial depreciation of a country's currency which may be met by action under paragraph 2. By 'multiple currency practices' is meant practices by governments or sanctioned by governments.

Paragraph 6 (b)

Waivers under the provisions of this sub-paragraph shall be granted only on application by the contracting party proposing to levy an anti-dumping or countervailing duty, as the case may be.]

Article XI*

General Elimination of Quantitative Restrictions

1. No prohibitions or restrictions other than duties, taxes or other charges, whether made effective through quotas, import or export licences or other measures, shall be instituted or maintained by any contracting party on the importation of any product of the territory of any other contracting party or on the exportation or sale for export of any product destined for the territory of any other contracting party.

2. The provisions of paragraph 1 of this Article shall not extend to the following:

(a) Export prohibitions or restrictions temporarily applied to prevent or relieve critical shortages of foodstuffs or other products essential to the exporting contracting party....

Article XVI*

Subsidies

Section A—Subsidies in General

1. If any contracting party grants or maintains any subsidy, including any form of income or price support, which operates directly or indirectly to increase exports of any product from, or to reduce imports of any product into, its territory, it shall notify the Contracting Parties in writing of the extent and nature of the subsidization, of the estimated effect of the subsidization on the quantity of the affected product or products imported into or exported from its territory and of the circumstances making the subsidization necessary. In any case in which it is determined that serious prejudice to the interests of any other contracting party is caused or threatened by any such subsidization, the contracting party granting the subsidy shall, upon request, discuss with the other contracting party or parties concerned, or with the Contracting Parties, the possibility of limiting the subsidization.

Section B—Additional Provisions on Export Subsidies*

2. The contracting parties recognize that the granting by a contracting party of a subsidy on the export of any product may have harmful effects for other contracting parties, both importing and exporting, may cause undue disturbance to their normal

commercial interests, and may hinder the achievement of the objectives of this Agreement.

3. Accordingly, contracting parties should seek to avoid the use of subsidies on the export of primary products. If, however, a contracting party grants directly or indirectly any form of subsidy which operates to increase the export of any primary product from its territory, such subsidy shall not be applied in a manner which results in that contracting party having more than an equitable share of world export trade in that product, account being taken of the shares of the contracting parties in such trade in the product during a previous representative period, and any special factors which may have affected or may be affecting such trade in the product.*

4. Further, as from 1 January 1958 or the earliest practicable date thereafter, contracting parties shall cease to grant either directly or indirectly any form of subsidy on the export of any product other than a primary product which subsidy results in the sale of such product for export at a price lower than the comparable price charged for the like product to buyers in the domestic market. Until 31 December 1957 no contracting party shall extend the scope of any such subsidization beyond that existing on 1 January 1955 by the introduction of new, or the extension of existing, subsidies.*

5. The Contracting Parties shall review the operation of the provisions of this Article from time to time with a view to examining its effectiveness, in the light of actual experience, in promoting the objectives of this Agreement and avoiding subsidization seriously prejudicial to the trade or interests of contracting parties.

Annex I
Notes and Supplementary Provisions
Ad *Article XVI*

The exemption of an exported product from duties or taxes borne by the like product when destined for domestic consumption, or the remission of such duties or taxes in amounts not in excess of those which have accrued, shall not be deemed to be a subsidy.

Section B

1. Nothing in Section B shall preclude the use by a contracting party of multiple rates of exchange in accordance with the Articles of Agreement of the International Monetary Fund.
2. For the purposes of Section B, a 'primary product' is understood to be any product of farm, forest or fishery, or any mineral, in its natural form or which has undergone such processing as is customarily required to prepare it for marketing in substantial volume in international trade.

Paragraph 3

1. The fact that a contracting party has not exported the product in question during the previous representative period would not in itself preclude that contracting party from establishing its right to obtain a share of the trade in the product concerned.
2. A system for the stabilization of the domestic price or of the return to domestic producers of a primary product independently of the movements of export prices,

which results at times in the sale of the product for export at a price lower than the comparable price charged for the like product to buyers in the domestic market, shall be considered not to involve a subsidy on exports within the meaning of paragraph 3 if the Contracting Parties determine that:

(a) the system has also resulted, or is so designed as to result, in the sale of the product for export at a price higher than the comparable price charged for the like product to buyers in the domestic market; and
(b) the system is so operated, or is designed so to operate, either because of the effective regulation of production or otherwise, as not to stimulate exports unduly or otherwise seriously to prejudice the interests of other contracting parties.

Notwithstanding such determination by the Contracting Parties, operations under such a system shall be subject to the provisions of paragraph 3 where they are wholly or partly financed out of government funds in addition to the funds collected from producers in respect of the product concerned.

Paragraph 4

The intention of paragraph 4 is that the contracting parties should seek before the end of 1957 to reach agreement to abolish all remaining subsidies as from 1 January 1958; or, failing this, to reach agreement to extend the application of the standstill until the earliest date thereafter by which they can expect to reach such agreement.]

Article XX
General Exceptions

Subject to the requirement that such measures are not applied in a manner which would constitute a means of arbitrary or unjustifiable discrimination between countries where the same conditions prevail, or a disguised restriction on international trade, nothing in this Agreement shall be construed to prevent the adoption or enforcement by any contracting party of measures:

(a) necessary to protect public morals;
(b) necessary to protect human, animal or plant life or health;
(c) relating to the importations or exportations of gold or silver;
(d) necessary to secure compliance with laws or regulations which are not inconsistent with the provisions of this Agreement, including those relating to customs enforcement, the enforcement of monopolies operated under paragraph 4 of Article II and Article XVII, the protection of patents, trade marks and copyrights, and the prevention of deceptive practices;
(e) relating to the products of prison labour;
(f) imposed for the protection of national treasures of artistic, historic or archaeological value;
(g) relating to the conservation of exhaustible natural resources if such measures are made effective in conjunction with restrictions on domestic production or consumption;
(h) undertaken in pursuance of obligations under any intergovernmental commodity agreement which conforms to criteria submitted to the Contracting Parties

and not disapproved by them or which is itself so submitted and not so disapproved;*

(i) involving restrictions on exports of domestic materials necessary to ensure essential quantities of such materials to a domestic processing industry during periods when the domestic price of such materials is held below the world price as part of a governmental stabilization plan; Provided that such restrictions shall not operate to increase the exports of or the protection afforded to such domestic industry, and shall not depart from the provisions of this Agreement relating to non-discrimination;

(j) essential to the acquisition or distribution of products in general or local short supply; Provided that any such measures shall be consistent with the principle that all contracting parties are entitled to an equitable share of the international supply of such products, and that any such measures, which are inconsistent with the other provisions of the Agreement shall be discontinued as soon as the conditions giving rise to them have ceased to exist. The CONTRACTING PARTIES shall review the need for this sub-paragraph not later than 30 June 1960.

Annex I
Notes and Supplementary Provisions
Ad *Article XX*

Sub-paragraph (h)

The exception provided for in this sub-paragraph extends to any commodity agreement which conforms to the principles approved by the Economic and Social Council in its resolution 30 (IV) of 28 March 1947.

Appendix C

General Agreement on Trade in Services*

(Extracts)

Members,

Recognizing the growing importance of trade in services for the growth and development of the world economy;

Wishing to establish a multilateral framework of principles and rules for trade in services with a view to the expansion of such trade under conditions of transparency and progressive liberalization and as a means of promoting the economic growth of all trading partners and the development of developing countries;

Desiring the early achievement of progressively higher levels of liberalization of trade in services through successive rounds of multilateral negotiations aimed at promoting the interests of all participants on a mutually advantageous basis and at securing an overall balance of rights and obligations, while giving due respect to national policy objectives;

Recognizing the right of Members to regulate, and to introduce new regulations, on the supply of services within their territories in order to meet national policy objectives and, given asymmetries existing with respect to the degree of development of services regulations in different countries, the particular need of developing countries to exercise this right;

Desiring to facilitate the increasing participation of developing countries in trade in services and the expansion of their service exports including, *inter alia*, through the strengthening of their domestic services capacity and its efficiency and competitiveness;

Taking particular account of the serious difficulty of the least-developed countries in view of their special economic situation and their development, trade and financial needs;

Hereby *agree* as follows:

Article I
Scope and Definition

1. This Agreement applies to measures by Members affecting trade in services.
2. For the purposes of this Agreement, trade in services is defined as the supply of a service:

(a) from the territory of one Member into the territory of any other Member;
(b) in the territory of one Member to the service consumer of any other Member;
(c) by a service supplier of one Member, through commercial presence in the territory of any other Member;
(d) by a service supplier of one Member, through presence of natural persons of a Member in the territory of any other Member.

* Text available at: http://www.wto.org.

3. For the purposes of this Agreement:

(a) 'measures by Members' means measures taken by:
   (i) central, regional or local governments and authorities; and
   (ii) non-governmental bodies in the exercise of powers delegated by central, regional or local governments or authorities;

   In fulfilling its obligations and commitments under the Agreement, each Member shall take such reasonable measures as may be available to it to ensure their observance by regional and local governments and authorities and non-governmental bodies within its territory;

(b) 'services' includes any service in any sector except services supplied in the exercise of governmental authority;
(c) 'a service supplied in the exercise of governmental authority' means any service which is supplied neither on a commercial basis, nor in competition with one or more service suppliers.

Article II
Most-Favoured-Nation Treatment

1. With respect to any measure covered by this Agreement, each Member shall accord immediately and unconditionally to services and service suppliers of any other Member treatment no less favourable than that it accords to like services and service suppliers of any other country.
2. A Member may maintain a measure inconsistent with paragraph 1 provided that such a measure is listed in, and meets the conditions of, the Annex on Article II Exemptions.
3. The provisions of this Agreement shall not be so construed as to prevent any Member from conferring or according advantages to adjacent countries in order to facilitate exchanges limited to contiguous frontier zones of services that are both locally produced and consumed.

Article VI
Domestic Regulation

1. In sectors where specific commitments are undertaken, each Member shall ensure that all measures of general application affecting trade in services are administered in a reasonable, objective and impartial manner.
2. (a) Each Member shall maintain or institute as soon as practicable judicial, arbitral or administrative tribunals or procedures which provide, at the request of an affected service supplier, for the prompt review of, and where justified, appropriate remedies for, administrative decisions affecting trade in services. Where such procedures are not independent of the agency entrusted with the administrative decision concerned, the Member shall ensure that the procedures in fact provide for an objective and impartial review.
   (b) The provisions of subparagraph (a) shall not be construed to require a Member to institute such tribunals or procedures where this would be inconsistent with its constitutional structure or the nature of its legal system.

3. Where authorization is required for the supply of a service on which a specific commitment has been made, the competent authorities of a Member shall, within a reasonable period of time after the submission of an application considered complete under domestic laws and regulations, inform the applicant of the decision concerning the application. At the request of the applicant, the competent authorities of the Member shall provide, without undue delay, information concerning the status of the application.
4. With a view to ensuring that measures relating to qualification requirements and procedures, technical standards and licensing requirements do not constitute unnecessary barriers to trade in services, the Council for Trade in Services shall, through appropriate bodies it may establish, develop any necessary disciplines. Such disciplines shall aim to ensure that such requirements are, *inter alia*:

(a) based on objective and transparent criteria, such as competence and the ability to supply the service;
(b) not more burdensome than necessary to ensure the quality of the service;
(c) in the case of licensing procedures, not in themselves a restriction on the supply of the service.

5. (a) In sectors in which a Member has undertaken specific commitments, pending the entry into force of disciplines developed in these sectors pursuant to paragraph 4, the Member shall not apply licensing and qualification requirements and technical standards that nullify or impair such specific commitments in a manner which:
   (i) does not comply with the criteria outlined in subparagraphs 4(a), (b) or (c); and
   (ii) could not reasonably have been expected of that Member at the time the specific commitments in those sectors were made.
(b) In determining whether a Member is in conformity with the obligation under paragraph 5(a), account shall be taken of international standards of relevant international organizations[1] applied by that Member.

6. In sectors where specific commitments regarding professional services are undertaken, each Member shall provide for adequate procedures to verify the competence of professionals of any other Member.

Article VIII
Monopolies and Exclusive Service Suppliers

1. Each Member shall ensure that any monopoly supplier of a service in its territory does not, in the supply of the monopoly service in the relevant market, act in a manner inconsistent with that Member's obligations under Article II and specific commitments.
2. Where a Member's monopoly supplier competes, either directly or through an affiliated company, in the supply of a service outside the scope of its monopoly rights and which is subject to that Member's specific commitments, the Member shall

[1] The term 'relevant international organizations' refers to international bodies whose membership is open to the relevant bodies of at least all Members of the WTO.

ensure that such a supplier does not abuse its monopoly position to act in its territory in a manner inconsistent with such commitments.

3. The Council for Trade in Services may, at the request of a Member which has a reason to believe that a monopoly supplier of a service of any other Member is acting in a manner inconsistent with paragraph 1 or 2, request the Member establishing, maintaining or authorizing such supplier to provide specific information concerning the relevant operations.

4. If, after the date of entry into force of the WTO Agreement, a Member grants monopoly rights regarding the supply of a service covered by its specific commitments, that Member shall notify the Council for Trade in Services no later than three months before the intended implementation of the grant of monopoly rights and the provisions of paragraphs 2, 3 and 4 of Article XXI shall apply.

5. The provisions of this Article shall also apply to cases of exclusive service suppliers, where a Member, formally or in effect, (*a*) authorizes or establishes a small number of service suppliers and (*b*) substantially prevents competition among those suppliers in its territory.

Article IX
Business Practices

1. Members recognize that certain business practices of service suppliers, other than those falling under Article VIII, may restrain competition and thereby restrict trade in services.

2. Each Member shall, at the request of any other Member, enter into consultations with a view to eliminating practices referred to in paragraph 1. The Member addressed shall accord full and sympathetic consideration to such a request and shall cooperate through the supply of publicly available non-confidential information of relevance to the matter in question. The Member addressed shall also provide other information available to the requesting Member, subject to its domestic law and to the conclusion of satisfactory agreement concerning the safeguarding of its confidentiality by the requesting Member.

Article XIII
Government Procurement

1. Articles II, XVI and XVII shall not apply to laws, regulations or requirements governing the procurement by governmental agencies of services purchased for governmental purposes and not with a view to commercial resale or with a view to use in the supply of services for commercial sale.

2. There shall be multilateral negotiations on government procurement in services under this Agreement within two years from the date of entry into force of the WTO Agreement.

Article XIV
General Exceptions

Subject to the requirement that such measures are not applied in a manner which would constitute a means of arbitrary or unjustifiable discrimination between countries where like conditions prevail, or a disguised restriction on trade in services, nothing in this Agreement shall be construed to prevent the adoption or enforcement by any Member of measures:

(a) necessary to protect public morals or to maintain public order;[2]
(b) necessary to protect human, animal or plant life or health;
(c) necessary to secure compliance with laws or regulations which are not inconsistent with the provisions of this Agreement including those relating to:
  (i) the prevention of deceptive and fraudulent practices or to deal with the effects of a default on services contracts;
  (ii) the protection of the privacy of individuals in relation to the processing and dissemination of personal data and the protection of confidentiality of individual records and accounts;
  (iii) safety;
(d) inconsistent with Article XVII, provided that the difference in treatment is aimed at ensuring the equitable or effective[3] imposition or collection of direct taxes in respect of services or service suppliers of other Members;
(e) inconsistent with Article II, provided that the difference in treatment is the result of an agreement on the avoidance of double taxation or provisions on the avoidance of double taxation in any other international agreement or arrangement by which the Member is bound.

Article XV
Subsidies

1. Members recognize that, in certain circumstances, subsidies may have distortive effects on trade in services. Members shall enter into negotiations with a view to developing the necessary multilateral disciplines to avoid such trade-distortive

[2] The public order exception may be invoked only where a genuine and sufficiently serious threat is posed to one of the fundamental interests of society.

[3] Measures that are aimed at ensuring the equitable or effective imposition or collection of direct taxes include measures taken by a Member under its taxation system which:

(i) apply to non-resident service suppliers in recognition of the fact that the tax obligation of non-residents is determined with respect to taxable items sourced or located in the Member's territory; or
(ii) apply to non-residents in order to ensure the imposition or collection of taxes in the Member's territory; or
(iii) apply to non-residents or residents in order to prevent the avoidance or evasion of taxes, including compliance measures; or
(iv) apply to consumers of services supplied in or from the territory of another Member in order to ensure the imposition or collection of taxes on such consumers derived from sources in the Member's territory; or
(v) distinguish service suppliers subject to tax on worldwide taxable items from other service suppliers, in recognition of the difference in the nature of the tax base between them; or
(vi) determine, allocate or apportion income, profit, gain, loss, deduction or credit of resident persons or branches, or between related persons or branches of the same person, in order to safeguard the Member's tax base.

Tax terms or concepts in paragraph (d) of Article XIV and in this footnote are determined according to tax definitions and concepts, or equivalent or similar definitions and concepts, under the domestic law of the Member taking the measure.

effects.[4] The negotiations shall also address the appropriateness of countervailing procedures. Such negotiations shall recognize the role of subsidies in relation to the development programmes of developing countries and take into account the needs of Members, particularly developing country Members, for flexibility in this area. For the purpose of such negotiations, Members shall exchange information concerning all subsidies related to trade in services that they provide to their domestic service suppliers.

2. Any Member which considers that it is adversely affected by a subsidy of another Member may request consultations with that Member on such matters. Such requests shall be accorded sympathetic consideration.

Article XVI
Market Access

1. With respect to market access through the modes of supply identified in Article I, each Member shall accord services and service suppliers of any other Member treatment no less favourable than that provided for under the terms, limitations and conditions agreed and specified in its Schedule.[5]

2. In sectors where market-access commitments are undertaken, the measures which a Member shall not maintain or adopt either on the basis of a regional subdivision or on the basis of its entire territory, unless otherwise specified in its Schedule, are defined as:

(a) limitations on the number of service suppliers whether in the form of numerical quotas, monopolies, exclusive service suppliers or the requirements of an economic needs test;

(b) limitations on the total value of service transactions or assets in the form of numerical quotas or the requirement of an economic needs test;

(c) limitations on the total number of service operations or on the total quantity of service output expressed in terms of designated numerical units in the form of quotas or the requirement of an economic needs test;[6]

(d) limitations on the total number of natural persons that may be employed in a particular service sector or that a service supplier may employ and who are necessary for, and directly related to, the supply of a specific service in the form of numerical quotas or the requirement of an economic needs test;

(e) measures which restrict or require specific types of legal entity or joint venture through which a service supplier may supply a service; and

[4] A future work programme shall determine how, and in what time-frame, negotiations on such multilateral disciplines will be conducted.

[5] If a Member undertakes a market-access commitment in relation to the supply of a service through the mode of supply referred to in subparagraph 2(a) of Article I and if the cross-border movement of capital is an essential part of the service itself, that Member is thereby committed to allow such movement of capital. If a Member undertakes a market-access commitment in relation to the supply of a service through the mode of supply referred to in subparagraph 2(c) of Article I, it is thereby committed to allow related transfers of capital into its territory.

[6] Subparagraph 2(c) does not cover measures of a Member which limit inputs for the supply of services.

(f) limitations on the participation of foreign capital in terms of maximum percentage limit on foreign shareholding or the total value of individual or aggregate foreign investment.

Article XVII
National Treatment

1. In the sectors inscribed in its Schedule, and subject to any conditions and qualifications set out therein, each Member shall accord to services and service suppliers of any other Member, in respect of all measures affecting the supply of services, treatment no less favourable than that it accords to its own like services and service suppliers.[7]
2. A Member may meet the requirement of paragraph 1 by according to services and service suppliers of any other Member, either formally identical treatment or formally different treatment to that it accords to its own like services and service suppliers.
3. Formally identical or formally different treatment shall be considered to be less favourable if it modifies the conditions of competition in favour of services or service suppliers of the Member compared to like services or service suppliers of any other Member.

Article XVIII
Additional Commitments

Members may negotiate commitments with respect to measures affecting trade in services not subject to scheduling under Articles XVI or XVII, including those regarding qualifications, standards or licensing matters. Such commitments shall be inscribed in a Member's Schedule.

Article XIX
Negotiation of Specific Commitments

1. In pursuance of the objectives of this Agreement, Members shall enter into successive rounds of negotiations, beginning not later than five years from the date of entry into force of the WTO Agreement and periodically thereafter, with a view to achieving a progressively higher level of liberalization. Such negotiations shall be directed to the reduction or elimination of the adverse effects on trade in services of measures as a means of providing effective market access. This process shall take place with a view to promoting the interests of all participants on a mutually advantageous basis and to securing an overall balance of rights and obligations.
2. The process of liberalization shall take place with due respect for national policy objectives and the level of development of individual Members, both overall and in individual sectors. There shall be appropriate flexibility for individual developing

[7] Specific commitments assumed under this Article shall not be construed to require any Member to compensate for any inherent competitive disadvantages which result from the foreign character of the relevant services or service suppliers.

country Members for opening fewer sectors, liberalizing fewer types of transactions, progressively extending market access in line with their development situation and, when making access to their markets available to foreign service suppliers, attaching to such access conditions aimed at achieving the objectives referred to in Article IV.
3. For each round, negotiating guidelines and procedures shall be established. For the purposes of establishing such guidelines, the Council for Trade in Services shall carry out an assessment of trade in services in overall terms and on a sectoral basis with reference to the objectives of this Agreement, including those set out in paragraph 1 of Article IV. Negotiating guidelines shall establish modalities for the treatment of liberalization undertaken autonomously by Members since previous negotiations, as well as for the special treatment for least-developed country Members under the provisions of paragraph 3 of Article IV.
4. The process of progressive liberalization shall be advanced in each such round through bilateral, plurilateral or multilateral negotiations directed towards increasing the general level of specific commitments undertaken by Members under this Agreement.

Article XX
Schedules of Specific Commitments

1. Each Member shall set out in a schedule the specific commitments it undertakes under Part III of this Agreement. With respect to sectors where such commitments are undertaken, each Schedule shall specify:
(a) terms, limitations and conditions on market access;
(b) conditions and qualifications on national treatment;
(c) undertakings relating to additional commitments;
(d) where appropriate the time-frame for implementation of such commitments; and
(e) the date of entry into force of such commitments.

2. Measures inconsistent with both Articles XVI and XVII shall be inscribed in the column relating to Article XVI. In this case the inscription will be considered to provide a condition or qualification to Article XVII as well.
3. Schedules of specific commitments shall be annexed to this Agreement and shall form an integral part thereof.

Article XXI
Modification of Schedules

1. (a) A Member (referred to in this Article as the 'modifying Member') may modify or withdraw any commitment in its Schedule, at any time after three years have elapsed from the date on which that commitment entered into force, in accordance with the provisions of this Article.
(b) A modifying Member shall notify its intent to modify or withdraw a commitment pursuant to this Article to the Council for Trade in Services no later than three months before the intended date of implementation of the modification or withdrawal.

2. (a) At the request of any Member the benefits of which under this Agreement may be affected (referred to in this Article as an 'affected Member') by a proposed modification or withdrawal notified under subparagraph 1(b), the modifying Member shall enter into negotiations with a view to reaching agreement on any necessary compensatory adjustment. In such negotiations and agreement, the Members concerned shall endeavour to maintain a general level of mutually advantageous commitments not less favourable to trade than that provided for in Schedules of specific commitments prior to such negotiations.
   (b) Compensatory adjustments shall be made on a most-favoured-nation basis.
3. (a) If agreement is not reached between the modifying Member and any affected Member before the end of the period provided for negotiations, such affected Member may refer the matter to arbitration. Any affected Member that wishes to enforce a right that it may have to compensation must participate in the arbitration.
   (b) If no affected Member has requested arbitration, the modifying Member shall be free to implement the proposed modification or withdrawal.
4. (a) The modifying Member may not modify or withdraw its commitment until it has made compensatory adjustments in conformity with the findings of the arbitration.
   (b) If the modifying Member implements its proposed modification or withdrawal and does not comply with the findings of the arbitration, any affected Member that participated in the arbitration may modify or withdraw substantially equivalent benefits in conformity with those findings. Notwithstanding Article II, such a modification or withdrawal may be implemented solely with respect to the modifying Member.

5. The Council for Trade in Services shall establish procedures for rectification or modification of Schedules. Any Member which has modified or withdrawn scheduled commitments under this Article shall modify its Schedule according to such procedures.

Article XXVIII
Definitions

For the purpose of this Agreement:

(a) 'measure' means any measure by a Member, whether in the form of a law, regulation, rule, procedure, decision, administrative action, or any other form;
(b) 'supply of a service' includes the production, distribution, marketing, sale and delivery of a service;
(c) 'measures by Members affecting trade in services' include measures in respect of
   (i) the purchase, payment or use of a service;
   (ii) the access to and use of, in connection with the supply of a service, services which are required by those Members to be offered to the public generally;
   (iii) the presence, including commercial presence, of persons of a Member for the supply of a service in the territory of another Member;
(d) 'commercial presence' means any type of business or professional establishment, including through

(i) the constitution, acquisition or maintenance of a juridical person, or
(ii) the creation or maintenance of a branch or a representative office,
(iii) within the territory of a Member for the purpose of supplying a service;

(e) 'sector' of a service means,
(i) with reference to a specific commitment, one or more, or all, subsectors of that service, as specified in a Member's Schedule,
(ii) otherwise, the whole of that service sector, including all of its subsectors;

(f) 'service of another Member' means a service which is supplied,
(i) from or in the territory of that other Member, or in the case of maritime transport, by a vessel registered under the laws of that other Member, or by a person of that other Member which supplies the service through the operation of a vessel and/or its use in whole or in part; or
(ii) in the case of the supply of a service through commercial presence or through the presence of natural persons, by a service supplier of that other Member;

(g) 'service supplier' means any person that supplies a service;[8]

(h) 'monopoly supplier of a service' means any person, public or private, which in the relevant market of the territory of a Member is authorized or established formally or in effect by that Member as the sole supplier of that service;

(i) 'service consumer' means any person that receives or uses a service;

(j) 'person' means either a natural person or a juridical person;

(k) 'natural person of another Member' means a natural person who resides in the territory of that other Member or any other Member, and who under the law of that other Member:
(i) is a national of that other Member; or
(ii) has the right of permanent residence in that other Member, in the case of a Member which:
1. does not have nationals; or
2. accords substantially the same treatment to its permanent residents as it does to its nationals in respect of measures affecting trade in services, as notified in its acceptance of or accession to the WTO Agreement, provided that no Member is obligated to accord to such permanent residents treatment more favourable than would be accorded by that other Member to such permanent residents. Such notification shall include the assurance to assume, with respect to those permanent residents, in accordance with its laws and regulations, the same responsibilities that other Member bears with respect to its nationals;

(l) 'juridical person' means any legal entity duly constituted or otherwise organized under applicable law, whether for profit or otherwise, and whether privately-owned or governmentally-owned, including any corporation, trust, partnership, joint venture, sole proprietorship or association;

[8] Where the service is not supplied directly by a juridical person but through other forms of commercial presence such as a branch or a representative office, the service supplier (i.e. the juridical person) shall, nonetheless, through such presence be accorded the treatment provided for service suppliers under the Agreement. Such treatment shall be extended to the presence through which the service is supplied and need not be extended to any other parts of the supplier located outside the territory where the service is supplied.

(m) 'juridical person of another Member' means a juridical person which is either:
   (i) constituted or otherwise organized under the law of that other Member, and is engaged in substantive business operations in the territory of that Member or any other Member; or
   (ii) in the case of the supply of a service through commercial presence, owned or controlled by:
      1. natural persons of that Member; or
      2. juridical persons of that other Member identified under subparagraph (i);

(n) a juridical person is:
   (i) 'owned' by persons of a Member if more than 50 per cent of the equity interest in it is beneficially owned by persons of that Member;
   (ii) 'controlled' by persons of a Member if such persons have the power to name a majority of its directors or otherwise to legally direct its actions;
   (iii) 'affiliated' with another person when it controls, or is controlled by, that other person; or when it and the other person are both controlled by the same person;

(o) 'direct taxes' comprise all taxes on total income, on total capital or on elements of income or of capital, including taxes on gains from the alienation of property, taxes on estates, inheritances and gifts, and taxes on the total amounts of wages or salaries paid by enterprises, as well as taxes on capital appreciation.

Appendix D

1993 Statement by the Governments of Canada, Mexico, and the United States*

The governments of Canada, the United States and Mexico, in order to correct false interpretations, have agreed to state the following jointly and publicly as Parties to the North American Free Trade Agreement (NAFTA):

The NAFTA creates no rights to the natural water resources of any Party to the Agreement.

Unless water, in any form, has entered into commerce and become a good or product, it is not covered by the provisions of any trade agreement including the NAFTA. And nothing in the NAFTA would oblige any NAFTA Party to either exploit its water for commercial use, or to begin exporting water in any form. Water in its natural state in lakes, rivers, reservoirs, aquifers, water basins and the like is not a good or product, is not traded, and therefore is not and never has been subject to the terms of any trade agreement.

International rights and obligations respecting water in its natural state are contained in separate treaties and agreements negotiated for that purpose. Examples are the United States-Canada Boundary Waters Treaty of 1909 and the 1944 Boundary Waters Treaty between Mexico and the United States.

* Statement is available at http://www.scics.gc.ca/cinfo99/83067000_e.html.

Appendix E
International Joint Commission

Protection of the Waters of the Great Lakes: Final Report to the Governments of Canada and the United States, 22 February 2000
(Extracts)*

Section 8—Legal and Policy Considerations

...

The International Legal Context

...

International Trade Law. One issue raised by the governments in the Reference was whether international trade obligations might affect water management in the Basin. To address this issue, the Commission, with the assistance of the study team, reviewed the relevant World Trade Organization (WTO) agreements, including the General Agreement on Tariffs and Trade (GATT) as well as the Canada–United States Free Trade Agreement (FTA) and the Canada–United States–Mexico North American Free Trade Agreement (NAFTA), and relevant case law. The Commission and its study team also consulted experts in the field.

The Commission believes it is unlikely that water in its natural state (e.g., in a lake, river, or aquifer) is included within the scope of any of these trade agreements since it is not a product or good. This view is supported by the fact that the NAFTA parties have issued a statement to this effect. When water is 'captured' and enters into commerce, it may, however, attract obligations under the GATT, the FTA, and the NAFTA.

The key GATT provision with possible significance for water exports is the prohibition of quantitative restrictions in Article XI. The GATT, however, creates a number of exceptions. Of these, the most relevant to trade in water would appear to be those related to measures 'necessary to protect human, animal, or plant life or health' (the 'health exception') or 'relating to the conservation of exhaustible natural resources if such measures are made effective in conjunction with restrictions on domestic production or consumption' (the 'conservation exception').

With respect to the former, there has been some debate as to whether this provision should be read broadly, so as to in effect create an 'environmental' exception to the GATT, or narrowly, so as to embrace essentially traditional concerns related to sanitary and phytosanitary measures.

With respect to the latter, there may be a question as to whether water is an exhaustible natural resource, although this raises less of a problem in the case of

* Text available at http://www.ijc.org/php/publications/html/finalreport.html.

a discrete ecosystem such as the Great Lakes Basin, where only a small part of the resource is replenished annually. Both exceptions are qualified by a requirement that they '[not] be applied in a manner which would constitute a means of arbitrary or unjustifiable discrimination between countries where the same conditions prevail, or a disguised restriction on international trade.'

Although dispute-settlement panels considering these GATT exceptions have affirmed, in principle, that trade interests may have to give way to legitimate environmental concerns, it is also true that the same panels have questioned very closely whether measures nominally taken for environmental reasons have underlying protectionist elements. Clearly, then, the achievement of a coherent and consistent approach to water conservation and management in the Great Lakes Basin—an approach clearly grounded in environmental policy—would be an important step in addressing any trade-related concerns with respect to the use of Basin waters.

The NAFTA trade obligations with respect to goods, while rooted in the GATT, appear to constrain the availability of certain GATT exceptions—including the conservation exception—in some important ways, in effect making it more difficult to 'turn off the tap' once trade in water has been established. These constraints do not, however, apply to the health exception, and the NAFTA wording of that exception specifically provides that it is understood by the parties to include environmental measures. NAFTA also makes provision for certain trade obligations in environmental/conservation agreements to prevail in the event of a conflict. Finally, it should be recalled that following the signing of NAFTA, the three parties issued a joint declaration that NAFTA creates no rights to the natural water resources of any party; that unless water, in any form, has entered into commerce and has become a good or product, it is not covered by the provisions of any trade agreement, including NAFTA; and that international rights and obligations respecting water in its natural state are contained in separate treaties, such as the Boundary Waters Treaty, negotiated for that purpose.

Many people who made presentations during the Commission's hearings in September and October 1999 believed that the NAFTA and WTO agreements could prevent or at least impede the United States and Canada from prohibiting the export of Great Lakes waters and the diversion of those waters. Several noted that to date, in all the cases before the WTO involving issues of protecting environmental or natural resource interests, the WTO had ruled against those interests. Some observed that the WTO decision-making process was not transparent.

Since issuing its Interim Report, the Commission has received a letter dated November 24, 1999, from the Deputy United States Trade Representative concerning the implications of international trade agreements for the protection of the waters of the Great Lakes Basin. A copy of this letter is attached (Appendix 8). The Commission has also received a document entitled Bulk Water Removal and International Trade Considerations from the Canadian Department of Foreign Affairs and International Trade (Appendix 9). These submissions generally are consistent with the Commission's views regarding the effect of international trade law on the ability of the two countries to protect the water resources of the Great Lakes Basin.

The Commission also received legal opinions from several experts. The following points synthesize the thrust of these opinions received and are intended to take into account the uncertainties and the caution expressed with respect to international trade law. They are similar to the views expressed by the Canadian and U.S. governments.

- The provisions of NAFTA and the WTO agreements do not prevent Canada and the United States from taking measures to protect their water resources and preserve the integrity of the Great Lakes Basin ecosystem where there is no discrimination by decision-makers against individuals from other countries in the application of those measures.
- NAFTA and the WTO agreements do not constrain or affect the sovereign right of a government to decide whether or not it will allow natural resources within its jurisdiction to be exploited and, if a natural resource is allowed to be exploited, the pace and manner of such exploitation.
- Moreover, even if there were sales or diversions of water from the Great Lakes Basin in the past, governments could still decide not to allow new and additional sales or diversions in the future.
- The NAFTA and WTO agreements contain provisions that prohibit export restrictions and discrimination between nationals and foreigners who are entitled to national treatment under those treaties. Sales of water that are allowed could not be restricted to the domestic market unless they fit within the health and conservation exceptions referred to above (i.e., restrictive measures would be necessary for the protection of human, animal, or plant life or health or for the conservation of an exhaustible natural resource and are not applied in a way that constitutes arbitrary or unjustifiable discrimination or a disguised restriction of international trade). Recent decisions of the appellate body of the WTO may raise concerns about the circumstances in which environmental measures will meet the test of not constituting arbitrary or unjustifiable discrimination or a disguised restriction of international trade, even though they may otherwise relate to the conservation of an exhaustible natural resource or may be necessary for the protection of life or health. The WTO decisions have tended to focus on whether measures are arbitrary or discriminatory. In the light of these decisions, it appears that it would be desirable, whenever possible, for environmental measures to be based on an international agreement or arrangement.
- If governments in Canada and the United States want to avoid falling within the investment provisions of the NAFTA, they should avoid creating undue expectations by clearly articulating their water-management policies in a fully transparent manner, by acting in a manner that is entirely consistent with their stated policy, and by limiting the time for which authorizations are valid. Moreover, the governments should make it clear that authorizations do not give rise to any continuing entitlement or expectation on the part of the holder of the authorization, that, if the holder of the authorization were to reapply after the expiry of the authorization, there is no guarantee that that person would be given treatment any more favorable than any other person who might apply, and that it is within the government's jurisdiction to decide whether or not even to permit an authorization to be issued again.
- Actions with respect to water diversions or sales that nationalize or expropriate an investment of a foreigner may lead to a claim under Chapter 11 of NAFTA, which gives private investors of one country the right to commence proceedings against

> another country for injuries to the rights accorded private investors under the agreement. In all other cases, claims under the WTO agreements or the NAFTA must be brought by a Party to the agreement (i.e., by the government of one of the countries).

Other experts, while not suggesting international trade law made it impossible to regulate exports of water, cautioned that trade law could make the process more complicated.

Appendix F

North American Free Trade Agreement Between the Government of the United States of America, the Government of Canada, and the Government of the United Mexican States*

Chapter 11

(Extracts)

North American Free Trade Agreement

PART FIVE

INVESTMENT, SERVICES AND RELATED MATTERS

Chapter Eleven: Investment

Section A—Investment

Article 1101: Scope and Coverage

1. This Chapter applies to measures adopted or maintained by a Party relating to:

(a) investors of another Party;
(b) investments of investors of another Party in the territory of the Party; and
(c) with respect to Articles 1106 and 1114, all investments in the territory of the Party.

2. A Party has the right to perform exclusively the economic activities set out in Annex III and to refuse to permit the establishment of investment in such activities.
3. This Chapter does not apply to measures adopted or maintained by a Party to the extent that they are covered by Chapter Fourteen (Financial Services).
4. Nothing in this Chapter shall be construed to prevent a Party from providing a service or performing a function such as law enforcement, correctional services, income security or insurance, social security or insurance, social welfare, public education, public training, health, and child care, in a manner that is not inconsistent with this Chapter.

* Text available at: http://www.nafta-sec-alena.org/DefaultSite/index.html (last visited on 28 May 2004) and reprinted in 32 *ILM* 289 (1993), at 289.

Article 1102: National Treatment

1. Each Party shall accord to investors of another Party treatment no less favorable than that it accords, in like circumstances, to its own investors with respect to the establishment, acquisition, expansion, management, conduct, operation, and sale or other disposition of investments.
2. Each Party shall accord to investments of investors of another Party treatment no less favorable than that it accords, in like circumstances, to investments of its own investors with respect to the establishment, acquisition, expansion, management, conduct, operation, and sale or other disposition of investments.
3. The treatment accorded by a Party under paragraphs 1 and 2 means, with respect to a state or province, treatment no less favorable than the most favorable treatment accorded, in like circumstances, by that state or province to investors, and to investments of investors, of the Party of which it forms a part.
4. For greater certainty, no Party may:

(a) impose on an investor of another Party a requirement that a minimum level of equity in an enterprise in the territory of the Party be held by its nationals, other than nominal qualifying shares for directors or incorporators of corporations; or
(b) require an investor of another Party, by reason of its nationality, to sell or otherwise dispose of an investment in the territory of the Party.

Article 1103: Most-Favored-Nation Treatment

1. Each Party shall accord to investors of another Party treatment no less favorable than that it accords, in like circumstances, to investors of any other Party or of a non-Party with respect to the establishment, acquisition, expansion, management, conduct, operation, and sale or other disposition of investments.
2. Each Party shall accord to investments of investors of another Party treatment no less favorable than that it accords, in like circumstances, to investments of investors of any other Party or of a non-Party with respect to the establishment, acquisition, expansion, management, conduct, operation, and sale or other disposition of investments.

Article 1104: Standard of Treatment

Each Party shall accord to investors of another Party and to investments of investors of another Party the better of the treatment required by Articles 1102 and 1103.

Article 1105: Minimum Standard of Treatment

1. Each Party shall accord to investments of investors of another Party treatment in accordance with international law, including fair and equitable treatment and full protection and security.
2. Without prejudice to paragraph 1 and notwithstanding Article 1108(7)(b), each Party shall accord to investors of another Party, and to investments of investors of another Party, non-discriminatory treatment with respect to measures it adopts or maintains relating to losses suffered by investments in its territory owing to armed conflict or civil strife.
3. Paragraph 2 does not apply to existing measures relating to subsidies or grants that would be inconsistent with Article 1102 but for Article 1108(7)(b).

Article 1106: Performance Requirements

1. No Party may impose or enforce any of the following requirements, or enforce any commitment or undertaking, in connection with the establishment, acquisition, expansion, management, conduct or operation of an investment of an investor of a Party or of a non-Party in its territory:

(a) to export a given level or percentage of goods or services;
(b) to achieve a given level or percentage of domestic content;
(c) to purchase, use or accord a preference to goods produced or services provided in its territory, or to purchase goods or services from persons in its territory;
(d) to relate in any way the volume or value of imports to the volume or value of exports or to the amount of foreign exchange inflows associated with such investment;
(e) to restrict sales of goods or services in its territory that such investment produces or provides by relating such sales in any way to the volume or value of its exports or foreign exchange earnings;
(f) to transfer technology, a production process or other proprietary knowledge to a person in its territory, except when the requirement is imposed or the commitment or undertaking is enforced by a court, administrative tribunal or competition authority to remedy an alleged violation of competition laws or to act in a manner not inconsistent with other provisions of this Agreement; or
(g) to act as the exclusive supplier of the goods it produces or services it provides to a specific region or world market.

2. A measure that requires an investment to use a technology to meet generally applicable health, safety or environmental requirements shall not be construed to be inconsistent with paragraph 1(f). For greater certainty, Articles 1102 and 1103 apply to the measure.

3. No Party may condition the receipt or continued receipt of an advantage, in connection with an investment in its territory of an investor of a Party or of a non-Party, on compliance with any of the following requirements:

(a) to achieve a given level or percentage of domestic content;
(b) to purchase, use or accord a preference to goods produced in its territory, or to purchase goods from producers in its territory;
(c) to relate in any way the volume or value of imports to the volume or value of exports or to the amount of foreign exchange inflows associated with such investment; or
(d) to restrict sales of goods or services in its territory that such investment produces or provides by relating such sales in any way to the volume or value of its exports or foreign exchange earnings.

4. Nothing in paragraph 3 shall be construed to prevent a Party from conditioning the receipt or continued receipt of an advantage, in connection with an investment in its territory of an investor of a Party or of a non-Party, on compliance with a requirement to locate production, provide a service, train or employ workers,

construct or expand particular facilities, or carry out research and development, in its territory.
5. Paragraphs 1 and 3 do not apply to any requirement other than the requirements set out in those paragraphs.
6. Provided that such measures are not applied in an arbitrary or unjustifiable manner, or do not constitute a disguised restriction on international trade or investment, nothing in paragraph 1(b) or (c) or 3(a) or (b) shall be construed to prevent any Party from adopting or maintaining measures, including environmental measures:

(a) necessary to secure compliance with laws and regulations that are not inconsistent with the provisions of this Agreement;
(b) necessary to protect human, animal or plant life or health; or
(c) necessary for the conservation of living or non-living exhaustible natural resources.

Article 1108: Reservations and Exceptions

1. Articles 1102, 1103, 1106 and 1107 do not apply to:

(a) any existing non-conforming measure that is maintained by
  (i) a Party at the federal level, as set out in its Schedule to Annex I or III,
  (ii) a state or province, for two years after the date of entry into force of this Agreement, and thereafter as set out by a Party in its Schedule to Annex I in accordance with paragraph 2, or
  (iii) a local government;
(b) the continuation or prompt renewal of any non-conforming measure referred to in subparagraph (a); or
(c) an amendment to any non-conforming measure referred to in subparagraph (a) to the extent that the amendment does not decrease the conformity of the measure, as it existed immediately before the amendment, with Articles 1102, 1103, 1106 and 1107.

2. Each Party may set out in its Schedule to Annex I, within two years of the date of entry into force of this Agreement, any existing nonconforming measure maintained by a state or province, not including a local government.
3. Articles 1102, 1103, 1106 and 1107 do not apply to any measure that a Party adopts or maintains with respect to sectors, subsectors or activities, as set out in its Schedule to Annex II.
4. No Party may, under any measure adopted after the date of entry into force of this Agreement and covered by its Schedule to Annex II, require an investor of another Party, by reason of its nationality, to sell or otherwise dispose of an investment existing at the time the measure becomes effective.
5. Articles 1102 and 1103 do not apply to any measure that is an exception to, or derogation from, the obligations under Article 1703 (Intellectual Property National Treatment) as specifically provided for in that Article.
6. Article 1103 does not apply to treatment accorded by a Party pursuant to agreements, or with respect to sectors, set out in its Schedule to Annex IV.
7. Articles 1102, 1103 and 1107 do not apply to:

(a) procurement by a Party or a state enterprise; or

(b) subsidies or grants provided by a Party or a state enterprise, including government supported loans, guarantees and insurance.

8. The provisions of:

(a) Article 1106(1)(a), (b) and (c), and (3)(a) and (b) do not apply to qualification requirements for goods or services with respect to export promotion and foreign aid programs;
(b) Article 1106(1)(b), (c), (f) and (g), and (3)(a) and (b) do not apply to procurement by a Party or a state enterprise; and
(c) Article 1106(3)(a) and (b) do not apply to requirements imposed by an importing Party relating to the content of goods necessary to qualify for preferential tariffs or preferential quotas.

Article 1110: Expropriation and Compensation

1. No Party may directly or indirectly nationalize or expropriate an investment of an investor of another Party in its territory or take a measure tantamount to nationalization or expropriation of such an investment ('expropriation'), except:

(a) for a public purpose;
(b) on a non-discriminatory basis;
(c) in accordance with due process of law and Article 1105(1); and
(d) on payment of compensation in accordance with paragraphs 2 through 6.

2. Compensation shall be equivalent to the fair market value of the expropriated investment immediately before the expropriation took place ('date of expropriation'), and shall not reflect any change in value occurring because the intended expropriation had become known earlier. Valuation criteria shall include going concern value, asset value including declared tax value of tangible property, and other criteria, as appropriate, to determine fair market value.
3. Compensation shall be paid without delay and be fully realizable.
4. If payment is made in a G7 currency, compensation shall include interest at a commercially reasonable rate for that currency from the date of expropriation until the date of actual payment.
5. If a Party elects to pay in a currency other than a G7 currency, the amount paid on the date of payment, if converted into a G7 currency at the market rate of exchange prevailing on that date, shall be no less than if the amount of compensation owed on the date of expropriation had been converted into that G7 currency at the market rate of exchange prevailing on that date, and interest had accrued at a commercially reasonable rate for that G7 currency from the date of expropriation until the date of payment.
6. On payment, compensation shall be freely transferable as provided in Article 1109.
7. This Article does not apply to the issuance of compulsory licenses granted in relation to intellectual property rights, or to the revocation, limitation or creation of intellectual property rights, to the extent that such issuance, revocation, limitation or creation is consistent with Chapter Seventeen (Intellectual Property).
8. For purposes of this Article and for greater certainty, a non-discriminatory measure of general application shall not be considered a measure tantamount to an

expropriation of a debt security or loan covered by this Chapter solely on the ground that the measure imposes costs on the debtor that cause it to default on the debt.

Article 1114: Environmental Measures

1. Nothing in this Chapter shall be construed to prevent a Party from adopting, maintaining or enforcing any measure otherwise consistent with this Chapter that it considers appropriate to ensure that investment activity in its territory is undertaken in a manner sensitive to environmental concerns.

2. The Parties recognize that it is inappropriate to encourage investment by relaxing domestic health, safety or environmental measures. Accordingly, a Party should not waive or otherwise derogate from, or offer to waive or otherwise derogate from, such measures as an encouragement for the establishment, acquisition, expansion or retention in its territory of an investment of an investor. If a Party considers that another Party has offered such an encouragement, it may request consultations with the other Party and the two Parties shall consult with a view to avoiding any such encouragement.

Section B—Settlement of Disputes between a Party and an Investor of Another Party

(Articles 1115–1139) not reproduced

Appendix G
Bibliography

Aljundi, H., LEGISLATIONS OF IRRIGATION WATER USE IN SALAMIEH, MIMEO (2003).

Allan, J. A., *Virtual Water–the Water, Food, and Trade Nexus: Useful Concept or Misleading Metaphor?*, 28 WATER INT'L 4 (2003).

Anaya, S. J. and Grossman, C., *The Case of Awas Tingni v. Nicaragua: A New Step in the International Law of Indigenous Peoples*, 19 ARIZ. J. INT'L & COMP. L. 1 (2002).

Anderson, B. D., *Selling Great Lakes Water to a Thirsty World: Legal, Policy & Trade Considerations*, 6 BUFFALO ENVTL. L. J. (1999).

Anderson, T. L. (ed.), *Continental Water Marketing*, Pacific Research Institute for Public Policy, San Francisco (1994).

Arnold, C. A., *The Reconstruction of Property: Property as a Web of Interests*, 26 HARV. ENVTL. L. REV. 281 (2002).

Bauer, C. J., SIREN SONG: CHILEAN WATER LAW AS MODEL FOR INTERNATIONAL REFORM (2004).

Benvenisti, Eyal, SHARING TRANSBOUNDARY RESOURCES. INTERNATIONAL LAW AND OPTIMAL USE (2002).

Buergenthal, Thomas, *To Respect and to Ensure: State Obligations and Permissible Derogations*, in THE INTERNATIONAL BILL OF RIGHTS: THE COVENANT ON CIVIL AND POLITICAL RIGHTS (Louis Henkin ed., 1981).

Beuscher, Jacob, *Appropriation Water Law Elements in Riparian Doctrine States*, 10 BUFFALO L. REV. 448 (1961).

Boisson de Chazournes, L., *The Aral Sea Basin: Legal and Institutional Aspects of Governance*, in THE MULTI-GOVERNANCE OF WATER THROUGH FOUR CASES (Matthias Finger and Ludivine Tamiotti eds, 2001).

Boisson de Chazournes, L., LES RESSOURCES EN EAU ET LE DROIT INTERNATIONAL [WATER RESOURCES AND INTERNATIONAL LAW] 17 (Centre for Studies and Research in International Law and International Relations, Hague Academy of International Law, 2001).

Boisson de Chazournes, L., *Public Participation in Decision-Making: The World Bank Inspection Panel*, in THE WORLD BANK, INTERNATIONAL FINANCIAL INSTITUTIONS, AND THE DEVELOPMENT OF INTERNATIONAL LAW 84 (Brown Weiss, E., Rigo Sureda, A., and Boisson de Chazournes, L. eds, 1999).

Boyle, A. E. and Anderson, M. R., HUMAN RIGHTS APPROACHES TO ENVIRONMENTAL PROTECTION (1996).

Brans, E. H. P. et al., THE SCARCITY OF WATER: EMERGING LEGAL AND POLICY RESPONSES (1997).

Brown, F. Lee and Ingram, Helen, WATER AND POVERTY IN THE SOUTHWEST (1988).

Brown, Lester R., *Water Deficits Growing in Many Countries: Water Shortages May Cause Food Shortages*, EARTH POLICY INSTITUTE: ECO-ECONOMY UPDATES, August 6, 2002, available at http://www.earth-policy.org/Updates/Update15.htm.

Brubaker, E., PRIVATIZING AND REGULATING CANADA'S WATER UTILITIES (2002).

Butler, Lynda, *Allocating Consumptive Water Rights in a Riparian Jurisdiction: Defining the Relationship Between Public and Private Interests*, 47 U. PITT. L. REV. 95 (1987).

Cameron, J. and Mackenzie, R., *Access to Environmental Justice and Procedural Rights in International Institutions*, in HUMAN RIGHTS APPROACHES TO ENVIRONMENTAL PROTECTION 129 (Boyle, A. and Anderson, M. eds, 1996).

Chichilnisky, Graciela, *North-South Trade and the Global Environment*, 84 (4) AMERICAN ECONOMIC REVIEW 851 (1994).

Center for International Environmental Law (CIEL), *Going With the Flow: How International Trade, Finance and Investment Regimes Affect the Provision of Water to the Poor* (2003), available at http://www.ciel.org/Publications/Waterbrief_3Sept03.pdf.

Coase, Ronald, *The Problem of Social Cost*, 3 JOURNAL OF LAW AND ECONOMICS 1 (1960).

Committee on the Future Demands of Irrigation in the Face of Competing Demands, Water Science and Technology Board, Commission on Geosciences, Environment, and Resources, National Research Council, A NEW ERA FOR IRRIGATION (1996).

Cottier, T., *The Challenge of Regionalization and Preferential Relations in World Trade Law and Policy*, 2 EUR. FOREIGN AFF. REV. 149 (1996).

Daoudy, M., *Entre le Tigre et l'Euphrate: Une Négociation en EauxTtroubles*, in LES CAHIERS DE L'ORIENT 44 (4th Trimestre 1996).

Dasgupta, P. and Heal, G., ECONOMIC THEORY AND EXHAUSTIBLE RESOURCES (Cambridge University Press, 1979).

De Haan, E. J., *Balancing Free Trade in Water and the Protection of Water Resources in GATT*, in THE SCARCITY OF WATER: EMERGING LEGAL AND POLICY RESPONSES (Edward H. P. Brans et al. eds, 1997).

Deen, T., *Privatisation No Answer to Water Scarcity*, UN, INTERNET PRESS SERVICE NEWS AGENCY, 18 March 2004, available at http://www.ipsnews.net/interna.asp?idnews=22931.

Delmon, J., WATER PROJECTS—A COMMERCIAL AND CONTRACTUAL GUIDE (2001).

Dinar, A., *Political Economy of Water Pricing reforms in Irrigated Agriculture*, in THE POLICITAL ECONOMY OF WATER PRICING REFORMS (A. Dinar, ed., 2000).

Dolatyar, M., *Water Diplomacy in the Middle East*, in THE MIDDLE EASTERN ENVIRONMENT (Eric Watkins ed., 1995).

Doremus, H. and Tarlock, A. D. *Fish, Farms, and the Clash of Cultures in the Klamath Basin*, 30 ECOLOGY L. Q. 279 (2003).

DuMars, Charles T. and Minnis, Michele, *New Mexico Water Law: Determining Public Welfare Values in Water Right Allocation*, 31 ARIZ. L. REV. 817 (1989).

Ebbesson, J., *The Notion of Public Participation in International Environmental Law*, 8 Y.B. INT'L ENVTL. L. 51 (1997).

Ethier, Wilfred, J., *Unilateralism in a Multilateral World*, Tinbergen Institute Discussion Papers 01-033/2 (Tinbergen Institute, 2001).

Fearon, J., *Rationalist Explanation for War*, 49 INTERNATIONAL ORGANIZATION 3, 379 (1995).

Ferrell, J. R., THE BIG DAM ERA: A LEGISLATIVE AND INSTITUTIONAL HISTORY OF THE PICK-SLOAN MISSOURI BASIN PROGRAM (1993).

Finnegan, W., *Leasing the Rain*, THE NEW YORKER, 8 April 2002.

Fisher, F., *The Economics of Water Dispute Resolution*, in PROJECT EVALUATION AND MANAGEMENT: AN APPLICATION TO THE MIDDLE EAST WATER RESOURCES DEVELOPMENT (1995).

Food and Agricultural Organization (FAO), PREPARING NATIONAL REGULATIONS FOR WATER RESOURCES MANAGEMENT: PRINCIPLES AND PRACTICE, FAO Legislative Study No. 52 (1994).

Foster, S., *Essential Concepts For Groundwater Regulators*, in GROUNDWATER LEGAL AND POLICY PERSPECTIVES (S. M. A. Salman ed., 1999).

Freyfogle, E., *Water Rights and the Common Wealth*, 26 ENVTL. L. 27 (1996).

Fudenberg, D. and Tirole, J., GAME THEORY (1992).

Gaillard, E., *Centre International pour le règlement des différends relatifs aux investissements: chronique des sentences arbitrales*, JOURNAL DU DROIT INTERNATIONAL 230 (2003).

Gardner, J., HUMAN RIGHTS AS GENERAL NORMS AND A STATE'S RIGHT TO OPT OUT 185-207 (J. Gardner ed., 1997).

Geyer, B., Besançon, Y. Calvet, and Debaine, F., *Les marges arides de la Syrie du Nord: résultats préliminaires d'une prospection géo-archéologique*, B.A.G.F 75/2 (1998).

Girouard, R. J., *Water Export Restrictions: A Case Study of WTO Dispute Settlement Strategies and Outcomes*, 15 GEORGETOWN INT'L ENVTL. L. REV. 247 (2003).

Gleick, P. H., *Basic Water Requirements for Human Activities: Meeting Basic Needs*, 21 WATER INT'L 83 (1996).

Gleick, P. H., *The Changing Water Paradigm: A Look at Twenty-First Century Water Resources Development*, 25 WATER INT'L 127 (2000).

Gleick, P. H., *The Human Right to Water*, 1 WATER POL'Y 487 (1998).

Gleick, P. H., WATER IN CRISIS (1993).

Gleick, P. H. et al., THE NEW ECONOMY OF WATER—THE RISKS AND BENEFITS OF GLOBALIZATION AND PRIVATIZATION OF FRESH WATER (Pacific Institute for Studies in Development, Environment and Security, 2002).

Gomez, S. and Loh, P., *Communities and Water Markets: A Review of the Model Transfer Act*, 4 HASTINGS WEST-NORTHWEST J. ENVIR. L. AND POLICY 63 (1996).

Gould, E., *Water in the Current Round of WTO Negotiations on Services*, Canadian Centre for Policy Alternatives Briefing Paper Series: Investment and Trade, Vol. 4, No. 1 (2003), available at http://www.policyalternatives.ca/publications/brief4-1.pdf.

Gould, G., *Water Rights Transfers and Third-Party Effects*, 23 LAND & WATER L. REV. 1 (1988).

Gowlland G., A., *The Environmental Accountability of the World Bank to Non-State Actors: Insights from the Inspection Panel*, 72 BRIT. Y.B. INT'L L. 213 (2001).

Gray, B. E., *The Role of Laws and Institutions in California's 1991 Water Bank*, in SHARING SCARCITY: GAINERS AND LOSERS IN WATER MARKETING 133 (Harold O. Carter, Henry Vaux, Jr., and Ann F. Securing eds, 1994).

Grimeaud, D., *The EC Water Framework Directive—An Instrument for Integrating Water Policy*, 13(1) REV. EUR. COMMUNITY & INT'L ENVTL L. [RECIEL] 27 (2004).

Güner, S., *The Turkish–Syrian War of Attrition: The Water Dispute*, 20 (1) STUDIES IN CONFLICT AND TERRORISM 105 (1997).

Gutierrez, E. et al., *New Rules, New Roles: Does PSP Benefit the Poor?* Synthesis Report (WaterAid and Tearfund, 2003).

Hanak, E., Who Should be Allowed to Sell Water in California? Third Party Issues and the Water Market (Public Policy Institute of California, 2003).

Hardin, G., *The Tragedy of the Commons*, 162 Science 1243 (1968).

Hart, John, Storm Over Mono: The Mono Lake Battle and California's Water Future (1996).

Hartman, L. and Seastone, D., Water Transfers (1970), National Water Commission, Water Policies for the Future (1973).

Hefti, T., La protection de la propritrangère en droit international public 40 (Zurich, 1989).

Hettena, S., *State's Rice Farmers Evolve From Foe to Friend*, Associated Press, December 12, 2003.

Hey, E. *Sustainable Use of Shared Water Resources: The Need for a Paradigmatic Shift in International Watercourses Law*, in The Peaceful Management of Transboundary Resources 127 (Gerald H. Blake et al. eds, 1995).

Higgins, R., *Introduction*, in Human Rights as General Norms and a State's Right to Opt Out xv, xxvi–xxviii (Christine Chinkin et al. eds, 1997).

Hishleifer, J., *From Weakest Link to Best Shot: The Voluntary Provision of Public Goods*, 41 Public Choice 371 (1983).

Holmes, B. H., A History of federal Water Resources projects, 1800–1960 (U.S. Dept. of Agriculture, Misc. Pub. No. 1233, 1972).

Horsman, S., Water in Central Asia: Regional Cooperation or Conflict? (Roy Allison and Leana Jonson eds, 2001).

Howitt, R. et al., A Retrospective on California's 1991 Emergency Drought Water Bank: A Report Prepared for the California Department of Water Resources (March, 1992).

Inter American Development Bank, *El proceso de transformación del sector de agua potable y saneamiento en Argentina*, July 1996.

International Joint Commission, *Protection of the Waters of the Great Lakes: Final Report to the Governments of Canada and the United States*, February 22, 2000.

Isaac, J., et al., *Water Supply and Demand in Palestine*, ARIJ (1994) (unpublished, on file with the Harvard Middle East Water Project).

Isaac, J., *The Palestinian Water Crisis*, Information Brief, n. 4, Center for Policy Analysis on Palestine, Washington, D.C. (1999).

Isaac, J. and Selby, J., *The Palestinian Water Crisis—Status, Projections and Potential for Resolution*, 20(1) Natural Resource Forum 17 (1996).

Jaubert, R. and Debaine, F., *Spatial Division and Territorial Control in the Syrian Steppe*, Arab World Geographer, Toronto (2002).

Jaubert, R., Geyer, B., Debaine, F. and Dbiyat, M., *L'exploitation des eaux de subsurface des marges arides de Syrie: dégradation ou transformation?*, Scheresse Vol. 13 No. 1 (2001).

Kingsbury, B., *Operational Policies of International Institutions as Part of the Law-Making Process: The World Bank and Indigenous Peoples*, in The Reality of International Law: Essays in Honour of Ian Brownlie 323 (G. S. Goodwin-Gill and S. Talmon eds, 1999).

Klasing, A., *The Common Commercial Policy in the Constitution for Europe—A Step Forward for the Environment?*, Ecologic Briefs: A Sustainable Constitution for Europe (Ecologic, September 2003).

Krafft, M.-C., *Les accords bilatéraux sur la protection des investissements conclus par la Suisse*, in FOREIGN INVESTMENT IN THE PRESENT AND A NEW INTERNATIONAL ECONOMIC ORDER (Detlav Dicke ed., 1987).

Krajewski, M., NATIONAL REGULATION AND TRADE LIBERALIZATION IN SERVICES (2003).

Krajewski, M., *Public Services and Trade Liberalization: Mapping the Legal Framework*, 6(2) JOURNAL OF INTERNATIONAL ECONOMIC LAW 341 (2003).

Krutilla, J. and Eckstein, O., MULTIPLE PURPOSE RIVER BASIN DEVELOPMENT (1958).

Lewis, N., NOMADS AND SETTLERS IN SYRIA AND JORDAN 1800–1980 (1987).

Lowi, M., WATER AND POWER (1993).

Lucero, L. and Tarlock, A. D., *Water Supply and Urban Growth in New Mexico: Same Old, Same Old, or New Era*, 43 NAT. RES. J. (2003).

Luterbacher, U. and Wiegandt, E., *Social Dimensions of Resource Use: The Freshwater Case*, 1(4) SWISS POL. SCI. REV. 131 (1995).

Luterbacher, U. and Wiegandt, E., *Water Control and Property Rights: An Analysis of the Middle East Situation*, in CLIMATIC CHANGE: IMPLICATIONS FOR THE HYDROLOGICAL CYCLE 379 (Martin Beniston ed., 2002).

MacDonnell, L. J., THE WATER TRANSFER PROCESS AS A MANAGEMENT OPTION FOR MEETING CHANGING DEMANDS (Natural Resources Law Center, University of Colorado School of Law, 1990).

MacDonnell, L. J., *Transferring Water Uses in the West*, 43 OKLA. L. REV. 119 (1990).

Maurhofer, R., *The quest for the lesser evil: Great Britain, Switzerland and the decision to create EFTA*, Working Paper 286 (Institut für Politikwissenschaft, Universität. St. Gallen, 2000).

Mbaria, J., *Uganda, Kenya Sign Water, Sanitation Deal*, THE EAST AFRICAN (Nairobi), April 12, 2004.

McCaffrey, S. C., *A Human Right to Water: Domestic and International Implications*, 5 GEORGETOWN INT'L ENVTL. L. REV. 1 (1992).

McCaffrey, S. C., THE LAW OF INTERNATIONAL WATERCOURSES: NON-NAVIGATIONAL USES (2001).

McEntire J., *Water Farms and Transfer Conflicts in Arizona, USA: A proposed Resolution Process*, 13 ENVTL. MGMT. 287 (1989).

Mehta, L., *Problems of Publicness and Access Rights: Perspectives from the Water Domain*, in GLOBAL PUBLIC GOODS: MAKING GLOBALISATION WORK FOR ALL (Inge Kaul et al. eds, 2003).

Mehta, L., *Water for the Twenty-First Century: Challenges and Misconceptions*, IDS Working Paper, 111, Institute of Development Studies (2000), available at http://www.ids.ac.uk/ids/bookshop/wp/wp111.pdf.

Mehta, L., and La Cour Madsen, B., *Is the WTO After your Water? The General Agreement on Trade and Services (GATS) and the Right to Water*, Institute of Development Studies, University of Sussex (August 2003).

Meron, T., *Extraterritoriality of Human Rights Treaties*, 89 AJIL 78 (1995).

Meyers, C. J. et al., WATER RESOURCE MANAGEMENT 434–5 (3rd edn, 1988).

Moulin, H., GAME THEORY FOR THE SOCIAL SCIENCES (1986).

Nahal, I., *L'homme et la désertification au Proche-Orient*, SCHERESSE, Vol. 4 No. 2. (1991).

National Research Council, ENDANGERED AND THREATENED FISHES IN THE KLAMATH RIVER BASIN: CAUSES OF DECLINE AND STRATEGIES FOR RECOVERY (2003).

National Research Council, PRIVATIZATION OF WATER SERVICES IN THE UNITED STATES—AN ASSESSMENT OF ISSUES AND EXPERIENCE (2002).

Nell, P. G., *Extension of the European Union/EFTA Regional Trading Bloc to Central and Eastern Europe*, 20 WORLD COMPETITION—LAW AND ECON. REV. 131 (1997).

Nowrot, K. and Wardin, Y., *Liberalisierung der Wasserversorgung in der WTO—Rechtsordnung-Die Verwirklichung des Menschenrechts auf Wasser als Aufgabe einer transnationalen Verantwortungsgesellschaft* in BEITRÄGE ZUM TRANSNATIONALEN WIRTSCHAFTSRECHT, Heft 14 (2003).

OECD, *Improving Water Management—Recent OECD Experience* (OECD Paris, 2003).

OECD, *Environmental Goods and Services, The Benefits of Further Global Trade Liberalization* (OECD Paris, 2001).

OECD, *Improving the Environment Through Reducing Subsidies*, Part III, Case Studies (OECD Paris, 1999).

OECD, *Industrial Water Pricing in OECD Countries*, ENV/EPOC/GEEI(98)10/FINAL (OECD Paris, 1999).

OECD, *Agricultural Water Pricing in OECD Countries*, ENV/EPOC/GEEI(98)11/FINAL (OECD Paris, 1999).

OECD, *Household Water Pricing in OECD Countries*, ENV/EPOC/GEEI(98)12/FINAL (OECD Paris, 1999).

OECD, *Improving the Environment Through Reducing Subsidies*, Part I, Summary and Conclusions (OECD Paris, 1998).

OECD, *Improving the Environment Through Reducing Subsidies*, Part II, Analysis and Overview of Studies (OECD Paris, 1998).

Office of Technology Assessment, PREPARING FOR AN UNCERTAIN FUTURE: SUMMARY 32 (1993).

Oggins, C. and Ingram, H., DOES ANYBODY WIN? THE COMMUNITY CONSEQUENCES OF RURAL-TO-URBAN WATER TRANSFERS: AN ARIZONA PERSPECTIVE (Udall Center Issue Paper No. 2, 1990).

Ostrovksy, A., Speed, R., and Tuerk, E., *GATS, Water and the Environment—Implications of the General Agreement on Trade in Services for Water Resources*, A CIEL and WWF International Discussion Paper (October 2003), available at http://www.panda.org/downloads/policy/gatswaterenvironment.pdf.

Parden, S., *The Milagro Beanfield War Revisited in Ensenada Land & Water Association v. Sleeper: Public Welfare Defies Transfer of Water Rights*, 29 NAT. RESOURCES J. 861 (1989).

Parker, M. P. and Man, S. B., *Water Management: Mission Impossible?*, 70 FLORIDA BAR J. 20, 28 n. 9 (1996).

Perrier, E. R. and Salkini, A. B. SUPPLEMENTAL IRRIGATION IN THE NEAR EAST AND NORTH AFRICA (E. R. Perrier and A. B. Salkini, eds, 1991).

Peterson, L. E., *Emerging Bilateral Investment treaty Arbitration and Sustainable Development*, Research Note, available at www.iisd.org/pdf/2003/trade_bits_disputes.pdf.

Piaget, J., *Limits in Water Concession Contracts: the case of Aguas del Aconquija (Argentina)*, Master of International Management, University of Lausanne, 11–25 (2003).

Pisani, D., To Reclaim a Divided west: Water, Law and Public Policy, 1848–1902 (1992) and Water, Land, Law in the West: The Limits of Public Policy (1996).

Pontifical Council for Justice and Peace, *Water, An Essential Element for Life*, Vatican City, March 2003, available at http://www.vatican.va/roman_curia/pontifical/councils/justpeace/documents/rc_pc_justpeace_doc_20030322_kyoto-water_en.html.

Popovic, N. A. F., *In Pursuit of Environmental Human Rights: Commentary on the Draft Declaration of Principles on Human Rights and the Environment*, 27 Colum. Hum. Rts. L. Rev. 487, 528 (1996).

Porter, G., *Subsidies and the Environment: The State of Knowledge*, paper presented to the OECD Workshop on Environmentally Harmful Subsidies, Paris, 7–8 November 2002.

Postel, S., Dividing the Waters: Food Security, Ecosystem Health, and the New Politics of Scarcity (1996).

Public Citizen, Water Heist, How Corporations are Cashing in on California's Water (December 2003), available at www.citizen.org/california/water/heist.

Repetto, R., *Skimming the Water: Rent-Seeking and the Performance of Public Irrigation Systems*, Research Report No. 4 (Washington D.C., World Resources Institute, 1986).

Romano, C. P. R., The Peaceful Settlement of International Environmental Disputes: A Pragmatic Approach (2000).

Russell, B. K., The Promise of Water: The Legacy of Pick-Sloan and Irrigation in North Dakota, available at http://www.nd-humanities.org/html/russell.html.

Salman, M. A., *Groundwater. Legal and Policy Perspectives*, Proceedings of a World Bank Seminar (Technical Paper n° 456, Washington D.C., 1999).

Salman, M. A. and McInerney-Lankford, S., *The Human Right to Water. Legal and Policy Dimensions* (The World Bank, Washington D.C., 2004).

Salman, M. A. and Boisson de Chazournes, L., *International Watercourses: Enhancing Cooperation and Managing Conflict*, Proceedings of a World Bank Seminar (Technical Paper n° 414, Washington D.C., 1998).

Sand, P. H., *Information Disclosure as an Instrument of Environmental Governance*, 63 Zeitschrift für Ausländisches öffentliches Recht und Völkerrecht 487 (2003).

Sand, P. H., Mackenzie, R. and Shany, Y., Manual on International Courts and Tribunals (1999).

Sauvé, P., *Regional versus Multilateral Approaches to Services and Investment Liberalization: Anything to Worry About?*, in Regionalism and Multilateralism after the Uruguay round (P. Demaret et al. eds, 1997).

Sax, J. L., *Understanding Transfers: Community Rights and the Privatization of Water*, 1 HASTINGS WEST-NORTHWEST J. ENVIR. L. AND POLICY 13 (1994).

Sax, J. L., et al., LEGAL CONTROL OF WATER RESOURCES (2000).

Scanlon, J., Cassar, A., and Nemes, N., *Water as a Human Right?*, IUCN Environmental Policy and Law Paper No. 51 (2004).

Schaufelberger, P., LA PROTECTION DES INVESTISSEMENTS INTERNATIONAUX DANS LES PAYS EN DÉVELOPPEMENT (1992).

Schecter, M., Becker, N. and Zeitouni, N., *Reallocating Water Resources in the Middle East through Market Mechanisms*, 12(1) WATER RESOURCES DEV. 17 (1996).

Schlemmer-Schulte, S., *The Impact of Civil Society on the World Bank, the International Monetary Fund and the World Trade Organization: The Case of the World Bank*, 7 ILSA J. INT'L & COMP. L. 399 (2001).

Shany, Y., THE COMPETING JURISDICTIONS OF INTERNATIONAL COURTS AND TRIBUNALS (2003).

Smets, H., *The Right to Water as a Human Right*, 30 ENVTL. POL'Y & L. 248 (2000).

Sohnle, J., LE DROIT INTERNATIONAL DES RESOURCES EN EAU DOUCE: SOLIDARITE CONTRE SOUVERAINETE (La Documentation française, Paris, 2002).

Sorensen, M., MANUAL OF PUBLIC INTERNATIONAL LAW (1968)

Sornarajah, M., THE INTERNATIONAL LAW ON FOREIGN INVESTMENT (1994).

Squillace, M. and Zellmer, S., *Managing Interjurisdictional Waters Under the Great Lakes Charter Annex*, 18 NATURAL RESOURCES & ENVIRONMENT 8 (2003).

Steenblick, R., *Subsidy Measurement and Classification: Developing a Common Framework*, paper presented to the OECD Workshop on Environmentally Harmful Subsidies, Paris, 7–8 November 2002.

Sur, M., Umali-Deininger, D., and Dinar, A., *Water-Related Subsidies in Agriculture: Environmental and Equity Consequences*, paper presented to the OECD Workshop on Environmentally Harmful Subsidies, Paris, 7–8 November 2002.

Tanzi, A. and Arcari, M., THE UNITED NATIONS CONVENTION ON THE LAW OF INTERNATIONAL WATERCOURSES. A FRAMEWORK FOR SHARING (2001).

Tanzi, A. and Pitea, C., *Emerging Trends in the Role of Non-State Actors in International Water Disputes*, in RESOLUTION OF INTERNATIONAL WATER DISPUTES (Peace Palace Papers, 2003).

Tarlock, A. D., LAW OF WATER RIGHTS AND RESOURCES (1988).

Tarlock, A. D., *New Water Transfer Restrictions: The West Returns to Riparianism*, 27 WATER RESOURCES RESEARCH 987 (1991).

Tarlock, A. D., *Western Water Law: Global Warming, and Growth Limitations*, 24 LOYOLA OF LOS ANGELES L. REV. 979 (1991).

Tarlock, A. D., *What the Report of the World Commission on Dams Might mean for the United States Water Community*, 5 U. Denver Water Law Rev. 225 (2001).

Tarlock, A. D., et al., WATER RESOURCE MANAGEMENT: A CASEBOOK IN LAW AND PUBLIC POLICY (5th ed., 2002).

Taylor, C. R., *The Right of Participation in Development Projects*, in SUSTAINABLE DEVELOPMENT AND GOOD GOVERNANCE 205 (Konrad Ginther et al. eds, 1995).

Thompson, B. H., Jr., *Institutional Perspectives on Water Policy and Markets*, 81 CAL. L. REV. 671 (1993).

Tolba, M.K. and El Kholy, O.A., THE WORLD ENVIRONMENT 1972–1992 (M.K. Tolba and O.A. El Kholy eds, 1992).

Toope, S.J. and Brunee, J., *Freshwater Regimes: The Mandate of the International Joint Commission*, 15 Arizona J. Int. & Comp. L. 273 (1998).

Trindade, A. and Cancado, A., *The Parallel Evolutions of International Human Rights Protection and of Environmental Protection and the Absence of Restrictions on the Exercise of Recognized Human Rights*, 13 REVISTA IIDH 35 (1991).

United Nations Conference on Trade and Development (UNCTAD), *Transnational Corporations and Export Competitiveness*, World Investment Report 2002.

United Nations Economic Commission for Europe (UNECE), THE AARHUS CONVENTION: AN IMPLEMENTATION GUIDE (United Nations, New York, and Geneva, 2000).

United Nations Environment Programme (UNEP), Food and Agriculture Organization (FAO), Oregon State University, and Transboundary Freshwater Dispute Database, ATLAS OF INTERNATIONAL FRESHWATER AGREEMENTS (2002).

United Nations High Commissioner for Human Rights (UNHCHR), Economic, Social and Cultural Rights, *Liberalisation of Trade in Services and Human Rights*, Report of the High Commissioner E/CN.4/Sub.2/2002 (June 2002).

United States Bureau of Reclamation, RECLAMATION'S STRATEGIC PLAN: A LONG-TERM FRAMEWORK FOR WATER RESOURCES MANAGEMENT, DEVELOPMENT AND PROTECTION (June 1992).

U.S. Department of Interior, FINAL ENVIRONMENTAL IMPACT STATEMENT, WATER RIGHTS ACQUISITION FOR LAHONTAN VALLEY WETLANDS, CHURCHILL COUNTY, NEVADA, Vol. 1, 1-5 (September 1996).

Veiga da Cunha, L., *The Aral Sea Crisis: A Great Challenge in Transboundary Water Resources Management*, NATO Advanced Research Workshop on Transboundary Water Resources Management: Technical and Institutional Issues, Skopelos, Greece, May 1994.

Wälde, T.W., *ICSID Annulment Committee*, OIL, GAS & ENERGY LAW INTELLIGENCE, Vol. I, Issue 02 (March 2003).

Wälde, T.W. and Weiler, T., *Investment Arbitration under the Energy Charter Treaty in the Light of the New NAFTA Precedents: Towards a Global Code of Conduct for Economic Regulation*, in INVESTMENT TREATIES AND ARBITRATION, ASA Special Series No. 19 (Gabrielle Kaufmann-Kohler/Blaise Stucki eds, 2002).

Water Science and Technology Board, National Academy of Sciences/National Research Council, WATER TRANSFERS IN THE WEST: EQUITY, EFFICIENCY, AND THE ENVIRONMENT (1992).

Western Water Policy Review Advisory Commission, WATER IN THE WEST: CHALLENGE FOR THE NEXT CENTURY (1998).

Whincop, M. and Rowland, S., *Markets and Corporate Law*, in WHO BENEFITS FROM PRIVATISATION? (1998).

Wilcox, C., SUGAR WATER: HAWAII'S PLANTATION DITCHES (1996).

Willey, Z., ECONOMIC DEVELOPMENT AND ENVIRONMENTAL QUALITY IN CALIFORNIA'S WATER SYSTEM (Institute of Governmental Studies, 1985).

Wirth, D.A., *Reexamining Decision-Making Processes in International Environmental Law*, 79 IOWA L. REV. 769 (1994).

World Bank, Syrian Arab Republic Irrigation Sector Report, Rural Development, Water, and Environment Group, Middle East and North Africa Region, Report No. 22602-SYR, Washington D.C. (2001).

World Bank Inspection Panel, ACCOUNTABILITY AT THE WORLD BANK: THE INSPECTION PANEL 10 YEARS ON (Washington D.C., 2003).

World Commission on Dams, DAMS AND DEVELOPMENT—A NEW FRAMEWORK FOR DECISION-MAKING (Earthscan, 2000).

World Health Organization (WHO), THE GLOBAL WATER SUPPLY AND SANITATION ASSESSMENT 2000 (WHO, 2000).

WORLD HEALTH ORGANIZATION (WHO), THE RIGHT TO WATER (WHO, 2003).

World Water Council, Third World Water Forum, Global Water Partnership, FINANCING WATER FOR ALL, Report of the World Panel on Financing Water Infrastructure (2003).

Ziegler, A., TRADE AND ENVIRONMENTAL LAW IN THE EUROPEAN COMMUNITY 199 (1996).

Zillman, D., Lucas, A., and Pring, G., HUMAN RIGHTS IN NATURAL RESOURCE DEVELOPMENT: PUBLIC PARTICIPATION IN THE SUSTAINABLE DEVELOPMENT OF MINING AND ENERGY RESOURCES (2002).

Appendix H
Water-related Websites

Académie de l'Eau
http://www.oieau.fr/academie/

Centre on Housing Rights and Evictions (COHRE)—Right to Water Programme
http://www.cohre.org/water.htm

Commission on Environmental Cooperation under the North America Free Trade Agreement (NAFTA)
http://www.cec.org/

Dams and Development Project
http://www.unep-dams.org/

Dialogue on Water and Climate
http://www.waterandclimate.org/

Dialogue on Water, Food and Environment
http://www.iwmi.cgiar.org/dialogue/index.asp

Environment Canada: Freshwater Website
http://www.ec.gc.ca/water/index.htm

Food and Agriculture Organization (FAO)
http://www.fao.org/english/newsroom/focus/2003/water.htm

Global Environment Monitoring System
http://www.gemswater.org/

Global International Waters Assessment
http://www.giwa.net/

Global Water Partnership
http://www.gwpforum.org/servlet/PSP

Great Lakes Commission
http://www.glc.org/

Green Cross International
http://www.greencrossinternational.net/index.asp

International Commission on Irrigation and Drainage (ICID)
http://www.icid.org/

International Joint Commission (United States and Canada)
http://www.ijc.org/

International Hydrologic Programme (IHP)
http://www.unesco.org/water/ihp/index.shtml

International Network of Basin Organizations (INBO)
http://www.riob.org/riobang.htm

International Office for Water
http://www.oieau.fr/

International River Basins of the World
www.transboundarywaters.orst.edu.register

International Rivers Network
www.irn.org

International Secretariat for Water
http://www.irc.nl/content/view/full/6670

International Water Academy
www.thewateracademy.no

International Water History Association
www.iwha.net

International Water and Sanitation Centre
http://www.irc.nl/

International Water Law Project
www.internationalwaterlaw.org

International Water Law Research Institute
http://www.dundee.ac.uk/law/iwlri/index.php

International Water Management Institute (IWMI)
http://www.iwmi.cgiar.org/

International Water Resources Association (IWRA)
http://www.iwra.siu.edu/

Murray—Darling Basin Commission—
www.mdbc.gov.au

Stockholm International Water Institute
http://www.siwi.org/

The Water Page—International Water Law
www.thewaterpage.com/int_water_law

The World's Water
www.worldwater.org

UN-HABITAT United Nations Human Settlements Programme
http://www.unhabitat.org

United Nations Children's Fund (UNICEF)
http://www.unicef.org/wes/

United Nations Commission on Sustainable Development (CSD)
http://www.un.org/esa/sustdev/csd/csd12/csd12.htm

United Nations Development Programme (UNDP)
http://www.undp.org/

United Nations Education, Scientific and Cultural Organization (UNESCO)
http://www.unesco.org/water/

United Nations Environment Programme (UNEP)
http://www.unep.org/themes/freshwater/

Water Issues Announcement List
http://www.iisd.ca/email/water-L.htm

Water Resources Information—American Water Resources Association
www.awra.org

Water Supply and Sanitation Collaborative Council (WSSCC)
http://www.wsscc.org/

World Bank Group—Water Resources Management
http://lnweb18.worldbank.org/essd

World Commission on Dams
http://www.dams.org/

World Conservation Union (IUCN)
http://www.iucn.org/

World Health Organization (WHO)—Water Sanitation and Health (WSH)
http://www.who.int/water_sanitation_health/en/

World Meteorological Organization (WMO)
http://www.wmo.ch/index-en.html

World Water Assessment Programme (WWAP)
http://www.unesco.org/water/wwap/index.shtml

World Water Council
http://www.worldwatercouncil.org/

World Water Forum
http://worldwaterforum.net

World Resources Institute
http://www.wri.org/

WWF Freshwater Programme
http://www.panda.org/about_wwf/what_we_do/freshwater/index.cfm

Index